The Joan Palevsky Imprint in Classical Literature

In honor of beloved Virgil—

"O degli altri poeti onore e lume . . ."

—Dante, *Inferno*

The publisher and the University of California Press Foundation gratefully acknowledge the generous support of the Joan Palevsky Imprint in Classical Literature.

REASON AND REVELATION IN BYZANTINE ANTIOCH

THE BERKELEY SERIES IN POSTCLASSICAL ISLAMIC SCHOLARSHIP

Series Editors

Asad Q. Ahmed, University of California, Berkeley

Margaret Larkin, University of California, Berkeley

1. *The Light of the World: Astronomy in al-Andalus*, by Joseph Ibn Naḥmias and edited, translated, and with a commentary by Robert G. Morrison
2. *Language between God and the Poets: Maʿnā in the Eleventh Century*, by Alexander Key
3. *Reason and Revelation in Byzantine Antioch: The Christian Translation Program of Abdallah ibn al-Fadl*, by Alexandre M. Roberts

REASON AND REVELATION IN BYZANTINE ANTIOCH

The Christian Translation Program of Abdallah ibn al-Fadl

Alexandre M. Roberts

UNIVERSITY OF CALIFORNIA PRESS

University of California Press

Oakland, California

Library of Congress Cataloging-in-Publication Data

Names: Roberts, Alexandre M., 1986- author.
Title: Reason and revelation in Byzantine Antioch : the Christian translation program of Abdallah ibn al-Fadl / Alexandre M. Roberts.
Other titles: Berkeley series in postclassical Islamic scholarship ; 3.
Description: Oakland, California : University of California Press, [2020] | Series: Berkeley series in postclassical islamic scholarship ; 3 | Includes bibliographical references and index.
Identifiers: LCCN 2019040181| ISBN 9780520343498 (cloth) | ISBN 9780520974821 (ebook)
Subjects: LCSH: Antaki, Abd Allah ibn al-Fadl, -approximately 1052—Influence. | Christianity and other religions. | Christian philosophy—Translating into Arabic—History—11th century. | Philosophy, Ancient—Translating into Arabic—History—11th century.
Classification: LCC BR127 .R56 2020 | DDC 270.3092—dc23
LC record available at https://lccn.loc.gov/2019040181

Manufactured in the United States of America

29 28 27 26 25 24 23 22 21 20
10 9 8 7 6 5 4 3 2 1

CONTENTS

ILLUSTRATIONS

MAPS

TABLES

ACKNOWLEDGMENTS

This book and its author owe much to Maria Mavroudi, for pivotal conversations and her detailed marginalia on earlier stages of this project. A student's debt to such a teacher can never be fully reckoned. For their constructive comments and corrections, I also thank Asad Ahmed, Michael Cooperson, and Susanna Elm. Samuel Noble and Alexander Treiger were generous with their unpublished work as I embarked on this project. Along the way, I benefited from conversations about the project with Joe Glynias, Katerina Ierodiakonou, Richard Janko, Pavlos Kalligas, Harvey Lederman, Eleni Perdikouri, and others.

Libraries, public and private, in Berkeley, Los Angeles, Basel, Paris, Athens, Rome, Venice, Berlin, New York, Florence, and Genoa shaped this book and made it possible. Marie-Geneviève Guesdon at the Bibliothèque nationale de France, Susy Marcon at the Biblioteca Marciana, Ida Giovanna Rao at the Biblioteca Laurenziana, and the staff of the Biblioteca Apostolica Vaticana and the Universitätsbibliothek Basel made possible my consultation of manuscripts in their care. For furnishing me with reproductions of particular manuscripts, I would also like to thank the Bibliothèque Orientale de l'Université Saint-Joseph in Beirut, the Cadbury Research Library of the University of Birmingham, Makarios Haidamous of the Basilian Salvatorian Order, Joun, Lebanon, Polykarpos Avva Mena of the Monastery of Mār Mīnā, Maryūṭ, Egypt, and the Beinecke Library at Yale University

This project was researched and completed with the support of the Dolores Zohrab Liebmann Fellowship, the M. Alison Frantz Fellowship at the Gennadius Library of the American School of Classical Studies at Athens, and the Dean's Normative Time and Mellon Sawyer Graduate Fellowships at the University of California, Berkeley; and aided by research funding from a Lenfest Junior Faculty

Development Grant at Columbia University and from the University of Southern California. Asad Ahmed and Margaret Larkin facilitated publication of the result in the series where it now appears. Comments and corrections from an anonymous reviewer, Alexander Treiger, and Eric Schmidt greatly improved the manuscript. Austin Lim helped prepare the manuscript for production. Francisco Reinking shepherded the book through the production process. David Fussner, Michal Hoftich, and other coders and maintainers of LaTeX offered technical assistance. Gordie Thompson drafted the maps, and Marian Rogers copyedited the full book manuscript. Roberta Engleman produced the General Index.

Love of intellectual labor I owe to my parents, Carla and John, and to my brothers. Malika Maskarinec and Anthony Mahler offered exemplarity. The final stages of work on this book took place under Sibylline supervision. Without Maya, this book would not exist.

NOTE ON CONVENTIONS

Throughout, I spell the Arabic name ʿAbd Allāh without a space (ʿAbdallāh) and write *ibn* (not *b.*) for both *bn* and *ʾbn*.

For Greek names, I use the English form (often identical to the Latinized form) when it is widely familiar (e.g., Aristotle, Democritus), but otherwise opt for a non-Latinized transliteration (e.g., Theodoulos, Psellos).

Standard bio-bibliographical information is drawn from *OCD*^{3}, *Brill's New Pauly*, *ODB*, or *EI*^{2} unless otherwise noted. English translations are mine unless otherwise indicated by citation of a translation in the notes.

To cite a manuscript's folio 1 recto, line 2 from the bottom (i.e., second-to-last line), I write fol. $1^{r}_{\triangle 2}$. Sigla for manuscripts of Ibn al-Faḍl's works, used in the footnotes and the critical apparatus to the Arabic text, can be found in the bibliography. In the Arabic text and apparatus, I employ the following marks:

<. . .>	editorial insertion
{. . .}	editorial deletion
[. . .]	editorial completion of text damaged in manuscript
[[. . .]]	deletion marked in manuscript
‘. . .’	insertion marked in manuscript
(. . .)	editorial note

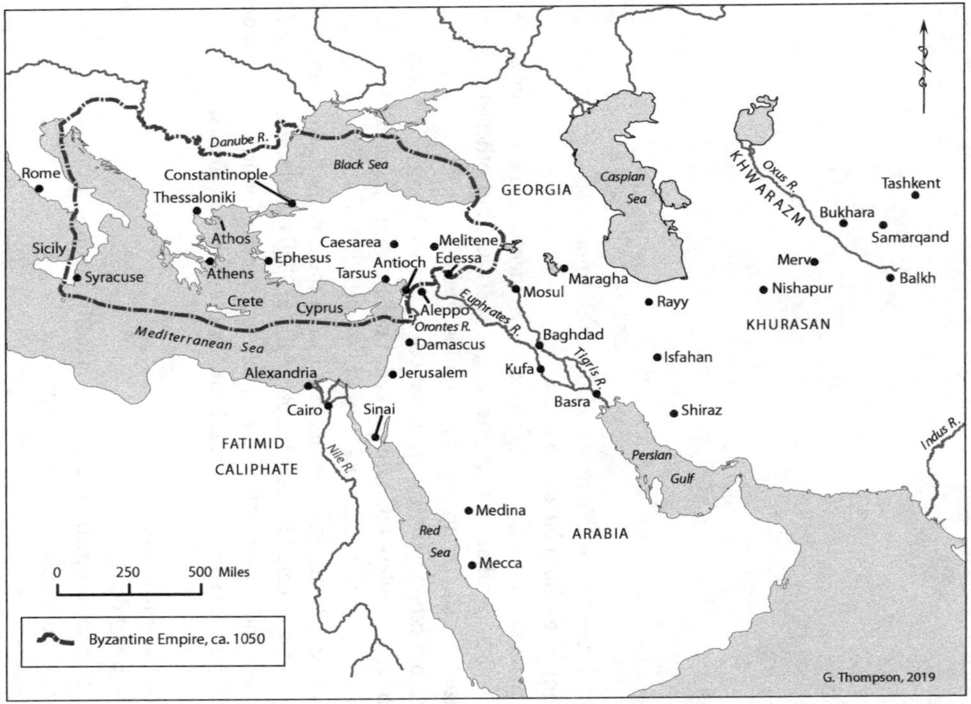

MAP 1. The Byzantine Empire and the Near East, ca. 1050. Map by Gordie Thompson, after *ODB*, vol. 1, p. 354; and John Haldon, *The Palgrave Atlas of Byzantine History* (New York, 2005), map 6.4.

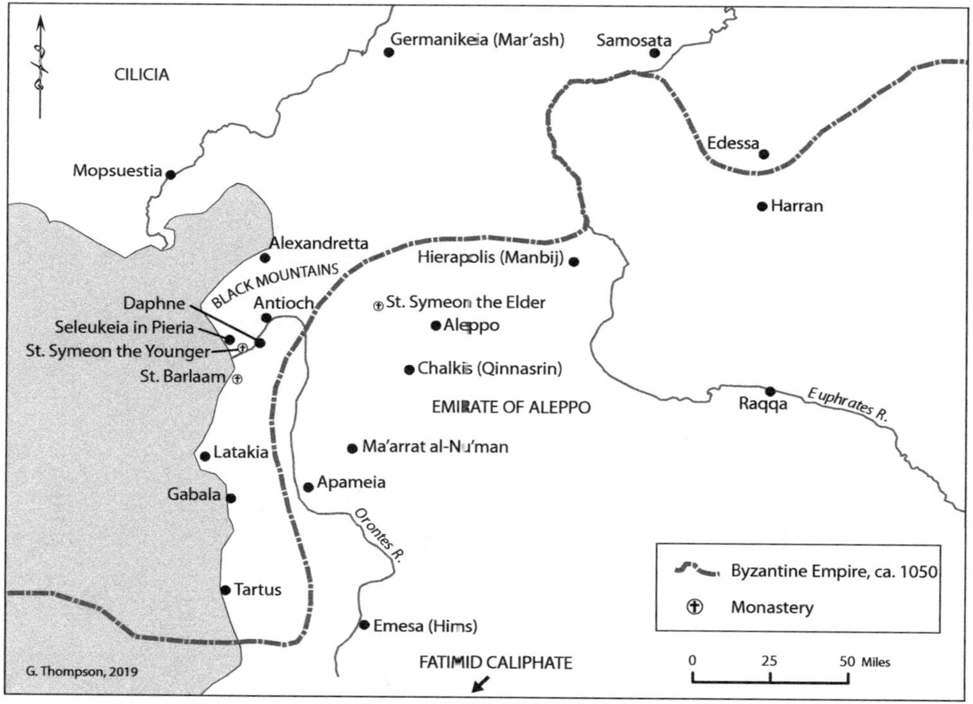

MAP 2. Northern Syria, ca. 1050. Map by Gordie Thompson, after Todt, “Region,” 267; and Honigmann, *Die Ostgrenze*, map 3.

INTRODUCTION

I have seen a group of Christians today who have devoted themselves to understanding the works of erring outsiders. . . . Sometimes they start to go on about literature, sometimes about another of the sciences. . . . They cling to [these] things . . . which bring no reliable advantage. . . .

Whoever reads the sciences has done philosophy, and whoever does philosophy has come to know God the Mighty and Exalted to some extent.

—ʿABDALLĀH IBN AL-FAḌL AL-ANṬĀKĪ

This book is about the Greek-into-Arabic translation program of an Arabic-speaking Christian who lived in northern Syria under Byzantine rule in the mid-eleventh century: ʿAbdallāh ibn al-Faḍl of Antioch. Ibn al-Faḍl was a theologian and deacon in the Byzantine Church. His ambitious translation program focused on Christian texts by ecclesiastical authors well known in the Byzantine world.

Ibn al-Faḍl's translation program is part of a much larger story, the story of how ancient philosophy was cultivated, adapted, and reconceived in medieval Byzantine and Middle Eastern scholarly culture and religious education. The texts Ibn al-Faḍl translated are all what today we typically call religious texts: homilies on books from the Old and New Testaments, disquisitions on correct Christian doctrine, laudatory speeches honoring Christian saints, and guides to reforming the self in order to approach a Christian moral ideal and become more similar to God. Ibn al-Faḍl's own account of his translation program frames it in opposition to ancient philosophy and indeed any teachings outside of Christianity.

And yet Ibn al-Faḍl's own annotations on his translations regularly interpret these Christian texts through the lens of an ancient philosophical tradition of treatises, commentaries, education, speculation, and debate grounded in the works of Aristotle. A close examination of Ibn al-Faḍl's annotations reveals the translator's simultaneous engagement with ancient Greek and contemporary Byzantine and Arabic philosophy, science, and literary culture. The language of his translations, moreover, attests to his immersion in Arabic Aristotelian philosophical vocabulary. The picture of Ibn al-Faḍl that emerges is of a scholar who applied his own philosophical and philological education to the task of reading the classics of Byzantine Christianity.

What are we to make of this apparent contradiction? How could Ibn al-Faḍl be at once so parochial in his religiosity, so committed to his faith tradition, so dead set against ancient, pagan philosophy, and at the same time so eager to discuss ancient philosophy in practice, and not just anywhere, but in the margins of the very texts whose Christian worth and validity he contrasted with philosophy's pagan vapidity and error? By watching Ibn al-Faḍl at work, we will see that he objected to philosophy when it was cultivated for its own sake but had no problem with it, indeed promoted it, when it was directed to a higher purpose, above all reading the Christian classics that he translated.

This book seeks to uncover how Ibn al-Faḍl mobilized his knowledge of ancient philosophy to explicate these Christian texts. His methods and aims tell us about how he, and other medieval scholars (Muslim, Christian, Jewish, and other), understood the relationship between reason and revelation, between the system of formal knowledge they inherited from the late antique Alexandrian synthesis of ancient Greek thought and the living truth they inherited from the prophets and apostles of God. I argue that Ibn al-Faḍl's attitudes and approaches were coherent and emblematic of the scholarship of his age: universal in its ambitions, parochial in its articulation, cosmopolitan in its practice. This was a shared scholarly culture of robust intellectual curiosity *in the service of tradition* that had an enduring role in Eurasian intellectual history, for it forged a mode of critical inquiry driven by confessional concerns and universalizing ethical aspirations.[1]

Throughout the eleventh century, Byzantium and the Middle East were hardly worlds apart, nor was their contact restricted to war and diplomacy. On the contrary, scholars, texts, and ideas circulated widely across their political boundaries, in both directions.[2] Antioch, where Ibn al-Faḍl lived and worked around the year 1050, was a critical meeting-point for this circulation.

In the tenth and eleventh centuries, the Byzantine Empire expanded both militarily and economically, especially during the reigns of Nikephoros II Phokas (963–969), John I Tzimiskes (969–976), and Basil II (976–1025). In this era, territories in southern Italy, the Balkans, the Mediterranean islands, and northern Syria and Mesopotamia fell once again under Byzantine control (maps 1–2). Among the most celebrated Byzantine conquests was the ancient city of Antioch. Antioch would remain in Byzantine hands for over a century, from 969 to 1084.[3]

In their new eastern territories, Byzantine administrators encountered Byzantine Chalcedonian Christians but also Syrian and Armenian Miaphysite Chris-

1. For the close relationship between natural philosophy and improvement of the self in early modern Europe, see Jones, *Good Life*.

2. Gutas, *Greek Thought, Arabic Culture* (hereafter *GTAC*); Condylis-Bassoukos, *Stéphanitès;* Mavroudi, *Byzantine Book;* Mavroudi, "Greek Language"; Mavroudi, "Translations."

3. Ostrogorsky, *History*, ch. 4; Kazhdan, *History*, 2:1–5; Harvey, *Economic Expansion*.

tians (locals and new immigrants alike), Muslims, and others.[4] Constantinople was transformed by the influx of peoples, wealth, and ideas. Prayers were said for the Fatimid caliph (with occasional interruptions) in Constantinople's mosque.[5]

When compared to the vast empire the Arab Muslim conquerors had amassed by the year 700, the Islamic world of the eleventh century was politically fragmented. Yet even as states splintered, Islamic religious and scholarly institutions transcending state boundaries flourished.[6] Fatimid Cairo, a center of learning, was also the headquarters for missionary activity throughout the Islamic world aimed at convincing Muslims to recognize the legitimacy of the Ismaili Shiite imams (the Fatimid caliphs) and to accept Ismaili doctrines on law, the natural world, cosmology, and theology.[7] At the same time, Sunni Muslim religious scholars (*ʿulamāʾ*) were consolidating their authority across the Islamic world as legal and religious experts and arbiters of political legitimacy, which allowed them to develop symbiotic relationships with regional military leaders (emirs) like the Buyids, Mirdāsids, and Seljuks. Well-endowed Sunni educational institutions and their emblematic architectural setting, the *madrasa*, prestigious and entrenched in subsequent centuries, were taking shape in the tenth and eleventh centuries, drawing students and professors from across the Islamic world.[8]

In the mid-eleventh century, Byzantine relations with neighboring Muslim states—the Arab Mirdāsid rulers of Aleppo (about 100 km east of Antioch) and the Fatimid caliphs based in Cairo and in control of Palestine and southern Syria—were generally peaceful and open to travel and trade.[9] Nor was it unusual for merchants, scholars, and professionals to arrive at Antioch, Cairo, and Constantinople from at least as far as Baghdad, where the Persian Shiite dynasty of the Buyids ruled (as the nominal servants of the Sunni-aligned Abbasid caliphs) until 1055, when they were replaced by the Seljuk Turks.[10]

Non-Muslim scholars in the eastern Mediterranean and Middle East were generally as active and mobile as their Muslim counterparts. Christian ecclesiastical institutions of various confessions flourished in Baghdad, northern Mesopotamia, Palestine, and Egypt, although aberrant rulers disrupted this scholarly activity through their violent treatment of non-Muslims. These rare occasions temporarily replaced the peaceful circulation of scholars with their rapid flight: when the Fatimid caliph al-Ḥākim (r. 996–1021) enacted particularly harsh policies,

4. Dagron, "Minorités."

5. Reinert, "Muslim Presence," 135–40; *EI*², s.v. "Fāṭimids," 2:855.

6. Hodgson, *Venture,* 2:8–11, 17.

7. Halm, *Fatimids and Learning.*

8. Hodgson, *Venture,* 2:46–52. Later developments: Chamberlain, *Knowledge.*

9. *EI*², s.v. "Mirdās, Banū or Mirdāsids"; Hodgson, *Venture,* 2:21–28; *EI*², s.v. "Fāṭimids," 2:855; Goitein, *Mediterranean Society,* 1:42–59.

10. Hodgson, *Venture,* 2:42–46.

Christians fled Egypt; many Chalcedonians ended up in Antioch, such as the historian Yaḥyā ibn Saʿīd al-Anṭākī (ca. 980–after 1033).[11]

If we consider when and where Ibn al-Faḍl lived, then, it is not difficult to see how he came into contact with the wide range of perspectives, languages, and ideas that played a role in his thinking. In the eleventh century, they were all to be found in Antioch.

This book's investigation will proceed as follows. Part 1 will examine Ibn al-Faḍl's translation program in detail. First, we consider Ibn al-Faḍl's intellectual milieu and the multilingual city where he produced his translations (chapter 1). Next, we will seek to characterize his translation program (chapter 2): Which texts did he translate? The next step will be to consider the list of translated texts taken as a whole (chapter 3): What sort of texts were they? What was their resonance and relevance in the eleventh century? Who wanted to read such texts, and who wanted them to be read?

Building upon this foundation, part 2 will then investigate the role of philosophy and philosophical education in how Ibn al-Faḍl read and taught the texts he translated. We will begin by turning to a crucial witness for understanding why Ibn al-Faḍl translated these texts: Ibn al-Faḍl himself. In the manuscripts of a number of his translations, Ibn al-Faḍl's prefaces are preserved. These will allow Ibn al-Faḍl to tell us what motivated his work (chapter 4). We will then shift from Ibn al-Faḍl's stated purpose to consider how he used his own translations and meant them to be used, by closely analyzing a selection of his marginalia on these same translations (chapter 5).

In the subsequent chapters, Ibn al-Faḍl's translations and marginalia will allow us to investigate the intersections of his translation program with logic (chapter 6), physics (chapter 7), cosmology (chapter 8), and astronomy (chapter 9). The aim will be to glimpse the medieval world's interlocking philosophical and scientific disciplines through the lens of Ibn al-Faḍl's project to translate and teach the classics of Byzantine Christianity.

Ibn al-Faḍl was part of a vibrant intellectual community in Antioch. The Byzantine and Islamic educational traditions to which his translations attest were to have a long afterlife, and his translations themselves had an enduring place in Arabic-language Christian libraries. Through these translations, this book seeks to recover something of Ibn al-Faḍl's era, its multicultural roots, its creative adaptations of past and present, and its lasting legacy.

11. *EI*^{2}, s.v. "Fāṭimids"; Swanson, "Yaḥyā ibn Saʿīd."

PART I

TRANSLATION

1

A SCHOLAR AND HIS CITY

Who was Ibn al-Faḍl? What was it like to live in his city when he did, and how might it have shaped his work? The present chapter considers these questions to the extent possible given the current state of research on both the scholar and his city. This will set the stage for investigating Ibn al-Faḍl's translations and annotations in the rest of the book.

First the scholar, then his city.

1 ʿABDALLĀH IBN AL-FAḌL OF ANTIOCH

Ibn al-Faḍl's modern biographers are forced to infer much from a few words.[1] The only date we possess from his life is ca. 1051 CE, in which he completed two of his translations, according to manuscripts of those works.[2] One of the richest sources for his life is his name. A particularly detailed version of his name appears in an early thirteenth-century manuscript containing one of his translations; there he is called "the most exalted sheikh and most noble deacon Abū l-Fatḥ ʿAbdallāh of Antioch, the Melkite, son of al-Faḍl, son of ʿAbdallāh the metropolitan."[3]

1. Treiger, "ʿAbdallāh"; Graf, *Geschichte der christlichen arabischen Literatur* (hereafter *GCAL*), 2:52–64; Nasrallah, *Histoire,* 3.1:191–229. In this section I especially draw and build upon Treiger's work, based on my own reading of Ibn al-Faḍl's works, especially his prefaces and marginalia (see chs. 4 and 5).

2. Ibn al-Faḍl, translations of Basil, *Homilies on the Hexaemeron,* and pseudo-Kaisarios, *Questions and Answers:* Nasrallah, *Histoire,* 3.1:193.

3. Jerusalem, Holy Sepulcher, ar. 35 (1227 CE), fol. 440^{r} (colophon to Ibn al-Faḍl, translation of John Chrysostom, *Homilies on Genesis*); Koikylides, *Κατάλογος,* 40: *al-shaykh al-ajall wa-l-shammās al-anbal Abī l-Fatḥ ʿAbdallāh al-Anṭākī al-malakī ibn al-Faḍl ibn ʿAbdallāh al-Muṭrān* (I am grateful

The epithet "sheikh" implies that he was deeply learned,[4] and perhaps a respected teacher as well. Elsewhere he is called "learned."[5] One text even calls him "the peerless philosopher."[6] "Abū l-Fatḥ"—literally, "father of victory"—is probably a metaphorical epithet or second name (rather than a reference to his offspring).[7] He is explicitly identified as a Melkite (*malakī*)[8]—that is, an "imperial" Christian in communion with the Byzantine Church—and an Antiochian (*Anṭākī*), if not by birth, at least by residence.[9]

His grandfather, we can infer, was a metropolitan bishop.[10] Metropolitan bishops were among the highest hierarchs in the church. Ibn al-Faḍl must therefore have come from an influential, possibly wealthy family, or at least one with a distinguished past.

Ibn al-Faḍl's full name was a good Arabic name, with nothing foreign about it. At the same time, his name was easily transferable to a Greek context. His given name, ʿAbdallāh, meaning "slave of God," has its exact equivalent in the common Byzantine name Theodoulos. Meanwhile his *kunya*, "Abū l-Fatḥ," could

---

to Maria Mavroudi for the opportunity to consult a reproduction of this manuscript). Instead of *Abī l-Fatḥ* (not good Classical Arabic but otherwise unproblematic), Koikylides (followed by Nasrallah, *Histoire*, 3.1:191–92) reads *Ibn al-Fatḥ*, clearly spurious. The manuscript admits both readings. In Sinai ar. 156 (1316 CE), fol. 247ʳ (ascription of John Chrysostom, *Homilies on Hebrews*, trans. Ibn al-Faḍl), and in his *Refutation of Astrology* (ed. Graf, "Die Widerlegung," 340), Ibn al-Faḍl's *kunya* appears as Abū l-Fatḥ.

4. Nasrallah, *Histoire*, 3.1:192; Féghali, "ʿAbdallāh," 96.

5. In Jerusalem, Holy Sepulcher, ar. 24 (1565 CE), fol. 144ᵛ (introducing an abbreviation of Ibn al-Faḍl's preface to Isaac the Syrian); see Koikylides, *Κατάλογος*, 32; Nasrallah, *Histoire*, 3.1:211–12: *al-mutarjim al-fāḍil al-shammās ʿAbdallāh ibn al-Faḍl.* I thank Asad Ahmed for pointing out this sense of *fāḍil*.

6. See ch. 2, pp. 68–69 and n. 167.

7. Nasrallah, *Histoire*, 3.1:192. See *EI*², s.v. "Kunya."

8. I will generally avoid using the term "Melkite" because of its confusingly similar but distinct meaning in modern usage. In Ibn al-Faḍl's day "Melkite" referred to Christians in communion with the Roman-Byzantine Church, Chalcedonian, Dyothelete, and Dyoenergist by doctrine, whose highest-ranking prelates were the pope of Rome and the patriarch of Constantinople (followed by the Chalcedonian patriarchs of Antioch, Jerusalem, and Alexandria). By contrast, in modern times, when the Roman Catholic pope and the Greek Orthodox patriarch of Constantinople are no longer in communion with one another, and after early modern efforts to convert Arab Christians to Catholicism, "Melkite" has come to refer to certain Arab Christian communities in communion with the Catholic Church.

9. Ibn al-Faḍl's contemporary Yaḥyā ibn Saʿīd al-Anṭākī was originally from Egypt but later acquired the *nisba* of his adopted city.

10. Treiger, "ʿAbdallāh," 89. Nasrallah (*Histoire*, 3.1:192) suggests that al-Muṭrān is a family name derived from an earlier ancestor who bore the title. One might have expected in that case for there to be an *ibn* before *al-Muṭrān*. Atiya ("St. John Damascene," 77) mistakenly thought that Ibn al-Faḍl was an archbishop. Féghali ("ʿAbdallāh," 96) raises the possibility that Ibn al-Faḍl's *father* was a bishop but cites no evidence.

have been understood as equivalent to Greek names referring to conquest (*fatḥ* ~ *nikē*), such as the popular middle Byzantine names Nikephoros, Niketas, and Nikon.

He was not only a sheikh but also a *shammās*—a deacon. Thus he was a member of the hierarchy of the Byzantine Church at Antioch.

The chronology of Ibn al-Faḍl's life, as already mentioned, is restricted to the dates of his works. But very few of Ibn al-Faḍl's translations are dated in the manuscripts: two or three, depending on how we count. The first is his translation of Basil of Caesarea's *Hexaemeron.*[11] At the beginning, before the table of contents, the text invokes the eternal God and names the translated work: "The Book of the Explication of the Six Days of Creation" (i.e., *Hexaemeron*). It then says when and by whom it was translated:[12]

ونقله[1] من اللغة اليونانية والرومية[2] إلى لغة الأعراب[3] عبد الله بن[4] الفضل الأنطاكي لطلب الأجر والثواب، وذلك في التاريخ الرابع من جملة السنين في عام ستة آلاف وخمسمائة وستّين[5].

[1]ونقله: ب د ق؛ نقله: ذ [2]والرومية: ب د ق؛ ـــ ذ [3]لغة الأعراب: ب د ذ؛ اللغة الاعراب: ق [4]بن: ق؛ ابن: ب د ذ [5]وذلك في التاريخ . . . وستّين: ب د ق؛ ـــ ذ

> ʿAbdallāh ibn al-Faḍl al-Anṭākī translated it from the Greek and Roman language into the language of the Arabs (*aʿrāb*) to seek recompense and reward. That was in the fourth indiction (*taʾrīkh*) of the group of years,[13] in the year six thousand and five hundred and sixty.

The two dates given are off by one year. The year 6560, reckoned from the creation of the world, corresponds to 1 September 1051–31 August 1052 CE, but the fourth year of this indiction cycle corresponds to 1 September 1050–31 August 1051 CE.[14] The indiction year was the standard dating system familiar to those living under Byzantine rule, while the Anno Mundi, or Year of the World, date was rather bookish, so it is likely that Ibn al-Faḍl got the indiction year right.[15] This would make the date of translation 1050–1051 CE (not 1052, as often reported on the basis of the Anno Mundi date).[16]

The very fact that Ibn al-Faḍl used the indiction year combined with the year reckoned from the creation of the world (Anno Mundi) is itself evidence that helps us situate Ibn al-Faḍl within the cultural landscape of his time. In Byzantine literature and inscriptions it was standard to use these two ways of reckoning in

11. See ch. 2, §2.

12. Ibn al-Faḍl, translation of Basil's *Hexaemeron*, **B** 2, **D** unnumbered, **E** title page, **Q** title page.

13. This formula refers to the Roman-Byzantine indiction year. It is not, as Haddad suggested (*Manuscrits*, 96), part of the Anno Mundi date.

14. Alexander Treiger first pointed out this discrepancy to me.

15. See Grumel, *La chronologie*, 193–203; *ODB*, s.v. "Indiction." For favoring the indiction in cases of disagreement, see also Theophanes, *Chronicle*, trans. Mango and Scott, lxiv–lxv (introduction).

16. For example, Graf, *GCAL*, 2:56; Nasrallah, *Histoire*, 3.1:193, 204.

combination.[17] In the Islamic world, by contrast, Muslims and Christians alike used the Hijri calendar, which was the prevalent system in administration. For example, Yaḥyā ibn Saʿīd of Antioch, a Byzantine Chalcedonian Christian like Ibn al-Faḍl but originally from Cairo who moved to Antioch around 1015, used Hijri years in his historical work.[18]

Manuscripts also assign the exact same date verbatim (6560 AM and the fourth indiction) to Ibn al-Faḍl's *Joy of the Believer* and his Arabic translation of pseudo-Kaisarios's *Questions and Answers* (incorporated into the *Joy of the Believer*).[19] One way to read this evidence would be that 1050–1051 CE was a productive year for Ibn al-Faḍl. Alternatively, perhaps only one of Ibn al-Faḍl's works originally bore this date, and then later scribes added the date to another, undated text.[20] Either way, we may confidently conclude that Ibn al-Faḍl was active in the year 1050–1051.

The ascription also emphasizes that Ibn al-Faḍl made his translation of Basil's *Hexaemeron* from the original Greek. This is a frequent assertion made about Ibn al-Faḍl's translations and seems to have been an important selling point.[21] The way the Greek language is described in this particular ascription in Basil's *Hexaemeron* may be intended to stress a continuity between the ancient Greek and contemporary Byzantine language: the text's original language is called "the Greek (*yūnānīya*) and Roman (*rūmīya*) language," or, in (anachronistic) modern parlance, "the ancient Greek and Byzantine language."[22] This usage is not unique to Ibn al-Faḍl: an Arabic manuscript copied no later than the tenth century and an Arabic translation dated to 772 CE (and preserved in manuscripts copied as early as the ninth

17. E.g., (1) in the colophon of Vat. gr. 463 (a homily collection): "December of the first indiction, in the year 6571 [1062 CE]," trans. Anderson, "Vat. gr. 463," 178; and (2) in the *Life of Saint Symeon the (New) Theologian* by Niketas Stethatos (1005?–ca. 1090), where the numeral 5 miraculously appears and is interpreted as an indiction year presaging the return of the saint's relics to the capital "when the fifth indiction had come to an end, in the year 6560 [August 1052 CE]": §129.2, ed. and trans. (modified) Greenfield, 312–13.

18. He probably did so, despite living under Byzantine rule, because he was continuing the chronicle of Eutychios of Alexandria, who used the Hijri dating system.

19. Vat. ar. 164, fol. 1^r; Vat. Sbath 45, fol. 1^v.

20. I owe this suggestion to Alexander Treiger; see further Roberts, "Re-Translation," 202 and n. 20, 204.

21. E.g., his Arabic translations of the Psalter (Vat. ar. 4 [1711 CE], fol. 1^v), Chrysostom's *Homilies on Hebrews* (Paris ar. 96, fol. 2^v), Isaac the Syrian (Vat. Sbath 649, fol. 3^r), and in his adaptation of Sophronios's *Synodical Letter* (Vat. Sbath 44, fol. 81^v). The word "Roman" (*rūmīya*) is often dropped. These attributions also share other features, such as the phrase "in order to seek recompense and reward."

22. One of the three manuscripts (**E**) omits *rūmīya*, which may represent a later emendation, especially since **E**'s text frequently shows signs of reflecting a scribe's emendations. *Yūnān* (Ionia) in medieval Arabic tends to refer to ancient Greece, while *Rūm* (Ῥωμαῖοι) was used to describe those who are now called Byzantines. See Samir, "Quelques notes"; cited by Treiger, "Earliest Dated Translation," 31 n. 13.

century) refer to the Greek language with the adjective *rūmī*.[23] In a precise parallel with Ibn al-Faḍl's expression, the preface to a collection of texts on divination, in the voice of the astrologer Muḥammad ibn Khālid, declares that the collection that follows was translated (in the mid-ninth century) "from Greek and *rūmīya*" into Arabic.[24]

Nikolaj Serikoff has argued that when applied to language the terms *yūnānī* and *rūmī* referred not only to a chronological distinction (ancient versus contemporary medieval Greek) but also to technical versus demotic registers of Greek.[25] These two senses (chronology and register) are closely related (the high register of Greek cultivated by Byzantines was much closer to certain ancient dialects of Greek than medieval spoken Greek), but making this distinction allowed Serikoff to make an important linguistic observation: words described by Arab authors as *yūnānī* tended to be transliterated from written versions (often via Syriac translations) of technical literature, while words described as *rūmī* tended to reflect contemporary Byzantine pronunciation and occasionally even distinct vocabulary. So perhaps when Ibn al-Faḍl is said to have translated from *yūnānī* and *rūmī*, we are meant to understand it as "written and spoken Greek." In other words, perhaps a translation labeled this way was advertising itself as being based not only on the ancient Greek text but also on knowledge of contemporary spoken Greek. This would correspond especially well to a consistent feature of Ibn al-Faḍl's translations: Arabic transliterations of Greek words and names reliably reproduce the Byzantine pronunciation of those words rather than providing letter-by-letter transliterations or standard Arabic forms—for example, *Iflāṭun*, with emphasis on the penultimate syllable, as in Greek Πλάτων, rather than *Iflāṭūn*, with emphasis on the last syllable.[26]

Patrons and Teachers

Manuscripts of Ibn al-Faḍl's works occasionally preserve the names of those who commissioned them: Ibn al-Faḍl's patrons. These names have been gathered and discussed by Alexander Treiger, who argues that they allow us to glimpse, if dimly, Ibn al-Faḍl's social world and the sort of person who supported his intellectual

23. Binggeli, "Graeco-Arabica," 237; Treiger, "Earliest Dated Translation," 30 n. 5, 31 and n. 13, with references.

24. Trans. Mavroudi, "Translations," 40 n. 53 bottom: *Kitāb al-Dhakhīra* (*The Treasury*).

25. Serikoff, "*Rūmī* and *Yūnānī*," esp. 182; cited by Treiger, "Earliest Dated Translation," 31 n. 13.

26. E.g., in a marginal note on Basil's *Hexaemeron* (where Aristotle's name is also spelled phonetically, *Arisṭāṭālīs*, stress on the penult, as in Greek, rather than the conventional *Arisṭū*); see ch. 8, §1, p. 235. (**E** contains the standard spelling of Plato's name and a variant on Aristotle's, *Arisṭūṭālīs*, the latter probably meant to reflect the omicron in Ἀριστοτέλης; both are probably scribal emendations.) Likewise Ibn al-Faḍl's *Joy of the Believer* (at least in one manuscript): Wakelnig, "Al-Anṭākī's Use," 307–8.

projects.[27] Many were churchmen: a deacon, officials at the patriarchate of Antioch, and a bishop. One was a physician.[28] It is worth taking a closer look at these patrons for what they can tell us about Ibn al-Faḍl and his work.

Ibn al-Faḍl's most distinguished known patron was John (Yūḥannā), metropolitan bishop of Manbij, who commissioned Ibn al-Faḍl's dogmatic work refuting Jacobites and Nestorians, the *Exposition of the Orthodox Faith* (*Sharḥ al-amāna al-mustaqīma*).[29] The town of Manbij (Syriac Mabbûg, Greek Hierapolis) was situated between Aleppo to the southwest and Edessa to the northeast.[30] Its metropolitan status gave the bishopric of Manbij a high rank in the ecclesiastical hierarchy under Antioch's jurisdiction, even though the city was not under Byzantine imperial control in the 1050s.[31] (It is possible that Ibn al-Faḍl received this commission from the bishop of Manbij in the brief period when it was again under Byzantine control, 1068–1071.) John of Manbij was thus an illustrious patron. He may have commissioned Ibn al-Faḍl's work as part of an attempt to establish and defend Chalcedonian Christian dogma in an area where the West-Syrian (Miaphysite) Church was active and influential.[32]

Two further patrons may be clearly identified as church functionaries. First is Nīkīfūr[33] Abū l-Naṣr ibn Buṭrus al-Qubuqlīs, whom Ibn al-Faḍl names as the commissioner of his translation of Isaac the Syrian.[34] As Treiger pointed out, "qubuqlīs" is a transliteration of the Greek ecclesiastical title *kouboukleisios,* held by the patriarch's chamberlain.[35] The *kouboukleisios* was a very high-ranking official within Antioch's patriarchal administration. The patriarch took a personal interest in appointments to this high office, as we may infer from the displeasure that Peter III, patriarch of Antioch (ca. 1052–1057),[36] expressed in a letter to Michael Keroularios, patriarch of Constantinople, when Keroularios unilaterally conferred the title of *kouboukleisios* upon a deacon of Antioch, one Christodoulos Hagio-

27. Treiger, "Christian Graeco-Arabica," 207–8; Treiger, "ʿAbdallāh," 90.

28. Treiger, "Christian Graeco-Arabica," 208.

29. Wannous, "Abdallah," 262–64.

30. Goossens, *Hiérapolis,* 4.

31. Manbij was captured by Emperor John I Tzimiskes (r. 969–976) in 974; the Mirdāsids of Aleppo in 1025; Romanos IV Diogenes (r. 1068–1071) in 1068; and the Seljuk ruler Alp Arslan in 1071. *EI*², s.v. "Manbij," 6:379; Goossens, *Hiérapolis,* 184; Todt and Vest, *Syria,* 1264–81.

32. This would be a plausible motivation even if it should turn out that John of Manbij was residing in Antioch (rather than his episcopal see) at the time he commissioned this work. I thank Maria Mavroudi for raising this possibility.

33. Nasrallah does not give this part of his name, but Treiger ("ʿAbdallāh," 90) does. "Nīkīfūr" transliterates Νικηφόρος. "Abū l-Naṣr" translates the same name: Graf, *GCAL,* 2:58.

34. See ch. 4, §4, pp. 141–42, 143.

35. Treiger, "ʿAbdallāh," 90; Treiger, "Christian Graeco-Arabica," 208 n. 84 with references; *ODB,* s.v. "Kouboukleisios." Cf. "al-Qabqalīs": Graf, *GCAL,* 2:58; Nasrallah, *Histoire,* 3.1:193.

36. Martin-Hisard, "Pierre III."

stephanites.[37] Attested *kouboukleisioi* include a legate sent on a difficult mission to Georgia by Patriarch Theodore III of Antioch (r. 1034–1042),[38] the honoree of an epitaph dated 1046 and preserved in the Museum of Antakya,[39] and the scribe of a Greek manuscript completed ca. 1050–1052.[40] One version of Ibn al-Faḍl's preface to Isaac the Syrian also mentions two brothers of this Nikephoros Abū l-Naṣr the *kouboukleisios:* Abū l-Ḥasan Simʿān (Symeon) and Abū l-Khayr Mīkhāʾīl (Michael).[41] They too may have commissioned or otherwise supported Ibn al-Faḍl's work in some capacity.

The second *kouboukleisios* known to have been a patron of Ibn al-Faḍl is "the sheikh" Abū l-Faḍl Salāma ibn al-Mufarraj, a deacon, *kouboukleisios,* and physician (*mutaṭabbib*), who commissioned Ibn al-Faḍl's translation of John Chrysostom's *Homilies on Matthew* (or perhaps the Gospel of Matthew alone), according to Ibn al-Faḍl's preface.[42] That this *kouboukleisios* was also a physician suggests the profile of a "professional" (as Treiger puts it), not a learned aristocrat but someone who used his education to earn a living. It is not unusual to see churchmen trained in medicine.[43]

About two other patrons we lack specific titles or other details. Abū l-Fatḥ ʿĪsā ibn Idrīs (or, in another manuscript, Darīs) commissioned Ibn al-Faḍl's translation of John of Thessaloniki's *Encomium to Saint Demetrios.*[44] Ibn al-Faḍl refers to him

37. Grumel et al., *Les regestes,* fasc. 3, nos. 860–61; cited by *ODB,* s.v. "Koubouleisios"; Noble and Treiger, "Christian Arabic Theology," 374 n. 14; Todt, "Region," 261 and n. 124. See also Darrouzès, *Recherches sur les Offikia,* 39–44; cited by Dagron and Feissel, "Inscriptions," 461.

38. Basil the Grammarian: Todt, *Region,* 665 and n. 131.

39. 2 January, AM 6554; ed. Dagron and Feissel, "Inscriptions," 460–61.

40. Theophylact; Oxford, Bodleian, Holkham gr. 6: Jenkins and Mango, "Synodicon," 231, 233; cited by Noble and Treiger, "Christian Arabic Theology," 374 n. 14.

41. Ch. 4, §4, p. 142; Noble and Treiger, "Christian Arabic Theology," 374 n. 13; Treiger, "Christian Graeco-Arabica," 208.

42. Sinai ar. 76 (thirteenth century), fol. 8r: "*saʾalanī tarjamata kitābika*"; cited by Treiger, "Christian Graeco-Arabica," 207–8. (In the manuscript I read "Mufarraj" instead of "Muʿarraj.") This manuscript contains a preface (where this patron's name is mentioned) that is labeled as Ibn al-Faḍl's preface to his translation of Chrysostom's *Homilies on Matthew.* But, as Joe Glynias kindly pointed out to me, the rest of the manuscript does not contain Chrysostom's homilies but rather the four Gospels. See Atiya, *Fahāris,* 150–53. The preface is addressed entirely to Christ and speaks of Ibn al-Faḍl being the "translator" (*nāqil*) of "your book" (fol. 7v; see also the passage already cited). Only at the very end does the preface mention Chrysostom (fol. 8v), after first mentioning Matthew. The final line about Chrysostom could have been added by a later scribe. On the other hand, the preface, despite its focus on the Gospel of Matthew rather than Chrysostom's exegesis, may nonetheless have been intended for Chrysostom's homilies, as the manuscript says it was.

43. Other contemporary examples include Ibn al-Ṭayyib (Graf, *GCAL,* 2:160) and his student Ibn Buṭlān (ibid., 2:191).

44. The fact that Ibn al-Faḍl translated this text was only recently discovered by Treiger, "Christian Graeco-Arabica," 208 and n. 86 (who also published the patron's name); see ch. 2, p. 72, n. 186.

respectfully as "my lord the wise and learned sheikh."[45] Thus Ibn al-Faḍl portrays this patron as a scholar. The absence of an ecclesiastical title suggests a layman. Likewise, Ibn al-Faḍl names Abū Zakariyā' ibn Salāma[46] in his preface to the Psalter as the one who commissioned the translation.[47] Ibn al-Faḍl does not mention a title or anything else about this patron but portrays him as a pious Christian and addresses him with respectful expressions of the sort typically found in Arabic formal letters.[48]

All this situates Ibn al-Faḍl in prominent social circles of Byzantine Antioch, primarily urban and ecclesiastical rather than monastic.[49] The two *kouboukleisioi* suggest a close connection between the patriarchate of Antioch and Ibn al-Faḍl's translation activities.

Two further names can be linked to Ibn al-Faḍl: his teachers of Arabic and Greek. Samuel Noble and Alexander Treiger discovered these names in the marginalia that Ibn al-Faḍl added to his translations.[50] (We will return to marginalia in chapter 5.)

First, his teacher of Greek. Ibn al-Faḍl, in a note on his *Book of the Garden* (a translation of a Greek wisdom collection known today as the *Loci communes*),[51] names this teacher as one Simʿān (Symeon) al-'bmysqn (probably a title)[52] ibn al-Shanīḥī (?),[53] or "Symeon the [. . .] son of [. . .]." Treiger has recently conjectured that this might in fact be the Byzantine intellectual Symeon Seth (fl. second half of the eleventh century), a native of Antioch who was himself a translator—from Arabic into Greek.[54] Should this tantalizing identification prove correct, it would link Ibn al-Faḍl to the highest intellectual circles of Constantinople. Whoever this Symeon was, the way Ibn al-Faḍl refers to him is indicative of how he studied Greek texts with this teacher. After a quotation from "the Theologian" (Gregory of

45. Ch. 4, pp. 138–39 and n. 42.

46. Or Zakhariyā *and* Yūḥannā ibn Salāma, the reading of New Haven, Yale Beinecke, ar. 349, fol. 181ᵛ, as Samuel Noble observed; cited by Treiger, "ʿAbdallāh," 90; Noble and Treiger, "Christian Arabic Theology," 374 n. 12. As I read the evidence, the original preface probably referred to only one patron named Abū Zakariyā' Yūḥannā ibn Salāma. See ch. 4, p. 127, n. 11.

47. Treiger, "Christian Graeco-Arabica," 207.

48. Ch. 4, p. 127, n. 12.

49. Treiger, "Christian Graeco-Arabica," 208.

50. Treiger, "ʿAbdallāh," 89.

51. For Ibn al-Faḍl's *Book of the Garden*, his translation of the *Loci communes*, see ch. 2, §4, pp. 62–64.

52. Treiger reads *al-'ymsyqn*. The two, *'ymsyqn* and *'bmysqn*, differ in their consonant skeletons only by inverting the positions of the *s* and the *y*: *-sy-* versus *-ys-*.

53. Or al-Sabīḥī, or al-Sabnakhī (Treiger, tentatively).

54. Emending Shanīḥī to Sīthī: Συμεὼν ὁ (τοῦ) Σήθ. I am grateful to Alexander Treiger for this suggestion. Arabic-Greek translator: Condylis-Bassoukos, *Stéphanitès*. Other alternate readings of the consonantal skeleton: al-Manbijī, or a toponymic referring to Shīḥa, "[a] village near Cyrrhus" in northern Syria: Thomas A. Carlson, "Shīḥa," *The Syriac Gazetteer*, http://syriaca.org/place/1503.html (entry published 30 June 2014).

Nazianzos), Ibn al-Faḍl remarked, in a note on his translation, that this quotation was from Gregory's eulogy for Saint Basil of Caesarea, a text that he had read and studied in Greek with his teacher Symeon. As Ibn al-Faḍl's note makes clear, Symeon was no longer alive when the note was written.[55] Ibn al-Faḍl's emphasis on the fact that he read the text *in Greek* suggests that this was not his native language.

Ibn al-Faḍl's teacher of Arabic was named Abū l-ʿAlāʾ. In a different note on the same translation, Ibn al-Faḍl mentions that he studied Ibn al-Sikkīt's *Correct Diction* (*Iṣlāḥ al-manṭiq*), on Arabic morphology, with one Abū l-ʿAlāʾ.[56] Treiger has suggested that this teacher may well be the famous blind poet Abū l-ʿAlāʾ al-Maʿarrī (973–1057),[57] who lived near Antioch in Maʿarrat al-Nuʿmān (southeast of Antioch and southwest of Aleppo), and who is said to have visited Antioch as a young man.[58] Abū l-ʿAlāʾ al-Maʿarrī also visited a monastery near Latakia (even closer to Maʿarrat al-Nuʿmān), where, as the bio-bibliographer Ibn al-Qifṭī (d. 1248) relates, the poet learned philosophy from a monk, an experience that exposed him to "doubts" that he was unprepared to counter.[59]

Treiger's plausible inference that the name Abū l-ʿAlāʾ refers here to the famous Muslim poet nevertheless rests for the time being on circumstantial evidence and the relative rarity of the name Abū l-ʿAlāʾ.[60] It is therefore worth noting that while the name is uncommon, it is not unique to the Muslim poet. The index to Georg Graf's handbook on Christian Arabic literature lists four individuals by that name, of whom one (a Nestorian Christian physician named Abū l-ʿAlāʾ Ṣāʿid ibn al-Ḥasan) was certainly Ibn al-Faḍl's contemporary.[61]

55. This note by Ibn al-Faḍl is discussed further (with transcription and translation) in ch. 5, §1, p. 157, at n. 23.

56. Treiger, "ʿAbdallāh," 89; Treiger, "Christian Graeco-Arabica," 208. See ch. 5, §1, pp. 153–54.

57. Smoor says that he died in 1058 (*EI*², s.v. "al-Maʿarrī"). Ibn al-Qifṭī, *Inbāh*, ed. Ibrāhīm, 1:109: Friday 13 Rabīʿ I 449, but this Hijrī date is equivalent to Tuesday 20 May 1057. Ibn al-ʿAdīm, *Bughya*, ed. Zakkār, 908: the night of Friday 3 Rabīʿ I 449 = Saturday 10 May 1057. Ibn al-ʿAdīm's date seems more plausible since the Friday-Saturday discrepancy is a single day.

58. Treiger, "ʿAbdallāh," 89; Noble and Treiger, "Christian Arabic Theology," 375–76; Treiger, "Christian Graeco-Arabica," 208.

59. Ibn al-Qifṭī, *Inbāh*, ed. Ibrāhīm, 1:84. The monastery in Latakia was the Monastery of the Shroud, Dayr al-Fārūs. As the editor notes, this was "among the [monastic] houses of the Byzantines" (*min diyārāt al-Rūm*). Ibn al-ʿAdīm insists that Abū l-ʿAlāʾ would not have sought out libraries there or in Antioch: *EI*², s.v. "al-Maʿarrī."

60. The case is strengthened, as Alexander Treiger has pointed out to me, by Abū l-ʿAlāʾ's own reference to Ibn al-Sikkīt's *Iṣlāḥ al-manṭiq*: Noble and Treiger, "Christian Arabic Theology," 376 nn. 19, 20.

61. Graf, *GCAL*, 5:4 (index), 2:324, 195, 178–79, 435–36, respectively. (1) Abū l-ʿAlāʾ Saʿīd: a.k.a. Gabriel ibn Tarīk, Coptic Patriarch, r. 1131–1145; (2) Abū l-ʿAlāʾ Ṣāʿid ibn al-Ḥasan: Nestorian physician, d. 1072; (3) Abū l-ʿAlāʾ Ṣāʿid ibn Sahl: another eleventh-century Nestorian physician, brother of Elias of Nisibis, addressee of a letter from Elias about a theological debate before a vizier in 1026; (4) Abū l-ʿAlāʾ al-Ṣāʾigh: a Jewish scholar with whom Abū l-Fakhr, who was born Jewish but converted to (Coptic) Christianity, corresponded.

If Ibn al-Faḍl was indeed the student of the famous Muslim Arab poet Abū l-ʿAlāʾ al-Maʿarrī, he may have known other elite Muslims, as well as Nestorian Christians (as Noble and Treiger observe), such as the Antiochian philosopher and physician Ibn al-Ṭayyib (active in Baghdad), whose student Ibn Buṭlān traveled extensively and eventually retired to a monastery near Antioch. Ibn Buṭlān knew Abū l-ʿAlāʾ well and may have been at the poet's side during his final hours.[62]

Beyond this, we are more or less in the dark about Ibn al-Faḍl's intellectual interactions with contemporaries, at least for now. Did the learned deacon of Antioch know personally or read the work of an ascetic author like Nikon of the Black Mountain, who spent time at the Monastery of Saint Symeon on the Wondrous Mountain?[63] What sort of contact did Ibn al-Faḍl have with other translators and bilingual intellectuals in the region like the abbot Antonios of Saint Symeon, the *protospatharios* Ibrāhīm ibn Yūḥannā al-Anṭākī, or—whether or not he was his Greek teacher—Symeon Seth?[64]

Influences

Ibn al-Faḍl was a prolific theologian and translator.[65] His theological works, such as his *Discourse on the Holy Trinity,* were conceptually sophisticated and drew extensively on the Greek and Arabic philosophical tradition, ancient and contemporary.[66] At various points throughout his works he cites a range of Greek and Arabic philosophers, including John Philoponos (d. after 567), Abū Bakr al-Rāzī (d. 925 or 935), al-Fārābī (d. 950), and Ibn al-Ṭayyib (d. 1043).[67] Ibn al-Faḍl quotes and paraphrases passages from Philoponos's lost book *Against Aristotle on the Eternity of the World,*[68] Philoponos's partially extant book *Against Proklos on the Eternity of the World,*[69] and al-Fārābī's *Enumeration of the Sciences* (*Iḥṣāʾ al-ʿulūm*).[70]

62. Noble and Treiger, "Christian Arabic Theology," 376 and n. 21.

63. Doens, "Nicon."

64. Todt, "Antioch," 184–87.

65. For his works, see Noble and Treiger, "Christian Arabic Theology," 377–79; Treiger, "ʿAbdallāh"; Graf, *GCAL,* 2:52–64; Nasrallah, *Histoire,* 3.1:191–229; Samir, "Bibliographie (2)," 210–14; "Bibliographie (corr.)," 306.

66. Noble and Treiger, "Christian Arabic Theology," 379–85; Noble, "Doctrine."

67. Noble, "Doctrine," 293. Ibn al-Ṭayyib: Faultless, "Ibn al-Ṭayyib."

68. In his *Book of Benefit,* §14, as shown by Rashed, "Problem."

69. In his *Joy of the Believer,* as discovered by Wakelnig, "Al-Anṭākī's Use." (I owe this reference to Samuel Noble.) The beginning of Philoponos's *Against Proklos* is lost in the original Greek; one of Ibn al-Faḍl's quotations comes from this lost beginning: Wakelnig, "Al-Anṭākī's Use," 297.

70. In his *Book of Benefit,* as Maroun Aouad has recently discovered: Aouad et al., "Les manuscrits de philosophie," 195 and n. 4. I am grateful to Emma Gannagé for alerting me to Aouad's work on Ibn al-Faḍl. See also Treiger, "ʿAbdallāh," 95.

Similarly, as Rachid Haddad has observed, Ibn al-Faḍl was open to citing the arguments of more recent Christian authors of different confessions (that is, not only fellow Byzantine Chalcedonians but also Miaphysites and Nestorians, for example). In addition to Ibn al-Ṭayyib (a Nestorian), he cites Abū Rā'iṭa al-Takrītī (a probably eighth/ninth-century defender of Christianity against Muslim critiques, and refuter of Chalcedonian doctrines) and the *Apology of al-Kindī* (a probably pseudonymous treatise possibly written in the eighth/ninth century whose confession is unclear but may have been Nestorian or Miaphysite).[71] This should not be taken as a sign that Ibn al-Faḍl (the author of a refutation of Miaphysite and Nestorian doctrines) approved of non-Chalcedonian theology, of course. Instead he was simply engaging in a practice typical of Byzantine and medieval Middle Eastern scholars, drawing on the ideas of other scholars, past and present, where they were in agreement (Miaphysite, Nestorian, Muslim, or pagan though they might be).[72]

Later Legacy

Though few English-speaking readers will have heard of Ibn al-Faḍl, he was and is an important author in the Arabic-speaking Christian communities of the Near East.

The thirteenth-century Coptic-Miaphysite Egyptian scholar Ibn al-Rāhib (in the autograph copy of his Arabic *Book of Demonstration*) quotes Ibn al-Faḍl approvingly, calling him "learned" (*fāḍil*).[73] Though Ibn al-Rāhib does not say where the quotation is from, we may identify it with the end of one of Ibn al-Faḍl's comments on his translation of the *Encomium to Demetrios* by John of Thessaloniki.[74] This underscores Ibn al-Faḍl's legacy not only as a translator but also as a commentator.

Another thirteenth-century Coptic-Miaphysite scholar, Ibn al-ʿAssāl, refers to Ibn al-Faḍl in such a way that suggests that his translations were well known and well regarded. Ibn al-ʿAssāl characterizes the translation style of Theophilos ibn Tawfīl (a Damascene bishop of Cairo who, on Ibn al-ʿAssāl's testimony, translated the Gospels from Greek into Arabic before 1046–1047 CE) by comparing him to Ibn al-Faḍl: Theophilos "was skilled in the Arabic language, and I think," he continues, "that Ibn al-Faḍl imitated him in his exposition (*īrād*)."[75] This passage

71. Haddad, *La Trinité*, 75; cited by Noble, "Doctrine," 293. Keating, "Abū Rā'iṭa"; Bottini, "*Apology*."

72. Mavroudi, "Licit," 433–36. I am grateful to Maria Mavroudi for sharing this article with me before publication.

73. Vat. ar. 104, fol. 4v. Nasrallah (*Histoire*, 3.1:229) reports that Ibn al-Rāhib called Ibn al-Faḍl a "sage" (*al-ḥakīm*). On Ibn al-Rāhib, see Sidarus, "Ibn al-Rāhib."

74. See ch. 5, §3, p. 170, n. 71.

75. MacDonald, "Ibn al-ʿAssāl's Arabic Version," 377 (text), 385 (trans., modified); cited by Graf, *GCAL*, 2:51.

seems to presuppose that Ibn al-Faḍl's style is famous and well known, for Ibn al-ʿAssāl's aim here is to introduce Theophilos and his style, not Ibn al-Faḍl. To help the reader imagine Theophilos's style, he explains that it was probably the model for Ibn al-Faḍl's approach to translating. By the thirteenth century, we may conclude, Ibn al-Faḍl was a well-known translator of Greek texts into Arabic even among non-Chalcedonians.

The seventeenth-century Greek-Orthodox patriarch of Antioch Makarios III ibn al-Zaʿīm (r. 1647–1672), himself a Greek-Arabic translator, was especially full of praise for Ibn al-Faḍl and saw him as a crucial figure in the revival of Greek letters under Muslim rule.[76] His interest in preserving and copying the works of Ibn al-Faḍl is part of why so many of them survive.[77]

Even today Ibn al-Faḍl continues to attract attention from Arabic-speaking Christians, as attested by a recent notice about Ibn al-Faḍl in the bulletin of the Chalcedonian-Orthodox Archdiocese of Mount Lebanon.[78]

2 BYZANTINE ANTIOCH

There has been growing interest among historians, archaeologists, and philologists in the century that Antioch and its hinterland spent under Byzantine rule (969–1084).[79] This has resulted in a number of foundational studies on aspects of Byzantine Antioch, from administration (civil and military), politics, diplomacy, and the Byzantine Church[80] to urban infrastructure and city layout,[81] cultural ties between Antioch and Constantinople,[82] and Antioch's Greek-Arabic translation movement itself.[83] These past studies make it possible to sketch the outlines of the city where Ibn al-Faḍl lived and worked.

In 1051 CE, Antioch lay, as it always had, on the left bank of the Orontes River, spreading up to the nearby slopes of Mount Silpion and Mount Staurin. Across the

76. Walbiner, "Preserving the Past," 436–38; cited by Noble and Treiger, *Orthodox Church*, 37 n. 145. On Makarios ibn al-Zaʿīm, see also Rassi, "Le 'Livre de l'abeille.'" For his many words of praise for Ibn al-Faḍl, see Nasrallah, *Histoire*, 3.1:191 n. 1. I thank Maria Mavroudi for pointing out the connection between Makarios III's translation activities and his appreciation of Ibn al-Faḍl's.

77. Noble and Treiger, *Orthodox Church*, 37.

78. Bulletin of 17 September 2017; posted and translated by Samuel Noble, http://araborthodoxy.blogspot.com/2017/09/the-deacon-abdallah-ibn-al-fadl-al.html (18 September 2017), accessed 26 April 2018.

79. Byzantine Antioch's historical importance: Mavroudi, "Occult Sciences," 52–53; Mavroudi, "Greek Language," 304–5.

80. Todt, *Region;* Todt, "Region"; Todt, "Antioch"; Todt and Vest, *Syria*, 539–663.

81. Eger, "(Re)Mapping Medieval Antioch"; see also *Antioch-on-the-Orontes.*

82. Kontouma, "Jean III"; trans. in Kontouma, *John of Damascus*, ch. 2. I owe this reference to Maria Mavroudi.

83. Treiger, "Christian Graeco-Arabica."

river to the north and east sprawled the Amuq Plain, dotted with marshland around a central lake with an abundant stock of freshwater eel.[84] To the north rose the Amanus Mountains (a.k.a. the Black Mountain), laced with rising valleys and mountain passes leading to the town of Alexandretta and on to the region of Cilicia. Following the Orontes southwest and downstream from Antioch, one sailed by Daphne (present-day Harbiye) perched to the left on a plateau, with its ancient spring and country villas, then continued through canyons leading past the Wondrous Mountain on the right and the foothills of Mount Kasion on the left, then out through a small plain to the Mediterranean Sea.

From the vantage point of 1051, Antioch was an ancient city, founded over 1,300 years earlier in 300 BCE by Seleukos I Nikator, a Hellenistic successor to the great Alexander. Antioch gradually took over the role of regional capital from Seleukeia in Pieria by the sea and other competitors, drawing the surrounding territory into its administrative embrace. Hellenistic kings left their mark on the city in the form of building projects, elegant and useful monumental propaganda for the ages. Roman administrators did much the same. Antioch became an important Roman provincial capital, attracting visitors, official and unofficial, from afar.[85]

The centuries had left their mark on Antioch. The rectilinear grid of the Hellenistic, then Roman city was still in use, but no longer in the same way.[86] After a major earthquake in 528 CE Justinian renamed the city Theoupolis—City of God.[87] In manuscripts copied half a millennium later we still find the city being called *madīnat Allāh Anṭākiya*, "Antioch, City of God."[88]

First-millennium CE Antioch is perhaps best known as a major center of Christianity—a result of its prominence as a Roman city. The apostles Peter and Paul were active in Antioch, and early on, Antioch's bishop acquired the title of patriarch, along with the bishops of Rome and Alexandria. (In the fifth century, Constantinople and Jerusalem also acquired patriarchal rank.) Under Muslim rule, during middle Byzantine rule, after falling to the Seljuks and then the Crusaders, and up until the present day (under the Mamluks, Ottomans, European colonial powers, and Turkey), Antioch has remained an important ecclesiastical reference point for Chalcedonian and non-Chalcedonian Christians alike.[89]

After the Byzantines surrendered the city to Arab-Muslim conquerors in 638 CE,[90] the new rulers gradually reshaped Antioch according to a late-antique

84. De Giorgi, *Ancient Antioch*, 71.
85. De Giorgi, 71; Matthews, *Journey*.
86. Kennedy, "Antioch"; De Giorgi, *Ancient Antioch*.
87. Malalas, *Chronographia*, 18.29, ed. Thurn, 371 = Bonn 443; cited by De Giorgi, *Antioch*, 67 n. 4.
88. Sinai ar. 452 (twelfth or thirteenth century), fols. 6^v–7^r.
89. Papadopoulos, *Ἱστορία τῆς Ἐκκλησίας Ἀντιοχείας*.
90. Eger, "(Re)Mapping Medieval Antioch," 98.

urban model familiar from other early Islamic cities in Syria, Palestine, and Iraq.[91] This model favored orchards and urban gardens within the walls, softening the hard pavement of city life with the comforts and pleasures of the countryside.[92] This granted the city a certain "self-sufficiency," though plenty of grain, oil, wine, and other fruits of the land continued to make their way through local markets to the hungry metropolis.[93]

Under Muslim rule, Antioch's administrative prominence diminished as other cities eclipsed it in the caliphate's administrative structure. Damascus became the capital not only of Syria but of the entire Islamic empire under the Umayyads. Antioch was placed under the control of a regional administration seated in Emesa (Ḥimṣ), and then Chalkis (Qinnasrīn).[94] Northern Syria itself became a border region as the fluctuating frontier between the Islamic and Byzantine empires gradually stabilized around Cilicia and northern Syria and Mesopotamia under the early Abbasids.[95] Within this region other towns like Manbij rose to prominence.[96] As the Abbasid caliphate gradually disintegrated in the late ninth and tenth centuries, Antioch passed into the hands of the Ṭulūnids of Egypt (in 878) and the Ḥamdānids of Aleppo (in 944–945).[97] Throughout, Antioch never lost its strategic importance as a trading hub on the road from Syria to Cilicia and Anatolia,[98] a road that led, eventually, to the great capital city that loomed large in the minds of medieval populations, from western Europe to the Middle East: Constantinople, the New Rome.[99]

In the tenth and early eleventh centuries, Byzantine power and prestige were growing. Antioch, taken by a Byzantine army in 969, was a crowning achievement of Byzantine military expansion. It would remain under Byzantine control for over a century, until it fell to the Seljuk Turks in 1084—and fourteen years later to the Crusaders in 1098. Under Byzantine rule, the city and its hinterland flourished, continuing its major commercial role, while imperial resources flowed to the city to support the army, administration, and a civic building program.[100]

The imperial government exerted careful control over Antioch. Nonetheless, the city maintained close informal ties with the lands of Muslim Syria, Palestine,

91. Kennedy, "From Polis."

92. Eger argues against reading intramural "green space" as evidence of decline by comparing it to parks and urban gardens in modern cities: "(Re)Mapping Medieval Antioch," 123, 125–26.

93. Eger, "(Re)Mapping Medieval Antioch," 104–5, 127–28.

94. Eger, 98.

95. Vasiliev, *Byzance et les Arabes;* Honigmann, *Die Ostgrenze;* Sivers, "Taxes."

96. Todt, "Antioch," 173.

97. Todt, 173.

98. Eger, "(Re)Mapping Medieval Antioch," 98–99; Jacoby, "Silk Economics," 231.

99. Ciggaar, *Western Travellers,* ch. 2; El Cheikh, *Byzantium Viewed.*

100. Eger, "(Re)Mapping Medieval Antioch," 103–5.

Egypt, and Iraq. It received Christian visitors from throughout the Near East, and Muslims too. Trade with Aleppo (under Muslim rule) was encouraged.[101]

Government

Byzantine Antioch was governed by a military governor (δοῦξ, from Latin *dux*, whence English "duke") appointed by the emperor.[102] This governor governed a district (δουκάτον) stretching from Cilicia and Marʿash (Germanikeia) to the west and north, and down along the coast past Alexandretta, Antioch, and Latakia to Ṭarṭūs, with its southern extremity not far from the present-day border between the nation-states of Syria and Lebanon. Antioch was the district's capital (map 2).[103] Emperors tended to appoint their most competent generals to govern the district, attesting to its pivotal place in the Byzantine imperial system.[104] Many of Antioch's other top-level administrators were also appointed by the emperor, and the rest of the government tended to be staffed by bureaucrats from or at least trained in Constantinople.[105] The governing class in Constantinople took great interest in events and developments in Antioch, and Byzantine officials remained in close contact with the capital.[106]

Byzantine governors of Antioch made major investments in the city's fortifications, as well as basic infrastructure, such as pipes, aqueducts, and city streets.[107] For a century and more they defended Antioch from various attacks and, using the city as a base, engaged in diplomatic and military campaigns with and against the Muslim rulers of Aleppo (the Ḥamdānids and after them the Mirdāsids),[108] the Ismaili-Shiite Fatimid caliphs (based in Cairo but with an empire extending from North Africa to Palestine, Syria, and Arabia),[109] and the Kingdom of Georgia (a.k.a. Iberia).[110] Byzantine imperial officials in Antioch and other eastern districts were also confronted with the question of how to approach conflicts that arose between Byzantine Chalcedonian churchmen and the Armenian- and Syriac-speaking Christians of the conquered territories, many of whom were Miaphysites of the West-Syrian Jacobite Church and the Armenian Church.[111]

101. Eger, 103.
102. Todt, "Antioch," 176–79.
103. Todt, 178–79.
104. Todt, 177; Cheynet, "Michel Psellos," 412, 420.
105. Cheynet, 412.
106. Cheynet, 412. Cheynet's main evidence is Psellos's correspondence with officials in Antioch, along with lead seals.
107. Todt, "Antioch," 180.
108. Canard, *Histoire;* Cheynet, "Michel Psellos," 418.
109. Walker, "Byzantine Victory"; Cheynet, "Basil II," 97.
110. Cheynet, 98–102.
111. Dagron, "Minorités"; Mavroudi, "Licit," 433–34.

The Patriarchate of Antioch

In the eleventh century, the Byzantine Chalcedonian patriarchate of Antioch was a large and complex organization, administered by a hierarchy of bishops. Theoretically, the patriarch's authority stretched from Syria to Georgia to Damascus to Baghdad to "Romagyris" in central Asia.[112] The head of the organization—the patriarch of Antioch—was such a crucial figure that the Byzantine emperor and the patriarch of Constantinople made every effort to control the selection of new patriarchs of Antioch, and occasionally to depose patriarchs to be replaced by candidates of their own choosing. In this they vied with the bishops under Antioch's jurisdiction.[113]

In part because of this rivalry between Syrian and Constantinopolitan control over the patriarchate, there has been a tendency in modern scholarship to see the Antiochian Church and churchmen as not only politically but also culturally different from the Byzantine churchmen, administrators, and bureaucrats pulling strings from Constantinople.[114] This difference is implicitly emphasized by the prevailing use of "Melkite" to refer to Arabic-speaking Christians, in contradistinction to Greek-speaking Byzantine Chalcedonian Christians, who are in this modern nomenclature typically referred to using either the neologism "Byzantine" or else the self-description "Orthodox" ("correctly believing," a term applied by just about every medieval Christian confession to itself).

On the one hand, it is true that many Syrian churchmen were native speakers of Arabic or Syriac while their Constantinopolitan counterparts were native speakers of Greek, and that this linguistic difference was not lost on eleventh-century churchmen. Chalcedonian Christians in Syria and Palestine, in the absence of close ties to Constantinople over centuries of Muslim rule, had maintained divergent local traditions, most prominently in the liturgy.[115] Nevertheless, this approach risks treating "Byzantine" and "Melkite" as essential, immutable categories. Certainly the Byzantine conquest of Antioch resulted in a dramatic shift of power dynamics in the patriarchate of Antioch. But it seems more plausible to imagine

112. Perhaps Nishapur or Merv in Khurāsān or Tashkent in Transoxania. Using a range of contemporary sources, Klaus-Peter Todt ("*Notitia*," 177–83) has offered a reconstruction of Antioch's episcopal hierarchy.

113. Todt, "Region," 256–66.

114. Kennedy ("Melkite Church," 339) wrote of a "loss of identity" among "Melkites" after the Byzantine conquest of northern Syria, whose signs were that "the native hierarchy were replaced by Greeks while the local liturgy was replaced by Constantinopolitan forms." He concluded, "It is a measure of the independent identity of the Melkite church that it thrived when the Muslims were in the ascendant but was threatened by Byzantine successes."

115. For the Byzantine Chalcedonian Church of Antioch under early Islamic rule, see Papadopoulos, *Ἱστορία τῆς Ἐκκλησίας Ἀντιοχείας*, 736–812; Kennedy, "Melkite Church"; Griffith, *Church in the Shadow*.

that at least some local Arabic-speaking clergy (whether out of pragmatic opportunism or a preexisting appreciation for the Byzantine Church and Byzantine culture) were in favor of cultivating closer ties with Constantinople. In any case, as we shall see in chapter 3, by the mid-eleventh century Arabic-speaking "Melkites" like Ibn al-Faḍl could commit their careers to actively promoting an intellectual program grounded in Byzantine culture and the contemporary Byzantine ecclesiastical curriculum. Was that impulse a new development caused by Byzantine initiatives? Or were there simply more resources under Byzantine rule to support the work of people like Ibn al-Faḍl, or like the Syriac-speaking Byzantine Chalcedonian compiler of the fine parchment manuscript now at the Vatican containing a Syriac synaxarion and produced at the Monastery of Panteleemon on the Black Mountain near Antioch in 1041 CE as part of an effort to import Constantinopolitan liturgical practices to Antioch?[116] This seems to me an open question.

What is clear is that imperial officials in the capital kept in close contact with ecclesiastical administrators, just as they did with civil and military administrators. From Psellos's letter collection, we learn that the Byzantine scholar and bureaucrat was in correspondence with two patriarchs of Antioch, Theodosios III Chrysoberges (before August 1057–ca. 1059) and Aimilianos (ca. 1059–1078 or 1079).[117]

Around the time Ibn al-Faḍl was active (ca. 1050), the patriarch of Antioch was Basil II (1042–ca. 1051; not to be confused with the emperor of the same name). We know almost nothing about Patriarch Basil II, only that like several of his predecessors he would later come to be venerated in Antioch as a saint, and that his lead seals bore the inscription "Basil, patriarch of the City of God, Antioch the Great."[118]

Because of the limited sources, there is some confusion about who succeeded Basil on the patriarchal throne. Most lists of patriarchs of Antioch say that the next patriarch was Peter III (ca. 1052–1057).[119] This straightforward narrative of succession, however, is complicated by a Synodikon manuscript copied in Antioch in 1050–1052.[120] Produced by an official at the patriarchate of Antioch, it refers to "our patriarch Sophronios."[121] However we may explain the unique appearance of this

116. Vat. syr. 21; Brock, "Syriac Manuscripts," 61; cited by Todt, "Region," 263 n. 133. Adoption of the Byzantine liturgy in Antioch under Byzantine rule: Sauget, *Premières recherches,* 21–22. Byzantine liturgical influences on Syriac Miaphysite liturgy: Varghese, "Byzantine Occupation."

117. Grumel, "Le patriarcat," 142–45, corrected by Martin-Hisard, "Pierre III"; Cheynet, "Michel Psellos," 413–14.

118. Todt, *Region,* 665 and n. 136.

119. Martin-Hisard, "Pierre III," where the insertion of a Patriarch "John IV" after Peter III is shown to be spurious.

120. See n. 40.

121. Jenkins and Mango, 233–34.

Sophronios,[122] we are left with the sense that the patriarchate of Antioch around 1051 was at a moment of transition.

If Ibn al-Faḍl's career continued into the following years, then it overlapped with the episcopate of Peter III of Antioch, known among historians for his correspondence with the patriarch of Constantinople concerning the conflict with the Latins—the so-called Schism of 1054—over the use of unleavened bread for the Eucharist and other doctrinal and canonical issues.[123] Peter was appointed by Emperor Constantine IX Monomachos (r. 1042–1055), a native of Antioch like Peter himself.[124] Peter, in a letter written on the occasion of his consecration as Antioch's bishop, made much of his Antiochian origins.[125] Even if we know that Ibn al-Faḍl had already been producing translations before Peter arrived in Antioch as its new chief prelate, we may wonder whether the new patriarch played some role in encouraging the work of Greek-Arabic translators like Ibn al-Faḍl. It is of particular interest in this connection that in his letter Peter writes that when he was young he left Antioch for Constantinople out of "love of letters" and there in the capital received a well-rounded "general education" (*enkyklios paideusis*).[126]

As the next two chapters argue, the character of Ibn al-Faḍl's translation program suggests close affinities with the cultural priorities of patriarchs like Peter appointed from Constantinople. And in light of Ibn al-Faḍl's erudition in Greek and Arabic letters, Ibn al-Faḍl must have had access to some significant libraries, perhaps at the patriarchate, perhaps at one or more of the many monasteries in the region.

Ecclesiastical Landscape

Traveling by foot or camel through Antioch and the surrounding countryside in 1051, one would have encountered an impressive concentration of churches and

122. Jenkins and Mango, 234; Todt, "Region," 259–60; Todt, *Region*, 665–67, esp. 666 n. 141. Jenkins and Mango suggested that Sophronios might have been chosen by Syrian bishops but rejected by Constantinople or vice versa. Todt has proposed a third option: that Patriarch Sophronios II *of Jerusalem* (who may have been patriarch of Jerusalem in 1050–1052 when the manuscript was copied) is the Sophronios in question, perhaps because he temporarily directed Antioch's affairs between the death of Patriarch Basil II and the arrival of his successor Peter III.

123. Bacha and Cheikho ("ʿAbdallāh," 952) consider whether Ibn al-Faḍl supported Keroularios in 1054, concluding that he couldn't have, since the patriarch of Antioch opposed Keroularios's move, and since Ibn al-Faḍl's exegesis of a line from the Gospel of John stresses Saint Peter's precedence. This conclusion may have been particularly tempting to Arab Catholic scholars in light of the modern Catholic argument that there had never been a schism between the patriarchate of Antioch and the pope, so that it was perfectly natural for modern Chalcedonian Christians of the Middle East to "renew" their allegiance to the Roman Catholic Church against the Greek Orthodox Church.

124. Todt, *Region*, 670 and n. 154; Todt, "Antioch," 185.

125. Todt, *Region*, 670–71.

126. §3.1, ed. Michel, *Humbert und Kerullarios*, 2:432–39, lines 28–30. Todt, *Region*, 671 and n. 158. *Enkyklios paideia: ODB*, s.v. "Paideia."

monasteries. To imagine this landscape of holy places, historians must piece together the fragments offered by medieval descriptions and archaeological remains.[127] Foremost among these sources is the description of Antioch by Ibn Buṭlān. In the early 440s of the Islamic calendar, or around 1048–1051 CE, Ibn Buṭlān wrote a letter from Antioch to a high-ranking official at the Buyid court in Baghdad, the octogenarian Buyid secretary Hilāl ibn al-Muḥassin (969–1056), a Muslim convert from the star-venerating religion of the Harranian Sabians.[128]

In Antioch, wrote Ibn Buṭlān, "there are innumerable churches, all wrought in gold, silver, colored glass, and *opus sectile* (*al-balāṭ al-mujazzaʿ*)."[129] His account gives particular prominence to the cathedral church dedicated to Saint Peter, known as *kanīsat al-Qasyān*, the Church of Cassian. Noting its size and its impressive water clock, Ibn Buṭlān describes the "porticoes where judges would sit in judgment, along with students (*mutaʿallimū*) of grammar and language."[130] His report also portrays it as a bustling institution with "countless paid servants" that housed "a chancellery (*dīwān*) for revenues and expenses, with over ten secretaries."[131] These secretaries were apparently church functionaries in charge of overseeing the finances of the patriarchate of Antioch.

When Emperor Basil II pressured Patriarch Agapios of Antioch (978–996) to resign,[132] he appointed the *chartophylax* (chief archivist) of Hagia Sophia to replace him, ordering this new patriarch (John III Polites, r. 996–1021) to "put in order (*yurattib*) the Church of Cassian according to the model of Hagia

127. Eger, "(Re)Mapping Medieval Antioch."

128. Ibn Buṭlān, Letter to Abū l-Ḥusayn Hilāl ibn al-Muḥassin al-Ṣābī, *apud* Yāqūt, *Buldān*, 1:266b$_{\Delta 3}$–268b$_{13}$; trans. Le Strange, *Palestine*, 370–75. On Hilāl's conversion, see Roberts, "Being a Sabian," 271–75; van Bladel, *Arabic Hermes*, 104–9. Hilāl's *kunyā* was Abū l-Ḥusayn, not Abū l-Ḥasan as printed in Yāqūt, *Buldān*, 1:266b$_{\Delta 3\text{-}\Delta 2}$. Yāqūt dates the letter to the early (*nayyif wa-*) 440s AH = ca. 1048–1051 CE.

129. Ibn Buṭlān *apud* Yāqūt, *Buldān*, 1:267a$_{\Delta 5\text{-}\Delta 4}$.

130. Ibn Buṭlān *apud* Yāqūt, *Buldān*, 1:267a$_{15-26}$; Eger, "(Re)Mapping Medieval Antioch," 104. The name of the church in Arabic is often voweled with a *u*, Qusyān, e.g., by Le Strange, *Palestine*, 371; Todt, "Antioch," 189. Lamoreaux ("Ibrāhīm," 2:613), discussing the successive burial places of Patriarch Christopher (killed in 967) described by Ibrāhīm ibn Yūḥannā al-Anṭākī the *protospatharios* (d. after 1025) in his *Life of Christopher*, describes the last two as, secondly, "the Cathedral Church of Antioch" and, thirdly, "the House of St Peter itself." This would seem to distinguish between the cathedral and St. Peter's, but in the *Life*, the second burial place is named as *al-kanīsa al-kubrā;* Sinai ar. 405, fol. 129$^{r}_{4}$; Zayat, "Vie," 358. This "Great Church" may be distinct from the cathedral; it may even refer to the octagonal church known in late antiquity as the Great Church (also as Apostolica and Domus Aurea), which Troupeau ("Les églises d'Antioche," 320) describes as unmentioned by Arab sources. (Troupeau infers from this that the Great Church was gone by the medieval period, but if the *Life of Christopher* is indeed referring to it, then it was still around in the tenth century.)

131. Ibn Buṭlān *apud* Yāqūt, *Buldān*, 1:267b$_{4-6}$.

132. Todt, "Greek-Orthodox Patriarchate," 36.

Sophia."[133] John's previous administrative position as *chartophylax* of the patriarchal church of Constantinople made him an appropriate choice to reshape Antioch's central ecclesiastical administration according to a Constantinopolitan model.

From the *protospatharios* Ibrāhīm ibn Yūḥannā of Antioch (second half of the tenth century) we know of two "sanctuaries," perhaps churches or chapels, built in Antioch under the middle Byzantine administration.[134] One of them was dedicated to Saint John Chrysostom. The other dedication is difficult to discern because the non-Arabic (apparently Greek) name appears to have been corrupted in manuscripts.[135] By calling the sanctuaries "beautiful," Ibrāhīm implies that he has seen them. They may still have been standing a half century later, in the 1050s.

The names of many other churches are known from a range of medieval sources, especially the lists of the Shiite-Muslim scholar al-Masʿūdī (d. 956 CE), who visited Antioch in the 940s, and the Miaphysite Christian Abū l-Makārim, who wrote an account of churches and other sites of supernatural phenomena in and around Antioch.[136] The names of churches in their reports corroborate Ibn Buṭlān's testimony that Antioch's churches were "innumerable." In the mid-eleventh century, Antioch, like other Christian metropolises, teemed with new and ancient churches.

Monasteries

Throughout the Byzantine Empire, the tenth and eleventh centuries were an era of great monastic foundations and renovations.[137] Northern Syria was no exception. Byzantine funds bolstered this revival, helping to rebuild and renovate monasteries in the region, like Saint Symeon the Younger on the Wondrous Mountain and

133. Yaḥyā of Antioch, *Histoire*, ed. Kratchkovsky, 445–46. This passage has led some to believe that Basil II ordered John to rebuild or renovate the church; e.g., Todt, "Antioch," 189. Already Cheynet ("Basil II," 74 and n. 10) expressed doubt about reading *yurattib* (trans. Micheau and Troupeau: "mettre en ordre"; but cf. Pirone, 212 = §11.25: "risistemare") as referring to the church's "reconstruction," reasoning that "this could also be understood as the re-organisation of the church's property after the model of St Sophia." Both cited by Eger, "(Re)Mapping Medieval Antioch," 103.

134. *Life of Patriarch Christopher of Antioch* (d. 967), ed. Zayat, "Vie," 336: after Christopher's murder, his close ally Theodoulos, who had since become archbishop of Seleukeia, "built two beautiful sanctuaries in Antioch" (*wa-banā bi-Anṭākiya haykalayn ḥasanayn † . . . † wa-Fam al-Dhahab*). Cited by Todt, "Antioch," 190 n. 74; Kennedy, "Antioch," 189; Eger, "(Re)Mapping Medieval Antioch," 103. For Ibrāhīm, see Graf, *GCAL*, 2:45–48.

135. Zayat's edition reads *al-ʾzks ʿwṭs*. A more promising reading is found in Sinai ar. 405, fol. $121^{r}_{\Omega 2}$: *li-l-ʾksyr ʾtyqws*. Dmitry Morozov, on the NASCAS listserv (24 January 2018 in response to Josh Mugler), relayed the plausible suggestion that the church was dedicated to Michael the Archangel, referred to as the ἀρχιστράτηγος (*li-l-arkistrātīghūs*). For the title, see Lampe s.v. ἀρχιστράτηγος 2–3.

136. Troupeau, "Les églises de Syrie"; Hacken, "Description," with English translation, 195–215. Abū l-Makārim's dependence on the Anonymous Description of Antioch: Troupeau, 581. Abū l-Makārim and his text are difficult to date.

137. Darrouzès, "Le mouvement."

Saint Barlaam on Mount Kasion.[138] Indeed by the eleventh century the region around Antioch had become a major Byzantine Chalcedonian monastic center.[139]

The Monastery of Saint Symeon the Younger on the Wondrous Mountain was one of the most prominent and prestigious monasteries around Antioch.[140] Situated less than 20 km southwest of Antioch, it was well known throughout the Byzantine Empire, as attested by a letter written by Psellos to the empress Eudokia Makrembolitissa (r. 1067, d. after 1078) on behalf of the monastery.[141] The monastery housed a library, to which Patriarch Theodore III of Antioch (1034–1042) donated many volumes,[142] and served as a center for intellectual activity.[143] This included Greek-Arabic translation. One of the monastery's abbots, Antonios (active in the late tenth/early eleventh century; d. before 1053), was himself an important translator of Greek Christian literature into Arabic.[144] Among other texts, he translated John of Damascus's *Dialectica* and *Exposition of Faith,* parts of the Damascene's *Fountain of Knowledge,*[145] both extremely popular in Byzantium.[146]

Alongside the large community of Arabic- and Greek-speaking monks, there were also Georgians, who controlled some of the monastery's land. They had their own church within the monastery by the first half of the eleventh century. Two Georgian inscriptions from the monastery survive, and several others attested by

138. Todt, "Antioch," 190.

139. Todt, *Region,* 903–47; Djobadze, *Materials;* Djobadze, *Archeological Investigations;* Brock, "Syriac Manuscripts."

140. Van den Ven, *La vie;* Djobadze, *Archeological Investigations,* ch. 2; De Giorgi, *Antioch,* 149–50.

141. Cheynet, "Michel Psellos," 415.

142. Todt, *Region,* 664 and n. 129.

143. Todt and Vest, *Syria,* 1768–75.

144. Graf, *GCAL,* 2:41–45; Nasrallah, *Histoire,* 3.1:273–89; Treiger, "Christian Graeco-Arabica," 206–7, 209–18. The tenth-century *floruit* given for Antonios depended on Nasrallah's observation that one of his translations was produced after the death of Emperor Constantine VII (d. 959), and that another was produced no later than 379 AH = 989–990 CE, which date is how Nasrallah read the colophon of Vat. ar. 436 (1581 CE), as saying that it was copied from a manuscript "dating from before" (*qad taqadamma tārīkhuhā ʿan tārīkh . . .*) 379 "lunar years" (i.e., Hijrī years = 989–990 CE). But Alexander Treiger (who kindly shared his observation with me) has proposed a subtly but crucially different reading of this colophon: "dating from before *it* [i.e., this sixteenth-century manuscript] *by*" (*. . . ʿan tārīkhihi bi- . . .*) 379 "lunar years," which would put it 379 years before 989/1581, in 610/1213–1214. For firmer evidence for Antonios's *floruit,* see now Ibrahim, "Some Notes on Antonios," 165–66: at least in part after ca. 1000 (the date of a Greek text Antonios translated) and *terminus ante quem* of 1053 (the date of a manuscript in which he is referred to as one refers to the deceased).

145. John of Damascus, *Die Schriften,* ed. Kotter, vols. 1–2. Kontouma ("*Fount,*" esp. 15) argues that the *Fountain of Knowledge* as John of Damascus composed it consisted only of the *Dialectica* and the *Exposition of Faith* (typically transmitted together in Greek manuscripts) but did not include *On Heresies* (less commonly appearing together with the other two in manuscripts).

146. Kotter, *Die Überlieferung;* cited by Papaioannou, *Psellos,* 56, who writes that the *Fountain of Knowledge* was "the most popular theological work in Byzantium."

visitors appear now to be lost.[147] In the 1050s there were about fifty Georgian monks; they may have had their own scriptorium.[148] The Georgian translator George the Athonite spent time at Saint Symeon and worked on his Greek-Georgian translations there.[149] This Georgian presence had a long past: the Greek *Life of Saint Symeon the Younger* attests to many Georgian pilgrims who visited the sixth-century saint while he was still alive.[150]

Saint Symeon the Younger (521–592, a stylite saint who had perched on a column on the Wondrous Mountain much as the elder Symeon had lived on one outside of Aleppo) had a significant following among local Syriac-speaking Chalcedonians, as attested by a ninth-century Syriac *Life of Saint Symeon the Younger* produced by "a Chalcedonian monk of the Black Mountain."[151] Likewise, a Georgian manuscript copied near the monastery in 1040 CE invokes "the intercession of . . . Saint Symeon the wonder-worker."[152]

The Monastery of Saint Barlaam on Mount Kasion, originally founded in the sixth century like Saint Symeon, was revived under Byzantine rule, recolonized by Georgian monks.[153] Georgian inscriptions were found in the ruins of the monastery during modern excavations.[154] There was a Georgian scriptorium, where several extant medieval Georgian manuscripts were copied.[155]

Finally, we may briefly mention the Black Mountain to the northwest of Antioch. The Black Mountain was home to a range of monasteries whose monks spoke Arabic, Syriac, Greek, Georgian, and Armenian.[156] In addition to Chalcedonian monasteries, there were a number of non-Chalcedonian communities on the Black Mountain, in particular Miaphysites, both Syrian-Jacobites and Armenians.[157]

There were thus many and diverse monasteries flourishing in the environs of Antioch by the mid-eleventh century. Like the patriarchate within the city itself, the wealthiest of these monasteries had libraries, scriptoria, and scholars producing translations and new works, and attracting the attention of prominent individuals, from the Byzantine empress to the patriarch of Antioch.

147. Djobadze, *Archeological Investigations*, 210–11.
148. Djobadze, *Materials*, 87–89.
149. George the Small, *Life of George the Athonite*, §§16–17, trans. Djobadze, *Materials*, 52.
150. Djobadze, *Materials*, 65.
151. Alpi, "Le paysage," 153, citing a recent discovery by Sebastian Brock.
152. Trans. Djobadze, *Materials*, 7.
153. Djobadze, *Materials*, 86. On the monastery's history and archeology, see Djobadze, *Materials*, 4–5; Djobadze, *Archeological Investigations*, ch. 1; De Giorgi, *Antioch*, 146–47.
154. Djobadze, *Archeological Investigations*, 206–10.
155. Djobadze, *Materials*, 90.
156. Brock, "Syriac Manuscripts," 59.
157. Doens, "Nicon," 133.

Languages and Religious Confessions

Situated at a border between the Byzantine and Islamic worlds, Antioch in the eleventh century was home to a rich variety of languages, including Greek, Syriac, Arabic, Georgian, and Armenian. Greek, the primary language spoken in the Byzantine Empire, had a long and ancient history in Syria as well. Though it is often assumed that Greek had ceased to be an important language in the Near East long before the eleventh century, this is not the case.[158] Greek learning had never entirely disappeared from Antioch in the centuries of Muslim rule. Even as Greek waned as a common spoken and literary language of the city, Byzantine ideas, habits of thought, and terms of discussion lived on in Syriac and Arabic.[159]

Georgian and Armenian, commonly spoken in the Byzantine Empire,[160] are also attested for Byzantine Antioch and its hinterland, especially Georgian. Georgians had a prominent place in the Byzantine Chalcedonian Church. Theophilos, Byzantine metropolitan of Tarsus in the mid-eleventh century, for example, was "a Georgian by birth" according to the *Life of George the Athonite.*[161]

The most common languages in northern Syria were Syriac and Arabic. Based on liturgical manuscripts from Antioch, it appears that these two were the main liturgical languages during the middle Byzantine period.[162] In a study of twelve Syriac liturgical manuscripts from the region around Antioch, Sebastian Brock suggested that they were produced by Syrian-Chalcedonian Christians as part of an effort to introduce Byzantine liturgical practices into Antioch and its region. The rite previously used by Chalcedonian Christians in Antioch—known as "the rite (*ṭeksā*) of the Syrians (*Suryāye*)"—continued to be used alongside the new Byzantine one—"the rite of the Greeks (*Yawnāye*)."[163]

Georgians too used the Syro-Palestinian liturgy at least until the tenth century, when Euthymios the Athonite produced an abridged translation of the *Synaxarion of Constantinople* in Georgian. In the eleventh century, George the Athonite retranslated the same Byzantine *Synaxarion* into Georgian.[164] This parallels the adoption of the Byzantine liturgy by Syriac-speaking Chalcedonians around Antioch under Byzantine rule.

There does not appear to have been any Byzantine attempt linguistically to "re-Hellenize" Antioch after the conquest.[165] At the same time, Greek is far from absent. A marble gravestone for one Bardas dated 1063 CE is handsomely inscribed

158. Mavroudi, "Greek Language."
159. Tannous, "Syria," 25–30.
160. Dagron, "Formes."
161. §18, trans. Djobadze, *Materials*, 56.
162. Todt, "Antioch," 186 and n. 57.
163. Brock, "Syriac Manuscripts," 66.
164. Djobadze, *Materials*, 68, 83; Martin-Hisard, "La Vie de Jean et Euthyme," 105 n. 113.
165. Todt, "Antioch," 186.

with Byzantine lettering familiar from contemporary Byzantine inscriptions elsewhere, and uses the standard Byzantine dating system combining the indiction and the Year of the World.[166] Another gravestone from a cemetery in Antioch was inscribed (in 1041–1042 CE) on the back of an Arabic gravestone dated to the early years of Byzantine rule over Antioch.[167]

Sometimes one inscription used both Greek and Arabic at once, such as the bilingual epitaph for one Basil who died in 999 CE. With Greek on top and Arabic below, it commemorates the deceased using the same standard Byzantine dating system: Basil, "slave of God," passed away (ἐκοιμήθη) on the sixth of June, a Tuesday, in the 12th Indiction, Year of the World (*li-l-ʿālam*) 6507—that is, in 999 CE.[168] This shows that a single Antiochian might hope to reach both Greek and Arabic audiences. As Gilbert Dagron and Denis Feissel, who published this inscription, remark, personal bilingualism did not always carry over onto one's gravestone: when a certain Nicholas of Antioch, son of Abū l-Faraj (ὑὸς Ἀπολφαρατζί), was laid to rest in Mopsuestia in Cilicia, in 1052 CE, his tomb, bearing an Arabic name, was inscribed only in Greek.[169]

It seems that much of the local population under Byzantine rule was Chalcedonian Christian by confession. These Chalcedonian Christians spoke as wide a range of languages as the population at large: Greek, Syriac, Arabic, Georgian, and Armenian.[170] Most of them probably spoke Arabic.[171] There were also Miaphysite Christians in the region, whose relationship with the Byzantine authorities and the Byzantine Church was uneasy and often tense; they were primarily speakers of Syriac and Armenian.[172]

There was a Jewish community in medieval Antioch (though attested only in the Crusader period)[173] and probably also a Muslim community. In any case, there seem to have been significant numbers of Muslims in the coastal cities of Latakia and Gabala to the south, both within Byzantine territory: the chronicler Ibn

166. Dumbarton Oaks Museum, BZ.1938.78: ἐκοιμήθη ὁ δοῦλος τοῦ θ(εο)ῦ / Βάρδας ἡμέρας β πρώτου δε- / κεμβρίου μηνὸς ἰν(δικτιῶνος) β ἔ(τους) ςφοβ.

167. Eger, "(Re)Mapping Medieval Antioch," 119.

168. Dagron and Feissel, "Inscriptions," 457–58 and figure 5; cited by De Giorgi, *Antioch*, 167. The right side of the inscription (containing the ends of Greek lines and beginnings of Arabic lines) is missing.

169. Dagron and Feissel, "Inscriptions," 458; Dagron and Marcillet-Jaubert, "Inscriptions," 378. For the spelling ὑός, see LSJ s.v. υἱός.

170. For these languages, see Todt, "Antioch," 182–88. Greek: Mercati, "Origine antiochena" (on two eleventh-century Greek codices from Antioch). Syriac: Desreumaux, "La paléographie," 560. Armenian: Todt, "Antioch," 188 n. 65, with references.

171. Todt, "Antioch," 182.

172. Todt, 188.

173. Todt, 188.

al-Athīr (1160–1233) reports that the Byzantine administration permitted Muslim judges to be active in those two cities.[174]

In Byzantine Antioch, as in any other medieval city, the existence of soldiers, bureaucrats, churchmen, and monks was sustained and made possible by a whole range of laborers, especially in the industrial sectors,[175] and peasants bringing agricultural products from the countryside. Merchants, pilgrims, and other travelers, even from the Latin West, were constantly passing through.[176] Although a scholar like Ibn al-Faḍl probably cultivated relationships with patrons and fellow scholars most attentively, we must imagine that his daily life brought him into constant contact with these other residents and visitors. Perhaps we may even imagine him at work by a window, seeing and hearing the bustle of the city outside, not unlike the vignette of urban life that the late eleventh-century Georgian scribe Iona saw fit to record. "Fathers," wrote Iona in a manuscript he had finished copying, "if there are mistakes [in this manuscript] do not reproach me. My house in Antioch was above the springs where many boys and girls came with jugs on their shoulders, and my mind was distracted by them."[177]

Visitors to Antioch also included Christian and Muslim scholars from the Islamic world. Ibn Buṭlān has already been mentioned above for his description of Antioch's churches and monasteries. He is a good example of the sort of versatile traveling intellectual who passed through Antioch.[178] A native of Baghdad, Ibn Buṭlān left the Abbasid capital in 1049 and made his way, via Syria (including Aleppo, where he advised the Mirdāsid ruler, and Antioch), to Cairo. After a stay of several years and a bitter rivalry with Ibn Riḍwān, the Muslim chief physician at the Fatimid court, Ibn Buṭlān proceeded to Constantinople, arriving in the middle of 1054, where he became involved in the theological controversy between the papal legate Cardinal Humbert and Patriarch Michael Keroularios of Constantinople. After a year in Constantinople, Ibn Buṭlān spent the next decade serving rulers in Antioch and Aleppo, then retired to an Antiochian monastery, where he was buried when he died.[179]

The eleventh-century Muslim scholar Ibn al-Qāriḥ, in his letter to the Muslim poet Abū l-ʿAlāʾ al-Maʿarrī that prompted the latter to write his *Epistle of Forgiveness* (ca. 1033 CE), mentions that he went to Antioch and then to Melitene (also within Byzantine territory), where he was hosted by al-Māyisṭirīya Khawla,

174. Todt, 188.

175. Eger, "(Re)Mapping Medieval Antioch," 117, 119–20, 122–23.

176. Cheynet, "Basil II," 80. Latins: Todt, "Antioch," 188.

177. Jerusalem, Holy Sepulcher, Georgian 2 (copied at the Monastery of Ckʾarotʿa), fol. 255ʳ; trans. Djobadze, *Materials,* 49.

178. Mavroudi, "Licit."

179. Conrad, "Ibn Buṭlān."

"daughter of Saʿd al-Dawla."[180] Khawla's title must be based on the Greek title *magistros,* or the feminine version, *magistrissa,* which she presumably bore.[181] This casual reference attests to the ease with which elites moved across political boundaries in this region: a Ḥamdānid princess married to a Byzantine provincial official offered hospitality to a Muslim man of letters visiting Byzantine territory. Ibn al-Qāriḥ likewise writes as if there were nothing particularly remarkable about an elite Muslim like him visiting Byzantine Antioch.

When a Seljuk army captured Antioch in 1084, the Byzantine Empire had controlled the city for almost 115 years, energetically seeking to integrate the ancient city into Byzantine imperial culture and administration. In histories of Byzantium and the Middle East, it is typical to treat the Byzantine rule of Antioch as a mere interlude. Philip Hitti's classic history of Syria gave it one sentence.[182] Even more recent scholars who have made important contributions to our understanding of middle Byzantine Antioch have characterized Byzantine rule of Antioch as a "brief occupation."[183] But 115 years is a long time.

By the 1050s, when we know Ibn al-Faḍl was active, Antioch had already been under Byzantine rule for just about "four score and seven years"—a lifetime. With hindsight, we can look for signs that imperial rule of Antioch and the eastern territories would soon come to an end. But in the mid-eleventh century, this would have seemed like a remote possibility. Byzantine armies had successfully repelled repeated attempts on Antioch, and Byzantine administration and the Byzantine Church had taken root. The result was a relatively peaceful, stable microcosm, where intellectuals with Byzantine ecclesiastical patronage could thrive. Byzantine rule must have seemed like it was there to stay.

180. In Maʿarrī, *Epistle of Forgiveness,* ed. and trans. van Gelder and Schoeler, 48–49.
181. *ODB,* s.v. "Magistros." Trapp, *Lexikon,* s.v. μαγίστρισσα.
182. Hitti, *History of Syria,* 565.
183. Eger, "(Re)Mapping Medieval Antioch," 103.

2

A TRANSLATION PROGRAM

What texts did Ibn al-Faḍl translate into Arabic, and what sort of texts were they? Only once we have a sense of the contours of his translation program may we begin to assess why he undertook it and what he did with it. This chapter approaches the list of texts that Ibn al-Faḍl translated as a partial reading list, a coherent set of texts that give insight into the body of literature that Ibn al-Faḍl and his patrons wished to make available in Arabic translation. Along the way, the examination of these texts will occasion some general remarks about their place in Byzantine culture. Chapter 3 will then return to the Byzantine context by focusing on the cultural resonance of these texts in the eleventh century.

The texts that Ibn al-Faḍl translated or retranslated into Arabic are known only from Arabic manuscripts containing them. There is no master list compiled by Ibn al-Faḍl or his students. The best we can do is compile a working list and update it with each new discovery. An up-to-date list (based on previous lists) can be found in table 1, organized roughly in chronological order according to when the authors of the original texts lived.[1] Quite a number of other translations have been ascribed to Ibn al-Faḍl with varying degrees of certainty—for example, translations that seem to be in his style or that bear a preface like those that introduce many of his known translations, or translations contained in manuscripts that also contain some of his known translations. Many of these may well turn out to be his translations, but my list (and this book) concentrates on translations that we can confidently ascribe to Ibn al-Faḍl.

1. Bacha and Cheikho, "ʿAbdallāh"; Cheikho, *Kitāb al-makhṭūṭāt,* 142–44, 240; Graf, *GCAL,* 2:52–64; Nasrallah, *Histoire,* 3.1:191–229; Noble and Treiger, "Christian Arabic Theology," 377–78; updated by Treiger, "Christian Graeco-Arabica," 208 and n. 86.

TABLE 1 Works translated by Ibn al-Faḍl, based on Noble and Treiger, "Christian Arabic Theology," 377–78

	Author	Date	Work		*CPG*	N/T
1			Psalms			1
2			Gospel Lectionary			2
3			Epistolary	?		2
4			Prophetologion	?		2
5	Basil of Caesarea	d. ca. 379	*Homilies on the Psalms*		2836	4.1
6			*Homilies on the Hexaemeron*		2835	4.2
7	Gregory of Nyssa	d. ca. 394	*On Making Man*	?	3154	5.1
8			*Apology on the Hexaemeron*	?	3153	5.2
9			*Homilies on the Song of Songs*	?	3158	5.3
10	John Chrysostom	d. 407	*Homilies on Genesis*		4409	3.1
11			*Homilies on Matthew*	?	4424	3.2
12			*Homilies on John*	?	4425	3.3
13			*Homilies on First Corinthians*	?	4428	3.4
14			*Homilies on Hebrews*		4440	3.5
15			*Homilies on Romans*		4427	3.6
16			Collection of 87 homilies	?		3.7
17			*Exhortation to Penitence*	?		3.8
18	Pseudo-Kaisarios	?mid-6th c.	*Questions and Answers* (partial)		7482	12
19	John of Thessaloniki	6th/7th c.	*Encomium to St. Demetrios*		7925	
20	Sophronios	d. ca. 638	*Synodical Letter* (adaptation)		7635	10
21	Maximos Confessor	d. 662	*Disputation with Pyrrhos*		7698	6.1
22			*Chapters on Love*	?	7693	6.2
23			*Chapters on Knowledge*	?	7694	6.3
24	Pseudo-Maximos	ca. 10th c.	*Loci communes*		7718	11
25	Isaac of Nineveh	7th/?8th c.	*Ascetic Homilies* (35 of 82)		7868	9.1
26			*Chapters on Knowledge*	?		9.2
27	Andrew of Crete	d. 740	*Encomium to St. Nicholas*		8187	7
28	John of Damascus	d. ca. 750	*Statement on Correct Thought*		8046	8

NOTE: Translations whose attribution I question are marked with ?. The column N/T provides cross-references to the list in Noble and Treiger.

Other than several translations of parts of the Bible, the texts in this list are all patristic—that is, they are works by authors remembered in the later ecclesiastical tradition as "fathers" of the church. These texts were retroactively designated by that subsequent tradition as doctrinally correct and authoritative. But the men who wrote these texts were embedded in their own cultural contexts and had their own particular intellectual concerns. These included controversies within the church and broader debates shared by Christians and non-Christians alike. The fourth-century Cappadocian Fathers (Basil of Caesarea, Gregory of Nyssa, and Gregory of Nazianzos) wrote strenuously in defense of the doctrines declared orthodox at the Council of Nicea in 325, but they also sought to articulate a model of Christian leadership to rival their pagan peers, like the emperor Julian, whose culture and education they shared.[2] Accordingly, they constantly engaged with the Hellenic pagan tradition they inherited, using it to construct a coherent account of their revealed mystery religion in terms palatable to the Graeco-Roman elite (including themselves). In this, they followed in the footsteps of writers like the Jewish scholar Philo of Alexandria (d. ca. 50 CE), who had done much the same for Judaism. Even in the eleventh century, with the benefit of historical distance, a reader of these texts could not have avoided absorbing some of that context, and some of those concerns, and appropriating them.

In the following overview of Ibn al-Faḍl's translation program, I cannot hope to do justice to each of the rich texts on the list. Instead, I aim to offer a sense of the texts' genre and content, as viewed from the vantage point of the eleventh century. Such a discussion could be arranged in various ways—for example, by the genres typical in modern scholarship on ecclesiastical literature,[3] or in chronological order, or by their primary theological or philosophical concerns. The approach taken here will combine a roughly chronological criterion with an equally rough generic criterion, moving from Scripture to the exegetical work of three celebrated church fathers and champions of Nicene dogma, Basil of Caesarea (fourth century), his brother Gregory of Nyssa, and John Chrysostom (fourth–fifth century); dogmatic and polemical works by Sophronios of Jerusalem, Maximos the Confessor, and John of Damascus in defense of their own understanding of Chalcedonian theology produced soon before and after the rise of Islam (sixth–seventh century); encomia to Saints Demetrios and Nicholas by John of Thessaloniki (sixth/seventh century) and Andrew of Crete (eighth century), respectively; and, finally, collections of brief sayings compiled by Maximos the Confessor and Isaac of Nineveh (seventh/?eighth century), along with two pseudonymous collections ascribed to Maximos and Kaisarios.

As we will see, each set of texts offered an alternative to pagan literature and philosophy. In most cases, this was a self-conscious aim of the texts.

1 SCRIPTURE AND LITURGY

Ibn al-Faḍl produced Arabic versions of the book of Psalms, most accompanied with extracts from patristic commentaries; of a Gospel lectionary (readings selected from the Gospels); and possibly of an epistolary (readings from New Testament epistles) and prophetologion (readings from Old Testament prophets).[4]

2. Elm, *Sons;* Elm, "Priest and Prophet."

3. Beck's classic handbook of ecclesiastical literature (*Kirche*) follows the following classification: dogmatics and polemic, asceticism and mysticism, homilies, hagiography, exegesis, canon law, liturgical poetry, prayers. For such divisions, see Mavroudi, "Occult Sciences," 41–42 and n. 6.

4. Graf, *GCAL,* 1:116–20, 186–87, 189–91; Nasrallah, "La liturgie," 170–71. Naṣrallah (based on the testimony of Patriarch Makarios ibn al-Zaʿīm, d. 1672) came to believe that Ibn al-Faḍl also produced an Arabic synaxarion, but the evidence is very slim.

Biblical texts had been translated into Arabic centuries before. The Monastery of Saint Catherine at Mount Sinai preserves two early Arabic New Testament manuscripts, one dated to the ninth century and another that dates the Arabic translation it contains to 867 CE.[5] The Rabbinic Jewish scholar Saʿadya Gaon (882–942) translated the Hebrew Bible into Arabic.

The Psalter had already been translated into Arabic long before Ibn al-Faḍl produced his Arabic version. The famous parchment fragment known as the Violet fragment, found in 1900 in a sealed storage space (the *qubbat al-khazna*) at the Umayyad Mosque in Damascus and probably dating, on paleographical grounds, to the late ninth or early tenth century, preserves part of Psalm 77(78) in Arabic translation written in Greek script.[6] A number of ninth- and tenth-century Sinai manuscripts contain the same Arabic translation (in Arabic script).[7] Ibn al-Faḍl's version is based on this earlier Arabic translation.[8] He indicates his use of an earlier translation in his preface to the text, where he speaks of what "moved me to correct the Psalter . . . and extract its sense from Greek into Arabic." That is, he corrected an *Arabic* Psalter that was already available, revising it based on his reading of the Greek (Septuagint) Psalter.[9]

To accompany his Arabic version of the Psalms, Ibn al-Faḍl translated extracts from a number of Greek patristic commentaries on the Psalms. We know about these extracts from two manuscripts, one containing the passages of commentary on the Psalms, the other containing a preface to Ibn al-Faḍl's Arabic Psalter that describes the commentary's source.[10] The first says little about where the commentary comes from, and the second contains only the preface, not the commentary itself. Graf, with access only to the first manuscript, believed the commentary to be Ibn al-Faḍl's own original work.[11] The preface of the second manuscript, however, explains that "the Greek copy from which we extracted these explications com-

5. Sinai New Finds Parch. ar. 14+16 (dated not 859 but rather 873 CE, as Alexander Treiger kindly informed me) and Sinai ar. 151, respectively: Kashouh, *Gospels*, 86 n. 9; Vollandt, *Pentateuch*, 27, 54; Treiger, "From Theodore," 40 n. *c*.

6. Mavroudi, "Arabic Words."

7. Vollandt, "Beyond Arabic"; I thank Alexander Treiger for this reference.

8. Vollandt, "Beyond Arabic."

9. See ch. 4, §1, pp. 125, 126. Cf. Graf, *GCAL*, 1:116. For translating *maʿānī*, see Key, *Language*.

10. Vat. ar. 145, fols. 74ʳ–93ᵛ: commentary. New Haven, Yale Beinecke, ar. 349: preface. See also ch. 4, §1, esp. p. 124, n. 2.

11. Graf, *GCAL*, 2:59; followed by Nasrallah, *Histoire*, 3.1:217. This judgment was presumably based on the manuscript's heading (Vat. ar. 145, fol. 74ʳ): "From marginalia on the Psalms extracted by Ibn al-Faḍl" (*min ḥawāshī* [*sic*] *ʿalā mazāmīr ikhrāj Ibn al-Faḍl*). But "extracted" (a word also found in the other manuscript's preface) does not mean "written by" but suggests rather translating or excerpting (or both).

prises opinions of a number of commentators.... I abbreviated it as much as possible."[12]

The Psalter was a fundamental text for Byzantine primary education. Just as early memorization of the Qur'an was a standard marker of a Muslim boy's precocious talent (the historian al-Ṭabarī says that he managed the feat by age seven),[13] getting the Psalter by heart was an early sign of a Christian child's brilliance. The hagiographical *Life of Sabas the Younger,* written in Greek by Patriarch Orestes of Jerusalem (r. 986–1006) and preserved in at least three middle Byzantine manuscripts, reports that when Sabas "reached the age of education, his parents determined that he should frequent schoolteachers and be occupied with divine studies. Since he was naturally well suited for learning, it was not long before he had thoroughly learned the utterances of David [i.e., the Psalms]."[14] The Psalter also played a public role in the Christian liturgy.

Ibn al-Faḍl's Arabic Psalter enjoyed widespread popularity not only among Chalcedonian Christians like Ibn al-Faḍl but also among other Arabophone Christians, such as Coptic Miaphysites. And while very few of Ibn al-Faḍl's translations have appeared in print, his Psalter was included in the Arabic Bible printed in Rome in 1671.[15]

More exclusively associated with the liturgy than the Psalter were lectionaries, bound collections of excerpts from the Bible to be read during the liturgy on specific days, in particular from the Old Testament prophets (prophetologion), New Testament epistles (epistolary), and the Gospels ("evangeliary" or Gospel lectionary). By the early modern period, the Arabic lectionaries used in the liturgy had been standardized in the (Greek Orthodox) patriarchate of Antioch; these are often called the "Melkite" lectionaries. Some manuscripts of these "Melkite" lectionaries ascribe them to Ibn al-Faḍl.[16]

Ibn al-Faḍl's name is attached to the "Melkite" Gospel lectionary in at least one manuscript.[17] The "Melkite" epistolary appears with a preface by Ibn al-Faḍl on the

12. New Haven, Yale Beinecke, ar. 349 (absent from Vat. ar. 145): *anna l-nuskhata l-yūnānīyata lladhī [sic] stakhrajnā minhā hādhihi l-tafāsīra fa-tashtamilu ʿalā ārāʾi ʿiddatin mina l-mufassirīn ... wa-khtaṣarnā dhālika ḥasaba mā amkana.*

13. *EI*², s.v. "al-Ṭabarī, Abū Djaʿfar," 10:11.

14. *BHG* 1611; Orestes, *Life of Sabas the Younger* 2.1, in *Historia et laudes*, ed. Cozza-Luzi, 7; cited by Kazhdan and Talbot, *Database,* Key 29,572 (accessed 29 July 2013). The middle Byzantine manuscripts date from the tenth (Vat. gr. 826) and eleventh (Vat. gr. 823; Vat. gr. 2072) centuries; cited in *Pinakes.*

15. Graf, *GCAL,* 1:117–18.

16. Nasrallah, "La liturgie," 170–71: Ibn al-Faḍl translated "the liturgical lectionaries: Epistolary, Evangeliary, Psalter, and perhaps the *propheteiai.*"

17. Sinai Porph. ar. 67; Graf, *GCAL,* 1:188.

Pauline Epistles in some manuscripts.[18] It therefore seems likely that Ibn al-Faḍl produced the Arabic epistolary, or else that it was produced based on Ibn al-Faḍl's translations of the Pauline Epistles with Chrysostom's commentary. The "Melkite" prophetologion, or lectionary of Old Testament prophets, may or may not be by Ibn al-Faḍl; there is no firm evidence.[19]

That Ibn al-Faḍl was *re*-translating, producing new Arabic versions of biblical texts that had already been translated into Arabic, should make clear from the outset that there was more to Ibn al-Faḍl's translation program than making texts available to a population that no longer understood Greek, or at least preferred Arabic. The nature of the translation itself mattered too.

2 LATE ANTIQUE BIBLICAL EXEGESIS

The bulk of Ibn al-Faḍl's known translation program is devoted to works by the late antique church fathers Basil of Caesarea (ca. 330–?379) and John Chrysostom (d. 407), and perhaps also Basil's brother Gregory of Nyssa (ca. 335–394 or thereafter).[20] In their own day, these three men, along with Gregory of Nazianzos (d. ca. 390), were all bishops and leading figures among elite Christians with a Hellenic education. They sought to articulate what it meant to be a Graeco-Roman Christian, promoting their own visions of monasticism, church leadership, and Christian doctrine, vehemently opposing pagans and Christians who rejected the Council of Nicea or otherwise disagreed with their theological positions.[21]

The particular texts of Basil and Chrysostom that Ibn al-Faḍl translated, as well as those by Gregory of Nyssa that he might have translated, are overwhelmingly works of biblical exegesis: Basil's *Homilies on the Psalms*[22] and *Homilies on the Hexaemeron;* possibly Gregory of Nyssa's *Homilies on the Song of Songs, On Making Man,* and *Apology on the Hexaemeron;* and Chrysostom's homilies on Genesis,

18. Graf, *GCAL,* 1:189. The incipit of this preface in Birmingham, Mingana, Christian Arabic Add. 220 = cat. no. 138 (printed in Mingana, *Catalogue of the Mingana Collection,* 3:8) indicates that it is the same as the preface in Paris ar. 96 and other manuscripts; see ch. 4, §5.

19. Bacha and Cheikho ("ʿAbdallāh," 947) thought it was. Graf (*GCAL,* 1:187) calls this ascription groundless.

20. Quasten, *Patrology,* 3:204–7, 254–55, 424–28; Rousseau, *Basil.*

21. Elm, *Sons.*

22. Nasrallah, *Histoire,* 3.1:204. The evidence for attributing this translation to Ibn al-Faḍl is somewhat slim and rather more complicated than Nasrallah lets on. Nasrallah only says explicitly of one manuscript that it attributes the translation to Ibn al-Faḍl: Sinai ar. 271 (1233 CE). Ibn al-Faḍl is indeed named as translator in the colophon on fol. 229ᵛ. Upon closer inspection, however, it seems that the colophon did not originally mention Ibn al-Faḍl at all, but rather the attribution was later added by someone writing over part of the original colophon.

Hebrews, Romans, and perhaps Matthew, John, and First Corinthians.[23] (Ibn al-Faḍl is also sometimes said to be the translator of a certain collection of eighty-seven of Chrysostom's homilies, and of an *Exhortation to Penitence* by Chrysostom, but there is little evidence for either attribution.)[24] These works, while framed as close readings of the Bible, were also occasions for these late antique authors to stake out their positions on a variety of issues, from ancient philosophy to the nature of Christ.

These men were towering figures in Byzantine culture. Three of the four were given special epithets, indicating their prominence in the Byzantine tradition. Basil was Basil "the Great"; "Chrysostom" means "the Golden-Mouthed"; and Gregory of Nazianzos was "the Theologian." The ancient orator Dio was also called "the Golden-Mouthed," and John the Evangelist was also called "the Theologian." But when Byzantine authors referred to "the Golden-Mouthed" and "the Theologian" without further specification, they meant John Chrysostom and Gregory of Nazianzos.

John Chrysostom

What sort of texts were these late antique works of biblical exegesis? Let us begin with the author whose works represent the greatest proportion of Ibn al-Faḍl's known translation work, John Chrysostom.

Chrysostom delivered his homilies to an audience of Christians. Each homily usually treats a very short excerpt from the text being studied, often a single biblical verse. A typical homily by Chrysostom begins with an exhortation, seeking to rouse his audience out of their torpor, urging them to concentrate on his exegetical

23. Graf, *GCAL*, 2:56; Nasrallah, *Histoire*, 3.1:201. Graf expressed uncertainty regarding the ascription of the homilies on 1 Corinthians to Ibn al-Faḍl appearing in "Sbath Fihris 398." This is a reference to Sbath, *Fihris*, 1:51, item no. 398. This publication is notoriously unreliable. Nasrallah declares that Ibn al-Faḍl translated this text, with no further explanation; he refers to this manuscript, and to two others—Paris ar. 94 (1236 CE) and Sinai ar. 289 (thirteenth century), fols. 243ʳ–316ʳ—neither of which appears to mention Ibn al-Faḍl. As for the Arabic translations of Chrysostom's homilies on Matthew and John, Nasrallah's ascription of them to Ibn al-Faḍl derives from late manuscripts and is contradicted by the testimony of much earlier manuscripts containing the *same* Arabic translations of these works but ascribing them to Antonios of Saint Symeon; see Ibrahim, "Some Notes on Antonios," 161–63, where the homilies on 1 Corinthians are also discussed. For a preface by Ibn al-Faḍl that is labeled as a preface to Chrysostom's *Homilies on Matthew*, see ch. 1, p. 13, n. 42.

24. For the eighty-seven homilies, see Graf, *GCAL*, 1:341; Nasrallah, *Histoire*, 3.1:203. As for the *Exhortation to Penitence*, Nasrallah (*Histoire*, 3.1:203) says that the Arabic translation of a work by Chrysostom with this title "is attributed by name to Ibn al-Faḍl" in a single manuscript, Florence, Laurenziana, or. 99 (item no. 3). This information presumably derives from the eighteenth-century catalog of the Laurenziana's oriental manuscripts by Assemani (*Bibliothecae Mediceae Laurentianae*, 130, no. 76), who asserts that Ibn al-Faḍl translated this and several other works contained in the manuscript, along with "the rest" of Chrysostom's works. The Florence manuscript in question (which I examined on 30 October 2017), written in Garshuni (Arabic in Syriac script), does not in fact appear to mention Ibn al-Faḍl's name anywhere.

lesson, and berating them to read the week's assigned reading multiple times throughout the week in preparation for his lessons. The middle of the typical homily is then devoted to a close reading of the assigned text, phrase by phrase, with detailed discussion. Chrysostom's homilies then end with an appeal to his audience to improve themselves, to turn their attention away from their daily lives, and to shun the pointless and corrupting entertainment of the theater and the stadium; the last line is reserved for praise of God.

Chrysostom's exegetical homilies are often lyrical and consistently put his deft oratory on display while considering doctrinal and philosophical problems. He emphasizes the distance between "Hellenic" (pagan) philosophers and the "true philosophy" of the Bible—by which he means not that the Gospels are a (nonrational) alternative to philosophy but that they are philosophy done right. Thus Chrysostom describes John the Evangelist as speaking the truth plainly (as Socrates said one should) and says that when he wrote, "In the beginning was the Logos," he clearly meant that God transcends time altogether—a doctrine that Chrysostom regards as "true philosophy" in contrast to the incoherent Hellenic teaching that some gods are older than others.[25]

Chrysostom's books of homilies are voluminous and discuss a wide range of concepts and doctrinal positions that Chrysostom himself was instrumental in establishing. They often refer openly to the major ideological debates in which he was engaged, seeking to counter Jewish, Marcionite, Arian, Manichaean, and other doctrinal opponents. The sixty-seven homilies on Genesis present a detailed exegesis of the first book of Moses. In the ninety homilies on the Gospel of Matthew, Chrysostom is particularly concerned to condemn Manichaean teachings and to insist, against the Arian doctrine, that the Son is equal to the Father.[26] The eighty-eight homilies on John, which are much shorter than those on Matthew, seek to counter Arian attempts to read passages in the Gospel of John as support for their heteroousian, anomoian Christology—that is, for their view that the Son's substance is not identical to the Father's substance, nor even *like* the Father's.[27] The homilies on First Corinthians likewise attack the anomoians.[28] In his homilies on the Pauline Epistles, Chrysostom's impassioned enthusiasm for the apostle to the Gentiles resounds throughout; the city of Rome, he writes in his homilies on Romans, is not glorious for its gold or its columns but rather because of "these pillars of the Church," Peter and Paul.[29]

25. Chrysostom, *Homilies on John*, homily 2, PG 59:30–35, at 34. Briefly discussed by Féghali, "ʿAbdallāh," 108–9.

26. Quasten, *Patrology*, 3:437.

27. Quasten, 3:439; Féghali, "ʿAbdallāh," 101–2.

28. Quasten, *Patrology*, 3:445.

29. Trans. Quasten, 3:442–44.

Many of Chrysostom's concerns continued to be relevant long after he wrote his homilies. This is partly because the outcomes of these debates were codified in church councils, whose teachings, especially the Nicene Creed, continued to be a key part of a Christian education. It is also because some of the same christological debates were still alive in the eleventh century.[30] Muslims, for instance, held that Christ was a prophet, not God, and so would have agreed with Arians, who said that Christ was not even similar to God (the Father) in substance. Chrysostom was, furthermore, one of a number of authorities whose christological statements were adduced in debates between Chalcedonian, Nestorian, and Miaphysite Christians.

While most of Ibn al-Faḍl's translations are known only from manuscripts that contain them, he does refer to his translation of Chrysostom's homilies on Genesis in his book *The Joy of the Believer* (dated 1050–1051 CE).[31] In that passage, Ibn al-Faḍl seems to suggest that he also translated Chrysostom's commentaries on the other four books of the Pentateuch, translations that are otherwise unknown—a reminder of how many of his translations must still await, undetected, in manuscripts.

Basil

Ibn al-Faḍl translated two sets of homilies by Basil of Caesarea: the *Homilies on the Psalms* and the *Homilies on the Hexaemeron*.[32] Ibn al-Faḍl's translation of Basil's *Hexaemeron* is a revised translation based on an earlier Arabic translation as well as the original Greek (though only the Greek is mentioned in manuscripts of the translation).[33] As in many of his translations, Ibn al-Faḍl added his own marginal commentary; we will return to these particularly lengthy marginalia on the *Hexaemeron* in later chapters.

Basil's homilies on the Psalter cover only a dozen or so psalms. These homilies are in a sense a guide to improving the soul using this small set of psalms. "A psalm is the serenity of souls," writes Basil, "author of peace, calming the tumult and swell of thoughts."[34] The audience for these homilies included ordinary people; "a psalm," continues Basil,

30. I thank Maria Mavroudi for stressing this point.

31. Féghali, "ʿAbdallāh," 100; Ibn al-Faḍl, *Joy of the Believer*, question 83, Cairo COP Theol. 112 (= Graf 638 = Simaika 238), p. 77, lines 8–9: "This is what . . . Saint John Chrysostom said in his explication of the Pentateuch, which we translated from Greek into Arabic" (*hādhā qawlu abīnā l-muʿaẓẓami l-qiddīsi Yūḥannā l-dhahabīyi l-fami fī tafsīri l-Tawrāt, naqalnāhu mina l-lughati l-yūnānīyati ilā l-ʿarabīya*). The date typically reported for this text is 1052 CE, based on an Anno Mundi and indiction date given by the manuscripts, but these are best understood as 1050–1051 CE. For the identical date given in manuscripts of Ibn al-Faḍl's translation of Basil's *Hexaemeron*, see ch. 1, §1, p. 9.

32. According to Nasrallah (*Histoire*, 3.1:204), Ibn al-Faḍl may also have translated a number of Basil's homilies transmitted in Paris ar. 133 after his translation of Basil's *Homilies on the Psalms*.

33. Roberts, "Re-Translation." Ibn al-Faḍl's style is neither overly loose nor strictly literal. Cf. Graf, *GCAL*, 2:56 ("kompilatorische Uebersetzung"); Daiber, "Graeco-Arabica," 7 ("free rendering").

34. Basil, *On the Psalms* 1.2, PG 29:212C.

> is a refuge from demons, a means of inducing help from the angels, a weapon in fears by night, a rest from toils by day, a safeguard for infants, an adornment for those in their prime, a consolation for the elderly, a most fitting ornament for women. It colonizes deserts; it teaches the marketplaces moderation; it is the elementary exposition of beginners, the improvement of those advancing, the solid support of the perfect, the voice of the Church.[35]

Psalms, and so Basil's homilies too, are directed not merely at the elite biblical scholar but also at students, those who frequent markets, and those who spend their days in manual labor. We may guess at the typical occupation of Basil's audience when he declares, "Today you have cultivated the earth, tomorrow another will do so, and after him another."[36] By translating this work, Ibn al-Faḍl made available an accessible guide to improving the self, built upon a text that Christians with any education at all were expected to know well.

Basil's *Homilies on the Hexaemeron,* a series of nine homilies delivered during Lent before 370, is an extended commentary on the six-day creation narrative (known as the "hexaemeron") in Genesis 1:1–26.[37] In an accessible but artful style, the homilies portray the cosmos as God created it. They address the origin of the cosmos (homily 1), the earliest moments of the universe before anything was fully formed (homily 2), the nature of time and eternity (homily 3), elements and their qualities (homily 4), plant life (homily 5), ordinary versus "true" light, the sun and moon (homily 6), sea animals (homily 7), land animals (homily 8), and the human being, pinnacle of creation and most similar to God (homily 9). The result is a scriptural commentary arranged according to its "focus text" that at the same time builds a natural-philosophical argument about what the universe is and how it is structured.[38]

As he delivered these homilies, Basil periodically exhorted his audience to trust completely in the literal truth of the first book of Moses, even as he led them through fairly detailed discussions of the theories that philosophers and "external" (non-Christian) authors had developed about the universe. In the process, Basil took positions on the most influential theories, dismissing some and accepting others, even as he claimed to avoid speculation about unknowable things. Basil also advanced positive cosmological arguments, building upon an existing exegetical tradition focused on the hexaemeral creation narrative, especially Philo of Alexandria's *On the Making of the World According to Moses.*[39] Basil's own exegesis

35. *On the Psalms* 1.2; trans. based on Way, 152–53.

36. *On the Psalms* 1.5; trans. Way, 159.

37. See Quasten, *Patrology,* 3:216; Callahan, "Greek Philosophy."

38. I adopt the term "focus text" (in the sense of *matn*) from Ahmed, "Post-Classical Philosophical Commentaries."

39. Περὶ τῆς τοῦ κατὰ Μωυσέα κοσμοποιΐας, a.k.a. *De opificio mundi;* Robbins, *Hexaemeral Literature.*

was to have a lasting impact not only on hexaemeral exegesis in the Greek and other "eastern" traditions but also in the Latin West.

Several of the positions Basil (like other hexaemeral authors) takes are prominently and self-consciously in opposition to Platonic, Aristotelian, Epicurean, Stoic, and other Hellenic doctrines. But much of Basil's cosmological description takes their conceptual framework for granted, even though he insists that "simplicity of faith" and the word of God should count for more than "rational demonstrations."[40] His periodic show of refusing to stoop to debating is best seen as a rhetorical strategy to distance himself from the theorists he mocks.[41] It is hardly to be taken as an accurate description of his relation to their ideas.

Basil's cosmological framework comes out especially clearly in homilies 1, 2, 3, 6, and 9. He begins (homily 1) with the moment of creation, of cosmogony, asserting God as the cause of all (1.1), contrasting this view with various false Hellenic theories that assert "matter" or "atoms" as the principle or cause of the universe's generation (1.2). The world has a clear beginning in time, rather than being beginningless and thus coeternal with God, as some (e.g., Platonists and Aristotelians) would have it (1.3). Indeed, time itself is part of the world that God created (1.4). This world consists of unseen intelligible things as well as ordinary visible things, such that the intelligible is prior to the visible; the beings that exist outside of time already existed, and then "the present world" was "brought in as an addition" to them, at the beginning of time (1.5).[42] Basil is at pains to emphasize that God was not merely a cause but rather an *intelligent* cause. The world was created with a purpose, as a school for souls (1.5).[43] The word *archē* (beginning, origin, principle) can mean various things (1.5). God's role as the "origin" of the world is analogous to that of human craftsmen (1.7).

The world's creation was instantaneous (1.7). Basil argues that the scriptural "firmament" is not something holding up the earth from below—for then you would need to posit something that holds *it* up, and so on, ad infinitum—but instead that it is God's power alone that keeps the earth motionless at the center of the cosmos (1.8–9). Finally, Basil discusses various theories about the elemental composition of the sky (1.11).

In homily 2, he evokes the early world, created but as yet unformed. "The earth was invisible and formless" (Genesis 1:2). To interpret this passage, he considers whether the earth was impossible to see with ordinary eyes of matter but judges instead that the earth was merely hidden from view (2.1), for it was under water (2.3). Matter is *not*

40. Basil, *Hexaemeron,* 1.10 end, ed. Amand de Mendieta and Rudberg, $18_{10\text{–}11}$ = PG 25A.

41. E.g., 1.11, ed. Amand de Mendieta and Rudberg, $19_{23\text{–}24}$ = PG 28A. For Basil's claim that he avoids speculating beyond what he can know, see Basil, *Hexaemeron,* ed. Giet, 211 n. 3.

42. Ed. Amand de Mendieta and Rudberg, 9_{11}.

43. Ed. Amand de Mendieta and Rudberg, 9_{12}.

uncreated or coeternal with God, but rather God created matter along with forms and bound it all together with an affinity that ensures hidden connections, or *sympatheia*, between even distant material objects (2.2).[44] God's active power is the antithesis of matter's passivity (2.3). The shadows covering the abyss (Genesis 1:2) are not evil but simply the absence of light; evil is not from God but is merely the absence of good (2.4). A shadow does not subsist in itself, but is instead caused by something opaque blocking light. What light? The light in which "the hosts above heaven" (αἱ ἐπουράνιοι στρατιαί) are bathed. What blocks this "light above the cosmos" (ὑπερκοσμίῳ φωτί), casting the shadow? The sky, which must be opaque (2.5).

Basil's rationalizing approach to Scripture can also be seen in homily 3, where he distinguishes between sky and "firmament" (3.3) and proposes a physical-geometric model to fit the puzzling biblical description of "a firmament in the midst of the water" acting as "a divider between water and water" (3.4). There is so much water in the world in order to counter the abundant elemental fire in the universe; by the end of the world, the fire will consume all of the water (3.5). Basil seems to construe the region above the firmament as both physically and ontologically higher; in the lower region is earth and matter (3.9). Despite this placement of the intelligible realm in *physical* relation to the visible realm, Basil ends the homily by urging his audience, in good Platonic form, to progress "from visible things" to an awareness of "the invisible one," God (3.10).

Further along, in homily 6, Basil again lingers upon the (Platonic) distinction between the visible and the invisible. From "visible things" we can extrapolate to "the Unseen One" as from "the sun that is subject to decay" to "the true light" (6.1)—very Platonic notions indeed, even if couched in biblical language.[45] Light existed before the luminaries (the sun and moon), which are material vehicles for light (6.2–3). This is also an opportunity for Basil to emphasize that the Bible offers no pretext for astrology (6.5–6) with its deterministic implications (6.7).

These examples are enough to illustrate how Basil avails himself of Hellenic thought while claiming to reject not only the conclusions of Hellenic, pagan philosophers but also their basic assumptions and principles in favor of a literal reading of the Bible.[46] This was not hypocrisy. Rather it is a single case of the general rule that old habits of thought die hard. Much of what we may call Platonic or Aristotelian had by the fourth century, in elite Graeco-Roman circles, become basic common sense.[47]

44. For *sympatheia*, see Ierodiakonou, "Greek Concept."

45. See Plato's allegory of the sun, *Republic* 6, 508a4–509b9. Comparable biblical passages, Malachi 4:2 ("sun of justice") and John 1:9 ("true light"), are cited by Amand de Mendieta and Rudberg, 89.

46. Ancient Greek influence on the hexaemeral tradition more broadly: Robbins, *Hexaemeral Literature*, 1–23. See also Courtonne, *Saint Basile;* Quasten, *Patrology*, 3:217.

47. Elm, *Sons*. See also Karamanolis, *Philosophy*.

Gregory of Nyssa

Basil's brother Gregory of Nyssa engaged with the ancient philosophical tradition in a way that was particularly sustained and integral to the way he thought about God, the human being, and the cosmos.[48]

Ibn al-Faḍl may have translated Gregory of Nyssa's *Homilies on the Song of Songs,* which explicates part of the Song of Songs (a.k.a. Song of Solomon) in fifteen homilies.[49] Gregory articulates his commentary's interpretive framework from the beginning: the text is to be read as referring to the wedding between the human soul and Christ, a model of transcendence and salvation with a long tradition before and after Gregory.[50]

Ibn al-Faḍl may also have translated Gregory of Nyssa's *On Making Man* (a.k.a. *De hominis opificio*) and *Apology on the Hexaemeron* (a.k.a. *Liber in Hexaemeron*). Arabic translations of these two texts consistently circulated along with Ibn al-Faḍl's translation of Basil's *Hexaemeron,* forming an Arabic "Hexaemeron Corpus." The *same* Arabic translations of these two works by Gregory are, however, also found in manuscripts of a different, earlier Arabic translation of Basil's *Hexaemeron.*[51] Until the translation styles are "fingerprinted" and compared (or a manuscript with clear ascriptions is found), we cannot be sure whether Ibn al-Faḍl produced the Arabic translation of these two hexaemeral texts by Gregory.[52] Still, because the three texts (Basil's *Hexaemeron* and Gregory's two texts) circulated as a corpus in Greek, Arabic, and other manuscripts, it is worth briefly describing Gregory's contributions to this corpus here. Even if Ibn al-Faḍl did not translate them, he must have known the texts and had them in mind as he translated Basil's *Hexaemeron.*

Gregory of Nyssa's *On Making Man* picks up where Basil left off, when God created man in his own image (Genesis 1:27).[53] Accordingly, this is one of the principal works in which Gregory of Nyssa articulates his understanding of "likeness to God" (ὁμοίωσις τῷ θεῷ), an important concept in late antique Platonism,

48. Drobner, "Gregory of Nyssa." See also Dörrie et al., *Gregor von Nyssa;* Bedke, *Anthropologie.*

49. On Song of Songs 1:1–6:8. Nasrallah's assertion that Ibn al-Faḍl translated this text rests on a single manuscript: Ḥarīṣā, Saint Paul, 36. The catalog entry for that manuscript was written by Nasrallah himself: *Catalogue,* 1:66. There he transcribes the title of the text and says that the text "is preceded by a preface." He then asserts that the text's "translator is ʿAbdallāh Ibn al-Faḍl." Nasrallah prints the scribe's colophon. Nowhere does he explain what evidence there is for his assertion that Ibn al-Faḍl translated the text.

50. Quasten, *Patrology,* 3:266. For this tradition, see Pagoulatos, *Tracing the Bridegroom.*

51. Roberts, "Re-Translation."

52. Fingerprinting: Treiger, "Christian Graeco-Arabica," 209–18.

53. In Arabic, *Fī khilqat al-insān wa-sharaf maʿānīh* (Dayr al-Mukhalliṣ 114, p. 235, following Ibn al-Faḍl's translation of Basil's *Hexaemeron*), or *Fī khilqat al-insān fī l-yawm al-sādis* (Paris ar. 134, fol. 103ʳ, following the Anonymous Translation of Basil's *Hexaemeron*).

Christian and pagan alike.[54] This likeness lends humanity its special place in the cosmos, and recovering this original similarity to God is salvation. Much of Gregory's explication dwells on human physiology and his theory of the human being (anthropology).[55]

The work begins by placing man's creation in the context of the world's creation. Man is the pinnacle of the visible world (§§1–3). The entire human being, soul and body, were made to rule the world (§4), for man is a likeness of God (§5). Various aspects of the human body are evaluated. Why does man lack the natural equipment of claw, fang, wing, and so on? So that he focuses his attention on harnessing the power of other animals (§7). The upright human body corresponds to an elevated nature and the possibility of contemplating intellectual rather than corporeal things (§§8–9). Gregory then considers the mind, its connection with the senses, its invisible inscrutability in accordance with *its* being a likeness of God, and the question of where in the body the mind resides and how it relates to matter (§§10–12). Dreams and sleep receive considerable attention (§13). Returning to the question of where the mind is located, Gregory concludes that it pervades the entire body (§14). This is a fact difficult to grasp, since it would be wrong to say that an incorporeal thing is *contained* within a body; instead it is ineffably associated with the body such that when the body ceases, so does the mind (§15). Now if man was made "in God's image and likeness," why arc there male and female? (§16). Indeed, how would humans have multiplied had they remained without sin in paradise? Answer: however angels multiply (§17). Passions and the question of appetites in paradise (§§18–20) lead Gregory to the resurrection (§§21–22). The end of time is a logical necessity if one admits a beginning (§23). Matter is not coeternal with God (§24). Gregory now discusses resurrection and objections to it in considerable depth, especially the question of how the matter of bodies that have decayed or entirely dissolved can be put back together again (§§25–27). If a carnivorous fish, say, devours a man's body and then is caught and eaten by a fisherman (§26.1), God still knows where all the pieces of the first man's body are (§26.2), and the soul recognizes all the parts that belong to it (§27.2), so that they come back together like quicksilver poured out in the dust (§27.6)—a very metallurgical analogy. Souls are created simultaneously with bodies, and the transmigration of souls is absurd (§§28–29). Finally, Gregory concludes with "a more medical consideration" of the human body (§30).[56]

Throughout, the body's materiality is a central concept. As Gerhart Ladner puts it in his study of this treatise, the underlying question for Gregory is

54. For this concept in Gregory of Nyssa (contrasted with Gregory of Nazianzos), see Elm, "Priest and Prophet," 169, 180.

55. Quasten, *Patrology*, 3:263. Use of the Greek medical tradition: Wessel, "Reception."

56. Ed. Forbes, 1:292.

> why, if man was created according to the image and likeness of God and at the same time was made a spiritual-corporeal compound, should his God-given bodily condition be an occasion for so much suffering and evil? The relationship of the material body to the immortal spirit and the position of the soul and mind between the two were . . . principal problems of Gregory of Nyssa's philosophical anthropology.[57]

In this way, Gregory's influential work stressed the need to take seriously the human body's role in Christian spiritual progress and salvation.

The other hexaemeral text by Gregory (which, again, Ibn al-Faḍl may or may not have translated) is his *Apology on the Hexaemeron.*[58] Not a series of homilies (like Basil's *Hexaemeron*) or divided into chapters (like *On Making Man*), the *Apology* instead proceeds through its subject matter in one unbroken text. Returning to the five days prior to the creation of the human being, it was meant to supplement Basil's *Hexaemeron,* ostensibly by defending it, in practice by dealing with many of the problems Basil had left unexplained; Gregory's readings are not always in agreement with his brother's.[59] In particular, Gregory seeks to move away from Basil's antiallegorical stance to allow for more flexibility in interpreting certain scriptural statements about the physical world, and in doing so to integrate the biblical hexaemeron more closely with fourth-century Neoplatonic philosophy.[60] Thus where Basil considers the world above the firmament to be distinct in its brightness but physically continuous with our own world, only separated from us by a material barrier, Gregory posits a world "up there" that is absolutely divided from ours, the intelligible world; it is only "up there" in a figurative sense, since it is not located in space but rather transcends it.[61]

Some of the exegetical solutions Gregory comes up with are quite striking. To explain how God, who is immaterial, could have created a world made of matter, Gregory proposes that matter itself is a complex of qualities, each of which alone is an immaterial idea: as Richard Sorabji put it, for Gregory "the material world is a bundle of God's thoughts."[62]

The Hexaemeron Corpus

The joint circulation of these three hexaemeral texts in Arabic—Basil's *Hexaemeron* and Gregory's *On Making Man* and *Apology on the Hexaemeron*—follows the model of the Greek manuscript tradition. There too the three frequently appear

57. Ladner, "Philosophical Anthropology," 62.

58. *Iḥtijāj Ghrīghūriyūs . . . ʿan al-khalīqa fī l-sittat ayyām* (*sic;* Dayr al-Mukhalliṣ 114, p. 401).

59. Callahan, "Greek Philosophy," 31, 44 n. 63, 47.

60. Gil-Tamayo, "Hex."

61. Callahan, "Greek Philosophy," 47.

62. Gil-Tamayo, "Hex," 388; Sorabji, *Philosophy of the Commentators,* 2:158–61. See also ch. 7, p. 209, n. 39.

together in manuscripts, providing a detailed exegesis of the Genesis creation narrative: (1) Basil's *Hexaemeron*, on the first five days of creation; (2) Gregory's *On Making Man*, on the sixth and final day; and (3) Gregory's *Apology on the Hexaemeron*, again on the first five days.

The Greek manuscript tradition of these works attests to three common groupings of texts:[63]

1. Small Hexaemeron Corpus: Basil, *Hexaemeron* (nine homilies); two homilies on the sixth day of creation, attributed to Basil (or, sometimes, to his brother Gregory);[64] and the *On Paradise*, also attributed to Basil.[65]
2. Normal Hexaemeron Corpus: Basil, *Hexaemeron* (nine homilies); Gregory, *On Making Man*; Gregory, *Apology on the Hexaemeron*.
3. Large Hexaemeron Corpus, containing all of these texts: the Small Corpus, followed by the second and third works in the Normal Corpus.

It is the second of these, the Normal Corpus, which circulated in Arabic.[66] We may refer to it here simply as the "Hexaemeron Corpus."

Ibn al-Faḍl certainly produced a revised translation of the first work of this corpus, Basil's *Hexaemeron*. Even if he did not translate the other two parts of the corpus, he may well have intended his retranslation of Basil to circulate with Arabic versions of Gregory's hexaemeral texts. In Greek, the three texts circulated together by the eleventh century.[67] Already when he composed them, Gregory clearly intended these two works to be associated with his brother's *Hexaemeron*.[68]

The Hexaemeron Corpus, taken together, offers a cosmological exposition that proceeds in stages culminating in the creation of man, and then turns back to consider the first five days in light of the noblest of God's creatures. The ensemble, carrying all the authority of the Cappadocian Fathers, conjured before the eleventh-century reader the world's earliest moments, raising and addressing a range of physical and cosmological questions and encouraging readers to use it as a focus text for their own natural philosophical commentaries.[69]

63. Amand de Mendieta and Rudberg, *Basile*, 3.

64. PG 30:9–72, edited as Basil's homilies 10 and 11 by Smets and van Esbroeck; as dubia by Hörner. Considered dubious: Quasten, *Patrology*, 3:217. Spurious: Amand de Mendieta and Rudberg, *Basile*, 3. Plausibly authentic: Rousseau, *Basil*, 363. They are absent from Arabic manuscripts containing Ibn al-Faḍl's translation of Basil's *Hexaemeron*, and from the Armenian version: Thomson, *Saint Basil*, 19.

65. Ed. Hörner.

66. In Arabic manuscripts, Gregory's *Apology on the Hexaemeron* is typically presented as the last chapter (*bāb* 32) of *On Making Man*, so some manuscript catalogs list only Basil's *Hexaemeron* and Gregory's *On Making Man* under Arabic manuscripts that in fact contain all three.

67. Amand de Mendieta and Rudberg, *Basile*, entries on eleventh-century manuscripts.

68. Gregory of Nyssa, *On Making Man*, preface, PG 44:124–28.

69. Robbins, *Hexaemeral Literature*; Pasquali, "Doxographica."

3 PRO-CHALCEDONIAN DOGMA AT THE DAWN OF ISLAM

Basil, the Gregorys, and Chrysostom loomed large in the Byzantine Chalcedonian tradition, as well as the other Nicene traditions (Nestorian, Miaphysite, Monothelete, and so on). After these traditions formally parted ways in the fifth century, their own great ecclesiastical writers continued to join the ranks of the fathers of their own respective churches.

In this section, we will consider several later Chalcedonian church fathers from the following centuries whose works on Byzantine ecclesiastical teachings Ibn al-Faḍl translated: Sophronios of Jerusalem (b. ca. 560, Damascus; d. perhaps ca. 638, Jerusalem), Maximos the Confessor (580–662), and John of Damascus (b. ca. 650; d. ca. 750 or before 754).[70] To the theological issues of the fourth century—especially Christ's divinity—were added new concerns: If Christ was God, how was he at the same time a human being? In the fifth century, a series of fierce debates carried out largely by bishops in the imperial political arena resulted in the emergence of several parties, each with their own answers: Nestorians, that Christ's human and divine nature are quite separate from each other, such that the Virgin Mary was the mother not of God but of Christ; Miaphysites, that to the contrary the human and divine in Christ are so inextricably connected as to be a single nature; and Chalcedonians, that the two natures simultaneously exist in Christ, inseparable from each other but at the same time clearly distinguishable from one another.[71]

Sophronios, Maximos, and John of Damascus were Chalcedonian thinkers of a later age, writing after centuries of debate and conflict among these parties within the empire. They were active at a time when the Roman (Byzantine) Empire was increasingly unstable. The invasion and occupation of Syria, Palestine, and Egypt by the Persian Sasanid Empire (610–629) was followed by a triumphant reconquest by the Byzantine emperor Heraclius (r. 610–641) and his recovery of the True Cross in 630—and then the stunning defeat of Byzantine and Persian armies alike at the hands of new Arab Muslim conquerors (beginning 634). These critical developments rattled the imperial elite.[72] In this climate, in 638, Heraclius and his allies took the side of those who accepted Chalcedonian doctrine on Christ's two natures but further argued that he had only one will (Monotheletes) and one activity (Monenergists).[73]

70. Louth, "Maximus"; Studer, "John of Damascus," 228. For conflicting information concerning the date of Sophronios's death, see Booth, *Crisis*, 243–44; cited by N. Marinides, NASCAS listserv, 10 July 2013.

71. Dvornik, *Ecumenical Councils*, 13–29.

72. Booth, *Crisis*, esp. 4–5.

73. Dvornik, *Ecumenical Councils*, 29–36. For grassroots support for Monotheletism in Syria, see Tannous, "In Search of Monotheletism."

Maximos and Sophronios fought the imperial adoption of these doctrines, which fell short, as they saw it, of the radical position that Christ was meaningfully human and divine at once. And so Dyotheletism (the explicit doctrine that Christ has two wills) was born.[74] Maximos in particular was a tireless champion of Dyotheletism.

In the Byzantine Empire (and the Latin West), their views eventually triumphed. John of Damascus, writing about three generations later, a Byzantine Christian under Islamic rule, sought to systematize and defend this Chalcedonian Dyothelete orthodoxy while vigorously opposing a new Byzantine ecclesiastical and imperial policy that sought to purge the church of any hint of idolatry: iconoclasm.[75] His pro-icon stance and his philosophical systematization of Chalcedonian theology also eventually became established Byzantine orthodoxy.

Sophronios

A disciple of John Moschos (d. 619 or 634), Sophronios was the patriarch of Jerusalem (634–638) who negotiated the city's surrender in 638 to the caliph ʿUmar ibn al-Khaṭṭāb (r. 634–644). When he became patriarch of Jerusalem, he promulgated a *Synodical Letter* affirming Chalcedonian Dyothelete dogma.[76]

Ibn al-Faḍl produced an Arabic adaptation of Sophronios's *Synodical Letter.* This text, entitled *The Book of Proof on the Confirmation of Faith,* was previously thought to be the translation of a spurious work falsely attributed to Sophronios.[77] A comparison of manuscripts of Ibn al-Faḍl's Arabic text to the Greek of Sophronios's *Synodical Letter,* however, shows that the Arabic consists of excerpts adapted and translated from the *Synodical Letter.*[78] Various collections of theological excerpts from the *Synodical Letter* circulated in Greek.[79] To judge from their similar content, it seems likely that one of these was the basis for Ibn al-Faḍl's translation.[80]

74. Jankowiak, "Invention."

75. Dvornik, *Ecumenical Councils,* 36–40; Brown, "Dark-Age Crisis."

76. PG 87:3148–200; ed. as part of the Acts of the Quinisext Council: ed. Riedinger in *ACO*², 2.1:410–94; trans. (with Riedinger's text on facing pages) Allen, *Sophronius,* 65–157.

77. *Kitāb al-Burhān fī tathbīt al-īmān.* Graf (*GCAL,* 2:57) calls the Arabic a work "of unknown origin," noting the ascription to Sophronios. Nasrallah (*Histoire,* 3.1:207) holds essentially the same opinion on the matter, although he does list it under the heading "Œuvres de Saint Sophrone." Noble and Treiger ("Christian Arabic Theology," 378) call it a work by "Pseudo-Sophronius."

78. This was my conclusion from comparing the text in Vat. Sbath 44 (seventeenth century) to the *Synodical Letter.* As Alexander Treiger has kindly informed me, there is now an edition of Ibn al-Faḍl's translation, ed. Khūrī, with a detailed comparison (introduction, part 2, ch. 6 = pp. 203–17) of *Burhān* 1–3 with a modern Arabic translation of the *Synodical Letter.*

79. Riedinger, "Die Nachkommen."

80. E.g., the adaptation in Paris gr. 1371 begins (fol. 9ʳ) with the same prefatory remarks as *Burhān* 1.1, ed. Khūrī, 252 (χρὴ πάντα χριστιανὸν . . . καθὰ καὶ ὑποτέτακται = *yanbaghī li-kulli masīḥī* . . .

The heading for the Arabic version reads:

> Book/Letter (*kitāb*) of Proof on the Confirmation of Faith, by Saint Sophronios, given the honorific "Mouth of Christ," which he sent to Rome, on the faith of the Six Holy Councils—he referred to six councils only because he departed from this world before the seventh council took place. The deacon ʿAbdallāh ibn al-Faḍl ibn ʿAbdallāh al-Muṭrān al-Anṭākī translated it from Greek into Arabic, to seek recompense and reward; it is twenty-eight chapters.[81]

This heading emphasizes the letter's profession of faith and agreement with—and thus suitability as a guide to—the doctrine of the ecumenical councils, which, for the Byzantines, were seven in number. Sophronios's text, the heading is quick to point out, did not intentionally leave out the pro-icon Seventh Ecumenical Council of 787 but was simply written before it took place.

Sophronios's *Synodical Letter* articulated with precision and detail what set Miaphysites in Byzantine's eastern reconquered territories apart from the Byzantine Chalcedonian hierarchy. The version that Ibn al-Faḍl translated, by highlighting the six ecumenical councils—of which Miaphysites accept only the first three—and generally rearranging the letter under doctrinal headings, is even better suited for this purpose.

Maximos's Debate with Pyrrhus

Sophronios's student Maximos the Confessor (580–662) is one of the most important theologians in the Chalcedonian Dyothelete (and modern Greek Orthodox) tradition. Not only did he subscribe to the doctrine of two natures inextricably bound yet distinct in Christ, but he also fought vehemently against Monotheletism. Monotheletes accordingly held him in contempt, as attested by a defamatory *Life of Maximos* written in Syriac in the seventh/eighth century at the latest.[82] In exasperation at Maximos's Dyothelete (two-will) stance, the *Life* mocks Maximos for thinking that everything about Christ was "doubled" (*ʿfîfā*) except his hypostasis.[83]

As a young man, Maximos pursued a career at the imperial court in Constantinople, before giving it up to become a monk nearby. In 626 he fled the Sasanian

---

wa-hādhā sharḥuhā), then likewise continues with *Synodical Letter* 2.2.1, where, like the *Burhān*, it is missing a phrase (ἀλλ' οὐδὲ ἄλλοθέν ποθεν ἢ ἐκ τοῦ πατρὸς τὴν ὑπόστασιν ἔχοντα).

81. Vat. Sbath 44, fol. 81v, repeated fol. 83r. Now ed. Khūrī, 248, 251.

82. Brock, "Early Syriac Life," 300: the *Life* is preserved in a single manuscript, British Museum Add. 7192, fols. 72v–78v, in the second part, which is "in a seventh/eighth century hand." It is entitled *The story of impious Maximos of Palestine, who blasphemed against his Creator and whose tongue was cut out* (*tašʿîtā d-ʿal Maksîmûs rašîʿā d-men Palesṭîniʾ d-gaddep ʿal bārûyeh w-etpseq lešāneh*), ed. Brock, 302, trans. (modified) 314.

83. §9, ed. and trans. Brock, 306, 316.

invasion into Asia Minor, settling in North Africa. It was there that he took up his vocal opposition to Heraclius's Monothelete edict of 638, the *Ekthesis*. Maximos's stance, supported by Pope Martin at the Lateran Council of 649, eventually led to Maximos's arrest, exile, and subsequent condemnation for treason, for which his tongue and right hand were severed. He died in 662, exiled to Lazika, by the Black Sea.[84]

Maximos's objections to Monotheletism centered around its incompatibility with his theory of the human being. He believed that the will attached not to the person but to the nature, so that someone with both a human and a divine nature must have both a human and a divine will, for human nature without the human will would hardly in his view be human nature at all. Thus his theory of the human being had manifest theological implications.[85]

Maximos wrote works ranging from philosophically sophisticated treatises to more accessible articulations of doctrine and spiritual instruction. Those translated or possibly translated by Ibn al-Faḍl are reasonably accessible: *Disputation with Pyrrhos* (certainly translated by Ibn al-Faḍl) and the *Chapters on Love* and *Chapters on Knowledge* (possibly: see §4 below).

The *Disputation with Pyrrhos*—or, in Arabic, *A Debate between Pyrrhos Patriarch of Constantinople and Saint Maximos the Confessor on Ecclesiastical Opinions*[86]—is a dialogue on whether Christ has one or two wills or activities. It presents arguments in favor of the two-will position in a dialogue narrating Maximos's debate in North Africa in 645 with the Monothelete Pyrrhos, who had recently resigned from his Constantinopolitan see. Maximos's refutation of the one-will position eventually convinces even Pyrrhos.[87]

This debate was of clear importance to the eleventh-century Byzantine Church, since it focused on a doctrine that distinguished that church from contemporary Monotheletes in Syria, the Maronites, whose community was still significant.[88] It also distinguished the Byzantine Church from the influential Syrian Miaphysites, since the Miaphysite position that Christ's human and divine natures were combined into a single nature precludes the possibility of Christ having two separate wills.

John of Damascus

John of Damascus (ca. 650–ca. 750) was a monk at the Monastery of Mar Saba outside of Jerusalem. He wrote on a range of subjects, including the theory of

84. Louth, "Maximus," 135–36; *ODB*, s.vv. "Ekthesis," "Maximos the Confessor."

85. Tatakis, *La philosophie*, 82, 86–87.

86. *Maqāla li-l-qiddīs Maksīmus wa-sharḥ al-munāẓara allatī jarat fīmā baynahu wa-bayn Bīrrus baṭrak al-Qusṭanṭīnīya fī l-ārāʾ al-bīʿīya.* Abbreviated title in Jerusalem, Holy Sepulcher, ar. 12 (twelfth/thirteenth century), fol. 75r; longer title on the next page, fol. 75v, and in Vat. ar. 125 (1716 CE), fol. 1v.

87. Louth, "Maximus," 136; *ODB*, s.v. "Pyrrhos."

88. Tannous, "In Search of Monotheletism"; Graf, *GCAL*, 2:94–102.

images used to justify the veneration of icons (especially icons of Christ). His extremely popular *Dialectica* (an elementary introduction to Aristotelian logic)[89] and *Exposition of Faith* (on natural philosophy and theology) offered a synthesis of and introduction to Peripatetic philosophy and how it can be used to defend Chalcedonian Christian theological positions.

The *Dialectica* and *Exposition of Faith* were already available in Arabic when Ibn al-Faḍl was active, since both had been translated by the abbot Antonios of the Monastery of Saint Symeon the Younger near Antioch.[90] There does not seem to be any evidence that Ibn al-Faḍl produced his own translation or retranslation of these important works.[91] Still, he was certainly familiar with Antonios's Arabic translation at least of the *Exposition of Faith,* since he excerpted it in his *Joy of the Believer.*[92]

Ibn al-Faḍl translated John of Damascus's brief creed, or statement of orthodox doctrine: the *Statement on Correct Thought.*[93] It is a compact confession of doctrine and statement of obedience to conciliar canons, his bishop (addressed directly), and Saint Basil (probably a reference to his monastic *Rules*).

It begins with a short preface, framed in the humble manner expected of a monk, followed by a first-person confession of belief in (§1) God, the Trinity, creation, and God's attributes; (§2) the Son, his incarnation for human salvation, his consubstantiality with both the Father and with humans (antiheteroousian, i.e., anti-Arian), his two natures (anti-Miaphysite) but single hypostasis (anti-Nestorian), since otherwise the Trinity would be a quadrinity; why all this must be; (§3) that both natures coexist in the Son, who has two wills (anti-Monothelete) and two activities (anti-Monenergist)—with an explanation of why this must be so—and the Son's perfection despite his human will and activity; (§4) two wills, two activities (reiterated), that the Son "performed divine acts and, theandrically,[94] human acts," that God became man, as is clear from the episode in which Peter tells Jesus that he is the messiah and Son of God (Matthew 16:13–18); (§5) that there are three hypostases of the Divinity, as the Trisagion hymn says. John further rejects "the

89. See ch. 6, esp pp. 184–85.

90. See ch. 1, p. 27.

91. Nasrallah, *Histoire,* 3.1:209.

92. Kotter, *Die Überlieferung,* 217, reporting Graf's unpublished observations.

93. Λίβελλος περὶ ὀρθοῦ φρονήματος: PG 94:1421–32; *CPG* 8046, where the Latin title given is *De recta sententia liber.* It is also known as *Libellus de recta fide* and *Libellus de recta sententia*—not to be confused with the Damascene's *Expositio fidei* (*CPG* 8043), called *De fide orthodoxa* in the Latin version.

94. A Dionysian term, especially with *energeia:* ps.-Dionysios, *Epistle* 4 (end), ed. Ritter in ps.-Dionysios the Areopagite, *Corpus Dionysiacum II,* 161, line 9 = PG 3:1072C; cited by Lampe s.v. θεανδρικός 2. The term is also used by Gregory of Nyssa and pseudo-Kaisarios; in addition to Lampe, see Allen, "Pseudo-Caesarius," 99.

addition of the empty-minded Peter the Fuller" and (§6) Origen's doctrine of the preexistence of souls, metempsychosis, and "the portentous restoration,"[95] while (§7) accepting "the six holy councils." He methodically names those condemned by each council, then ends with an oath: (§8) "I swear . . . to be of such a mind," and not to have anything to do with those who believe otherwise, especially Maronites; not to accept "clerical bigamy"; "to obey the most holy and catholic and apostolic Church of our Christ-loving metropolis of Damascus, and in all things to obey and follow Your Holiness, and not to accept any of the Manichaeans cast out by Your Holiness," and to follow "the holy canons of the holy apostles, the holy synods, and the holy and God-revealing Basil."

Ibn al-Faḍl translated this concise confession of orthodoxy and obedience under the title *Dustūr fī l-amāna al-mustaqīma,* a literal translation of the Greek title.[96] (Ibn al-Faḍl's translation as preserved in manuscripts replaces Damascus with Constantinople in §8: "our Christ-loving city, known as Constantinople."[97] Perhaps Ibn al-Faḍl's Greek exemplar contained a recension of the creed produced in the Byzantine capital.) Ibn al-Faḍl thus made available to Arabic readers a basic template for right belief, which would steer them away from the errors that might lead them to fall away from Nicene, Chalcedonian, and other conciliar doctrine. Obedience to Basil (of Caesarea) likely refers to Basil's monastic *Rules,* which were widely used among Byzantine Chalcedonians, especially since John of Damascus was a monk—a fact noted in manuscripts of his work.[98]

A "brief" confession of faith follows Ibn al-Faḍl's translation of the *Statement* in some manuscripts.[99] Graf states that Ibn al-Faḍl is named as the *translator* of this text but that no author is mentioned, while Joseph Nasrallah offers the tentative suggestion that Ibn al-Faḍl himself compiled the text.[100] But the testimony of the manuscript Graf used should leave little doubt, for it opens:

95. John of Damascus refers here to Origen's theory of universal "restoration" (*apokatastasis*), as described in a text sometimes ascribed to Leontios of Byzantium (d. ca. 543), that "when the body is punished (κολαζομένου) the soul is gradually purified and thus is restored (ἀποκαθίσταται) to its former rank, and . . . that the demons and angels are also restored": *De sectis* 10.6 = PG 86:1265C; cited by Lampe s.v. ἀποκατάστασις B.3. See Ramelli, *Christian Doctrine of Apokatastasis.*

96. Not all Greek manuscripts have this title; see the "Admonitio" at PG 94:1421. On the translation: Graf, *GCAL,* 2:57–58; Nasrallah, *Histoire,* 3.1:208–9. Although Sbath asserts that Ibn al-Faḍl is the translator of John Damascene's other works, Nasrallah rightly expresses caution about following this unsubstantiated assertion.

97. Sinai ar. 352, fol. 97ᵛ; Vat. ar. 79, fol. 325ʳ: *madīnatinā al-muḥibba li-l-masīḥ al-maʿrūf bi-l-Qusṭanṭīnīya.*

98. Quasten, *Patrology,* 3:212–14. It could also be a reference to the liturgy attributed to Saint Basil: ibid., 3:226–228; Taft, *ODB,* s.v. "Liturgy."

99. I use the text in Vat. ar. 79 (1223 CE), fols. 325ᵛ–326ʳ.

100. Graf, *GCAL,* 2:58; Nasrallah, *Histoire,* 3.1:208.

In the name of God the Father, the Son, and the Holy Spirit. The Very Brief Creed. It is sound for the one from among the Orthodox who has no learning at all. ʿAbdallāh ibn al-Faḍl ibn ʿAbdallāh al-Muṭrān extracted it from the words of the Holy Fathers and translated it into Arabic.[101]

In other words, Ibn al-Faḍl constructed this brief creed from patristic excerpts and translated them (presumably from Greek) into Arabic. The rest of the text reads, in its entirety:[102]

بارك أيّها السيد. أؤمن بإلاه واحد، ضابط الكل، أزلي لا مبدأ له بالكلّيّة، صانع الكل ممّا يُرى وما لا يرا (كذا)، معلوم في ثلاثية الأقانيم، أعني أباً وابناً وروحاً قدوساً، وبرئاسة واحدةٍ ا<ل>لاهوت الواحد، وملك واحد، وسلطان واحد، وقوة واحدة، وفعل واحد، وإرادته واحدة وطبيعته واحدة. وأؤمن بربنا وإلاهنا إيسوع المسيح، أحد الثالوث القدوس الطاهر، كلمة الله الأب وابنه الوحيد الذي قبل الدهور، وأعترف أنّه لأجل رحمته التي لا توصف لهفوتنا البشرية بإيثاره طوعاً وإرادة الله والده ومسرّة الروح القدس الإلهية تجسد خلواً من زرع من والدة الله الكلّيّة القدس مريم البتول، وصار بعينه إنساناً كاملاً، كما أنه إلاه بالطبع كاملٌ قنوماً واحداً مركّباً من طبيعتين، وهو طبيعتان وله فعلان طبيعيّان و<إر>ادتان طبيعيتان. وأقبل المجامع الستة القدوسة الجارية في العالم وأؤثر وأرتضي بكل ما جددوه وأفرزوا بعد كل خلاف ثار على بيعة المسيح إلاهنا الطاهر. هذا كله أعتقد وإيّاه أحفظ، ومع هذا (كذا) الأمانة المستقيمة المرضية لله تعالى، أؤمّل وأضرع أن أمثل لدى منبر المسيح تعالى في يوم الدينونة وأحظى بخلاصةٍ بجوده الذي له يليق المجد والإكرام والسجود مع أبيه الذي لا مبدأ له وروحه الكلي القدس والمحيي، الآن، دائماً، وإلى آباد الدهور، آمين. نجوت.

Lord, bless. I believe in one god, master of the universe, pre-eternal, with no beginning at all, maker of the universe, seen and unseen, known in the triplicity of the hypostases, I mean a father, a son, and a holy spirit, and with one rulership the one godhead, and one kingship, and one might, and one power, and one activity (*fiʿl* ~ ἐνέργεια); his will is one, and his nature is one. And I believe in our lord and god Jesus Christ, one of the chaste holy trinity, the word of God the Father and his only son, who is before the ages; and I confess that on account of his compassion, which is indescribable, towards our human lapse, by his love (*īthār*), voluntarily, and by the will of God his father and the divine pleasure (*masarra*) of the Holy Spirit, without seed he acquired a body from the All-Holy Mother of God, the Virgin Mary, and he became in himself a complete man, just as he is a complete god by nature, one hypostasis composed of two natures, being two natures and having two natural activities and two natural wills. And I accept the six holy councils that took place in this world, and I love and cherish all that they added and clarified after each controversy that erupted against the Church of Christ our chaste god. I believe all this and memorize it, and with this correct creed, pleasing to God Almighty, I hope and beseech that I may stand before the pulpit (*minbar*) of Christ Almighty on the day of judgment (*daynūna*) and obtain salvation by his goodness; to him belongs majesty and honoring and worship

101. Vat. ar. 79, fol. 325v: *bismi llāhi l-abi wa-l-ibni wa-l-rūḥi l-qudus, al-amānatu <l->mukhtaṣaratu jiddan, taṣluḥu li-man lā darra lahu bi-l-ʿilmi mina l-urthudhuksīyīn, istakhrajahā min kalāmi l-ābāʾi l-qiddīsīn ʿAbdallāh ibn al-Faḍl ibn ʿAbdallāh al-muṭrān wa-tarjamahā ilā l-lughati l-ʿarabīya.*

102. Vat. ar. 79, fols. 325v–326r. There follow three lines added later. For scribal notes written in Greek by non-Greek scribes on fol. 327v (which was once the end of the manuscript), see Roberts, "Writing." Like John of Damascus, Ibn al-Faḍl mentions only six councils.

> along with his father, who has no beginning, and his holy and life-giving universal spirit, now and forever, and until the eternities of the ages. Amen. May I be saved.

This text was produced by Ibn al-Faḍl, as the title notes, for the ignorant among Christians of his own confession. It stands in contrast to much of the rest of his translation program, perhaps being closest in its audience to his translation of the Psalter. This, if anything, was a text for pastoral purposes—placing his translations of more sophisticated texts in relief. Even his translation of John of Damascus's creed was at a register too high to expect the Arabic-speaking Christian flock of Antioch's churches to study and too long for them to memorize.

This document, though simple in style, promoted the Byzantine Chalcedonian answers to a series of complex theological and christological questions. Together they amounted to a vision of orthodoxy espoused by the Byzantine hierarchy, against Nestorian, Miaphysite, Monothelete, and other doctrinal positions that were articulated and defended in the eastern territories of the Byzantine Empire.

4 COLLECTED WISDOM

Two closely related genres of texts Ibn al-Faḍl translated, "chapters" (*kephalaia*) and "questions and answers" (*erōtapokriseis*), offer the reader carefully curated collections of pithy wisdom, brief statements, and sayings that could easily be studied and memorized on the road to self-perfection.

The Christian genre of *kephalaia,* or short "chapters," can be traced back to Evagrius of Pontus (d. 399), who modeled his *kephalaia* on earlier Greek wisdom literature, proverbs, and collections of sayings.[103] (His works often circulated under others' names because of his condemnation as a heretic at the Second Council of Constantinople in 553.) Each "chapter" offered a succinct distillation of spiritual instruction for monks, culled from scriptural or patristic sources and varying in length from a single line to a modest paragraph.

Belonging to this genre are two collections of "chapters" by Maximos the Confessor, the *Chapters on Love* and the *Chapters on Knowledge,* probably translated by Ibn al-Faḍl,[104] and another collection, certainly translated by Ibn al-Faḍl, that sometimes circulated under Maximos's name but was not the work of his pen,

103. Kalvesmaki, "Evagrius"; Géhin, "Les collections," esp. 2, 8–12. Wisdom literature: Gutas, *Greek Wisdom;* Gutas, "Classical Arabic Wisdom Literature."

104. Nasrallah, *Histoire,* 3.1:207. Graf does not mention either as a translation by Ibn al-Faḍl. Nasrallah mentions both, with no explicit evidence. For the *Chapters on Love,* one of the manuscripts Nasrallah cites is from the "Collection Naṣrī Wakīl à Alep," listed under Ibn al-Faḍl's name in Sbath, *Fihris,* 1:52, no. 404. The other manuscripts listed by Nasrallah would need to be examined to confirm the ascription to Ibn al-Faḍl, since Sbath's catalog is unreliable. Likewise, one of the manuscripts

known to modern scholars as the *Loci communes*. Isaac of Nineveh's *Ascetic Homilies*, partially translated by Ibn al-Faḍl, are related to this genre. Isaac's *Chapters on Knowledge*, which Ibn al-Faḍl *may* have translated (see below), fit squarely within it, even bearing the same title as one of Evagrius's works.[105]

"Questions and answers" (*erōtapokriseis*) likewise gather brief wise statements, framing them not as a simple numbered list (as in collections of "chapters") but rather as the answers to a series of questions. In this genre, Ibn al-Faḍl translated the *Questions and Answers* ascribed in the Greek tradition to Kaisarios (Caesarius), the brother of Gregory of Nazianzos (fourth century).

Maximos the Confessor: *Kephalaia*

Maximos's collections of "chapters" were carefully crafted, arguing through the selection and arrangement of (mostly unattributed) quotations for specific theories of the human being and its relation to divinity while guiding the Christian ascetic in his or her quest of self-perfection. They thus participate in a long tradition of "practical philosophy"—theories of ideal human action and its close connection to interior psychological states.

The *Chapters on Love* consist of a preface followed by four sets of 100 chapters each (whence each is called a "century," ἑκατοντάς), most of them quite short (several lines), on the theme of love (*agapē*). While occasionally making reference to Chalcedonian theological positions such as the "homoousian Trinity,"[106] these chapters focus not on what the community should believe but rather on how the individual wishing to live a spiritual life of love should go about it.[107] The Arabic version that Ibn al-Faḍl may have produced circulated under the title *Book on Love, which is the most noble and exalted of the commandments*.[108]

Stressing that the thoughts are not his own, Maximos explains in the preface that he has plucked ideas from the works of "the Holy Fathers" and phrased them concisely as an aid to memorization.[109] He then concludes by saying that the chapters are difficult to understand fully and should be read with an "uncomplicated mind"; the

---

Nasrallah cites for the *Chapters on Knowledge* is from the "collection des héritiers ʿAbdallah Ṣaqqāl à Alep," also listed under Ibn al-Faḍl's name in Sbath, *Fihris*, 1:52, no. 405. Again, we can only be sure of the ascription to Ibn al-Faḍl if other manuscripts corroborate it.

105. Géhin, "Les collections," 3.

106. *Chapters on Love* 4.77$_{1-2}$.

107. Balthasar, *Kosmische Liturgie*, 410; Louth, "Maximus," 138.

108. *Kitāb fī l-maḥabbati llatī hiya ashrafu l-waṣāyā wa-ajalluhā*. Arabic title from Nasrallah, *Histoire*, 3.1:207. Nasrallah also lists two other titles sometimes given to the text. In Vat. Sbath 176, the title mentions an additional 200 chapters; these are Maximos's *Chapters on Knowledge*.

109. Maximos, *Capitoli sulla carità*, ed. Ceresa-Gastaldo, 48$_{6-10}$ = PG 90:960A; Arabic translation, Vat. Sbath 176, fols. 1^{v}–2^{r}. On this preface, see Kalvesmaki, "Evagrius," 267–69. On Maximos's method of compiling such chapters to be "artfully interlocking," see Balthasar, *Kosmische Liturgie*, 485.

one who reads only to find fault with Maximos "will never receive any profit from anywhere."[110] The chapters themselves draw on a wide variety of patristic writers as advertised.[111] They are approachable but leave Maximos's ideal simplehearted reader with much to contemplate.[112]

The text is arranged roughly by spiritual progress. The first "century" defines love early on in negative terms. Esteem for the body before the soul and God's creation before God is "idolatry," and whoever turns his mind from love of God is an idolater (1.7–8). But faith alone is not enough to earn salvation, "for even demons believe" in God and fear him (James 2:19); one must love him as well (1.39). Next, the text elaborates on how to free oneself from passions and come to know God: "Not from his substance (*ousia*) do we know God, but from his great work (*megalourgia*) and providence for existent beings; for through these things, as if through mirrors, do we contemplate his boundless goodness and wisdom and power" (1.96).

The second "century" focuses on the demons and passions that keep one chained "to material things" (2.3). To be "perfect in love," one must tear down the boundary between the self and others (2.30), thus defeating self-love (*philautia*), "the mother of passions" (2.8). The "century" offers advice to the one seeking this difficult transformation of the self, such as what to do "when you see your mind pleasurably occupied with material things" (2.51). The reader is taught to exercise control over the passions.

Such lessons pave the way for the third "century," which encourages the reader to question what was taken for granted in earlier stages when passions reigned. Things (food, procreation, glory, and money) are not evil in themselves, but rather their abuse (gluttony, fornication, vainglory, and greed), caused by mental negligence (3.4). Evil itself, as Dionysios the Areopagite says, is merely deprivation of the good (3.5). The "century" goes on to contrast God's knowledge of himself and of his creation, with the knowledge by which angels ("the holy powers") know him and his creation (3.21–22).[113] The category of "rational and intellectual substance" is divided into angelic and human; the angelic substance may in turn be holy or sinful, while the human substance may be pious or impious (3.26).

110. Ed. Ceresa-Gastaldo, 48_{19-24} = 960B, 961A; trans. Berthold, 35.

111. E.g., the fifth-century Alexandrian exegete Ammonios's commentary on Matthew, which survives in fragments, is quoted verbatim at 4.96 (quoted from PG 85:1389C, ad loc. Matthew 27:46; cited by Lampe s.v. ἐγκατάλειψις B.2.e). Likewise, Dionysios the Areopagite is explicitly cited at 3.5 for the argument that evils are simply "deprivations" (στερήσεις) of the good.

112. Louth ("Maximus," 138) calls the work "the most attractive of Maximus' ascetical writings"; Balthasar (*Kosmische Liturgie*, 408) calls it "dieses liebenswürdigste und leichteste aller Werke des Bekenners."

113. For the history of the notion that the same term when applied to different beings can mean the same things but have a different force, see Treiger, "Avicenna's Notion."

In this way, the reader is invited to lift his[114] thoughts beyond the material world—"bodies composed of opposites," that is, of the elements "earth, air, fire, water"—to contemplate that which is "rational and intellectual and capable of receiving opposites, like virtue and evil and wisdom and ignorance," being "incorporeal and immaterial" (3.30). At the same time, the chapters continue to circle back to the problem of sin, but now the discussion is more abstracted and generalized; where previously sins were individually combated, the text now offers advice on how to preserve a state of near or total sinlessness. The one without passion for worldly things loves silence, it proclaims, as the one who loves no human thing "loves all men"; knowledge of God and divine things comes to the one who is sinless in deeds and thoughts (3.37). There is, as another chapter relates, a causal chain of sins, leading from "self-love" to "the three most general thoughts of desire": gluttony, avarice and vainglory, which in turn give rise to further sins (3.56). By averting such chain reactions, the soul and mind can become perfect. This perfection is expressed now in positive terms that echo the negative with which the first century began: the perfect soul has turned all its "affective faculty" toward God, and the perfect mind has transcended knowledge "through true faith," to know the unknowable (3.98–99). Just as a rejection of passions leads to detachment from the pettiness of a material existence, so too can the mind itself be set free from the constraints of this world.

Such a mind exists in a state of awe and amazement (4.1). The fourth 'century' concerns this state and the philosophical considerations which provoke and justify it, seeking to lay out guidelines for the meaning of transcendence. "The incorporeal substance provides wellbeing through speech, action, and being contemplated; the corporeal, only through being contemplated" (4.12). Such contemplations are interrupted by the warning that the one who fails to persevere and who abandons "love of spiritual brothers" when tried by hardship does not yet have "perfect love" or "deep knowledge of God's Providence" (4.16). The chapters repeatedly stress the need to maintain the state of perfection and of "perfect love" and the dangers of turning toward the material and worldly.[115] The "century" builds slowly to the final purpose of self-perfection, communion with God. "Love for God is always wont to give the mind wings to fly toward divine communion" (4.40),[116] and "the way to knowledge is dispassion (*apatheia*) and humility, without which no one will see the Lord" (4.58).[117] The latter half of the fourth "century" is then a denouement that links the mystic's goal to the radical warmth of universal Christian love. True knowledge gives rise to, and requires, love (4.59–62). Love all men,

114. There are occasional signs that the text is addressed to men in particular, e.g., 4.49–50.

115. E.g., 4.39, 41, 54, 65, 81.

116. The wings that love gives to the mind echo a similar conceit in Plato's *Phaedrus* (e.g., 249c4–6).

117. Cf. Stoic *apatheia*.

or at least hate none of them until you are able to love them (4.82). It is Christ's will that you love even the blasphemer (4.83–84). Maximos ends his collection with a scriptural aphorism of whose meaning the entire text is an elaboration: "*God is love* [1 John 4:8]. Glory to him forever. Amen."

In these four "centuries," then, Maximos constructs a way for the seeker, a path for the one ignited by a thirst for God.[118] In the final chapter of the first "century," which cites two great late antique writers, Gregory of Nazianzos and Dionysios the Areopagite, the ideal mystic is described in terms that were to become familiar in Sufi accounts of the quest for God. He is "burning with longing" and can "find no relief" as he struggles to articulate God's very being, an impossible task (1.100).[119]

Who is this seeker? There are indications throughout that the text is addressed to a monastic audience. Many passages refer to the challenges of getting along with and helping one's "brothers."[120] Others seem to speak to the specific challenges that a monk faces.[121] Occasionally, the text refers specifically to a monk, as when it tells the reader what a true monk is (2.54), and once the reader is addressed directly as a monk (2.63).[122]

This was a guide to contemplative practice built upon the Christian heritage. Learning to speak directly and frankly to God (*parrhēsia*), keeping the mind trained upon "frankness towards God" (1.50), cultivating "amorous frankness" (4.32), the reader could learn to be like the martyrs and confessors who boldly declared their faith, like the bishops who openly advocated before emperors what was best for their cities, but also like the philosophers who told the powerful not what they wanted to hear but the truth.[123]

The eleventh-century Antiochian audience for an Arabic translation of Maximos's *Chapters on Love*, as in other times and places, would have been those with

118. In sum: (1) awareness of one's passions and connection to material things, (2) liberation from self-love and the demons chaining one to this world, (3) contemplation of higher, immaterial, incorporeal things, and (4a) the encounter with God, an experience that finally gives way to (4b) love for all mankind.

119. Cf. the Sufi concepts of *ʿishq* and *maḥabba*.

120. The first "century," for example, reminds the reader that it is bad to "bear a grudge against one's brother" (1.56) or to "slander a brother" or "condemn" him (1.57). The fourth and last "century" contains a series of injunctions about how to relate to one's brothers (4.19–32), who are "spiritual" brothers (4.26).

121. For example, the fantasies that 2.68 suggests the reader will have (of food, of women, etc.) are reminiscent of the apparitions that monks face in ascetic literature, such as in the *Life of Saint Anthony*. Combating demons (2.71) is one of a monk's main occupations.

122. Louth, "Maximus," 137; Balthasar, *Kosmische Liturgie*, 408.

123. Brown, *Power and Persuasion*, 61–62, 77–78. Rabbinic parallels: Siegal, "Shared Worlds," 453–54. Later, in the ninth century, Theodore of Stoudios linked *parrhēsia* closely with martyrdom in his letters to a secret network of iconodules: Hatlie, "Politics of Salvation."

a desire to "philosophize" as Christians (4.47), to live model lives, to contemplate the hidden meaning behind the material curtain of this world, and to be divinized, to become like God. Such readers were mostly monks and perhaps churchmen and laymen who sought, in some way, to model their lives on those of monks.[124] Translating the text in the major monastic center of Antioch would have made perfect sense.

The case with the *Chapters on Knowledge* is quite similar. These "chapters" are organized into two sets of 100. The Arabic title of this work is *Book on the Creator and His Attributes and Perfections.*[125] Like the *Chapters on Love,* these two "centuries" focus on a particular aspect of the ascetic's quest: approaching divinity. All human beings are equally endowed with a "rational soul" made in the creator's image, but only some will seek and be granted insight and intimacy with God, being "judged worthy to lie with the Logos-Bridegroom in the inner chamber of the mysteries"; others may be jealous because they wish to be wise only for the sake of receiving praise (1.11–21).[126] These chapters thus offer a method for bringing the human soul closer to God by realizing the rational soul's potential for true knowledge.

The text distinguishes between two spiritual stages, roughly corresponding to the English terms "ascetic" and "mystic," both of whom might be called "renunciants": "Sense-perception accompanies the one concerned with action (πρακτικῷ), who succeeds in the virtues with difficulty. Freedom from sense-perception (ἀναισθησία) accompanies the one concerned with knowledge, who has drawn his mind away from the flesh and the world and towards God" (1.99).[127] Crucially, the distinction hinges upon "sense-perception," which should be understood as the perception of the material world by means of the sense organs. Becoming "blind" to everything other than God is the only way to receive wisdom from him (2.9). The text explicitly and persistently promotes the pursuit of secret wisdom usually obscured by workaday knowledge. It defines two types of knowledge (*gnōsis*): passively acquired knowledge versus knowledge "active in actuality, which brings . . . true apprehension (κατάληψιν) of beings through experience" (1.22). To seek the latter is to seek true illumination (1.30–35).

These two centuries offered much to a reader concerned with the body, the soul, the location of the transcendent world and its relation to our own, and how

124. Monks and laymen were closely connected in Byzantine society. In Maximos's day (seventh century): Hatlie, *Monks,* 233–48; in subsequent centuries: ibid., 289–311. Nor were laymen and monks "castes" apart from one another in the middle Byzantine period: ibid., 90. Laymen often adopted monastic aims and practices and had monks as spiritual advisers: ibid., 74, 92–94. There must have been a similarly complex relationship between monasteries and lay institutions in Byzantine Antioch.

125. *Kitāb fī l-bārī ʾi wa-ṣifātihi wa-kamālātihi:* Nasrallah, *Histoire,* 3.1:207.

126. Translations in this and the following two paragraphs are from Berthold, often modified. Bridegroom: see n. 50 above.

127. "Renunciant," "ascetic," "mystic": Kinberg, "What Is Meant by *Zuhd.*"

the soul could approach God. The ascent is conceived as a grueling, even violent struggle to "slay the bodily passions" and "destroy the passionate thoughts of the soul" (2.97). One must be trained "manfully to engage in the divine struggles according to practical philosophy" in order to dispel the passions and so "go over" to the calm stillness of "theoretical (*gnōstikē*) philosophy" (2.94). Body and soul come to be in harmony through virtue and knowledge, inspired by the Spirit, inhabited by the Logos (2.100). This is as close as one can come to true knowledge of all things. And yet, even the human being who is perfect in deed and thought has only partial access to "knowledge and prophecy" while still in an "earthly state." Only "at the end of the ages" will "those who are worthy" encounter "the truth as it is in itself" (2.87). Even the holiest person will have only partial knowledge before encountering "the Truth"—an epithet of Christ.[128] But, as this "chapter" implies, his partial knowledge will include some measure of prophecy. It is fairly common in hagiographical literature to find saints accurately predicting the future, a gift that could earn them considerable attention.[129] Here we have an articulation of how the contemplative might acquire this gift as an incidental consequence of his spiritual ascent and approximation to the divine model (even if true foreknowledge belongs to God alone).[130]

Pseudo-Maximos: *Loci communes*

The ecclesiastical concern with orthodoxy—in Byzantium as elsewhere—rarely meant a total rejection of non-Christian culture. The Greek collection of sayings and quotations known as the *Loci communes* (a.k.a. *Capita theologica*), which circulated under Maximos's name, is a good example of the synthesis between pagan and Christian culture in the sphere of wisdom.[131] This collection seamlessly combines what modern scholars often call "sacred" or "religious" (i.e., Christian) and "profane" or "secular" (i.e., non-Christian), openly drawing on authors both Christian and pagan. It cites church fathers alongside ancient pagan authors, including philosophers (Socrates, Plato, Aristotle, Epicurus), orators, and playwrights.[132] This is

128. John 14:6. Cf. the later Sufi name for God, *al-ḥaqq*.

129. For example, Saint Luke of Stiris in Phokis (d. 953) predicted the Byzantine conquest of Crete "about twenty years" before it took place, according to his *Life* (PG 111:469A), *quasi si fuisset homo bulla*. The fulfillment of this prophecy in 961 ensured steady imperial interest in him and later in his cult. The Monastery of Hosios Loukas bears the imprint of imperial patronage, and as Carolyn Connor argued ("Hosios Loukas"), the Katholikon of the monastery (or at least elements of its decorative program) may have been built to commemorate the conquest.

130. For God's exclusive possession of foreknowledge (in the sense of perfect knowledge of the future), see Beck, *Vorsehung*, 216. I owe this reference to Maria Mavroudi.

131. Ed. Ihm. On Ibn al-Faḍl's translation, see Noble and Treiger, "Christian Arabic Theology," 378 n. 26; Treiger, "ʿAbdallāh," 100–103.

132. Treiger, "ʿAbdallāh," 101.

emphasized by its Greek title (in some manuscripts): *Sayings from Various Poets and Rhetors, Both External and from Our Own Holy and God-Beloved Paideia.*[133] As usual, "external" here means non-Christian.

Ibn al-Faḍl's Arabic translation of the *Loci communes* situates his translation program in this Byzantine pattern of adapting the Hellenic pagan past to the Christian present. The known manuscripts of the translation call it the *Book of the Garden* (*Kitāb al-Rawḍa*) and make no mention of Maximos. The translation is anonymous in some manuscripts, while one manuscript says that Ibn al-Faḍl translated it from Greek.[134] The commentary included in Arabic manuscripts of the text gives further evidence that Ibn al-Faḍl was the translator.[135]

This collection of *Loci communes* bears some resemblance to the collections of sayings compiled by Maximos the Confessor: like Maximos's authentic *kephalaia* in the Evagrian tradition, the collection of *Loci communes* seeks to edify its readers with short, memorable "chapters" on a given theme. Occasionally the selections in Maximos's compilations even sound like they could come from a gnomonology like the *Loci communes,* such as the apophthegmatic "Many are we who speak, few who do," from the *Chapters on Love,*[136] which sits well beside "Let every man be quick to listen and slow to speak," from the *Loci communes.*[137]

There are also considerable differences. In the *Loci communes,* each "chapter" is usually attributed to an author. Where Maximos's collections are programmatic, leading their readers on through progressive spiritual stages, the collection of *Loci communes* allows its reader to consult specific topics of interest, for it is organized thematically. Beginning with "virtue and wickedness" (§1), it then moves through particular virtues (§§2–8) and "sovereignty and power" (§9), then to other themes like "wealth and poverty and avarice" (§12), on to "education and philosophy and childrearing" (§17), "silence and secrets" (§20), sin (§26), sleep (§29), drunkenness (§30), frankness (*parrhēsia*) and disputation (§31), truth and falsehood (§35), beauty (§37), "judgement to come" (§38), providence (§41), physicians (§43), the soul (§46), the command "Know thyself" (§49), and so forth, down to death (§65), hope (§67), women (§68), old age and youth (§70), ending with "endurance and patience" (§71).

133. Ed. Ihm, 7: Ἀπομνημονεύματα ἐκ διαφόρων ποιητῶν καὶ ῥητόρων ἔκ τε τῶν θύραθεν καὶ τῆς καθ' ἡμᾶς ἱερᾶς καὶ φιλοθέου παιδείας.

134. Beirut BO 545 (1851 CE), according to Graf, *GCAL,* 2:63. Graf, unaware that the text is a translation of a preexisting Greek collection, the *Loci communes,* took the manuscript's testimony to mean that Ibn al-Faḍl was the translator *and* compiler of the sayings. Van Esbroeck ("Les sentences," 13–16) identified it as a translation of the *Loci communes:* Noble and Treiger, "Christian Arabic Theology," 378 n. 26.

135. See ch. 5, pp. 153, 160, 161, esp. the reference to Ibn al-Faḍl's *Book of Benefit.*

136. *Chapters on Love* 4.85, ed. Ceresa-Gastaldo, 232.

137. Ed. Ihm, 20.2/2 (James 1:19).

Though ostensibly a miscellaneous collection of sayings on various topics, each section is in fact a coherent composition that was probably intended to be read as a unified whole. So, for example, in the section on physicians (§43), the biblical and patristic quotations include metaphors about medicine and salvation. In this light, the subsequent "profane" quotations criticizing and mocking bad physicians could be read as a comment on those who falsely promise salvation.

While Maximos's *Chapters on Love* and *Chapters on Knowledge* draw primarily upon patristic works, pagan authors provide the bulk of the *Loci communes*. This does not mean that the collection is inattentive to the distinction between Christians and Hellenes, for each section is carefully arranged in the following order: New Testament, Old Testament, church fathers, and only then the non-Christian Hellenic authors.[138] This organization implicitly argues that Christian and Hellenic philosophy are in harmony, similar to the placement of Nonnos's *Paraphrase of the Gospel of John* and Gregory of Nazianzos's epigrams at the beginning of the tenth-century *Anthologia Palatina*, or the tendency in classical Arabic literature to open treatises, books, and chapters with qur'anic and then prophetic quotations, followed by the book's main subject of investigation. Their inclusion is an authoritative moral anchor that implies the harmony between this authoritative Christian (or Muslim) starting point and the pagan wisdom that follows.[139]

By translating this collection of pagan and Christian wisdom, Ibn al-Faḍl (in keeping with a long tradition) implied that the ancient pagan past could provide valuable wisdom as part of a Christian education, and indeed that Christians were the true heirs of classical Greek literature. This may have troubled some medieval readers, or at least failed to interest them: a scribe working no later than 1266 CE seems to have cut the number of pagan sayings dramatically when copying Ibn al-Faḍl's *Book of the Garden*.[140] But had one asked Gregory of Nazianzos, he would not have hesitated to claim the classics as his own.[141] His eleventh-century Byzantine admirers would have agreed.[142]

138. Ed. Ihm, I. Quotations from Philo (and pseudo-Philo) in particular: Parker and Treiger, "Philo's Odyssey," 136–38. Ibn al-Faḍl's translation of Maximos's *Chapters on Knowledge* (if indeed he is the translator) would be another avenue for Philo's ideas (albeit unattributed) to enter Arabic; see Balthasar, *Kosmische Liturgie*, 516–17, 585–87.

139. I thank Maria Mavroudi for this interpretation.

140. Sinai ar. 66 (1266 CE) omits most of the selections from pagan authors (especially from chapter 26 onward, where pagan sayings are "practically eliminated"), while Vat. ar. 111 keeps most of them; van Esbroeck, "Les sentences," 14.

141. Elm, *Sons*, 11 and n. 33.

142. Papaioannou, *Psellos*, 17–19.

Isaac of Nineveh

The Syriac-speaking Nestorian Christian Isaac of Nineveh (seventh/?eighth century), also called Isaac the Syrian (especially in the Greek and other non-Syriac traditions), was a major ascetic writer, not only in the Nestorian (East-Syrian) tradition but also among non-Nestorians. Sources for Isaac's life place his origins in a region called Bêth Qaṭrāye, possibly to be identified with Qaṭar. He was made bishop of Nineveh sometime between 660 and 680 CE, abdicated soon afterward, and was quite old when he died.[143]

In the Syriac tradition, Isaac's works are divided into at least three parts.[144] The "first part" (Isaac I) is often referred to as the *Ascetic Homilies* (eighty-two homilies).[145] Isaac I was translated into Greek in the ninth century.[146] The "second part" (Isaac II) was thought lost except for fragments, but the discovery of a complete manuscript allowed Sebastian Brock to publish an edition of II.4–41—that is, all but sections 1–3.[147] An edition of the remaining sections of Isaac II is being prepared by Paolo Bettiolo.[148] The "third part" (Isaac III) has been edited by Sabino Chialà.[149]

The subdivisions of Isaac II can be particularly confusing because the first three sections (II.1–3) are much longer than the rest of the sections: together, they are roughly equal in length to the rest of the sections (II.4–41, edited by Brock). Furthermore, the third section (II.3 = *Chapters on Knowledge*) is considerably longer than the first two (II.1–2). Finally, the *Chapters on Knowledge* are (like Maximos's *Chapters on Love*) divided into four "centuries" or sets of 100 "chapters" (*rîše* ~ κεφάλαια).[150]

To summarize, the first three parts of Isaac's corpus can be visualized as follows:

- Isaac I ("first part") = *Ascetic Homilies*, edited by Bedjan; translated into Greek in the ninth century (eighty-two homilies), edited by Pirard
- Isaac II ("second part")
  II.1–3: edition in preparation by Bettiolo

143. Khalifé-Hachem, "Isaac," 2041–42; Louth, "Isaac," 225–26.

144. The Syriac tradition sometimes counts only two, rather than three of them. Sometimes it counts more than three. For these further parts, especially the "Fifth Part," see Chialà, "Due discorsi"; and Kessel's 2018 article listed by Kessel and Seleznyov, "Bibliography," 301–2. I owe my awareness of these fourth and fifth parts to Alexander Treiger. For simplicity, I will omit mention of all but the first three parts in what follows.

145. Isaac I Bedjan. English translation: Isaac I_{eng} Wensinck.

146. Critical edition: Isaac I_{gr} Pirard.

147. Isaac II.4–41 Brock.

148. See Isaac II.4–41 Brock, 1:introduction.

149. Isaac III Chialà, with Italian translation. English: Isaac III Hansbury.

150. Kessel, "Isaac of Nineveh's *Chapters*," with translations of a selection, 255–80.

- II.1–2
- II.3.a–d = *Chapters on Knowledge* (in four "centuries")

II.4–41 (i.e., to the end): edited by Brock

- Isaac III ("third part"): edited by Chialà

Ibn al-Faḍl translated at least one and possibly two selections from this corpus. The first was from Isaac I (the *Ascetic Homilies*), which had been translated into Greek in the ninth century. Of the eighty-two homilies, Ibn al-Faḍl translated thirty-five.[151] His preface to this translation will be discussed in chapter 4.

Ibn al-Faḍl may also have translated the third section of the "second part" (II.3), known as the *Chapters on Knowledge* (a recurring title in the Evagrian tradition and, as we have seen, the title of one of Maximos's works) under the Arabic title *Fī ruʾūs al-maʿrifa,* literally *Concerning the head(ing)s of knowledge.*[152] Since the "second part" (Isaac II) is not known to have been translated into Greek, this would have been a translation directly from the Syriac original. But the evidence that Ibn al-Faḍl translated the *Chapters on Knowledge* is quite slim. Nasrallah cites a single manuscript in Lebanon that contains an Arabic version (in Syriac script) of Isaac's *Chapters on Knowledge.*[153] The catalog entry for that manuscript was written by Nasrallah himself, and while it states that Ibn al-Faḍl is the translator, the entry does not say whether the translation is explicitly attributed to Ibn al-Faḍl, or indeed whether Ibn al-Faḍl's name appears anywhere in the manuscript.[154]

To summarize, Ibn al-Faḍl translated (1) thirty-five homilies from Isaac I = *Ascetic Homilies;* and (2) possibly, pending further investigation, Isaac II.3.a–d = *Chapters on Knowledge.*[155]

In his *Ascetic Homilies,* Isaac, building, like Maximos, upon Evagrian foundations,[156] advocates an ascetic path of quiet and self-isolation. For Isaac too, passions and "thoughts" must be quelled to allow the soul to recover its "natural" state; for him too love "burns up" the solitary, who through his ascetic practice obtains (as

151. In some manuscripts, the thirty-five homilies are entitled "the book of Mār Isaac *On the Ascetic Life* (*al-ḥayāt al-nuskīya*)": Nasrallah, *Histoire,* 3.1:210, with several other titles in n. 89.

152. Only one manuscript containing this translation is known: Nasrallah, *Histoire,* 3.1:211. Noble and Treiger ("Christian Arabic Theology," 378) have plausibly suggested that the Arabic title *Fī ruʾūs al-maʿrifa* derives from the phrase *kephalaia gnōstika,* "Chapters on Knowledge." (The Greek word for "chapter," like the Latin from which English *chapter* is derived, is related to the word for "head.") Indeed, the Arabic translation of Maximos's preface to his *Chapters on Love* cited in n. 108 above also refers to the *kephalaia* as "heads" (*ruʾūs*): Vat. Sbath 176, fol. 2^r. The four "centuries" in Isaac II.3.a–d are known in Syriac as *Rîše d-îdaʿtā* (Isaac II.4–41 Brock, 1:XI), quite literally the same as *ruʾūs al-maʿrifa.*

153. Nasrallah, *Histoire,* 3.1:211.

154. Dayr al-Banāt 23a (Garshuni, paper); Nasrallah, *Catalogue,* 2:178–80.

155. Several other brief texts by Isaac are grouped with the thirty-five *Ascetic Homilies* in Arabic manuscripts. Ibn al-Faḍl might (or might not) have translated them as well.

156. Louth, "Isaac," 226.

one of Isaac's translators puts it) "the spiritual silence of knowledge."[157] These homilies provide detailed instructions for the improvement of the self through contemplative asceticism. As for Isaac's *Chapters on Knowledge*, four sets of a hundred or so brief sayings, their overarching purpose is to teach human beings to live a spiritual life, guided by the Holy Spirit.[158]

Although Isaac was a Nestorian author, he was firmly a part of the Byzantine heritage, having been appropriated in the ninth century, when Patrikios and Abramios, monks at the Monastery of Mar Saba near Jerusalem (the same center of Greek Chalcedonian Christianity where John of Damascus had been a monk), translated the *Ascetic Homilies* (Isaac I) into Greek.[159] In Latin, Isaac's popularity rested in part on a mistaken identification of him with an Isaac whom Gregory the Great mentions, but Patrikios and Abramios seem to have been well aware of whose work they were translating.[160] Isaac's *Ascetic Homilies* have been influential in the Greek monastic tradition ever since. Gregory Palamas (d. 1359) included Isaac among the very few authors it is worth one's time to read. Already in Ibn al-Faḍl's lifetime, Paul Evergetinos (d. 1054) included Isaac's writings in his florilegium known as the *Evergetinon*.[161] In this light, Ibn al-Faḍl's choice of Isaac's *Ascetic Homilies* was in impeccable Byzantine taste.[162]

Manuscripts of Ibn al-Faḍl's translation of thirty-five of the *Ascetic Homilies* record that he translated them from the Greek.[163] This confirms that Ibn al-Faḍl's translation was not an "importation" of an East-Syrian author from outside the Byzantine canon. In Ibn al-Faḍl's day the *Ascetic Homilies* were part of the Byzantine ecclesiastical heritage.

If Ibn al-Faḍl did in fact translate Isaac's *Chapters on Knowledge* (presumably from the Syriac original), the choice to do so would have represented more of an "importation," since no Greek translation of the text is known to have existed, nor was it a standard text of the Byzantine ecclesiastical tradition. This would suggest—again, if indeed Ibn al-Faḍl should turn out to be the translator of the Arabic version identified by Nasrallah—that Chalcedonian Christians in Syria had already been reading Isaac's *Chapters on Knowledge* in Syriac and wished to continue this tradition of reading in Arabic. This would be the only text on the list of Ibn al-Faḍl's translations not readily available to elite Greek-speaking scholars in the Byzantine Empire.

157. Bettiolo, "Syriac Literature," 482.

158. Kavvadas, *Isaak*, 1–2.

159. Louth, "Isaac," 226.

160. Hausherr, "Dogme," 154–55.

161. Hausherr, 157; Cross and Livingstone, "Evergetinos."

162. The Syrian Miaphysites too adopted him and sometimes merged him with a Miaphysite Isaac: Hausherr, "Dogme," 161–64.

163. Title, **ṬV** (not in **A**); cf. Nasrallah, *Histoire*, 3.1:210 n. 87.

Pseudo-Kaisarios: *Questions and Answers*

As part of his book of answers to 365 questions, the *Joy of the Believer* (*Kitāb Bahjat al-muʾmin*), Ibn al-Faḍl translated 100 questions (and answers) selected from the 218 *Questions and Answers* of pseudo-Kaisarios (Caesarius). These 100 questions from pseudo-Kaisarios became numbers 101–200 of Ibn al-Faḍl's 365 questions.[164] The Greek original, though ascribed to Gregory of Nazianzos's brother Kaisarios (d. 369), was probably composed in the mid-sixth century by a Miaphysite (to judge from internal evidence). The text, however, avoids the crux of the Chalcedonian-Miaphysite debate by speaking of neither one nor two natures in Christ. The questions deal with a range of theological, meteorological, and astronomical topics and include anti-Jewish, anti-Arian, and anti-Origenist polemics.[165] In the Byzantine tradition, the *Questions and Answers* were generally treated as the work of Kaisarios, whose orthodoxy was beyond doubt.

5 IN PRAISE OF SAINTS

Ibn al-Faḍl translated at least two hagiographical encomia, elegant discourses in praise of saints: one for the bishop-saint Nicholas and the other for the soldier-saint Demetrios. Both saints were extremely popular in the middle Byzantine period. Such high-literary praises for saints were an important fixture of middle Byzantine reading lists. Their elaborate style (and, in the case of Demetrios, detailed theological vocabulary) called for the skill of a translator like Ibn al-Faḍl.

Andrew of Crete on Saint Nicholas

Ibn al-Faḍl translated the *Encomium to Saint Nicholas* by Andrew of Crete (b. ca. 660, Damascus; d. 740, Lesbos).[166] The text begins with a prefatory encomium by Ibn al-Faḍl, followed by his translation of Andrew's encomium. Ibn al-Faḍl's preface appears under the heading "An epistle which the peerless philosopher ʿAbdallāh ibn al-Faḍl ibn ʿAbdallāh composed specifically for his translation from Greek into

164. Riedinger, *Pseudo-Kaisarios,* 63. I refer here to Recension A (with 365 questions); Recension B (in Vat. ar. 164, thirteenth century) has 111 questions: Treiger, "ʿAbdallāh," 103–5.

165. Riedinger, *Pseudo-Kaisarios,* 444, 447; Allen, "Pseudo-Caesarius," 100; *ODB,* s.v. "Kaisarios, Pseudo-." On one occasion Ibn al-Faḍl (or his Greek exemplar, or a later Arabic scribe) omits a line that equivocates on whether the Magi-star may represent a city; Riedinger suggests that Ibn al-Faḍl may have omitted it because it seemed too astrological: Riedinger, *Pseudo-Kaisarios,* 66 (with several other divergences).

166. *CPG* 8187; *BHG* 1362; PG 97:1192–1205; ed. Anrich, *Hagios Nikolaos,* 1:419–28. Anrich doubted the authenticity of the ascription of this work to Andrew of Crete, but as he admits, none of his evidence is conclusive. A close examination of Anrich's evidence convinces me that none of it should lead us to doubt Andrew of Crete's authorship.

Arabic of an encomium for Saint Nicholas, may his prayers be with us. Amen."[167] After the preface, Andrew's encomium then appears under the following heading:

> Encomium of Saint Andrew, chief of the bishops of Crete, for our father, great among the saints, Nicholas, (worker) of many signs and miracles, which ʿAbdallāh ibn al-Faḍl ibn ʿAbdallāh translated from Greek into Arabic, [thereby] coming closer to God and to the precious saint, asking for his intercession, may God grant forgiveness to the one who says [of Ibn al-Faḍl] "God have mercy on him!" Amen.[168]

This last line gives the impression of having been added by a scribe copying the text soon after Ibn al-Faḍl's death—or by Ibn al-Faḍl himself, with an eye to readers of the future.

The great Saint Nicholas (of Sion and of Myra—by the tenth century the two saints had become one) was already immensely popular by the eleventh century.[169] He and his encomiast Andrew of Crete were models of Christian episcopal leadership.

Ibn al-Faḍl's translation of Andrew's *Encomium* indicates interest not only in Saint Nicholas but perhaps also in Andrew of Crete himself and the generation that witnessed the momentous Arab conquests of the seventh century. Andrew spent his youth as a monk in Jerusalem until he traveled to Constantinople in 685 as one of the envoys declaring Jerusalem's support for the anti-Monothelete council that had taken place in the Byzantine capital in 680–681 (at which Maximos had been posthumously vindicated). Afterward, Andrew stayed on, became a deacon, and took up an administrative post. After about fifteen years in Constantinople, he was made archbishop of Gortyna, Crete, where he became a patron of "charitable institutions" and of a church dedicated to the Virgin. He died on Lesbos on the way back to his see after a visit to Constantinople, which he had undertaken to seek relief for Crete from a famine.[170]

His life alone might have been reason enough for eleventh-century interest in Andrew among Byzantine churchmen of Antioch. He had ties with Antioch's two neighboring patriarchates, Jerusalem and Constantinople. He was a model monk, who traveled from the Levant to the capital to preach orthodoxy to the powerful. As a deacon, he had been a true servant (*diakonos*) of those in need. And but for a moment of doctrinal weakness as a Byzantine Christian might see it (his acquiescence to a short-lived imperial initiative favoring Monotheletism), Andrew had

167. Noble, "Saint Nicholas," ¶2: *Risālatun anshaʾahā l-faylasūfu l-awḥadu ʿAbdallāh . . . maqṣūratan ʿalā naqlihi mina l-lughati l-yūnānīyati ilā l-lughati l-ʿarabīyati madīḥa<n> li-l-qiddīsi Nīqūlāwus, ṣalātihi maʿnā, āmīn.*

168. Noble, "Saint Nicholas," ¶4: *Madīḥu l-qiddīsi Andhrāwus raʾīsi asāqifati Iqrīṭish* [read *Iqrīṭī*] *li-abīnā l-muʿaẓẓami fī l-qiddīsīn Nīqūlāwus dhī l-āyāti wa-l-muʿjizāt, tarjamahu . . . ʿAbdallāh . . ., taqarruban ilā llāhi wa-l-qiddīsi l-nafīs, wa-stishfāʿan bihi, ghafara llāhu li-man taraḥḥama ʿalayhi, āmīn.*

169. *ODB*, s.v. "Nicholas of Sion"; *V.Nich.Sion.*

170. Studer, "Andrew."

been the ideal bishop, caring for his flock and petitioning the emperor on their behalf in the face of Muslim aggression. His struggles against Arab invaders made him a convenient symbol of Crete's Byzantine past in the decades after the celebrated Byzantine conquest of Crete in 961.

An interest in Byzantine leaders from immediately before the rise of Islam may be indicated by the Arabic translation of songs praising the Virgin for liberating Constantinople from Chosroes in the time of Heraclius, bound with Ibn al-Faḍl's translation of the Psalms in an early modern Florence manuscript, although of course we cannot be sure that this interest predates the manuscript itself.[171] Andrew's fame in the eleventh century must also have stemmed from the liturgical poetry he composed, especially the penitential canon, which became a permanent part of the Byzantine rite.[172] He also wrote homilies (about fifty are ascribed to him), including encomia of saints. His encomium to Saint Nicholas is one of them. The specific choice to translate this encomium suggests an interest in Nicholas himself and a desire to promote the saint, his cult, and his example.

Nicholas was an episcopal saint. A tenth-century representation of Nicholas in the Leo Bible, a manuscript commissioned in Constantinople by the holder of the lofty Byzantine imperial post of treasurer (*sakellarios*), shows him standing, head uncovered, clothed in white vestments, including a bishop's omophorion, holding a Bible in his left hand and blessing with his right.[173] Similar iconography is found in the eleventh-century frescoes of Saint Nicholas in the Church of Holy Wisdom in Kiev[174] and the provincial Church of Episkopoi in Evrytania (central Greece).[175]

Some of Nicholas's most prominent miracles were his intervention on behalf of three officials falsely condemned by the emperor Constantine, his successful appeal for tax exemption for the city of Myra, and his rescue of a ship sailing through a storm; he also amassed an impressive list of healing miracles.[176] Such a

171. Florence, Laurenziana, or. 396 (= 607 = Pizzi 178); Assemani, *Bibliothecae Mediceae Laurentianae,* no. 34. On 30 October 2017, I examined this tiny manuscript (108 × 76 mm). After the Arabic Psalter come ten "glorifications" (*tasābīḥ*) of God (129ʳ–138ᵛ), then the hymn to the Virgin (139ʳ–148ʳ) by "Eugene the Philosopher of Constantinople" (*hādhihi l-madāʾiḥu l-muqaddasatu min ʿamali Iwjāniyūs al-Qusṭanṭīnī al-faylasūf*). This is the *Akathistos Hymn,* said to commemorate the 626 Persian-Avar siege of Constantinople, in the Arabic translation edited by Peters, "Eine arabische Uebersetzung"; cited by Graf, *GCAL,* 1:631.

172. Studer, "Andrew," 162.

173. The "Leo Bible," Vat. Reg. gr. 1, fol. 1ʳ. Mango, "Date of Cod. Vat. Regin. Gr. 1," 122: "The manuscript was commissioned by Leo, patrician, *praepositus* and *sakellarios,* and donated by him to a monastery of St. Nicholas that had been founded by his deceased brother, Constantine the protospatharios." Date: ibid., 126. Iconography: Del Re and Celletti, "Nicola," col. 941; *ODB,* s.vv. "Nicholas of Myra," "Omophorion." See also Canart, *La Bible du patrice Léon.*

174. Reproduced at Del Re and Celletti, "Nicola," col. 930.

175. Now in the Byzantine Museum, Athens, BXM 1363.

176. Anrich, *Hagios Nikolaos,* vol. 1.

saint would have appealed to the patriarchate of Antioch, with its complex relationship to the imperial center. Having long defined itself while under Muslim rule as the "imperial" (*malakī*) church in opposition to East-Syrian Nestorians and West-Syrian and Armenian Miaphysites, the Chalcedonian community in Antioch now had the chance to prove its loyalty to a distant imperial center that was eager to impose its policies and prelates upon the reconquered patriarchate. For churchmen performing this balancing act, Nicholas, with his ability to stand up to coercive imperial authority, would have been an appealing patron.

Andrew of Crete's *Encomium* praises the saint as someone who can get things done in times of need, someone accomplished in "practical philosophy."[177] He is like the Old Testament prophets (Abel, Enoch, Noah, Abraham, Isaac, Jacob, Job, Joseph, Moses, David) in his justice, self-sacrifice, and otherworldliness, his perseverance in rooting out heresy, his teaching, and his dissuasion of others from error. Fighting heresy and impiety is particularly emphasized: like Job, he endures in the face of the heretics' attacks; like David, he fights with spiritual arms, driving off the "wolves" from "Christ's spiritual (*logikē*) flock."[178] He is a successor to Christ's disciples as well.[179] He is, as it were, a farmer, a builder, a soldier, an angel.[180] He aids those in need and is gentle even when debating a heretical bishop.[181] He is close to God, as a teacher, an "interpreter of the Word and guide to ineffable things," and as someone with the intimacy to speak frankly (*parrhēsia*) with God and who in turn receives divine illumination.[182] Andrew praises the city that had Nicholas as its bishop, then addresses his audience, declaring that they should celebrate this holy man and "cast far away from ourselves any pleasure in any worldly pomp or festival or deceptive ornaments, anything with a pretense to the evil-spirited error of Hellenic secrecy (*echeomythia*), and any of those plays (*paignia*) that depend upon base confusion and a make-believe stage."[183]

The text that Ibn al-Faḍl translated, then, stresses this famous saint's exemplarity as an effective leader who fights heresy, "speaks frankly" (*parrhēsia*) with the powerful (perhaps the emperor as well as God), and protects his flock.[184] Promoting

177. §1, ed. Anrich, *Hagios Nikolaos,* 1:420_{9} = PG 97:1193B.

178. §2. The flock: ed. Anrich, 422_{13} = PG 1196C.

179. §3, ed. Anrich, 422_{18-21} = PG 1196D–97A.

180. §§4–6, ed. Anrich, 423–25 = PG 1197A–1201A.

181. §7, ed. Anrich, 425–26 = PG $1201A_{8}$–B.

182. §8. Teacher: ed. Anrich, 426_{12} = PG 1201C. Cf. "ineffable" (*arrhētos*) in Psellos: Magdalino and Mavroudi, *Occult Sciences,* 15–20. Frankness (mentioned earlier, in §2, ed. Anrich, 421_{10}) and illumination: ed. Anrich, 427_{1-2} = PG 1204A.

183. §§9–10. Quote: ed. Anrich, 427_{25}–428 = PG 1204C. Migne's text is quite different at this point. Cf. Ibn al-Faḍl's translation (ed. Noble, "Saint Nicholas"), esp. "*al-ḍalāl al-ḥanīfī wa-kharaf al-ṣābiʾīn.*"

184. Perhaps his church-building was also relevant to Antiochian Chalcedonians: Eger, "(Re)Mapping Medieval Antioch," 103–5.

Nicholas in Antioch meant promoting a highly popular Byzantine bishop-saint who represented episcopal power so great that it could exercise oversight over imperial excess. Such a model would surely have had an appeal for the patriarch of Antioch. The miniature in the Leo Bible, in which an imperial official and an abbot kneel before Nicholas, illustrates how a bishop might have liked to imagine his relations with other holders of worldly power.

John of Thessaloniki on Saint Demetrios

Ibn al-Faḍl's interest in rhetorical hagiography extended beyond Saint Nicholas. Thanks to Alexander Treiger's recent discovery, we now know that Ibn al-Faḍl also produced an annotated Arabic translation of the Greek *Encomium to Saint Demetrios* by John of Thessaloniki (d. ca. 620).[185] The Arabic translation was carried out at the request of one Abū l-Fatḥ ʿĪsā ibn Idrīs.[186]

John was archbishop of Thessaloniki in the early seventh century and played a central role in warding off the siege of Thessaloniki by the Avaro-Slavs in ca. 618, aided by a dream vision of Saint Demetrios. His other works included a collection of miracles performed by Saint Demetrios.[187] By the eleventh century, he was himself considered a saint.

John of Thessaloniki's *Encomium to Saint Demetrios,* like Andrew of Crete's later *Encomium to Saint Nicholas,* is at a high literary register. The structure of John's text is, however, quite different, with most of it devoted to a narrative. After an extended prologue (§§1–4), John spends most of the piece imagining a confrontation between the saint and a series of doctrinally misguided interlocutors: Hellenes from Athens, Jews from Jerusalem, Manichaeans of Mesopotamia, Arians of Alexandria, and others (§§5–16). This detailed and technical debate, vividly narrated, was surely a key to the text's appeal, as much in the eleventh century as in the seventh.

In the prologue, John of Thessaloniki begins his encomium in the usual way, by praising Saint Demetrios and his excellent qualities.[188] Demetrios's renown is such that when one uses the martyr's epithet, "the Prizewinner," without mentioning a name, everyone knows that Demetrios is meant; his solicitude for us is great (§1). He brings peace to the city (of Thessaloniki) and offers protection against death and the plague, victory in battle, safe passage for ships, and so on (§2). He was raised "among us" and preached against Jews, Hellenes (pagans), and heretics (§3).

185. *CPG* 7925; *BHG* 547h; ed. Philippidis-Braat, "L'enkômion," with detailed summary.

186. Treiger, "Christian Graeco-Arabica," 208 and n. 86: preserved in Sinai ar. 350, fols. 237ᵛ–270ᵛ, and Sinai ar. 352, fols. 98ʳ–114ʳ, along with Ibn al-Faḍl's translations of Isaac the Syrian.

187. Lemerle, *Les plus anciens recueils,* 2:184; Philippidis-Braat, "L'enkômion," 399; Louth, "John," 118, 120–21. The *Encomium* is preserved in Paris gr. 1517, a twelfth-century collection of Demetrios.

188. My summary, especially of §§1–4, follows that of Philippidis-Braat, "L'enkômion," 400–405.

John's language is artful and performative, with many rhetorical questions, interjections, and other figures of speech. In his translation, Ibn al-Faḍl too is attentive to language, as is typical for his translations. In these introductory sections, for example, he translates an apostrophized question in such a way as to preserve its rhetorical force in Arabic while making clear to the Arabic reader that the question is supposed to be raised by someone other than John. The Greek reads, "By whom was he brought up?" while the Arabic reads, "If you ask, sir, about his upbringing, I answer . . ."[189] Again in §4, when the Greek asks, "What then is the story?" the Arabic version reads, "If you ask, sir, about this report and seek to learn what it is, I answer that . . ."[190]

Ibn al-Faḍl's prose is rhythmic and often rhymes. When John asks, "How am I to pass over all his unseen acts of assistance in wars and acts of mercy out of love for his city?" Ibn al-Faḍl translates, "And how am I to delay in mentioning the many types of his acts of assistance in wars (*aṣnāfi muʿāḍadātihi fī l-ḥurūb*), and his lofty mercies in misfortunes and affairs (*wa-ʿālī tarāwufihi fī l-nawāʾib wa-l-khuṭūb*)?" rhyming *ḥurūb* with *khuṭūb*.[191] Likewise at the beginning of §4, Ibn al-Faḍl writes: "I answer that some men with penetrating contemplation (*al-naẓr al-thāqib*), and in divine matters conviction unswerving (*ṣāʾib*) . . ."[192] The ends of these two phrases rhyme, all the more so if we imagine someone pronouncing *qāf* as a *hamza* (ʾ), as in many modern Arabic dialects: *thāqib* and *ṣāʾib*. This rhythmic rhymed prose (*sajʿ*), typical in Arabic literature, is something Ibn al-Faḍl clearly wields intentionally. In this particular translation, he even uses the word *sajʿ* in a line about ornamented speech, in §13.[193] Here we also find Ibn al-Faḍl translating in his typical style—a loose translation that ensures the effectiveness of the Arabic while conveying the sense of the original.

This means that Ibn al-Faḍl's translation often introduces subtle shifts in meaning, making it more accessible in an Arabophone context. Where John wrote, "Jewish, Hellenic [pagan], and all other god-fighting heresy," Ibn al-Faḍl wrote, "the hypocrisy (*nifāq*) of the Jews and the pagans (*ḥunafāʾ*)." Thus the Arabic

189. §3 = 407_{16-17}: Ἐτράφη δὲ τίνι; **A** 245^{v}_{5-6}: *wa-in saʾalta yā ṣāḥ ʿan kayfīyati l-tarbīya, ajabtuka.*

190. 407_{37}: Τί δὲ καὶ τὸ διήγημα; **A** 247^{v}_{3-5}: *fa-in saʾalta yā ṣāḥ ʿan hādhā l-khabar, wa-stakshafta ʿam-māhīyatih, ajabtu anna.*

191. 406_{33-34}: Πῶς δὲ παρεάσω τὰς ἐν πολέμοις αὐτοῦ ἀοράτους συμμαχίας καὶ τοὺς φιλοπόλιδας οἰκτιρμούς. **A** 243^{v}_{13}–244^{r}_{2}: *wa-kayfa atakhallafu ʿan dhikri aṣnāfi muʿāḍadātihi fī l-ḥurūb, wa-ʿālī tarāwufihi fī l-nawāʾib wa-l-khuṭūb.* The last phrase suggests that Ibn al-Faḍl's exemplar might have read φιλοπόνους for φιλοπόλιδας.

192. **A** 247^{v}_{5-6} (~ Greek 407_{38}): *anna qawman min dhawī l-naẓari l-thāqib, wa-l-ifrār* [read *wa-l-iqrār*] *fī l-ilāhīyāti l-ṣāʾib. Ṣāʾib* evokes an arrow that "seeks out" its target; *iqrār* can connote effectively convincing someone of the truth: *Lisān* s.vv. *ṣwb, qrr.*

193. See n. 229 below.

focuses on the two categories of the Jews and the pagans and refers to their wrongdoing as *nifāq*, a term used in Muslim contexts to mean the act of pretending to accept Islam but secretly failing to be a believer.[194] The word Ibn al-Faḍl chooses to refer to the Hellenes also means pagan but transports it to a different semantic constellation: *ḥanīf*, derived from the Syriac word for "pagan," *ḥanpā*. A literal rendering of "Hellenic" as *yūnānī*, "Greek," would have failed to capture the religious sense of the word. But the term *ḥanīf* in Arabic had further connotations, since in the Qur'an it is used to refer to the original monotheists, most prominently Abraham; accordingly, Muslims used it to describe righteous Muslims, followers of the religion revealed so many times, to Abraham, to Moses, to Jesus, to Muḥammad. But this qur'anic term *ḥanīf* was also adopted as a self-description by practitioners of a star-venerating religion centered around the northern Mesopotamian city of Ḥarrān, who also called themselves by another qur'anic term, Sabians (*Ṣābi'a*)—which itself came to be used by Arabophone authors to refer to "pagans" like Plato.[195] In other words, Ibn al-Faḍl's choice as a translator here was perfectly natural and reasonable, and its meaning clear in the context, but it came with a very different set of connotations than "Hellene."

In this opening portion (§§1–3), John expects his audience to be familiar with at least some of the miracles ascribed to Saint Demetrios. A number of references in the *Encomium* to feats or qualities of Demetrios can be read as references to John's own collection of Demetrios's miracles.[196]

John introduces the centerpiece of his discourse, the narrative of Demetrios's methodical refutation of a range of opponents, by calling it a story he heard from certain "fathers." In the Greek, he says this as a sort of interjection:

> So then this god-given (θεοπάροχος)[197] champion of the Thessalonians preached; he who had been brought up with them was their teacher—for as the discourse proceeds to this I must also recall a wondrous tale that I heard fathers tell—and he filled the city with orthodoxy and heaped earth over those who disagreed.

Ibn al-Faḍl's translation makes the transition clearer by rearranging the clauses (all but necessary to make it comprehensible in Arabic) so that the reference to the story comes at the end of the sentence:

194. §3 = 407_{25-26}: ἰουδαϊκὴν καὶ ἑλληνικὴν καὶ πᾶσαν ἄλλην θεοπόλεμον αἵρεσιν. **A** 246^{v}_{1}: *nifāq al-yahūd wa-l-ḥunafā'*. According to the *Lisān* s.v. *nfq*, the term *nifāq* acquired this religious sense only in the Islamic period.

195. See de Blois, "*Naṣrānī* and *ḥanīf*"; van Bladel, *Arabic Hermes*, 190–91. Elsewhere, Ibn al-Faḍl uses both *ḥanīfī* (~Ἑλληνικός) and *Ṣābi'ūn* (~Ἕλληνες) to refer to pagans in the same breath; Ibn al-Faḍl, translation of Andrew of Crete's *Encomium to Saint Nicholas* (see n. 183 above).

196. See Philippidis-Braat, "L'enkômion," 406–7, footnotes.

197. Trapp, *Lexikon*, s.v. θεοπάροχος: "von Gott gespendet (verliehen)," citing a list of passages beginning with this one. Ibn al-Faḍl's translation agrees.

> But this learned saint and perfect teacher, pastor to the Thessalonians, of the same town (*balda*) and homeland (*waṭan*) as they, who was God's gift to them, did not cease exhorting the people to the luminous faith, to the point that [this faith] spread throughout the city and shone its rays on all parts of [the city], and error was refuted, falsehood and absurdity suppressed. Indeed I must mention the venerable, wondrous elucidation[198] that I heard from the fathers, an excellent promulgation, of great significance. For the discourse (*qawl* ~ *logos*) calls for me to proceed to that.[199]

Ibn al-Faḍl has considerably expanded the part about spreading the faith and combatting false belief in the city. This is an indication of what excited his interest in this text and in Saint Demetrios himself. Ibn al-Faḍl also magnifies the description of the story that is to follow: what was in Greek two words, "wondrous tale," has been expanded to three. Ibn al-Faḍl clearly recognized that this story, occupying the remainder of John's discourse, was the text's main act.

In §4, John finally takes it up. Those who are attentive will seek to understand how the saint's fame could have grown to such an extent that the tyrant (i.e., Roman emperor) heard tell of him.[200] They will realize that it wasn't so much the bodies he healed as the souls he purified through his teaching.[201] We see here concisely expressed what this text is all about: "For he roused, as if out of sleep, and cleansed, as if of filth, souls bound by stench and gloom in the pond of idolatry."[202] In this way "he introduced the noetic sunrise and the incense mixed in heaven—Christ, our true god—into their hearts."[203] Ibn al-Faḍl has replaced the somewhat obscure metaphor of Christ as the noetic sunrise with Christ as the noetic sun (*al-shams al-ʿaqlīya*).

John stresses Demetrios's fame and impact beyond the saint's hometown of Thessaloniki. This emphasis is especially pronounced in Ibn al-Faḍl's translation as he transitions to the heart of the narrative about refuting opponents with the final line of §4: "As for what magnified his importance, and raised his rank, and sent word of him flying *to lands other than his own*, this is what we will now recount."[204]

198. *sharḥ* ~ *diēgēma*. Later, Ibn al-Faḍl renders *diēgēma* as *khabar*, "report" (407_{37}; **A** 247^{v}_{4}).

199. §3, end = 407_{32-34}; **A** 246^{v}_{13}–247^{r}_{9}.

200. 407_{38-40}; **A** 247^{v}_{5-11}.

201. 407_{40-42}; **A** 247^{v}_{11}–248^{r}_{1}. The phrase διὰ διδαχῆς becomes a doublet: *bi-taʿālīmihi wa-talqīnih*, "by his teachings and his causing [souls] to understand."

202. 407_{42}–408_{1}. Cf. **A** 248^{r}_{1-5}: *wa-dhālika annahu ayqaḍa* [i.e., *ayqaẓa*] *l-nufūs min sinati l-ḍalāli wa-l-buhtān, wa-nashalahā min mahābiṭi ʿibādati l-awthān, wa-ghasalahā min ḥumāti l-ghayyi wa-l-jahl, wa-aʿtaqahā min masājini l-ẓulāmi wa-l-natn.*

203. 408_{1-3}; **A** 248^{r}_{5-8}: *wa-ashraqa fī qulūbi hādhihi l-ṭawāʾifi l-shamsu l-ʿaqlīya, wa-askanahā iyyāhā, wa-ʿaṭṭarahā bi-l-ʿiṭri l-samāwīyi lladhī huwa l-masīḥu ilāhunā l-ḥaqīqī.* Sunrise as a metaphor for Christ, based on Old Testament prophecy (Zacharias 6:12): Lampe s.v. ἀνατολή 1. Incense-making: Lampe s.v. σύνθεσις 3.

204. **A** 248^{v}_{9-12} (~ Greek 408_{8-10}): *fa-ammā lladhī ʿaẓẓama khaṭarahu, wa-rafaʿa makānahu, wa-ṭāra bi-khabarihi, ilā awṭāni ghayri waṭanihi, fa-hādhā l-amru lladhī hā nudhā{dhā}kiruhu* [**B** : *h-n-dhādhākiruhu* **A**] *al-ān* (emphasis added).

§5. The story begins with Demetrios confronted by debating opponents who visit him to tempt him: pagans (*ḥunafāʾ*), Jews, Manichaeans, and Arians. He is like Christ confronted by the Sadducees.

§6. The Hellene (pagan) speaks first. His manner of speech is soft and understated. He asks what the saint believes about God. The saint replies, paraphrasing the Nicene Creed, that there is one uncreated and eternal God, maker of all things seen and unseen, and that he rules over and manages all things. The Hellene remarks that in fact he agrees with much of that, since he is a Hellene of the Socratic, not Epicurean, variety. He believes in the one God, but also other gods, created by the first but also incorporeal and, by the will of the first god, also incorruptible. He also believes, like Plato, in a trinity of gods all of whom have the same divine essence: the first god, the Mind (*nous* ~ *ʿaql*)—"whom we also call God's Word (λόγον τοῦ θεοῦ ~ *kalimat Allāh*)"—and the Spirit (*pneuma* ~ *rūḥ*), "which some call the world-soul (*psychē tou kosmou* ~ *nafs al-ʿālam*)," and which is life-giving (ζωοποιοῦν, a reference to the portion on the Holy Spirit added to the Nicene Creed at the Council of Ephesus).[205] (The Hellene is clearly framing his own beliefs in a way that will be palatable to the Christian believer. There is a long Christian tradition of emphasizing how close Plato came to the truth.) There are, continues the Hellene, three hypostases (*aqānīm:* self-subsisting beings) according to Plato: the Good, the Demiurge-Mind, and the World-Soul. The first god created the rest of creation through these two gods (Mind and Spirit). The Hellene also agrees that the Mind and Spirit came from God's hypostasis but nevertheless are coeternal with it—but not equally wise or honored or powerful; the Father is superior to the other two, and the Mind is superior to the Spirit. He concludes his speech, saying, "Such is the doctrine of the eminent teachers among the Hellenes concerning God."[206]

§7. The saint weeps for the Hellene when he hears this.[207] Then he turns to the Arian "with a merciful eye" and asks him what penalty he will pay for being a disciple of Hellenic nonsense and ignoring Christ's pronouncement "I and the Father are one" (John 10:30), going on to explain how each aspect of what the Hellene says aligns with the Arian's theology, except that the Arian is even worse, since he, unlike the Hellene, denies that the Son and the Spirit are from the hypostasis of the Father and consubstantial and coeternal with him.

205. Philippidis-Braat refers here ("L'enkômion," 408 n. 24) to Porphyry, fragment 16 Nauck = Porphyry, *Opuscula tria*, 11–12, from Cyril, *Against Julian*.

206. Greek 408_{39-40}.

207. **B** 104^{v}_{3-4}: *fa-ammā l-mujāhidu l-sharīf, lammā samiʿa hādhā l-kalām, inhamalat ʿabarātuh, wa-tawāṣalat zafarātuh*. This line of rhymed prose seems to reflect archaicizing language on Ibn al-Faḍl's part. The word *ʿabra* makes one think immediately of the *muʿallaqa* of Imruʾ al-Qays: *wa-inna shifāʾī ʿabratun muharāqatun*. Indeed, this same line (with a variant ending to the hemistich) seems to be the first example that occurred to Ibn al-Manẓūr as well: *Lisān* s.v. *ʿbr*.

§8. Now a follower of Origen speaks up to agree that Son and Spirit are from God's essence, consubstantial and coeternal with him, but to add further that they were caused by him and so are inferior. The saint retorts that he's no better than a Platonist, and that being consubstantial implies having the same power, and so the same glory.

§9. The saint turns back to the Hellene, saying that the Hellene is wrong to call the inferior "intelligible and holy substances [οὐσίας ~ *jawāhir*]" gods. As the church teaches, they are not gods, since they came into existence and so, as the Arabic translation emphasizes, are subject to "coming-to-be" (γεγόνασι γάρ ~ *li-annahā dākhila taḥt al-kawn*).[208] They cannot be gods because they are not pre-eternal (*proaiōnion* ~ *azalī*). They are not consubstantial; they are creatures, nor do they share God's power. He then lists attributes of God, including foreknowledge (*to prognōstikon* ~ *annahu sābiq al-maʿrifa*), that belong to God but not to creatures. Created, incorporeal, immortal beings are best called "God's angels, his servants, not gods." It only makes sense to say "gods" in a metaphorical sense (*katachrēsis* ~ *istiʿāra*—a standard term of Arabic literary criticism),[209] not literally (*kyriolexia* ~ *taḥqīq*). (Ibn al-Faḍl addressed this line in the commentary on his translation.)[210] The Hellene replies by framing the saint's claim as being (or, in the Arabic, asking whether it is) that these incorporeal beings trick Hellenes[211] by pretending to be gods and claiming God's name and his glory for themselves. Saint Demetrios replies: No, only the ones who have fallen away from God, thus making themselves not angels but demons (ἑαυτοὺς ἐποίησαν δαίμονας ~ *tashayṭanū*).

§10. With the Hellene and the Arian refuted, now the Jew steps up, addressing the saint respectfully as "slave of God" (ὦ δοῦλε θεοῦ ~ *yā ʿabd Allāh*), and expressing full agreement with his proof of God's oneness and that he alone must be worshipped, and that all other beings, perceptible or noetic, are his creation. The saint replies: Don't be deceitful. You know that not only the Father is God but also the Son and the Holy Spirit, as the Mosaic law, the Prophets, and the Psalms say. God frequently refers to what "God" will do in the third person, so one entity (Father or Son) called God must be speaking of the other one. Also, God made man in God's image.[212] So there must be more than one Person (*prosōpon* ~ *qanūm*). As for

208. John of Damascus distinguishes between *agenētos* with one *nu* (unoriginated, uncreated) and *agennētos* with two (unbegotten); all three persons of the Trinity are *agenētoi,* but only the Father is *agennētos* (though only the Son is *gennētos,* while the Spirit is *ekporeuton*): *Exposition of Faith* 8, lines 123–41, ed. Kotter, 23–24. I thank Alexander Treiger for clarifying this point. Saint Demetrios here is saying that the Hellenes' gods fail to be *agenētoi.*

209. *EI*², s.v. "istiʿāra."

210. See ch. 5, pp. 167–68.

211. Reading "us," ἡμᾶς, not "you," ὑμᾶς, at 409_{37}; this reading is supported by Ibn al-Faḍl: **A** 253^{r}_{7} *tuṭghīnā* and **A** 254^{r}_{10} *tufīdunā.*

212. κατ' εἰκόνα θεοῦ 410_{11}; *ʿalā ṣūrat Allāh* **A** 255^{v}_{3}.

God's Spirit, it is mentioned in "almost every holy scripture" (Ibn al-Faḍl's translation has dropped the "almost").[213] These scriptural passages show that God's Spirit is everywhere, not spatially restricted.

The question of *where,* spatially, the Spirit and other incorporeal beings are located is apparently of great interest to Saint Demetrios (or to John of Thessaloniki), for the saint continues: Being everywhere at once (spatially unrestricted) is a trait not shared by any corporeal substances (*ousias*), nor by any incorporeal, noetic substances, since they are all created, and if in one place, they are not in another, even if they go from one place to another very fast, being incorporeal—or rather *subtle-bodied* (*leptosōmatoi* ~ *laṭīfat al-ajsām*). Only the Divine Nature is truly (*alēthōs*), or literally (*ʿalā l-taḥqīq*), incorporeal,[214] and only it fills all things but is not contained.[215]

Ibn al-Faḍl's careful translation of this passage, attentive to technical terms as usual, indicates his interest in its contents. An explanatory note (*tafsīr*) appearing at this point and discussing the corporeality of angels relative to the Spirit and to human beings would seem to confirm it; the note is almost certainly by Ibn al-Faḍl, though not labeled as such.[216]

The saint's response to the Jew continues: Scripture attests throughout to three divine Persons, not one (*prosōpon* ~ *wajh,* τῶν τριῶν ~ *al-thalātha al-aqānīm*).[217] In any case, how can you deny that God has speech/rationality (*logos* ~ *nuṭq*)[218] and a spirit, just like human beings, who were, after all, formed in God's image?[219]

§11. The Jew replies, addressing the saint as the "servant of the only [μόνου, or 'the one,' *al-wāḥid*] God." He begins by stressing his agreement with the saint's final statement that man was made in God's image. And so, he says, Jews observe that man's mind (*nous, ʿaql*) produces speech (*logos, nuṭq*), which exits the mouth through the mediation of the spirit/breath (*pneuma, rūḥ*), but only man's mind subsists (i.e., is a hypostasis, ὑφέστηκεν, *al-mutaqannim*), being the rational/articulate (*logistikon, nāṭiq*) part of the soul (*psychē, nafs*), while the utterance and the spirit/breath are dispersed in the air and cease to be. Since man was made in God's image, God too must be analogous, so that he too creates and rules over all using speech and spirit/breath, but there are not three subsisting parts or hypostases in the divinity (*theotēs, lāhūt*).

213. πάσης σχεδὸν τῆς ἁγίας γραφῆς 410_{14}; *fa-kullu kitābin muqaddasin* **A** 255^{v}_{8}.

214. 410_{22}; **A** 256^{r-v}.

215. ὑπ' οὐδενὸς περιεχομένη 410_{23}; *lā yaḥṣiruhā ḥāṣir* **A** 256^{v}_{3}.

216. Explication 3; see ch. 7, §3, esp. pp. 211–12. For the plausibility of Ibn al-Faḍl's authorship of this and the other two notes appearing without attribution in the manuscripts, see ch. 5, §3, ¶2, p. 166.

217. **A** 257^{r}_{2} = Greek 410_{26}; **A** 257^{r}_{3} = Greek 410_{27}.

218. **A** 257^{v}_{2} = Greek 410_{33}.

219. 410_{33-34}; **A** 257^{v}_{2}.

With a great show of patience, the saint sighs, prays to God, and replies that the Jew is insisting on making the analogy between God and man too exact. A depiction (*apeikonisma*) of a mortal emperor is quite different from the emperor himself; the image shares only some of the characteristics of the prototype. Otherwise, the image would be the emperor himself.[220] Likewise, if man's speech and spirit/breath were substantial (ἐνυπόστατα; i.e., were a hypostasis) and incorruptible, then man would not be in God's image but God himself—an image lacking nothing relative to its archetype.[221] Instead, the situation is as follows. God the Father is incorporeal and uncreated and ungenerated by nature, so his speech and spirit are self-subsisting, though inseparable from him. But in the case of man, only man's mind (not his speech or spirit) is self-subsisting, for his speech and breath disappear "with the action itself."[222] This is not the case with God. His speech and spirit are neither activities (ἐνεργεῖαι, *fiʿlayn*) nor actions (ἐνεργήματα, *mafʿūlayn*)—that is, neither the doing nor the thing done—but rather living, substantial hypostases (ὑποστάσεις οὐσιώδεις καὶ ζῶσαι, *qanūmayn jawharayn ḥayyayn*); they act but are not acted upon. Scripture attributes many actions to them, making them agents in their own right. These actions prove their substantial subsistence (*al-qanūmīya . . . al-jawharīya*). An agent acting by (its own) will (αὐτοθελῶς, *bi-irādatin*) must be a living substance; every living substance acts. Therefore man's speech and spirit are not living hypostases, substances, since if you (being human) say, Let there be such and such, nothing happens as a result of your speech alone, whereas when God says it, it happens.

§12. The Jew is sufficiently convinced to acknowledge that God has three persons.[223] But he asks how this position can be compatible with the monotheism to which Scripture enjoins us.

The saint replies[224] that the three persons are also well attested in Scripture, and there can be no contradictions between different parts of the same divinely inspired Scripture. The text (now using indirect discourse) says that the saint went on to relate that Scripture, when it speaks of confessing one god, must not mean it in the sense of one person,[225] but rather it means that the three persons are a single divinity, "that is, one substance, one power, one knowledge," and so on. They thus share in all these things and agree on everything and are closely linked; it is in this sense that they are one god. This is quite different from those beings that Hellenes (*ḥunafāʾ*) call gods, since the gods of the Hellenes are creatures; and even if the

220. ἀλλ' αὐτὸ βασιλεύς 411_4; *bal hiya l-maliku bi-ʿaynih* **A** 258^v_2.

221. ἀρχέτυπον 411_8; *al-ʿunṣur* **A** 258^v_9.

222. ἅμα τῇ ἐνεργείᾳ 411_{14}; *maʿ nafsi l-fiʿl* **A** 259^r_8 (following the reading supplied in the margin of **A,** to replace *al-ʿaql* in the main text).

223. πρόσωπα 411_{25}; *aqānīm* **A** 260^r_1.

224. 411_{27}.

225. πρόσωπον 411_{29}; *qanūman* **A** 260^r_{11}.

Hellenes were to claim that their gods are all a single substance, this cannot be the case because they are all different from each other just as different human beings are different from each other. Thus the universal apostolic church (*al-kanīsa al-jāmiʿa al-rasūlīya*) rightly confesses that God is one in three persons. (Here another explication appears, this one on number, alterity, and divine attributes.)[226]

§13. A great throng of others crowds around. Here John's language alludes to Homer: they are crowding "like many thronging swarms of flies, as someone said"—or, as Ibn al-Faḍl's translation specifies, as *the poet* said.[227] (Later readers of this text in Arabic were interested in the source of this quotation; someone, perhaps the scribe, wrote in the margin of one ca. thirteenth-century manuscript that it was Homer.)[228] The throng thanks the saint for these illuminating teachings on the Trinity, which they accept. They then ask him to resolve the disagreements they have with one another regarding the dispensation (*oikonomia, siyāsa*) of God's Logos. The saint replies that he is happy to do so. The measure (μέτρον) of good speech is not its vigorous style (εὐτονία) but rather that it is easy on listeners.[229] To save time, he proposes not answering their questions one by one but rather hearing their positions, and then addressing them all at once.

§14. There follows a series of objections to Nicene-Chalcedonian theology (each labeled in the margins of manuscripts with the name of the one who raised the objection).[230] God's Logos couldn't become corruptible flesh (margin: Manichaeans); God only appeared to be a man, as he appeared to Abraham and Isaac (margin: Markion, in the Greek manuscript); contrariwise, Christ was a mere man, not divine at all, and "received the origin of his being only from the Virgin" (margin: Photinians);[231] God the Word took on flesh, "but flesh not from the Virgin, consub-

226. See ch. 5, p. 169.

227. ὡς ἔφησέ τις 411_{42-43}; *ka-qawli l-shāʿir* **A** 261^{v}_{4}. Homer, *Iliad* 2.469; Philippidis-Braat, "L'enkômion," 411 n. 41. Ibn al-Faḍl translates the Homeric line as *ka-qabāʾila jammatin mina l-dhubābi l-mutaṭāyiri maʿan.*

228. **A** 261ᵛ.

229. 412_{6-7}; **A** 262ʳ. Ibn al-Faḍl seems to have interpreted this line rather differently (or had a different version of the Greek before him): "We learned . . . that with [speech] one does not seek to adorn one's expression or employ *sajʿ*" (*ʿalimnā kayfa . . . fī l-kalām . . . wa-annahu laysa yuqṣadu bihi taḥsīnu l-ʿibārati wa-stiʿmālu l-sajʿ*). Perhaps *sajʿ* is meant to translate μέτρον (in a very different sense than I have construed it), or perhaps *sajʿ wa-taḥsīn al-ʿibāra* is a doublet for εὐτονία, construed as meaning something like "fine sound."

230. Manichaeans: in both the Greek manuscript (Paris gr. 1517) and **A** 262ᵛ. Photinians: Greek and **A** 263ʳ (*al-Fātīnī*), though the Arabic label is misplaced, coming one sentence too early. Eutychians: Greek and **A** 263ʳ. Arians: Greek and Arabic (*al-Āriyūsīya*). Apollinarians: Greek and Arabic. Origenists: Greek and Arabic. Nestorians: not in Greek manuscript, only in Arabic, **A** 265ᵛ (*al-Nasāṭira*).

231. According to George the Hieromonk, Photeinos held beliefs similar to those of Paul of Samosata, for "he too taught that the son had taken the beginning of his existence from Mary"; *To Epiphanius On Heresies*, XI.5, ed. Richard, "Le traité," 265; cited by Philippidis-Braat, "L'enkômion," 412 n. 45.

stantial with ours, but from heaven and consubstantial with the Word," so that Christ has only one nature (margin: Eutychians); Christ took on human flesh but no human soul, God the Logos taking the place of the human soul (margin: Arians); Christ has a soul but not a rational one,[232] and so is not a complete human being and consequently has two natures, one pertaining to the Logos, the other to the human being (margin: Apollinarians); Christ has a rational soul that was created in time but before the world was created, along with all incorporeal beings like angels and human souls, which were created simultaneously before the world, and then later God the Logos took on that soul and took only his flesh from the Virgin (margin: Origenists); the Virgin gave birth to a human being into whom God the Logos then entered, making her not Theotokos (Mother of God) but Christotokos (Mother of Christ). Those who make this last objection believe that there are two persons in Christ, "even if they are ashamed to say it" (this clause is omitted in the Arabic),[233] "for they confess two natures of the same hypostasis, bound together by a relation alone, not by hypostasis" (margin: Nestorians). (After the reference to the Apollinarian objection appears another explanatory note.)[234]

Finally, the last group to speak offers the "correct" Christology (so labeled in the margin of the Arabic):[235] the Logos, accompanied by the Holy Spirit as always, took flesh from the Virgin that was already endowed with a rational soul, then added to it his own hypostasis, so that the Virgin is the Mother of God, of God made human and made flesh.

Then they ask the saint: Which one of us is right?

§15. In a grand finale, Saint Demetrios responds to them all at once. He begins by lamenting humanity's "excessive curiosity" (*periergia*) that was not satisfied by exercising itself upon "matter" or even "incorporeal and noetic substances" but had to try out its methods on the creator as well.[236] But he will not hold back the orthodox truth from them. The last group to speak was correct. He then proceeds to spell out their position in great detail, careful to address each of the other positions implicitly in his elaboration of the orthodox (i.e., Chalcedonian) position. For example, he stresses that the divine and human parts of Christ share in both the miracles and the suffering (rather than one being the prerogative of the divine part, the other of the human part) on account of their "unity" (*henōsis*).[237]

Though he professes not to use human reason to work out the correct position, he does in fact offer logical arguments. For example, Christ is one hypostasis in two

232. ἄνουν καὶ ἄλογον 412_{21-22}; *ghayr nāṭiqa wa-lā ʿāqila* **A** 263^{v}_{3-4}.
233. **A** 266^{r}_{6}.
234. See ch. 5, pp. 170–71.
235. **A** 266^{v}: *hāʾulāʾ aṣḥāb al-raʾy al-qawīm.*
236. 413_{17-20}.
237. 413_{32-38}.

natures, so you can say that his hypostasis is composite but not that his nature is composite, since then he would be consubstantial neither with the Father (whose divine nature is not composite) nor with us (whose human nature is also not composite).[238]

§16. The saint ends his speech. The crowd acclaims him joyfully. Christ, whom the saint "blamelessly preached," spreads the saint's fame throughout the earth.

This whole text would have resonated well in the eleventh century, when Arabic texts on religious debates were popular. Saint Demetrios's (and John's, and Ibn al-Faḍl's) theological tour de force combined the beauty of rhetorical language and the competitive thrill of partisan debate with detailed theological argumentation—interconfessional polemics executed in a philosophical framework.

6 CONCLUSION

The texts we have surveyed in this chapter were all in a sense Christian answers to facets of the old Hellenic-pagan curriculum. The Psalter and other Scripture could stand in as a preferable corpus of edifying poetry and "true" stories about the divine, to take the place of all the pretty but misleading literature that Socrates had wished to ban from his ideal polity because it mendaciously attributed vices to the gods.[239] Patristic masterpieces offered doctrinal authority from the pens of esteemed bishops and, perhaps more importantly, rhetorical models and intellectual frameworks for justifying their vision of God, humanity, and the cosmos. Later doctrinal syntheses developed language and methods for responding to challenges to this worldview in the wake of the conquest of vast swaths of Eurasia, including most of the Roman (Byzantine) Empire, by monotheists claiming to bear a new scriptural revelation from the same god. Encomia to saints continued the rhetorical tradition and bolstered saints who could offer protection to the downtrodden and whole cities, as well as the intellectual firepower to debate doctrinal opponents. Collections of wise sayings in the form of *kephalaia* or "chapters" could be used to shape the self in accordance with Christian philosophical virtues—a challenge to Hellenic-pagan claims to teach the virtue that leads to a life well lived.

But who, precisely, was interested in such texts in the eleventh century?

238. 414_{11-15}.
239. Plato, *Republic* 2, 376e1–378e4.

3

A BYZANTINE ECCLESIASTICAL CURRICULUM

Now that we have surveyed the character and content of the texts Ibn al-Faḍl is known to have translated (table 1), we are in a position to ask who else was reading these texts in the eleventh century. The answer the present chapter offers is that these texts together formed part of a Byzantine ecclesiastical curriculum. Much read by elite Byzantines (not only churchmen or monks but also laypeople), they were a core part of eleventh-century Byzantine literary culture. These same texts were also read by Chalcedonian Christian speakers of other languages in the Byzantine Empire. In particular, Ibn al-Faḍl's list taken as a whole bears striking similarities to the lists of texts translated by contemporary Georgians working at the Iviron Monastery ("of the Georgians") on Mount Athos and in Antioch's hinterland. More broadly, Georgian book culture overlapped considerably with what we can glean from Ibn al-Faḍl's translations about Arabic book culture in Byzantine Antioch. This allows us to see Ibn al-Faḍl's translation program as part of a concerted effort to promote a Byzantine ecclesiastical curriculum in Antioch.

1 GREEK MANUSCRIPTS

As a first step in assessing the Byzantine popularity of the texts Ibn al-Faḍl translated, we may estimate how many Greek manuscripts containing each text survive from the eleventh century. There is no complete list of all extant Greek manuscripts. Instead, I will use the online database *Pinakes*, which has entries on roughly 40,000 Greek manuscripts. (By comparison, Elpidio Mioni estimated that about 44,000 Greek manuscripts are extant today, of which 24,000 are premodern.)[1] Many, many Greek manuscripts have been lost or destroyed over the centuries, so even the extant Greek manuscripts are only a small fraction of all the Greek manuscripts ever *produced.* This means that tallies from *Pinakes* can only go so far in indicating the circulation of a given text. Caution is especially necessary in the case of texts with very few surviving manuscripts: small numbers of extant manuscripts do not necessarily prove limited circulation in centuries past. In the case of relatively large numbers of extant manuscripts, we can be more confident in concluding that the text enjoyed a relatively wide circulation.

The results of a tally of the relevant manuscripts on *Pinakes* are given in table 2. Only manuscripts dated to the tenth/eleventh, eleventh, or eleventh/twelfth century are included in the tally; in some cases there are many, many more extant manuscripts, most of them later than the eleventh century. As the results indicate, many of the texts Ibn al-Faḍl translated are extremely well attested in the contemporary Greek manuscript tradition.

Some of the best-attested texts are those of late antique biblical exegesis. Chrysostom's *Homilies on Matthew* (206 manuscripts) and *Homilies on Genesis* (171 manuscripts) were clearly extremely popular in the eleventh century. Also widely copied were his *Homilies on John* (81 manuscripts) and Basil of Caesarea's *Homilies on the Psalms* (55 manuscripts) and *Homilies on the Hexaemeron* (32 manuscripts). Other genuine patristic works attested in over ten ca. eleventh-century manuscripts include Chrysostom's homilies on Roman, Hebrews, and First Corinthians; Gregory of Nyssa's *On Making Man;* and Maximos's *Chapters on Love.*

This wide circulation corresponds to the fame of these saints and church fathers in Byzantium. Indeed, Basil and Chrysostom are just the sort of authors one might expect an educated medieval Greek-speaking Christian to be interested in reading. Perhaps more striking is the popularity of a work less well known today, the *Loci communes* (81 manuscripts). Though the pseudonymous ascription to Maximos the Confessor may have helped its success, the text's popularity suggests that its synthesis of Christian and pagan wisdom held great appeal for Byzantine readers. Something similar might be said about the *Questions and Answers* ascribed to Kaisarios (25 manuscripts). Collections of concise sayings or answers to questions that could be used in education were popular. These two collections were particularly popular in eleventh-century Byzantium. Could this explain why Ibn al-Faḍl translated them?

Similarly, the attestation for Andrew of Crete's *Encomium to Saint Nicholas* (16 manuscripts) helps explain Ibn al-Faḍl's choice. If one supposes an interest in the genre of elegant literary discourses on saints, then translating this particular representative of the genre into Arabic made perfect sense—perfect sense, that is, if one also assumes that Byzantine literary tastes were an important factor behind

1. Mioni, *Introduzione,* 111.

TABLE 2 Tally, according to *Pinakes*, of extant ca. 11th-century Greek manuscripts (including those dated to the 10th/11th, 11th, and 11th/12th centuries)

	Author	Work		*CPG*	Tally
1		Psalms			
2		Gospel Lectionary			
3		Epistolary	?		
4		Prophetologion	?		
5	Basil of Caesarea	*Homilies on the Psalms*		2836	55
6		*Homilies on the Hexaemeron*		2835	32
7	Gregory of Nyssa	*On Making Man*	?	3154	25
8		*Apology on the Hexaemeron*	?	3153	8
9		*Homilies on the Song of Songs*	?	3158	3
10	John Chrysostom	*Homilies on Genesis*		4409	171
11		*Homilies on Matthew*	?	4424	206
12		*Homilies on John*	?	4425	81
13		*Homilies on First Corinthians*	?	4428	17
14		*Homilies on Hebrews*		4440	18
15		*Homilies on Romans*		4427	22
16		Collection of 87 homilies	?		
17		*Exhortation to Penitence*	?		
18	Pseudo-Kaisarios	*Questions and Answers* (partial)		7482	25
19	John of Thessaloniki	*Encomium to St. Demetrios*		7925	0
20	Sophronios	*Synodical Letter* (adaptation)		7635	4
21	Maximos Confessor	*Disputation with Pyrrhos*		7698	4
22		*Chapters on Love*	?	7693	30
23		*Chapters on Knowledge*	?	7694	9
24	Pseudo-Maximos	*Loci communes*		7718	81
25	Isaac of Nineveh	*Ascetic Homilies* (35 of 82)		7868	6
26		*Chapters on Knowledge*	?		
27	Andrew of Crete	*Encomium to St. Nicholas*		8187	16
28	John of Damascus	*Statement on Correct Thought*		8046	0

NOTE: This table contains each text in table 1 (including translations whose attribution to Ibn al-Faḍl I question, again marked with ?). These numbers should be taken as rough preliminary estimates; they are far from a definitive tally.

Ibn al-Faḍl's choice of texts. Indeed, these manuscript counts, rough as they are, make it difficult to avoid the conclusion that they were.

To underscore this, let us return for a moment to Ibn al-Faḍl's abundant translations of works by Chrysostom. These translations show just how central Byzantine tastes (and perhaps an appreciation of Chrysostom's role in the history of the Antiochian Church) were to the Antiochian Chalcedonian milieu. The brilliant orator of Antioch and onetime patriarch of Constantinople was extraordinarily popular in Byzantine culture.[2] While the works of Basil and Gregory of Nyssa are

2. See Quasten, *Patrology*, 3:424–32.

well attested in eleventh-century manuscripts, Chrysostom's homilies are *phenomenally* well-attested. In his 1907 study on Chrysostom's works, Chrysostomus Baur surveyed manuscript catalogs available to him at the time, omitting manuscripts later than the sixteenth century; he counted 1,917 manuscripts containing Chrysostom's homilies, including 512 dated to the eleventh century.[3] Thanks to the manuscript catalogs published in the past hundred years, the same survey today would doubtless come up with even more.[4]

These numbers are truly astounding. Given the overall survival of Greek manuscripts—manuscripts from the eleventh century and earlier are much less likely to survive than those dating to the twelfth century or later—it is highly significant that over a quarter of the extant pre-seventeenth-century manuscripts of Chrysostom's homilies date to the eleventh century. This may in part be due to the production and use of such books in monasteries and patriarchates with institutional continuity from the eleventh century to the present, but we cannot escape the conclusion that this was a period in which Chrysostom's homilies were copied and studied with particular intensity. That these homilies make up the bulk of the works Ibn al-Faḍl translated is a clear sign that contemporary Byzantine culture was a major factor behind his translation program.

Individual Byzantine libraries held multiple works (in Greek) from the list of Ibn al-Faḍl's known translations. Among the books that Michael Attaleiates listed in his will, drawn up in 1077, were three books by Chrysostom: his "Hexaemeros," probably referring to his sixty-seven homilies on Genesis (perhaps only the first ten homilies covering the six-day creation narrative); a book *On the Statues* (*CPG* 4330); and "a parchment book written in minuscule script (*monokairon*) containing a work of Chrysostom" and several saints' lives. Among the other books Attaleiates listed along with these were a manuscript of Basil's *Hexaemeron*, "a theological book" by John of Damascus, and a Psalter with commentary.[5] In the second half of the twelfth century, a single scribe, George Lolenos, annotated a tenth-century manuscript containing Basil's *Hexaemeron* and another manuscript containing Chrysostom's *Homilies on Matthew*, homilies 1–45 (out of ninety), according to Sofia Kotzabassi (on circumstantial and paleographical grounds).[6] Further research would probably turn up much more evidence that the texts Ibn al-Faḍl translated circulated together in the middle Byzantine period and were housed together in the same libraries. It might well turn up evidence that these texts were diffused widely

3. Baur, *S. Jean Chryosostome*, 29; cited by Quasten, *Patrology*, 3:431. Given the relatively low survival rate of Greek manuscripts, these are very high numbers.

4. The project of cataloguing all Greek Chrysostom manuscripts is still ongoing: *Codices Chrysostomici Graeci*.

5. Gautier, "La diataxis," 93–95, lines 1254–67.

6. Kotzabassi, "Miscellanea," 135–36.

not only in the Byzantine capital but also in the imperial peripheries. For now, there is this suggestive example: in the 1050s there was at least one copy of Basil's *Hexaemeron* in a library not far from Edessa (in northern Mesopotamia), the private collection of the Cappadocian Eustathios Boïlas, who listed it in his will.[7]

2 CHRYSOSTOM AND THE CAPPADOCIAN FATHERS

If these texts were popular in eleventh-century Byzantium, what was their cultural resonance? Who read such texts in Byzantium and why? Though much of the following applies to other chronological stages of the Byzantine tradition, the focus is on the eleventh century.

As we have seen from the Greek manuscript tradition, works by John Chrysostom ("the Golden-Mouthed") and the Cappadocian Fathers Basil of Caesarea ("the Great") and Gregory of Nyssa were very popular in eleventh-century Byzantium, including the particular works Ibn al-Faḍl translated. This is also true of the third Cappadocian Father, Gregory of Nazianzos ("the Theologian"), whose works are not among Ibn al-Faḍl's known translations but who will be considered alongside the late antique authors who are. As we shall see, these hierarchs were revered in Byzantium as exegetical authorities, literary models, authors of the words pronounced at the Divine Liturgy, and holy bishops—saints honored in public ceremonies by the patriarch of Constantinople, and by the emperor himself.

Biblical Exegetes

There are many places we could look for an illustration of their exegetical authority. Outside of the manuscript tradition, the influence of their interpretations is attested in the later commentary tradition, the authority accorded to their works by all sides in doctrinal disputes among (Nicene) Christians, and citations of their interpretations in other Byzantine literary works. Here a brief look at a text that succinctly captures this influence should suffice: a catena.

A catena is a series or "chain" of excerpts from authoritative (patristic) sources on a biblical passage (the term "catena" dates to the early modern period).[8] Rather than offer one author's interpretation of a text, a catena compiles a diachronic snapshot of the exegetical tradition by compiling selections deemed relevant and appropriate by their (anonymous) editor. Catenae provided a scholarly apparatus for studying Scripture and its interpretation by juxtaposing prominent commentators' interpretations of each passage. The prominence of Chrysostom especially, but the other three as well, vividly illustrates the weight that their exegetical opinions carried.

7. Lemerle, *Cinq études*, 25, line 157: Ἑξαήμερος τοῦ ἁγίου Βασιλείου. Cited by Fedwick, *Bibliotheca Basiliana*, 4.1:220. The will is dated April 1059.

8. *ODB*, s.v. "Catenae."

As an example, consider an eleventh-century Greek manuscript containing a catena on Genesis now in Basel at the University Library.[9] Given the popularity of Basil's *Hexaemeron* (on the opening lines of Genesis), we would expect Basil to be particularly prominent here in the portion covered by his homilies (the first thirty folios). And so he is. The very first authority quoted after the first line of Scripture is "Saint Jo(hn) Chrysostom, from his discourse on the Fortieth [Day of Lent]."[10] Then come several other excerpts from Chrysostom, then, on the next page, a brief excerpt from Basil, then one from Chrysostom's homilies on Hebrews, then a page and a half from "Basil bishop of Caesarea" (fols. 2^{v}–3^{r}). Then come others, often quoted at length—Theodoret, Severian of Gabala, "Hippolytos bishop of Rome," Apollinaris, Cyril of Alexandria, Eusebius of Emesa—but Basil maintains his prominence. Less so Chrysostom, but he will return.

"And God said: Let us make man according to our image and likeness . . ." (Genesis 1:26, fol. 25^{r}). Here we reach a critical passage for the commentary tradition. It receives a significant amount of treatment in the manuscript, beginning with two pages of Basil, then about a page of Severian (fols. 25^{r}–26^{v}). Then new authorities appear: Gregory of Nyssa, back to Basil, then "Gregory the Theologian" (of Nazianzos), then back to Gregory of Nyssa from his *On Making Man*, "chapter 4," and so on (fol. 26^{v}). In a couple of pages, Gregory of Nyssa is back, and then we hear again from "Jo(hn) archbishop of Constantinople," that is, Chrysostom (fol. 27^{v}). And the chain continues.[11]

Of course if we were to dip into Greek catenae on a different corner of the Bible, we might come up with a different balance of citation. On the creation of the world, Basil was particularly authoritative, and likewise Gregory of Nyssa's views on the human being and what it meant to be created in God's image carried particular weight in the tradition. But the overall configuration would be similar: we have a relatively small club of authoritative exegetes, of whom some, like Chrysostom, were such towering figures as to be afforded prominence even when the tradition might have been more interested in the interpretations of others on a given matter. How could one fail to cite Chrysostom?[12]

9. Basel, Universitätsbibliothek AN III 13. See Omont, *Catalogue des manuscrits grecs*, 6, no. 1.

10. Basel, Universitätsbibliothek AN III 13, fol. 2^{r}: τοῦ ἁγίου Ιω(άννης) τοῦ χρυσοστόμου, ἐκ τοῦ λόγου τοῦ εἰς τὴν τεσσαρα(κοστήν). The reference is to *Sermones in Genesim* (*CPG* 4410), sermon 1 (of nine), delivered on the fortieth day of Lent, that is, the day before Easter.

11. The manuscript refers to them as familiar authorities. Sometimes they are given episcopal epithets, but usually they are simply referred to by their given names (Basil, John, Theodoret, etc.), or even a quick shorthand, e.g., Βα for Basil, ΙΩ for John Chrysostom.

12. For a more comprehensive view of the Greek catenae on Genesis, see Petit, *La chaîne sur la Genèse*. The catenae contained in Basel, Universitätsbibliothek AN III 13 (and other manuscripts) are edited in Petit, *Catenae graecae in Genesim et in Exodum*.

Literary Models

These men were very much "fathers of the church." In the eleventh century Symeon the (New) Theologian portrays them as successors to the apostles, bearers of the word of God.[13] But they were also influential models for Byzantine rhetoric—a field embracing discursive theory but also belles lettres, wit, public speaking, and philology (in the broad sense of "love of letters" and mastery of a venerable literary tradition), always at a high literary register.[14] As a rhetor, Gregory of Nazianzos outshone the others, to judge from the middle Byzantine rhetorical tradition, just as Basil and Chrysostom were giants in the Byzantine exegetical tradition.[15] This case could be made for any period in Byzantine history; in what follows, I will focus on the middle Byzantine period, beginning with Photios, whose *Bibliotheca* is a unique source for how an elite Byzantine scholar read and evaluated what he read.

The erudite Patriarch Photios (d. after 893) attests to a learned Byzantine appreciation for these authors *as authors*. In his collection of book reviews known as the *Bibliotheca*,[16] Photios discusses Chrysostom's letters (codex 86), *Encomium to the Forty Martyrs* (codex 274), individual homilies on various topics (codex 277),[17] and an excerpt from an otherwise unknown text, *On Saint Paul* (codex 270), which Photios ascribes to Chrysostom.[18] He also reviewed a book by Chrysostom that we know Ibn al-Faḍl translated—namely, the *Homilies on Genesis*. (Photios remarks that his copy called them "discourses," *logoi*, but that they read like homilies.) Photios praises Chrysostom's "customary clarity and purity," his "brilliance and fluency," in these homilies, which "display at once a variety of thoughts and a most fitting abundance of examples." Photios found the homilies' language too humble and so preferred the style of Chrysostom's *Homilies on Acts* but emphasized the brilliance of all of Chrysostom's writings. Of works Ibn al-Faḍl translated, Photios also read Chrysostom's *Homilies on the Apostle*, that is, his homilies on the letters of Saint Paul.[19] In all, Photios devotes more attention to Chrysostom than to any other writer.[20]

13. Symeon the New Theologian, *Hymn* 19, lines 78–82, ed. Kambylis, 155.

14. For rhetoric, Byzantine *logoi* more broadly, and their middle Byzantine social context, see Papaioannou, *Psellos*, 20–24.

15. Papaioannou, 17 n. 45, 46 n. 71, 56.

16. Photios, *Bibliothèque*, ed. Henry. On the work, see Treadgold, *Nature*.

17. Including an *Exhortative Discourse on Penitence*, possibly the same text whose Arabic translation has sometimes been ascribed to Ibn al-Faḍl.

18. Henry says he could not find anything matching Photios's description of *On Saint Paul* in the standard Chrysostomic corpus: *Bibliothèque*, ed. Henry, 8:277, note for p. 78, line 28. Treadgold, *Nature*, 166: "unattested?"

19. Codices 172–74, ed. Henry, 2:168–70. Cited by Baur, "Chrysostomus," 230. (Of these, Ibn al-Faḍl is only known to have translated the homilies on Hebrews, Romans, and possibly First Corinthians.)

20. Treadgold, *Nature*, 108–9.

Photios also had a very high opinion of Basil as a writer. He reviewed Basil's *Hexaemeron, Moralia,* letters, and *Ascetica* (codices 141–44, 191). The letters he considered a reasonably good model for writing one's own letters in fine style.[21] The *Hexaemeron* he found outstanding:

> Have read the divine Basil's commentaries on the hexaemeron. The great Basil is excellent in all of his literary works, for with his pure, clear, and authoritative diction, he is entirely equipped for political and panegyric speech, if anyone is. In the arrangement and purity of thoughts he takes first place and seems to be second to none. A lover of persuasion and sweetness as well as brilliant clarity, his speech flows, causing the stream to gush forth as if spontaneously. He makes use of persuasion to such a degree that if one should take his works as a model for political speech and learn them thoroughly, and assuming he is not inexperienced in the relevant laws [of the genre], I think he would need no other model, neither Plato nor Demosthenes, with whom the ancients recommend one to become familiar in order to become a political and panegyric rhetor.[22]

In these homilies, Photios clearly appreciates both the style and the content—pure diction and pure thoughts—of Basil's writing. He rates him so highly as a rhetor, at least as concerns public speeches and praising, that he believes Basil can in these respects replace two of the most celebrated and imitated writers in the Byzantine rhetorical tradition, Plato and Demosthenes.

We get a similar picture from subsequent comments on these authors. The teacher, courtier (under Emperor Constantine IX Monomachos), bishop, and then monk John Mauropous (b. ca. 1000, d. ca. 1075–1081) wrote an essay on Basil, Gregory of Nazianzos, and Chrysostom, arguing that God had inspired not only the content of their works but also their rhetorical form.[23] In the mid-eleventh century, John Doxapatres, in the introduction to his commentary on a rhetorical treatise by Aphthonios (fourth/fifth century), compares the styles of Lykophron (a poet and scholar at the court of Ptolemy Philadelphos in Alexandria, third century BCE), Gregory of Nazianzos, and John Chrysostom (in order to help him characterize the subject of his commentary, Aphthonios). Doxapatres finds that while the ancient orator Lykophron is overblown in his language and short on substance, and Gregory is understated though strong on substance, Chrysostom strikes a balance most of the time, communicating important ideas in artful but not pompous words.[24] Elsewhere, Doxapatres, speaking of how a rhetorical form (*idea*) such as solemnity (*semnotēs*) is analogous to an abstract Platonic Form (*idea*) that com-

21. Ed. Henry, 2:109–10.

22. Codex 141, ed. Henry, 2:109, translation after Henry's.

23. *Discourse on the Three Holy Fathers and Teachers;* see Papaioannou, *Psellos,* 71 and n. 68.

24. John Doxapatres, *Rhetorical Homilies on Aphthonios's Progymnasmata,* introduction, ed. Rabe, *Prolegomenon,* 141. On Doxapatres, see Papaioannou, *Psellos,* 71.

prises individual instances of solemnity, gives as his two examples Thucydidean and Chrysostomic solemnity.[25] A bit further along when he reaches for examples of solemnity and brilliance (σεμνότης καὶ λαμπρότης), his examples are "Theological" (i.e., of Gregory of Nazianzos) and "Chrysostomic."[26]

John Mauropous's famous student Psellos built on a growing Byzantine appreciation for the church fathers as rhetorical models, writing several essays on these authors' rhetorical merits.[27] One of them is comparative: *The Styles of Gregory the Theologian, Basil the Great, Chrysostom, and Gregory of Nyssa.*[28] He also wrote individual essays on Gregory of Nazianzos and Chrysostom.[29]

In his essay on Chrysostom (analyzed by Wolfram Hörandner), Psellos compared Chrysostom to ancient Greek orators, defending Chrysostom against the charge that his style is not artful enough.[30] In fact, Psellos insists, there are two kinds of rhetoric, one bombastic and over the top, the other natural and restrained in its use of verbal ornamentation. Chrysostom's rhetoric is of the latter, natural type, which is superior. In this he is superior even to ancient orators like Lysias and Plato (whose style Byzantine writers continued to admire and emulate). Chrysostom finds the mean between "weighty" and "trivial" speech, between using too many words and too few. He digresses in order to vary the subject matter agreeably, but never strays too far from the overarching argument he is making. The result, Psellos contends, is clear, straightforward, but subtly artful speech—rhetorically superior, even by ancient standards, to most, if not all ancient authors.

Psellos has a preference for the Theologian. As Stratis Papaioannou discusses, Psellos praises Gregory of Nazianzos's rhetoric in his *Improvised Discourse to Pothos the Vestarches . . . on the Theologian's Style,* entirely devoted to the subject, but also at various points in his commentary on Gregory's *Orations.*[31] Still, Psellos ultimately sees all four rhetors as outstanding in their own way, such that the ideal

25. John Doxapatres, *Prolegomena on Hermogenes's Book on Literary Forms,* ed. Rabe, *Prolegomenon,* 420–26, here 424_{16-17}. For the translation "solemnity," I follow Papaioannou, in Psellos, *Literature and Art,* 21.

26. Ed. Rabe, *Prolegomenon,* 425_{5-6}.

27. Papaioannou, *Psellos,* chs. 1–2.

28. Ed. Boissonade in Psellos, *De operatione daemonum,* 124–31 = Moore 1013. ("Moore" refers to the numbering system of Moore, *Iter Psellianum.*) Now trans. Papaioannou in Psellos, *Literature and Art,* ch. 7. For *charaktēres* as "styles," see Papaioannou, *Psellos,* 54.

29. On Gregory: ed. Mayer, "Psellos' Rede"; ed. Levy = Moore 1011. On Chrysostom: ed. Levy = Moore 1012.

30. My discussion of this text closely follows the summary and analysis given by Hörandner, "Literary Criticism."

31. Papaioannou, *Psellos,* 55. *On the Theologian's Style:* Moore 1011. Now trans. Papaioannou in Psellos, *Literature and Art,* ch. 8. Commentary on seventy-three passages from Gregory's *Orations:* Moore 543–615 = THE.1–73; in Psellos, *Theologica I,* ed. Gautier; and *Theologica II,* ed. Westerink and Duffy.

rhetor might combine qualities of all four. He sums up his comparative essay *The Styles of Gregory the Theologian, Basil the Great, Chrysostom, and Gregory of Nyssa* with an oft-quoted aspiration:

> And so I, at any rate, would wish, indeed would love, to be able to praise like Gregory the Theologian, speak with a clear and resounding voice like Basil the Great, interpret divine oracles like Gregory of Nyssa, and approach the deliberative genre and sweeten my speech with simple and indescribable grace like the golden lyre of the Spirit [Chrysostom].[32]

The aspiring writer could not hope for better models.[33]

These church fathers could stand in for the best of Byzantine civilization, emblematic of its civilizing mission. Theophylact, bishop of Ohrid (b. ca. 1050, d. after 1126), in a letter to one Nicholas Anemas, sympathizes with the younger man's complaints about living in barbaric Bulgaria. Theophylact, who was born in Greek-speaking Euboea, writes that he has lived for many years in Bulgaria surrounded by boorishness and yearning for wisdom. Anemas, at least, has "just yesterday" had books in his hands; their wisdom still echoes in his ears. And now, continues Theophylact, "I have sent you a book by Chrysostom." This unspecified work by John Chrysostom, Theophylact suggests, should be at least some consolation to Anemas: a taste of civilization, now far away.[34] Clearly implied is an opposition between Byzantine civilization (urban culture) and Bulgarian barbarity (rusticity). Chrysostom represents civilization.

As we have already seen from these examples, divine authority and rhetorical exemplarity were not mutually exclusive. Indeed, in the Byzantine view, these virtues were closely linked.[35] This is reflected in a brief epigram "on Saint John Chrysostom" by the eleventh-century poet Christopher of Mytilene (b. ca. 1000, d. after 1050 or 1068):

> The words from your lips are truly pearls,
> adorning not throats nor breadths of breasts,
> but rather the forms, O John, within.
> For they adorn not bodies but souls.[36]

32. In Psellos, *De operatione daemonum,* 130–31; trans. (modified) Hörandner, "Literary Criticism," 338–39.

33. For both essays, see Papaioannou, *Psellos,* 54–55, with references.

34. Theophylact, *Lettre* 34, ed. Gautier. See Mullett, *Theophylact,* 275–76.

35. Papaioannou, *Psellos,* ch. 2.

36. Ed. Groote, 137 = no. 141: Ναὶ μαργαρῖται χειλέων σῶν οἱ λόγοι, / οὐκ αὐχένας κοσμοῦντες, οὐ στέρνων πλάτη, / μορφὰς δὲ μᾶλλον, Ἰωάννη, τὰς ἔσω· / ψυχῶν γάρ εἰσι κόσμος, οὐχὶ σωμάτων. For another epigram that calls his words "pearls," see Krause, "Göttliches Wort," 162 and n. 96.

Chrysostom's words are the pearls of the Sermon on the Mount (Matthew 7:6), something precious not to be "cast before swine," perhaps because they are a divine revelation. Indeed, this reading is supported by Chrysostom himself, who, in reconciling this exclusivist pronouncement with Christ's injunction to proclaim his teachings "from the rooftops" (Matthew 10:27), explains that the swine are "those who continually live an undisciplined life, who are all, said [Christ], unworthy of such instruction." They are unworthy because their "corruption" (διαφθορὰν) prevents them from accepting "such perfect doctrines" (τὰ τελειότερα δόγματα), and learning only makes them more audacious (θρασύτεροι).[37] At the same time, when the poem calls the words of the Golden-Mouthed orator pearls, their beauty is also clearly intended; they adorn the soul with rhetoric just as pearls adorn the body. Style and substance alike are pearls, indeed the same pearls, Chrysostom's literary production, his *logoi.*

Liturgists and Preachers

The *logoi* of these fathers of the church were not only read with pleasure by Byzantine elites. They were also read aloud regularly as part of the Divine Liturgy carried out in churches great and small, in the capital and in the provinces, with primarily lay congregations, and in monasteries, throughout the empire and beyond its borders. Many of these texts were genuine works of Chrysostom, Basil, and the two Gregorys. Even those that modern scholars judge to be later ascriptions to them contributed to their reputations in eleventh-century Byzantium.

Most prominently, the texts of two major liturgies of the Byzantine Church were attributed to Basil and Chrysostom. The *Liturgy of Saint John Chrysostom* was said (and is still said) on most days of the year; on some occasions the *Liturgy of Saint Basil* or another text was pronounced instead.[38] The earliest surviving ascription of the *Liturgy of Chrysostom* to Chrysostom seems to be from the eleventh century.[39] Before ca. 1000, the *Liturgy of Basil* had been more frequently used.[40] In the eleventh-century fresco program of the Church of Holy Wisdom in Ohrid, Basil is depicted performing the liturgy, carrying a scroll bearing a line from the

37. Chrysostom, *Homilies on Matthew,* 13.3, PG 57:310–11.

38. Philias, "Eucharistie," 99.

39. The ascription appears in Vat. gr. 1970 (eleventh century): Philias, "Eucharistie," 100, 105. Philias argues that the failure of pre-eleventh-century sources to mention Chrysostom's authorship of the liturgical text, especially in contexts where other liturgies like those of Saint Basil, the Apostles, and Saint James are mentioned as being widespread, strongly suggests that the ascription was new in the eleventh century. As Philias notes (ibid., 102), however, an apparently genuine text by John the Faster (patriarch of Constantinople, 582–595 CE) says that Chrysostom was responsible for an abridged version of Basil's liturgy.

40. Schellewald, "Chrysostomos," 183–84.

Liturgy of Basil.[41] Elsewhere in the same church, Chrysostom too is depicted as a liturgical celebrant.[42]

In addition to these liturgical texts, orations and homilies of authoritative authors were selected to be read on specific days of the liturgical year. Collections of such "liturgical homilies" of Basil, Gregory of Nazianzos, and Chrysostom had been assembled by the tenth century. Manuscripts of these collections were widespread in the tenth and eleventh centuries, indicating that their use in the liturgy was probably quite common in Byzantium.[43]

Monasteries and churches also had homiliaries, collections of homilies to be read during the liturgy arranged not by author but according to the day of the liturgical year when each was to be read. Such homiliaries gave great prominence especially to selections from Chrysostom's homilies.[44] Basil of Caesarea and Gregory of Nyssa occasionally appear, as well as various others, including Andrew of Crete and John of Damascus.[45]

This may have been part of the purpose Ibn al-Faḍl or his patrons had in mind in translating exegetical homilies, especially those of Chrysostom, who figures so prominently in homiliaries. But if so, it was only part of their aim, and only a marginal one. After all, the texts we know Ibn al-Faḍl translated are not homiliaries (with readings selected and arranged for the liturgical year) but rather complete sets of homilies on entire biblical books (or, in the case of the hexaemeral texts, a well-known part customarily chosen as a focus text for exegesis).

To illustrate this, we may consider two Greek manuscript homiliaries described by Albert Ehrhard: one from the mid-eleventh century (Athos, Skētē Kausokalybion, Kyriakou 3); the other, representing a different strand of the tradition, from the ninth century (Thessaloniki, Vlatadōn Monastery, 6).[46] A large proportion of the homilies in both homiliaries are ascribed to authors whose works Ibn al-Faḍl translated, mainly Chrysostom: twenty-four out of thirty-six (two-thirds), of which nineteen (53 percent) are ascribed to Chrysostom, in the eleventh-century Athos manuscript; and twenty-nine out of sixty (48 percent), of which twenty-

41. Schellewald, 182, 184, figs. 37, 42 (on pp. 458, 463): κ(ύρι)ε ὁ θ(εὸ)ς ἡμῶν ὁ κτίσας ἡμᾶς.

42. Schellewald, 182–83.

43. Papaioannou, *Psellos*, 46 n. 71, with references.

44. *ODB*, s.v. "Sermon."

45. Basil: e.g., Paris gr. 757 (mid-eleventh century); Ehrhard, *Die Überlieferung*, 2:251, nos. 5, 6 (two homilies on fasting). Gregory of Nyssa: e.g., in a ninth-century manuscript homiliary, Thessaloniki, Vlatadōn Monastery, 6: Ehrhard, ibid., 2:246, no. 46 (homily on Easter). Andrew of Crete: Thessaloniki, Vlatadōn Monastery, 6; Ehrhard, ibid., 2:246, no. 55. Athos, Skētē Kausokalybion, Kyriakou 3 (mid-eleventh century); Ehrhard, ibid., 2:249, no. 8; 250, nos. 25, 28. John of Damascus: Athos, Skētē Kausokalybion, Kyriakou 3, described by Ehrhard, ibid., 2:249, no. 3; Paris gr. 757, described by Ehrhard, ibid., 2:251, no. 4.

46. Ehrhard, *Die Überlieferung*, 2:243–46, 249–51.

seven (45 percent) are ascribed to Chrysostom in the ninth-century Thessaloniki manuscript. Nevertheless, if we identify the texts contained in those homiliaries based on the beginnings of each text printed by Ehrhard, we find that none, or at least none of those easy to identify, derives from texts Ibn al-Faḍl is known to have translated. Instead, they are almost all free-standing homilies often transmitted in manuscripts arranged according to the liturgical year, like these two manuscripts in Thessaloniki and Mount Athos. (They are also often "spurious" homilies—that is, wrongly ascribed, and usually wrongly ascribed to Chrysostom—but that need not concern us here, since we are interested in how the tradition viewed these texts, not how their view compares to modern assessments.)[47] Of the texts in these two homiliaries, the only ones that even sound like they might be identical with texts translated by Ibn al-Faḍl are four homilies in the Thessaloniki manuscript on specific verses of Matthew, but upon closer inspection, these do not appear to derive from Chrysostom's ninety homilies on Matthew possibly translated by Ibn al-Faḍl (and certainly translated by Antonios of Saint Symeon).[48]

We may therefore conclude that while liturgy contributed to the reputations of Chrysostom and the others in Byzantium and Byzantine Antioch, Ibn al-Faḍl's translation activities were not primarily geared toward producing texts to be read to an Arabic-speaking congregation during the liturgy.[49]

47. To identify the works, I looked up each incipit given by Ehrhard in the index of the *CPG*. Incipits that did not match exactly I consider uncertain (marked with ?). Texts that I failed to identify are those whose incipits did not appear in the index at all. For the present purposes this preliminary survey of the texts should be sufficient, especially since Ehrhard indicates what the homilies are about, further strengthening the impression that they are not excerpted from works Ibn al-Faḍl is known to have translated. In the following two lists of identifications, for each homily I give the number as listed in Ehrhard, followed by *CPG* number (or — if I failed to identify the text), then the *ascribed* author *when not Chrysostom*, skipping entirely those homilies that are not ascribed to an author whose works Ibn al-Faḍl translated.

Athos, Skētē Kausokalybion, Kyriakou 3: (1) 4200?; (2) 4577; (3) 8112 John of Damascus; (4) 4595; (5) —; (7) 5057?; (8) 8192 Andrew of Crete; (9) —; (10) —; (16) —; (19) —; (20) 4186 Severian of Gabala; (21) —; (22) 4590; (24) —; (25) 8177 Andrew of Crete; (26) 4643; (27) 4602; (28) 8178 Andrew of Crete; (29) 4415; (30) —; (31) 4199? Severian of Gabala; (32) —; (36) —.

Thessaloniki, Vlatadōn Monastery, 6: (1) 4658; (3) 4591; (4) 4716c; (5) 4577; (7) 5529 ps.-Eusebius of Alexandria; (8) 4693 (cf. 4007); (10) — (no incipit: beginning missing in manuscript); (11) 4562; (12) 5057?; (14) —, on Matthew 11:28; (16) 4601; (22) —, on Matthew 20:18; (23) —, on Matthew 20:21; (27) 4588; (28) 4415; (29) —; (34) —; (35) 4654, on Matthew 26:39; (36) 4604; (42) 4408; (43) 5527; (44) 4673; (46) 3174 Gregory of Nyssa; (48) —; (49) 5055; (51) 4739; (52) 5528; (53) 4342; (55) 8192.

48. The four homilies are no. 14 on Matthew 11:28, but homily 38 (or 39) of ninety (*CPG* 4424) is on Matthew 11:25 while the next homily is on Matthew 12:1; no. 22 on Matthew 20:18 and no. 23 on Matthew 20:21, but homily 65 (or 66) is on Matthew 20:17 and the following homily is on Matthew 20:29; no. 35 on Matthew 26:39, which can be positively identified as a distinct text, *CPG* 4654.

49. This conclusion is contrary to Nasrallah's view that the primary motive for Ibn al-Faḍl's translation activity was the need "to offer to the faithful, who had less knowledge of Greek, the tool necessary to better participate in the liturgical offices"; Nasrallah, *Histoire*, 3.1:194.

Holy Bishops

Finally we turn to the most visible aspect of Chrysostom and the Cappadocian Fathers in middle Byzantine culture: their holiness.[50] These late antique authors were also venerated as major saints, often in public ceremonies by public officials of the highest rank, including the Byzantine emperor and the patriarch of Constantinople.

Icons and frescoes depicting these holy authors were ubiquitous in churches. One icon of Chrysostom inspired this tenth-century two-line epigram:

> Before when you were alive, only spirit (*pnoē*) was present.
> Now that you are painted, only your breath (*pnoē*) is missing.[51]

This plays on the commonplace description of statues and images as being so lifelike that they could almost be breathing, in order to depict Chrysostom as so holy, so spiritual, as almost to be incorporeal.

In the first half of the eleventh century, mosaics in the Monastery of Hosios Loukas (in Phokis, Greece), apparently funded by the imperial purse, present a unified middle Byzantine decorative program that gives great prominence to Basil and Chrysostom (niches in the naos) and Gregory the Theologian (in the sanctuary under the dome depicting Pentecost), while also including Gregory of Nyssa in a less prominent position along with another saint known for his interest in Plato, Dionysios the Areopagite, and two other saints, Hierotheos and Philotheos. All are dressed as bishops.[52]

Hagiographical encomia (high-style laudatory discourses in honor of saints, like those for Saints Nicholas and Demetrios translated by Ibn al-Faḍl) were written for Chrysostom by John of Damascus (d. ca. 750), Kosmas Vestitor (eighth/ninth century), Emperor Leo VI the Wise (r. 886–912), and Niketas-David the

50. For bishop-saints, see Rapp, *Holy Bishops*.

51. John Geometres (tenth century), ed. Cougny, *Epigrammatum*, 3:337 = Appendix, Epigrammata demonstrativa, no. 284: Σοὶ ζῶντι τὸ πρὶν ἡ πνοὴ παρῆν μόνη, / γραφέντι δ' αὖ νῦν ἡ πνοὴ λείπει μόνη. Note the rhyme on the fifth, pre-caesura syllable (*prin*/*nyn*).

52. Chronology: Oikonomides, "First Century." Imperial patronage: see also ch. 2, p. 62, n. 129. Floor plan of the *katholikon* (with errors): Diez and Demus, *Byzantine Mosaics*, after 117. On that plan, the mosaics are located at nos. 65 (Basil), 62 (John Chrysostom, not the Forerunner), 4 (Gregory the Theologian), 15 (Gregory of Nyssa). Basil and Chrysostom are in niches at the east ends of the north and south walls, respectively, of the nave, under the eastern squinches. Perhaps the choice to place Gregory the Theologian under the depiction of the twelve apostles receiving the Holy Spirit with flames above their heads is related to the traditional description of Gregory as "breathing fire" from being so infused with the Spirit, an image that Nicholas Mesarites invokes in his description of Gregory's tomb, wrought of a fiery red stone, in the Church of the Holy Apostles in Constantinople: Downey, "Nikolaos Mesarites," 890 (trans.), 915 (text) = §38.4.

Paphlagonian (fl. tenth century, first half).[53] Gregory of Nazianzos received similarly high-profile attention, including encomia by Niketas-David (*BHG* 725) and John Geometres (*BHG* 726) in the tenth century. Basil was celebrated in high rhetorical style especially in late antiquity in orations by Gregory of Nazianzos (*BHG* 245) and Gregory of Nyssa (*BHG* 244), and in twelve funerary epigrams by Gregory of Nazianzos (*BHG* 245b), which were commented on in the tenth century by Niketas-David (*BHG* 245c).[54] Other late antique works recount Basil's life and miracles. An encomium for Basil is attributed to Ephrem the Syrian (fourth century).[55] Andrew of Crete (seventh/eighth century) wrote an oration on the Circumcision of Christ and on Saint Basil (since both feasts were celebrated on the same day, 1 January).[56]

Basil's younger brother Gregory of Nyssa had a somewhat more modest saintly profile. Still, Gregory of Nazianzos dedicated an oration to Gregory of Nyssa (*BHG* 716).[57] A *Life of Gregory of Nyssa* dating anywhere from the eighth to the tenth century emphasizes his fight against heresy. It also contains a vivid passage in which the anonymous author describes how, late one night, he read a work of Gregory that seemed to support the (heretical) doctrine of universal "restoration" (*apokatastasis*) and so went to sleep deeply troubled but then in a dream saw a vision of Gregory himself, who explained that the apparently heretical bits were introduced by wicked interpolators.[58] In the eleventh century, John Mauropous's *Discourse on the Three Holy Fathers and Teachers* (*BHG* 747) does not include the younger Gregory.[59]

The respect and veneration with which Chrysostom and Basil especially were read is exemplified by the early medieval *Life of Gregory of Agrigento* by one Leontios, abbot of the Monastery of San Saba in Rome.[60] In this eighth-/ninth-century

53. John of Damascus (*BHG* 879), ed. Kotter, 5:359–70. Kosmas: Dyobouniotes, "Κοσμᾶ Βεστίτωρος ἀνέκδοτον ἐγκώμιον." Leo VI: *Homiliae*, homily 38, ed. Antonopoulou. Niketas: Dyobouniotes, "Νικήτα."

54. See *BHGNovAuct.*

55. *BHG* 246 = *CPG* 3951. "Est dubiae authenticitatis": Geerard, in *CPG*, 2:400.

56. *BHG* 262; PG 97:913–32, on the circumcision (913A–24A) and Basil (924B–32A), with the latter portion (e.g., 930) also weaving in themes from the first part on circumcision.

57. It was once thought that Chrysostom wrote an encomium for Gregory of Nyssa (*BHG* 717c), but this turned out to be a compilation of excerpts from Gregory of Nyssa's encomium for Basil, as shown by Lackner, "Ein angebliches Enkomion"; cited in *BHGNovAuct.*

58. *BHG* 717. Edited and studied by Lackner, "Ein hagiographisches Zeugnis"; cited in *BHGNovAuct.* Date: Lackner, ibid., 75; the dream episode, §§3–4, pp. 55–59; summary, pp. 45–46. One of the manuscripts containing the text dates to the tenth century (pp. 46–47). *Apokatastasis*: ch. 2, p. 54, n. 95.

59. Mauropous, in Vat. gr. 676, ed. Lagarde, 106–19 = no. 178. Mauropous wrote a second encomium on the same subject, *BHG* 747b.

60. Leontios, *Das Leben des Heiligen Gregorios*, ed. Berger; trans. Martyn, with different section numbering. For the author and date (in part based on dating the Donation of Constantine), see Berger, 23, 41–43, 47–48.

text, the protagonist Gregory reads a *Life of Saint Basil* and yearns to visit the sites where Basil "received the grace of the Holy Spirit" during his lifetime.[61] Later, in Antioch, he is thrilled to stay in the room "where our holy father Basil the Great wrote some of his commentary on the *Hexaemeron*."[62] Then, in Constantinople, he reads Chrysostom's books at the Monastery of Saints Sergios and Bacchos.[63] These books are framed as part of the saint's advancing education, erudition, and sophistication. During one phase of his education in a monastery in the desert near Jerusalem, he is taught "rhetoric," "grammar," "philosophy," and "astronomy," and so becomes "a new man, a second Chrysostom."[64] The result is that Gregory, who becomes bishop of Agrigento, is not only respected as a self-controlled ascetic of unimpeachable integrity (despite what wicked enemies might say) and a wonder-worker, but also as an inspired intellectual. The *Life* narrates that Gregory of Agrigento wields the "Scripture . . . and all ecclesiastical and rhetorical knowledge (*epistēmē*)" as he elucidates and refutes numerous heresies.[65] (As we shall see, this is just the sort of learned ecclesiastical scholar that Ibn al-Faḍl seems to be trying to educate with his translations and annotations.) Thus Chrysostom and Basil are at once exemplars of rhetorical lucidity and ecclesiastical leadership. Their writings are also imbued with an almost miraculous power, as if the saints' words, like relics, could serve as vehicles for the saints' presence.

Actual relics of Chrysostom and Gregory of Nazianzos—the remains of their bodies—rested in the Church of the Holy Apostles in Constantinople in the eleventh century. This was a significant fact. Hagiographical texts often discuss it. For example, the translation of Chrysostom's relics prominently concludes John of Damascus's *Encomium to John Chrysostom:* Chrysostom cared so much for his "bride" (his episcopal see of Constantinople, from which he had been exiled) and his "children" (its population) that even in death he returned, his body going to the "visible" imperial abode, his spirit to the "invisible" kingdom of heaven.[66] There seems to have been particular interest in the translation of Chrysostom's relics in the middle Byzantine period. Kosmas Vestitor (ca. eighth century), Emperor Leo VI (r. 886–912), and his son Emperor Constantine VII Porphyrogennetos (r. 945–959) wrote or commissioned accounts of how Emperor Theodosios II

61. $3_{26–32}$, ed. Berger, 148 (see also commentary, 344–45); trans. Martyn, 125 (§6).

62. $28_{1–6}$, ed. Berger, 179 (see also commentary, 359); trans. Martyn, 156–57 (§30).

63. $28_{8–10}$, ed. Berger, 179; trans. Martyn, 157 (§30). For the monastery of Sergios and Bacchos as a "well-known place for monks from Italy to stay" in Constantinople "in the tenth/eleventh century," see Berger, 360.

64. $27_{15–18}$, ed. Berger, 178 (see also commentary, 358); trans. Martyn, 156 (§29).

65. $35_{7–8}$, ed. Berger, 187; trans. Martyn, 165 (§36).

66. §19, ed. Kotter, 5:370.

(r. 408–450) moved Chrysostom's relics to the Church of the Holy Apostles in Constantinople.[67]

Constantine VII also celebrated the translation of Gregory of Nazianzos's relics, which he himself undertook early in his reign as sole emperor. He did so by delivering an oration (perhaps on 19 January 946) composed for the occasion, perhaps by Constantine himself or else by a member of his literary circle.[68] A letter written in the voice of the emperor by Theodore Daphnopates, one such member of the emperor's literary circle, was directed to Saint Gregory before his relics had been translated and beseeched the saint to "return" to Constantinople.[69]

This is evidence not only of the generally high profile of Chrysostom and Gregory of Nazianzos, but also of a Byzantine emperor's concerted efforts to promote their cults and associate himself with them in the tenth century. As Bernard Flusin has argued, Constantine VII modeled his translation of Gregory's relics on the translation of Chrysostom's relics centuries earlier. Gregory's tomb was placed facing Chrysostom's in the sanctuary of the Church of the Holy Apostles, and the liturgical date of Gregory's translation to the Church of the Holy Apostles (19 January) was chosen to line up with the feast day of the apostle Timothy (22 January, at the Holy Apostles), Gregory's own feast day (25 January), and the commemoration of the translation of Chrysostom's relics to the Holy Apostles (27 January).[70] Joint cultivation of these holy hierarchs became part of the legacy that future emperors of the Macedonian Dynasty (867–1056), still ruling when Ibn al-Faḍl was active, would inherit. By the mid-eleventh century, the feast of the Three Hierarchs (Chrysostom, Basil, and Gregory of Nazianzos) had been added to the cycle (30 January).[71]

The tombs of Chrysostom and Gregory in the Church of the Holy Apostles were deliberately woven into the imperial ceremonial fabric. Constantine VII's *Book of Ceremonies* describes the imperial procession that took place each year on Easter

67. Kosmas (*CPG* 8145): Dyobouniotes, "Κοσμᾶ Βεστίτωρος ἀνέκδοτα ἐγκώμια." Leo VI (*BHG* 877h): *Homiliae,* homily 41, ed. Antonopoulou. Constantine VII (*BHG* 878d): Dyobouniotes, "Λόγος ἀνέκδοτος." For the interrelation of the texts ascribed to Leo VI and Constantine VII, and others, see Flusin, "Le panégyrique," 26–29. *BHG* 878d is not literally the work of Constantine VII's pen but appears to be a revision (perhaps one he commissioned) of Leo VI's account of the translation of Chrysostom's relics (*BHG* 877h): Ševčenko, "Re-reading Constantine Porphyrogenitus," 187 n. 49; Flusin, ibid., 25 and n. 92.

68. *BHG* 728; Flusin, "Le panégyrique," 6–7, 12. Flusin argues that *BHG* 728, transmitted without the name of an author but written in the voice of an emperor who translated Gregory of Nazianzos's relics to Constantinople, may well have been written by Constantine VII himself, or else commissioned by him.

69. *BHG* 727: Sakkelion, "Κωνσταντίνου Ζ' Πορφυρογεννήτου ἐπιστολή"; Daphnopates, *Correspondance,* no. 11, ed. Darrouzès and Westerink. For the authorship of the letter, see their introduction, 18; cited by Flusin, "Le panégyrique," 7 n. 8.

70. Flusin, 11, 21–31.

71. Krause, "Göttliches Wort," 154 and n. 63.

Monday.[72] It began in the palace, where the court would assemble, greet the emperor, and process. The emperor and patriarch met and entered the Great Church of Hagia Sophia together. Eventually, the emperor and his retinue set out again. By way of the Milion and Constantinople's central boulevard (Mesē), the emperor reached the church of Saint Constantine, where the patriarch met him to continue the prayers and ceremonies. Again, the emperor set out, continuing along the Mesē, through the quarters of the Bakers and the Bull, to the Church of the Mother of God Diakonissa, then on to Saint Polyeuktos, then finally to the Church of the Holy Apostles. When the patriarch arrived with the rest of the procession, the bishops bowed to the emperor "without falling to the ground," and the emperor and patriarch embraced. The patriarch recited the opening prayer of the liturgy. The emperor venerated the Gospel, the Holy Cross, and the altar. Here, finally, the emperor and patriarch prayed at the tombs of Saints John Chrysostom and Gregory the Theologian, on either side of the altar.[73] After appropriately venerating these two great hierarchs, they would pray at the tombs of Emperor Constantine I and the pro-icon patriarchs Nikephoros (r. 806–815, d. 828) and Methodios (r. 843–847). The liturgy, and the day's processing, would then continue.[74]

The prominence of the cults of Chrysostom and Gregory of Nazianzos is further exemplified by the famous and extremely popular Menologion of saints' lives rewritten by Symeon the Metaphrast (d. after 982).[75] This collection, arranged in calendrical order of the saints' feast days, contains a *Life of Gregory the Theologian* (*BHG* 723) and a *Life of John Chrysostom* (*BHG* 875), as well as an account of the translation of Chrysostom's relics to Constantinople (*BHG* 877).[76] Lives of Basil and Gregory of Nyssa do not appear, although Gregory of Nyssa does appear as an *author* of hagiography: the title of the *Life of Gregory the Wonder-Worker* in the Menologion says that it was written by Gregory of Nyssa (*BHG* 715), and the title of an encomium for Stephen the Protomartyr, ascribing authorship to Gregory as well, calls him a saint, "our father among the saints Gregory of Nyssa" (*BHG* 1654).[77] Of all these, only the *Life of Chrysostom* and the account of the translation of Chrysostom's relics are consistently claimed as the work of Symeon the Metaphrast himself.[78]

72. Chapter 10, ed. Vogt, 1:65–77; trans. Moffatt and Tall, 1:71–86.

73. Ed. Vogt, 1:69$_{23}$.

74. On Basil's feast day, 1 January, an imperial procession ended with the Gospel readings in a palace chapel dedicated to Saint Basil: *Book of Ceremonies*, ch. 33 (24), ed. Vogt, 1:127; trans. Moffatt and Tall, 1:136–37.

75. On Symeon the Metaphrast, see Papaioannou, *Psellos*, 17, 46–48.

76. On the relation of *BHG* 877 to earlier discourses on the translation of Chrysostom's relics, see Flusin, "Le panégyrique," 26–29.

77. *BHG*, 2nd ed., p. 286.

78. See the index to the Menologion of Symeon the Metaphrast compiled by Hippolyte Delehaye in *BHG*, 2nd ed., pp. 267–92; cited by Paul Halsall, *Medieval Sourcebook: Symeon Metaphrastes (10th*

Part of the reason that Chrysostom and Gregory of Nazianzos received particularly high-profile veneration in eleventh-century Constantinople may have been that they had come to be model patriarchs of Constantinople—even if both were deposed from the episcopal see in their own lifetimes. In his funeral oration for Patriarch Michael Keroularios (d. 1059), Psellos places the deceased in the company of "the trumpet of the Theologian" and "the grace of Chrysostom," as well as bishops of other sees who willingly stepped down.[79] This was clearly meant to resonate with the fact that Emperor Isaac I Komnenos (r. 1057–1059) had had Patriarch Keroularios arrested and brought to a site on the Hellespont to face trial so that he could be deposed. (Psellos had been prepared to deliver a prosecutorial accusation at the trial against him.) But Keroularios died before he could be put on trial. Given these events, it was appropriate to cast him in the role of persecuted patriarch.[80] Chrysostom and Gregory of Nazianzos had come to be emblematic of that role.

3 ORTHODOXY, EDUCATION, AND ORATIONS FOR SAINTS

I have dwelt upon the late antique church fathers because of their extraordinary popularity in middle Byzantine culture. I will now offer brief indications of how the rest of the curriculum Ibn al-Faḍl translated was being read in Byzantium. These remaining texts represented several facets of Byzantine (mainly elite) culture. First, they offered doctrinal statements certified by ecclesiastical authorities as True Statements—orthodoxy—that offered boundaries for what could acceptably be said and thought. At the same time, they were a firm foundation upon which one could build: within the broad boundaries they delineated, later authors could give themselves over to intellectual exploration. Second, many of the texts served educational purposes and were used by teachers or the self-taught as textbooks and guides to self-improvement. Third, other texts, especially the two hagiographical encomia, were used in high ecclesiastical and imperial contexts to cultivate saints who kept cities and the empire safe from its enemies, from armies and heretics alike.

Orthodoxy

Sophronios's seventh-century *Synodical Letter* was, in the eleventh century, a historical document: an official letter from the newly elected patriarch of Jerusalem

Century): Lives of the Saints: Index, https://sourcebooks.fordham.edu/source/metaphrast1.asp, accessed 8 September 2017. The relic translation was edited by Halkin, *Douze récits,* no. IX.

79. §60, lines 90–95, in *Orationes funebres I,* ed. Polemis, 74; trans. Polemis in Psellos, *Psellos and the Patriarchs,* 121.

80. For Keroularios's life and death, see Tinnefeld, "Michael I. Kerullarios."

to his colleagues in Rome, Antioch, Alexandria, and Constantinople.[81] The letter was a work of unquestionable authority, for it had been officially approved by the Quinisext Council (in Constantinople, 692) and incorporated into the official record of its proceedings.

At the same time, Byzantines could read it critically, as a text appealing to a reader's aesthetic and ethical judgment. Photios read the *Synodical Letter,* along with the dossier of patristic excerpts that followed it.[82] Of the letter, he observes that it is "full of piety but frequently innovates in its words, like a foal proud of its leaps"; it offers a most precise exposition of orthodoxy and "displays uncommon knowledge of the holy doctrines."[83] Still, what interested Photios most, to judge from the remainder of his comments on the letter, was the list of heretics that it condemns. The last of these whom he notes is Jacob the Syrian, "from whom the community (σύστημα) of the Acephalous heretics [i.e., Jacobites] derive their name."[84] The Jacob in question is Jacob Baradaeus (ca. 500–578), bishop of Edessa, a prominent Miaphysite active in Syria during the reign of Emperor Justinian.[85] This appears on the face of it to be a reference to how the Miaphysites (frequently called the Akephaloi, or the "Headless," by Byzantine Chalcedonians) referred to themselves—that is, as Jacobites. Indeed, we find Michael of Tanis, a Coptic Miaphysite Christian, referring to them as "the Jacobite Orthodox" (*al-yaʿāqiba al-urthudhuksīyīn*).[86] Finally, Photios notes that Sophronios asks Pope Honorius of Rome to supplement and correct the letter if anything is amiss.[87] In sum, Photios was interested in the letter, despite its style, as a succinct starting point for discussing not only doctrine but also questions of ecclesiastical authority (both the question of which bishops and other churchmen should be condemned as heretics and the question of how much deference should be shown to the bishop of Rome) and the de facto divisions within the church (for he sees Jacob Baradaeus not only as a heretic, but as the eponym of a continuing ecclesiastical community).

If we look to the manuscript tradition of Sophronios's *Synodical Letter,* we see that by the eleventh century the letter had come to be read and excerpted primarily

81. Only versions of the letter directed to Rome and Constantinople survive.

82. Reviewed in his *Bibliotheca,* codex 231, ed. Henry, 5:64–65.

83. Ed. Henry, 5:64.

84. Ed. Henry, 5:65.

85. Henry's note on this passage identifies "Jacob the Syrian" as Jacob of Sarugh, but Jacob Baradaeus is more plausible. On the other hand, some traditions link the name "Jacobites" to Jacob of Sarugh: Seleznyov, "Jacobs."

86. Michael of Tanis, *apud* Severus, *History,* ed. ʿAbd al-Masīḥ and Burmester, 2:142. In the thirteenth century, the Coptic Miaphysite author Ibn al-Rāhib (*K. al-Burhān,* Vat. ar. 104 [autograph], fol. 1^{v}) similarly refers to "the Coptic Jacobite Egyptians" (*al-qibṭ al-yaʿāqiba al-miṣrīyīn*); the context, specifying the community that owns a specific church in Fusṭāṭ, helps explain the absence of "orthodoxy" from his phrase.

87. Lines 28–34.

for its dogmatic content, rather than as a literary whole—an impulse consistent with Photios's primary interest in the text's discussion of heresies. Some manuscripts transmit the letter in versions directed to Pope Honorius and Patriarch Sergios of Constantinople, respectively.[88] (Evidently Photios was reading the version addressed to Pope Honorius.) Other manuscripts (not counted in the tally in table 2) offer collections of excerpts from this letter organized according to topic.[89] Ibn al-Faḍl's adapted translation, with its many thematic headings, showed a similar impulse.[90] In these collections—including Ibn al-Faḍl's adapted Arabic translation—the original context has faded into the background; instead, the original document has been mined, adapted, and supplied with headings, rendering it a useful work of reference on orthodox doctrine.

By contrast, John of Damascus's *Statement on Correct Thought* was already composed to be a relatively succinct confession of orthodoxy, enumerating the ecumenical councils (like Sophronios's *Synodical Letter*) and thus rejecting the "heretical" doctrines each council rejected. As we saw in the previous chapter, John of Damascus was a highly respected authority whose *Dialectica* and *Exposition of Faith* were deeply influential in Byzantium. To read a creed by the Damascene, like the one Ibn al-Faḍl translated, and to adapt it to compose one's own (shorter) creed, as Ibn al-Faḍl did, was to stand on a well-known bedrock of Byzantine orthodoxy and to extend to the unlearned the prospect of this security and the salvation that it promised.

Maximos the Confessor's *Disputation with Pyrrhos* was a different sort of doctrinal statement, framed as a dialogue, a genre used in the Byzantine period (as in earlier Greek literature) to teach philosophy and doctrine in an entertaining and digestible form.[91] Remembered by Chalcedonian Dyotheletes as a confessor for standing up for the anti-Monothelete, anti-Monenergist position against the emperor, Maximos offered in his dialogue with Pyrrhos an interactive model for refuting positions deemed heretical by the Byzantine Church. In contrast to straightforward confessions and creeds, this dialogue form encouraged the reader to think of heresy not as something to be unthinkingly rejected but rather critically examined and refuted on rational grounds, even if Pyrrhos's side of the argument is not exactly portrayed in an evenhanded way (the same could be said of Plato's portrayal of Socrates's interlocutors—for example, Thrasymachus in the *Republic*).

Photios read the *Disputation with Pyrrhos*, describing it as a dialogue in which Pyrrhos at first represents the "heretical" position but then is forced "by the

88. See ch. 2, p. 50.

89. Riedinger, "Die Nachkommen."

90. Perhaps further research will reveal that his translation was based on an extant Greek adaptation.

91. *ODB*, s.v. "Dialogue."

orthodox arguments and doctrines" to admit that he was wrong. Photios remarks that the dialogue is composed in a very humble style, perhaps to capture the improvisatory quality of their conversation, but that even so, the intellectual "contest" it narrates is "useful to the pious."[92] Photios's description has an agonistic overtone throughout, using language reminiscent of a duel (συνεχόμενος, συνελαυνόμενος) to describe the conversation. Photios concludes that the dialogue's style is simple but that it is useful reading "for the pious" all the same.[93]

Asceticism and the Self

The educational aspect is even more pronounced in didactic collections of "chapters" and questions and answers translated (or, in the case of some of them, possibly translated) by Ibn al-Faḍl.[94] The precise educational context for each of these texts varied, from specifically monastic, as with Maximos's *Chapters on Love* and *Chapters on Knowledge* and the works of Isaac the Syrian, to less closely associated with a monastic milieu (though also not excluding monks).

Photios read Maximos's *Chapters on Love* and *Chapters on Knowledge*. Photios says that in the *Chapters on Knowledge*, "knowledge of God (*theologia*) shines forth, and the orderly arrangement of the dispositions (*ēthē*) is outstanding."[95] Of the *Chapters on Love* he observes that it contains discussions "by which knowledge of God (*theologia*) is strengthened and which produce the holy and pure way of life," such that "those who industriously follow along" with the text will benefit from it considerably. Its style tends to be "bright and polished," with no flaws other than a failure to prefer Attic forms.[96] Photios's copy of the *Chapters on Love* was bound together with another work by Maximos, an "ascetic" work, arranged as questions and answers. What Photios says about it might also be applied to other ascetic texts of this sort: it is "useful to all, but especially to those whose government (*politeia*) is asceticism, for it teaches and cultivates dispositions by which one might become a citizen of heaven (*ouranopolitēs*)," especially helping one acquire "the knowledge and practice of love (*agapē*)."[97] Such ascetic texts, ethical and in a sense even political in their significance, were thus "useful to all"—potentially to be read by anyone—but especially directed at those who had chosen to devote themselves to the monastic way of life.

The *Loci communes* (sometimes ascribed to Maximos in manuscripts) was useful for a different part of a well-rounded Byzantine education. In drawing on a

92. Photios, *Bibliotheca*, codex 195, ed. Henry, 3:88–89; cited by Treadgold, *Nature*, index.
93. Ed. Henry, 3:89.
94. *ODB*, s.vv. "Chapters," "Erotapokriseis," "Literature, Didactic."
95. Codex 194_{18-28}, ed. Henry, 3:84–85; cited by Treadgold, *Nature*, index.
96. Codex 193, ed. Henry, 3:84; cited by Treadgold, *Nature*, index.
97. Codex 193, ed. Henry, 3:83–84; cited by Treadgold, *Nature*, index.

sample of Christian and non-Christian texts typical of Byzantine literary culture, it could serve as a distilled and digested version of "the classics" (by which I mean those works that Byzantines treated as classics). So for example in §5, "on justice" (περὶ δικαιοσύνης), one could quickly brush up on what Christ, Isaiah, Basil, Gregory the Theologian, Chrysostom, Gregory of Nyssa, Evagrius, Plato, the Seven Sages, Socrates, Epictetus, Pythagoras, Menander, and others had to say about it. (Jesus declared blessed the poor who feed on justice; Isaiah recommended everyone learn it; Basil said it was very easy to be corrupted by money or swayed by friendship or enmity and thus fail to do the right thing; and so on.)[98]

The question-and-answer genre was commonly used for education in Byzantium. Pseudo-Kaisarios's *Questions and Answers* offered useful didactic material for such a purpose. In his review of the book, Photios highlights the combination of Christian and non-Christian material, saying of the author that "he seems to be a young man and at the height of his strength in begetting literary offspring and in his learning, of both external (*thyrathen*) wisdom and our own."[99]

Saints

Doctrine and education were important aspects of John of Thessaloniki's *Encomium to Saint Demetrios.* This is clear from how much of the text is devoted to the saint's refutation of the doctrines of "the Hellene," "the Jew," and various "heretics" and the careful articulation of Chalcedonian teachings on Christ and the Trinity. In this way it resembles Maximos's *Disputation with Pyrrhos,* teaching doctrine to the Byzantine reader in the form of a dialogue. At the same time, it is, especially at the beginning, an elegant rhetorical oration in praise of a saint who, by the eleventh century, had come to be seen as a defender of Thessaloniki and the empire as a whole. In John of Thessaloniki's *Encomium,* Demetrios appears as a teacher, and this is how Photios in the ninth century also describes him in his review of a *Life of Demetrios,* as "a herald and teacher of piety" martyred under Emperor Maximian. Nevertheless, in the middle Byzantine period Demetrios came to be depicted in Byzantine art, and lead seals, as a soldier-saint.[100] For this reason, eleventh-century Byzantines listening to or reading John's *Encomium* probably pictured Demetrios in their minds as a soldier. As for readers of Andrew of Crete's *Encomium to Saint Nicholas,* they undoubtedly pictured him as a bishop, for this is how he appears in middle Byzantine iconography and hagiography, as well as the *Encomium* itself.

Demetrios and Nicholas, a soldier and a bishop, could be praised by anyone, from the humblest peasant or laborer to the patriarch or emperor. But the high

98. *Loci communes,* ed. Ihm, 92–106; PG 91:749B–53D.

99. Codex 210, ed. Henry, 3:115; cited by Treadgold, *Nature,* index.

100. Photios, *Bibliotheca,* cod. 255, ed. Henry, 7:213; cited in *ODB,* s.v. "Demetrios of Thessalonike." Lead seals: Cotsonis, "Contribution," 462–63.

style of these encomia suggests that they were used by elite Byzantines: for rhetorical training, enjoyable reading, and public performance.

To underscore how much Saints Nicholas and Demetrios resonated with Byzantine sensibility in the eleventh century, it is worth taking a brief look at the lead seals surviving from this period. Byzantine lead seals (small pieces of lead used to seal letters and other documents, stamped on both sides with a design and inscription particular to their owner) survive in the greatest numbers from the eleventh century. This reflects a mix of factors, of which the most significant was probably the expansion of the Byzantine civil, military, and ecclesiastical administration—and thus the swelling ranks of literate officials, posted throughout the empire and corresponding with one another about official and personal business.[101] At the same time, a preference for seals depicting saints rose from the ninth to the tenth century, then jumped dramatically in the eleventh, when about four out of five seals bear "religious figural iconography."[102] This means that the data for eleventh-century Byzantine lead seals bearing images of saints are particularly abundant; John Cotsonis's analysis of 7,284 published seals shows that while a large range of saints appear occasionally, a small set of saints dominate in the extant sigillographic record.

By this measure, Nicholas was extraordinarily popular.[103] In discussing depictions of bishop-saints, Cotsonis remarks on "the enormous number of seals that portray . . . Nicholas." Indeed, "Nicholas is by far the most popular of all the saints," appearing on 664 seals. "He is surpassed only by the Virgin." Most of the seals for Nicholas are from the eleventh century, with 368 dated to the eleventh and 70 and 93 dated, respectively, to the tenth/eleventh and eleventh/twelfth century.[104] Seals depicting Nicholas (in all periods, though this mostly means the eleventh century) were most likely to belong to civil administrators (43 percent), followed by military officials (7.6 percent), ecclesiastical leaders (7.5 percent), "lower clergy" (5.4 percent), and monks (4.5 percent). The remaining third of the seals do not clearly identify an official title or rank.[105]

After Nicholas, military saints enjoyed the most popularity, and "after Michael [the archangel], the three most popular military saints found on seals" were George, Theodore, and Demetrios; Demetrios is found on 259 of the seals.[106] On seals, as in other artistic representations, Demetrios underwent a dramatic shift from the tenth to the eleventh century. In the earliest seals (seventh/eighth to

101. Cotsonis, "Contribution," 389.

102. Cotsonis, 391, chart 2.

103. I owe my initial awareness of Nicholas's popularity on eleventh-century seals of civil officials to a passing remark in Nesbitt and Seibt, "Anzas Family," 192.

104. Cotsonis, "Contribution," 396, 433–34. On p. 434, "646" is a misprint for "664"; chart 3 (p. 396) prints the correct figure. Percentages on p. 437 are based on the misprinted total.

105. Cotsonis, 437; I have recalculated the percentages based on a total of 664 seals.

106. Cotsonis, 447; see also 494.

ninth/tenth century) he appears in the clothing of a civilian. Among seals dated to the tenth or the tenth/eleventh century, just over half (8 of 14) still depict him this way, while the rest depict him in military attire. But among seals dated to the eleventh century, the vast majority, 98 percent (142 of 145), clothe him in military attire; the seals showing him in civilian garb have become a tiny minority (only 3, or 2 percent). Seals from later centuries always depict Demetrios as a soldier.[107] In the eleventh century, this new military Demetrios is most often "found on seals belonging to members of the civil, military and ecclesiastical bureaucracies."[108]

The extraordinary popularity of Nicholas and Demetrios among Byzantine officials could not have been lost on Ibn al-Faḍl. Given that he was a deacon in the Byzantine Church in Antioch, we can be particularly confident that the tastes of Byzantine ecclesiastics would have been known to him. We may plausibly speculate that documents bearing seals portraying Nicholas and Demetrios might have passed through his hands.

Both saints were also prominently venerated in Constantinople. The cult of Saint Nicholas had been prominent in Constantinople from at least the sixth century onward, and it remained so through the eleventh century and later.[109] Emperor Justinian I renovated a church at Blachernae, dedicating it to Priskos and Nicholas; by the mid-seventh century, it was known as the church of Saint Nicholas alone.[110] It seems that Nicholas's feast was also celebrated in Hagia Sophia.[111] In the time of Anna Komnene, there was, right by Hagia Sophia, a church to Saint Nicholas, called the "refuge" (προσφύγιον) because it served as a sanctuary for those fleeing the law. It had by then the appearance of considerable age, since according to the *Patria* it was built in the time of Justinian.[112] In the ninth century, the emperor Basil I dedicated a chapel lavishly built within his palace to Christ, the Virgin, Elijah, Saint Nicholas, and the archangels Michael and Gabriel, as the eleventh-century historian John Skylitzes reports.[113] Another church for Saint Nicholas, in the monastery "of the leaded [?church]" (τοῦ Μολιβώτου) outside the Golden Gate, was a prominent site of imperial patronage in the eleventh century, and Constantine X Doukas (r. 1059–1067) was

107. Cotsonis, 462–63. Cotsonis argues (463–64) that this shift in representations of Demetrios began in Thessaloniki, and then spread to Constantinople and the rest of the empire; he suggests that the sack of Thessaloniki in 904 may have led Demetrios to "take on a military character."

108. Cotsonis, 465.

109. The fame of Saint Nicholas was as long-lasting in the East as in the West. A seventeenth-century Greek manuscript of pseudo-Kaisarios's *Erotapokriseis* (translated in part by Ibn al-Faḍl) contains a nine-line encomium of Saint Nicholas of Myra; Riedinger, *Pseudo-Kaisarios*, 16.

110. Janin, "Les églises byzantines," 404–6.

111. Janin, 407, who draws this information from synaxaria, without specifying a time frame for when the feast came to be celebrated there.

112. Janin, 408; *ODB*, s.v. "Patria of Constantinople."

113. Janin, 414.

buried there.[114] At least one non-Greek community in Constantinople embraced this Byzantine saint as well: from a miracle collection contained in eleventh-century manuscripts, a church "of the great archpriest Nicholas" at the monastery "of the Georgian(s)" (τῶν Ἰβήρων/τῶν Ἰβήρου) in Constantinople is known.[115]

The cult of Demetrios was also quite prominent in the Byzantine capital. In the tenth century, Constantine VII's *Book of Ceremonies* includes Demetrios's feast day as one of the occasions whose imperial ceremonies are described in detail. Encomia for the saint were composed by many middle Byzantine authors, often archbishops of Thessaloniki, including the archbishops John (our John of Thessaloniki), Plotinos, and Joseph, and Emperor Leo VI (three homilies).[116]

The materials John of Thessaloniki assembled and composed regarding Saint Demetrios are well attested in middle Byzantine manuscripts. Among the manuscripts described by Paul Lemerle containing part or all of John's collection of Demetrios's miracles, thirteen date to the tenth/eleventh, eleventh, or eleventh/twelfth century, some of provincial provenance.[117]

The Byzantine resonance of these two rhetorical pieces, then, would have been manifold. The appeal of these texts to elite Byzantines would only have increased their addressees' great popularity (including among Byzantine officials), highly visible veneration in the imperial capital, and respective profiles as bishop (Nicholas) and teacher-soldier (Demetrios). These were benevolent and mighty protectors in times of need, and the encomia of Andrew of Crete and John of Thessaloniki offered the sophisticated reader—from Thessaloniki to Antioch—fitting words and thoughts with which to honor them.

4 CONTEMPORARY GEORGIAN TRANSLATORS

Many of the texts that Ibn al-Faḍl translated had already been translated into a number of other languages, especially Latin, Syriac, Slavonic, Armenian, and Georgian.[118] As far as the historical context of Ibn al-Faḍl's translation program is concerned, late tenth- and eleventh-century Georgian translations are particularly telling.[119] In what follows I aim to show how closely Ibn al-Faḍl's Arabic translation program parallels the Georgian translation activity, and how their aims and methods

114. Janin, 412. Janin suggests that the name might have derived from siding on the church made of lead; Janin, *Géographie ecclésiastique*, 3:373.

115. Janin, "Les églises byzantines," 414–15.

116. Lemerle, *Les plus anciens recueils*, 1:10–11.

117. Lemerle, 1:13–30. Lemerle consulted a total of thirty-four manuscripts, including palimpsests. Of these, two were tenth/eleventh century: F, W. Eight were eleventh century: G, H, J, K, Q, X, Y, Λ. Three were eleventh/twelfth century: N, Θ, Ξ.

118. See the relevant entries in the *CPG*, including the Supplementum.

119. Noble and Treiger, *Orthodox Church*, 28.

were more or less the same.[120] To do so I consider the prolific and better-documented translation programs of three Georgian scholars: Euthymios the Athonite (d. 1028), George the Athonite (d. 1065), and Ep'rem Mc'ire (d. ca. end of eleventh century).

These roughly contemporary Georgian translators are a relevant comparison to Ibn al-Faḍl for a number of reasons. First, they were Chalcedonian Christians working within the Byzantine Empire, but often on its peripheries, much like Ibn al-Faḍl and his fellow Arabic-speaking Chalcedonian Christians of Antioch. Second, some of their Georgian translation and literary production took place in Antioch and its hinterland at precisely the same time, in one case with the patronage of the patriarchate, such that it is quite likely that Ibn al-Faḍl's circle of acquaintances overlapped with that of Georgian translators. Third, parts of Georgia had recently been annexed by Emperor Basil II around the year 1000,[121] much as Antioch had been conquered decades earlier. Elite Georgians in the Byzantine Empire, who were in communion with the Byzantine ecclesiastical hierarchy, were thus in a similarly privileged position vis-à-vis the Byzantine imperial center in comparison to "heterodox" Christian communities but at the same time sought to defend their own cultural heritage and political interests.

Euthymios the Athonite (Mt'ac'mindeli = Hagiorites, a.k.a. the Iberian; d. 1028) was the second abbot (1005–1019) of the Iviron Monastery ("of the Georgians") on Mount Athos, after his father John Varazvačc (a.k.a. the Iberian, abbot 980–1005).[122] Euthymios translated many works from Greek into Georgian. A *Life* of this pair, father and son, was written in Georgian around 1045 by George the Athonite (Mt'ac'mindeli; d. 1065), a translator in his own right. This *Life* includes a list of Euthymios's translations, preceded by an account of why Euthymios translated.[123] For this reason it is possible to draw up a more comprehensive list of his translations than for Ibn al-Faḍl.

George the Athonite (1009–1065), a Georgian born in Trialeti, was a student in Constantinople. In 1034, he became a monk on Mount Athos; about ten years later he was abbot of the Iviron Monastery. He traveled "back to Georgia, to the Black Mountain [just north of Antioch], and to Jerusalem." He had close ties with a hermit of the Black Mountain also named George, who encouraged his Greek-Georgian translations.[124] A list of his translations is also preserved, in the anonymous *Life of George*.[125]

120. I am grateful to Maria Mavroudi for suggesting a comparison with Georgian activities.

121. *ODB*, s.vv. "David of Tayk'/Tao," "Iberia," "Tayk'/Tao"; Tarchnišvili, *Geschichte der kirchlichen georgischen Literatur* (hereafter *GKGL*), 183.

122. *ODB*, s.v. "Iveron Monastery."

123. *ODB*, s.vv. "Euthymios the Iberian," "George Mt'ac'mindeli." *Life*, trans. Peeters, "Histoires," no. 1 (Latin); Martin-Hisard, "La Vie de Jean et Euthyme" (French).

124. Tarchnišvili, *GKGL*, 155.

125. Trans. Peeters, "Histoires," no. 2; Martin-Hisard, "La Vie de Georges l'Hagiorite."

Ep'rem (d. end of eleventh century) was the son of a wealthy Georgian who cooperated with the Byzantines after the annexation of Tayk' in 1027 and took up residence in Constantinople. Ep'rem went to Antioch, probably after 1057, and settled on the Black Mountain. There he was in close contact with educated Greeks. The patriarch of Antioch himself granted Ep'rem access to the excellent library of the Monastery of Saint Symeon the Younger, where he met Nikon of the Black Mountain and the Michael who wrote the Arabic *Life of John of Damascus*, a work that Ep'rem would later translate.[126] He also came to know a circle of Georgian scholars, including George the Athonite. He was abbot of the Kastana Monastery in 1091 and had died by 1103.[127]

The translations of Euthymios and George overlap considerably with those of Ibn al-Faḍl. Those of Ep'rem do not, but it is still valuable to consider him as well. For comparison, I will first present a concise summary of their translation activities, arranged in approximate chronological order by the author's lifetime. For this summary, I depend upon Michael Tarchnišvili's *History of Ecclesiastical Georgian Literature* (in German, based on the relevant portion of Kekelidze's Georgian-language handbook).[128]

Euthymios was a prolific translator. The Psalter, Apocalypse of John, and the four Gospels are not named in lists of Euthymios's translations, but evidence from tenth- and eleventh-century manuscripts suggests that he may have translated them.[129] He translated a number of apocryphal acts.[130] He produced Georgian versions of works by Basil of Caesarea,[131] Gregory of Nyssa,[132] Gregory of Nazianzos,[133]

126. Tarchnišvili, *GKGL*, 183. On this milieu, see Kontouma, "Jean III," 144.

127. Tarchnišvili, *GKGL*, 183–84.

128. Tarchnišvili, 131–54, 161–74, where detailed discussion with references (arranged by genre, rather than by author) may be found. Cross-references to Tarchnišvili's presentation take the form of a Roman and an Arabic numeral.

129. Psalter: I.3. Apocalypse: I.1. Gospels: I.2 (revision of previous translations). It is not clear to me what evidence there is in favor of his authorship of the Psalter translation, manuscript or otherwise; for the Psalter, Tarchnišvili refers (*GKGL*, 132 n. 1) to Džanašvili's book "Das georgische Schriftum" (*K'art'uli Mc'erloba*, Tbilisi, 1900), which is, however, inaccessible to me.

130. The Legend of Abgar (II.1), Acts of John the Evangelist (II.3), Acts of Peter (II.4), Acts of Andrew (II.5), and the *Pearls* (II.6—"a compilation of Apocrypha"; cf. VI.5).

131. *Homilies on the Psalms* (III.4, translated before 1014); *Apocalypse of Melchisedech* (III.7—possibly from a work by Basil); *Moralia*, translation organized in fifty-three chapters (V.18.a); "Homily on the sevenfold revenge of Cain" (V.18.b); twenty-one homilies (VI.6). Euthymios's translation of the *Homilies on the Psalms* includes all homilies in the Greek plus homilies on Psalms 37 and 115, which are considered spurious: Tarchnišvili, *GKGL*, 137 and n. 5.

132. *On the Our Father* (III.6.a); *The Life of the Holy Prophet Moses* (III.6.b = *CPG* 3159); "Considerations about the Soul and Resurrection with His Sister Macrina" (IV.4 = *CPG* 3149); "On the Beginning of Lent" (V.19.a); "On Virginity and the Divine Transformation" (V.19.b = *CPG* 3165); *On the Life of His Sister Macrina* (VI.2.a = *CPG* 3166?); *Encomium to Basil the Great* (VI.2.b = *CPG* 3185?); *On Fasting* (VI.2.c).

133. Twenty-five texts, trans. 983–991 CE (III.8; IV.1.a–c; V.1.a–b; VI.1.a–q); see Tarchnišvili, *GKGL*, 139.

Chrysostom,[134] Andrew of Caesarea (563–614),[135] Maximos the Confessor,[136] Pope Gregory the Great,[137] Abbot Zosimos (sixth century), Abbot Dorotheus (sixth century), John of the Ladder, Makarios the Egyptian,[138] John of Damascus,[139] Michael Synkellos,[140] Ephrem the Syrian,[141] Isaac "the Hermit,"[142] Andrew of Crete,[143] and Symeon of Mesopotamia.[144] He also produced Georgian translations of excerpts from Andrew of Crete, Theodore of Caesarea, Chrysostom, Isaiah the Priest, Neilos the Hermit, Mark the Hermit, Cassian the Roman, an anonymous work addressed to a monk of the Thebaid (in Egypt) concerning how one should occupy oneself in one's cell, and a *Book of Holy Men.*[145] In addition to these, Euthymios translated texts of hagiography, liturgy, and canon law.[146]

Of these works translated by Euthymios, quite a number are among Ibn al-Faḍl's translations as well, in particular the Psalter; Basil of Caesarea's *Homilies on the Psalms;* Chrysostom's homilies on Romans, Hebrews (Euthymios translated excerpts from Chrysostom's homilies on Hebrews, but Ibn al-Faḍl translated them in full), and, if Ibn al-Faḍl translated them, on John and Matthew; Maximos the Confessor's *Disputation with Pyrrhos;* and Andrew of Crete's *Encomium to Saint Nicholas.* Furthermore, several of the "capita" and "excerpts" from Maximos's works that Tarchnišvili mentions may also be related to the two sets of *kephalaia,*

134. Homilies on John (III.2, trans. 980 CE or before); homilies on Matthew (III.3, trans. near the end of the life of Euthymios's father, John); homilies on Galatians, 1 and 2 Thessalonians, and Romans, or perhaps excerpts therefrom (III.5—Ibn al-Faḍl translated the homilies on Romans); perhaps excerpts from homilies on 1 and 2 Corinthians, Ephesians, Philippians, Colossians, Hebrews, 1 and 2 Timothy, 1 and 2 John, Jude, and 1 Peter (III.5—Ibn al-Faḍl translated the homilies on Hebrews).

135. *Commentary on the Apocalypse of John* (III.1—translated 975–977 CE).

136. *Quaestiones ad Thalassium* (III.9.a—*CPG* 7688); an *erōtapokrisis* (III.9.b); a discussion of difficult words in Gregory of Nazianzos's homily on the Nativity (III.9.c = part of *CPG* 7705—namely, PG 91:1039–60); the *Disputation with Pyrrhos* (IV.2.a); "'15 Capita' (theologica)" (IV.2.b); "Considerations about the Passions to Father Thalassios" (V.2.a); 97 "Spiritual Teachings" (V.2.b—probably all but three of one of Maximos's various "centuries"); another *erōtapokrisis* (V.2.c); other excerpts (V.2.d); "Lecture to . . . Sergios the Magistros" (V.2.e); ps.-Maximos, *Glorification and Exaltation . . . of the Panagia . . .* (II.2).

137. *Dialogues,* translated from Greek (V.3).

138. Zosimos: V.4. Dorotheus: V.5.a–c. John of the Ladder: V.6 (previously translated in 983). Makarios: V.7.

139. "On Belief" (IV.3.a—excerpts from the *Fountain of Knowledge* and other works by the same author); "Of Christ's Two Natures" (IV.3.b); "On the Birth of the Virgin" (VI.3).

140. *Symbolum,* included (without attribution) in Euthymios's *Life of Maximos the Confessor* (IV.5).

141. Five works (V.8.a–e): "To the Monk and Abbot John" (a); "To the Monk Neophytos" (b); "On the Salvation of Ascetics" (c); "Friday Prayers" (d); "Admonition to Himself and Confession" (e).

142. Tarchnišvili describes the work as "ascetic lectures in 42 chapters" (V.9).

143. *Encomium to Saint Nicholas* (VI.4—translated by Ibn al-Faḍl).

144. "Homilies on Death" (V.20).

145. V.10–17, 21.

146. Hagiography: VII.1.a–v, VII.2.a–g. Liturgy: VIII.1–7. Canon law: IX.1–4.

or "chapters," that Ibn al-Faḍl may have translated. The text by John of Damascus given the title "On Belief" and apparently excerpted from the Damascene's works may (or may not) include the creed that Ibn al-Faḍl translated, the *Statement on Correct Thought.* If Isaac "the Hermit" is Isaac of Nineveh, then the "ascetic lectures in 42 chapters," as Tarchnišvili describes them, may be a selection from the *Ascetic Homilies* (Isaac I), of which Ibn al-Faḍl also translated a selection.[147] Overall, the overlap is striking. The common decision to translate Basil's *Homilies on the Psalms* and Chrysostom's works could have been coincidental, given the abundance of eleventh-century Greek manuscripts containing them. But Maximos's *Disputation with Pyrrhos* and Andrew of Crete's *Encomium to Saint Nicholas* are less well attested in contemporary manuscripts. In such cases, the overlap would seem to point to a closer connection between Euthymios's translation activities on Mount Athos and Ibn al-Faḍl's in Antioch.

With George the Athonite, such a connection becomes more plausible, given his close ties to Antioch and long stays there. George produced Georgian versions of the Psalter, the Gospels, and the Acts and Letters of the Apostles, as well as two apocryphal texts.[148] He produced translations of Ignatios of Antioch's letters (authentic and inauthentic);[149] Basil of Caearea's *Homilies on the Hexaemeron* (revised translation) and *Letter to the Noblewoman Simolikia;*[150] Gregory of Nyssa's *On Making Man* (revised translation),[151] *Homilies on the Song of Songs,* and *Encomium to Saint Theodore;*[152] Chrysostom's *Homilies on Genesis;*[153] Sophronios's *Homilies on the Annunciation;*[154] a homily by John of Damascus;[155] Theodore the

147. If this identification should be correct, there would be a discrepancy between the forty-two sections in Euthymios's version and the thirty-five in Ibn al-Faḍl's. This difference of seven could be related to the eight-homily discrepancy between the Eastern and Western recensions of the Syriac version of Isaac I; see Alfeyev, *Spiritual World,* 29.

148. Psalter, Gospel, Acts, Letters: I.1–3 (all revised translations). Apocrypha: the Legend of Abgar (II.1, different version from what Euthymios translated) and an account of Jesus's resurrection, etc., narrated by Joseph of Arimathaea (II.2).

149. IV.8.

150. III.1 and IV.9, respectively.

151. III.2. Tarchnišvili (*GKGL,* 164) notes that George "also edited a new redaction of the same work" under the title "That which the description of the Hexaemeron, which Saint Basil the Great had already written, was missing because he had left the genesis of humankind incomplete Gregory correctly and with divine beauty brought to completion." Might one or the other of these recensions include Gregory's *Apology on the Hexaemeron*? It is as a final chapter of *On Making Man* that the Arabic version of the *Apology* circulated.

152. *Homilies on the Song of Songs:* III.3 (ends at ch. 6, verse 8). *Encomium to Saint Theodore:* VI.3.

153. III.5.

154. VI.2.

155. IV.7.

Stoudite's fifty-seven Lenten homilies;[156] a Symbolon (or creed) by Photios;[157] several other creeds;[158] *Questions and Answers* ascribed to Athanasios and discussing church councils;[159] and *On Virginity* likewise ascribed to Athanasios.[160] He also translated an anonymous commentary on the Sermon on the Mount (Matthew 5–7),[161] as well as liturgical and hagiographical works.[162]

Several of these were also translated by Ibn al-Faḍl into Arabic (at roughly the same time): Basil's *Hexaemeron* (also a revised translation), Chrysostom's *Homilies on Genesis,* and possibly Gregory of Nyssa's *On Making Man* and *Homilies on the Song of Songs.* Chrysostom's homilies are extremely well attested in extant eleventh-century Greek manuscripts, but the other three are somewhat less so, especially Gregory's *Homilies on the Song of Songs.*

Given our fragmentary knowledge of Ibn al-Faḍl's translations (since we do not have lists of his translations, as we do for Euthymios and George), the overlap could be even more than what is apparent. For example, saints' lives are absent from our list of Ibn al-Faḍl's known translations (Andrew of Crete's *Encomium to Saint Nicholas* and John of Thessaloniki's *Encomium to Saint Demetrios* are about saints but are not saints' lives), but hagiographical literature is often transmitted without the name of its author or translator. Without lists for Euthymios and George, would we have known that they translated so much hagiography? Other translations may wait unrecognized in manuscripts or may simply not survive. Again, a number of known translations of Euthymios and George seem no longer to be extant.[163]

The translation activities of Ep'rem Mc'ire overlap much less with Ibn al-Faḍl's, although the authors and genres of the texts he translated were much the same. He translated, inter alia, the homilies of Gregory of Nazianzos, Basil of Caesarea's *Asketikon,* Chrysostom's homilies on Paul's epistles (here there is overlap with Ibn al-Faḍl), Theodoret of Cyrrhus's *History,* John of Damascus's *Fountain of*

156. VI.1.

157. IV.6. Tarchnišvili notes that this text is similar to "the 5th chapter" of Photios's letter to Pope Nicholas I, beginning "So glaube ich und bekenne die katholische Kirche," by which I take him to be referring to PG 102:592A (Οὕτω φρονῶν . . .).

158. Niceno-Constantinopolitan Creed (IV.1); Creed of Gregory the Wonderworker (IV.2, *CPG* 1764); Athanasian Creed (IV.3).

159. IV.4.

160. IV.5.

161. *Explications of the Hypomnemata:* III.4.

162. Liturgy: V.1–13. Hagiography: VII.1–5.

163. For example, no manuscript containing Euthymios's translation of Chrysostom's homilies on Paul's letters to the Galatians, Thessalonians, and Romans was known to Tarchnišvili, who notes, however, that the translations in question may actually be translations of *excerpts,* which do survive: *GKGL,* 137–38.

Knowledge, and the Dionysian Corpus.[164] As someone active in Antioch and its monasteries and with close ties to the patriarchate, Epʿrem must have known many of the same people and places as Ibn al-Faḍl. They may even have met. The various teachers, mentors, and patrons whom Tarchnišvili mentions[165] give the overall impression of a milieu in which those with Epʿrem's literary and linguistic ability were encouraged and given the resources to work. The patriarch of Antioch, as well as this circle of Georgians, all promoted and participated in a shared agenda to reproduce and engage with the Byzantine ecclesiastical curriculum in Georgian.

Tarchnišvili's description of Epʿrem's translation style is quite reminiscent of Ibn al-Faḍl's. Tarchnišvili writes:

> Epʿrem created his own method of translation, which became the permanent model in the subsequent period. For he represented the view that the translation of a work must be complete, with no gaps, exact, and faithful, but not slavish. At the same time, the spirit and independence of the language into which the translation was carried out needed to be preserved, lest it be inferior in beauty and euphony to the original text.[166]

He would employ many lexica at once to arrive at the precise meaning of a Greek word, only then seeking out the best way to express it in Georgian. Occasionally he would transliterate untranslatable words.[167] This last practice was different from Ibn al-Faḍl's, who usually coined a new term and then explained it in a comment, only employing transliteration in his comment. Like Ibn al-Faḍl, Epʿrem too included comments on difficult words.[168]

Retranslation—producing updated versions of older translations—was a major part of all three of these Georgian translators' work. That is, much of what they translated had already been translated into Georgian previously. They must have been aware of the previous translations. They often used them and sometimes even indicated their debt to previous translators explicitly. In a colophon to his translation of Basil's *Hexaemeron*, George acknowledged his predecessors with the words "May God also bless the first translations; they have been extremely beneficial to me."[169] George, we are told, prepared his translation of the Psalter by carefully collating various Greek and Georgian versions.[170] Epʿrem was criticized for attempting to improve translations or retranslate works already translated by

164. For Epʿrem's translation of the Dionysian Corpus into Georgian only several decades after it was translated into Arabic, see Mavroudi, "Licit," 435–36.

165. Tarchnišvili, *GKGL*, 183–84.

166. Tarchnišvili, 184.

167. Tarchnišvili, 184.

168. Tarchnišvili, 197.

169. Tarchnišvili, 164.

170. Tarchnišvili, 161.

Euthymios and George.[171] This all suggests that we should understand the translations in question as doing more than simply making a text accessible to Georgians. They were part of a continuing scholarly and educational tradition that emphasized the original Greek texts by periodically returning to them.

The translations they produced were not only meant to be accurate, but beautiful as well. Stressing Euthymios's "wondrous style of writing," Tarchnišvili's handbook declares:

> Never had a Georgian spoken and written as he: What clarity of thought, how transparent the veil of his language! Reading Euthymios's writings one has the impression of standing before a meadow full of flowers, bathed in a gleaming light. Euthymios was right when he said of himself: "Everything I write turns to light." It is no wonder that this language was regarded as a supernatural gift. This is why one learnt his writings by heart, as with the Bible. The powerfully eloquent Ep'rem Mc'ire did so, and many other Georgians after him.[172]

Tarchnišvili reports that Georgians believed that the Virgin Mary Mother of God (who had been a missionary in Georgia according to Georgian tradition) had given Euthymios the gift of the Georgian tongue.[173]

This context allows us to imagine Ibn al-Faḍl's translations, and the characteristics of his translations (balancing style and accuracy, texts often previously translated, and as a rule popular in contemporary Byzantine culture), in a wider context. This context included not only fellow Arab Christians, but a whole sphere of Chalcedonian Christians, churchmen and monks, patrons and fellow translators working in several languages. The patriarchate's significant role in Georgian translation activities is further circumstantial evidence that the patriarch may have had a hand in Ibn al-Faḍl's translation program as well.

5 GEORGIAN BOOK CULTURE

Not only the choices and method of translation but also the reception of the work of these Georgian translators parallels the case of Ibn al-Faḍl.

A number of notes in eleventh-century Georgian manuscripts from the region around Antioch make a point of the Greek origin of the texts, translated "from Greek into Georgian," and often mention the name of the translator. This is the same practice we see in many of Ibn al-Faḍl's translations, which use standardized language to say that 'Abdallāh ibn al-Faḍl translated the text "from Greek into Arabic," as we have seen. One manuscript copied near the Monastery of the Mother

171. Tarchnišvili, 185.
172. Tarchnišvili, 154.
173. Tarchnišvili, 154.

of God at Kalipos (to the west of Antioch) in 1040 CE names "the holy father Ek'vt'ime [Euthymios] who translated this book [*Life* and orations of Gregory the Theologian] from Greek into Georgian."[174] Another, copied near the Monastery of Saint Symeon the Younger on the Wondrous Mountain (also to the west of Antioch) in the early 1040s, exhorts the readers (or listeners), "Pray, you Christ-loving people, for humble David, who translated this [book] from Greek into Georgian."[175] In 1050 CE, a proud scribe on the Wondrous Mountain declared of his handiwork, "Both [volumes] are good and beautifully done and [both] derive from Greek, and their Georgian translations are close to the original in meaning."[176] At the Monastery of the Holy Romana, in the mid-eleventh century, one Iovane Djibisdze, upon finishing a copy of George the Athonite's translation of the *Great Synaxarion*, stressed that "it was translated from the Greek language into Georgian by Giorgi [George]. . . . I beseech all of you who will copy [this book]: do not change the words or dots, for it is faithful to the original. The names are extremely difficult. Write what you see as it is." Here the challenges of copying a translated text are foregrounded, as is the newness of the translation, for he refers to "Giorgi" familiarly but without the usual prayers for the deceased, meaning that he is still alive and perhaps still active in the region.[177] In the second half of the eleventh century, at the Monastery of the Reed Valley on the Black Mountain by the coast near Seleukeia in Pieria, Zak'aria finished copying the Gospels and noted, "I copied from [Nicholas the priest's] original, which he had copied from the gospel of Giorgi the Athonite, which Giorgi the Athonite collated with the Greek gospel" three times.[178] Zak'aria traces the text's laborious history, from the Greek to George the Athonite's Georgian (based on unmentioned earlier Georgian translations), painstakingly collated three times *with the original Greek* in order to avoid any error in this most sacred of Christian texts, then copied by one scribe, Nicholas the priest, before finally Zak'aria's own work could be completed.

Elsewhere, too, careful collation signals a concern for the quality of a translated text. The scribes who in 1054 CE at the Georgian monastery at Kalipos copied Euthymios's Georgian translation of the Gospels are careful to note that it was

174. Petersburg, Institute of Oriental Studies, Georgian 3; trans. (modified slightly) Djobadze, *Materials*, 5.

175. Athos, Iviron, Georgian 84 (1042–1044 CE), fol. 124r; trans. Djobadze, *Materials*, 31.

176. Athos, Iviron, Georgian 45 (1050 CE, on the Wondrous Mountain near the Monastery of St. Symeon the Younger, by the scribe Giorgi Ḥucesmonazoni); trans. (modified slightly) Djobadze, *Materials*, 35.

177. Tbilisi, Institute of Mss., ex coll. Historical and Ethnographical Society, 2211 (1042–1065 CE, perhaps the late 1040s); trans. Djobadze, *Materials*, 45. Djobadze uses the observation that George must be alive to date the manuscript to before George's death in 1065 CE; ibid., 96–97.

178. Tbilisi, Institute of Mss., ex coll. Ecclesiastical Museum, 845 (eleventh century, second half); trans. Djobadze, *Materials*, 48 (slightly modified).

collated with the Georgian exemplar and the Greek original: "Holy fathers who will use this Holy Gospel, know that it is truthful, and pure, collated with the Gospel [translated] by Ek'vt'ime [Euthymios]. It has been collated twice with the Greek and Georgian text, and it is totally faultless in numbers and canons."[179] The Gospels may be the most obvious place to look for concern for textual exactitude, but it appears elsewhere too. In a manuscript copied by the recluse George near the Monastery of Saint Symeon the Younger in 1042–1044 CE and donated to the nearby Monastery of the Mother of God, George writes, "Forgive [me] for my ignorant writing, but what I found in the original, I collated carefully and set down in writing."[180]

This interest in the Greek origin of translations is not, of course, restricted to manuscripts around Antioch,[181] nor to Georgians. Indeed, these few examples help to underscore just how much Ibn al-Faḍl's project shared with similar activities around him.

An interest in up-to-date Byzantine versions of saints' lives can be detected in an eleventh- or twelfth-century manuscript containing Georgian translations by Ep'rem Mc'ire of Metaphrastic saints' lives—that is, of the revised and stylistically updated version produced by Symeon the Metaphrast. The manuscript emphasizes that the Georgian text was "translated anew" by Ep'rem "from the Greek metaphrase." Colophons to individual saints' lives within the volume repeat the translator's name, and one reads, "Be it known that this Life of St. Theoktistos was translated from Greek into Georgian by Step'ane Sananoisdze," thus not only mentioning the different translator but also emphasizing that he too was working with the original Greek.[182] Here an interest in the translator and method of translation is compounded with an emphasis on *re*-translation, in this case of texts (the Metaphrastic lives) that were themselves rewritings of old texts. Here the Byzantine Metaphrastic project blends seamlessly into the ongoing Georgian project of translating and retranslating old texts to meet the expectations of demanding readers.

Such Georgian manuscripts, though written in a language other than Greek, are redolent of Byzantine culture—much like Ibn al-Faḍl's translations. The Georgian Gospel book copied in 1054 CE already mentioned dates itself to the reign of

179. Tbilisi, Institute of Mss., ex coll. Ecclesiastical Museum, 484, fol. 314^v; trans. Djobadze, *Materials*, 17.

180. Athos, Iviron, Georgian 84, fol. 124^r; trans. (modified slightly) Djobadze, *Materials*, 31. This note occurs immediately after his note about the translator David, cited in n. 175 above.

181. Tbilisi, Institute of Mss., ex coll. Ecclesiastical Museum, 135 (1035 CE, Šatberdi, Tao-Klarjeti, present-day Turkey), fol. 215^r; trans. Djobadze, *Materials*, 4: Basil's commentary on the Psalms, "translated from the Greek by Ek'vt'ime At'oneli."

182. Tbilisi, Institute of Mss., ex coll. Society for the Promotion of Learning among Georgians, 384; trans. Djobadze, *Materials*, 23–24.

"Constantine Monomachos, the patriarchate of Peter in Antioch," when "the *novelissimos* King Bagrat of the Abkhazians was visiting the metropolis [i.e., Constantinople]."[183] These chronological reference points are Byzantine: the emperor reigning in Constantinople, Constantine IX Monomachos (r. 1042–1055); the Byzantine appointee to the see of Antioch, Peter III (r. ca. 1052–1057); and the whereabouts of a Georgian king bearing a Byzantine title, *nōbelissimos* (pronounced "novelissimos" in Greek, from Latin *nobilissimus*). The manuscript's scribe also places himself in this Byzantine constellation, calling himself "Ivane [John] the Proedros, son of the *proedros* and *prōtoarchōn* Liparit Iese" and saying he wrote when "the mighty king of the Abkhazians and the Georgians and the *novelissimos* of all the Orient brought me from Constantinople."[184]

We also encounter the Byzantine reckoning of the year by the indiction in a Georgian hagiographical manuscript copied in 1040 CE near Antioch, possibly near the Monastery of Saint Symeon the Younger on the Wondrous Mountain, and donated to the Monastery of the Holy Cross near Jerusalem. The manuscript mentions the Georgian K'ronikon but also the indiction (8th Indiction).[185] This indiction method (often paired with the Year of the World) is common in middle Byzantine manuscripts and inscriptions, as we have seen, also appearing in manuscripts containing Arabic translations by Ibn al-Faḍl and other Antiochian scholars.

Georgians had ties to communities outside of Georgia and the Byzantine Empire, as illustrated by another manuscript also copied in 1040 CE near the Monastery of Saint Symeon the Younger and also donated by its scribes to the Monastery of the Holy Cross near Jerusalem.[186]

These colophons give us a sense of an atmosphere in which patronage and support for translations and copies of them were relatively abundant, but this was not always the case. The scribe Zak'aria, already mentioned, concludes his colophon by saying, "Forgive me for my idle, careless, and ignorant copying; I did not have another remedy; I had little money and without payment no one would write for me. Pray for me, the miserable."[187] Without the necessary resources to pay a professional scribe, those who sought or wished to distribute copies of such books had to do the work of a scribe themselves.

183. Tbilisi, Institute of Mss., ex coll. Ecclesiastical Museum, 484, fol. 314^r; trans. (modified slightly) Djobadze, *Materials*, 16.

184. Tbilisi, Institute of Mss., ex coll. Ecclesiastical Museum, 484, fol. 315^r; trans. Djobadze, *Materials*, 18.

185. Jerusalem, Holy Sepulcher, Georgian 156, fol. 100^r; discussed and translated by Djobadze, *Materials*, 25, 27.

186. Petersburg, Institute of Oriental Studies, Georgian 3; Djobadze, *Materials*, 10–11.

187. Trans. (slightly modified) Djobadze, *Materials*, 48–49.

6 CONCLUSION

The texts that Ibn al-Faḍl translated correspond closely to the "core texts" of eleventh-century literary culture, as Papaioannou characterizes them: the Psalter and other biblical texts; biblical exegesis, especially that of Chrysostom; "moral advisory texts, theology, and canon law" from John of the Ladder to Chrysostom, Basil, Anastasios of Sinai, and John of Damascus; saints' lives and other narrative in low (widely accessible) style; and high-style "speeches and hagiographical encomia," poetry, and hymnography.[188] In surveying Ibn al-Faḍl's translations, we have encountered a cross section of this Byzantine "core." Ibn al-Faḍl's known translations omit only a few of these categories, especially canon law, poetry, hymnography, and low-style (but not high-style) hagiography. As I have already emphasized, there may well be other texts he translated that have not yet come to light, but as it stands, the list is weighted toward texts at a relatively high linguistic register.

Some of the texts, especially Isaac's *Ascetic Homilies,* were intended primarily for use by monks (including members of the elite who had retired to monasteries). Many others, even those that may seem to modern readers like exclusively "religious" texts, were at the heart of the "classical tradition" by which elite Byzantine readers—lay, ecclesiastical, and monastic alike—cultivated themselves, and upon which Byzantine authors built their own work.

The material Ibn al-Faḍl translated includes not only Byzantine Chalcedonian authors but also Isaac the Syrian (Nestorian), pseudo-Kaisarios (Miaphysite), and the material extracted from pagan authors in pseudo-Kaisarios and the *Loci communes.* But even this foreign material had been assimilated into Byzantine ecclesiastical culture earlier.

This Byzantine curriculum bore a striking resemblance to the material that contemporary Georgians were translating into their own language. Interest in many of these texts individually had a long history. Ibn al-Faḍl, his Georgian contemporaries, and their Greek-speaking Byzantine neighbors all participated in long-standing literary microtraditions with each individual translation that they made. Taken as a whole, their similar translation programs reflect the particular tastes and reading lists of eleventh-century Byzantine literary culture, a culture that belonged to learned churchmen, monks, and laymen alike. For eleventh-century Byzantines, this was in a sense their literature, read for edifying content but also aesthetic pleasure, and perhaps even to wonder at the autonomous, creative force that modern readers call the author.[189]

188. Papaioannou, *Psellos,* 16–17 (I follow Papaioannou's description closely).
189. Papaioannou, chapter 2.

This helps explain Ibn al-Faḍl's efforts—shared by his Georgian contemporaries—not only to translate but also to *re*-translate works from this tradition or revise earlier translations. It was not enough simply to access the cosmological, ethical, or theological content of these texts in whatever form was available. The Arabic (or Georgian) translation needed to capture some of the rhetorical brilliance of the originals.

PART II

PHILOSOPHY

4

PURPOSE IN THE PREFACES

In part 1 we examined Ibn al-Faḍl's translation program. Now we turn to the words of the translator himself. We have considered the individual works he translated, the resonance of the curriculum as a whole in Byzantine culture, and its overlap with contemporary translations and retranslations from Greek into Georgian. What does Ibn al-Faḍl himself have to tell us about the works he chose and why he dedicated himself to the demanding task of rendering them into literary Arabic?

Fortunately, we are in a position to answer this question, for many of Ibn al-Faḍl's translations are accompanied by prefaces in the manuscripts. These prefaces, usually in the elegant rhymed prose of Classical Arabic highbrow literature, and employing the arsenal of Arabic rhetoric, delighting the reader with recherché vocabulary, clever turns of phrase, and long rhetorical periods, offer precious insight into the translator's motivations. Indeed, that is precisely the subject matter to which he repeatedly returns in these prefaces: what led him to translate these works.

In this chapter, we will examine a number of these prefaces. The aim is not to be comprehensive or exhaustive. There are surely many other elegant and revealing prefaces to be explored in the manuscripts of Ibn al-Faḍl's works and translations.[1] Instead, we will consider a selection of prefaces from a sample of his translations: of Scripture, of late antique biblical exegesis, of praise for saints, of wisdom, both anthologies (the *Loci communes* and pseudo-Kaisarios's *Questions and Answers*) and a single author's asceticism (Isaac's *Ascetic Homilies*).

The aim is to let the translator speak, as much as possible, for himself.

1. See, for example, Ibn al-Faḍl's preface to his anti-Jacobite, anti-Nestorian *Exposition of the Orthodox Faith* (*Sharḥ al-amāna al-mustaqīma*), discussed by Wannous, "Abdallah," 262–64.

1 THE PSALTER

We begin with Ibn al-Faḍl's elaborate preface to his translation of the book of Psalms accompanied by extracts of commentaries on the Psalms.[2] The ascription of the translation to Ibn al-Faḍl is clear and explicit in the scribe's opening lines:[3]

نبتدئ بعون الله تعالى وتأييده بكتابة المزامير الداوودية، أخرجه من اللغة اليونانية إلى اللغة العربية الشمّاس عبد الله ابن الفضل الأنطاكي، لطلب الأجر والثواب. ذلك فاتحة الخطاب، والله سبحانه الهادي للصواب، وإليه المرجع والمآب[١]، آمين.

[١]والمآب: والمأب: ف

> We begin, with the help and assistance of God Almighty, to write out the Davidic Psalms. The deacon ʿAbdallāh ibn al-Faḍl al-Anṭākī extracted [i.e., translated] it from Greek into Arabic, to seek recompense and reward. That is the opening of the discourse, and God, praise be to him, is the one who guides to correctness. To him is the return and the coming back. Amen.

The quite different ascription in another manuscript is equally explicit.[4]

Immediately following this is Ibn al-Faḍl's preface. (There are at least two different recensions of this preface. I focus here on the longer recension.) In order to give a sense of his rhymed prose, I present the greater part of the preface with my translation, followed by a summary of the rest.[5]

(١) *الحمد لله الّذي نبّأ الأنبياء القدّيسين، واصطفى رسلاً وبعثهم إلى العالم باسمه كارزين، ليرشدوا الناس إلى الصواب والحق اليقين، ويعرّفوهم بأنّه تعالى خالق الخلق أجمعين، وديّان العالمين، له الشكر على الدوام، إلى يوم البعث والقيام.*

(٢) *أمّا بعد: لما رمقت بعيني إلى الكتب المقدّسة العتيقة، وشاهدت كتاب الزبور المنسوب إلى النبي والملك داوود جدّ المسيح، وعاينتُ ما فيه من الترنم والتهليل والتسبيح، رُمْتُ أنْ أَمْدَحَ لأقواله وَأُطْنِبَ، وَأُقَرِّضَ لمعانيه الفاضلة وَأُسْهِبَ[١].*

(٣) لكن لما[٢] أجريت في خاطري، واخترت[٣] لناظري، قول القدّيس الجليل غريغوريوس الأثير الفيلسوف الحاذق الخطير[٤]، المتكلّم في اللاهوت، والمبرهن عن عظمة الله تعالى[٥] ذي العزّة والجبروت، حيث قال إنّ[٦] الطاهر لا يَدْنَا منه إلّا بطاهرٍ، والنّدّ[٧] الذّكيّ لا يُوْدَعُ إلّا في الإناء الرضي[٨]؛ وتصوّرت ما شرطه فأفحم وأحسن، وما قدّمه وجرمه فأفتن[٩]، أنقبض[١٠] اتّباعاً للواجب، معتضد[١١] رجوعاً إلى الأب[١٢]، وكيف لا أسلك هذا الأسلوب[١٣] الرضي، وأتنشق[١٤] هذا العرف[١٥] السني، المتعارف عند الأفاضل، والمشهور لدى[١٦] القوم الأماثل، *إذ سَبَبُ الاتّصال التناسب[١٧] والمشاكلة، وعلة الاتحاد التجاوز والمماثلة*

2. Contained in Vat. ar. 4 (**V**); copying completed in Rome on Friday 20 February 1711 CE, according to the colophon at fol. 101^{r-v}. New Haven, Yale Beinecke, ar. 349 (**Y**) does not contain the Psalter but does contain Ibn al-Faḍl's *preface* to the Psalter.

3. Ibn al-Faḍl, *Psalter,* **V** 1^{v} (with no *basmala*).

4. **Y,** beginning: "We are copying the beginning and front (*fātiḥat wa-ṣadr*) of the book, an apology to (*bi-maʿnā ʿtidhār*) the philosopher [i.e., Gregory of Nazianzos] by the exemplary learned deacon and perfect saint ʿAbdallāh ibn al-Faḍl the Orthodox, who extracted (*al-mukhrij*) this noble book, the Psalms, from Greek into Arabic, and who explicated (*wa-l-mufassir*) its obscure meanings, may God Almighty reward him."

5. Ibn al-Faḍl, *Psalter,* **V** 1^{v}–4^{r} (longer recension), here fols. 1^{v}–3^{r}; in **Y** (shorter recension). **Y**'s lengthy omissions are placed between asterisks in the text below (but not the translation).

(٤) إنّني[١٨] إذا ما أنعمت[١٩] النظر فيما أصدره[٢٠] داوود النبي المترنّم بالإلهيّات، والواصف لصنوف المعجزات، *في المزمور السابع والتسعون، الرافع هَدِيدُهُ شَدَّ الأعداءِ الماكِرين: «خلّصته يمينه وذراعه القدوس الطاهر»، أَتَجَاسَرُ على الإقدام، ولا أستجير مباشرة الإحجام،* وأدخل إلى روضة[٢١] المعاني الروحانية، وُلُوجَ[٢٢] اللِّصِّ إلى[٢٣] الجنّة الإلهيّة، بعد الإقرار[٢٤] بوخيم[٢٥] الأعمال، والاعتراف بذميم الأفعال[٢٦]، وأَقْطِفُ من زَهْرِها البَهِيِّ الكَرِيم[٢٧]، وَأَضُمُّ من ثَمَرِها العاليَ الجَسِيم[٢٨]. وهذا السبب، يعلم الله[٢٩] الواحد جوهراً، المثلّث أقانيم[٣٠]، *يخترع أنواع أعيان الجوهر، لا من مادّة تقدّمت، وسائس[٣١] الكلّيّات والجزئيات[٣٢] بقدرةٍ قد أبهرت وأدهلت،* هو الذي حرّكني على تصحيح كتاب الزبور، ذي[٣٣] البهاء الساطع النور[٣٤]، والحديقة[٣٥] التي نباتها[٣٦] فوائد ربّانيّة، والكنز الذي جواهره منافع[٣٧] روحانية، واستخراج تفاسير[٣٨] معانيه من اللغة اليونانية إلى اللغة العربية. وينضاف إلى ذلك ثلثـ<ـة> أسباب وكيدة[٣٩]:

(٥) أولها[٤٠]: اغتنام ثواب من[٤١] الله تعالى وإنعامه بِصَفْحِ ذنوبي الفظيعة[٤٢]، والتغافل[٤٣] عن هفواتي الشنيعة، وَنَشْلِي[٤٤] من الغَرَقِ العالميّ، والإتيان[٤٥] بي إلى المِيناء الصاحِي الشَّهِيِّ البَهِيّ[٤٦].

(٦) وثانيها[٤٧]: سؤال أبي زكرياء[٤٨] بن[٤٩] سلامة، الراغب[٥٠] في خلاص نفسه[٥١]، أدام الله كفايته، وحرس نعمته[٥٢].

(٧) وثالثها[٥٣]: انتفاع الرهط المسيحي، والحزب الإلهي، *أشرف الأنام مذهباً، وأفخرهم مَطْلَباً، وألطفهم جلالاً، وأَغَرُّهُم قولاً،* سادتي[٥٤] المؤمنين، الأجلّاء[٥٥] الراشدين[٥٦]، أدام الله تمكينهم[٥٧]، *وحرص عليهم دينهم، وتحصيل الدعاء من نفوسهم الزكية التي لا تَجْحَد، واقتناء الابتهال من ألبابهم الثاقبة التي لا تَرْفُضُ ولا تَنْبِذ وكيف لا يَصُبُّ المريض إلى الشفاء، والظمآن إلى عُذُوْبَة الماء، والوَجِل إلى الأَمان الحميد، والغريب إلى أُنْسِ الرحمن المجيد. ولقد وَضَحَ البرهان، وأسفر البيان، واندحض المُحال، وتلاشى[٥٨] الضلال.*

[١] وَأُشهِبَ: صححته؛ وأشهب: ف [٢] لكن لما: ف؛ إنني كلما: ي [٣] واخترت: ف؛ واخضرت(؟) به: ي [٤] غريغوريوس الأثير الفيلسوف الحاذق الخطير: ف؛ والفيلسوف ذو الشرف الخطير غريغوريوس: ي [٥] تعالى: ف؛ —ي [٦] حيث قال إنّ: ف؛ لأن: ي [٧] والنّدّ: ي؛ والندا: ف [٨] الرضي: ي؛ الموضي: ف [٩] فأفحم وأحسن، وما قدّمه وجرمه فأفتن: ف (وممكن الصحيح: وجزمه، بالزاء)؛ وأحسن وأفتن: ي [١٠] أنقبض: المنقبض: ي [١١] معتضد: ي؛ وامتغص: ف [١٢] الأب: ي؛ الرب: ف [١٣] أسلك هذا الأسلوب: ف؛ سلك السلوك: ي [١٤] وأتنشق: ف؛ واقسي(؟): ي [١٥] العرف: ف؛ الفرع: ي [١٦] لدى: صححته؛ لذى: ف ي [١٧] التناسب: صححته؛ المتناسب: ف [١٨] إنّني: ف؛ إلا: ي [١٩] أنعمت: ف؛ نعمت: ي [٢٠] أصدره: ف؛ صدره: ي [٢١] روضة: ف؛ —ي [٢٢] وُلُوجَ: ف؛ دخول: ي [٢٣] إلى: ف؛ —ي [٢٤] الإقرار: ف؛ الاعتراف: ي [٢٥] بوخيم: ف؛ بواخيم: ي [٢٦] والاعتراف بذميم الأفعال: ف؛ وسيال الغيرات قبل فروع الآجال: ي [٢٧] البَهِيِّ الكَرِيم: ف؛ كرم البهاء: ي [٢٨] وَأَضُمُّ من ثَمَرِها العاليَ الجَسِيم: ف؛ —ي [٢٩] يعلم الله: ف؛ لله: ي [٣٠] المثلّث أقانيم: صححته؛ المثلّث أقانيماً ف؛ ذو الثلثة أقانيم: ي [٣١] وسائس: وسآيس (بنقطة فوق الياء أيضا): ف [٣٢] والجزئيات: والجزوّيات: ف [٣٣] ذي: ي؛ ذو: ف [٣٤] الساطع النور: ف؛ والنور: ي [٣٥] والحديقة: ف؛ والوسرة. ي [٣٦] نباتها. ي؛ بنايها (أي: بنّاؤها، أو: بناءها): ف [٣٧] منافع: ف؛ منافعاً: ي [٣٨] تفاسير: ي؛ —ف [٣٩] وينضاف . . . وكيدة: ف؛ —ي [٤٠] أولها: ف؛ الأول: ي [٤١] من: ي؛ —ف [٤٢] الفظيعة: صححته؛ الفضيعة: ف؛ الكثيرة: ي [٤٣] والتغافل: ف؛ والمتفضل: ي [٤٤] عن هفواتي الشنيعة، وَنَشْلِي: ف؛ بالتشالي: ي [٤٥] والإتيان: ي؛ والايتان: ف [٤٦] البَهِيّ: ف؛ —ي [٤٧] وثانيها: ف؛ والثاني [٤٨] أبي زكرياء: ف؛ سيّديّ زخريا ويوحنا (زخرياؤ يوحنا؟): ي؛ فأظن أن المقصود هو: سيّدِيّ أبي زكرياء يوحنا بن سلامة [٤٩] بن: ي؛ ابن: ف [٥٠] الراغب: ف؛ الراغبين [٥١] نفسه: ف؛ نفوسهم: ي [٥٢] أدام الله كفايته، وحرس نعمته: ف؛ —ي [٥٣] وثالثها: ف؛ الثالث: ي [٥٤] سادتي: ف؛ ساداتي: ي [٥٥] الأجلّاء: ف؛ —ي [٥٦] الراشدين: ف؛ الرشيدين: ي [٥٧] تمكينهم: +بها آمين: ي [٥٨] وتلاشى: صححته؛ وتلاشا: ف

[1] Praise be to God, who made proclamation (*nabba'a*) to the holy prophets (*anbiyā'*) and selected apostles, and sent them to the world preaching in his name, to guide mankind to correctness and the certain truth and to teach them to know that he, Exalted, is the Creator of all creation, and the Judge (*dayyān*) of the worlds; to him is unceasing gratitude until the Day of Raising Up and Resurrection.

[2] When I looked (*ramaqtu*) with my eye into the old holy books, and saw (*shāhadtu*) the Psalter ascribed to the prophet and king David, forefather of Christ, and eyed (*ʿāyantu*) the singing, praising,[6] and glorifying [of God], I sought to give praise to his utterances (*aqwāl*) and go on about them (*wa-uṭnib*), to laud his ideas (*maʿānī*) and speak at length (*wa-us-hib*).

[3] But when I ran over in my mind (*khāṭirī*), and fixed my eye (*nāẓirī*) upon, the saying of the sublime Saint Gregory, the excellent, the adept and eminent philosopher, the Theologian, who proved the greatness of God the Exalted, the Mighty and Powerful, where he says that the pure approach [God] only with what is pure, and fragrant

6. *tahlīl:* repeatedly saying, *lā ilāha illā llāh,* "There is no god but God!" Hava, *Farā'id,* 824.

incense is only placed in a pleasing vessel; and when I thought about (*taṣawwartu*) how he stipulated—indisputably well (*fa-afḥama wa-aḥsana*)—and how he laid down a premise then made his attractive [or: perfect] judgment,[7] I hasten to follow duty, and recover my strength by resorting to the Father. And how can I not follow this pleasing course (*al-uslūb al-raḍī*) and breathe in this sublime fragrance (*al-ʿarf al-sanī*), well known among the learned (*afāḍil*) and famous among the exemplary (*amāthil*), since the cause (*sabab*) of reaching [God] is relation[8] and resemblance, and the cause (*ʿilla*) of unification is remission [of deserved punishment] and becoming similar [to God].

[4] Indeed, whenever I applied my gaze to that which the prophet David uttered—David, who sings of the divine matters (*ilāhīyāt*) and describes the various miracles (*muʿjizāt*)—in the Ninety-Seventh Psalm, which thunderously removes the attack of the cunning enemies: "His right hand and his holy, pure arm have saved him,"[9] then I would dare to approach (*iqdām*) and would not seek refuge in immediate retreat (*iḥjām*) but would enter the garden of spiritual ideas as a thief penetrates into the divine paradise, after acknowledging his noxious deeds (*wakhīm al-aʿmāl*) and confessing his blameworthy acts (*dhamīm al-afʿāl*); and of its flowers I pick the finest and most precious (*al-bahīya l-karīm*), and of its fruit I gather the choicest and most plump (*al-ʿāliya l-jasīm*). This reason—so knows God, One in substance, Triplicate in hypostases, who creates the various species of the entities of substance (*anwāʿ aʿyān al-jawhar*), which did not emerge from preexisting matter, ruler over the universals and the particulars with a dazzling and amazing power—is what moved me to correct the Psalter—possessing luminescent splendor and the garden whose plants are lordly benefits (*fawāʾidu rabbānīya*) and the treasure whose jewels (*jawāhir*) are spiritual benefits (*manāfiʿu rūḥānīya*)—and to extract (the explications of) its sense[10] from Greek into Arabic. In addition to that there were three compelling reasons:

[5] First: to seek recompense from God the Exalted, and that he generously forgive my foul sins (*dhunūbī l-faẓīʿa*) and disregard my repulsive faults (*hafawātī l-shanīʿa*), whisk me away from the worldly shipwreck (*al-gharaqi l-ʿālamīy*) and bring me to the cloudless, longed-for, resplendent harbor (*al-mīnāʾi l-ṣāḥī l-shahīyi l-bahīy*).

7. *jazamahu fa-aftana,* reading *jazamahu* for *jaramahu.* Perhaps *aftana* (to be attractive) is to be emended to *atqana* (to be perfect) by transposition.

8. Reading *al-tanāsub* for *al-mutanāsib.* Alternatively, read *al-munāsaba,* since the phrase *al-mushākala wa-l-munāsaba* occurs in Ibn al-Faḍl's preface to the *Book of the Garden,* ¶2 (see below, §2, pp. 132 and 133).

9. Psalm 97(98):1.

10. "Explications" (*tafāsīr*) is from **Y**, since **V** omits the word and so reads "to extract its sense (*maʿānī*)." **Y**'s reading is supported by the note that follows the preface in **Y** (but not in **V**), which refers to the commentators (*mufassirīn*) whose commentaries were translated and abbreviated (presumably by Ibn al-Faḍl).

[6] Second: the request of Abū Zakariyā' ibn Salāma,[11] who desires the salvation of his soul, may God grant him lasting protection[12] and preserve his well-being.

[7] Third: to benefit the Christian people (*al-raht al-masīḥī*), the partisans of God (*al-ḥizb al-ilāhī*), most noble of mankind in their way of thinking,[13] most glorious in aim, gentlest in disputation, most eminent in speech, my gentlemen (*sādatī*) the believers, sublime and rightly guided, may God make their strength last and incite them to their religion and to performing prayer from their righteous souls that do not abjure their faith, and to acquiring supplication from their penetrating minds that do not reject nor neglect [it]. How can the sick not love the cure (*shifā'*), and the thirsty, sweet water (*mā'*), and the fearful, lauded safety (*al-amān al-ḥamīd*), and the stranger, familiarity with the Merciful, the Glorious (*al-raḥmān al-majīd*)? The proof has been made clear (*waḍaḥa l-burhān*), and the exposition unveiled (*asfara l-bayān*), the absurd has been refuted (*indaḥaḍa l-muḥāl*), and error abolished (*talāshā l-ḍalāl*).

The rest of Ibn al-Faḍl's preface takes up about one small page in the manuscript with the longer recension. Ibn al-Faḍl asks for the reader's prayers in hopes that his own punishment in the afterlife may be lightened in spite of all his shortcomings, for God pours out his goodness "upon the obedient and the disobedient." He closes by invoking Christ—whom he describes in explicitly Chalcedonian,

11. Samuel Noble observed that **Y** refers to two names: Zakhariyā and Yūḥannā. (See ch. 1, n. 46.) The text even refers to them with dual and plural forms (*sayyidayya*, with two *shaddas* in the manuscript; *al-rāghibīn*, or the identically spelled *al-rāghibayn; nufūsihim* etc.). In **V**, these are all singular. As I indicate in the apparatus to the text, I believe the original text was probably "my lord Abū Zakariyā' Yūḥannā ibn Salāma" (*sayyidī Abī* . . .). In this scenario, we may imagine that the *hamza* at the end of the name Zakariyā' was at some point written with a *waw*, which a later scribe could have mistaken for the conjunction *wa-* (and). Before or after that, the word Abū/Abī (father of) was dropped. The result was that one man's *kunya* (patronymic) and *ism* (given name) became two *isms*. *Sayyidī* (my lord) was re-voweled as *sayyidayya* (the dual form), and the other forms were "corrected" to dual or plural forms. As for the discrepant spelling of the name Zachary, that is easily explained by the similarity of the letters *kāf* and *khā'* in some Arabic scripts.

12. *adāma llāhu kifāyatahu*. I follow van Gelder and Schoeler in translating *kifāya* (sufficiency) as "protection" in this formulaic expression: Ibn al-Qāriḥ, *Epistle* to Abū l-ʿAlā' al-Maʿarrī, 1.2, ed. and trans. van Gelder and Schoeler in Maʿarrī, *Epistle of Forgiveness*, 1:2–3. For this and similar formulas in formal Classical Arabic epistolography, see al-Qalqashandī (d. 1418 CE), *Ṣubḥ al-aʿshā*, 12.1, Cairo ed., 7:72–73 (on opening formulas in formal letters).

13. *madhhaban*, perhaps "doctrinal affiliation," as Mark Swanson translated it in his talk "On the Beauty of Texts: Examples from the Christian Arabic Heritage, 8th–13th Centuries CE," at the Simposio Patrimonio Arabo Cristiano e dialogo Islamo Cristiano: Atto Accademico in onore del Rev. P. Samir Khalil Samir, SJ, in occasione del suo 80° compleanno, Pontificio Istituto Orientale, Rome, 25 May 2018. Nasrallah (*Histoire*, 3.1:194 n. 6) translated *madhhab* here as "rites" and construed this as a reference to the liturgy and thus as support for his claim that Ibn al-Faḍl's translation program was largely meant to allow an Arabophone congregation to understand the liturgy.

Dyoenergist, Dyothelete terms (as having "one hypostasis, two substances, two activities, and two wills")—and "the Virgin his Mother," and "all the saints."[14]

The opening praise of God (*taḥmīd*) is "ecumenical," so to speak: it could have been written by a Muslim, since Muslims too believed in the prophets (*anbiyāʾ*) and apostles or messengers (*rusul*) and referred to them with this same language, only disagreeing with Christians about precisely who was or was not an apostle. The same goes for the language Ibn al-Faḍl uses as he continues the praise: correct belief, God as the Creator, gratitude, the resurrection. His rhyming prose here even has a slight echo of the commonly recited opening chapter of the Qur'an (the *fātiḥa*): "judge of the worlds" (*dayyānu l-ʿālamīn*) where the Qur'an has "lord of the worlds" (*rabbi l-ʿālamīn*) and "master of the Day of Judgment" (*māliki yawmi l-dīn*).[15]

Then Ibn al-Faḍl sets out to explain why he produced this Arabic version of the book of Psalms. Here and throughout, the prose is densely packed with rhymes and makes abundant use of paired synonyms (and other closely related words). These are staples of Arabic rhymed prose (*sajʿ*).

Ibn al-Faḍl first describes the Psalter catching his eye as he read the Old Testament. Both the style (*aqwāl*) and the content (*maʿānī*) amazed him. He then moves to Saint Gregory the Theologian (of Nazianzos) to explain what impelled him to produce a translation of the Psalms: Gregory's pronouncements on the need to approach God with only the purest of gifts. Ibn al-Faḍl then quotes a specific line from the Psalms that gave him the courage to carry out this work. Why does he need courage? Because he feels awe at the garden, the paradise, that is the book of Psalms. He vividly depicts himself as a contrite criminal, a thief, fearful to approach, but given strength by the words of David himself. Once inside, he avails himself of the garden's bounty, its flowers, its fruit.

The way that Ibn al-Faḍl describes the experience of reading the Psalms suggests that it is spontaneous or emotional rather than a result of reasoning. In this way, it seems to play a role analogous to what Socrates describes as the good type of poetry that will be permitted in his ideal city, a poetry that leads the listener to correct and good beliefs.[16] For the Psalter to be effective, then, one must be able to experience it in a version that captures its beauty.

Enjoying this beauty, this bounty in the garden of the Psalms, he explains, is what motivated him "to correct the Psalter" and "to extract"—that is, translate—

14. V 3ʳ–4ʳ.

15. Mark Swanson ("On the Beauty of Texts"; see n. 13 on the previous page) has drawn attention to the Christian Arabic rhetorical strategy of expressing doctrinal statements that are not specifically Christian in rhymed prose that could almost be mistaken for qur'anic verses, in particular that of Buṭrus al-Sadamantī.

16. See ch. 2, p. 82, n. 239.

"explications of its sense from Greek into Arabic."[17] Ibn al-Faḍl's Arabic Psalter, then, apparently drew on an earlier Arabic translation, which he "corrected" with recourse to the Greek (which, as part of the divinely inspired Septuagint Greek translation of the Hebrew Bible, could serve as an authoritative "original"). This procedure was presumably similar to how he produced his Arabic retranslation of Basil's *Hexaemeron,* except that in the latter case at least, he not only made corrections based on the Greek but also rewrote much of the text, even when it was a perfectly acceptable translation of the Greek.

In the course of giving this reason for producing his Arabic Psalter, Ibn al-Faḍl includes two extensive asides. The second is a description of the Psalter as something shining, resplendent, filled with light, or a garden whose plants are benefits from the Lord, or a treasure filled with "spiritual benefits," which Ibn al-Faḍl playfully describes as the treasure's "jewels" (*jawāhir*). I say playfully because the word he uses, *jawāhir,* means "substances" in an Aristotelian context: that is, people or things that subsist on their own (like Socrates or the sun), in contrast to "accidents," which exist only when they "inhere" in a substance (like Socrates's baldness or the brightness of the sun: if you were to speak of "the brightness," I would ask: "The brightness of what?"). We will return to the vocabulary of Aristotelian logic in chapter 6.

We can tell that this Aristotelian meaning of "substance" is on Ibn al-Faḍl's mind because the other extensive aside is about God and uses the word *jawhar* in this Aristotelian sense. There he describes God as having a single substance (*jawhar* ~ οὐσία) but three hypostases (*aqānīm* ~ ὑποστάσεις). This is the standard (Nicene) Christian description of God. Next, Ibn al-Faḍl stresses God's exclusive role as Creator of all that exists. To describe those created beings, he again uses the term "substance" (*jawhar*) along with another Aristotelian term, "species": God created the various "species" (*anwāʿ* ~ εἴδη) of the *aʿyān al-jawhar.*

The term *aʿyān* is used in Arabic philosophy to refer to "entities" or "essences." The Muslim Aristotelian philosopher Avicenna (Ibn Sīnā, d. 1037) uses the term *aʿyān* to refer to "individual essences" existing in the world as opposed to "forms" that exist only in our minds.[18] Ibn al-Faḍl's precise phrase *aʿyān al-jawhar* would be used similarly over a century later by the Muslim philosopher and mystic Ibn ʿArabī (1165–1240) to mean something like "entities of substance."[19] Of course, Ibn ʿArabī was writing long after Ibn al-Faḍl; if there is any connection between their technical language, it is perhaps because Ibn ʿArabī and Sufis drew on and adapted

17. Only the shorter recension (in **Y**) includes the word "explications."

18. Ibn Sīnā, *Najāt,* Logic §17, ed. Dānešpažūh, 17, trans. Ahmed, 13.

19. Ibn ʿArabī (1165–1240), *Futūḥāt,* ch. 302, ed. Shams al-Dīn, 5:16: "For in created existence there is nothing but *aʿyān al-jawhar* and the relations that adhere to them." From the context, it is clear that by *nisab* he is referring to the Peripatetic accidents that inhere in a substance. Both Ibn al-Faḍl and Ibn ʿArabī seem to refer to individuals (particular substances) as *aʿyān al-jawhar,* insofar as they are instantiations of a universal substance called the *jawhar.* See also Chittick, "Ibn Arabi," §4.1.

Christian philosophical theology for their own purposes, or, alternatively, because both drew on Arabic Peripatetic thought. Ibn al-Faḍl himself makes clear his attentiveness to this particular term in his *Discourse on the Holy Trinity*, where he writes that God has "a substance that does not vary with respect to entity" (*jawharin ghayri mukhtalifi l-ʿayn*).[20]

As he continues, Ibn al-Faḍl stresses that God did not form the creatures out of preexisting matter (*mādda*)—a key Christian objection to certain ancient theories of the origin of the universe.

Finally, in this aside about God Ibn al-Faḍl makes yet another reference to a philosophical controversy: God's knowledge of particulars. Ibn al-Faḍl stresses that God rules over universals *and* particulars. This refers to a long-standing discussion in ancient and medieval philosophy about God's knowledge of and activity concerning particulars. According to Aristotle's way of thinking, we may call things that exist (this horse, that river) "particulars." At the same time, we can say of each one that it is "a such and such" (the Orontes is a river, the Barada is a river); that is, there is a general class of things that can all be described as "a river." "River" in that sense—the general notion of what a river is rather than a particular river—is called a "universal." Some philosophers held that God knew or concerned himself only with universals—the general, unchanging versions of the specific, particular things we see in the world—but paid no attention to particulars themselves.[21] Others, especially Christian, Jewish, and Muslim thinkers, objected to this. Ibn al-Faḍl's insistence on God's reign over universals *and* particulars points to his stance on the issue.

As has already become clear, Ibn al-Faḍl used this preface not only to showcase high Arabic style and describe his motivation for the work that followed, but also to make extremely concise references to philosophical doctrines and issues that he considered important.

In the next part of the preface, Ibn al-Faḍl offers three additional reasons that motivated him to produce his corrected Arabic Psalter. First, he frames his work as an act of penitence that he hopes will earn him salvation and forgiveness for his sins. His metaphor for salvation is nautical: from drowning in the chaotic shipwreck of this world, he hopes to be whisked away to the calmest and sunniest of harbors.

Second, he credits a patron, Abū Zakariyāʾ ibn Salāma, for asking for the work to be carried out.[22] Presumably this involved some sort of commission, probably including monetary support for the translator's work. The patron's request is likewise framed as a pious act for the salvation of his own soul.

20. Ibn al-Faḍl, *Holy Trinity*, §3, ¶2, ed. Noble and Treiger, "Christian Arabic Theology," 398 (or, as they translate it, 409: "a substance undifferentiated in itself"). Ibn al-Faḍl seems to mean that the (three) individuals falling under God's (universal) substance are not different in their divinity.

21. For the epistemology behind such views, see Adamson, "On Knowledge of Particulars."

22. Probably one patron, not two. See n. 11 above.

Finally, Ibn al-Faḍl reveals his hope that his translation will benefit Christians as a whole. This prompts an enthusiastic encomium for the collectivity of Christians that may perhaps be read not simply as a statement of fact about Christians but as an aspirational ideal that he hopes Christians will continue to follow. Comparing them implicitly to other religious communities (Muslims and Jews presumably being foremost in his mind), he says that Christians have the best religion, ultimate goal, and speech. He does not say that theirs is the *only* legitimate faith, only the best. Christians' goal—that is, the paradise that they seek—is a spiritual one. Perhaps Ibn al-Faḍl has in mind a contrast with the paradise of Muslims as depicted in Christian polemic: a place of corporeal pleasures, of food and sex.[23]

He then asks God to strengthen Christians in their faith, that they "not abjure their faith." This is perhaps the real heart of this third and final additional motivation: the corrected translation of the Psalms is meant to strengthen the faith of the Christian community. The end of the first millennium was a turning point in the gradual demographic shift in the Near East from a Christian to a Muslim majority.[24] Was there a sense among Christians like Ibn al-Faḍl that more needed to be done to teach elite Arabic-speaking Christians not only the doctrines but also the sublime beauty of their faith, lest they be seduced by a Scripture whose beauty and inimitability (*iʿjāz*) were celebrated by Muslims as the proof of Muḥammad's prophethood?

In this light, the subsequent lines too acquire an aspirational tone: Christians must long for God and his Scripture (mustn't they?) as the sick long to be cured and the thirsty long for water. The truth of the religion has been proven, Ibn al-Faḍl continues, and falsehood refuted. How has this been accomplished? Presumably through Scripture itself, perhaps, in the case of the Psalms, not only the foretelling of a divine messiah that Christians see in it, but also the divine beauty of its words. If elite Arabophone Christians were to see this beauty, this proof of the truth of their religion, they would need a beautiful Arabic Psalter, error-free.

What then can we conclude from this preface about Ibn al-Faḍl's motivations to produce his Psalter? His expressed aims are (1) to do penance for his sins, (2) to satisfy the request of a patron, and (3) to benefit the community of Christians. He offered his patron and other Christians a corrected Arabic Psalter to strengthen their faith and perhaps allow them to deepen their knowledge and understanding. This last motive is implicit in the allusions to the Peripatetic philosophical concepts that Ibn al-Faḍl and other Christians used in order to discuss what Aristotle called "first philosophy" or "theology": knowledge of divine matters, of existence itself. This conceptual vocabulary, which had never ceased to be a part of

23. See Roggema, "Job," 507–8. A poem by the Sabian and Buyid secretary Abū Isḥāq Ibrāhīm ibn Hilāl al-Ṣābī (d. 994) presupposes that the Muslim paradise is a pleasurable garden inhabited by houris: trans. van Bladel, *Arabic Hermes*, 107–8; Roberts, "Being a Sabian," 261.

24. Bulliet, *Conversion*.

Byzantine thought—John of Damascus's *Fountain of Knowledge* is a particularly influential example of its continued prominence—was now being expressed in the language of Arabic Aristotelianism, a language that Muslims used but Christian translators had, for the most part, created. As will become clear, this Arabic philosophical vocabulary—not only accurate translations and beautiful style—is a major part of what Ibn al-Faḍl sought to offer in his translation program.

2 THE GARDEN

Fine style and references to philosophical terminology are also to be found in Ibn al-Faḍl's preface to the *Book of the Garden,* a translation of the "sacro-profane" florilegium known as *Loci communes* and sometimes ascribed (falsely) to Maximos the Confessor.[25] At the same time, in this preface the importance of education becomes more prominent.

The preface was transcribed and translated into French by Michel van Esbroeck,[26] who was, as mentioned in chapter 2, the first to realize that the *Garden* was a translation and not an original compilation by Ibn al-Faḍl. By revisiting the manuscript van Esbroeck used, I have been able to make a number of improvements to the Arabic text, so I present it here anew. The preface in its entirety reads:[27]

(١) بسم الأب والابن والروح القدس. أما بعد حمدِ الله الجوهر العام، ذي الأشخاص الثلثة أب وابن وروح قدس، الذي انْتَاشَنَا من وَرْطَةِ[١] الظَّلَالَة، ورفعنا من وَهْدَةِ العَمَايَةِ تَرَاؤُفاً[٢]، وَقَادَنَا إلى الهداية تَعَطُّفاً، بما هو خفيّ به وخليق:

(٢) فإنه لما كان تبارك وتعالى قد قال في[٣] إنجيله المقدس:[٤] «مَن يَعْمَل وَيُعَلِّم ذلك هو العظيم في ملكوت السماء»، وَكُنَّا[٥] فاقدين لهذين الأمرين، وعارين[٦] من هاتين الخَلَّتَيْن، رأينا أن[٧] نتسبب في الحُظْوَةِ بِيَسِير[٨] منهما، فشرعنا في استخراج عدة من المعاني التي تَصُبُّ إلى سماعها أنفس[٩] أولي النظر، وَتَهُشُّ إلى التصفح لها همه[١٠] ذوي الخَطَر، من اللغة اليونانية إلى اللغة العربية. وسمينا هذا الكتاب الجامع لها[١١] «كتاب الروضة» لِما في ذلك من المناسبة والمشاكلة. وجرينا في نَقْلِهِ مَجْرَى[١٢] من تقدم من النَّقْلَة في استعمال الزيادة والحَذْف، والتقديم والتأخير، راغبين إلى الله ذي العزة والكمال، والقدرة والجلال، يَرْزُقنا جزيلَ الثواب، والخَلاص من أليم العِقاب، والإرشاد إلى الصواب، بِمَنِّهِ وطَوْله وجُوْدِه.

(٣) فمن انتفع[١٣] منه واعظاً أو رادعاً، أو آمراً أو زاجراً[١٤]، أو راعياً أو راهباً، بما يلتقطه[١٥] من ألفاظ الآباء القديسين، والفلاسفة العابدين[١٦]، فلا[١٧] يَحُلُّنا[١٨] من الذكر الرضي، إن كنا في دار الفناء، والترحم السني، إن كنا في رَبْع[١٩] البقاء، آخذاً بالأجمل، ورجوعاً إلى الأفضل. فإن الله يحب المحسنين، وهو حَسْبُنَا وعليه مُعْتَمَدُنَا.

[١] وَرْطَةِ: ورطة: س؛ ورتة: فن إسبرك [٢] تراؤُفاً: تراوقا: س؛ فقد يكون المقصود: تَرَؤُّفاً [٣] في: في {في}: س [٤] +[[فاقدين]]: س. [٥] وَكُنَّا: وكـ'ـد'ـا[[ن]]: س [٦] وعارين: س؛ وغارين: فن إسبرك [٧] أن: 'أن': س [٨] بِيَسِير: صححته؛ نيسير: س [٩] أنفس: س؛ انفوس: فن إسبرك [١٠] همه: س؛ همة: فن إسبرك؛ وقد يكون المقصود: هِمَمُ [١١] لها: {ا}لها: س؛ لها: فن إسبرك [١٢] نَقْلِهِ مَجْرَى: نقلة مجري: فن إسبرك [١٣] انتفع: صحّحه فن إسبرك؛ اتنفع: س [١٤] زاجراً: صححته؛ زاجزاً: س، فن إسبرك [١٥] يلتقطه: س؛ يلتقته: فن إسبرك [١٦] العابدين: س؛ الغاربين: فن إسبرك [١٧] فلا: س (وكأنه قد كان «ولا» ثم غيّره الناسخ)؛ ولا: فن إسبرك [١٨] يَحُلُّنا: س؛ يخلنا: فن إسبرك [١٩] رَبْع: [[ا]]ربع: س

25. See ch. 2, §4, pp. 62–64.
26. Van Esbroeck, "Les sentences," 15–16.
27. Sinai ar. 66 (S), fols. 260^{v}–261^{r}. The preface was published with a French translation by van Esbroeck, "Les sentences," 15–16. I follow the text of the Sinai manuscript, marking van Esbroeck's readings in the apparatus. My translation was made with reference to his, though I differ on a number of points of interpretation.

[1] In the name of the Father, the Son, and the Holy Spirit. As for what comes after praise of God, the Universal Substance that possesses the three Persons, Father, Son, and Holy Spirit, who took us from the plight (*warṭa*) of darkness and raised us up from the chasm (*wahda*) of ignorance mercifully (*tarāʾuffan/taraʾʾufan*), and led us to guidance compassionately (*taʿaṭṭufan*), by means of that which is mysterious and worthy of Him:

[2] He, the Blessed and Exalted, said in his holy Gospel, "He who performs and teaches it [i.e., the least of the commandments] is great in the kingdom of heaven [Matthew 5:19]," but we were bereft of these two things, and devoid of these two attributes. Therefore, we decided to be the cause of [others] obtaining a bit of them. And so we began by extracting [i.e., translating] a number of ideas (*maʿānī*) to which the souls of the contemplative love to listen, and to study which the zeal of the noble is delighted, from Greek into Arabic. We called this book that gathers them together the *Book of the Garden* because of its affinity and similarity [to a garden]. In translating it we proceeded as one who progresses in translation by expanding and shortening, moving things forward and backward, asking God, in his might and perfection (*kamāl*), his power and sublimity (*jalāl*), to provide us with abundant recompense (*thawāb*), and salvation from the painful punishment (*ʿiqāb*), and guidance to correctness (*ṣawāb*), by his grace, his might, and his generosity.

[3] Whoever benefits from it—whether a preacher or abstainer (*rādiʿ*), one who commands (*āmir*) or forbids (*zājir*), pastor or monk—by what he gleans from among the words of the holy fathers (*qiddīsīn*), and the worshipful philosophers (*ʿābidīn*), does not absolve us from invoking [God] in a manner pleasing [to him] (*al-dhikr al-raḍī*), if we are in the abode of annihilation (*fanāʾ*), nor from asking sublimely for [God's] mercy (*al-taraḥḥum al-sanī*), if we are in the dwelling-place of permanence (*baqāʾ*), adhering to what is more beautiful, resorting to what is more excellent. For God loves those who do good; he is all we need, and upon him do we depend.

As part of his opening praise of God (*taḥmīd*)—or rather his unusually long transition from the praise to the main subject of his text (usually performed with a simple *ammā baʿd*, "as for what comes after," but here executed by continuing the praise)—Ibn al-Faḍl calls God "the universal substance." "Universal substance" is Porphyry's term for Aristotle's "secondary substance"—that is, the kind of thing (man, river) that individual "primary substances" (this man, that river) can be said to be. Porphyry, commenting on Aristotle's rather cryptic statement that some things can be predicated of other things but cannot be in a subject (*Categories* 2, 1a20–22), defines the term "universal substance" (ἡ καθόλου οὐσία) and explains that this is what Aristotle's description refers to.[28]

This concept was important for Ibn al-Faḍl because it was key to his metaphysical argument for the coherence of the Christian doctrine of the Trinity. As

28. Porphyry, *Isagoge et in Aristotelis Categorias commentarium*, on *Categories* 1a20–24, ed. Busse, 71–74, esp. 71_{37}, 72_{30}–73_{2}, 73_{29-31}, 74_{5}.

Samuel Noble and Alexander Treiger have shown, Ibn al-Faḍl argued that God's oneness is not the oneness of the individual, that is, of a particular substance, to use Porphyry's term (for that would make a trinity impossible), but instead that God's oneness is akin to that of a species: God is a universal substance predicated of exactly three individuals or particular substances (Father, Son, and Holy Spirit).[29] Ibn al-Faḍl uses this same epithet for God—"universal substance"—when invoking God in other works as well.[30] Porphyry's term "universal substance" accords well with his Neoplatonic reading of Aristotle; where Aristotle's terminology implies the priority of individuals ("primary substances") over the abstract categories under which they fall ("secondary substances"), Porphyry shifts the priority toward the abstractions, identified with Plato's Forms. Likewise, it certainly seems more appropriate to refer to the Christian God as "universal" rather than "secondary." The rhetorical effect of using this Neoplatonic expression in the very opening of the preface is implicitly to justify the use of ancient philosophy, in this case the better to praise and to understand God.

As Ibn al-Faḍl continues his transition to the main subject matter (*ammā ba ʿd . . .*), he describes God's salvation of human beings as a process of illumination, lifting us out of darkness, out of ignorance. The stage is set for framing his translation as part of this process. Exactly how can be discerned from what comes next: a quotation from the Gospel of Matthew that foregrounds teaching and good action as activities favored by God. The context of the quotation restricts this favor to teaching and performing God's commandments (as revealed in the Hebrew Bible)—even the most insignificant of them—but in Ibn al-Faḍl's preface the scope is much broader. God's favor for teaching and action, he explains, are what led him to translate the anthology of sayings "from Greek into Arabic."

Ibn al-Faḍl may not have assembled the anthology himself, but he was, he tells us, responsible for the title: the *Book of the Garden*. This name echoes the ancient Hellenic practice of referring to a collection of brief texts as "a collection of flowers" (Greek *anthologion*, Latin *florilegium*). It also recalls his preface to the Psalms, where he described himself as approaching the Psalter in trepidation as if it were a garden and he a thief not worthy of entering it. But here in his preface to the *Garden*, he offers no such image and instead alludes to the laborious process of producing a worthy translation. From God he asks for guidance and salvation.

29. In his *Book of Benefit*, chapter 6: Noble and Treiger, "Christian Arabic Theology," 383; Noble, "Doctrine," 295–97, esp. 297.

30. For example, as Noble has observed, Ibn al-Faḍl uses this term with this same meaning in his brief *Refutation of Astrology*: "We shall clarify this with the help of God, the Universal Substance (*al-jawhar al-ʿāmm*) with three individuals, Father, Son, and Holy Spirit"; trans. Noble, "ʿAbdallah," 184 (translation modified slightly) and n. 35 printed on p. 320.

Ibn al-Faḍl then gives us a glimpse of his intended audience: priests—who, it should be remembered, included powerful members of the ecclesiastical hierarchy up to the patriarch of Antioch himself—and monks—who again, would have included some very learned and prominent individuals, including abbots of influential monasteries like the nearby Monastery of Saint Symeon the Younger. He also mentions those who "command" (*āmir*) and "forbid" (*zājir*). This pairing immediately calls to mind the notion in Islamic jurisprudence that Muslims are obliged to "command right and forbid wrong" (*al-amr bi-l-maʿrūf wa-l-nahy ʿan al-munkar*).[31] Ibn al-Faḍl's word for "forbid" (*zajara*) is distinct from the standard verb (*nahā*) but is equated with the latter in medieval lexica.[32] Michael Cook has argued that this notion—especially the aspect that involves critiquing rulers—has limited parallels in pre-Islamic Christian culture, in particular the charismatic ascetic's habit of speaking truth to power (*parrhēsia*), but that it became much more prominent in Islamic culture. Cook's focus for the Classical Islamic period is on Muslims, but he does observe that by the thirteenth century at least some Christians—in particular the Miaphysite Jacobite (West-Syrian) Christian Bar Hebraeus (d. 1286)—had adapted this notion for their own purposes.[33] This discursive background seems to be at least part of what is behind Ibn al-Faḍl's pairing of these words (though perhaps he is drawing on Christian precedents too). It is not clear to me whom precisely Ibn al-Faḍl is designating with this term (perhaps preachers?), but he seems to be echoing the Jesus saying he quoted earlier elevating those who teach (and perform) God's commandments.

These priests and monks, commanders and forbidders, will, he hopes, profit from reading the sayings assembled in this book that Ibn al-Faḍl has translated. He calls the authors of these sayings "holy fathers" (*al-ābāʾ al-qiddīsīn*)—saintly fathers of the church like Chrysostom, Basil, and the Gregorys—and "worshipful philosophers" (*al-falāsifa al-ʿābidīn*).[34] The second phrase is probably intended mainly as a synonym of the first: the fathers of the church are the philosophers. Indeed, it was standard Byzantine practice to refer to monks as philosophers, in

31. Cook, *Commanding Right.*

32. E.g., *Lisān* s.v. *zjr.*

33. Cook, *Commanding Right,* ch. 19 and appendix 2 (on the dependence of Bar Hebraeus's discussion of commanding right and forbidding wrong on al-Ghazālī's). Pre-Islamic Jewish rabbis, Cook shows, engaged in a similar discourse of individual responsibility to rebuke those who do wrong. Cook's consideration of Christian influence focuses on precedents, that is, pre-Islamic Christianity; perhaps further scrutiny of authors like Ibn al-Faḍl would reveal discourses among seventh- to eleventh-century Christians and Jews in Byzantium and the Middle East that developed in parallel and perhaps in dialogue with the Islamic one.

34. Van Esbroeck ("Les sentences," 16) interprets this phrase as the "philosophes de l'extérieur," that is, pagan philosophers, and prints the corresponding text: *al-falāsifa al-ghāribīn.* Since van Esbroeck based his text on the same manuscript as I have, Sinai ar. 66, this was presumably intended as an emendation.

light of their devotion to contemplation, perfection of the self, and attainment of true knowledge.[35] Still, since the *Garden* is in fact a collection of sayings of both church fathers and pagan authors (as well as scriptural quotations), another reading is possible: perhaps Ibn al-Faḍl means to refer to those pagan authors who made it into the *Garden* (many of whom were indeed considered philosophers). In this case, "worshipful" would imply that these pagan philosophers were aware of the Christian God and honored him. Christian writers portrayed Plato as having come very close to the truth, even intuiting the Trinity. Indeed, as we have seen, in a text Ibn al-Faḍl translated, John of Thessaloniki's *Encomium to Saint Demetrios,* the pagan (*hellēn, ḥanīf*)—who, as he makes sure to tell the saint, is a "Socratic," not "Epicurean," pagan—says that Demetrios's Nicene account of the Trinity is very similar to what he, the pagan, believes.[36]

In spite of any benefit Ibn al-Faḍl's translation may confer upon others, the translator insists that he must nevertheless invoke God and beg for mercy. This requirement is unending, both while he is still alive in this world of annihilation (*fanāʾ*) and when he passes on to the afterlife, the world of permanence (*baqāʾ*).[37]

3 DEMETRIOS

We may now turn to Ibn al-Faḍl's preface to a rather different sort of text: the hagiographical *Encomium to Saint Demetrios* by John of Thessaloniki, just mentioned. As we have seen, this text depicts Demetrios as a teacher, and most of it is devoted to describing the saint's successful refutation of a series of misguided doctrines.

This educational mission, though present in the form of references to proofs and demonstration, remains in the background of Ibn al-Faḍl's preface. Instead, his emphasis is on a series of dichotomies: truth and falsehood, light and darkness, spiritual and material. He expresses them using metaphors of clothing.

35. Podskalsky, *Theologie und Philosophie,* 34–48.

36. See ch. 2, §5, p. 76.

37. Van Esbroeck ("Les sentences," 16) interpreted this passage as an indication that Ibn al-Faḍl wrote this at the end of his life: "ne nous prive pas d'une bonne pensée car nous sommes aux portes de la mort et comblés d'années." This shaped how he translated the remainder of the preface: "Si nous faisons quelque profit pour ce qui reste en touchant le meilleur et en retournant aux vertus, alors Dieu aimera ceux qui se rendent bons et il tiendra compte de nous qui sommes baptisés en lui." While *iʿtimād* can mean "baptism" (Hava, *Farāʾid,* 491) and so *muʿtam(a/i)d* can theoretically mean "baptized" and "baptizer," respectively, the context renders this reading implausible.

I present here most of the preface, followed by a brief summary of the rest. Ibn al-Faḍl writes:[38]

(١) قال عبد الله بن الفضل[١]: لم أباشر يا قديس الله الكامل، ويا شاهده الباسل الفاضل، ترجمة خَبَرِكَ النافع ذي الضياء الساطع[٢]، والمُعجز الذائع، عَبَثاً، ولا أقدمت عليه مُجازَفَةً، بل بقياس لا غَلَطَ يَشُوْبُه، ولا خَلَلَ يُمَازِجُه، لكن قد تَجَلْبَبَ بِجِلبابِ الصواب، وعَرِيَ من حُلّة المَيْنِ والمعاب.

(٢) وذلك أنني قلت كما أن الرؤساء العالميين، والأكابر الأرضيين، يجودون على الوافد عليهم والمقرِّظ لهم، بما يصلون إليه من خِلَعٍ هيولانيةٍ يمضي فيها حُكم العناد، وجوائز تنقاد بِزمام الكون والفساد، هكذا ذوو الأقدار في عالم العقل يَمْنَحُون قُصّادَهم مِنَحاً عقلية، ويخوِّلونهم نعماً روحانية، لا يتخطّى[٣] إلى ديارها حُؤول، ولا يُلِمُّ بِمِصْبَاحِها خُمُودٌ وَدُثُور؛ الذين أنت يا ذمتريوس الخطير، والقديس المنير، من أجلّائهم وكبرائهم، وممّن قد فاز بلطيف المكان، بحسن فَتْكِهِ في قبائل الطغيان، وحصل له صورة الموضع الكريم عند البارئ ذي الجلال والتعظيم.

(٣) وإذا كان ذلك كذلك بالدليل الواضح، والبرهان اللائح، فتفضّل على نفسي البائسة الخاطئة، الجانحة عن الرَّشاد، المنصبّة إلى الغَيّ والفَساد، بما أنت أهله من إنارة جوهرها الذي قد كساه سربال الظلام، تواصلَ[٤] الذنوب والآثام بنورك المستمدّ من الخير الذي لا ضِدَّ له لِاعْتِلائِهِ عن الكيفيات، وإشفاءَ سَقَمِها بِطِبِّكَ الروحاني، وإزالةَ مرضها بِعِلاجِكَ الرَّبَّاني، وَدَفْعَ موبق العوارض عنها بِقُوَّتِكَ التي هي أقوى منها.

(٤) ولا تلتفت إلى استحقاقي، فلقد كان العدم أولى بي من الوجود، بل إلى جود الذي أنت عبده ومتشبّه به ومكين عنده، الذي ما قَنِعَ بالإيجاد، وإجراء بِحار خيراته على العباد، حتى أضاف إليه ما هو أعلى منه قدراً، وأجلّ محلّاً، بأن لبس حلّة عبدٍ لباساً ما خلعه ولا يخلعه آباد الدهور، وإنالة صفاتِهِ، وتخصّص هو بخواصّه من غير غيار[٥] دنا من طبيعته جلّ جلالها، وَقَايَضَ شريفاً بوضيع، واستبدل كثيفاً من لطيفٍ رفيع، فقيل له إنسان، وقيل للإنسان إلاه، إفراطاً في الكرم والتحنّن، وإغراقاً[٦] في التفضّل وإسداءِ المِنَن.

(٥) وتوسّل فيّ بأني إلى من إذا ما[٧] سألته، فكأنك قد أرفدته، وإذا ما استعطفته، فكأنك قد حَبَوْتَهُ تبرك اسمه وعلا جدّه، عساني أن أقدر على نَقْلِ خَبَرِكَ وأعاجيبك، ونشر محاسنك من اللغة اليونانية إلى اللغة العربية من غير غلطٍ يستمرّ ولا سهوٍ يبرّ، إذ كان الطاهر لا يجوز أن يَقْرَبَهُ إلّا طاهر، ومن ركب مركب الغرر والتجاهل أَوْشَكَ أن يُصْلى بنار العَطَبِ المتواصل. ولتكن هذه محسوبة في جملة جرائحك الباسرة، ومعدودة في آياتك المذسلة الطاسرة.

[١]قال عبد الله بن الفضل: 'قال عبد الله بن الفضل': أ؛ —ب [٢]الساطع: أ؛ الصاطع: ب [٣]يتخطّى: صححته؛ يتخطّا: أ ب [٤]تواصلَ: تواصل: ب؛ وتواصل: أ [٥]غيار: ب؛ عيار: أ [٦]وإغراقاً: وإعراقاً: أ ب [٧]إذا ما: ب؛ إذا: أ

[1] *ʿAbdallāh ibn al-Faḍl said:* O perfect saint of God, O fearless, excellent martyr (*shāhid*), I did not undertake to translate this narrative about you, with its shining illumination and famous miracle, on a whim; nor did I approach it recklessly but rather with reasoning (*qiyās*) that no mistake adulterates and no defect contaminates; on the contrary, it has been clothed with the garment of correctness and stripped of the garb of falsehood and imperfection.

[2] Namely, I said that just as worldly chiefs and earthly notables are generous toward the traveler who arrives before them and lavishes praise on them, giving him material robes upon which is passed the judgement of rebellion, and gifts that are led on by the bridle of generation and corruption (*al-kawn wa-l-fasād*); so too do those of rank in the world of the mind bestow upon their followers gifts of the mind and confer upon them spiritual favors whose abodes the years do not overtake and to whose lamp snuffing-out and oblivion do not pay a visit. Of them, O Demetrios, eminent and luminous saint, you are among the sublimest and greatest, and among

38. The full preface is contained in **A** = Sinai ar. 350, fols. 237^{v}_{8}–241^{r}_{11}; and **B** = Sinai ar. 352, fols. 98^{r}_{8}–99^{v}_{11}. The portion printed here is at **A** 237^{v}–239^{v}; **B** 98^{r}_{8}–99^{r}.

those who have won the finest rank by how well they have persevered amidst the tribes of impiety, and for whom has taken shape the place of honor in the presence of the Creator, to whom belongs sublimity and exaltation.

[3] And if that is so, by clear proof and manifest[39] demonstration, then grant to my miserable, sinful soul, deviant as it is from right guidance and flowing down towards error and corruption, by illuminating its substance clothed with the garment of darkness in that way familiar to you—grant it the joining of its sins and transgressions to your light that derives from the Good that has no contrary because it transcends the qualities; the healing of its disease with your spiritual medicine; the elimination of its sickness by your lordly treatment; and the casting away from it of the doom of accidentals (*ʿawāriḍ*).

[4] And do not pay attention to my merit, for I am more worthy of non-existence than of existence, but to the generosity of the one whose slave you are, whom you resemble, and in whose presence you are firmly established; who was not content to grant existence and to shower oceans of good things upon his slaves (*ʿibād*), to the point that he added to it something beneath his power and rank by donning the garment of a slave such that he has not nor will ever doff it for all eternity, and obtaining [the slave's] attributes. He took on [the slave's] traits without an exchange that comes close to his nature—sublime is its sublimity—and traded the noble for the humble and exchanged the lofty and subtle for the dense. And so he was called a human being, and the human being was called a god, in an excess of honor and compassion and superfluity of bestowing and granting favors.

[5] And on my behalf, please ask him who, whenever you ask him, it is as if you have granted it, and whenever you implore him, it is as if you have bestowed it, blessed be his name and exalted be his greatness, that I might be able to translate (*naql*) this narrative about you and your miracles, and disseminate (*nashr*) your beautiful deeds (*maḥāsin*), from Greek into Arabic with no mistake that endures nor lapse that persists (?). For the one who is pure cannot be approached except by one who is pure,[40] and he who rides the ship of heedlessness and ignorance is on the point of being roasted by the fire of continuous perdition. Let this be reckoned among your dazzling miracles (?)[41] and counted among your amazing pure signs.

In what remains of the preface, Ibn al-Faḍl asks Demetrios, martyr of Christ "son of God the pre-eternal (*azalī*) described as the one hypostasis (*qanūm*), two natures, two activities (*fiʿlayn*), and two wills," for help. Then he mentions who asked him to produce this translation: "my lord the wise and learned sheikh Abū

39. *lāʾiḥ*, "appearing" (like a star) or "flashing" (like lightning): Hava, *Farāʾid*, 700. One thinks of the first line of Ṭarafa's *muʿallaqa*.

40. Cf. the similar quotation from Gregory of Nazianzos in Ibn al-Faḍl's preface to the Psalms, ¶3 (see §1, pp. 124–26, above).

41. The translation "miracles" is entirely from the context (to pair well with *āyāt*, "signs"). Accordingly, we might emend *jarāʾiḥika* to the not so different-looking *muʿjizātika* (miracles).

l-Fatḥ ʿĪsā ibn Idrīs/Darīs," whom he praises for his deeds and his learning.[42] He closes by invoking Saint Demetrios, Christ, "our lady his mother"—whom he praises at some length—and all other saints.

Rational thought is given great prominence in this preface. Ibn al-Faḍl explains that his decision to translate the text was the result of careful consideration and in particular logical inference (*qiyās*). This reasoning, he says, is "clothed" in correctness and "stripped" of falsehood. It consists of an analogy between the gifts (especially robes) that those who rule over the material world bestow upon those who praise them and, on the other hand, the "gifts of the mind" and "spiritual favors" provided by "those of rank in the world of the mind" to their admirers. Demetrios is among the most honored in the "world of the mind," for God gives him a place of honor as a saint and martyr. Rationality is not contrasted to faith here. On the contrary, Ibn al-Faḍl presents rationality and piety as necessarily in concord: piety is a rational—*the* rational—disposition to cultivate in oneself.

Next he asks for the saint's help, stressing his own unworthiness, in achieving salvation. Ibn al-Faḍl's soul is clothed in a "garment of darkness" (*sirbāl al-ẓalām*); he asks the saint to illuminate it with a light that derives ultimately from "the Good," that is, from God. This recalls Plato's famous analogy between the Good and the sun:[43] Demetrios is something like the moon, illuminating by reflecting the source of all light. This is a standard Christian use of the Neoplatonic notion of ontological lightness and darkness. At the same time, Demetrios is depicted as a physician who is to heal Ibn al-Faḍl's soul with "spiritual medicine." Similarly, Ibn al-Faḍl's description of God as "the Good that has no contrary because it transcends the qualities" refers to a doctrine current in Arabic Peripatetic, Neoplatonic philosophy. This same position is expressed and justified in similar terms by al-Fārābī and Avicenna.[44]

It is appropriate in this context that Ibn al-Faḍl emphasizes a particular aspect of God's goodness: that he deigned to dress himself in matter, "the garment of a slave," doing so for all eternity. The material aspect of this act is stressed: God took "the dense" (*kathīf*), a material body, in exchange for "the subtle" or "fine" (*laṭīf*), that is, that which is not dense: an existence outside of matter. "Subtle" here is the opposite of "dense"; it refers to something immaterial or almost immaterial, like vapor or, as we have seen, an angel's body.[45] This standard Aristotelian and Neoplatonic opposition occurs frequently in Ibn al-Faḍl's prefaces and commentary,

42. *wa-huwa mawlāy al-shaykh al-fāḍil al-sadīd Abū* [**B** : *Abī* **A**] *l-Fatḥ ʿĪsā ibn Idrīs* [**B** : *ibn Darīs* **A**], *adāma llāhu tamkīnahu.*

43. See ch. 2, p. 44, n. 45; and cf. p. 75.

44. Fārābī, *Virtuous City,* 1.1.3, ed. and trans. Walzer, *Al-Farabi on the Perfect State,* 62–65; Ibn Sīnā, *Shifāʾ*, Metaphysics (Ilāhīyāt) 8.5.13–14, ed. and trans. Marmura, *The Metaphysics of the Healing,* 282–83. I am grateful to an anonymous reviewer for clarification and for these references.

45. Peers, *Subtle Bodies.* See above, ch. 2, p. 78, and below, ch. 7, §3, pp. 210–14.

always with the same preference (shared with Neoplatonists) for the immaterial or almost immaterial.

Ibn al-Faḍl's appeal for Demetrios's intercession with God stakes out one motivation for translating the text. He asks to be able to translate this text about Demetrios and his miracles (that is, to judge from the contents of the encomium, Demetrios's teaching, which miraculously convinced multitudes of the truth of his Christian doctrines) and to disseminate it. In other words, he wishes for the saint's wondrous teachings and deeds to be known. This literary project of honoring the saints is of course what hagiographical literature is all about.

In the final portion of the text, which I have summarized above, Ibn al-Faḍl reports his other motivation: a patron, Abū l-Fatḥ ʿĪsā ibn Idrīs/Darīs. His emphasis on this patron's learning suggests that he imagines a learned audience for this translation.

4 ISAAC THE SYRIAN

In the case of Ibn al-Faḍl's preface to the homilies of Isaac the Syrian, there are at least two extant recensions: a longer recension (which I will call "version 1") and a shorter recension ("version 2").[46] It is not clear to me which of the two was written first.

In both versions, the preface begins by speaking of precious perfume that transfers its fine fragrance to the one that takes hold of it. The "vessels of valuable perfume" of version 1 have become "vessels of valuable, robust (*jasīm*) perfume" in version 2. The new word makes the prose rhyme better: instead of *thamīn* with *karīm*, the rhyme is *jasīm* with *karīm*. Version 1's "heavy, fine (*laṭīf*) fragrance" has become version 2's "heavy, lofty (*munīf*) fragrance"; perhaps in revising the preface Ibn al-Faḍl decided that it seemed incongruous to describe something as both heavy and subtle (*laṭīf*; i.e., not dense).

The preface then continues to compare this perfume to Isaac's words: if perfume can transfer its fragrance to someone who touches it, then it is fitting for Ibn al-Faḍl to experience Isaac's words, to contemplate them, and to translate his ideas (*maʿānī*). One change here makes a clause about Isaac's "divine words" (*aqwālika l-ilāhīya*) in version 2 rhyme with the previous clause (*bāhira* with *ẓāhira*), rather than the subsequent clause (*ilāhīya* with *rabbānīya*) as it had in version 1; this improves the overall effect because the previous clause did not participate in the rhyming in version 1, while the subsequent clause was already followed by another that rhymed with it.

46. Version 1: **A** = Sinai ar. 350. (Version 1 is also in Sinai ar. 351; cited by Treiger, "Christian Graeco-Arabica," 208 n. 87. I have not used it to establish the text cited below.) Version 2: **Ṭ** = Vat. Sbath 646; **V** = Vat. Sbath 649.

Next, Ibn al-Faḍl addresses Isaac directly. In version 1, he calls Isaac "our holy father"; version 2 adds "Isaac." Version 1 calls him "the precious, lofty divine man"; version 2 changes this to "the precious divine-minded man."[47] He continues: "O you who cast off the tattered (*sakhīf*) garment of matter and are propped up by the support of the subtle, teaching spirit [version 1]/refined, consoling spirit [version 2]."

This praise for Isaac as a saint is striking when we recall that Isaac was a Nestorian, Ibn al-Faḍl a Chalcedonian. In the eleventh century (and earlier) Byzantine Chalcedonians may have felt they had more in common and less to dispute with Nestorians than with Miaphysites and Monotheletes, both because of shared doctrines (two natures in Christ) and because while Miaphysite churchmen inhabited the Byzantine Empire and sometimes competed with Chalcedonian bishops (for example, at Melitene), there were fewer Nestorians in the empire. On the other hand, Chalcedonians certainly considered Nestorians heretical, so it seems most likely that Ibn al-Faḍl's praise simply reflects the success of the earlier Greek translators' efforts to eliminate hints of Isaac's doctrinal affiliation.[48]

The minor differences between the versions continue as Ibn al-Faḍl proceeds with his address to the saint, saying that Isaac moves us from material to spiritual, temporary to eternal, earthly to heavenly. Ibn al-Faḍl refers to God as "existence per se" (perhaps read "the one who exists per se").[49] He describes Isaac as having an ardent love for "the first Good" (*al-khayr al-awwal*) and "the most honored and noble Beloved (*ma'shūq*)": God. Isaac is especially learned "in the divine philosophy" (*fī l-falsafati l-ilāhīya*). This "philosophy" is of course Isaac's ascetic thought, but we should not dismiss it as a "code word" or cipher for dogma or orthodoxy.[50] Indeed, the phrase "divine philosophy" recalls Aristotle's own terms for what we call his *Metaphysics:* "theology" and "first philosophy," and what Arabic Peripatetics like Avicenna called "divine matters" (*ilāhīyāt*).[51]

From this point on, the two versions diverge much more. Isaac "drank from the springs [version 1: *ma'īn;* version 2: *yanābī'/yanbū'*] of life." Version 1 had made the reference explicit, continuing: "the god who became man, our Lord Jesus Christ, son of God, the living," and so on; version 2 omitted this. Likewise, they have two different ways of bringing the praise for Isaac to a close.

The major difference is what follows: how Ibn al-Faḍl describes the patron or patrons of his work.[52] Version 2 mentions only one patron, Abū Naṣr Nikephoros. Version 1 calls Abū Naṣr Nikephoros a *kouboukleisios,* mentions his patronymic

47. *wa-l-muta'alliha l-'āliya* [v2: *l-'aqla*] *l-nafīs.*

48. See *ODB*, s.v. "Isaac of Nineveh."

49. *al-wujūd bi-dhātih* **A** : *'illat al-wujūd bi-dhātih,* "cause of existence-per-se," **ṬV.** The expected epithet would be *al-mawjūd bi-dhātih.*

50. See pp. 135–36 and n. 35 above.

51. See ch. 6, p. 181, n. 1.

52. On whom see Treiger, "Christian Graeco-Arabica," 208 n. 87.

(Ibn Buṭrus), and includes much more extensive praise of him. This passage in version 2 reads:

> For my lord (*sayyidī*) the learned Nīkīfūr Abū Naṣr the wise, the famous, asked me to translate your noble book and incited me to do it with his ardent request.

In version 1, the same point is made at much greater length:

> For my lord the learned saint (*al-fāḍil al-qiddīs*)[53] and precious spiritual benefactor (*mun ʿim*), beautiful in his virtues, noble in his splendors (*khalā ʾil*) and his ways of thought (*madhāhib*), pure in love (*al-ṣāfī al-mawadda*), true in friendship (*al-ṣādiq al-khulla*) . . . Abū Naṣr Nīkīfūr the *kouboukleisios* Ibn Buṭrus, may God continue to give him strength, asked me to do it and incited me to it.

This longer version is mainly longer because of additional praise for this patron with a Greek name and title, the *kouboukleisios* Nikephoros, son of Peter.

In both versions, the preface continues with Ibn al-Faḍl asking Isaac to help him as he begins to translate, acknowledging his own unworthiness. In version 2 he then asks for Isaac to beseech God on his behalf and on behalf of all humankind. In version 1, he inserts between himself and humankind mention of Nikephoros and his two brothers:

> the wise aforementioned one [Nikephoros], along with my two noble lords (*sayyidayya*) his brothers (*ṣinwayhi*) Abū l-Ḥasan Simʿān and Abū l-Khayr Mīkhāʾīl, may God continue to give them strength, these suns in appearance (*shumūs sīmā ʾan*), torrents in honor, preeminent (*muṣaddarayn*) in understanding, lofty in their religion, set apart (*mufradayn*) in seclusion (*taṣawwunan*).

The assertion that they are suns "in appearance" or "by sign" (*al-shumūs sīmā ʾan*) may indicate that they are bishops. In an Arabophone Byzantine Christian context, "sun" (*shams*, plural *shumūs*) can refer to the medallion (ἐγκόλπιον) worn by a bishop upon his breast.[54] Alternatively, perhaps they are deacons, as Treiger has suggested, if *shumūs* is meant to recall *shammūsīya*, "diaconate."[55] Finally, their "seclusion" could lead us to believe they were monks. Since none of this is said explicitly, it is possible that they were simply laymen.

The preface then closes by asking for God's help (each version in a different way) in the task of translating Isaac.

The primary metaphor in this preface is fragrance: the fine scent of Isaac's "divine words." The metaphor of clothing also appears here, as part of the claim that Isaac's discourses move us from the material to the spiritual. Isaac has discarded the garment

53. Perhaps read *al-qissīs*, "priest."

54. Graf, *Verzeichnis*, 68.

55. Graf, *Verzeichnis*, 67; Treiger, "Christian Graeco-Arabica," 208, who also mentions that Symeon and Michael are Nikephoros's brothers.

that is matter, the material body and all the distracting desires, needs, and other helpless reactions to stimuli that come with it. This garment is *sakhīf*, which, applied to clothing, means "tattered." Matter, then, is, on the one hand, dense (*kathīf*)—as he suggested in his preface to the *Encomium to Saint Demetrios* (see the previous section) and also a couple lines later in his preface to Isaac—as opposed to "subtle" or "fine" (*laṭīf*), a term that Ibn al-Faḍl also uses in the next clause of the preface to Isaac. On the other hand, it is porous, tattered (*sakhīf*), connoting its decay.[56]

As for how the two versions of the preface relate to each other, a reading of the two does not make it clear to me which was written first. When it comes to the opening of the preface, version 2 often seems like a revision of version 1, with improvements to the rhymes of the rhymed prose and other small details. On the other hand, Ibn al-Faḍl's praise for his patron is more effusive and mentions his ecclesiastical title of *kouboukleisios* in version 1, which also mentions two further individuals who may also be patrons or otherwise supporters of Ibn al-Faḍl's project. These would seem to be later additions—for example, because Nikephoros had in the interim been appointed to the office of *kouboukleisios*. An alternative hypothesis is that version 1 is what Ibn al-Faḍl wrote, and version 2 was the result of a later copyist's revisions and abridgments.[57] Ibn al-Faḍl himself might well have been the one to revise and abridge it, perhaps because he was presenting a copy at some later point to someone other than his patron.

In both versions, this preface suggests a similar set of aims. The request of a patron—in this case a powerful officeholder at the patriarchate of Antioch, the *kouboukleisios* Nikephoros—prompted the project. Another major purpose can be inferred from his praise for Isaac as a divine philosopher, whose words are to be made available in clear, appealing Arabic so that learned readers of Arabic may profit from them. The experiential path to knowledge of God prescribed by Isaac needed to be taught from an appropriately powerful translation. Ibn al-Faḍl supplied one.

5 CHRYSOSTOM AND PAUL

A similar set of motivations can be inferred from reading Ibn al-Faḍl's preface to his epistolary (with Chrysostom's commentary on the Pauline Epistle for each day), sometimes appearing in manuscripts as the preface to Ibn al-Faḍl's translation of Chrysostom's homilies on Paul's letter to the Hebrews.[58]

56. A similar play on the terms *laṭīf* and *sakhīf* when applied to *hayūlā* appears in the brief *rajaz*-poem on matter and the soul by the tenth-century Sabian secretary Abū Isḥāq Ibrāhīm al-Ṣābī: Roberts, "Being a Sabian," 258–59.

57. As a parallel, see the extremely abridged version of this same preface in **J** = Jerusalem, Holy Sepulcher, ar. 24 (1567 CE), fols. 144^{v}–145^{r}.

58. For this preface I consulted Paris ar. 96; Lebanon, Dayr al-Ḥarf 7 (1704 CE); and Sinai ar. 156.

The preface, at least in its present form, begins by noting that this book contains the Pauline Epistles that are read out during the liturgical year. This occasions much praise for Saint Paul himself. Paul is "the perfect apostle" (*al-salīḥ al-kāmil*). (Here Ibn al-Faḍl opts for a Syriac loanword for apostle, *salīḥ* from *šlîḥā*, rather than *rasūl*, the word he used in the preface to the Psalms—and which the Qur'an also uses—in speaking of God's messengers or apostles, *rusul*.) Paul's words guide one to righteousness and correct those who are in error (*al-ḍāllīn*) using "clear demonstrations and proofs" (*bi-wāḍiḥi l-maqāyīsi wa-l-barāhīn*), illuminating them with the light of truth (*bi-ḍiyāʾi l-ḥaqq*).

Paul, Ibn al-Faḍl goes on, has shown the folly of depending upon the wisdom of this world (*al-ḥikma al-ʿālamīya*). His letters "command and forbid" (*āmira zājira*). This expression recalls the similar "commander or forbidder" (*āmiran aw zājiran*) in his preface to the *Garden*.[59] Paul's teachings benefit the soul and relieve one of worries and cares.

Now Ibn al-Faḍl turns to Paul's interpreter: Saint John Chrysostom. Chrysostom, he says, brought forth the letters' true meaning, thus offering the rest of us "prosperity and success" (of course of the spiritual sort), opening doors to allow those with "penetrating minds" (*al-albāb al-thāqiba*, a favorite phrase of Ibn al-Faḍl's) to enter. Those best suited to absorb the benefits that come from reading Paul's exegete "do not pay attention to the material things but rather love the spiritual things." They "only acquire the lightest and subtlest of worldly bonds (*khiṭām al-dunyā*)." (Here again we encounter something subtle, as opposed to dense.) Instead, they have opted for a treasure whose quantity (*kammīya*) does not fall short, whose quality (*kayfīya*) does not change, whose substance (*jawhar*) is unmoving and unchanging—namely, the resurrection, which cures maladies that the art of medicine (*al-ṣināʿa al-ṭibbīya*) fails to cure, and which rhetorical inferences (*al-maqāyīs al-minṭīqīya*) fail to comprehend.[60]

These saintly men, Ibn al-Faḍl continues, urged the rest of humanity to believe (*īmān*) in God and avoid error (*ḍalāl*) and wrongdoing (*ṭughyān*). They warned people away from the errors of the pagans (*al-mughālaṭāt al-ḥanīfīya*). Here Ibn al-Faḍl uses the same word for "pagan" (*ḥanīf*) as he uses to translate *hellēn* in John of Thessaloniki's *Encomium to Saint Demetrios*. Their proofs include signs and miracles but also "divine (*ilāhī*) acts and lordly (*rabbānī*) deeds."

Finally, Ibn al-Faḍl asks for help in his task from Christ, whom he describes using part of the same phrase he used in his prefaces to John of Thessaloniki and Isaac the Syrian—"son of God the pre-eternal (*azalī*) described as the one hypostasis (*qanūm*)"—but instead of continuing to describe Christ's two natures, two

59. ¶3; see §2 above, pp. 132 and 133.

60. *Lisān* s.v. *nṭq*: "*wa-l-minṭīq: al-balīgh*." Perhaps to be emended to the more expected *al-maqāyīs al-manṭiqīya*, "logical inferences."

activities, and two wills, he now writes "and the two substances (*jawharayn*),"[61] going on to state that Christ is the same in substance (*jawharan*) as the other two persons of the Trinity, but "different in attribute (*ṣifatan*)." He closes his preface by invoking the Mother of God, John Chrysostom, and the rest of the saints.

6 KAISARIOS AND A LITANY OF PHILOSOPHICAL QUESTIONS

Let us consider one last preface: Ibn al-Faḍl's preface to his translation of pseudo-Kaisarios, *Questions and Answers*. In it, he offers an extraordinary list of philosophical questions that he finds pointless and hopes to replace with this collection of (philosophical) questions compiled by an authoritative figure: Saint Kaisarios, brother of Saint Gregory of Nazianzos.[62] The preface in full reads:[63]

إنني لما رأيت جماعة من المسيحيين الآن قد توفروا على تفهّم مصنفات البرّانيين الضالين[١]، وأفنوا الزمان في المناظرات في معناها، وجعلوا دأبهم[٢] التسائل[٣] منها، فهم يتفاوضون تارةً من الأدب، وتارةً من غيره من العلوم، حتى ترى النهشل[٤] منهم فضلاً عن الغُرانِق[٥] يسـ<ـأ>ل غيره طالباً بِعَنَتِه[٦] وخاطباً الفتك به، فيقول: (١) ما الفرق بين الأعضب والأصلم، (٢) وما هو العدد المسمى جماعاً والعدد الدوري والعدد المعروف بأثينا[٧]، (٣) وأيما هي الكيفيات الأولى، وأيما هي الثواني، (٤) وما الفرق بين الهيولى والموضوع، (٥) وكم هي علل الحركة المكانية، (٦) ولم كانت المبادئ أربعة، (٧) وما السبب الداعي إلى أن كان البردي ذا زبيرة(؟) وَحَبُّ السَّفَرْجَل ذا لُزُوْجَة، (٨) ولم إذا أخذ فرع من شجرة وغرس أجدب، (٩) وما هو الخط المستقيم، (١٠) وكم هي أصناف الخطوط، (١١) وما هو الجَيْب[٨] ولم كانت الزوايا ثلثاً، (١٢) وكيف يُستخرج الجذر والكعب، (١٣) ولم كان الجوهر جنسـ<ـاً> واحد<اً> والأعراض تسعة، (١٤) ولم كانت الفصول على ثلثة أقسام، (١٥) وأيما[٩] هي المقدمات البرهانية، (١٦) ولم لم يقترن السور بالمحمول، (١٧) وكم لوازم البرهان، (١٨) وكم أصناف الذاتي، (١٩) ولم كانت أشكال القياس ثلثة، (٢٠) ولم تَبِعَت النتيجة أخسَّ المقدّمات، وما شاكل هذه السؤالات، وهي كثيرة جدّاً، وإنّما أوردنا منها ما أوردنا على سبيل المثال.

وتجري بينهم الخصائم، وتشتعل فيهم نار الموجدة والإعجاب، فلا يتفـ<ـا>وض[١٠] مجلسهم إلّا عمّا لا يستحسنه ذوو[١١] الألباب الصافية والخلال العالية، غير ناظرين[١٢] إلى ما يداوون به عقولهم المريضة، ولا مكترثين بما يجلو إصداء[١٣] ألبابهم المظلمة، ويعيدها إلى مضارعة التشبه الكريم والـ<ـتـ>ـسامي (؟) العظيم، ويلمع لها الفوز والسعادة والنجاح والغبطة، أعني بأنْ يتطلّعوا في الكتب الإلهيّة، والمصنّفات الروحانية، وما نطق[١٤] به الآباء القدّيسون والرجال المتألّهون، ويستنيروا بضيائِها[١٥] ويُجروا أمورَهم بين أوامرها وزواجرها، بل متعكفين على ما تقدمنا بذكره ممّا لا يعود بطائل يعوّل عليه، ولا يثمر ثمراً يلتفت إليه، ولا يزيل عن العقل الآفة[١٦]، ولا يحثّهُ على العبادة لله تعالى، والزهد في العالم، وإن كانت العلوم لا تخلو[١٧] من فائدة، غير زاكنين أنّ هذه المفاوضات تحسن بالنافع إلى حدٍّ ما مع ملازمة البيعة المقدّسة، والعمل بمفترض الشريعة الإلهية الضَّوِيئة[١٨] وبالجملة كما رسم القديس باسيليوس، وكما تسير الآباء المتألّهون، لا أن يفنى الزمان فيها، وهذا شيء لا يدفعهُ عاقل بل غاوٍ[١٩] بالخرف جاهل.

ووقع لي[٢٠] كتاب نفيس يوناني يتضمن سؤالات عدّة[٢١] روحانية نافعة للنفس عدّتها مائة سؤال[٢٢] سألها قسطنتيوس[٢٣] وثاوخاريسطس وأندراوس واغريغوريوس[٢٤] ودمنس[٢٥] وإيسيدرس ولاونتيوس[٢٦] صاحب الديوان، للقديس الجليل كاساريوس أخي أبينا المعظم في القديسين اغريغوريوس[٢٧] المتكلم في اللاهوت حين كان يعلّم في القسطنطينية[٢٨] وذلك أنه أقام يفيد العلم بها مُدّة عشرين سنة. وجدلت غاية الجدل بذلك، ولم[٢٩] أتمالك دون أن شرعت في ترجمته إلى اللغة العربية لأسباب ثلثة: الأوّل منها أنه صادر عن هذا الرجُل المتألّه، والثاني أنّه

61. Perhaps he means that Christ belongs at once to two (universal) substances (i.e., genera), God and human being.

62. Riedinger called attention to this remarkable preface in his study of the Greek manuscript tradition of the *Questions and Answers* and offered a brief summary of it, along with a German translation of part of it (¶3 in my text presented below). See Riedinger, *Pseudo-Kaisarios*, 63–64.

63. **Q** = Cairo COP Theol. 112 (1622–1623 CE), pp. 89–92; **Ṭ** = Vat. Sbath 45 (1662–1663 CE), fols. 1ᵛ–3ʳ.

في أمور نافعة للنفس، والثالث ليشتغل به خِراف السيد[٣٠] المسيح تعالى عن الولع بما لا يجدي كثير نفع[٣١] بل ربّما آلَ إلى غاية الضَّرَر.

فأنا أسأل السيد المسيح جلّ وعزّ، وإن كنتُ غرير المآثم، وافر الجرائم، أن يمدّ لي[٣٢] بمعونته، وينير عَيْنَيْ قلبي المظلمتين بالذنوب، ويؤهِّلَني لهذا الأمر الجليل الشريف النبيل، ويـ{ـو}قيني الزلل في القول والعمل برحمته، إنّه وليّ ذلك والقادر عليه.

ويجب أن تعلم أننا قد نقلنا من هذا الكتاب ما أمكن إذ[٣٣] كان الخَلَل قد أُلِمَ به والعَوَز[٣٤].

[١]الضالين: ق؛ الضاليين: ط [٢]دأبهم: ق؛ اذا بهم: ط [٣]التسائل: أي: التساؤل [٤]النهشل: في ط شرح: الشيخ [٥]الغُرانِق: في ط شرح: الشاب [٦]بِعَنَتِه: ط؛ إعناته: ق [٧]بأثينا: ق؛ باثينا: ط [٨]الجَيِّب: ق؛ الحبيب: ط [٩]وأيما: ط؛ دايماً: ق [١٠]يتفـ<ـا>وض: في «ط» و«ق»: يتفوض [١١]ذوو: ق؛ ذو: ط [١٢]غير ناظرين: ق؛ غيرنا ضـ'ـا'رين: ط [١٣]إصداء: أو: أصداء [١٤]نطق: ق؛ نطقوا: ط [١٥]بضيائِها: بضياوها: ط ق [١٦]الآفة: ق؛ الامهُ (أي، الأُمّة): ط [١٧]تخلو: ط؛ تخلوا: ق [١٨]الضَّوِيئة: الضوية: ط ق [١٩]غاوٍ: ق؛ —ط [٢٠]لي: ق؛ في: ط [٢١]عدّة: ط؛ —ق [٢٢]عدّتها مائة سؤال: ق؛ —ط [٢٣]قسطنتيوس: ط؛ قسطنطينوس: ق [٢٤]واغريغوريوس: ق؛ و[[ا]]غريغوريوس: ط [٢٥]ودمنس: ط؛ ودومنس: ق [٢٦]ولاونتيوس: ق؛ ولانتيوس: ط [٢٧]اغريغوريوس: ق؛ [[ا]]غريغوريوس: ط [٢٨]في القسطنطينية: ط؛ بالقسطنطينية: ق [٢٩]ولم: ق؛ لم: ط [٣٠]السيد: ق؛ —ط [٣١]كثير نفع: ط؛ كبير نفع: ق؛ وفي «ط» قد صحّحه يد آخر بإضافة تنوينين: كثيراً نفعٌ (كذا) [٣٢]يمدّ لي: ط؛ يمدّني: ق [٣٣]إذ: ق؛ اذ[[ا]]: ط [٣٤]والعَوَز: والعَوز: ق؛ والعوُز: ط

I have seen a group of Christians today who have devoted themselves to understanding the works of erring outsiders [*barrānīyīn;* i.e., non-Christians]. These people have wasted time in debates about what they mean and have made a habit of interrogating such texts. Sometimes they start to go on about literature (*adab*), sometimes about another of the sciences, to the point that you see the old man (*nahshal*) among them—to say nothing of the young (*ghurāniq*)[64]—quizzing someone, seeking to give him grief, and talking him to death, saying: [1] What is the difference between the slit (*aʿḍab*) and the severed (*aṣlam*)?[65] [2] What is the number called an "aggregate" (*jammāʿ*) and the "circular number" and the number known as Athena (*āthīnā*)?[66] [3] Which are the primary qualities, and which the secondary? [4] What is the difference between prime matter (*hayūlā*) and substrate (*mawḍūʿ*)? [5] How many are the causes of locational motion? [6] Why are the principles (*mabādiʾ* ~ ἀρχαί) four?

64. This word connotes "young men": *Lisān* s.v. *gh-r-n-q*. Cf. Plato, *Republic* 7, 539a–d: the young bicker heatedly about all sorts of topics but are fickle when it actually comes to making any intellectual commitments; older men are not supposed to be so inconstant and impetuous.

65. *Aʿḍab* may refer to a domesticated animal whose ear has been slit. *Aṣlam* may refer to one whose ear or nose has been severed. On another level, they are both terms from Arabic prosody: *Lisān* s.vv. *ʿḍb, ṣlm*.

66. The "circular number" (*al-ʿadad al-dawrī*) is how Thābit ibn Qurra's translation of Nikomachos of Gerasa's Ἀριθμητικὴ Εἰσαγωγή renders the term ἀποκαταστατικοὶ ἀριθμοί, "recurrent numbers" (*Glossarium*, Nicom.Arithm. 1434), which are (natural) numbers whose final digit is the same raised to any (natural-number) power (e.g., 5, whose powers $5^2 = 25$, $5^3 = 125$, etc., all end in 5): LSJ s.v. ἀποκαταστατικός I. (I am grateful to Asad Ahmed for a suggestion that led me to this result.) Nikomachos notes that they are also called "spherical" numbers: ed. Hoche, 111_{7-8}; Thābit's translation, ed. Kutsch, 87.

The "number known as *āthīnā*" probably refers to the number 7, called "Athena" by Pythagoreans. Theon of Smyrna (early second century), in his book *Mathematics Useful for Reading Plato,* explains that the Pythagoreans named 7 "Athena" because if one considers only the numbers from 1 to 10, 7 is the only number that has no mother among the others nor is mother to any of them: ed. Hiller, 103_{1-6}; cited by LSJ s.v. Ἀθήνη 4. Ibn al-Faḍl's transliteration, *ātīnā* (or, with the addition of a single dot, *āthīnā*), even corresponds to the way Theon refers to the goddess, not as Ἀθήνη (pronounced Athīnī) but by her variant name Ἀθηνᾶ (from Ἀθηναία).

[7] What is the cause which leads the date[67] to have *zabīra* (?) and the quince seed to have stickiness (*dhā luzūja*)? [8] When the branch of a tree is taken and planted, why is it barren? [9] What is a straight line? [10] How many kinds of lines are there? [11] What is the sine, and why are the angles three? [12] How does one calculate the root and the cube [of a number]? [13] Why is substance (*jawhar*) a single genus while the accidents are nine? [14] Why are the specific differences (*fuṣūl*) divided into three types?[68] [15] Whatever are the demonstrative premises? [16] Why isn't the quantifier combined with the predicate?[69] [17] How many are the requirements of demonstration? [18] How many are the kinds of the essential (*al-dhātī*)?[70] [19] Why are there three syllogistic figures? [20] Why does the result follow the weaker (*akhass*) of the premises? and questions resembling these, of which there are very many; of them we only listed what we listed for the sake of example.

Quarrels break out between them, and the fire of passion and wonderment is kindled among them, so that when they meet they only confer[71] about subjects which those of pure minds (*al-albāb al-ṣāfiya*) and lofty dispositions do not find suitable, paying no attention to what they might use to treat their diseased minds (*ʿuqūl*), indifferent to what would dispel the echoing of their darkened hearts (*albāb*), return their hearts to the resemblance of noble similitude and the great contest,[72] and would make victory, happiness, success, and beatitude shine for them—by which I mean for them to consider attentively the divine books, the spiritual compositions, and the utterances of the holy fathers and divine men (*mutaʾallihūn*),[73] and to be illuminated by the glow of [these books], and to conduct their affairs between the commandments and chastisements of [these books]. Instead, they cling to the things we just mentioned, which bring no reliable advantage, nor bear any noteworthy fruit, nor remove infirmity[74] from the mind, nor incite it to worship of God Almighty and renunciation (*zuhd*) in the world (*ʿālam*)—even if the sciences are not devoid of usefulness—not thinking that these discussions are beneficial to a point (when combined) with adherence to the holy Church and doing what is enjoined by the luminous divine law (*sharīʿa*), and in general as Saint Basil prescribed and as the divine

67. *Burdī* can refer to a date, *bardī* to papyrus: *Lisān* s.v. *brd.*

68. Cf. Ibn Sīnā, *Najāt,* Logic §14, ed. Dānešpažūh, 16, trans. Ahmed, 12, where Avicenna mentions two kinds of specific difference: "abstracted" (e.g., rationality) and "compound" (e.g., rational).

69. That is, why are quantifiers applied to the subject and not the predicate? (I thank Asad Ahmed for emendation and discussion of this question.) For the term quantifier (*sūr*), see Ibn Sīnā, *Najāt,* Logic §38, ed. Dānešpažūh, 23, trans. Ahmed, 18.

70. Perhaps the reference here is to one of Porphyry's five "universal utterances" (*al-alfāẓ al-kullīya*), so called by Avicenna. In this case, the answer would be three: genus, species, and specific difference, all of which Avicenna describes as "essential" (*dhātī*) in contrast to property and accident: Ibn Sīnā, *Najāt,* Logic §§11–16, ed. Dānešpažūh, 14–17, trans. Ahmed, 10–13.

71. Reading *yatafāwaḍ* for *yatafawwaḍ.*

72. Reading *al-tasāmī* for *al-sāmī/al-shāmī.*

73. The Arabic participle *mutaʾallih,* more explicitly than the Greek adjective θεῖοι, implies a *process* of deification (θέωσις).

74. *Āfa.* Or, following a different manuscript, "forgetfulness" (*amah*): *Lisān* s.v. *ʾmh.*

fathers behaved, not when one wastes time on them. This is something which an intelligent person does not reject, but only someone misguided, ignorant in his feeble-mindedness.

I came across a precious Greek book containing numerous spiritual questions useful to the soul, whose number is one hundred questions,[75] which Constantius,[76] Theocharistos, Andrew, Gregory, Domnos, Isidore, and Leontios the *episekretos*[77] asked the exalted Saint Kaisarios, brother of our Father, great among saints, Gregory the Theologian,[78] when he was teaching in Constantinople, for he lived there offering knowledge for twenty years. And I was extremely joyful[79] and could not refrain myself from embarking on translating it into the Arabic language for three reasons: first, that it comes from this divine man; second, that it is about matters useful to the soul; and third, so that the sheep of the lord Christ Almighty (*al-masīḥ ta ʿālā*) would occupy themselves with it rather than craving that which does not provide much benefit but rather often leads to extreme harm.

I ask the lord Christ the Exalted and Mighty (*jalla wa- ʿazza*),[80] even if I am tempted by sins and abundant in offenses, to grant me his assistance, to illuminate the eyes of my heart, darkened by sins, to make me fit for this exalted, illustrious, and noble task, and to protect me from slipping in speech and in deed by his mercy; he is surely the master of that and the one who is capable of it. You should know that we translated as much of this book as possible, since it suffered from imperfection and defectiveness.

Ibn al-Faḍl here makes at least some of his motives very clear. Christians who engage with "profane" learning ask all kinds of questions deriving from this contact with non-Christian (in the first place, pagan) philosophy.[81] They bother others with such questions, about arithmetic, geometry, trigonometry, grammar, botany, physics, metaphysics, and logic,[82] and debate them endlessly with each

75. **Q**; Riedinger, *Pseudo-Kaisarios,* 63–64. Omitted in **Ṭ**.

76. This reading of the name agrees with the Greek: Κωνσταντίου. The variant reading "Konstantinos" (**Q**; ed. Riedinger, 9) may have resulted from a manuscript's mis-dotting (or a modern scholar's misreading) of the name: "Qusṭantinūs" for Qusṭantiyūs.

77. *ṣāḥib al-dīwān.* In fact, it is Kaisarios who is the *episekretos* according to the title of the Greek text. The error was helped along by the Greek word order, in which Leontios's name appears at the end of a list (in the genitive) followed by Kaisarios's name (in the dative): ". . . Λεοντίου ἐπισηκρήτῳ Καισαρίῳ . . ." All that one would need to do to assign the title of *episekretos* to Leontios would be to read it as a genitive instead of a dative. In fact, this is precisely the reading of codex P = Patmos, Monastery of St. John the Theologian, 161 (ninth/tenth century; see Riedinger, *Pseudo-Kaisarios,* 31): ἐπϊσηκρήτου (ed. Riedinger, 9). This suggests a possible affinity between Ibn al-Faḍl's translation and the manuscript family to which codex P belongs. The title *episekretos* appears to be an invention of the pseudonymous author: Riedinger, *Pseudo-Kaisarios;* cited by Perczel, "Finding a Place," 59.

78. The Arabic omits a further phrase in the Greek: "holy bishop of Nazianzos" (τοῦ ἁγίου ἐπισκόπου Ναvζιανζοῦ [*sic*], ed. Riedinger, 9).

79. Reading *jadhiltu ghāyata l-jadhal* for *jadaltu ghāyata l-jadl.*

80. Reversing the usual Muslim formula *ʿazza wa-jalla.*

81. Riedinger glosses the "erring outsiders" as Muslims.

82. See also Riedinger, *Pseudo-Kaisarios,* 63.

other. Such discussions distract Christians from what would truly improve them as human beings: Scripture, and the writings of the church fathers, who are becoming, or have become, divine (*muta ʾallihūn*). On the other hand, Ibn al-Faḍl does acknowledge that "the sciences are not devoid of usefulness," but they are only "beneficial to a point," and only when combined with obedience to the church and divine law, and self-comportment according to the models provided by holy men.[83] And so when he encountered this book that asks and answers *useful* (rather than pointless) questions, he studied it carefully and translated it into Arabic. He did so because of (1) the text's (pseudonymous) author, (2) its utility for the soul, and (3) to give Christians better questions and answers to which to apply themselves.

The first motive should remind us just how important the authorship of patristic texts was—that is what made them patristic. A work written by a saint could be trusted in a way that other texts could not. The saints taken together sketched out the contours of the universal church; to determine who was or was not a saintly author was to articulate a vision—such as Ibn al-Faḍl's Byzantine Chalcedonian vision—of that universal church.

The second and third motives go together: translating this text allowed Christians to apply their mental energy to something useful that would benefit them. This was part of a long and ongoing debate over the value of the classical tradition in middle Byzantine culture. On the one hand, it was studied and taught; on the other hand, there are signs that some monks and churchmen sought to suppress aspects of non-Christian learning (the trial of John Italos, for instance, is adduced in this connection). But this impulse was nuanced: as Ibn al-Faḍl states clearly, knowledge from the "outside" is not bad per se but rather risks being harmful to those who do not approach it in the proper frame of mind. Such attitudes toward pagan or other non-Christian learning were prevalent and persistent in late antique Christian culture and lived on throughout the Byzantine period; similar attitudes existed among elite Muslims as well. Ibn al-Faḍl translated the *Questions and Answers* attributed to Kaisarios, on dogmatic but also natural philosophical questions, as part of an attempt to encourage the proper approach to knowledge about the world. What seems to have bothered Ibn al-Faḍl about the bickering busybodies who "go on about literature" and "the sciences" was not the subject matter they quizzed each other about but their frivolous and heedless attitude toward it. In the following chapters, we will be confronted with Ibn al-Faḍl's interest in many of the very subjects implicated in his list of the questions they pointlessly pose to one another.

83. Brown, "Saint as Exemplar."

7 CONCLUSION

Variation between prefaces notwithstanding, there is a clear overarching message, Ibn al-Faḍl's own explanation for why he translated a Byzantine ecclesiastical curriculum into Arabic. Prompted and supported by patrons, he produced translation after translation, often of texts that were already available in Arabic, in order to offer elite Arabic readers access to a special sort of knowledge. This knowledge was often divinely inspired, but it was always correct, insightful, useful, and relevant to the human condition. Offering true knowledge and supported by rational demonstrations, these texts could help strengthen the resolve of wavering Christians in Ibn al-Faḍl's community. They could ward off error introduced by "outsiders" (non-Christians) and redirect the intellectual energies of elite Christians from idle sophistry to questions (and answers) of the utmost urgency.

5

EDUCATION IN THE MARGINS

The previous chapter considered Ibn al-Faḍl's stated motivations for his translation program. How do these claims measure up against the evidence of the translations themselves? What can we learn from the surviving manuscripts of his translations about the intellectual agenda they served and how they fit into the wider scholarly landscape of the eastern Mediterranean and Middle East around the turn of the millennium?

The present chapter addresses a crucial feature of Ibn al-Faḍl's translations: his annotations.[1] Manuscripts of his translations often preserve notes on the translated text, usually ascribed explicitly to Ibn al-Faḍl or, when not, sometimes identifiable as his by other evidence. The chapter begins by describing the manuscript contexts for his annotations and briefly contextualizing them within medieval Greek and Arabic book culture. The rest of the chapter will closely examine a selection of annotations to reveal what Ibn al-Faḍl hoped to achieve by including them as part of his translations. The chapters that follow will continue to draw on these annotations.

Since there are no critical editions of any of Ibn al-Faḍl's translations, we are nowhere close to being able to survey his annotations comprehensively. But we can begin to get a sense of them, as in the case of the translations themselves, by looking at some of the manuscripts.

1. My interest in and approach to Ibn al-Faḍl's marginalia owe much to recent work on commentaries and glosses in postclassical Islamic philosophy, especially Ahmed and Larkin, "*Ḥāshiya*"; Ahmed, "Post-Classical Philosophical Commentaries/Glosses"; and other contributions to the same special issue of *Oriens* 41.3–4 (2013).

In the manuscripts that I have consulted, Ibn al-Faḍl's annotations never appear in the margins. Instead, they are included in the main body of the text, usually immediately following the "focus text" upon which they comment.[2] The most common way to distinguish his annotations from the focus text is to introduce the note with a word such as *ḥāshiya*, "marginal note." The end of the note is then often signaled by another word, such as *al-naṣṣ*, "the text," or *al-faṣṣ*, "the [next] segment [of text]."[3] These boundary-words are usually rubricated (i.e., written in red ink). In Arabic book culture, this arrangement is a typical way to present the notes on a focus text.[4]

The terms used in manuscripts to describe Ibn al-Faḍl's comments are typical of Arabic book culture. Beyond *ḥāshiya* (marginal note), the labels *sharḥ* (commentary) and *tafsīr* (explication) occur frequently as well.[5]

Ibn al-Faḍl's marginalia do not provide a systematic commentary on the text. They are the notes of a learned translator that supply definitions of technical terms, explain translation decisions, expand upon ideas brought up in the translated text, and follow tangential lines of discussion that they happened to bring to mind. In this way, from their position in the margins of authoritative texts, Ibn al-Faḍl's annotations drew the words of the Byzantine fathers of the church into the eleventh century, for eleventh-century purposes. What were Ibn al-Faḍl's approaches to this authoritative Christian tradition?

1 THE GARDEN

We begin with the *Book of the Garden*, Ibn al-Faḍl's translation of a collection of brief quotations from a range of Christian and non-Christian texts, organized according to subject matter.[6] In Ibn al-Faḍl's translation, after many of the quotations there appear notes, each labeled simply "commentary" (*sharḥ*) or "explication" (*tafsīr*). Though they do not mention Ibn al-Faḍl's name, he most likely composed them as part of his translation. For one thing, the notes are not labeled "marginal notes" (*ḥawāshī*); such a label might have suggested that they were anonymous notes written in the margin and then later incorporated into the main

2. See ch. 2, p. 42, n. 38.

3. Cf. the rhymed expression *bi-naṣṣihi wa-faṣṣihi*, "verbatim."

4. Gacek, *Arabic Manuscripts*, 228–29.

5. The various Arabic terms used to describe commentaries (esp. on logic): Gutas, "Aspects," 32–43. More generally (esp. Islamic sciences): Gacek, *Arabic Manuscripts*, 79.

6. See ch. 2, §4, subsection "Pseudo-Maximos: *Loci communes*" (pp. 62–64). Manuscripts used: **V** = Vat. ar. 111; **S** = Sinai ar. 66. There are lacunas in the Sinai manuscript's text, perhaps related to the omission of pagan sayings; see ch. 2, p. 64 and n. 140. In **V**, fols. 138–139, the inner sheet of their quire, were misbound; the correct order of the pages is 137^v, 139^r, 139^v, 138^r, 138^v, 140^r. (There are notes in Arabic and Latin indicating this.)

body of the text. Labels like "commentary" and "explication" carry no such suggestion. As to authorship, some of the notes contain strong evidence that the whole set of them were written by the translator himself. One addresses the reader (of the translation) directly. Another, even more tellingly, refers to the *Book of Benefit*, a known work by Ibn al-Faḍl, as "our book."[7] In light of this evidence, in what follows I will treat these notes as the words of Ibn al-Faḍl.

We may also observe that the note in which Ibn al-Faḍl addresses the reader directly strongly suggests that he meant this commentary on the *Garden* to be read. That is, these notes on the *Garden* were not private notes to himself or notes by students who copied down what he said while they read the text with him. They were a commentary that he produced as part of his translation.

These annotations on the *Garden* primarily focus on grammar and language. Alexander Treiger has suggested, on the basis of these "extraordinarily erudite grammatical and lexicographical notes," that Ibn al-Faḍl's aim might have been "to instruct Arab Christian readers in Arabic grammar, possibly to counter Muslim accusations that Christians were unable to write correct Arabic."[8] The following analysis will lend support to this hypothesis; it will also reveal that Ibn al-Faḍl aimed in his learned commentary to teach not only Arabic but also Greek philology.

Ibn al-Faḍl certainly wished to deepen his readers' knowledge of Arabic. As Treiger has observed, in one note he even refers to his own teacher of Arabic. The main subject of this note is the interchangeability of two Arabic phonemes (*ẓ* and *ḍ*) in certain words:[9]

قال أورسنين[1] الشاعر: ينبغي لنا أن نضع جمعاً وَنَنْدِبَ على المولود إلى كم شرور تقدم، فأمّا الذي قد قَضَى[2] نَحْبَهُ، فاستراح من التعب، فيجب علينا أن ننقذه[3] من المنازل جذلين[4] مقرّظين[5].

<شرح:> يقال قرّضه إذا مدحه بالظاء[6] والضاد جميعاً، كما نقول فاضت نفسه وفاظت. هكذا قرأنا في إصلاح المنطق لابن السكيت على شيخنا أبي العلاء.

[1]أورسنين: ف؛ والصحيح: أوْرِيبِدِس [2]تقدم، فأمّا الذي قد قَضَى: 'تقدم فأما الذي قد قضى' قد قضى (كذا، مكرر): ف [3]ننقذه: والصحيح: ننفذه [4]جذلين: ف؛ وممكن المقصود: جاذِلين [5]مقرّظين: مُقرّطين: ف [6]بالظاء: بالطا (بلا نقطة الباء ولا نقطة الظاء): ف

The poet Euripides said: We must gather and wail over the newborn for how many evils are ahead. As for the one who has passed away, he has achieved rest from labor, so we should send him forth from our homes,[10] rejoicing and eulogizing (*muqarriẓīn*).

7. See below, pp. 160 ("O reader), 161 ("our book"). *Book of Benefit:* Treiger, "ʿAbdallāh," 92–97, who also views (101) the *sharḥ* of the *Garden* as Ibn al-Faḍl's own commentary.

8. Treiger, "ʿAbdallāh," 101.

9. Ibn al-Faḍl, *Garden*, §36 (*fī l-mawt*), **V** 139^{r}_{5-9} (**S** appears, on fol. 332ʳ, to be missing the latter portion of *bāb* 36 containing this passage) = *Loci communes*, §65/36 (περὶ θανάτου), no. 29/33, ed. Ihm, 962: "*Euripides*. For we must hold a gathering to lament the newborn for the evils to come, and in turn, joyfully eulogizing, to send forth from home the deceased who ceases from labors."

10. The Greek plural δόμων is often used to refer to a single home; see LSJ s.v. δόμος I.1.

<*Commentary:*> One says that someone *qarraḍa*s someone else if he praises him, with both *ḍād* [i.e., *qarraḍa*] and *ẓā*ʾ [i.e., *qarraẓa*], just as we say *fāḍat nafsuhu* [he gave up the ghost] as well as *fāẓat*. So did we read in the *Correct Diction* of Ibn al-Sikkīt when studying it with our teacher Abū l-ʿAlāʾ.

Ibn al-Faḍl here teaches a feature of Arabic morphology while casually situating himself—and his readers—in the Arabic philological tradition. Ibn al-Sikkīt was a grammarian and lexicographer of Baghdad (d. 858). His *Correct Diction,* listing word-forms that could easily be confused with one another or were liable to be mispronounced, was a popular textbook for those in the Islamic world who aspired to impeccable knowledge of Classical Arabic.[11] By describing his studies of Ibn al-Sikkīt's *Correct Diction* with a teacher of Arabic, Ibn al-Faḍl links himself to the mainstream Arabic grammatical tradition cultivated by Arab Muslims.

Moreover, as mentioned in chapter 1, Treiger has suggested that this Abū l-ʿAlāʾ is the famous Arab Muslim poet Abū l-ʿAlāʾ al-Maʿarrī, from the town of Maʿarrat al-Nuʿmān in Syria. This would be quite an intellectual lineage.

Other notes on the *Garden* also attest to Ibn al-Faḍl's interest in teaching Arabic grammar with his translation of the florilegium. In the following note on a quotation from Gregory of Nazianzos, Ibn al-Faḍl's focus is on Arabic syntax:[12]

قال الثاولوغس: إذا طاب سير سفينتك فعندها اتّقِ الغرق.

تفسيره: الهاء في «عندها» عائدة على شيء مُقدّر في الكلام، معناه الحال، أي فعند الحال. وهذا شيء تفعله العرب كثيراً، وتستعمل المُضْمَر١ قبل الظاهر٢. وقد أُفْتِنَ النحاة في إيراد سؤالات٣ في هذا المعنى.

١المُضْمَر: صححته؛ المضم: س ف ٢الظاهر: الظاهر: س؛ المطاهر(؟): ف ٣سؤالات: ف؛ سوا الادب: س

The Theologian said: When your ship is sailing well, in that [circumstance] (ʿ*indahā*) beware of drowning.

Explication of this: The *hā*ʾ in ʿ*indahā* goes back to something implicit in what was said. It means the circumstance (*ḥāl*), that is "in that circumstance." This is something that the Arabs do a lot, using the pronoun (*muḍmar*) before the noun (*ẓāhir*). The grammarians are fascinated by (?) furnishing questions on this topic.[13]

Rather than address the topic of the quotation from Gregory of Nazianzos (the Theologian), Ibn al-Faḍl explains an odd grammatical feature of the quotation as he has translated it—namely, that it uses the pronoun -*hā* with no obvious referent. This feminine pronoun, he explains, refers implicitly to the circumstance—the Arabic noun meaning "circumstance" is feminine—referred to by the clause "when your ship is sailing well." He further justifies this translation choice by reference to

11. *Islāḥ al-manṭiq,* ed. Shākir and Hārūn; reviewed by Lewin.

12. *Garden,* §18, **V** 120ʳ; **S** 303ʳ (beginning with *ittaqi l-gharaq,* since the beginning is lost or misbound) = *Loci communes,* 18.10/11, ed. Ihm, 433: Τοῦ Θεολόγου.Ὅτ' εὐπλοεῖς μάλιστα μέμνησο ζάλης.

13. In **S**, the final remark has become "The grammarians are fascinated by furnishing things other than education [? *siwā l-adab;* or 'correct paideia,' *sawīya l-adab?*] on this topic."

"the Arabs," meaning not contemporary speakers of Arabic but rather the linguistically authoritative Arab tribesmen whose poetry was a constant reference point for medieval Arabic lexicographers. In doing so, he uses technical terms of Arabic grammar, *muḍmar* (pronoun) and *ẓāhir* (noun).

The grammatical principle he invokes is not perfectly suited for the occasion, since the pronoun in the saying is referring *back* to something implicit rather than referring *forward* to something that has not *yet* been mentioned explicitly. A better example, as it turns out, is highlighted by Abū l-ʿAlāʾ al-Maʿarrī in his commentary on a line from the poet al-Mutanabbī, *u ʿīdhuhā naẓarātin minka ṣādiqatan* ("I pray to God to keep it true, that vision of yours"). Using much the same language as Ibn al-Faḍl's note, someone asked Abū l-ʿAlāʾ, "What does the 'it' go back to?" (*ilā mā taʿūdu l-hāʾ*). Abū l-ʿAlāʾ replied, "To vision" (*ilā l-naẓarāt*), and cited a grammarian who justified such forward-looking pronouns by adducing a qur'anic verse that makes use of one.[14]

Ibn al-Faḍl was also concerned to explain cases of unusual Arabic morphology. Thus in one brief gloss on the word *ṭīr* (birds), he explains this irregular plural:[15]

شرح: الطير جمع طائر. وفاعِلٌ يجمع على ثلثين صنفاً.

Commentary: *Ṭīr* is the plural of *ṭāʾir*. [Nouns of the form] *fāʿil* become plural in thirty [different] ways.

Ibn al-Faḍl discusses other aspects of Arabic grammar, too—for example, in another note on the usage of the Arabic preposition *li-*.[16]

Likewise, in yet another note Ibn al-Faḍl explains the phonetic difference between two orthographically identical words (*sanāʾ* and *sanā*, both spelled *s-n-ʾ* in manuscripts), one of which (*sanāʾ*) has occurred in a quotation from John Chrysostom:[17]

شرح: السناء بالمدّ: المجد والشرف، والسنا بالقصر: النور. وليس هذا من المتفقة أسماؤها[1]، وذلك أنّ بين الاسمين فصلاً[2] في الكمية والكيفية يعرف صحّته الثاقب الهِمَّة.

[1]أسماؤها: س؛ اسماها: ف [2]فصلاً: س؛ فضلاً: ف

Commentary: *S-n-ʾ* with prolongation [i.e., *sanāʾ*] means "glory and honor." *S-n-ʾ* with shortening [i.e., *sanā*] means "light." This is not a case of homonyms. That is

14. Maʿarrī, *Muʿjiz Aḥmad*, ed. Diyāb, 3:252 (on the *qaṣīda* beginning *wā-ḥarra qalbāhu* . . . *saqamu*). Another eleventh-century commentator on this line made much the same point: Wāḥidī (d. 1076), *Mutanabii carmina*, ed. Dieterici, 482–83.

15. *Garden*, §35, **V** 137r; **S** 330v = *Loci communes*, 35.4, ed. Ihm, 678.

16. *Garden*, §56, **V** 150v (not in **S** 358r because it is missing the second half of *bāb* 56, from **V** 150r 12 *qāla*, onward) = *Loci communes*, §49, no. –/26, ed. Ihm, 818, an excerpt from Xenophon's *Memorabilia*.

17. *Garden*, §63, **V** 155r; **S** 368r-v = *Loci communes*, 56.9, ed. Ihm, 881.

> because between the two nouns there is a distinction in quantity and quality whose correctness is known to the one whose eagerness is piercing.

Indeed, the two words are pronounced differently in Classical Arabic, one with a long *alif* followed by a glottal stop (*hamza*), the other with an *alif* (often pronounced short) and no glottal stop. But by the eleventh century both would typically have been pronounced in the second way. The modern student of Arabic can easily tell these words apart because the first has a written *hamza* while the other does not, but in Ibn al-Faḍl's own day (and earlier too) this sort of distinction would have been particularly confusing because written Arabic did not typically mark the *hamza*. This distinction between *sanāʾ* and *sanā* is among those which Ibn al-Sikkīt made a point of mentioning.[18]

At one point in the *Garden*, there is a lengthy quotation from Chrysostom about how one should not become angry when laughed at. This quotation happens to use the word "mouths," which in Arabic has an irregular plural (*fam*, plural *afwāh*). Ibn al-Faḍl focuses on the morphology of this word in his note:[19]

> شرح: أفواه جمع فوه، بفتح[١] الفاء، كما ذكر الخليل[٢]، ووزنه فَعلٌ[٣]، فأمّا فم[٤] فناقصٌ وخارج عن الأصل، ودليل ذلك يتجه[٥] من وجهين، أحدهما[٦] كونه على حرفين، والآخر أن الفاء لا تتصل[٧] بالميم من غير حاجز[٨] يفصل[٩] بينهما، وقد ذكر هذا ابن دُريد في كتاب الجمهرة.
>
> [١]بفتح: س؛ يفتح: ف [٢]الخليل: صححته؛ الجليل: س ف [٣]فَعَلٌ: صححته؛ فِعلٌ(؟): ف؛ فعّلٌ(؟): س [٤]فم: س؛ فُمّ(؟): ف [٥]يتجه: س؛ تتجه: ف [٦]أحدهما: ف؛ احدثها(؟): س [٧]تتصل: ف؛ يتصل: س [٨]حاجز: ف؛ خارج: س [٩]يفصل: ف؛ يفضل: س
>
> *Commentary*: *Afwāh* (mouths) is the plural of *fawah*,[20] with a short-*a* vowel on the *fāʾ*, as al-Khalīl[21] mentioned, and its form is *faʿalun*. As for *fam* (mouth), it is defective and deviates from its origin. The proof of this has two aspects. One of them is that it has two letters. The other is that the letter *fāʾ* does not attach to the letter *mīm* without a divider separating them.[22] Ibn Durayd mentioned this in the *Book of the Collection*.

Ibn al-Faḍl is referring to two influential Muslim philologists of Arabic: al-Khalīl ibn Aḥmad (eighth century, b. Oman, d. Basra) and Ibn Durayd (b. 837 CE, Basra; d. 933 CE, Baghdad), author of a dictionary entitled the *Collection* (*Jamhara*). In teaching students or readers to read the Classical Arabic of his translation, Ibn al-Faḍl drew on his own education in the Arabic philology studied by his Muslim peers.

At the same time, in a number of notes Ibn al-Faḍl discusses the *Garden*'s Greek original and, accordingly, *Greek* grammar. In one of these, as Treiger observed

18. Ibn al-Sikkīt *apud* Ibn Manẓūr, *Lisān* s.v. *snʾ*: *al-sanāʾu mina l-majdi wa-sharaf, mamdūd.*
19. *Garden*, §40, **V** 140^{r}; **S** 335^{v}–336^{v} = *Loci communes*, 69/40, no. 11/11, ed. Ihm, 1014.
20. Ibn al-Faḍl only mentions the vowel on the *fāʾ* (i.e., *fawh*). Ibn al-Manẓūr seems to vowel it *fawah*: *Lisān* s.v. *fwh*.
21. Reading *al-Khalīl* for *al-Jalīl*.
22. In other words, a plural for *fam* like **afmām* could not exist because (1) it has only two, not three, root letters (*f-m*, not *f-m-m*), and (2) Arabic tends not to juxtapose the consonants *f* and *m*.

(and as already mentioned in chapter 1), Ibn al-Faḍl also names his teacher of Greek, the late Symeon:[23]

قال الثاولوغس: . . .

وقال: الأشياء التي عرفت مدائحها قد علمت ببيان الزيادة فيها.

شرح: هذا الفصل يرد في المرثية التي صنّفها في القديس[١] باسيليوس، وقرأتها أنا كلّها باليوناني على سيدي سمعان الابميسقن[٢] بن الشنيحي[٣] النفيس والقديس رحمه[٤] الله، وفسّر لي هذا الموضع في جملة ما فسّره، وهو أن الفضائل الممدوحة من شأنها أن تجتذب الكل إليها، فهي تزيد بذلك، وقد اختلف الناس في تفسير هذا الموضع.

[١]القديس: س؛ القديسين: ف   [٢]الابميسقن: ف؛ الابمتسقن: س   [٣]الشنيحي: ف؛ السبيحي: س   [٤]رحمه: س؛ يرحمه: ف

[*The Theologian*] *says:* The things whose praises I have known—I have clearly known increase of/excess in them.

Commentary: This excerpt appears in the eulogy which he composed on Saint Basil. I myself read the whole [eulogy] in Greek with my teacher Simʿān al-ʾbmysqn (?) ibn al-Shanīḥī (?), the cherished and holy one, may God have mercy upon him, and he explicated this passage for me along with everything else that he explicated: that virtues when praised tend to attract everyone (*al-kull*) to them so that they thereby increase. People are in disagreement about how to explicate it.

Just as with the note about his Arabic teacher Abū l-ʿAlāʾ, so too with this note, Ibn al-Faḍl situates himself—and his own students and readers—within an educational tradition, in this case a tradition of Greek philology. If indeed this Symeon should turn out to be Symeon Seth, as Treiger has conjectured,[24] it would be a tradition to which we have some direct access.

Ibn al-Faḍl tells us that with Symeon he studied Gregory of Nazianzos's lengthy and highly rhetorical funeral oration for Basil of Caesarea.[25] Moreover, he cites Symeon's exegesis of this quotation, which, when removed from the context of Gregory's oration, may seem rather cryptic. Symeon's understanding of the line seems consistent with the context of the oration, where Gregory has expressed the hope that, for good people, the funeral oration that he is about to give will give pleasure and serve as a call to virtue:[26] it is reasonable to infer that the increase of virtues praised is due to those hearing the praise seeking to emulate those virtues.

23. *Garden*, §43, **V** 142^{r-v}; **S** 340^{v}–341^{r} = *Loci communes*, 36.7, ed. Ihm, 688: "For I know well that those who have praise also have progress" (Ὧν γὰρ τοὺς ἐπαίνους οἶδα τούτων σαφῶς καὶ τὰς ἐπιδόσεις). Gregory of Nazianzos, *Oration* 43.1, PG 36:496_{9-11}, ed. Bernardi, 118_{21-22}; cited by Ihm, 688. Trans. Bernardi: "Car là où il y a éloge, je sais bien qu'il y a aussi exercice d'une influence." Cf. McCauley's translation, in Gregory and Ambrose, *Funeral Orations*, 28.

24. See ch. 1, p. 14 and n. 54.

25. Gregory of Nazianzos, *Oration* 43, PG 36:493–605, ed. and trans. Bernardi, 116–307; trans. McCauley in Gregory and Ambrose, *Funeral Orations*, 27–99. The middle Byzantine manuscript tradition for this oration (like others by Gregory) is vast: *Pinakes*, https://pinakes.irht.cnrs.fr/notices/oeuvre/7597/.

26. *Oration* 43.1, PG 36:496A, ed. Bernardi, 118_{21-22}.

In the *Garden*'s chapter on "education" (*adab* in the sense of cultivation and good breeding as well as learning),[27] Ibn al-Faḍl included a note contrasting the semantic range of the Arabic and Greek words for "voice." The saying that sparked Ibn al-Faḍl's commentary and the note itself read as follows:[28]

ما ينبغي أن تطلب في[١] السمك صوتاً ولا في غير المتأدّبين فضيلة.

تفسيره: يجب أن تعلم أن العرب تستجيز أن تصف سائر الحيوان وأنواعه[٢] على اختلاف طبائعها وتباين[٣] جواهرها بالصوت، إلّا أنها تخص[٤] الإنسان[٥] به على التحقيق. فأما اليونانيون فلا يصفون به شيئاً من الحيوان إلّا الإنسان فقط.

والصوت[٦] هو ما احتملته[٧] الكتابة وجرى عليه حُكْم الهِجاء من القَطْعِ والوَصْلِ واختلاف كيفيات الحروف.

وهو مركّب من اسمين ناقصين، هما النور والعقل.

[١]في: [[من]] 'في': ف [٢]سائر الحيوان وأنواعه: ف؛ سائر أنواع الحيوان: س [٣]وتباين: ف؛ وتبا[[ر]]ين: س [٤]تخص: س؛ يخص: ف [٥]الإنسان: س؛ الإنسان (صفحة جديدة) الإنسان: ف [٦]والصوت: ف؛ الصوت: س [٧]احتملته: ف؛ احتمله: س

You should not look for a voice among fish nor virtue among the uneducated.

Explication of this: You should know that the Arabs permit themselves to describe all animals and their species, in contrast to their natures and in contradistinction with their substances, as having a voice, although they attribute it to the human being in particular when speaking precisely. As for the Greeks, they do not describe any other animal as having [a voice], only the human being.

Voice is carried by writing and is the basis for determining how to spell, such as disjunction (*qaṭ*ʿ) and connection (*waṣl*) [of *hamza*s] and difference in the qualities of letters.

It [i.e., the word for "voice"] is composed of two deficient nouns—namely, light and mind.

Can a fish have a voice? Ibn al-Faḍl explains that strictly speaking a voice is something that only a human can have (by definition), but that the semantic range of the word 'voice' is different in Arabic and in Greek. In Arabic, one can, speaking metaphorically, refer to the vocal sound that a non-human animal makes as its voice. In contrast, the semantic range of 'voice' in Greek is narrower: it simply makes no sense to speak of an animal's voice.[29]

This remark about comparative linguistics seems intended to help the Arabic reader understand the Greek saying a bit better. An Arabic reader, after all, might respond to the saying by pointing out that perhaps a fish does indeed have a voice; so is it possible that there might be virtue among the uneducated? Ibn al-Faḍl's

27. The original Greek entitles the chapter "On Education, Philosophy, and Child-Rearing" (περὶ παιδείας καὶ φιλοσοφίας καὶ παίδων ἀνατροφῆς). For *adab*, see *EI*², s.v. "Adab"; *EI*³, s.v. "Adab *a–b*."

28. *Garden*, §17, **V** 117ᵛ–118ʳ; **S** 299ʳ (beginning missing; the lacuna may be due to a binding error) = *Loci communes*, §17, no. 21/22, ed. Ihm, 405.

29. Counterexamples can surely be found to this rule in Classical Greek—e.g., in LSJ s.v. φωνή I.2—but it generally holds, as shown by most of the examples in LSJ s.v., I. In later Greek, Ibn al-Faḍl's observation is perhaps even more valid; see Lampe s.v.

remark stresses that this is not the case. A voice, in Greek, is something only a human being could have, so by analogy, the point is that only the educated could possibly be virtuous.

Ibn al-Faḍl follows this comparative observation by asserting that writing transmits information about "voice" (intelligible utterances), and rules of orthography are derived from "voice" (pronunciation). This line might seem to be strictly about Arabic grammar because its example is about Arabic orthography. But the semantic range of "voice" implicit in this remark is Greek. The Classical Greek word for voice, *phōnē,* can also mean "faculty of speech" and "phrase, saying"; in Christian texts it could mean a scriptural passage.[30] The Arabic word *ṣawt* has a semantic range closer to the modern English word *voice* (along with *sound*). Extended meanings of *ṣawt* and related words include shouting and calling but tend not to refer to articulate speech per se except in humorous or otherwise allusive contexts.[31] Ibn al-Faḍl is saying that writing carries information about articulate speech (*phōnē*), which is of course uttered by a human voice (*ṣawt*) but is, as a concept, distinct from it.

Ibn al-Faḍl's final line makes even clearer that he is continuing to talk about the Greek word for "voice." The concept of a "deficient noun" that he uses there comes straight out of the Greek grammarians, as part of their discussion of compound nouns. So, for example, Dionysios Thrax (ca. 170–ca. 90 BCE), in his *Art of Grammar,* explains that there are four types of compounds, formed (1) from two perfect nouns, like Cheirisophos (χειρί + σοφός, each a Greek word in itself); (2) from two deficient nouns, like Sophocles (neither σοφο- nor -κλῆς is on its own a Greek word); (3) from a deficient followed by a perfect noun, like Philodemos (only δῆμος is a word); and (4) from a perfect followed by a deficient noun, like Pericles (only περί is a word).[32] A deficient noun, then, is one part of a compound noun that is not a word on its own.

In what sense does Ibn al-Faḍl mean that "voice" is composed of two deficient nouns? Certainly not that the Arabic *ṣawt* (voice) is composed from deficient versions of *nūr* (light) and *ʿaql* (mind). Instead, he must be saying that the Greek *phōnē* is composed from deficient versions of *phōs* (light) and *nous* (mind): *phō-* plus *-nē.* If this etymology seems doubtful, this should not be taken as a sign of Ibn al-Faḍl's distance from Greek grammar; on the contrary, this fanciful etymology also comes straight out of the Greek grammatical tradition. The fifth-century

30. LSJ s.v., II–III; Lampe s.v., 3 (p. 1504a, line 3).

31. *Lisān* s.v. *ṣwt.* The example given there that comes closest to meaning "articulate speech" is a proverbial expression of the Arabs: "The Arabs say: I hear voice (*ṣawt*) and see omission (*fawt*), that is, I hear voice and do not see action (*fiʿl*)." In other words: all talk and no action. "Voice" here stands in for speech and promises but clearly in a way analogous to the English "all bark and no bite."

32. Dionysius Thrax, *Ars grammatica,* §12, ed. Uhlig, 29–30.

grammarian Orion of Thebes (a teacher of Proklos), in his book on Greek etymology, explains the origin of the word *phōnē* by saying that *phōnē* is "what illuminates (*phōtizousa*) the mind by speech."[33] The late antique commentary of Elias on Porphyry's *Eisagoge* refers to this same etymology as part of an account of how communication through speech works.[34] Commentaries on Dionysios Thrax's *Art of Grammar* exploited this same etymology,[35] as did the ninth-century Byzantine grammarian Theognostos, in his work on Greek orthography,[36] and the middle Byzantine *Etymologicum Gudianum*.[37]

In short, this example makes clear that Ibn al-Faḍl was concerned here to teach his readers not only about Arabic but also about Greek.

We have focused on Greek and Arabic grammar so far, but Ibn al-Faḍl's vision of education was broader and grander. Another comment by Ibn al-Faḍl in the *Garden* underscores his interest in what we might anachronistically call a liberal arts education, intellectual but also ethical:[38]

وقال اغليقون: إن الأدب أمر صالح[1] لا يُسْلَب.

شرح: لا تظن أيّها القارئ أنّ الأدب هو تحفّظ[2] الشعر واللغة والنحو والعروض واليقين في التعاليم، مع استعمال واحدة من الرذائل، أعني حَسَداً مَكْراً خُبّاً عُجْباً هزاً (أو: هُراء؟) فِسْقاً كَذِباً وما شاكل ذلك، هيهات هيهات[3]، بل ذلك سقوط. ولقد أحسن كل الإحسان أبونا المعظم في القديسين يوحنّا الذهبي الفم حين يقول: أما الفلاسفة فيزعمون أن حدّ الإنسان هو حيّ ناطق مايت، وأما نحن فنرى أن الإنسان هو المستعمل الفضيلة.

[1]صالح: س؛ [1]بصالح: ف [2]تحفّظ: ف؛ يحفظ: س [3]هيهات هيهات: ف؛ هيهات (مرة واحدة): س

Glykon said: Education (*adab, paideia*) is something good that cannot be stolen.

Commentary: Do not think, O reader, that education is memorizing poetry, vocabulary, grammar, and prosody or perfecting your knowledge of mathematics,[39] while acting according to one of the vices, by which I mean envy, deception, malice, pride, indecent speech (?),[40] fornication, lying, and the like—far from it! No, that is a lapse. Our father, great among the saints, John Chrysostom was completely right when he

33. Orion, *Etymologicon*, ed. Sturz, col. 160, line 12. In the following entry on φώς ("human being," not to be confused with φῶς, "light"), Orion links speech and light to the human being: "Φώς: the human being, who alone illuminates (*phōtizōn*) the intellect with speech; or from φῶ, to speak."

34. Elias, lecture 14, ed. Busse, 37, lines 1–3.

35. Collection of excerpts of commentaries found in two Vatican manuscripts, ed. Hilgard, *Scholia*, 175_{6-9}. Byzantine commentary from no later than the ninth century (the date of the earliest manuscript containing it), ed. Hilgard, ibid., 567_{26}.

36. Theognostos, *Kanones*, no. 538 (φλη′), ed. Cramer, *Anecdota Graeca*, 2:92.

37. Ed. Sturz, col. 560, lines 7–8. On this and similar texts, see *ODB*, s.v. "Etymologika."

38. *Garden*, §17, **V** 119^{r}; **S** 301^{r-v} = *Loci communes*, 17.45/54, ed. Ihm, 418.

39. Mathematics: *taʿālīm* ~ μαθήματα, e.g., in Ḥubaysh's Arabic translation of Galen, *That the Soul's Faculties Follow upon the Mixtures of the Body*, §10, in *Scripta minora*, ed. Helmreich et al., 2:72 (that when Plato says μαθήματα he means geometry and arithmetic); corresponding to the Arabic, ed. Biesterfeldt, 38_{2}; cited by *Glossarium*, Galen.An-virt.3111.

40. Reading *hurāʾ*.

said: "As for the philosophers, they claim that the definition of man is 'a living, rational, mortal being.' As for us, our opinion is that man is the being that acts according to virtue."

Knowledge of poetry, grammar, mathematics—all of this is worthless without a moral compass. The sort of education, mentioned by the ancient Greek poet Glykon,[41] that cannot be stolen—and is worth keeping—is one that also makes one good.

Ibn al-Faḍl also intended to teach his readers pertinent aspects of natural philosophy. The subsequent chapters will focus on Ibn al-Faḍl's philosophical interests, so here we will simply consider one example from the *Garden*. After a quotation from the playwright Menander (fourth/third century BCE), he picks up on the word "nature" to describe several of its philosophical and medical meanings.[42]

قالماندرس: يا كل المتعظّمين في نفوسهم، لَأَنْتُم المثلّث شَقَاوَكُم لأنكم لا تعرفون طبيعة الإنسان.

شرح: ينبغي أن تعلم أن الطبيعة تقال عند الفلاسفة على خمس جهات، وذلك أنهم يسمّون الهيولى طبيعة، ويسمون الصورة طبيعة، ويسمون الطريق إلى الكون طبيعة. وعند الأطباء تقال على أربع جهات، وهي القوة المديرة للبدن، والمزاج، وهيئة[1] البدن، وحركة النفس. وقد أوردنا رسمها في كتابنا المعروف بكتاب المنفعة.

[1]وهيئة: وهية: ف

Menander said: All you who magnify your own importance, verily you are triply wretched because you do not know man's nature.

Commentary: You should know that among the philosophers "nature" has five meanings. That is, [1] they refer to matter (*hayūlā*) as nature; [2] they refer to form as nature; and [3] they refer to the way something comes to be as its nature. Among physicians it has four meanings, namely [1] the faculty that rules over the body, [2] the [bodily] constitution, [3] the arrangement of the body, and [4] the soul's movement. We presented a diagram (*rasm*) of them in our book known as the *Book of Benefit.*

This note seems to be incomplete, since Ibn al-Faḍl says there will be five philosophical meanings for "nature," but the note as preserved in the Vatican manuscript lists only three. Nevertheless, the note in its original form was clearly written by Ibn al-Faḍl; indeed, as mentioned above, it is the strongest evidence that Ibn

41. Assuming the Glykon meant is the "poet of unknown date and place to whom the glyconic metre is attributed" described in *OCD*[3], s.v. "Glycon (1)."

42. *Garden*, §34, **V** 136^{v} (not in **S** because of a lacuna at fol. 330$^{r}_{7}$ between *al-wuda ʿā ʾ* and the beginning of *bāb* 35 corresponding to **V** 136$^{v}_{9}$[*qāla Diyūjānis*]–137$^{r}_{2}$[*hiya ṣūratu a ʿdā ʾī*]) = *Loci communes*, 34, no. 34/29, ed. Ihm, 676: "*Menander:* O thrice-wretched all who grandly puff up great things [greatly, Kassel and Austin] about themselves, for they do not know man's nature" (Μενάνδρου. Ὦ τρισάθλιοι / ἅπαντες οἱ φυσῶντες ἐφ' ἑαυτοῖς μεγάλα [μέγα Kassel and Austin]· / αὐτοὶ γὰρ οὐκ ἴσασιν ἀνθρώπου φύσιν). Menander, fragment 219 (251), ed. Kassel and Austin, *Poetae Comici Graeci*, 6.2:153.

al-Faḍl is the author of the notes on the *Garden*, since it is here that he cites "our book called the *Book of Benefit*."

The note itself speaks to Ibn al-Faḍl's practice of using and imparting philosophical terminology. Though we could call this note philological, focusing on the word "nature" as it does, it is also an introduction to the corresponding philosophical and medical concepts.[43]

How did philosophy fit into Ibn al-Faḍl's educational program? We may find an initial answer in a note referenced by Samuel Noble and Alexander Treiger as evidence (compelling in my view) of Ibn al-Faḍl's approval of philosophy.[44] In the chapter of the *Garden* on the old adage "Know thyself!" (*i'rif nafsaka*, γνῶθι σεαυτόν), Ibn al-Faḍl responds to a quotation on self-knowledge as follows:[45]

ثاليس[1]: ما أصعب معرفة الإنسان ذاته، إلا أن ذلك سعادة لأنه يعيش بحسب الطبيعة.

شرح: إنما[2] صعب على الإنسان أن يعرف ذاته لهذا السبب، وهو أنه مركب من صَوَرَيْنِ[3] متضادين في الكيفية، وذلك أن أحدهما بسيط والآخر مركب، وهذا معقول وذلك محسوس، وهذا باقٍ لا يزول وذاك فانٍ يَحُوْل. ولا سبيل إلى تعرُّفِ هذين على ما ينبغي إلا بِدرْس جميع العلوم، ولا توصُّل إلى ما لا[4] تراه العيون إلا بأعظم مَشَقَّة. ومن قرأ العلوم فقد تفلسف، ومن تفلسف فقد عرف الله عزّ وجلّ بعضَ المعرفة، ومن عرف البارئ تقدّس اسمه حسب الممكن، فهو السعيد. والأشياء التي تدل على أن الإنسان قد علم حسب الطوق هي استعمال الفضائل والابتعاد من الرذائل، والسلم.

وله معنى آخر غير هذا وهو ظاهر لا يحتاج إلى إبانة.

[1]ثاليس: صححته؛ ثالبيس (بلا نقط): ف [2]إنما: تريغر؛ إنه لما: ف [3]صَوَرَيْنِ: ف؛ قد يكون الصحيح «جزؤين» حسب تصحيح تريغر [4]ما لا: تريغر؛ ـف

Thales: It is very difficult for man to know his own self, but [to do so] is happiness because [in that case] he lives in accordance with his nature.[46]

Commentary: It is indeed difficult for man to know his own self for this reason, namely that he is composed of two inclinations [or: parts][47] contrary in quality. That is, one of them is simple and the other composite, one intelligible and the other perceptible, one persisting without perishing and the other being annihilated and changing. There is no way to come to know both as one should except by studying all of the sciences, and there is no way to attain what eyes do not see except by the greatest toil. Whoever reads the sciences has done philosophy, and whoever does philosophy has come to know God the Mighty and Exalted to some extent; whoever knows the Creator (may his name be sanctified) to the extent possible is happy. The things that indicate that a human being has acquired knowledge according to his [or her]

43. Cf. Aristotle's list in *Metaphysics* Δ.4, 1014b16–1015a19. I owe this reference to an anonymous reviewer.

44. Noble and Treiger, "Christian Arabic Theology," 380 n. 33.

45. *Garden*, §56, **V** 150^{r-v} (not in **S** because of a lacuna; see n. 15) = *Loci communes*, 49.18/19, ed. Ihm, 816. Alexander Treiger kindly sent me his new critical edition of this note ("Greek into Arabic in Byzantine Antioch," 230–31, cited in the apparatus) before it was published.

46. The *Souda* lexicon mentions that Thales said, "Know thyself": Wöhrle, *Milesians: Thales*, 416 (fragment Th 495_8).

47. Treiger has plausibly suggested emending *ṣawarayn* to *juz'ayn* ("two parts").

capacity are: acting according to the virtues and avoiding the vices, end of story (*wa-l-salām*).

It also has another, different meaning that is clear and requires no explanation.[48]

Here Ibn al-Faḍl presents a succinct account of how knowledge, philosophy, theology, and ethical behavior are related to one another: each one leads to the next. There is thus a very important place in Ibn al-Faḍl's educational vision for the sort of knowledge that one acquires by studying "external" disciplines. Grammar, logic, astronomy, and the other sciences that Ibn al-Faḍl refers to and discusses—as we will see in the following chapters—are indispensable for a better understanding of the self, God, and, ultimately, for living a good life. Like Plato and his followers, Christian and non-Christian alike, Ibn al-Faḍl saw philosophy and true knowledge as inextricable from the development of character, the embodiment of virtue, and the life worth living.

Ibn al-Faḍl's ostensible rejection of philosophy, which might have seemed incontestable as we read his prefaces in chapter 4, begins to seem less absolute.

2 SOPHRONIOS

We now turn to two notes that Ibn al-Faḍl added to his adapted translation of Sophronios's *Synodical Letter*, one on the terminology of divine ontology, the other on how to read Trinitarian theology into Scripture.[49] In manuscripts of this text, Ibn al-Faḍl's notes are each called an "explication" (*tafsīr*).

Our first example appears in chapter 19, which discusses several epithets of God. The first epithet is the "existing" or "pre-eternal" one (ὁ ὤν ~ *al-azalī*). In Ibn al-Faḍl's translation, Sophronios's discussion reads:[50]

إن الأزلي أولى أن[1] يكون اسماً لله تعالى، وأقرب في الدلالة على جوهره، إذ ليس لوجوده مبدأ، بل إنّما هو دائم[2]، فأما كل ما سواه من الموجودات فلوجودها مبدأ[3].

[1]أن: م؛ ما: ط [2]دائم: ط؛ دائماً: م [3]فلوجودها مبدأ: فلوجودها (وقد أدخل بخط حديثي: «مبدأ»): م؛ 'فلوجودها مبدأ': ط

Azalī is more worthy as a name for God Almighty and closer to indicating his substance (*jawhar*), since his existence (*wujūd*) has no beginning, but rather he is everlasting. As for everything that exists (*mawjūdāt*) other than him, their existence has a beginning.

At this point Ibn al-Faḍl decided to explain his choice to translate the Greek word for "existing" (ὤν) by the Arabic for "pre-eternal" (*azalī*):[51]

48. It is not clear to me what this last line refers to.

49. Sigla for manuscripts used: **M** = Jerusalem, Holy Sepulcher, ar. 12; **Ṭ** = Vat. Sbath 44.

50. Sophronios, *Burhān*, 19.1, **M** 128ʳ; **Ṭ** 101ʳ (now ed. Khūrī, 295).

51. **M** 128ʳ; **Ṭ** 101ʳ. **M** marks the end of the *tafsīr* with a large dot; **Ṭ** does so with the words *min hāhunā l-naṣṣ*. Both then continue with Sophronios's text, which had been interrupted midsentence.

تفسير[١] قال عبد الله بن الفضل المترجم لهذا[٢] الكتاب الإلهي الفاضل[٣]: إنّ الأزلي هو[٤] في اللغة اليونانية أون، ويقال له[٥] في اللغة اليونانية مطوخي[٦]، وفي اللغة العربية اسم الفاعل، وهو يدل على الزمان الحاضر[٧]، وقد يقال له في اللغة العربية الدائم. وقوم يترجمونه[٨] الموجود، وليس هو[٩] بالصواب.

[١]تفسير: م؛ —ط   [٢]لهذا: م؛ هذا: ط   [٣]الكتاب الإلهي الفاضل: م؛ الكتاب 'تفسيراً': ط   [٤]هو: م؛ —ط   [٥]له: +أيضاً: ط   [٦]مطوخي: م؛ مطوشي: ط   [٧]الحاضر: م؛ الحاظر: ط   [٨]يترجمونه: م؛ يترجمون: ط   [٩]هو: م؛ —ط

Explication: ʿAbdallāh ibn al-Faḍl, the learned translator of this divine book said: The word *azalī* in Greek is *ūn* [ὤν]. In Greek it is called a *mitūkhī* [μετοχή, "participle"]; in Arabic, an active participle, indicating the present time; in Arabic it can also be called *al-dāʾim* ["everlasting"; or: "continuous participle"]. Some people translate it [i.e., ὤν] as "that which exists" (*al-mawjūd*), but this is not correct.

Ibn al-Faḍl explains that ὤν is an active present participle that can have a continuous aspect (like the English present progressive). He rejects translating it here as "existent" (*mawjūd*). His implicit justification is that when applied to God the word means more than when applied to all other beings that exist in the world: applied to God, it means pre-eternal (*azalī*); that is, it means not only that God exists now but that he has always existed. Ibn al-Faḍl argues—again implicitly—for a less literal translation that better captures Sophronios's meaning.

This is a philological point with conceptual implications. Indeed, if one were to replace *azalī* with *mawjūd* in Ibn al-Faḍl's translation, the resulting Arabic would be odd, because then it would say that one of the most appropriate names for God is *al-mawjūd*, a term generally applied to all things that exist (*al-mawjūdāt* ~ τὰ ὄντα); and furthermore, that this epithet comes close to revealing what makes God God (his οὐσία ~ *jawhar*). Ibn al-Faḍl's choice, though straying from the literal meaning, does arguably reproduce the sense of this epithet for God.

Clearly Ibn al-Faḍl thought carefully about how he translated texts like Sophronios's. He did not always choose the most literal or even the most interpretively neutral option. And once he had translated these texts, notes like this one indicate that he taught them with close attention to the philosophical—in this case metaphysical (theological)—concepts contained in the Arabic and in the Greek upon which the Arabic was based.

Another "explication" (*tafsīr*), on the Christian Trinity, is explicitly ascribed to Ibn al-Faḍl in the Sbath manuscript but not in the Jerusalem manuscript. The previous "explication" (on *azalī* and ὤν, just discussed) *is* ascribed to Ibn al-Faḍl in both, so the scribe of the Jerusalem manuscript may be assuming that the reader will understand that Ibn al-Faḍl's commentary is continuing. The note appears at a point where Sophronios is speaking of those who say that God is a single hypostasis (instead of the three persons of the Trinity). He says that they support their position by quoting Moses when he says, "Listen, Israel! The Lord your God is one lord."[52] Here Ibn al-Faḍl inserted an explanation:[53]

> تفسير قال عبد الله ابن الفضل المترجم لهذا الكتاب الإلهي[١]: إنه يشير بالرب الإله[٢] والرب إلى الأقانيم الثلثة، وبالواحد إلى الجوهر.
>
> [١]قال عبد الله . . . الكتاب الإلهي: ط؛ ـــ م   [٢]الإله: ط؛ والإله: م

> *Explication: ʿAbdallāh ibn al-Faḍl, the translator of this divine book, said:* By "the Lord God" and "the Lord" he refers to the three hypostases, and by "the One," to the substance.

After Ibn al-Faḍl's note, Sophronios's text continues by explaining that Moses said this with reference to God's substance, not his hypostases.[54] Ibn al-Faḍl's note offers a slightly different interpretation: that in this passage Moses is referring both to God's substance and to his hypostases, to the substance when he says God is "one" and to the three hypostases when he says "the Lord." This implies a different parsing of the biblical quotation, also admissible from the Arabic (and indeed in the Greek): "The Lord your God is lord, he is one." Thus in Ibn al-Faḍl's reading, Moses's proclamation to the Israelites is to be decoded as a Trinitarian confession: "The Lord"—that is, the three hypostases—"is one"—that is, one substance. Alternatively, Ibn al-Faḍl may mean not that Moses *intended* to say that but simply that when he referred to "the Lord," whether he knew it or not he was referring to the three hypostases, and when he said that the Lord is "one," that this could only mean one substance. In this reading, Moses's statement would not *necessitate* the Trinitarian doctrine but only be *compatible* with it.

As this note shows, part of Ibn al-Faḍl's educational agenda was scriptural exegesis through the lens of his Trinitarian theology, known to us, for example, from his *Discourse on the Holy Trinity*.[55]

3 JOHN OF THESSALONIKI

John of Thessaloniki's *Encomium to Saint Demetrios* focused, as we have seen, on the saint's refutation of a series of heterodox interlocutors, from pagans to Nestorians.[56] Ibn al-Faḍl wrote five comments on this relatively short text, responding to

52. §23.24 end, **M** 134^{r}; **Ṭ** 112^{v} (now ed. Khūrī, 317): *Istamiʿ* [**M** : *ismaʿ* **Ṭ**] *yā Isrāʾīl, al-rabbu ilāhuka rabbun wāḥidun huwa*. Deuteronomy 6:4, end (LXX: ἄκουε Ἰσραήλ· κύριος ὁ θεὸς ἡμῶν κύριος εἷς ἐστιν). Perhaps Ibn al-Faḍl's exemplar had ὑμῶν (your) instead of the homophonous ἡμῶν (our).

53. §23.25, **M** 134^{r}; **Ṭ** 112^{v} (now ed. Khūrī, 318).

54. **Ṭ** signals the end of Ibn al-Faḍl's note with the words *narjaʿu ilā lafẓi l-naṣṣ*. **M** hardly signals the end of Ibn al-Faḍl's note at all, using a comma of the sort that typically divides one phrase from the next in the text.

55. Ed. and trans. Noble and Treiger, "Christian Arabic Theology."

56. **A** = Sinai ar. 350 (ca. thirteenth century); **B** = Sinai ar. 352 (ca. thirteenth century).

the narrative by explaining pagan doctrines (explications 1 and 2) and supporting Saint Demetrios's Chalcedonian teachings with discussions of physics (explication 3), metaphysics (explication 4), and grammar (explication 5). We will save the third for chapter 7 but examine the rest of them here.

Ibn al-Faḍl's comments on his translation of John of Thessaloniki's *Encomium to Saint Demetrios* are each labeled *tafsīr,* "explication," like the notes on Sophronios and some of the notes on the *Garden.* Only the first two (explications 1–2) are explicitly attributed to Ibn al-Faḍl. The other three (explications 3–5) are anonymous. Nevertheless, these are most likely part of Ibn al-Faḍl's commentary as well. Just as in the *Garden,* here too the scribe (or Ibn al-Faḍl himself) may have left off writing Ibn al-Faḍl's name after the first two, assuming it would be obvious that the same commentary was continuing. Further evidence suggesting Ibn al-Faḍl's authorship of the unattributed explications is the fact that explication 5 draws on the Greek grammarian Dionysios Thrax, just like one of Ibn al-Faḍl's notes on the *Garden.*[57] I will treat all five as Ibn al-Faḍl's annotations.

Even before we look at the annotations, the opening lines of Ibn al-Faḍl's translation give the impression that he was interested in comparative grammar. In §1 of the text, the original Greek speaks of the word *athlophoros* "with the article" (the people of Thessaloniki will recognize this bare epithet as a reference to Demetrios). Ibn al-Faḍl deftly translates the concept, referring to "*al-mujāhid* with *alif* and *lām* alone."[58] In Arabic prefixing the letters *alif* and *lām* to a word is roughly equivalent to the Greek article.

Let us now turn to the annotations. Recall that when the Hellene (pagan) asked Demetrios what he believed, Demetrios replied that he believed in an all-powerful, unseen god, creator of all. To that the Hellene replied that he was very much in agreement, since he was not an Epicurean but rather a follower of Socrates. In response, Ibn al-Faḍl stresses just how bad Epicurean paganism is:[59]

تفسير: قال عبد الله بن[1] الفضل ناقل هذا المديح: إنّ أبيقرس السخين العين كان يدفع وجود الإله تعالى ويرى أنّ كون العالم بالاتّفاق، وقد طابقه على ذلك ضُلّال غيره.

[1]بن: ب؛ ابن: أ

Explication: ʿAbdallāh ibn al-Faḍl, translator of this encomium, says: The afflicted [literally "hot-eyed"] Epicurus rejected the existence of the Almighty Deity. His opinion was that the world came into being by coincidence. Other erring people have agreed with him on this.

57. See pp. 159 above and 171 below. The note in question on the *Garden* is not explicitly attributed to Ibn al-Faḍl either, but there is strong evidence for viewing the whole commentary on the *Garden* as Ibn al-Faḍl's work; see pp. 152–53 and n. 7 above.

58. **A** 243^{v}_{1}. Philippidis-Braat, "L'enkômion," 406_{14}: μόνον σὺν τῷ ἄρθρῳ τὸν ἀθλοφόρον.

59. Explication 1 (**A** 250^{r}_{9-13}, **B** 103^{v}_{16-19}), in §6, on **A** 250^{r}_{8} *lā min aṣḥābi Ibīqurus wa-man yajrī majrāhu* = Greek 408_{24}.

Ibn al-Faḍl concludes this brief remark as he often concludes his doxographical notes, referring to the others, usually anonymous as here, who have been led astray by the philosopher in question. In this context, it is a warning: even though the particular Hellene in question rejected Epicurus's allegedly atheistic cosmology, Epicurus had had, and still had, followers.[60]

At the same time, we may observe another feature that is typical of Ibn al-Faḍl's translations and comments, as already mentioned: careful attention to the transliteration of Greek. Ibn al-Faḍl transliterates "Epicurus" (Ἐπίκουρος) such that an Arabic speaker would place the stress on the antepenult, where it would have fallen when pronounced by medieval speakers of Greek: I*bī*qurus.

A bit further along in the text, where Saint Demetrios says that the Hellene should not use the word "god" to refer to the intelligible (i.e., immaterial) beings, or "substances," Ibn al-Faḍl elaborated on the point:[61]

تفسير[1]: قال عبد الله بن الفضل الناقل لهذا المديح: إنّما[2] ناقض القديس لهؤلاء الضُّلّال في الاسم الذي هو إلاه التفاتاً منه إلى المعنى الذي يشيرون إليه في هذه الآلهة الزمنيّة على رأيهم. وذلك أنهم، وإن قالوا إنها زمنيّة، ليس يعتقدون أنها محدثة بل أزليّة، لأنّ الزمان على رأيهم قديم، ولا مبدأ له، ويأتون لذلك بحجج مُبَهْرَجَة ومحيّرات خَفِيّة، حتى كأنها وكيدة حسب أوضاعهم، لا حسب ما يشهد به الحقّ. وإنّني لَأَعجَب من خَرَفِهِم، وهو قولهم إنها مخلوقة وليست محدثة بل أزلية. وهذا الاسم الذي هو إلاه على ما يزعم الآباء القدماء والأئمّة المتألّهون ملائم للجوهر الإلهي، يكاد يدلّ عليه، فليس للمخلوقات فيه نصيب، إلا أن يكون على سبيل الاستعارة، فأمّا على التحقيق، فلا.

وعدد الآلهة عند هذه الأمّة الضالّة مختلف، وذلك أن أهل أثينا يرون أن الآلهة اثنا عشر إلاهاً، وغيرهم يعتقد أنها كثيرة جدّاً، حتى تكاد تكون بلا نهاية، ويزعمون[3] أنّ منها ما هو سماوي، ومنها ما هو ناري، ومنها ما هو هوائي، ومنها ما هو مؤسّي أي مالي، ومنها ما هو أرضي، ومنها ما هو بحري. وقد ذكر هذا الآباء الروحانيون.

[1]تفسير: أ؛ التفسير: ب [2]إنّما: ب؛ إنّ ما: أ [3]ويزعمون: ب؛ ويزعموا: أ

Explication: ʿAbdallāh ibn al-Faḍl, translator of this encomium, says: The saint has refuted these erring people concerning the noun "god," turning from it to the notion (*maʿnā*) they indicate concerning these "temporal gods," as they would have it. For even if they say they are temporal [i.e., subject to time], they do not believe them to be originated (*muḥdath*) but rather pre-eternal (*azalī*), since in their opinion time is pre-eternal (*qadīm*) with no beginning. To this claim they bring counterfeit arguments and hidden confusions, such that it's as if [their arguments] are strengthened by virtue of their manners, not by virtue of what the truth testifies. I am truly astounded at their stupidity, namely that they say that they [the gods] are created and [yet] not originated but rather pre-eternal. The noun "god," according to the ancient fathers and divine imams, is fitting for the divine substance and just about refers to it [i.e., "god" is all but synonymous with "the divine substance"], such that created

60. For his espousal of a doctrine that the gods are "images" in the human mind, Epicurus was often viewed as an atheist, despite his statements to the contrary: Long and Sedley, *Hellenistic Philosophers*, 1:144–49, esp. 147.

61. Explication 2 (**A** 253^{r}_{7}–254^{r}_{9}, **B** 106^{r}_{4}–106^{v}_{6}) in §9, following **A** 253^{r}_{7}, **B** 106^{r}_{3} *allatī tuṭghīnā* but actually addressing **A** 253^{r}_{1-5}.

> beings have nothing to do with it, except in a metaphorical way (*ʿalā sabīl al-istiʿāra*), not strictly speaking (*ʿalā l-taḥqīq*).
>
> The number of gods according to this erring community (*umma*) differs. That is, the Athenians opine that the gods are twelve, while others believe that they are very plentiful, almost to the point of being infinite. They claim that some [gods] are celestial, some are fiery, some airy, some *mawahī*, that is watery (*māʾī*), some earthy, and some marine. The spiritual fathers have mentioned this.

In the first part of this note Ibn al-Faḍl argues that it is incoherent to say, as pagans do, that the gods are both created and pre-eternal. For Ibn al-Faḍl, the word "god" is a signifier that could only signify the sort of created beings (supposedly) worshipped by pagans in a metaphorical sense. Strictly speaking, "god" can refer only to the uncreated, eternal divine substance. In the second part of the note, he goes on to describe the various pagan beliefs about the gods.

While primarily about pagan doctrine and the definition of the word "god," this note also manages to slip in an Arabic lexicographical lesson. Ibn al-Faḍl often used recherché vocabulary in his translations, then glossed it in a note.[62] Here even in his note, he deliberately uses a more obscure word for "watery," *mawahī*, then glosses it with the common word, *māʾī*. This morphological lesson reinforces one we already encountered above in Ibn al-Faḍl's note in the *Garden* on *fam* (mouth) and its plural, *afwāh*, presented as the plural of the unusual word *fawah*.[63] Just as *fawah* in this theory gave way to the defective word *fam*, another word ending in *-awah*, *mawah* (water), yielded to the common word for water, *māʾ*. Indeed, medieval Arabic lexicographers thought of *mawah* and *māʾ* as deriving from the same root.[64]

In addition to Arabic morphology, Ibn al-Faḍl uses a standard term of medieval Arabic literary criticism: "metaphor" (*istiʿāra*), opposed here to "strictly speaking" (*taḥqīq*). This accords with his use of these same terms in his translation of John of Thessaloniki's *Encomium* itself.[65]

This note points to Ibn al-Faḍl's interests in the cosmological question of whether time and the world are eternal. The pagans, according to Ibn al-Faḍl, do not have a problem with saying that the gods are created but have no beginning in time because they believe time itself has no beginning (and, we might add, that certain celestial phenomena closely associated with time like the sun's progression around the zodiac have no beginning either). Just like the sun or the moon, the gods have always existed, even though they are created beings. We will return to the eternity of the world in chapter 8.

62. Pointed out by Noble and Treiger, "Christian Arabic Theology," 375 n. 17; Noble, "ʿAbdallah," 172.

63. See §1 above, p. 156.

64. *Lisān* s.v. *mwh*.

65. See ch. 2, p. 77.

In this same note, Ibn al-Faḍl also makes striking use of the word "imams" (*aʾimma*) to refer to church fathers, wielding what might seem (at least to the modern reader) like distinctively Muslim vocabulary. In Arabic as Muslims used it, *imām* referred to the prayer leader in a mosque but also to the divinely inspired ruler of the community of believers, such that in the early Abbasid period the title could be applied to Abbasid caliphs, descendants of the Prophet's son-in-law ʿAlī, and charismatic jurists like Aḥmad ibn Ḥanbal.[66] For Ibn al-Faḍl, of course, the fathers of the church were the true models of leadership of one's community. Gregory of Nazianzos had envisioned the model leader as one who underwent deification (*theōsis, taʾalluh*).[67] This is precisely how Ibn al-Faḍl describes the fathers of the church: "imams" who are "divine" or "deified" (*mutaʾallihūn*).

Passing over Ibn al-Faḍl's third explication (for which see chapter 7), we turn now to his fourth commenting on Saint Demetrios's account of how belief in the Trinity can be compatible with monotheism. Demetrios's account is in the first place exegetical (the divinely revealed Scripture mentions each of the three persons of the Trinity, so they must exist) and logical, taking advantage of Aristotle's theory of predication (Scripture's injunction to worship only one god must refer not to a single *person* but rather to a single divinity, which we may define as a single divine substance). The second part is meant to demonstrate the logical *compatibility* of Scripture's monotheistic statements with Trinitarian doctrine; the first, exegetical part is meant to tip the scales in favor of this Trinitarian reading. To this, Ibn al-Faḍl responds:[68]

تفسير[1]: العدد دالٌّ على كمّيّة الأمور لا جوهرها، وسبب الكمية الفصول والغيرية، وما لا يقبل فصلاً ولا غيرية لا يقبل كمية، وما لا يقبل كمية لا يقبل عدداً[2]. والجوهر الإلهي بهذه صفة وكذا صفاته، فلذلك لا يجوز أن يُعَدّ لا هو ولا هي.

[1]تفسير: أ؛ التفسير: ب [2]لا يقبل كمية، وما لا يقبل كمية لا يقبل عدداً: ب؛ ولا [3]يقبل[3] عدداً: أ

Explication: Number refers to the quantity of things, not their substance. The cause of quantity is divisions and alterity. Whatever does not admit of division or alterity does not admit of quantity, and what does not admit of quantity does not admit of number. The divine substance fits this description (*ṣifa*), as do its attributes (*ṣifāt*). Therefore one can enumerate neither [it] nor [its attributes].

Ibn al-Faḍl's syllogism is intended to show that divine substance cannot be enumerated (i.e., cannot be more than one). To make this ancillary point he uses the same Arabic technical terms of Aristotelian logic as he did in his translation. This facility with and interest in Arabic logic is typical for Ibn al-Faḍl, as we will see in chapter 6. Logic—and not merely received dogma—was a crucial part of theology

66. Cooperson, *Classical Arabic Biography.*

67. Elm, "Priest and Prophet"; Elm, *Sons,* 413–32.

68. Explication 4 (**A** 261^{r}_{7-12}, **B** 109^{v}_{13-17}) immediately following the first four words of §13 (*fa-lammā stakmala l-qiddīsu l-khiṭāb*) but actually referring to §12.

(a.k.a. metaphysics) for Ibn al-Faḍl, as it had been for John of Thessaloniki and other fathers of the church.

For Ibn al-Faḍl (and John of Thessaloniki), not only logic but also grammar could be crucial for a theological argument. In Saint Demetrios's serial refutation of various objections to Chalcedonian doctrines (§14), John of Thessaloniki has Demetrios describe the position of Apollinaris of Laodikeia (d. ca. 390), who held that Christ had a human body and soul but a divine mind, or, as the text more polemically puts it, that Christ had a body and soul but a soul without rationality. Demetrios then suggests that this doctrine derives from an implicit analogy with grammar—namely, that Christ has a defective human part and a perfect divine part.[69] Ibn al-Faḍl's translation subtly changes the Apollinarian argument into an *explicit* appeal to grammar: "they adduce the opinion of the grammarians."[70]

In the comment that appears at this point, Ibn al-Faḍl carefully explains the link with grammar for those who have not had the benefit of Byzantine grammar school:[71]

تفسير[١]: إن النحاة اليونانيين يزعمون أن الاسم تلزمه خمسة أشياء، وهي الجنس والنوع والشكل والعدد[٢] والإعراب، يزعمون أن الشكل كون الاسم بسيطاً ومركباً، وأنّ أحد تراكيبه أن يكون من اسمين كاملين.

فهؤلاء الضُّلّال، وهم[٣] أصحاب أبوليناريوس (كذا) الطاغي، قاسوا هكذا فقالوا: كما أنّ الاسم المركَّب من كاملين يقال لِجُزوَيهِ اسمان، هكذا المسيح إن كان مركَّباً من إلاهٍ تام وإنسان تام، فإنه يقال لكل واحد من جُزْوَيهِ[٤] مسيح، فيصير مسيحين. فيجب أن تكون البشرية ناقصة حتى لا تكون البشرية[٥] مسيحاً.

وإنني لأعجب من هذا الخرف، والتشبيه الرديء، والقياس الفاسد من جهات عدّة. وأنا أذكر ما سنح منها بعون الله تعالى، وشفاعة القديسين ذمتريوس ويوحنّا المادح له.

فأقول وأوجز إنّ هؤلاء القوم بمنزلة المجانين في أنهم أجروا المماثلة بين متباعدين في الغاية القُصْيا. والدليل على ذاك[٦] أن الاسم من الكم، وهو جنس فلسفي يعطي اسمه وحدّه لأنواعه وأشخاصه. والمسيح تعالى قنوم ذو جوهرين، ثم مع هذا إن الاسم لمّا كان مركّباً من اسمين، قيل لجزؤيه اسمان، لا لما كان جُزآه كاملين قيل لهما اسمان، والمسيح تعالى ليس مُركّباً من مسيحين فَيُقالَ لجزؤيه مسيحان. ونقول أيضاً أن السيّد المسيح، وإن كان مركّباً، إلا أنه لا[٧] يجري مجرى المركّبات من مادّة وصورة فيحكم عليه بحكمها[٨]، بل حاله حال[٩] فوق مقاييس العقول، وهذا بيّن عند ذوي الألباب الثاقبة. وفي ما[١٠] ذكرنا مقنعٌ، ولله جزيل المنّة.

[١]تفسير: أ؛ وآخرون يقولون: ب [٢]والعدد: أ؛ والغمدد: ب [٣]وهم: ب؛ هم: أ [٤]جُزْوَيهِ: ب؛ جُزيه: أ [٥]البشرية: أ؛ —ب [٦]ذاك: أ؛ ذلك: ب [٧]لا: ابن الراهب؛ ما: أ ب [٨]فيحكم عليه بحكمها: فبحُكم (أو: فيحكُم؟) عليه نحكمها [٩]حال: أ ب؛ —ابن الراهب [١٠]ما: ب؛ —أ

69. John of Thessaloniki, *Encomium to Saint Demetrios,* 14, ed. Philippidis-Braat, "L'enkômion," $412_{21–26}$.

70. **A** $265^{v}_{11–12}$, **B** 111^{r}_{2}: *fa-ya'tūna bi-ra'yi l-nuḥāt.* Cf. Greek 412_{26}: γραμματικήν τινα τεχνολογίαν, ὡς ἔοικε, τοῖς παισὶν ἐξηγούμενοι.

71. Explication 5 (**A** 264^{r}_{1}–265^{r}_{8}, **B** 111^{r}_{4}–111^{v}_{8}) following §14, ed. Philippidis-Braat, "L'enkômion," 412_{26}, **A** 263^{v}_{13} *li-l-ṣibyān* and two words later in **B** 111^{r}_{3} after *wa-ākharūna yaqūlūna.* Part of this explication (just before the end) was quoted by Ibn al-Rāhib in his *Kitāb al-Burhān,* Vat. ar. 104, fol. 4^v (see apparatus): *wa-qāla l-fāḍilu ʿAbdallāh ibn al-Faḍl inna l-sayyida l-masīḥ, wa-in kāna murakkaban . . . al-thāqiba.*

> *Explication:* The Greek grammarians claim that five things are attached to the noun,[72] namely genus,[73] species,[74] form,[75] number, and case (*iʿrāb*). They claim that the form is the noun being simple or compound, and that one of the ways it can be compound is for it to be composed of two perfect nouns.[76]
>
> These erring ones—being the followers of Apollinaris the impious—drew the following analogy, saying: "Just as the two parts of the noun composed of two perfect [nouns] are called nouns, so too in the case of Christ, if he is composed of perfect god and perfect man, each one of his two parts is called a christ, so there come to be two christs. So his humanity must be deficient in order for humanity not to be a christ."
>
> Now really, I am astounded at such feeble-mindedness, at such a vile comparison, an analogy faulty from so many angles. Of these I will mention what comes to mind, with the help of God, may he be exalted, and the intercession of Saints Demetrios and his encomiast John [of Thessaloniki].
>
> I say, keeping it short, that these people are at the level of madmen in their use of a comparison of two things that are as far apart as can be. The proof of this is that the noun is a type of quantity, which is a philosophical genus that gives its name and definition to its species and individuals. Now Christ, may he be exalted, is a hypostasis (*qanūm*) with two substances. Furthermore, it is when the noun is composed of two nouns that its two parts are called nouns, not when its two parts are perfect that they are called nouns. Christ, may he be exalted, is not composed of two christs such that his two parts would be called christs. Also, we say that the Lord Christ, even if he is composite, nevertheless is not so in the manner of things composed of matter and form such that judgments about them would apply to him, but rather his status transcends the analogies that minds can make. This is clear to those with penetrating minds (*al-albāb al-thāqiba*). In what we have said there is enough to persuade. Generous is God's favor.

Ibn al-Faḍl's account of Greek grammar is straight from the textbooks. Indeed, it reads very much like an Arabic translation of several lines from the *Art of Grammar* by Dionysios Thrax.[77] As already described earlier in this chapter, Dionysios Thrax describes the four possible combinations of two nouns to form a compound noun: perfect-perfect, deficient-deficient, deficient-perfect, and perfect-deficient. The combination Ibn al-Faḍl refers to here is the first: a compound noun formed

72. For example, Dionysios Thrax, *Ars grammatica*, §12 (περὶ ὀνόματος), ed. Uhlig, 24. The following three notes refer to this section, ed. Uhlig, 24–46, esp. 24–32.

73. *jins* ~ γένος: gender.

74. *nawʿ* ~ εἶδος: whether a word is primitive (πρωτότυπον), like the word γῆ (earth), or a form derived from a primitive word (παράγωγον), like γαιήϊος (earthly).

75. *shakl* ~ σχῆμα: simple, compound, or formed from a compound (παρασύνθετον).

76. That is the first way mentioned by Dionysius Thrax; see p. 159, n. 32, above.

77. See nn. 72–76 above.

from two "perfect" nouns—that is, two strings of Greek letters each of which is on its own a full Greek word.[78]

In accordance with the way Ibn al-Faḍl tweaked the meaning in his translation, here in his note, he attributes to the followers of Apollinaris the explicit argument that Christ's two parts, human and divine, are analogous to the two parts of a compound, and so governed by the same rules. To refute this argument, Ibn al-Faḍl appeals to Aristotelian logic (predication) and physics (matter and form) and his own interpretation of Dionysios Thrax's descriptive account of compound nouns.

Thus Ibn al-Faḍl again uses Aristotelian philosophy to make his theological argument. But to be able to make sense of what argument Demetrios (or rather John of Thessaloniki) was referring to, Ibn al-Faḍl's readers needed to understand Greek grammar.

4 CHRYSOSTOM ON HEBREWS: SUBSTANTIAL IMAGES

A final example will serve to underscore the philosophical aspect of Ibn al-Faḍl's philology. This example appears in Ibn al-Faḍl's translation of Chrysostom's commentary (in thirty-four homilies) on Paul's letter to the Hebrews.[79] In a marginal note on this text, Ibn al-Faḍl describes how he self-consciously created new Arabic philosophical vocabulary to capture an important terminological distinction in Chrysostom's Greek.

Chrysostom's second homily on Hebrews focuses on Paul's description of Christ with the phrase "the radiance of [God's] glory and the imprint (*charaktēr*) of his being/subsistence (*hypostasis*), sustaining all things with the word (*rhēma*) of his power, when through himself he had expiated our sins . . ." (Hebrews 1:3).[80] The homily takes this passage as an opportunity to refute a series of theologians whom Chrysostom considers heretical: Markion (d. ca. 160), Sabellios (fl. 220), Paul of Samosata (deposed as bishop of Antioch in 268–269), Markellos of Ankyra (d. ca. 374), Photeinos of Sirmium (d. ca. 376), and Arius (d. 336). Some, according to Chrysostom, had identified the Father and Son too closely, such that they ceased to be distinct persons of a trinity (Sabellios, Markellos, Photeinos, and Markion). Others had debased the Son, making him not only generated by the Father but also of an inferior nature (Paul of Samosata, Arius).[81] For Chrysostom, the power of

78. See p. 159 above.

79. Manuscripts: **A** = Paris ar. 96 (before 1229 CE); **B** = Paris ar. 95 (1217–1218 CE); **S** = Sinai ar. 303 (1228 CE). On the two Paris manuscripts, see Troupeau, *Catalogue des manuscrits arabes*, 1:74–75. For the date of the Sinai manuscripts, see https://www.loc.gov/item/00279384738-ms/.

80. Trans. based on the NRSV and Frederic Gardiner's translation in JChrys-NPNF-John/Heb, 370.

81. For the beliefs ascribed to these "heresiarchs," see the following references. Sabellios (Father became his own son and suffered on the cross; Father, Son, and Spirit are just different manifestations

the passage from Paul is that it at once elevates and humbles Christ, refuting both "extremes" in favor of the "middle ground" that Chrysostom advocates: Christ is generated (begotten) but not created by God, of the same nature and substance but independently self-subsisting (i.e., having his own distinct hypostasis).

A crucial passage in Chrysostom's positive advocacy for his own position hinges on the term "imprint" (*charaktēr*) in the Pauline phrase "imprint of his being" (χαρακτὴρ τῆς ὑποστάσεως αὐτοῦ). Chrysostom writes:[82]

> Then [Paul] adds: "and the imprint (*charaktēr*)." For the imprint is something other than its prototype, yet it is not other in all respects, but as to being subsistent (*enhypostatos*),[83] since here too the term "imprint" indicates that it is indistinguishable from that of which it is an imprint, similar in all respects. So when [Paul] calls [Christ] both form (*morphē*) and imprint, what do [the heretics] say?—"But man too," they say,[84] "is called an image (*eikōn*) of God.[85] What then? [Does that mean that man is] just like the Son?"—"No," says [Paul], but rather [tells us] that an image does not indicate similarity (*to homoion*).—And yet, in that man is called an image, it shows that there is resemblance in man. For what God is in heaven, man is on earth, I mean as to dominion. And as he has power over all things on earth, so also God has power over all things in heaven and on earth. But in any event, man is not called imprint, he is not called radiance, he is not called form; this last term indicates the substance (*ousia*), or also similarity in substance. So just as "the form of a slave"

of the one God): Simonetti, "Sabellio," esp. 9, 15; *ODB*, s.v. "Monarchianism." Paul of Samosata (the human Jesus only "participated in" God's Logos): Lang, "Christological Controversy." Markellos (God's Logos is ingenerate, existed in the Father alone before Creation, and will again after redemption): *ODB*, s.v. "Markellos of Ankyra." Photeinos (the Logos became the Son at the incarnation and will remain the Son only until the redemption; otherwise it is simply God's Word, not distinct from God): Elm, *Sons*, 233–34. Arius (the Logos was created in time by the Father and so is not co-eternal with the Father): *ODB*, s.v. "Arius." Markion (the god of the Old Testament, who created the world, is distinct from the truly good Christian god of the New Testament; Christ is a manifestation of the Christian god): *Brill's New Pauly*, s.v. "Marcion"; Räisänen, "Marcion," 105–6. The relevant aspect of Markion's thought here seems to be that "Markion, holding the Creation to be evil, denied the Son's preserving power": JChrys-NPNF-John/Heb, 371 n. 2.

82. Chrysostom, *Homilies on Hebrews*, 2.2, PG 63:22; trans. based on JChrys-NPNF-John/Heb, 371–72. Because Migne's text is particularly unsatisfying at this point, I have collated it with Vat. gr. 1656 (twelfth century), fol. 13^r: PG lines 28 Εἶτα] καὶ || 28–29 ὅτι καὶ χαρακτῆρ] ὅτι χ. || 34–35 εἰκόνος εἴρηται] θεοῦ εἴρ. || 36 ἀλλ' ὅτι εἰκὼν] ἀλλ' ὅτι ἡ εἰκὼν || 39 τοῦτο ὁ ἄνθρωπος] τ. ἄνθρ. || 42 τῶν ἐν τῷ οὐρανῷ καὶ τῶν ἐπὶ τῆς γῆς] τ. ἐν οὐρ. κ. ἐπὶ γ. || 43–44 οὐκ εἴρηται ἀπαύγασμα] om. : not trans. by Ibn al-Faḍl or Gardiner || 45 ἢ καὶ ὁμοιότητα] ἢ καὶ οὐσίαν καὶ ὁμ.

83. That is, as I understand him, Chrysostom is saying that the only difference between an imprint and its prototype is that they are distinct self-subsisting entities: hence they differ with respect to being subsistent in that they are each independently subsistent.

84. Reading φασι for φησι, as I propose based on Ibn al-Faḍl's translation: *yaqūlūn*.

85. Vat. gr. 1656: Ἀλλὰ καὶ θεοῦ. Ibn al-Faḍl's translation is consistent with this reading: *inna l-insāna ṣūratu llāhi taʿālā* (**BS**), or *inna* [[*l-insāna*]] *ṣūrata l-insāni ṣūratu llāhi taʿālā* (**A**). I have followed this reading in my translation. Savilius (as reported in the PG) had proposed deleting εἰκόνος

[Philippians 2:6–7] indicates nothing other than invariable man (*anthrōpon aparallakton*), so also the form of God indicates nothing other than God.

In order to advance his reading of Paul, Chrysostom has carefully contrasted the terms "imprint" (*charaktēr*) and "form" (*morphē*), with the term "image" (*eikōn*). Comparison with his commentary on Paul's letter to the Philippians shows that this exegetical move was more broadly an important aspect of his attempt to square Scripture with how he conceptualized the relationship between God, Christ, and the human being.[86] Here this allows him to address an important objection to his interpretation that when Paul says that Christ is an "imprint" of God he means that Christ shares God's nature and everything else about him except actual identity. The objection, as Chrysostom outlines it, is as follows: Scripture also says that the human being was created "in God's image" (κατ' εἰκόνα θεοῦ, Genesis 1:27); if the human being is an image of God, then Paul's statement that Christ is also an image of God (assuming "imprint" and "image" are synonyms) either fails to elevate Christ to the status of God or else elevates human beings in general, not only Christ, to God's status (a conclusion that all parties would find absurd). Chrysostom's careful distinction between "imprint" and "image," then, allows him to distinguish between these two scriptural statements: Christ is an "imprint" of God (indistinguishable from God in all respects except his independent self-subsistence), but man is a mere "image" of God.

Ibn al-Faḍl's translation of this passage is attentive to Chrysostom's conceptual-philological point. At first he translates *charaktēr* (imprint) as *ṣūra jawharīya* (substantial image), rendering *eikōn* (image) simply as *ṣūra* (image). Then, when Chrysostom discusses these words and *morphē,* Ibn al-Faḍl transliterates the Greek words in Arabic letters. His translation of this passage reads:[87]

εἴρηται. See, however, Ladner, "Concept," 7–8, where the possibility is suggested that in Paul's view man is the image of *Christ,* who is the image of God, making man the image of an image. If this were to lead us to accept some modified version of the PG text, then perhaps we would also opt for some version of **A**'s reading, perhaps with the second *al-insān* crossed out instead of the first, making it "Man is the image of the image of God."

86. Chrysostom, *Homilies on Philippians,* 6.3–4, PG 62:223, where Chrysostom discusses Paul's words "the form of a slave," arguing that the word "form" (*morphē*) refers to something "true" and "perfect" (perhaps akin to a Platonic Form or an Aristotelian universal). He explains: "Form (*morphē*) refers to [something's] invariability, inasmuch as it is a form. It is not possible for something to be of one substance but have the form of another [substance]. For example, no human being has the form of an angel, and no irrational [animal] has the form of a human being. How then would the Son? Then in our case, since we are composite, form is [the form] of the body, but in the case of the simple and uncompounded, it is [the form] of its substance." Cf. the translation at JChrys-NPNF-Gal-etc., 209, col. 1, bottom.

87. Ibn al-Faḍl, translation of Chrysostom's *Homilies on Hebrews, maqāla* 2, **A** 14^{r-v}, **B** 27^{v}–28^{r}, **S** 20^{v}–21^{r}.

ردف ذلك بقوله: «وصورة قنومه الجوهرية»، لأن الصورة الجوهرية غير الأصل، إلّا أنّها ليست غيره في كل الجهات، بل في القنومية. فإنّ قوله هنا: «صورة جوهرية»، إنّما يدلّ على ارتفاع الخُلف فيما[١] بينها[٢] وبين ما هي له صورة، وأنّها مثله في كل الجهات. والمعترضون يتشكّكون على الرسول في قوله إنه صورة، ويقولون: «فقد قيل أيضاً إنّ الإنسان صورة الله تعالى[٣]، أفمحلّ الابن إذاً[٤] كَمَحَلِّ الإنسان؟» والرسول يُزيل الشُّبْهة الطارئة عليهم قائلاً: «لا ما الابن كالإنسان»، لأنّ صورة الإنسان لا تدلّ على الشِّبْهِ الجوهري، وإن كان قد قيل إنه شبيهُ الله، أي إنّ حالَه في الأرض كما حال[٥] الله تبارك وتعالى في السماء، أي إنه رئيسٌ مِثْلَهُ، وكما أنّ الإنسان ضابط ومالك ومُسَلَّطٌ على كلّ ما على الأرض[٦]، هكذا الله عزّ وجلّ ضابط كلّ ما في السماء وعلى الأرض. ونقول قولاً[٧] آخرَ وهو إن الإنسان ما وُصِفَ بأنه صورة الله الجوهرية، بل صورة فقط[٨]، أي أنه ما قيل فيه[٩] إنه خَرَكْتِير[١٠]، ولا مُرفِي، اللذان يَدُلّان على الجوهر وعلى الشبه الجوهري، وكما أنّ مُرفِي العبد، أي صورته الجوهرية، لا تدلّ على شيء[١١] آخر إلّا على الإنسان[١٢] لا خلاف في إنسانيته، هكذا ومُرفِي الله لا يدلّ على شيء[١٣] من الأشياء إلّا على الله تعالى.

[١]فيما: أ؛ ما: ب؛ 'ما': س [٢]بينها: ب؛ بينهما: أ س [٣]إنّ الإنسان صورة الله تعالى: ب س؛ إنّ [[الإنسان]] صورة الإنسان صورة الله تعالى: أ [٤]إذاً: ب س؛ إذٍ: أ [٥]كما حال: أ ب س؛ والمقصود: كحال، أو: كمحلّ، أو: كما كان حال (؟) [٦]كلّ ما على الأرض: س؛ كلّما على: ب؛ كلّ ما في: أ [٧]قولاً: ب؛ قول: أ س [٨]فقط: +حاشية: أ، بحبر أحمر [٩]فيه: أ س؛ عنه: ب [١٠]خَرَكْتِير: خركتير: أ؛ خَرَاكْتِرْ: ب؛ خراكتيز: س [١١]شيء: أ ب؛ شيًا: س [١٢]الإنسان: ب؛ إنسان: أ س [١٣]شيء: أ ب؛ شيًا: س

Then [Paul] follows this by saying: “and the substantial image of his hypostasis (*qanūm*),” for the substantial image is different from the original. But it is not distinct from it in all aspects but rather with respect to self-subsistence (*qanūmīya*). Indeed his phrase here “substantial image” refers in particular to the elimination of difference between it and that of which it is an image, and [to the fact] that [the image] is similar to [the original] in all respects. The opponents raise doubts against the Apostle [Paul] with respect to his statement that [Christ] is an image, saying: “It has also been said that man is the image of God Almighty, so is the Son’s status therefore like man’s status?” But the Apostle removes the uncertainty that has come over them, saying: “No, the Son is not like man.” For man’s “image” does not refer to substantial likeness, even if it has been said that [man] is like unto God, that is, that his condition on earth is like the condition of God Blessed and Exalted in heaven, that is, that [man] is in charge like [God], and just as man is the one who maintains order and the possessor and the one given power over all that is on earth, likewise God the Mighty and Exalted maintains order over all that is in heaven and on earth. We say further that man was not described as being the substantial image of God but merely the image, that is, he was not called *kharaktīr*, nor *murfī*, both of which refer to the substance and to substantial similarity. Just as the *murfī* of the slave, that is, his substantial image, does not refer to anything other than man with no divergence concerning his humanity, likewise the *murfī* of God does not refer to anything other than God Almighty.

At this point Ibn al-Faḍl wrote a marginal note explaining that in Greek there are separate terms meaning “substantial image” and “nonsubstantial image” and that to capture these meanings, he needed to coin a new term in Arabic:[88]

حاشية[١]: قال عبد الله بن[٢] الفضل الخاطئ المسكين[٣] المفسّر لهذه[٤] الرسالة الإلهية: إنّ في اللغة اليونانية أسماءً تَدُلُّ على الصورة[٥] الجوهريّة الذاتية مفردة، من ذلك خركتير[٦] ومرفي والخركتير[٧] هو الذي استعمله[٨] الرسول[٩] في هذا[١٠] الفصل من الرسالة؛ وأسماء تدلّ على الصورة التي ليست كذلك[١١]، من ذلك إيقون، وهذا الاسم هو الذي استُعمل في الإنسان[١٢]، فقيل إنّه صورةُ الله. فأمّا اللغة العربية فقد

88. **A** 14v–15r, **B** 28r. **S** does not transmit this note.

ضاقت في هذا الموضع حسب ما وصلتْ إليه معرفتي، ولم يوجد فيها اسمٌ يدلّ هذه الدلالة. فلذلك زِدتُ في الكلام لفظة[13] الجوهرية، فقلتُ: «وصورة قنومه الجوهرية»، ليتبين[14] المعنى، ويُمكن دحض حُجّة المناقض في هذه اللغة. ونحن نسـ<أ>ل الله[15] المعونة والإرشاد[16].

[1]حاشية: أ؛ –ب [2]بن: ب؛ ابن: أ [3]الخاطئ المسكين: أ؛ –ب [4]المفسّر لهذه: أ؛ مفسّر هذه: ب [5]الصورة: أ؛ الصور: ب [6]خركتير: أ؛ خَرَاكْتِيْر: ب [7]والخركتير: أ؛ وخَرَاكْتِيْر: ب [8]هو الذي استعمله: أ؛ هي التي استعملها: ب [9]+يدل على الصورة التي ليست الاسم هو الذي استعمل ماهيئة (كذا) الانسان: أ [10]هذا: ب؛ هذه: أ [11]وأسماء تدلّ . . . كذلك: ب؛ واسمى كذاك: أ [12]الاسم هو الذي استُعمل في الإنسان: ب؛ –أ [13]لفظة: أ؛ 'لفظة': ب [14]ليتبين: ب؛ ليبين: أ [15]الله: ب؛ الله تعالى: أ [16]المعونة والإرشاد: ب؛ حسن المعونة: أ

> *Marginal note: ʿAbdallāh ibn al-Faḍl the wretched sinner, interpreter of this divine letter, said:*[89] In Greek there are nouns that refer to substantial, essential images (*al-ṣuwar al-jawharīya al-dhātīya*) alone, such as χαρακτήρ (*kharaktīr*) and μορφή (*murfī*), which is what the Apostle [Paul] used in this section of the epistle; and nouns that refer to the image that is not like that, such as εἰκών (*īqūn*), which is the noun that was used concerning man when it was said that he is an image of God (*ṣūrat Allāh*). As for Arabic, it is limited in this respect, as far as I know, and it has no noun with this meaning. So I added to the phrase the word "substantial" and said, "and the substantial image of his hypostasis" (*wa-ṣūratu qanūmihi l-jawharīya*) so that the meaning would be clear. It is possible to refute the argument of one's opponent using this language. And we ask God for aid and guidance.

In this note, Ibn al-Faḍl self-consciously invents a new Arabic term to reproduce the distinct definitions that Chrysostom read into the Greek of Paul and the Septuagint version of Genesis. What was for Chrysostom an exegetical move (though one that he presented as the straightforward consequence of the obvious meanings of *charaktēr, morphē,* and *eikōn*) has now been encoded in Ibn al-Faḍl's Arabic.

In crafting new Arabic technical vocabulary, Ibn al-Faḍl was following in the footsteps of the Greek-Arabic translators before him. In his own day, the Syriac- and Arabic-speaking Nestorian Christian Elias of Nisibis (975–1046) remarked on Arabic's lack of technical vocabulary relative to Greek, Syriac, and Persian.[90] Fill-

89. The wording here strongly suggests that the scribe has preserved the words that Ibn al-Faḍl himself used to introduce his comment, for it is usual for a writer to call *himself,* not others, a "poor sinner." This would mean that Ibn al-Faḍl calls himself a *mufassir* as well, implying that he viewed his work as a *tafsīr*, an "explication" of the text, rather than a translation. Complicating this is the question of what the words "this divine letter/treatise" (*al-risāla al-ilāhīya*) refer to. They could refer to Chrysostom's commentary, but it seems more likely that they refer to Paul's epistle. This would seem to imply in turn that Ibn al-Faḍl considered his translation with commentary of Chrysostom's homilies on Paul's letter to the Hebrews to be an explication, not of the text translated, but of the text that *Chrysostom* had explicated. In other words, Ibn al-Faḍl does not present his work as a super-commentary, but as a first-level commentary on the focus text itself. This may be a clue as to how medieval translators—in particular in this Antiochian milieu—understood their own activities.

90. Elias of Nisibis, *Liber sessionum*, session 6, ed. Seleznyov, 127–28; Cheikho, "Majālis," 373; cited by Graf, *GCAL*, 2:125–26; Roggema, "Ḥunayn," 769; Bertaina, "Science," 203. Cheikho's edition presents the discussion of technical vocabulary as if it were a quotation from Ḥunayn ibn Isḥāq's *Kitāb al-nuqaṭ* (written two centuries earlier), and this is how the passage has typically been interpreted, but it seems

ing in these gaps was part of the translator's task when the texts in question—texts like Chrysostom's exegetical homilies—were highly technical or philosophical.

By the eleventh century, Chrysostom's classification of images might have taken on additional significance. The Byzantine theory of images had developed considerably in the eighth and ninth centuries as a result of the Iconoclast Controversy (εἰκονομαχία) in order to allow for a conceptual distinction between an image of Christ and Christ himself while nevertheless justifying the practice of venerating images of Christ.[91]

John of Damascus, famous for his defense of icon veneration, wrote a commentary on Paul's Epistles based on that of Chrysostom, as indicated by the title it bears in some manuscripts: *Abbreviated Selections from the General Commentary of John Chrysostom, Selected by John of Damascus.*[92] Discussing this same passage of Paul's letter to the Hebrews, the Damascene's commentary explains that Paul's statement that Christ is the *charaktēr* of God's subsistence (*hypostasis*) refers to the Gospel passage typically used to show that Christ is in some sense identical with God the Father: "The one who has seen me has seen the father [John 14:9]."[93] He thus carries over Chrysostom's reading in much abbreviated and much less explicit form. In the Damascene's text, the point is that seeing Christ is *the same as* (not merely *like*) seeing the Father, which is why Christ is called a *charaktēr* (not a mere image) of God. But the comparison of a *charaktēr* to a mere image is no longer explicit.

Elsewhere, the Damascene uses different terminology to talk about the same pivotal concept. In his third oration on images, he distinguishes six kinds of images.[94] The first kind of image he defines is the "natural image" (*eikōn physikē*). After a series of scriptural citations including the pivotal passage from Paul's letter to the Hebrews (that Christ is the "imprint" of God), the Damascene writes: "The Son is a natural image of the Father, invariable, similar in all ways to the Father except in ingenerateness and fatherhood."[95] (That is, Christ is generated—though pre-eternal and not created—by the Father, while the Father is not generated.) This kind of image is to be contrasted with the third kind of image, an image made by God by way of imitation

to me that the passage in question must be in Elias's own voice because it begins with no indication that it is a quotation but rather with a transition signaling that the text is returning to an issue raised by Elias's interlocutor, the vizier (*wa-mimmā yadullu ʿalā anna lughata l-ʿarabi laysat awsaʿa min sāʾiri l-lughāt*, Seleznyov, 128_1, responding to the vizier's assertion *lughatu l-ʿarabi awsaʿu min sāʾiri l-lughāt*, ibid., 126_7). Only what *precedes* Ḥunayn's name (the claim that Syriac has fewer synonyms than Arabic only for unappealing things that people would rather not talk about) is clearly attributed to Ḥunayn.

91. Ladner, "Concept"; Parry, *Depicting the Word*. I thank Andrew Griebeler for referring me to the latter.

92. Ed. Volk; see introduction, 1, 3.

93. On Hebrews 1:3, ed. Volk, 474.

94. *Oration* 3.18–23, ed. Kotter, 126–30. See Parry, *Depicting the Word*, 23 n. 10, 39–41.

95. *Oration* 3.18_{19-21}, ed. Kotter, 127.

(κατὰ μίμησιν)—namely, man created in God's image.[96] This is precisely Chrysostom's distinction between an "imprint" (*charaktēr*) and an "image" (*eikōn*).

Ibn al-Faḍl's new Arabic terminology, like the Damascene's, opts not for two independent words ("imprint" and "image") but rather two terms each framed as a type of "image" (*eikōn, ṣūra*). Perhaps this similarity was a conscious choice on Ibn al-Faḍl's part to align his terminology with the Damascene's (although if so, he chose to call the imprint a "substantial" rather than "natural" image). Alternatively, it may simply be a coincidence, the consequence, in each case, of generalizing from the particular exegetical context in which Chrysostom had found it expedient to make the distinction. In any case, the result was that the philosophical language advocated by Ibn al-Faḍl resonated well with the influential thought of John of Damascus.

Calling attention to his new Arabic technical term, Ibn al-Faḍl stresses its usefulness in debating an opponent—perhaps, we might speculate, one who accuses Christians of polytheism for their belief in the Trinity, or of idolatry for their veneration of icons. Such accusations were, of course, quite commonly leveled against Christians by Muslims. We know from the few original works of his that have received scholarly attention that Ibn al-Faḍl was indeed engaged in defending Christian doctrine against Muslim challenges.[97] Here, we see that Ibn al-Faḍl's approach to the task included the introduction of new Arabic philosophical vocabulary on the basis of Byzantine terminology.

Subsequent readers were to recognize Ibn al-Faḍl's terminological distinction as an important feature of his translation, to judge from the addition of the Greek terms—in a fine Byzantine minuscule—above their Arabic transcriptions in one thirteenth-century manuscript.[98]

This sort of attention to detail must have played a role in the popularity of Ibn al-Faḍl's translations. His decision to create new technical vocabulary in the target language represents a phenomenon familiar to Graeco-Arabists, for it was a major part of the task undertaken by translators of "secular" philosophy, medicine, and other technical subjects from Greek into Arabic in the eighth to tenth century, and this fact has been noted and appropriately highlighted as an important aspect of translators' intellectual contributions.[99] We thus see Ibn al-Faḍl here engaging in a practice of translation shared with translators in Baghdad like Ḥunayn ibn Isḥāq (808–873). Ibn al-Faḍl treats Chrysostom's text not simply as an edifying "religious" text to be consumed passively but as a philosophical argument that must be understood precisely and translated with an Arabic term that will allow

96. *Oration* 3.20, ed. Kotter, 128.

97. Treiger, "ʿAbdallāh," 95.

98. Paris ar. 96 (**A**), fol. 14ᵛ. For the manuscript, see n. 79 above. For this and similar examples, see Roberts, "Writing."

99. Rosenthal, *Classical Heritage*, 16–17; Gutas, *GTAC*, 149–50.

a crucial Chrysostomic concept to be salient in the Arabic—more salient than in the original Greek. This might allow one to refute one's opponents and certainly would make it intellectually worthwhile to study this text. In this example, we see clearly that Ibn al-Faḍl's translations and retranslations were meant to capture the philosophical ideas undergirding and driving the texts of a Byzantine ecclesiastical curriculum being taught from Mount Athos to Constantinople to Antioch.

5 CONCLUSION

The examples in this chapter begin to give a sense of the range of Ibn al-Faḍl's annotations on his translations, from Greek and Arabic philology to philosophy. Further examples could be given, such as his notes on Basil's *Hexaemeron* to explain that in Greek Sunday is called the Lord's Day (in Arabic it is simply "day one")[100] and to provide Euclid's definitions of "figure," "surface," "plane surface," and "circle."[101]

Even without exhaustively treating Ibn al-Faḍl's marginalia, we may divide them into several categories: (1) philological, (2) doxographical, and (3) philosophical. In philological notes, he explains the meaning of unusual Arabic words, offers grammatical explanations of tricky Arabic morphology and syntax, and, when relevant for understanding his translation choices or for interpreting the text, discusses the original Greek as well. Doxographical notes are concerned primarily with reporting the philosophical opinions of philosophers (such as Epicurus's alleged atheism). Philosophical notes primarily address philosophical topics themselves, such as how to define a concept in logic. Taking a sufficiently broad definition of philosophy, we may include notes on sciences like geometry, astronomy, and physics under this heading.

These three categories often overlap. Grammar and lexicography could be wielded to coin a new philosophical term and define its conceptual scope. Doxography could be followed in the same note by a discussion of the philosophical question at stake. Nevertheless, the three categories can help make sense of Ibn al-Faḍl's educational agenda as expressed in his marginalia.

Ibn al-Faḍl's annotations often give the appearance of notes for the purpose of education.[102] Many are abbreviated marginal notes of the sort that one might write in preparation for reading a text with students, to remind oneself of what points to raise with them. Others, at least in the form we have them, appear more formal and planned, as if written for inclusion as part of Ibn al-Faḍl's "published" Arabic version of the text. In all cases, the marginalia make clear that Ibn al-Faḍl intended

100. **B** 34_{14-16}, in homily 2, *faṣl* 9 = Greek 2.8, ed. Amand de Mendieta and Rudberg, 37_2, τετιμημένην.
101. **Q** 7, in homily 1, *faṣl* 1 = Greek 1.3, ed. Amand de Mendieta and Rudberg, 6_2, 6_6.
102. I thank Maria Mavroudi and Asad Ahmed for suggesting this interpretation.

readers to work through these texts carefully as part of a course of study that would train them not only in the specific texts but also in core subjects of ancient and medieval paideia: grammar, rhetoric, logic, and so on.

Philological marginalia served this aim by encouraging students, probably native speakers of colloquial Arabic or Syriac, to acquire excellent knowledge of high literary Arabic—a purpose that the elaborate Arabic of Ibn al-Faḍl's prefaces to his translations could also serve, as we have seen. Other philological notes allowed students who did not know Greek to glimpse features of the Greek language that would help them understand Arabic translations from Greek. Indeed, perhaps some students of such texts *were* learning or had learned Greek. Finally, the philological marginalia fostered an approach to the texts that was at once erudite and painstakingly meticulous. These were texts to be pored over. Every word mattered.

Doxographical and philosophical notes likewise helped the student of philosophical disciplines to review (or learn) those subjects as part of the vivid setting in which these foundational texts of Byzantine Christianity had been composed. Doxographical notes in particular (as we will see in the rest of part 2) helped situate the church fathers within the rich ancient tradition out of which they emerged.

Ibn al-Faḍl's marginalia thus reinforce the impression that his was not so much an attempt to make Greek texts available to the Christian Arab "masses," congregations of men and women without the time or the money or the inclination to learn the Greek that would allow them to read or listen to the original texts. It was, rather, a project to offer Arabic-speakers an elite scholarly education. Perhaps some who sought such learning were training (like the Cappadocian Fathers themselves) to be churchmen, administrators, or government officials; an updated Arabic version of the Byzantine curriculum would have allowed them to thrive in the Byzantine Empire in close proximity to cities under Muslim administration. Others might have been monks and laymen intent on preserving and participating in an ancient scholarly tradition, and on contemplating, through scholarship, something of the divine.

6

LOGIC

In the previous chapter, we saw that Ibn al-Faḍl's marginalia bear witness to how he thought about and taught the Greek Christian classics that he translated or retranslated into Arabic. This chapter and those that follow will explore how Ibn al-Faḍl, in his interpretation and teaching of this Byzantine ecclesiastical curriculum, engaged with several philosophical disciplines.

It is fitting to begin an investigation of philosophy's place in Ibn al-Faḍl's translations and annotations with logic, for logic was, in antiquity and the Middle Ages, the gateway to philosophy. This chapter begins with an abbreviated sketch of the history of Aristotelian logic in the eastern Mediterranean and Middle East from Aristotle to the eleventh century CE, and then turns to several passages from Ibn al-Faḍl's translations and annotations that attest to his interest in logic. The three chapters that follow will follow a similar pattern, each sketching the history of the discipline whose name it bears (physics, cosmology, and astronomy) before turning to what Ibn al-Faḍl had to say about it.

From the point of view of the eleventh century, logic began with Aristotle (384–322 BCE). Aristotle had laid out his theory of logic in a series of treatises grouped by the later tradition into a corpus known as the *Organon* (Tool) because it was conceived as a tool for formal thought and demonstration concerning the natural world (physics) and ontology ("metaphysics," or, as Aristotle called it, "theology" and "first philosophy").[1] The *Organon* introduces the student to Aristotle's theory of predication, that is, in what senses we say things about someone or something

1. Aristotle, *Metaphysics* E, 1026a19, 24: θεολογική (φιλοσοφία) ~ *ilāhīyāt;* ἡ πρώτη φιλοσοφία ~ *al-falsafa al-ūlā*. See Cohen, "Aristotle's Metaphysics," §1; Inwagen and Sullivan, "Metaphysics," §1.

(*Categories*); how to analyze strings of words (utterances), especially statements or "propositions," in order to understand how the parts of utterances interact with one another (*On Interpretation*); syllogisms, assertoric and modal, that is, the rules of valid inference (*Prior Analytics*); epistemology, causality, and scientific demonstration through inferences from true premises (*Posterior Analytics*); dialectic, that is, how to conduct a valid argument or debate, making sound inferences from premises that are not certain but only probable or generally accepted (*Topics*); and logical fallacies committed and debate tricks employed by those seeking to prove and refute arguments, especially in competitive debate settings (*Sophistical Refutations*). In the Greek commentary tradition of late antique Alexandria (and later among Arabic Aristotelians), Aristotle's treatises on nonmetrical (*Rhetoric*) and metrical (*Poetics*) discourse were also integral parts of the *Organon*.[2] Aristotle's system, notably modal logic, was further developed by his successors, especially Theophrastos (fourth/third century BCE) and Eudemos (fourth century BCE).[3]

The Stoics, especially Chrysippos (ca. 280–207 BCE), developed their own system of logic that impacted the later tradition mainly through the incorporation of their ideas by commentators on Aristotle's logical works.[4] The famous physician and Peripatetic philosopher Galen of Pergamon (second/?third century CE) wrote an *Introduction to Dialectic*, a book *On Demonstration*, and commentaries on Aristotelian and Stoic logical works; of these, only the *Introduction to Dialectic* survives.[5]

Many commentaries on Aristotle's logical works survive; many others, like Galen's, were composed and read in the past but do not survive today. This abundance of logical works in late antiquity and the Middle Ages is largely explained by the central role logic played in higher education. In order to teach logic, philosophers produced commentaries and paraphrases to help make sense of it for students, improve and systematize its exposition, and extend it, incorporating the logical insights of philosophers after Aristotle, Peripatetics and Stoics alike.[6] Commentators on Aristotle's logical works include the pagans Alexander of Aphrodisias (fl. ca. 200 CE, perhaps active in Athens); Porphyry (234–ca. 305), a Syrian who studied with the famous Platonist philosopher Plotinos in Rome; Ammonios (fifth/sixth century), a student of Proklos in Athens and teacher of philosophy in Alexandria, following in the footsteps of his father, Hermeias; the Christian John Philoponos (fifth/sixth century), active in Alexandria and a student of Ammonios and the pagan philosopher Olympiodoros of Alexandria (sixth century); and the

2. Black, *Logic*, chs. 1–2. I owe this observation and the reference to an anonymous reviewer.

3. Bobzien, "Ancient Logic," §3.

4. Bobzien, §3.

5. Εἰσαγωγὴ διαλεκτική [= *Institutio logica*], ed. Kalbfleisch; trans. Kieffer. See Bobzien, "Ancient Logic," §7.

6. Bobzien, "Ancient Logic," §7.

pagan Simplikios (sixth century), a student of Ammonios and Olympiodoros in Alexandria and the pagan Damaskios in Athens, where Simplikios was teaching when Emperor Justinian closed the Athenian school in 529.[7]

In addition to commenting on Aristotle's *Organon,* Porphyry composed an *Introduction* (*Eisagōgē*) to Aristotle's *Categories,* the first work of the *Organon.* Porphyry's *Eisagoge* discusses the various senses of five key terms of the Aristotelian theory of predication: genus, species, difference, property, and accident. The *Eisagoge* was extraordinarily influential in the later tradition, Greek, Latin, Syriac, and Arabic alike. It came to be the very first logical text to be read by the student embarking upon a philosophical education, serving as an introduction not only to the *Categories* but in practice to the entire *Organon.* As a result, it became the focus of numerous commentaries itself. Ammonios, Philoponos, Olympiodoros, Elias (sixth century), and David (sixth century) wrote commentaries on the *Eisagoge,* of which those by Ammonios, Elias, and David survive,[8] as well as part of a commentary edited under the name of "pseudo-Elias."[9]

The teaching of logic continued in Syria and northern Mesopotamia without a break, from the late Roman to the Islamic period.[10] Many of the commentaries on the *Organon* and Porphyry's *Eisagoge* were translated into Syriac and eventually into Arabic. For the sake of brevity, I will mention only the translations of commentaries on Porphyry's *Eisagoge.* Philoponos's commentary was translated into Syriac and perhaps Arabic as well. Ammonios's commentary was translated into Syriac by the Miaphysite Christian scholar and Jacobite patriarch of Antioch Athanasius of Balad (d. 686) and then into Arabic by Abū ʿUthmān al-Dimashqī (d. after 914).[11] Elias's commentary was available in Syriac; a Christian from a Persian family, Abū l-Khayr al-Ḥasan ibn Sawār ibn Bābā ibn Bahnām, known as Ibn al-Khammār (b. 942), who was a student of Yaḥyā ibn ʿAdī, translated it from Syriac into Arabic.[12] Syriac-speaking scholars produced at least four different Syriac translations of Porphyry's *Eisagoge* itself, with new Syriac commentary, from the fifth to seventh century. Multiple Arabic translations, from the Syriac

7. Bobzien, §7; Blank, "Ammonius"; Wildberg, "Olympiodorus"; Watts, *City,* esp. ch. 5.

8. See Ibn al-Ṭayyib, *Tafsīr Kitāb Īsāghūjī,* ed. Gyekye, xxv–xxvi; Wildberg, "Elias"; Wildberg, "David." Syriac excerpts from Philoponos's commentary may be preserved in manuscripts such as Vat. syr. 158, no. 9, beginning on fol. 107ʳ; see Assemani and Assemani, *Bibliothecae Apostolicae Vaticanae codicum manuscriptorum catalogus,* 3:307: "*In Isagogen Commentaria* . . . . Videtur esse *Ammonii,* aut potius *Johannis Philoponi.*" In describing Paris syr. 248, an apograph of Vat. syr. 158, Georr describes no. 9 (beginning on fol. 63ʳ) as "extraits de la version du commentaire . . . par Jean Philoppon [*sic*]": *Les Catégories d'Aristote,* 203; cited by Gyekye, ibid., xxvi n. 6.

9. Ps.-Elias, *Lectures on Porphyry's Isagoge,* ed. Westerink.

10. Gutas, "Aspects," 43.

11. *EI*³, s.vv. "Athanasius of Balad" and "Abū ʿUthmān al-Dimashqī."

12. Ibn Abī Uṣaybiʿa, *ʿUyūn,* 428–29; cited by Gyekye, in Ibn al-Ṭayyib, *Tafsīr Kitāb Īsāghūjī,* xxvi.

translations, were produced from the eighth to tenth century: by Ibn al-Muqaffaʿ (d. ca. 815), Ayyūb ibn al-Qāsim al-Raqqī (d. ca. 840), and Abū ʿUthmān al-Dimashqī (d. ca. 920).[13] Many Arabic commentaries were produced by both Christians and Muslims.[14]

Meanwhile, the *Organon* and *Eisagoge* and commentaries on them continued to be used and commented upon in Greek as well. Most prominently, John of Damascus (d. 749) wrote an introduction to philosophy, in particular elementary logic, known as the *Dialectica*.[15] To judge from the Greek manuscript tradition alone, this was, as already mentioned, a very popular work in the middle Byzantine period.[16] The Arabic translation by Antonios of Saint Symeon is also well attested.[17]

The first part of John of Damascus's *Dialectica* roughly parallels Porphyry's *Eisagoge*, Aristotle's *Categories*, and commentaries on both.[18] Using the Aristotelian conceptual framework, the Damascene addresses several particularly prominent Christian theological terms: "hypostasis" (self-subsisting existence), "person" (πρόσωπον, whose definition is similar to that of an "individual," ἄτομον, as he notes); *enhypostaton* (primarily meaning something that is not self-subsisting but subsists in a hypostasis not itself, e.g., human nature subsisting in an individual human being; or, similarly, soul and body, neither constituting a human being on its own, subsisting together in a human individual); *anhypostaton* (not existing or not self-subsisting). Most of the examples given are not specifically Christian, although one example of something *enhypostaton* is Christ's flesh.[19] Then the text returns to the *Categories* tradition, including a series of "chapters" on Aristotle's ten types of predication ("categories") themselves: substance, quantity, relation, quality, action, undergoing action, position, where, when, and condition.[20] John of Damascus's

13. Dimashqī's translation: ed. Badawī in Aristotle, *Manṭiq Arisṭū*, 3:1055–1104.

14. Ibn al-Ṭayyib, *Tafsīr Kitāb Īsāghūjī*, ed. Gyekye, xxvi–xxx.

15. Ierodiakonou and Bydén, "Byzantine Philosophy," §1.3. The work goes by various names in the manuscript tradition, including the title *Philosophers' Chapters* (Vat. gr. 490, twelfth/thirteenth century); ed. Kotter, in John of Damascus, *Institutio elementaris, Capita philosophica (Dialectica)*, 47.

16. Kotter (38) counts one tenth-century and nineteen eleventh-century manuscripts—along with 279 (!) other manuscripts. *Pinakes* (accessed 15 December 2017) lists five tenth-, one tenth/eleventh-, and seventeen eleventh-century manuscripts. See also ch. 1, p. 27 and n. 146.

17. Graf, *GCAL*, 2:43.

18. Shorter recension, §§1–25; longer recension, §§1–42. The two recensions organize the discussion somewhat differently; I cite section numbers for both recensions. My discussion of sources and parallels is based on Kotter's detailed *apparatus fontium*.

19. *Dialectica* §26/43_{5}, §27/$44_{10–11}$, §28/$45_{7–15}$, §29/46; ed. Kotter, 108–10. Krausmüller, "Enhypostaton." Cf. Ibn al-Faḍl's four definitions of *qanūm* (hypostasis): Noble and Treiger, "Christian Arabic Theology," 381–82.

20. §30/47 (parallel divisions of "existent being" and "substance"), §§31–32/48–49 (substance), §§33–40/50–57 (the other nine types of predication). Cf. Aristotle, *Categories* 4, 1b25–27.

subsequent discussion also overlaps with Aristotle's *Metaphysics*.[21] Continuing *Categories* material, the Damascene covers propositions, negation, and affirmation (based on Aristotle's *On Interpretation*) and definitions, premises, and syllogisms (based on the *Prior Analytics*).[22] Even within these sections, the parallels with commentaries on the *Categories* continue, showing how the later tradition wove these interrelated subjects into a new order of exposition, and how John of Damascus himself was part of that tradition, continuing the process by rearranging and revising for his own purposes. A list of definitions of "philosophy" near the end of the shorter redaction draws on Plato and Aristotle via Aristotelian and Neoplatonic commentaries.[23] Another rare explicitly Christian discussion "on hypostatic union" occurs near the end. Using the concepts laid out and discussed in the Damascene's thoroughly Peripatetic work, this section addresses specifically Christian concerns but in the abstract—for example, speaking of two natures coming together to form one hypostasis while preserving those two natures intact—but not mentioning Christ or human and divine natures. Instead, the Damascene's example of choice continues to be the soul and the body.[24] This was an introductory textbook on logic that helpfully discussed the concepts and terminology necessary for further philosophical study, illustrated with abundant examples—at the same time hinting at, but not engaging in, the specifically Chalcedonian Christian doctrinal arguments that Aristotelian logic might be used to make.

Although the Byzantine literary record is especially fragmentary for the seventh and eighth centuries, the teaching of Aristotelian logic in Greek seems to have continued uninterrupted.[25] Leo the Mathematician (d. after 869) probably taught and wrote about logic, but his works do not survive.[26] The scholar, teacher, and eventual patriarch of Constantinople Photios (d. after 893), whose book reviews we encountered in chapter 3, taught logic and wrote about Aristotle's *Categories*.[27] Arethas of Caesarea (d. after 932) assembled notes on Porphyry's *Eisagoge* and Aristotle's *Categories* and copied them into manuscripts that still survive.[28] In the eleventh century, Psellos composed interpretive paraphrases of *On Interpretation* and *Prior Analytics* book 1,[29]

21. §42/59 (on possession and deprivation); cf. *Metaphysics* Δ.20, 1022b4–14; 22, 1022b22–1023a7.
22. §§47–48/64–65.
23. §49/66.
24. §50/67: Περὶ τῆς καθ' ὑπόστασιν ἑνώσεως.
25. Ierodiakonou, "Psellos' Paraphrasis," 157; Ierodiakonou and Bydén, "Byzantine Philosophy."
26. Ierodiakonou and Bydén, "Byzantine Philosophy," §1.1.
27. Ierodiakonou and Bydén, §1.3.
28. Ierodiakonou and Bydén, §1.3.
29. Paraphrase of *On Interpretation* (Moore PHI.16): in Ammonios, *Ammonii Hermei Commentaria in Librum peri Hermeneias*, ed. Manutius, M1r–O6r. Paraphrase of *Prior Analytics* 1 (Moore PHI.18): unedited. For both texts, see Ierodiakonou, "Psellos' Paraphrasis."

along with other logical works.[30] In his paraphrase of *On Interpretation*, he largely follows Aristotle and earlier commentators (as, indeed, do most other commentaries) but occasionally offers new ways of expressing and defending received interpretations and even new interpretations of his own.[31]

Psellos's student and successor to the head professorship of philosophy in Constantinople, the southern Italian John Italos (ca. 1025–after 1082), wrote short works on logic. And although Eustratios of Nicea (fl. ca. 1100) wrote his commentary on the *Posterior Analytics* book 2 after Ibn al-Faḍl's lifetime, we may nevertheless mention it, since it suggests that this text on epistemology and scientific induction had continued to be studied in the eleventh century as well; otherwise within what tradition, and using what copy of the *Posterior Analytics*, would he have composed the commentary?[32]

As Katerina Ierodiakonou and Börje Bydén have stressed, logic was at the core of the "standard philosophical curriculum in Byzantium," which also included arithmetic and physics. The texts most used to teach logic were Porphyry's *Eisagoge*, Aristotle's *Categories, On Interpretation, Prior Analytics* 1.1–7, and *Sophistical Refutations* 1–7, covering predication, statements, syllogisms, and logical fallacies.[33] Along with John of Damascus's *Dialectica*, Byzantine textbooks on logic included the first part of the anonymous *Logic and Quadrivium* dated 1007–1008.[34]

The Byzantine logic curriculum is neatly mirrored by what we know of the seventh- to ninth-century Syriac curriculum in the Near East: Porphyry's *Eisagoge*, Aristotle's *Categories, On Interpretation,* and *Prior Analytics* 1.1–7.[35] Indeed, continuity in education during this period is attested not only for logic. If we correlate what we know about Greek, Syriac, and Arabic higher education from the sixth to ninth century or so, the picture that emerges is one of striking continuity.[36] The evidence for logic is especially good in this regard—as one would expect, given that logic, as the most elementary part of philosophy, would have produced the most literary evidence (introductory courses have more students, more students means more textbooks).

As demand for a philosophical curriculum among Muslims and other speakers of Arabic increased, Arabic translations of the Greek and Syriac logic curriculum

30. Ierodiakonou, "Psellos' Paraphrasis," 159–61.

31. Ierodiakonou, 172–79.

32. Ierodiakonou and Bydén, "Byzantine Philosophy," §1.3.

33. Ierodiakonou and Bydén, §1.1; Ierodiakonou, "Psellos' Paraphrasis," 159.

34. Ed. Heiberg. See Barnes, "Syllogistic in the anon Heiberg," esp. 97–100; Ierodiakonou and Bydén, "Byzantine Philosophy," §1.1.

35. Street, "Arabic and Islamic Philosophy of Language," §1.1.

36. Tannous, "Syria." Syriac logic tradition: Hugonnard-Roche, *La logique*, 6–20. Commentaries in particular: Brock, "Syriac Commentary Tradition."

were produced, mostly by Christian translators like Ḥunayn ibn Isḥāq (808–873), his son Isḥāq (d. 910–911), and other collaborators like Tadhārī (Theodore), who translated Aristotle's *Prior Analytics* into Arabic and gave it to Ḥunayn to revise, as Ibn al-Nadīm describes. Tadhārī was identified by Joep Lameer as the brother of Ḥunayn's collaborator Iṣṭifan (Stephen) ibn Basīl.[37] These same translators also continued to produce new Syriac translations, suggesting that the development of the Arabic logic curriculum was concurrent with the continued cultivation of the Syriac curriculum. The result was new Arabic and Syriac versions of the *Organon,* including a Syriac *Posterior Analytics;* other related texts were studied as well, such as Galen's *On Demonstration,* which, though lost today, was known to Ḥunayn.[38] At the same time, Ḥunayn's contemporary Yaʿqūb ibn Isḥāq al-Kindī (ninth century)—an Arab Muslim active at the Abbasid court in Baghdad—taught this curriculum. At least in part for this purpose, al-Kindī composed a synopsis of the *Organon.*[39]

This Aristotelian curriculum continued to be cultivated by Christians and Muslims alike. Mattā ibn Yūnus (d. 940), a Christian, and al-Fārābī (d. 950), a Muslim, promoted Aristotelian philosophy in Baghdad. Mattā translated the *Posterior Analytics* from Syriac into Arabic. The "Baghdad Peripatetics," as they and their associates are known, also commented on the *Organon.*[40] The Nestorian Christian Ibn al-Ṭayyib (d. 1043), active in Baghdad, wrote commentaries on the entire *Organon,* of which those on Porphyry's *Eisagoge* (edited, studied, and translated into English by Kwame Gyekye) and Aristotle's *Categories* survive.[41]

Avicenna's (d. 1037) adaptation and reworking of Aristotelian logic (and indeed of Aristotelian philosophy in general) was extremely influential in the later tradition. Avicenna shifted the focus away from interpreting Aristotle's words to adapting his ideas freely, without the constraint of explaining Aristotle's more obscure statements. Avicenna's reworking in many ways replaced Aristotle as a focus text for subsequent readers and commentators.[42] His systematic treatment of the subject can be found in the parts on logic in his three great philosophical summas: the

37. Lameer, *Al-Fārābī,* 3–4; cited by D'Ancona, *EI*³, s.v. "Aristotle and Aristotelianism," §1.2. I am grateful to Cristina D'Ancona for directing me to Lameer's argument.

38. Street, "Arabic and Islamic Philosophy of Language," §1.1.

39. Rescher, "Al-Kindī's Sketch"; cited by Street, "Arabic and Islamic Philosophy of Language," §1.1. See also Adamson, *Al-Kindī,* esp. 4–5, 26–27; Brentjes, "Teaching the Sciences."

40. Street, "Arabic and Islamic Philosophy of Language," §1.2. For an extant example (cited by Street), see al-Fārābī on the *De interpretatione,* in *Al-Farabi's Commentary,* trans. Zimmermann.

41. Ibn al-Ṭayyib, *Tafsīr Kitāb Īsāghūjī,* ed. Gyekye; trans. Gyekye as *Arabic Logic.* For Ibn al-Ṭayyib's life and works and a synopsis of his commentary, see Gyekye's edition, *Tafsīr Kitāb Īsāghūjī,* xxxi–xlviii.

42. Street, "Arabic and Islamic Philosophy of Language," §1.3; Gutas, "Aspects," 45 (§19).

Healing (*Shifāʾ*), the *Deliverance* (*Najāt*), and the *Pointers* (*Ishārāt*).[43] The last was especially influential. It was adopted as a teaching text in the madrasas and came to be, in the words of one detractor, "the philosophers' Qurʾan."[44]

This rapid survey of the Greek, Syriac, and Arabic tradition of Aristotelian logic does not begin to do justice to the richness of the tradition, but it should give us a sense of what to look for in a text that might signal a connection to this tradition. In what follows, we will see that in his translations and annotations, Ibn al-Faḍl displays knowledge of logic and Arabic logical terminology and an interest in emphasizing logic in his teaching of Christian texts.

1 MOSES CONTEMPLATING: BEINGS, SUBSTANCE, AND ACCIDENT

We begin with the first note that Ibn al-Faḍl wrote in the margin of his translation of Basil's *Hexaemeron*. The passage is in the first homily, near the beginning of Basil's text. Ibn al-Faḍl's brief exposition of the concept of an "existent thing" or "being" (*mawjūd*)—a topic discussed in the *Categories* and Porphyry's *Eisagoge*—ensures that from the beginning his students and readers encounter Basil's homilies with concepts from Aristotle's *Organon* in mind.

At the point where Ibn al-Faḍl's note appears, Basil has not yet begun his exegesis but is still engaged in introducing the text—the opening creation narrative of Genesis—and its divinely inspired author, Moses. Summarizing Moses's biography, at one point Basil recounts (in Ibn al-Faḍl's translation):[45]

وذهب إلى بلد الحبشة، وأقام هناك متجرداً للنظر، وملازماً[١] للبحث عن معرفة الموجودات مدة أربعين سنة كاملة.

[١]وملازماً: ق؛ وملازم: ب

> And he went to Ethiopia and settled there, isolated for contemplation, applying himself to seeking knowledge (*maʿrifa*) of existent beings (*al-mawjūdāt*) for a period of forty whole years.

Here appears Ibn al-Faḍl's marginal note:[46]

حاشية لعبد الله ابن الفضل: الموجودات جمع موجود. والموجود يَعُمُّ الجوهر والعرض، عمومَ اسمٍ مُشْتَرَكٍ على رأي قومٍ، وعلى رأي آخرين عمومَ جنس[١]، ولكل من الفريقين[٢] حجةٌ يحتج بها. واسم الموجود إنه القائم بذاته، والذي قيامه بغيره فهو العرض.

[١]جنس: ق؛ الجنس: ب [٢]الفريقين: ق؛ المفريقين: ب

43. Ibn Sīnā, *Shifāʾ*, ed. Madkūr; *Najāt*, ed. Dānešpažūh, logic portion trans. Ahmed, *Avicenna's Deliverance; Ishārāt*, ed. Dunyā.

44. Ibn Taymīya, *Darʾ*, ed. Sālim, 9:254, ¶5: "*muṣḥaf hāʾulāʾ al-falāsifa.*" Michot, "Vanités," 599; cited by Street, "Arabic and Islamic Philosophy of Language," §1.3.

45. **B** 9, **Q** 3_{5-7} = Basil, *Hexaemeron*, 1.1, ed. Amand de Mendieta and Rudberg, 3_{1-3}.

46. **B** 9, **Q** 3_{7-11}.

> *Marginal note by ʿAbdallāh ibn al-Faḍl:* "Existent beings" (*al-mawjūdāt*) is the plural of "an existent being" (*mawjūd*). "The existent being" (*al-mawjūd*) is common to substance and accident, as an equivocal term (*ism mushtarak*) according to some, and according to others as a genus. Each party has its arguments by which they argue. The name of the existent being is "the self-subsistent"; and that which subsists in another is accident.

Ibn al-Faḍl explains the word *mawjūd* (existent being) by noting that it is applied to both substances and accidents (that is, existence is "common to" both). (For example, substances like Socrates or this horse are said to exist, and accidents like the brownness of this horse or Socrates's location are also said to exist.) He then notes that some people believe that when we say that a substance exists, we mean something different by the word "exists" from what we mean by "exists" when we say that an accident exists. In this first view the existence of a substance like this horse or Socrates is quite different from the existence of an accident like brownness or being in Athens.

Ibn al-Faḍl then presents a second position, which views substances and accidents as subsets of a larger set, or "genus," of all things that exist. This view—rejected by Aristotle[47]—implies that the existence of substances and the existence of accidents are the same kind of existence.

Noting that each side of this debate produces its own arguments, he goes on to state definitions of "being" and "accident" that would seem to support the first position: he defines a being as something that is self-subsistent but an "accident" as something that subsists in another (and so is *not* self-subsistent).

The logical terms Ibn al-Faḍl uses are standard for Arabic Aristotelian logic (*jawhar, ʿaraḍ, ism mushtarak, jins, mawjūd*). The use of the verb *ʿamma* to express the notion that "being is common to substance and accident" is also a standard usage—for example, in Abū ʿUthmān al-Dimashqī's Arabic translation of Porphyry's *Eisagoge.*[48]

Ibn al-Faḍl's marginal note is only tangentially related to Basil's text. Basil refers to all things that exist—the object of Moses's contemplation—with the word "beings"; but to understand what Basil means one does not really need to know about substance, accident, self-subsistence, and so on. Here as elsewhere in his marginalia, it seems likely that such a note was prompted by a student's question, such as "Was Moses contemplating accidents or only substances?" Ibn al-Faḍl's answer addresses the concerns of a specific sort of reader of Basil's text: a student of philosophy.

47. In *Metaphysics* B.3, 998b22, as an anonymous reviewer kindly pointed out.

48. Ed. Badawī in Aristotle, *Manṭiq Arisṭū*, 3:1089: *wa-yaʿummu l-jinsa wa-l-faṣla annahumā ayḍan idhā rtafaʿā, irtafaʿa mā taḥtahumā.* Greek, ed. Busse, 14_{10-11}: κοινὸν δὲ καὶ τὸ ἀναιρεθέντος ἢ τοῦ γένους ἢ τῆς διαφορᾶς ἀναιρεῖσθαι τὰ ὑπ’ αὐτά (which does not use a verb to express the notion of commonality).

2 DOG LOGIC AND THE ARABIC ARISTOTLE

The logic curriculum at the background of the study of Christian texts like Basil's comes to the fore toward the end of Basil's *Hexaemeron,* in the ninth and last homily. There, Ibn al-Faḍl wrote a note on syllogistic logic. This note is particularly significant because it quotes (without attribution) a known Arabic translation of Aristotle's *Prior Analytics.*

Basil's ninth homily on the six-day creation narrative of Genesis focuses on the creation of land animals. At one point, Basil contrasts the rationality of humans, who stand upright, with the lack of reason in "quadrupeds," whose gaze is cast down "at the earth and . . . the belly."[49] But these four-footed animals do each have their own distinct traits: "The ox is steady, the ass is sluggish, the stallion is hot in its lust for the mare," and so on.[50] He especially dwells on the heightened sense-perception of the dog. His discussion, part of a long tradition of "Chrysippos's dog,"[51] runs as follows.

First, he says, the dog has powers of perception that stand in for reason, allowing him to intuit what sages have gone to great pains to learn—namely, the syllogistic figures.[52] Ibn al-Faḍl takes this as an opportunity to enumerate the syllogistic figures:[53]

حاشية لابن الفضل: إنّ أشكال القياس ثلثة. (١) الأول منها ما هو أن يكون الحدّ الأوسط موضوعاً[١] في المقدمة الكبرى، محمولاً[٢] في الصغرى، مثال ذلك: كل إنسان حيوان، وكل حيوان جوهر؛ فإن الحيوان هو الحد الأوسط. وضروب هذا الشكل أربعة، وهذه صورته[٣]. (٢) والثاني منها هو أن يكون الحدّ الأوسط محمولاً[٤] على الطرفين، مثال ذلك: ليس شيءٌ[٥] من الحِجار[٦] حياً، وكل إنسان حي؛ فالحي هو الحد الأوسط، وضروب هذا الشكل أربعة أيضاً، وهذه صورته[٧]. (٣) والثالث هو أن يكون الأوسط[٨] موضوعاً[٩] في الطرفين جميعاً، مثال ذلك: كل إنسان (ناطق)[١٠] وكل إنسان حي؛ فإن الإنسان هو الحد الأوسط، وضروب هذا الشكل ستة، وهذه صورته.

[١]موضوعاً: أثبتّه من ذ؛ موضوع: ب د ق [٢]محمولاً: أثبتّه من ذ؛ محمول: ب د ق [٣]وهذه صورته: ب د ق؛ –ذ [٤]محمولاً: أثبتّه من ذ؛ محمول: ب د ق [٥]شيءٌ: شيّ: د ذ ق؛ شيئاً: ب [٦]الحِجار: ذ ق؛ الحجارة: ب د [٧]وهذه صورته: ب د ق؛ وهو صورته: ذ [٨]الأوسط: ب د ق؛ الحد الأوسط: ذ [٩]موضوعاً: أثبتّه من ذ؛ موضوع: ب د ق [١٠](ناطق): +ذ

Marginal note by Ibn al-Faḍl: The syllogistic figures (*ashkāl al-qiyās*) are three. (1) The first of them is for the middle term to be subject in the major premise and predicate in the minor premise.[54] For example: "Every human is an animal, and every

49. Basil, *Hexaemeron,* 9.2, ed. Amand de Mendieta and Rudberg, 149_{1-2}. Cf. Basil-NPNF, 102.

50. §9.3, ed. Amand de Mendieta and Rudberg, 149_{14-15}; trans. based on Basil-NPNF, 102.

51. Floridi, "Scepticism and Animal Rationality," esp. 29, 35–39. I owe this reference to an anonymous reviewer.

52. §9.4 mid, ed. Amand de Mendieta and Rudberg, 153_{21-24}.

53. **B** 131_{6-15}, **D** 147_{1-10}, **E** 116_{10-17}, **Q** 219_{8}–220_{1}, *faṣl* 10; at Basil, *Hexaemeron,* 9.4, ed. Amand de Mendieta and Rudberg, 153_{24} πεπαιδευμένος.

54. Aristotle's "perfect syllogism," *Prior Analytics* 25b34–35; Tadhārī's translation, *al-qiyās al-kāmil,* ed. Badawī in Aristotle, *Manṭiq Arisṭū,* 1:113.

> animal is a substance." The animal is the middle term. This figure has four moods (*ḍurūb*); this is a picture of it. (2) The second of them is for the middle term to be predicated of the two extremes. For example: "No stone is living, and every human is living." "Living" is the middle term. This figure has four moods as well; this is a picture of it. (3) The third of them is for the middle term to be the subject of both extremes. For example: "Every human (is rational), and every human is living."[55] "Human" is the middle term. This figure has six moods; this is a picture of it.

This typology of syllogisms—three figures, with four, four, and six moods, respectively—is the standard Aristotelian account (*Prior Analytics* 1.4–6). Likewise, the Arabic terminology Ibn al-Faḍl uses for "syllogism," "figures," "moods," "middle term," "major/minor premise," "subject," "predicate," and so on is standard and current. For example, Avicenna uses the same terms in his *Deliverance*.[56]

Today, a comparably technical and elementary logic lesson on Ibn al-Faḍl's note might look something like the following. Let *A, B,* and *C* be the three terms; let *B* be the middle term. Furthermore, let *AaB* mean "every *A* is *B*" (universal affirmative); let *AeB* mean "no *A* is *B*" (universal negative); let *AiB* mean "some *A* is *B*" (particular affirmative); and let *AoB* mean "some *A* is not *B*" (particular negative).[57] Ibn al-Faḍl's example of the first figure is *AaB, BaC,* omitting the conclusion: *AaC* (where *A* is "human," *B* is "animal," and *C* is "substance"). To use the mnemonic developed in the Latin West, this syllogism is *Barbara.* Likewise, his example of the second figure is *AeB* and *CaB,* omitting the conclusion: *CeA* (where *A* is "stone," *B* is "living," and *C* is "human"): *Cesare.* Finally, his example of the third figure is *BaA* and *BaC,* omitting the conclusion: *CiA* (where *A* is "rational," *B* is "human," and *C* is "living"): *Darapti.*

Ibn al-Faḍl's original marginal note must have included diagrams, for after each figure he adds, "And this is a picture of it" (*wa-hādhihi ṣūratuhu*). These would presumably have summarized the moods—a helpful guide for the student of logic of the sort still presented to students of Aristotelian logic today.[58] Indeed, the entire note reads like a basic review or exposition of Aristotle's syllogistic.

55. In most of the manuscripts I consulted, the minor premise reads simply "Every human," which is clearly missing a predicate, since we would expect "Every human is *X*; and every human is living." The conclusion would then be "Therefore some living beings are *X*" (*Darapti*). In one of the manuscripts, **E,** whose text often reflects a later scholar's (perhaps the scribe's) emendations, the minor premise has been completed: ". . . is rational."

56. §§61–64, ed. Dānešpažūh, 52–64; trans. Ahmed, 43–50.

57. For this convention, as opposed to Aristotle's way of phrasing propositions as "*B* applies to all *A*," etc., see Lagerlund, "Medieval Theories," §2.

58. E.g., Smith, "Aristotle's Logic," §5.4. Ibn al-Faḍl's diagram may have looked like those found in Byzantine manuscripts of logical and philosophical texts, on which see Roberts, "Byzantine-Islamic Scientific Culture," esp. nn. 76–78, with references.

Apparently Ibn al-Faḍl regarded a session on this Byzantine classic by a father of the church as an excellent opportunity to refresh his students' memories about Aristotelian logic.

Basil continues by providing an example of his claim that dogs use instincts instead of syllogisms. Basil observes that when hunting, the dog instinctually follows a process of elimination to find its prey:

> When the dog is on the track of game and sees (the path) divide in several directions, he approaches the paths leading in each direction, and he all but gives voice to the deduction guiding his action. The creature, he says, turned here or there or in another direction. It is neither here nor there; what remains is that it has rushed in that direction. And thus, eliminating falsehoods, he discovers the truth.[59]

Commenting on this description of the dog's process of elimination, Ibn al-Faḍl identifies the syllogism that the dog's nature is effortlessly replicating:[60]

> القياس الذي قد أورده القديس باسيليوس رحمنا الله بصلواته في معنى الكلب قياسٌ شرطيّ، والقياس الشرطيّ جنسٌ تحته خمسة أنواع، وهذا من النوع الخامس.

> The syllogism which Saint Basil has presented—may God have mercy on us through his prayers—on the theme of the dog is a conditional syllogism. The conditional syllogism is a genus under which are five species; this one is of the fifth species.

This note continues the logic lesson by discussing a different sort of syllogism not part of Aristotle's basic exposition of assertoric syllogisms. Here too Ibn al-Faḍl uses the same logical vocabulary as Avicenna.[61]

At this point, Basil finishes his analogy with a scoff at the logicians: "What more remarkable thing is done by those who, reverently setting themselves before diagrams, trace lines upon the dust, rejecting two of three propositions and discovering the truth in the one that remains?"[62] Ibn al-Faḍl's translation here intensifies the scorn by comparing not only human logic to canine behavior but the logicians

59. Basil, *Hexaemeron,* 9.4, ed. Amand de Mendieta and Rudberg, 153_{24}–154_{1}. Trans. based on Basil-NPNF, 104. Arabic: **D** 147_{10-16}, **E** $116_{\Omega6-\Omega2}$, *faṣl* 10.

60. **B** 131_{22-24}.

61. As Asad Ahmed observed in a marginal note on a draft of this section, the type of conditional syllogism to which Ibn al-Faḍl refers is the "exceptive syllogism." See Ibn Sīnā, *Najāt* (*Deliverance*), Logic 60 "on exceptive (*istithnāʾī*) syllogisms," §78 "on conditional (*sharṭīya*) propositions," and Logic 83.5 on this sort of disjunctive deduction (where indeed this is the fifth and last type of *istithnāʾī* syllogism that Avicenna discusses); ed. Dānešpažūh, 52, 79, 91–92; trans. Ahmed, 43 ("repetitive" for "exceptive"), 62, 72. For translating *al-qiyās al-istithnāʾī* as "the exceptive syllogism," see Shehaby, *Propositional Logic,* 183, translation of Ibn Sīnā, *Shifāʾ*, Logic 8.4, ed. Madkūr, 1.2:389.

62. Basil, *Hexaemeron,* 9.4, ed. Amand de Mendieta and Rudberg, 154_{1-3}. Trans. based on Basil-NPNF, 104.

themselves to the dog: "On what basis are the masters of [syllogistic] figures preferable who trace out diagrams on the ground . . . ?"[63] (Scorn for drawing diagrams is particularly striking coming immediately after Ibn al-Faḍl's note that, as we just saw, originally included diagrams.) Ibn al-Faḍl's next note then glosses the logical terms that Basil used, providing a definition of the word "premise" (πρότασις ~ *muqaddima*).[64] He quotes from an extant Arabic translation of Aristotle's *Prior Analytics* to do so (quoted text in italics):[65]

«المقدمة[1] هي قول موجب شيء[2] لشيء وسالب[3] شيئاً عن شيء»، ولا تخلو من أن تكون «إمّا كلية، وإمّا جزئية، وإما مهملة»، وهي تتركب من موضوع ومحمول على أقلّ الأمر، والقياس لا ينتظم من أقلّ من مقدّمتين.

[1]المقدمة: ب د؛ فالمقدّمة: تذاري [2]شيء: ب د؛ شيئا: تذاري [3]وسالب: ب د؛ أو سالب: تذاري

> *The premise is speech which posits something for something or negates something of something,* and it must be *either universal, particular, or indefinite.* It is composed of a subject and a predicate at least; a syllogism cannot be put together from fewer than two premises.

Ibn al-Faḍl, it would seem, was working with a standard Arabic version of Aristotle, produced by Theodore (Tadhārī) and checked over by Ḥunayn ibn Isḥāq. Either the text—or an excerpt from it—was in front of him, or else he was quoting these standard definitions from memory. Either way, he was reading and teaching what students of philosophy in Baghdad and throughout the Islamic world were reading.

Basil's purpose in this whole passage on the instinctually syllogizing dog is to meditate upon the nature of rationality by comparing the rational animal to an irrational one, while at the same time questioning reason's exclusive access to truth and mocking those who take the rational apparatus of logic too seriously. Ibn al-Faḍl clearly appreciated Basil's take on this ancient thought-experiment, to judge not only from his marginal notes but also from his quotation of this same passage from Basil in a different book, his philosophical compendium, the *Joy of the Believer.* (Strikingly, Ibn al-Faḍl there quotes not from his own Arabic translation of the *Hexaemeron* but rather from the anonymous Arabic translation upon which he based his own translation. This suggests that he wrote

63. **D** 147_{19-21}: *fa-yā layta shiʿrī bi-mādhā yufaḍḍalūna* [*sic*] *aṣḥābu l-ashkāli lladhīna yakhuṭṭūna fī l-arḍi ṣuwarahā.* I thank Asad Ahmed for pointing out the distinct meaning of Ibn al-Faḍl's translation and suggesting the translation of *bi-mādhā yufaḍḍalūn,* that I have adopted.

64. Basil, *Hexaemeron,* 9.4, ed. Amand de Mendieta and Rudberg, 154_{2} (προτάσεων).

65. **B** $131_{\text{Ω1}}$–132_{3}, **D** 147_{21-24}. Parts that are quoting Theodore's (Tadhārī's) translation of Aristotle's *Prior Analytics* 24a16–17, ed. Badawī in Aristotle, *Manṭiq Arisṭū,* 104, I have placed in italics; the variants, all minor, I give in the Arabic, though ignoring *hamza* discrepancies.

the *Joy of the Believer* before carrying out his retranslation of Basil's *Hexaemeron* in ca. 1051.)[66]

At the same time, Ibn al-Faḍl's marginal notes on this passage have a very different purpose from the passage itself. Where Basil mocked the syllogizers, Ibn al-Faḍl enthusiastically details their art, even inserting into the margin just the sort of diagram that Basil ridiculed as "lines [traced] in dust." As we have seen, Byzantines distinguished between "external" (secular) and "our" (Christian) sciences.[67] In this example, Ibn al-Faḍl propounds logic—one of the "external" sciences—and even quotes Aristotle to do so, all safely within a page from the homilies of Saint Basil. Seeking to remain within the realm of "our" science, Ibn al-Faḍl brings the "external" into this realm by lodging it within the confines of the page.

3 LOGIC IN THE GARDEN

Now we turn to the *Book of the Garden,* Ibn al-Faḍl's translation of the wisdom collection *Loci communes.* As we saw in the previous chapter, the *Garden* includes many notes that may plausibly be assigned to Ibn al-Faḍl's pen.[68]

Two Witnesses, Two Premises

In the section of the *Garden* "On Law," the following quotation appears (John 8: 16–17):[69]

قال الإنجيل: الحكم الذي لي حقّ هو، لأنّي لستُ وحدي، لكن أنا والذي أرسلني. وقد كتب في شريعتكم أن شهادة إنسانين حقّ هي.

> *The Gospel says:* The judgment that is mine is true, because I am not alone, but rather I and the one who sent me [judge together]. It has been written in your law that the testimony of two people is true.

In the Arabic version, a comment follows, ascribed to "a certain scholar." Here it appears that Ibn al-Faḍl is referring to another scholar's interpretation, possibly transcribed from an anonymous source such as a marginal note in the Greek manuscript

66. Ibn al-Faḍl, *Joy of the Believer,* Recension A (see Treiger, "ʿAbdallāh," 103–7), question no. 53, Cairo COP Theol. 112 (= Graf 638 = Simaika 238), pp. 44–46, esp. p. 45 (fol. 23^{v})$_{4-16}$: *qāla l-qiddīsu Bāsīliyūs: al-kalbu lladhī lā nuṭqa lahu . . .* Cf. Basil, *Hexaemeron,* Anonymous Translation (see Roberts, "Re-Translation"), **P** 98^{r}, **S** 131^{v}–132^{r}.

67. See ch. 2, pp. 62–63.

68. See ch. 5, §1, pp. 152–53.

69. Ibn al-Faḍl, *Garden,* §58 (*fī l-sharīʿa*), **V** 151^{v} (and **S** 359^{v}–360^{v}) = *Loci communes,* 51.1/1 (περὶ νόμου), ed. Ihm, 830.

he was using to produce his Arabic translation.[70] The scholar's interpretation attests to a striking intellectual reflex, to invoke logical concepts to justify the words of Jesus:

شرح بعض العلماء: إنّما نفذت شهادة الاثنين وقُبلت لأجل أن كلّ ما يطلب معرفته بالعقل لا يصحّ علمه ما لم يسبقه علم مقدّمتين قبله. وقد أجمع المنطقيون[1] على أنّ النتيجة أقلّ ما يكون من مقدمتين صحيحتين، وهي تابعة لأخسّ المقدمتين. ومثال ذلك: بعض الناس طبيب، وكلّ طبيب ناطق، فبعض الناس إذاً ناطق. وقولنا: فبعض الناس إذاً ناطق، هي النتيجة، وقد تبعت للمقدمة الجزئية التي هي: بعض الناس طبيب، وهي أخسّ[2] من المقدمة القائلة: كلّ طبيب ناطق، لأنّ هذه كلّيّة، والكلّيّ أشـ<ـر>ف من الجزئي وهذا من الشكل الأول من القياس.

[1]المنطقيون: صحّحته؛ وفي الأصل: المنطيقيون [2]أخسّ: صحّحته؛ وفي الأصل: أحسن

Commentary by a certain scholar: The testimony of two [witnesses] is valid and accepted because all knowledge of things that require reason to be understood is only valid if two premises are known beforehand. Logicians are in agreement that the conclusion is the least of what can be derived from two sound premises and follows the baser (*akhass*) of the two premises. For example: "Some human being is a physician, and every physician is rational, so some human being is therefore rational." When we say "so some human being is therefore rational," that is the conclusion, which has followed the particular premise, which is "some people are physicians." This is baser[71] than the premise that says "every physician is rational" because that one is universal, and the universal is nobler[72] than the particular. This is a syllogism of the first figure.

This note sets out to read Jesus's reference to a legal rule requiring two witnesses to establish a fact in court through the lens of Aristotelian logic. It first rationalizes the legal rule by making an analogy with syllogisms, in which two premises (like the testimony of two witnesses) must be known in order to generate a new piece of knowledge.

The note then quickly moves on from the analogy to discuss logic itself, stating the syllogistic rule that the quantity (all/none versus some/not-all) of the conclusion is determined by the quantity of the premise with narrower scope. This is a standard Aristotelian observation about syllogisms: for a syllogism to have a universal conclusion, it is a necessary (but not sufficient) condition that it have two universal premises.[73] The Arabic note's phrasing, in particular "the weaker of the

70. It is at least possible that the phrasing *sharḥ baʿḍ al-ʿulamāʾ* instead of *sharḥ* alone reflects a later scribe's attempt to distinguish between the text's running commentary by Ibn al-Faḍl and the scribe's own addition from a different source. Still, I find it more likely that this commentary's presence in the text goes back to Ibn al-Faḍl.

71. Reading *akhass* for *aḥsan.*

72. Reading *ashraf* for *ashaff.* The word *shiff* can mean "excess," "profit," or "extra amount," and the comparative *ashaff* can have the sense of "a bit more," as in "so-and-so is *ashaff* than so-and-so," meaning he is a bit older: *Lisān* s.v. *šff.* So it is not impossible that it could be used here to mean "broader in scope." But *ashraf* is attested in Arabic logic with precisely this usage: Ibn Rushd (Averroes, twelfth century), *Talkhīṣ Kitāb al-Burhān* [= *Middle Commentary on the Posterior Analytics*], 1.31, ed. Jihāmī in Ibn Rushd, *Talkhīs manṭiq Arisṭū*, 5:445$_{15}$: *anna l-kullī ashraf min al-juzʾī.*

73. Aristotle, *Prior Analytics* 1.24, 41b22–24; Smith, "Aristotle's Logic," §5.5, no. 5.

two premises," is often used in discussing the *modality* (necessary, actual, possible) rather than the quantity of propositions.[74]

Universal Propositions without Quantifiers

This eagerness to raise logical topics not explicitly present in the main text is also apparent elsewhere in the *Garden*. In one note, Ibn al-Faḍl even references Aristotle's *On Interpretation* explicitly in response to a quotation from Basil under the heading "On Honoring One's Parents":[75]

قال باسيليوس: الأولاد الوفيّون يصنعون محامد الآباء جسيمةً.
شرح: هذه مقدمة كُلِّيّة، لم يكن بسورٍ لأن حرف التعريف يقوم مقام السور، فكأن قوله: الأولاد، عِوَض من قوله: كلّ ولد. وهذا قد نبّه عليه <أ>رسطاطاليس في الفصل الخامس من كتابه الثاني في العبارة.

Basil said: Loyal children cause their parents' praiseworthy actions to be embodied.

Commentary: This is a universal proposition. It is not [expressed] with a quantifier because the definite article stands in the place of the quantifier. So it is as if his phrase "children" is a substitute for saying "every child." Aristotle brought attention to this in the fifth section of his second book, *On Interpretation*.[76]

The quotation from Basil must have seemed logically ambiguous to Ibn al-Faḍl or one of his students. Did Basil mean that *some* loyal children have this embodying effect, or all such children? Ibn al-Faḍl responds to this query by explaining that the meaning is universal (*all* loyal children), even though Basil omitted the quantifier "all."

In order to support this claim, Ibn al-Faḍl refers to the passage from Aristotle's *On Interpretation* that discusses universal propositions formulated without using the word "every" or "all" (πᾶς).[77] For example, one may say "man is mortal" to

74. The rule about modality is attributed by the commentators to Theophrastos; fragment 106, ed. and trans. Fortenbaugh et al., 1:206–23; cited by Bobzien, "Ancient Logic," §3.1. Ibn Rushd (following Themistios's paraphrase) uses the same standard Arabic term for the "weaker" premise (*akhass*): *Middle Commentary on Aristotle's Prior Analytics*, 1.9, 30a33–b6 = Theophrastos fragment 106H, ed. Fortenbaugh et al., 1:218: "The mode of the conclusion follows the weaker of the two modes" (*anna jihata l-natījati tābiʿun li-akhassi l-jihatayn*). For Themistios as Ibn Rushd's source, see Huby, *Theophrastus*, 124.

75. Ibn al-Faḍl, *Garden*, §23 (*fī karāmat al-wālidayn*), **V** 127ʳ (also **S** 315ʳ) = *Loci communes*, §2<3>, no. 5/5, ed. Ihm, 531.

76. *On Interpretation* may be considered Aristotle's "second book" in the sense that it is second after the *Categories* in standard collections of his work. For example, the important ninth-century codex Milan, Ambrosiana, gr. L 93 contains (1) Porphyry, *Eisagoge;* (2) Aristotle, *Categories* with commentary by Ammonios; (3) Aristotle, *On Interpretation;* (4) Aristotle, *Prior Analytics* with commentary by Simplikios; (5) Aristotle, *Posterior Analytics* with commentary by Simplikios: Martini and Bassi, *Catalogus codicum graecorum bibliothecae Ambrosianae*, 591–92, no. 490.

77. §7, 17b5–12. Aristotle's example of a universal subject in the passage just before is "man," without an explicit quantifier (§7, 17a39–b1).

mean "*every* human being is mortal." This is similar to how al-Fārābī interprets the same Aristotelian passage.[78]

In his interpretation, al-Fārābī, like Ibn al-Faḍl, uses the technical term *sūr* to mean "quantifier." Avicenna also uses it.[79] This is a term that Aristotle lacked, at least in *On Interpretation*. There, Aristotle refers to "universal" and "particular" subjects without a term for "quantifier." Discussing these same concepts, the Greek tradition also developed a term referring to the quantifiers collectively. The fourth-century philosophers Dexippos and Ammonios (fifth century) both speak of the four *prosdiorismoi*—namely, universal affirmative (all), universal negative (none), particular affirmative (some), particular negative (not all).[80] In the eleventh century, Psellos, in his paraphrase of Aristotle's treatise, uses the same terminology.[81] We may therefore conclude that Ibn al-Faḍl, though referring to Aristotle himself, also drew on the logic tradition of his own day to elucidate this patristic quotation.

Propositions and Erudition

In another brief note in the *Garden* (coming soon after the note about his Arabic teacher discussed in chapter 5), Ibn al-Faḍl responds to a quotation ascribed to the Athenian playwright Sophocles by analyzing it logically and defining an obscure Arabic word:[82]

قال سوفقليس: ولا واحد من الناس خليلا للرَّيْم.
شرح: هذه مقدمة كلّيّة صادقة سالبة، وينبغي أن تعلم أنّ الرَّيْم من المتّفقة أسماؤها لأنّه يَقَعُ على القبر، والفضل، والعَظْم من عِظام الجَزُور.

Sophocles said: No human being is a friend of the grave.[83]

Commentary: This is a true negative universal proposition. You should know that *raym* is a case of [different things with] names that coincide, for it can mean "grave," "surplus," or "one of the bones of the slaughter-camel."

78. *Sharḥ Kitāb al-ʿibāra*, ed. Kutsch and Marrow, 69–70; trans. Zimmermann, 63–64. I owe this reference to an anonymous reviewer.

79. See ch. 4, p. 147 and n. 69.

80. Dexippos, *In Aristotelis Categorias commentarium*, ed. Busse, 12_{22}; Ammonios, *In Porphyrii Isagogen*, ed. Busse, 28_{18}.

81. Psellos, *Paraphrase of On Interpretation*, §2, in Ammonios, *Ammonii Hermei Commentaria in Librum peri Hermeneias*, ed. Manutius, M5ʳ, lines 11ff. This usage of προσδιορισμός does not appear in LSJ s.v., nor is there an entry for the word in Lampe or Trapp, *Lexikon*.

82. Ibn al-Faḍl, *Garden*, §36 (*fī l-mawt*, which begins on fol. 137ᵛ), **V** 139^{r}_{12-15} = *Loci communes*, §65/36 (περὶ θανάτου), ed. Ihm, 962. Ihm notes that although it is sometimes marked as a quotation from Sophocles (as in Ibn al-Faḍl's version), this is in fact a fragment of Euripides (no. 1081 Nauck).

83. *Khalīl:* an apt rendering of "loyal friend" (πιστὸς . . . φίλος). Elsewhere in the *Garden*, a comment states that the word *aḥad*, rather than *wāḥid*, is used in negative statements (see below, p. 199), so it is striking that the Arabic text of Sophocles here reads *wa-lā wāḥid*.

The brief comment has two parts, one logical, one lexicographical. The logical part is the simple observation that the quotation from Sophocles constitutes a certain type of "proposition" or statement. It is universal in that its subject is a complete set, the set of all human beings, and negative in that it asserts that the predicate, "friend of the grave," is *not* predicated of any member of that set. The additional observation that the proposition is "true" is a judgment that indeed no human being is fond of death. Ibn al-Faḍl, in this commentary, may have seen fit to add this qualification to help the student of logic to distinguish between a negative proposition and a false statement. Aristotle himself seems in part to be emphasizing this point when he says that "affirmative and negative propositions must be either true or false."[84]

The second part of the comment points out that the relatively obscure Arabic word Ibn al-Faḍl used to render Sophocles's "grave," *raym*, has several distinct meanings. The definitions Ibn al-Faḍl lists appear in Ibn al-Manẓūr's lexicon *Lisān al-ʿarab.*[85]

Taken together, these two separate observations—logical and lexicographical—illustrate the educational tradition to which Ibn al-Faḍl belonged, a tradition emphasizing knowledge of high-style language, on the one hand (whether Greek or Arabic), and logic, on the other. There is a well-known anecdote in which an eloquent Arabic grammarian and a tongue-tied Christian logician (Mattā ibn Yūnus, mentioned above) debate the respective merits of their disciplines before the vizier in tenth-century Baghdad.[86] The entrenched images of logicians and grammarians implicit in this account, especially their mutual antagonism, are nowhere to be seen in Ibn al-Faḍl. For him (as for al-Fārābī), grammar and logic were two important disciplines to be cultivated simultaneously.

Substance, Accident, and Arabic Grammar

Indeed, language (or grammar) and logic were so closely linked in Ibn al-Faḍl's annotations that even in discussing (Arabic) grammar, he makes abundant use of logical terminology. In the section of the *Garden* "On Old Age and Youth," we read:[87]

قال اغريغوريوس نيسس: في كل شيء على أكثر الأمر الشيبية رأيٌ خَطِرٌ، وليس أحد من ذوي الشبيبة يَثقَف[1] شيئاً[2] من الفضائل بسهولة له.

[1]يَثقَف: س؛ يثقف: ف [2]شيئاً: شيا: س؛ شي: ف

84. *On Interpretation* 9, 18a29–30.

85. *Lisān* s.v. *rym* (baheth.info): ¶8 end (*al-qabr*); ¶7 (*al-ziyāda wa-l-faḍl*); ¶8 beginning (*ʿaẓmun yabqā baʿdamā yuqsamu laḥmu l-jazūri wa-l-maysir*).

86. Recounted in Street, "Arabic and Islamic Philosophy of Language," §1.2. For the broader impact of the tenth-century grammar-logic debate in the Islamic world, see Gutas, "Aspects," 45 nn. 76 and 77, with references.

87. Ibn al-Faḍl, *Garden*, §41, **V** 141ʳ; **S** 337ᵛ–338ʳ = *Loci communes*, §70.15/17, ed. Ihm, 1026.

> *Gregory of Nyssa said:* In all things, most of the time youth is [or: has; i.e., gives][88] dangerous advice, and no one possessing youth masters any of the virtues with ease.

The grammatical note that follows picks up on the use of the word *aḥad* (here the "one" in "no one") in Ibn al-Faḍl's rendering of this quotation:

قال شرح: ينبغي أن تعلم أن أحداً لا يستعمل إلّا في السلب دون الإيجاب، وقد دلّ ذلك ابن[1] السكيت في إصلاح المنطق، وهو يخصّ في اللغة العربية الناطق فقط دون سائر الموجودات من الجواهر والأعراض.

[1] ابن: ف؛ بن: س

> *Commentary:* You should know that the word *aḥad* is only used in negation, not in affirmation, as Ibn al-Sikkīt indicated in [his book] *Good Diction* (*Iṣlāḥ al-manṭiq*). In the Arabic language it is used only of rational beings, to the exclusion of all other existent beings, both substances and accidents.

The point is that the Arabic word *aḥad* is used of rational beings (like English "no one," in contrast to "nothing," which is used of all other entities) and only in negative statements, in contrast to the other word for "one," *wāḥid,* which is used in affirmative statements.[89] This note was probably articulated as a response to a student's question about why the word *aḥad,* not *wāḥid,* was used in this passage of the *Garden.*

Ibn al-Faḍl's reference to the grammarian Ibn al-Sikkīt (d. 858) puts on display his own training in the Classical Arabic language and attests to his emphasis on imparting Classical Arabic to his students. We have already seen from another note on the *Garden* that Ibn al-Faḍl studied this very book of Ibn al-Sikkīt with his teacher Abū l-ʿAlāʾ.[90]

Although this is primarily a grammatical note, it incidentally uses logical terminology such as negation (*salb*) and affirmation (*ījāb*). It also uses the term "rational" (*nāṭiq*), which is very common in examples of logic (all men are rational; all men are animals; therefore some animals are rational) and Aristotle's theory of predication in *Categories* (rationality is man's specific difference relative to other animals). The terms "substance" (*jawhar*) and "accidents" (*aʿrāḍ*) are at the core of Aristotle's *Categories.*

4 CONCLUSION

From the foregoing, it is clear that Ibn al-Faḍl not only had studied Aristotelian logic himself but also emphasized it when he taught the Christian texts he translated from

88. Reading *li-l-shabība* for *al-shabība.*

89. This ignores another common use of *aḥad*—namely, in referring to one of two or more things as part of an *iḍāfa*-construction, e.g., *aḥad al-baytayn,* "one of the two houses." But clearly the commentator's focus here is on why *aḥad,* not *wāḥid,* is being used *here.*

90. Ch. 5, §1, pp. 153–54.

Greek into Arabic. He encouraged students to analyze patristic passages using the framework of logic. When texts like Basil's *Hexaemeron* referred to logical concepts, Ibn al-Faḍl used the opportunity to offer a review of Aristotelian syllogistic. Sometimes his explanations of logic came straight out of the Arabic Aristotle.

In the following chapters, we will continue to scour Ibn al-Faḍl's translations and annotations for telltale signs of this philosophical tradition beyond logic. But already from logic alone we may suggest that at least as taught in Byzantine Antioch, the Greek philosophical tradition and Greek ecclesiastical tradition went hand in hand.

7

PHYSICS

Throughout his translations and annotations, Ibn al-Faḍl displays repeated interest in the natural world. This interest is consistent with the Christian philosophical tradition he inherited. The Cappadocian Fathers, for example, had devoted considerable energy to assessing, critiquing, and adapting ancient theories of matter, especially where these had potential consequences for important parts of the Christian worldview. They associated Epicurean atomism, for example, with the primacy of matter (atoms) as the origin of the visible world, and with a denial of God's active role in creating and continuing to influence and guide the material world. To these late antique Christian authors, this made Epicurus unacceptable.

Church fathers were only some of the many scholars in the first millennium CE who continued to explore ancient physical theories, especially Aristotle's, and to propose revisions to these theories. Aristotle's *Physics* attracted Greek commentators in late antiquity: Alexander of Aphrodisias (second/third century), Themistios (d. 388), Simplikios (sixth century), and John Philoponos (d. after 567). Ibn al-Faḍl's contemporaries in Constantinople, such as John Italos, also concerned themselves with issues raised in the *Physics* tradition.[1] Philoponos also wrote a commentary on Aristotle's *On Generation and Corruption*.[2] A similar tradition of studying and

1. Hunger, *Die hochsprachliche profane Literatur,* 1:27, 31–34. Alexander of Aphrodisias, fragments: ed. and trans. Rashed. Italos: Trizio, "Late Antique Debate"; I owe this reference to Asad Ahmed. The *Physics* commentary ascribed to Psellos in a number of manuscripts was in fact composed by George Pachymeres (1242–ca. 1310) in the margins of Florence, Laurenziana, gr. 87.5 (thirteenth century, end): Golitsis, "Un commentaire."

2. *Commentaria in Aristotelem Graeca* 14.2; cited by Hunger, *Die hochsprachliche profane Literatur,* 1:27.

commenting on the *Physics* existed in Arabic. The Arabic translation of the *Physics* was extensively commented upon by the Baghdad Peripatetics; the unique Leiden *Physics* manuscript (copied in 1130 CE, but copied from a 1077 CE manuscript, itself copied from a 1004 CE manuscript) contains the Arabic translation of the Nestorian Christian Isḥāq ibn Ḥunayn (d. 910–911, son of the famous Greek-Arabic translator Ḥunayn ibn Isḥāq) and the commentaries of the Miaphysite Christian Yaḥyā ibn ʿAdī (d. 974), the Christian Abū ʿAlī Ibn Samḥ (d. 1027), and the Nestorian Christians Mattā ibn Yūnus (d. 940) and Ibn al-Ṭayyib (d. 1043).[3] Muslim "theologians" (*mutakallims*, "dialecticians" to be precise, whose interests ranged far beyond the science of the divine, *theologia,* to include physics as well) developed their own elaborate, rigorous physical model based in part on Epicurean atomism.[4] The great Muslim Aristotelian Avicenna (d. 1037) wrote extensively on physics.[5]

These philosophers took various approaches to physics and did so out of a range of motives. What was Ibn al-Faḍl's approach? What motivated his interest? How did he draw on predecessors and contemporaries? Such are the questions addressed in this chapter.

1 TYPES OF CAUSES

When modern physicists speak of the cause of an event, they usually mean what makes the event happen: when I drop this pencil, it accelerates downward *because of* a gravitational force. By contrast, Aristotle spoke of four types of causation: material, formal, efficient, and final cause.[6] The third, "efficient cause," corresponds to the modern physicist's "cause."

The other three are foreign to the modern scientific paradigm. An object's "material cause" is the matter that underlies it (without which it would not exist): the wood and graphite out of which my pencil is made. Likewise, the "formal cause" is the form—the matter's particular configuration—that makes something what it is: the arrangement of the graphite in a cylinder encased in a tube of wood and sharpened to a point. Finally, there is the "final cause," perhaps most foreign to the modern paradigm. This is the "end" or purpose for which something exists and which, in the Aristotelian paradigm, is a *reason* that it exists: my pencil, and any pencil like it, exists so that one may use it to write.[7]

3. Leiden, Univ. Library, Warner or. 583 (233 folios, 23 lines per page); ed. Badawī in Aristotle, *Arisṭūṭālīs: al-Ṭabīʿa*. On the manuscript, see Badawī, 1:26–27; Stern, "Ibn al-Samḥ"; Giannakis, "Structure."

4. Dhanani, *Physical Theory;* Dhanani, "Kalām Atoms."

5. For example, in the physics sections (*ṭabīʿiyāt*) of his three summas, the *Healing* (*Shifāʾ*), *Deliverance* (*Najāt*), and *Pointers* (*Ishārāt*).

6. Aristotle, *Physics* 2.3, 194b24–195a3; *Metaphysics* Δ.2.1–3, 1013a24–b3; Falcon, "Aristotle on Causation," §2.

7. Aristotle, *Physics,* 2.3, 194b23–35; Shields, "Aristotle," §7; Falcon, "Aristotle on Causation," §2.

The final cause is an essential feature of Aristotle's teleological way of thinking about natural phenomena. To understand and explain the natural world, the Aristotelian must explain *for what purpose* things exist and processes occur. (In principle, the modern scientific paradigm ignores this question. Biology in the Darwinian framework often addresses it in explaining certain features of organisms—not only *how* certain populations of finches came to have such large beaks but also, as an ancillary question, *what purpose* such beaks might serve—while nevertheless tending to hold that no overarching purpose drives evolution.)

Ibn al-Faḍl, in a note on a saying of Solomon from the *Garden* (Ibn al-Faḍl's translation of the *Loci communes*), offers an expanded version of this typology of causes. After Solomon's saying on honoring one's father (in the chapter on honoring one's parents), Ibn al-Faḍl wrote:[8]

تفسير: إنّما وجبت كرامة الوالدين لأنهما[١] السبب في إيجاد[٢] الولد بعد تفضُّل الله عزّ وجلّ. ويجب أن تعلم أنّ الأسباب عند الحكماء ستة: (١) فاعل، بمنزلة النجار[٣] للباب، (٢) وصورة، كصورة الباب التي يُوْجِدُهَا النجار في مادته[٤]، (٣) والخشب[٥] القابل[٦] لصورة الباب[٧]، (٤) وغاية، وهي[٨] ضربان، (٤/ ١) أول، كإنجاد[٩] صورة الباب في مادته[١٠]، (٤/ ٢) وثان، وهي منفعة الباب وهي إحراز المَتاع ودفع أذى الحرّ والبرد، (٥) وأداة بمنزلة القَدُوم للنجار، (٦) ومثال، كما في نفس النجار من صورة الباب.

[١]لأنهما: س؛ لأنهم: ف [٢]إيجاد: ف؛ اتحاد: س [٣]النجار: ف؛ [[التحلـ]] التجار: س [٤]مادته: س؛ مادّية: ف [٥]والخشب: س ف؛ وممكن الصحيح: ومادة كالخشب [٦]القابل: ف؛ للقابل (مصحَّح: القابل): س [٧]الباب: +[[في مادته وبان هي منفعة]]: س [٨]وهي: ف؛ 'و'هي: س [٩]كإنجاد: ف؛ كاتحاد: س [١٠]مادته: س؛ مادّية: ف

Explication: Now, honoring one's parents was imposed as a duty because they are the cause of the child's being made to exist, after the favor of God the Mighty and Exalted. You should know that according to the sages there are six causes: (1) maker (*fāʿil* ~ ποιητής), such as the carpenter with respect to a door; (2) form, like the door's form which the carpenter causes to exist in its matter; (3) the wood that receives the form of the door; (4) purpose (*ghāya* ~ τέλος), which is of two types, (4.1) a first, like producing the form of the door in its matter, and (4.2) a second, which is the utility of the door, namely protecting one's property and warding off the harm of heat and cold; (5) tool, corresponding to the carpenter's axe with respect to the carpenter; (6) model, such as the form of the door in the soul (i.e., mind) of the carpenter.

This comment begins by explaining Solomon's saying in terms of causality: parents are the cause of the child. Here the text already hints at the need to specify the type of causality by emphasizing that God's favor, as a cause, is prior to the parents as a cause.

The types of causes that follow correspond to the four Aristotelian causes—efficient, material, formal, and final. The "maker" (1) is Aristotle's efficient cause. "Form" (2) is his formal cause. The "wood" (3) corresponds to material cause;

8. Ibn al-Faḍl, *Garden*, §23, **V** 126ᵛ–127ʳ; **S** 314ʳ ᵛ = *Loci communes*, 23.3, ed. Ihm, 528. The Arabic translation of the saying is missing the final line of the Greek about the remission of sins.

indeed, the original note may well have called this "matter," as would be expected, with "wood" as its example.[9] "Purpose" (4), then, is the final cause.

That leaves "tool" (5) and "model" (6). Both concepts appear in Aristotle's discussion of the types of causes alongside the four overarching types of causes. To introduce the formal cause, Aristotle says that cause can mean "the form (εἶδος) and the *model* (παράδειγμα)."[10] Likewise, after describing the final cause, Aristotle goes on to say that when there are intermediate steps leading to a desired goal, those steps are also done for the sake of that final goal; such steps can be *tools* (ὄργανα) or actions (ἔργα).[11] For example, if a scholar writes a book, perhaps the "final cause" (purpose) is to share the results of historical investigation and advocate for an interpretation of those results; in that case, necessary tools like a pen (or text editor) are also ultimately for the purpose of sharing knowledge, as are the required actions like reading other books and writing a line of text.

Ibn al-Faḍl's two types of "purpose" (4) also correspond to this discussion. The second (the anticipated benefit of having a door) is the end goal, while the first (the carpenter's immediate aim of producing a material object in the shape of a door) could be understood as an intermediate step toward that final purpose.

Ibn al-Faḍl's note on the types of causes is thus thoroughly Aristotelian. The formulation he was working with seems to have counted six rather than four causes by treating model and tool, both discussed by Aristotle, as separate causes.

2 QUALITIES AS BODIES OR NOTHING AT ALL

"Quality" (ποιότης or τὸ ποιόν, *kayfiya*) refers to what something is like. Is it red, blue, sweet, bitter, wet, dry, hot, cold? But what exactly *are* such things as redness and blueness and heat and cold? Are they things that actually exist? They certainly seem to exist, even if they are always attached to other things: redness does not exist on its own but rather always in poppies and pomegranates and other red things. In those things, it seems quite real. But is it? And if so, what sort of thing is it?

Such questions exercised natural philosophers in the Greek tradition quite early, in part because qualities were typically seen as elemental in some way (usually in contrary pairs like hot and cold)—that is, that the natural world was somehow constructed out of them. Thus, for example, the Aristotelian tradition viewed the four elements as each bearing two elemental qualities: fire, hot and dry; air, hot

9. The original might have been *mādda ka-l-khashab* . . . instead of simply *al-khashab*. The previous word is *māddatihi*, so a scribe might easily have dropped another *mādda* immediately following it (by haplography). A later scribe might then have emended the text by dropping the preposition *ka-* to make it make sense.

10. *Physics* 194b27; *Metaphysics* 1013a26–27.

11. *Physics* 194b35–195a4; *Metaphysics* 1013a35–b3.

and wet; water, cold and wet; earth, cold and dry.[12] Qualities thus often occupied a central place in ancient physical theories.

Aristotle, as already mentioned, identified "quality" as one of his ten "categories" (types of predicates), and later Aristotelians like John of Damascus followed him.[13] For them, redness or another quality was something that you could say about other things, much like quantity, position, and so on. But they were not substances (οὐσίαι, *jawāhir*) like this poppy or that strawberry. Instead they, and all the other categories other than substance, were "accidents," which could not subsist on their own but had to inhere in a substance.

Not everyone agreed with this account. Prior to Aristotle, Democritus (fifth century BCE) seems to have concluded from his doctrine of a material world made up exclusively of atoms that macroscopic qualities like color or bitterness were unreal because they were not inherent characteristics of atoms but rather simply by-products of the *configuration* of atoms and a much smaller set of intrinsic atomic properties. So when we think we taste something bitter, what we call bitterness is *really* just atoms with the inherent quality of sharpness making microscopic tears in the tongue's flesh.[14]

The atomist materialist philosopher Epicurus (341–270 BCE) adopted aspects of Democritus's theory but made important revisions that let him avoid denying the reality of qualities. As Timothy O'Keefe argued, Epicurus allowed for the existence of qualities by considering the by-products of atomic properties and configurations as *real,* even if not intrinsic to atoms themselves. In particular, Epicurean qualities are *dispositional:* atomic properties and configurations have the potential to interact with our sense-organs to produce a particular sensory experience. An object's redness is the potential of its assembled atoms to produce a sensation of redness to our eyes under certain circumstances (e.g., in the light).[15]

Thus whereas the Aristotelian would say that bitterness is inherent in horseradish, Epicurus would say that bitterness is our (real) experience, which we should rationally interpret as the side effect of intrinsic properties of atoms and their interactions with the atoms that make up our tongues. Democritus, however, might have concluded from this that bitterness is not real at all.

The Stoics, on the other hand, believed that the qualities were corporeal. In Stoic physics, only "bodies" (physical objects) can act and be acted upon, cause and be caused, and thus be considered part of reality. Since qualities do seem to be real, they must be bodies.[16] For the Stoics, horseradish's bitterness was not only real; bit-

12. *EI*³, s.v. "Elements."
13. Ch. 6, p. 184, n. 20.
14. O'Keefe, "Ontological Status," 120.
15. O'Keefe, 126–34. See also Sedley, "Hellenistic Physics," 379–82.
16. Kupreeva, "Qualities," 300–302; Long and Sedley, *Hellenistic Philosophers,* 1:162–76 (§§27–28).

terness was itself a corporeal constituent of horseradish, pervading the horseradish, according to one formulation (that of Chrysippus) as spirit (πνεῦμα).[17]

Arguments defending and critiquing these various positions were often quite elaborate. We have already encountered the debate, reported by Ibn al-Faḍl in his first marginal note on Basil's *Hexaemeron*, about whether "existence" means the same thing when applied to substances and accidents[18]—a more general discussion of the particular question of the sense in which a quality (as an accident) may be said to exist.

Basil, in his first homily on the *Hexaemeron*, suggests that this sort of deliberation about the ontological status of qualities was wasted effort. In discussing the two parts of the world mentioned in the opening line of Genesis—"In the beginning God made the sky and the earth"—Basil is quick to dismiss the physicist's attempt to discover the substance of sky and earth. He declares himself satisfied with Isaiah's comparison of sky to smoke.[19] About the earth, he says,

> Let us resolve not to busy ourselves finding out what its substance (οὐσίαν ~ *jawhar*) is, nor to weary ourselves with thoughts by seeking out the substrate (ὑποκείμενον ~ *mawḍū'*) itself,[20] nor to seek some nature which is devoid of qualities, quality-less by definition.[21]

Instead, explains Basil, everything we conceptualize as qualities of earth (like its texture and density) are essential parts of its substance (συμπληρωτικὰ τῆς οὐσίας, *mutammim li-jawharihā*).[22] Theoretically stripping earth of its qualities will leave nothing at all.[23]

In the margin beside Basil's discussion of qualities, substance, and underlying substrate of earth, Ibn al-Faḍl wrote a loosely related note describing two philosophical positions on the ontological status of qualities:[24]

إنّ طائفة من الفلاسفة الضلّال[1] دفعوا وجود الكيفيات، وكابروا ما يشهد بصحّته الحِسّ، ومن جملتهم ابيقورس؛ وطائفة اعتقدت أنّها أجسام، فضلّوا أيضاً، ومن[2] جملتهم اكسناغورس[3].

[1]الضلّال: الضلال: ب د؛ الضالّين: ذ؛ وإنما في ب د «أصعب القراءتين» [2]ومن: د ذ؛ وفي: ب [3]اكسناغورس: ب د؛ اكستاغورس: ذ

17. Long and Sedley, 1:172.
18. See ch. 6, p. 181, n. 1.
19. Basil, *Hexaemeron*, 1.8, ed. Amand de Mendieta and Rudberg, 14_{22}. Arabic: **B** 19_{2}.
20. Cf. *hādhā l-mawḍū'* in Ibn al-Faḍl's Arabic translation, which seems to read the nonattributive αὐτὸ in the medieval and modern vernacular sense of the demonstrative pronoun, rather than the ancient meaning, "itself."
21. Basil, *Hexaemeron*, 1.8, ed. Amand de Mendieta and Rudberg, 15_{3-5}; trans. based on Basil-NPNF, 56. Arabic: **Q** $21_{⌂1}$–22_{14}. Here in the manuscripts, Ibn al-Faḍl's note (discussed below) intervenes.
22. LSJ s.v. συμπληρωτικός 1.
23. Basil, *Hexaemeron*, 1.8, ed. Amand de Mendieta and Rudberg, 15_{6-12}. Arabic: **Q** 22_{6-8}.
24. **B** 19_{7-10}, **D** 13_{14-17}, **E** $11_{⌂1}$–12_{3}. Ibn al-Faḍl's note appears in-line in manuscripts after the part where Basil speaks of a "nature devoid of qualities, quality-less by definition."

> One group of erring philosophers rejected the existence of qualities, contradicting what sense-perception testifies to be right; among them is Epicurus. Another group held that [the qualities] are bodies, and they are also in error; among them is Anaxagoras.[25]

Ibn al-Faḍl here introduces a discussion that was not addressed in Basil's text. Basil had not even mentioned the notion that the qualities might not exist, or the notion, equally foreign to Aristotelian physics, that they are material bodies.[26]

The two doctrines in question are well attested in antiquity, as we have seen. Epicurus did indeed believe that qualities did not inhere in bodies, since for him they were simply the result of atoms' elemental properties and configuration (as modern chemists and physicists might agree). Still it is perhaps not quite fair to say that Epicurus thought they did not exist at all; that is closer to Democritus's view. But already in antiquity, the first-century Platonist philosopher Plutarch (in a passage that has played an important role in reconstructing the Epicurean theory of sense-perception) sought to lump Epicurus together with Democritus, concluding that since Epicurus espoused atomism just like Democritus, he must also have denied the existence of the qualities perceived by the senses.[27] Ibn al-Faḍl's note seems to be in this tradition of viewing Epicurus as a quality-denier.

The doctrine that Ibn al-Faḍl ascribes to Anaxagoras, that the qualities are bodies, is best known as the Stoic view. It does not correspond precisely to any of the known fragments or doxographical statements of Anaxagoras.[28] However, this doctrine is consistent with the notion, which appears to emerge from the published Anaxagoras fragments, that matter is made up of "seeds" (σπέρματα, which could have been transformed by a scribal error into σώματα) that have inherent qualities, or else that they are the qualities themselves, "the hot," "the cold," and so forth, although the word "qualities" is never used.[29] Perhaps, then, Ibn al-Faḍl was articulating Anaxagoras's "seed" doctrine in Aristotelian terms, or else was drawing it from another source, such as one of the notes in Greek manuscripts. A Greek note on an earlier passage in this same homily, contained in a fourteenth-century manuscript, displays a similar interest in Anaxagoras's conception of matter.[30]

25. *Aksanāghūras;* read *Anāksaghūras.*

26. See Studtmann, "Aristotle's Categories," §2.2.4.

27. O'Keefe, "Ontological Status," 129–31.

28. Ibn al-Faḍl's note may thus be a new piece of evidence about Anaxagoras's physical doctrine. There are no explicit statements among the Anaxagoras fragments that the qualities (ποιότητες) are bodies (σώματα): ed. in Diels-Kranz, §46A; Anaxagoras, *Fragments,* ed. and trans. Sider, ch. 2; *Anaxagoras of Clazomenae,* ed. and trans. Curd, pt. 1. I thank Richard Janko for a helpful conversation about these fragments.

29. Anaxagoras, *Fragments,* e.g., B4a, B7, B15, A43, A44–46, A48. See the comments in the editions by Curd, 163–64, and Sider, 131.

30. Pasquali no. 3; see n. 89 below. The Greek note appears in Vat. gr. 1857 (Amand de Mendieta and Rudberg's B8, Pasquali's y), at Basil, *Hexaemeron,* 1.2, ed. Amand de Mendieta and Rudberg, 4_8. The

Why this interest? Ibn al-Faḍl ostensibly agrees (or in any case does not disagree) that speculation about the qualities is pointless. Still, even more than Basil, he clearly considers these theories worthy of some discussion. Perhaps this is in part because there continued to be proponents of such doctrines in his own day.

For example, on the one hand, some Muslim *mutakallims* refused to see qualities as existent entities in themselves. According to the influential Muslim *mutakallim* Abū l-Ḥasan al-Ashʿarī (d. 935–936, Baghdad), the Muʿtazilī-inclined *mutakallim* al-Aṣamm (d. ca. 816),[31] whose works are now lost, declared, "I affirm nothing but the long, wide, deep body" (as opposed to length, width, depth, or any other abstract attributes of bodies).[32] Al-Ashʿarī likewise reports that some nominally Muslim materialists (in particular Dahrī *aṣḥāb al-ṭabāʾiʿ*) denied the existence of accidents like blackness, whiteness, sweetness, sourness, and so on, saying that only qualified things (e.g., black things) exist, not the abstract qualities themselves.[33]

On the other hand, Abū Isḥāq al-Naẓẓām (d. ca. 836), an early Muʿtazilī author whose doctrines were rejected by later Muslim thinkers (and whose works do not survive), seems to have held that the qualities are subtle, interpenetrating bodies, as David Bennett has argued on the basis of the doxographical statements of al-Ashʿarī, the Muslim intellectual and man of letters al-Jāḥiẓ (d. 868–869, Basra), and the Nestorian Christian scholar and Greek-Syriac translator Job of Edessa (active in Baghdad; d. after 832).[34] Al-Naẓẓām made qualities the basis of his ontological system, such that "the ultimate constituents of nature," as Bennett puts it, "are simple properties and *rūḥ*,"[35] where *rūḥ* (spirit) is like Stoic *pneuma*. In particular, according to Job of Edessa, al-Naẓẓām thought of qualities not as accidents but as substances.[36]

Basil's own position, that stripping a thing of its qualities leaves no substrate at all, seems somewhat similar to the view of the Muʿtazilī Ḍirār ibn ʿAmr (d. ca. 815).[37] As Bennett describes, Ḍirār believed that bodies were composed of "bits"

---

note, on what different philosophers considered the elements (τὰ στοιχεῖα) to be, reports that Anaxagoras called them the "like-parts" (ὁμοιομερείας)—a term known from extant Anaxagoras testimonia (A1, A15, A44–46, A104, B5).

31. G. Schwarb, *EI*³, s.v. "al-Aṣamm."

32. Ashʿarī, *Maqālāt,* ed. Ritter, 343_{12}.

33. Ashʿarī, *Maqālāt,* ed. Ritter, 348_{11}–349_{2}. See Crone, "Excursus II," 118 and n. 50, and, on Dahrīs and other "ungodly" people, 104–8.

34. Bennett, "Spirit of Ahypokeimenonical Physics," 2; Bennett, "Abū Isḥāq," 211. (I thank Michael Cooperson for referring me to Bennett's work.) Biographical information: Bennett, "Abū Isḥāq," 207; Roggema, "Job." See also Crone, "Excursus II," 118 and n. 48.

35. Bennett, "Spirit of Ahypokeimenonical Physics," 2.

36. Roggema, "Job," 507; Langermann, "Islamic Atomism," 286.

37. Ḍirār's life and death: van Ess, *Theologie und Gesellschaft,* 3:32–34 (§1.3.1); *EI*², s.v. "Ḍirār b. ʿAmr," 12:225.

(*ab ʿāḍ*) that are themselves qualities. A particular body is nothing but a particular assemblage of these "property-parts," as Bennett calls them, though Ḍirār does not seem to have believed that such property-parts could exist on their own.[38] Both Basil and Ḍirār seem to consider physical objects to be made up of properties with no underlying substrate.[39]

Ibn al-Faḍl's note does not explicitly challenge Basil's physical theory (presented as common sense). Still, by sidestepping Basil's point about the *substrate*'s nonexistence to focus instead on qualities' nonexistence (or corporeality), Ibn al-Faḍl certainly does not endorse Basil's theory. Furthermore, Ibn al-Faḍl's rejection of two extremes, qualities' absolute unreality or nonexistence and their perfect reality to the point of being (self-subsisting) bodies, could be read to imply that his own view was the standard Aristotelian one, that qualities exist but only as accidents inhering in bodies (and other substances).

Indeed, Ibn al-Faḍl's translation of this passage suggests that he wished to weaken Basil's claim to make it more compatible with Aristotelian ontology. Where Basil says that nothing is left behind if one seeks to strip away the qualities *in theory* (τῷ λόγῳ), Ibn al-Faḍl's translation crucially speaks of doing so *in practice* (*bi-l-fi ʿl*). This is a much weaker claim—namely, that if you take an object and seek to remove its redness, density, and so on, you will be left with nothing in the end, presumably because you will have failed to separate these qualities from the unqualified prime matter in which they inhere. Aristotle does not claim that qualities and other accidents are separable from the substance in which they inhere *in practice*, only that they are *theoretically* separable. So in Ibn al-Faḍl's version, Basil is no longer contradicting Aristotle.[40]

A circa tenth-century Greek manuscript now in Genoa containing Basil's *Hexaemeron* (and with some textual affinity to Ibn al-Faḍl's translation) includes a Greek note that displays a similar tendency to sidestep Basil's non-Aristotelian ontology. It defines one of the words Basil used, "substrate," as "the qualified substance that underlies the qualities."[41] This apparently innocent gloss subtly undermines Basil's claim that nothing is left after stripping away the qualities; if that is

38. Bennett, "Abū Isḥāq," 209.

39. Basil's view could be compatible with that of his brother Gregory of Nyssa that material bodies are simply the confluence of qualities, which are pure concepts: *In hexaemeron* [= *Apology on the Hexaemeron*], §7, PG 44:69, ed. Drobner, 15_{10}–16_{11}. This is a key passage for Sorabji's argument (*Time*, 287–94) that Gregory came up with an idealism like Berkeley's idealism, critiqued by Hibbs ("Gregory") and defended and refined by Hill ("Gregory").

40. An equivalent Greek expression (τῷ ἔργῳ), not attested in the apparatus of the Greek edition, may nevertheless have been present in a Greek exemplar not used for the edition.

41. G2 = Genoa, Franzoniana, gr. 17, fol. 11^r; apparatus to Basil, *Hexaemeron*, 1.8 τὸ ὑποκείμενον, ed. Amand de Mendieta and Rudberg, 15, scholion on line 5; Cataldi Palau, "Complemento," 351 (scholion R).

what a substrate *is*, then it would seem that something *would* be left after stripping away the qualities: the Aristotelian substance that underlies them all and in which qualities inhere, thus "qualifying" the substance. Likewise, the next note in the same manuscript explains that by "a nature devoid of qualities," Basil is referring to "so-called matter."[42] This note does not contradict Basil by claiming that unqualified matter exists, but, like Ibn al-Faḍl's note, makes a point of explaining Basil's references using the appropriate Aristotelian (and Platonic) technical terms. The ultimate effect of these two Greek notes together is to support the plausibility of the Aristotelian claim, rejected by Basil, that stripping away all qualities in theory *does* leave something behind, the ultimate substrate: prime matter.

In this way, Basil's rejection of speculative attempts to mentally analyze earth and sky into substrate and qualities was a liability that could become an opportunity for Ibn al-Faḍl (and other commentators) to pivot to the problem of what kind of thing qualities actually are. This allowed Ibn al-Faḍl to consider answers that ancient philosophers had given to the question and implicitly stake out a space for his own answer.

3 RELATIVE CORPOREALITY OF ANGELS

At the background of this discussion about the corporeality of qualities was a basic aspect of Aristotelian and Platonic ontology: a division between the material and the immaterial, the corporeal and the incorporeal. In this view, there is a whole world of things that exist that is independent of matter. Thus, for example, a human being is made up of a material body and an immaterial soul: the soul is a real thing that interacts with material things—namely, the parts of the body that the soul controls and that affect it in turn—but is not itself material or corporeal.

An "explication" in Ibn al-Faḍl's translation of John of Thessaloniki's *Encomium to Saint Demetrios*—the only one not already discussed in chapter 5—engages with this feature of Aristotelian and Platonic physics in response to John's placement of spiritual beings like angels on a continuum between corporeality and incorporeality.

In the text (§10), Saint Demetrios has just been berating his Jewish interlocutor for pretending to share the saint's position on the oneness of God, whereas in fact, says the saint, they differ because the saint believes there are three entities that all share a single divine substance. He eventually turns to the all-pervasiveness of the Holy Spirit, distinguishing it from all other beings, corporeal (like human beings) and incorporeal (like angels). Even incorporeal beings, he says, are not in fact entirely incorporeal, so that even though they can move very fast, they are never in more than one place at once; it would, he says, make more sense to call them

42. G2, fol. 11ʳ; apparatus to Basil, *Hexaemeron,* 1.8 τινα φύσιν ἔρημον ποιοτήτων, ed. Amand de Mendieta and Rudberg, 15, scholion on lines 5–6; and Cataldi Palau, "Complemento," 351 (scholion S).

subtle-bodied (λεπτοσώματοι ~ *laṭīfat al-ajsām*). Only God's nature is truly incorporeal such that it is all-pervasive and nothing can confine it in space.[43]

Biblical angels were made of fire and wind (Psalm 104:4, Hebrews 1:7). John of Thessaloniki's contention (placed in the mouth of Saint Demetrios) that angels have subtle bodies was one answer (not without precedent) to the question of how to square scriptural statements about the nature of angels with the Aristotelian and Neoplatonic division of all being into the corporeal and the incorporeal. Some early Christian scholars insisted that angels were entirely incorporeal; others that they were nearly incorporeal, much less corporeal than human beings. John's own views—this very passage—were excerpted in the Acts of the pro-icon Second Council of Nicea (787 CE), and so his view that angels have "subtle bodies" became the official teaching of the Byzantine Church.[44]

John's formulation resembles certain pre-Socratic theories of the soul discussed by Aristotle in his treatise *On the Soul,* which was translated into Arabic by Isḥāq ibn Ḥunayn (d. 910–911). One theory says that the soul is composed of the "most subtle-parted" element (λεπτομερέστατον ~ *daqīqat al-ajzāʾ*); another, that it is itself "a subtle-parted body" (σῶμά τι λεπτομερές ~ *jism laṭīf al-ajzāʾ*).[45] The Stoics too considered the soul to be a subtle body: breath. Perhaps most tellingly, the Epicurean soul was a thinly spread collection of atoms that interpenetrated the human body; Epicurus himself called the soul "a subtle-parted (λεπτομερές) body."[46] John's doctrine of "subtle bodies" thus responded to an exegetical problem with a physical theory grounded in the ancient philosophical tradition, including potentially problematic parts of it like atomism, Epicurean or otherwise.

We have seen how low an opinion Ibn al-Faḍl held of "hot-eyed" Epicurus.[47] Indeed in responding to John's account of "subtle bodies," Ibn al-Faḍl seems to have been seeking to avoid such atomistic associations. At this point in his Arabic translation of John's text, the manuscripts include an "explication" (*tafsīr*). While the two previous explications on this text are attributed to Ibn al-Faḍl, this one and the following two are simply labeled "explication" without an explicit attribution. As already discussed, it is nevertheless likely that all five explications were written by Ibn al-Faḍl.[48] This explication on angels' subtle bodies reads:[49]

43. See also ch. 2, §5, p. 78 (within description of John of Thessaloniki, *Encomium*, §10).

44. Peers, *Subtle Bodies*, 1–3, 194. For the relevance of angels' subtle bodies for pro-icon arguments, see also Parry, *Depicting the Word*, ch. 9.

45. Aristotle, *De anima*, 1.2, 1.5 = 405a–b, 409a–b; Arabic ed. Badawī, *Fī l-nafs*, 10, 22; cited in Roberts, "Being a Sabian," 259.

46. Long and Sedley, *Hellenistic Philosophers*, 1:65–72, 315, 320; 2:64 (Epicurus).

47. See ch. 5, §3, p. 166.

48. See ch. 5, §3, ¶2, p. 166.

49. Ibn al-Faḍl, translation of John of Thessaloniki's *Encomium to Saint Demetrios*, Explication 3, **A** 256^{v}_{4-9}, **B** 107^{v}_{7-10}; following **A** 256^{v}_{3}, **B** 107^{v}_{6} (*lā yaḥṣiruhā ḥāṣiruni l-battata*).

إنّ الملائكة إذا ما قيسوا بالبارئ تعالى، كانوا كثيفين لأجل[1] بساطته في الغاية القصوى، وإذا ما قيسوا بنا نحن معشر الأنام كانوا بسيطين، لأنّهم ليسوا مثلنا منسحبين مع الهيولى[2].

[1]لأجل: أ؛ لأنّ: ب [2]+«هذا ما أفدناه وتَلَقَّناه من الكتاب المقدس»: أ؛ وهذا من المتن، لا من التفسير.

> When angels are compared to the almighty creator, they are dense (*kathīf*) on account of his most extreme simplicity (*basāṭa*). When they are compared to us, mankind, they are simple (*basīṭ*), because they are not drawn out, like us, with matter (*hayūlā*).[50]

This note seeks to explain Demetrios's gradient of incorporeality by adding terminology to the discussion: "dense" (*kathīf*) and "simple" (*basīṭ*, the opposite of "compound"). Ibn al-Faḍl here inversely correlates density with simplicity.

This formulation has several consequences. First, it treats simplicity as a matter of degree (rather than a dichotomy between simple and composite).[51] Second, and more significantly, it shifts away from Demetrios's claim that angels are not incorporeal but rather subtle-bodied, which could be read to mean that they have some very fine and insubstantial material component, by stressing that in *contrast* to angels we are mixed with matter. The overall effect is to interpret away Demetrios's claim about relative *corporeality*, transforming it into a discussion of relative *simplicity*.

Ibn al-Faḍl's comparison of humans, angels, and God finds a close parallel in John of Damascus's discussion of the topic in the *Exposition of Faith*, which was translated into Arabic by Antonios of Saint Symeon, as already mentioned. In that text, in the chapter "on God's location and that only the divine is uncircumscribable," the Damascene says that God is "not in a location" because he is immaterial and uncircumscribable. After considering scriptural passages and expressions that might seem to suggest that God is localizable in space, the Damascene notes that "the divine is without parts" (that is to say, simple) but is in everything all at once, rather than having one part here and another part there.[52] He then contrasts God with angels:[53]

> The angel is not confined corporeally in a way that would give it form and outline. Nevertheless, it is said to be in a location because it is present [there] intellectually, acts according to its own nature, and is nowhere else but is circumscribed intellectually in the same place where it also acts. For it is not able to act in two different places at the same time, since only God can act everywhere at the same time. Whereas the angel can act in different places by its speedy nature and its instant and speedy trans-

50. Perhaps "drawn out" refers to spatial extension. **A** includes another line as if it were part of the *tafsīr*: "This is what we gathered and learned from the Holy Bible." This is not part of the *tafsīr* but the next line of the *Encomium* (Philippidis-Braat, "L'enkômion," 410_{23-24} Ταῦτα . . . μεμαθήκαμεν).

51. Cf. the Neoplatonic ontology in which the One is absolutely simple, and lower spheres of being are characterized by increasing multiplicity: Merlan, *From Platonism*, 1.

52. John of Damascus, *Exposition of Faith*, §13 (= 1.13), lines 9–29, ed. Kotter, 38, esp. lines 27–29. Arabic (Antonios): Vat. ar. 177, fol. 49^{v}_{5-7}.

53. §13, lines 30–38, ed. Kotter, 38–39; trans. after Peers, *Subtle Bodies*, 108. Arabic (Antonios): Vat. ar. 177, fol. 49^{v}_{7-15}.

location, the divine (τὸ θεῖον, *Allāh*) . . . performs different activities in different places at the same time by a single, simple activity.

In this way, the Damascene explains that angels are incorporeal but are still restricted to being in only one place at once. They are localized in that place "intellectually," that is, as an "intelligible" or "noetic" being (as opposed to a material being): even though they have no material body, their immaterial being nevertheless occupies place much as a body does. Thus while focusing on location in space, he implies that angels are immaterial beings whose immateriality is quite different from God's, since he is everywhere at once and not localized in space. The key to this difference is simplicity. Note in particular that God's universal, unlocalizable *activity* is described here as "simple," just as Ibn al-Faḍl focuses in his description on God's simplicity.

Later in the same *Exposition of Faith,* in the chapter "on angels," the Damascene addresses the question of angels' relative corporeality head-on:[54]

> The angel is furthermore an intelligible substance (οὐσία νοερά ~ *jawhar ʿaqlī*) in perpetual motion, of free will, incorporeal, serving God, endowed by grace with an immortal nature. . . . It is said that an angel is incorporeal and immaterial but only in relation to us. For everything compared to God, who alone is incomparable, is found dense and material, for only the divine is in reality immaterial and incorporeal.

In other words, angels are incorporeal (subtle, immaterial) *compared to us* but seem quite corporeal (dense, material) *compared to God.* Thus the Damascene, while retaining the concept of corporeality, adds density and matter—two concepts that Ibn al-Faḍl's note favors—to the discussion.

Finally, in one of his treatises focused specifically on the cult of icons, the Damascene puts it succinctly:[55]

> God is by nature completely incorporeal. Meanwhile, angel, soul, and *daimōn*, when compared to God, are bodies; but when compared to material bodies, they are incorporeal.

Here we see most clearly how the distinction is supposed to work: we have material bodies, angels have (or are) immaterial bodies, and God does not have a body at all. Immaterial bodies, it should be noted, are at a safe distance from the atomism that might be associated with "subtle bodies."

54. §17 (= 2.3), ed. Kotter, 45; trans. after Peers, *Subtle Bodies,* 109. Arabic (Antonios): Vat. ar. 177, fol. 52^{v}_{4-9}.

55. John of Damascus, *Third Oration on Images,* 3.25, ed. Kotter, 132; trans. after Parry, *Depicting the Word,* 81. Antonios translated a portion of the Damascene's *Orations on Images*, but apparently not this section: Graf, *GCAL,* 2:44; Nasrallah, *Histoire,* 3.1:278 and n. 171; Ibrahim, "Some Notes on Antonios," 177, who clarifies that Antonios translated a single continuous portion, seemingly the only portion available to him.

John of Damascus's analysis of human, angelic, and divine relative corporeality was influential in the later Byzantine tradition. The indefatigable abbot Theodore of the Stoudios Monastery in Constantinople (b. 759, d. 826) follows the Damascene's account closely in his own writings on the subject.[56] Both John of Damascus and Theodore the Stoudite were key pro-icon intellectuals whose writings in defense of the cult of icons were canonized in the wake of the "Triumph of Orthodoxy" of 843, as the end of official Iconoclast policies is known in the Byzantine Church. Defending icons was certainly a motivation for their articulation and defense of this theory of angelic corporeality.[57] But it was also a compelling physical theory on its own terms, carefully distinguishing between two features of existent beings, materiality and spatial boundedness (both inversely related to simplicity). The Damascene's physics was apparently current in the eleventh century, for it is a lens through which Ibn al-Faḍl read John of Thessaloniki's officially sanctioned but troubling claim that angels are subtle bodies.

4 MATTER AND ATOMS, PLENUM AND VOID

What happens when you divide material objects, or "bodies," repeatedly? If you keep dividing, do you reach a minimal building block, or can you keep dividing indefinitely? From very early on in the Greek philosophical tradition, this question was an important strand of speculation about the natural world often linked to ethical and political questions that gave it additional urgency. Such associations continued throughout antiquity and the Middle Ages. Basil addressed the problem head-on in his *Hexaemeron,* and Ibn al-Faḍl's translation and a brief note of clarification indicate his interest in it—and also let us further characterize the sort of contemporary philosophy he was reading.

As remembered by the later tradition, Democritus and Leucippus (fifth century BCE) proposed that physical bodies are not infinitely divisible, but rather that repeated division eventually results in "uncuttable" parts (atoms) out of which all bodies are composed.[58] These smallest bodies inhabit empty space (void) and are unchanging and indestructible; decay and generation of macroscopic bodies, in this theory, are due to atoms detaching from one another and recombining. In this way, at least according to Aristotle (*On Generation and Corruption* 1.8, 325a2–9), atomism was meant to explain the world's obvious mutability without having to say that something (a new phenomenon) comes from nothing. Aristotle, who argued vigorously against atomism, also opposed Plato for his theory, elaborated in the *Timaeus* (53c–57d), that all physical bodies are constructed out of fire, air, water, and earth, each

56. Parry, *Depicting the Word,* 81.
57. Peers, *Subtle Bodies;* Parry, *Depicting the Word.*
58. My account of ancient Greek atomism is based upon Berryman, "Ancient Atomism," here §2.

corresponding to a regular solid (fire to tetrahedron, air to octahedron, water to icosahedron, earth to cube), themselves built from two sorts of triangles that could recombine (in a way analogous to Democritean atoms) to change from one element to another.[59] Aristotle himself argued for a different view of the material world, in which bodies are infinitely divisible—that is, that no matter how much a body is divided, its parts can always be further divided in theory. Thus matter is not discrete (as in atomism); it is, rather, a continuum. In response to critiques of atomism, especially Aristotle's, Epicurus (341–270 BCE) refined the theory. Aristotle had argued that atomism is incoherent because it posits bodies without parts (atoms) but then speaks about their orientation in space and attachment to each other, implying that an atom has parts after all (e.g., upper and lower parts, or in a string of atoms attached to each other, a side attached to the atom before it, and another side attached to the atom after it). In part to resolve such problems, Epicurus argued that atoms have theoretical parts, but that these minimal parts do not have parts, not even in theory.[60]

Theories different from both of these seem to have been espoused by Herakleides of Pontus (fourth century BCE) and Asklepiades of Bithynia (second century BCE).[61] A perusal of the Herakleides fragments collected by Fritz Wehrli allows us to characterize his views, at least roughly.[62] Galen (second/?third century) lumped Herakleides and Asklepiades together, saying they both "posit fragile molecules as the principles [i.e., starting points or building blocks] of the universe."[63] Sextus Empiricus (second or third century?) said much the same, in a long doxographical list of doctrines on what the "material principles" (*hylikai archai*) are.[64] He also attributed to Herakleides and Asklepiades the belief that their "fragile molecules" were subject to change, unlike Democritean and Epicurean atoms.[65] According to the Christian bishop Eusebius of Caesarea (b. ca. 260, d. 339–340 CE), Herakleides called the basic constituents of the material world "bulks" or "molecules" (ὄγκοι). Eusebius thought that Asklepiades took the term "molecules" from Herakleides (Herakleides no. 118), but it was already used widely with various meanings—for example, by Aristotle and Epicurus—so it is unnecessary to posit this dependence.[66] Asklepiades in particular seems also to have believed that running between

59. Berryman, "Ancient Atomism," §§2–3.

60. Berryman, §7; Long, *Hellenistic Philosophy*, 33.

61. Berryman, "Ancient Atomism," §8.

62. Wehrli, *Herakleides Pontikos*, 38–39, commentary at 101–3.

63. Fragment no. 119a. For the interpretation that ἄναρμοι ὄγκοι means "fragile corpuscles," see Vallance, *Lost Theory*, 18–22.

64. Fragment no. 119b = Sextus Empiricus, *Outlines of Pyrrhonism*, 3.32. See also Vallance, *Lost Theory*, 14.

65. Fragment no. 120 = Sextus Empiricus, *Against the Physicists*, 2.318.

66. Fragment no. 118 = Eusebius, *Praeparatio evangelica*, 14.23. On the term ὄγκος, see Vallance, *Lost Theory*, 16–18.

the microscopic molecules were "pores," which could at least be interpreted as "interstitial void"—that is, microscopic empty space or "micro-voids."[67] Such a theory would be similar to what Heron of Alexandria (fl. 62 CE), in the preface to his *Pneumatics,* seems to presuppose in his discussion of compression of air, artificial vacuums, and other observable phenomena. Heron stresses that while void (τὸ κενόν) cannot exist "all together" in a continuum (ἀθροῦν), it certainly does exist "interspersed" throughout matter "in small parts."[68]

Still, we should perhaps not read too much into the similarity of wording. There seem to have been various theories, quite different from one another, that imagined "pores" running through matter; for example, Sylvia Berryman argues that the "pores" proposed by Aristotle's and Theophrastos's successor Straton of Lampsakos (ca. 287–269 BCE) were straight tunnels cutting through transparent matter, meant to explain how light can pass through (in a straight line), in contrast to Heron's interstitial voids, which he compared to the gaps between grains of sand in a pile of sand (not arranged in a straight line, and meant to explain the compression of air, not transparency).[69] Even when the two words are paired—"molecules and pores"—this need not mean that the theory behind them is the same. Already Epicurus (b. 342–341 BCE, d. 271–270 BCE) used both terms.[70] It is not entirely clear what physical theory Diogenes Laertius ascribes to Diogenes of Sinope (the Cynic) when he reports (in a textually problematic passage where the various proposed emendations alter the doctrine in question) that the Cynic held that "everything is in everything and through everything," such that "in bread there is some meat, and in vegetable there is some bread, and some of all simple bodies is in all things, since through certain unseen pores molecules penetrate and are joined in vaporous form."[71] Then there is Empedocles's theory explaining the action of one body on another by way of pores (void passageways interrupting the continuity of matter), which Aristotle had sought to refute. But even Aristotle (in *Meteorologica* book 4, whose authenticity has been questioned) uses the term "pores" for a similar purpose, to explain how one body can act upon another. The sixth-century Aristotelian commentator Olympiodoros, drawing on his own teacher Ammonios, explains away this apparent inconsistency quite plausibly by claiming that in

67. "Interstitial void": Vallance, *Lost Theory*, 49, 54. "Microvoid": Berryman, "Evidence for Strato," 279.

68. Ed. Schmidt, 4_{3-4}, 16_{21-23}, 28_{2-3}: bodies are made "from bodies with subtle parts, between which are interspersed voids smaller than the parts." See Berryman, "Evidence for Strato"; Berryman, "Ancient Atomism," §8; Vallance, *Lost Theory*, 48–54.

69. Berryman, "Evidence for Strato," 288–89.

70. By ὄγκος Epicurus refers to the tiny masses out of which matter is built; by πόρος, he refers to "openings." See LSJ s.v. ὄγκος (B) III.

71. Diogenes Laertius, 6.73, ed. Marcovich, 420–21. Materially significant emendations were proposed by Gigante, "Su un insegnamento"; Basta Donzelli, "Del 'Tieste.'"

this latter passage Aristotle uses "pores" merely in the sense of parts of a material body that are more receptive to another body's action than others (that is, they are *not* voids tunneling through matter).[72]

In any case, it has been argued that the doxographical literature is back-projecting Asklepiades's theories onto Herakleides.[73] Since we are interested in the later tradition as it might have been read and experienced by Ibn al-Faḍl and his contemporaries, this question need not concern us here. Of the various sources for these theories, the best-represented in the later tradition is Galen. Galen's works were influential in Byzantium and were a major component of the literary heritage translated in the Greek-Arabic translation movement of eighth- to tenth-century Baghdad, most famously by Ḥunayn ibn Isḥāq. So it is worth looking at how Galen characterizes Asklepiades in particular.

Galen, writing in a polemical vein against Asklepiades, who was also a physician, tars him as an atomist, saying that he believed in "molecules and pores" (*onkoi kai poroi*), which Galen says are just new names for Epicurus's atoms and void.[74] Elsewhere he writes sarcastically of Asklepiades's "miraculous molecules and pores," suggesting Asklepiades used his theory to justify his medical approach—an approach that Galen refutes at length.[75] While Epicurus did indeed speak of "molecules" and "pores," Galen's equation of Asklepiades's theory with atomism may not be quite right, since it appears that Asklepiades's "molecules" might have been infinitely divisible.[76] All the same, it is certainly the case that Galen sought to associate Asklepiades's "molecules and pores" with two doctrines vehemently opposed by Aristotelians: atomism and the existence of void.

The stakes were high, not only for the specific medical arguments Galen wished to make, but also for natural philosophy. Galen, strongly committed to teleological explanations in nature and especially in medicine, closely associated continuum theory (the Aristotelian position that matter is infinitely divisible) with "beneficent teleology," and the belief that matter is discrete with "blind necessity."[77] This was a polemical oversimplification, but nevertheless Galen, and the later tradition, found it plausible.

Still, Galen's rough contemporary Alexander of Aphrodisias (second/third century) could approach the general question with more nuance. Alexander, in a

72. Viano, "Le commentaire d'Olympiodore," 71–72.

73. Vallance, *Lost Theory*, 10–12.

74. Galen, *To Pison on Theriac*, in *Opera omnia*, ed. Kühn, 14:250; cited by Vallance, *Lost Theory*, 38–39. Arguments against authenticity: Leigh, "On Theriac," 19–53, who concludes that Galen was probably not its author. The Arabic translation, like the Greek text, circulated under Galen's name: Richter-Bernburg, "Eine arabische version."

75. Galen, *On the Elements*, §12, ed. De Lacy, 146 = Kühn, 1:499. Cited by LSJ s.v. ὄγκος (B) III.

76. Berryman, "Ancient Atomism," §8; Vallance, *Lost Theory*, 20–24, 42–43.

77. Berryman, "Ancient Atomism," §8; von Staden, "Teleology and Mechanism."

fragment of his lost commentary on Aristotle's *Physics,* says that Democritus and Epicurus believed in void *within bodies,* in between atoms, which Democritus thought were themselves continuous. In another fragment, Alexander notes that Democritus said that all continuous bodies (for him, atoms) are indivisible; that Stoics believed that the whole universe is continuous; and that Democritus and Stoics agree that outside of the universe there is an infinite void.[78] Thus Alexander, carefully distinguishing between macro- and micro-voids, describes continua *as a feature of atomism,* at least of the Democritean variety.

Many Muslim thinkers situated themselves squarely within the Aristotelian-Galenic tradition, but others developed a theory of atoms with striking parallels to Epicurean atomism. For example, some *mutakallim*s held that the smallest body (analogous to Epicurus's "atom") is made up of some minimum number of "parts without parts" that are not themselves bodies but only *parts* of bodies. Each non-corporeal part without parts is called a *jawhar* (usually translated as "atom" in the *kalām* context, in contrast to the Aristotelian *jawhar,* which means "substance," οὐσία).[79] These *jawāhir* are sometimes thought to have magnitude, sometimes not.[80] They can be viewed as analogous to the *minimal parts* of an Epicurean atom, which do have magnitude.[81]

Less evidence survives for Christians espousing atomism, but enough does survive to make clear that some did.[82]

How do the Arabic Aristotelian tradition and the *kalām* tradition relate to one other? Y. Tzvi Langermann has argued that Galen was viewed by the Muslim practitioners of *kalām* as a major figure whose philosophical system they opposed, and that the atomism they developed can be read as part of a response to Galen, an attempt to defend atomism against his critiques.[83] Thus we should not imagine that in the world of Arabic philosophy, Aristotelians and non-Aristotelians were sequestered from one another and unaware of each other's activities. Instead these traditions developed in dialogue with one another, as they had in Greek, even when they do not alert us to this relation. The dialogue continued. Avicenna was clearly concerned to refute arguments by more recent atomists, and Fakhr al-Dīn al-Rāzī, trained in Aristotelian doctrines, developed an appreciation for atomism, presumably by thinking through atomists' arguments.[84]

78. Fragments 88 and 89, ed. Rashed, 227–28.

79. See Dhanani, *Physical Theory,* 57, ch. 4, and elsewhere. See also Bennett, "Abū Isḥāq," 208–9.

80. Dhanani, "Kalām Atoms," 162–66.

81. Ed. Long and Sedley, *Hellenistic Philosophers,* 2:32 = 9A.9 (from Epicurus, *Letter to Herodotus*), with commentary, ibid., 1:41–42. Dhanani, "Kalām Atoms," esp. 166–70; Crone, "Excursus II," 113–14.

82. Crone, "Excursus II," 113.

83. Langermann, "Islamic Atomism."

84. Lettinck, "Ibn Sina on Atomism"; Dhanani, "Impact."

Against this background, we may turn to a passage from Basil's first homily on the six-day creation narrative of the book of Genesis (Basil, *Hexaemeron*, 1.2), Ibn al-Faḍl's translation of that passage, and a note he wrote beside it in the margin.

In Basil's view, cosmological theories that omit God's role in creating the material world are critically flawed. To illustrate this point, he goes on to mention some of those theories. To aid a comparative examination of Basil's original Greek with the two Arabic translations (Ibn al-Faḍl's translation and the Anonymous Translation), we will consider all three, beginning with Basil's Greek:[85]

> (1) Οἱ γὰρ θεὸν ἀγνοήσαντες αἰτίαν ἔμφρονα προεστάναι τῆς γενέσεως τῶν ὅλων οὐ συνεχώρησαν, (2) ἀλλ' οἰκείως τῇ ἐξ ἀρχῆς ἀγνοίᾳ τὰ ἐφεξῆς συνεπέραναν. (3) Διὰ τοῦτο οἱ μὲν ἐπὶ τὰς ὑλικὰς ὑποθέσεις κατέφυγον, τοῖς τοῦ κόσμου στοιχείοις τὴν αἰτίαν τοῦ παντὸς ἀναθέντες· (4) οἱ δὲ ἄτομα καὶ ἀμερῆ σώματα καὶ ὄγκους καὶ πόρους συνέχειν τὴν φύσιν τῶν ὁρατῶν ἐφαντάσθησαν.

> (1) For, being ignorant of God, they did not concede that an intelligent cause presided at the generation of the universe, (2) but in accordance with their original ignorance they concluded the things that follow [from it]. (3) Because of this, some had recourse to material premises (*hypotheseis*), attributing the cause of the universe to the world's elements; (4) others imagined that bodies uncuttable (*atoma*) and without parts (*amerē*), and molecules and pores, comprised the nature of visible things.

Basil further describes that in such a theory, coming to be and ceasing to be happen because of the combination and recombination of these bodies-without-parts with each other, and some bodies are more durable simply because they are made of more tightly bound atoms.[86]

The physics tradition we have been surveying is clearly at the background of this passage. Basil, like Galen, associates theories about atoms, as well as "molecules and pores," with the doctrine that the world's generation (and so presumably worldly events in general) has only material causes: the collisions and combinations of material particles. Basil's passing mention of these theories also recalls the doxographical tradition on "material premises" or "material principles (*archai*)," beginning with Aristotle, who says that most earlier thinkers posited as principles only things that are "in the form of matter."[87] For example, Sextus Empiricus's list of doctrines on material principles mentioned above begins with various theories that they are one or some or all four (or five) of the elements, then atoms, then several others, then the "fragile molecules" discussed above, then a few more.[88]

85. Basil, *Hexaemeron*, 1.2, ed. Amand de Mendieta and Rudberg, 4_{4-9}; trans. based on Basil-NPNF, 53.

86. Amand de Mendieta and Rudberg, 4_{9-12}.

87. Aristotle, *Metaphysics* A.3, 983b6–11; cited by Amand de Mendieta and Rudberg, 4, apparatus.

88. Sextus Empiricus, *Outlines of Pyrrhonism*, 3.30–32.

This fits Basil's mention of "elements," on the one hand, and "atoms . . . and molecules and pores," on the other. This doxographical background was apparent to Byzantine readers. As a Greek marginal note on this passage in manuscripts of Basil's *Hexaemeron* explains,

> It is clear that all sages among the Hellenes [i.e., pagans] said that the world and matter are composed out of many things. For example, Pythagoras calls the elements of the principles numbers, Straton calls them qualities, Alkmaion antitheses, Anaximander the indefinite, Anaxagoras like-parts, Epicurus atoms, Diodoros things without parts, Asklepiades molecules.[89]

The note then continues with two more such doctrines before moving to various single elements (water, fire, air, earth), all four elements (Zeno, Empedocles, Plato), and finally all four plus a nameless fifth (Aristotle). Such lists are standard in the doxographies upon which modern scholars have based their reconstructions of these ancient theories.

So much for the state of the tradition when Basil was writing in the fourth century. What about seven centuries later, when Ibn al-Faḍl translated this passage in the eleventh? As already mentioned, Ibn al-Faḍl's Arabic version of Basil's *Hexaemeron* is a revision, made with recourse to the original Greek, of an earlier, anonymous Arabic translation.[90] This allows us to compare Ibn al-Faḍl's version to the earlier Arabic version, considering differences in vocabulary and phrasing to be Ibn al-Faḍl's deliberate choice. Considering what motivated those choices gives insight into the conceptual and terminological background against which Ibn al-Faḍl produced his new Arabic translation. (To aid comparison, passages identical in the two Arabic versions are printed in boldface.)

The Anonymous Translation, which Ibn al-Faḍl used as a basis for his own, renders this passage as follows:[91]

(١) وذاك أنهم لمّا جهلوا الله تعالى، لم يطلقوا علة مفهومة لكون الكل، (٢) بل الذي بنوه على ما تقدّم يضاهي جهلهم من الابتداء بأصل. (٣) ففيهم من لجأ إلى الأسباب الهيولانية فجعل علة الكل اسطقسات العالم، (٤) ومنهم من جعلها أجساما لا تنقسم ولا تتجزأ[١]، وجعلوا أجراماً ومسالكَ تشتمل على طبيعة المبصرات.

[١]تتجزأ: صححته؛ تتجزئ: س

89. Pasquali, "Doxographica," 195–96 = no. 3. Pasquali gathered scholia on Basil's *Hexaemeron* from four manuscripts: A3 [Pasquali's F] = Florence, Laurenziana, gr. 4.27, parchment, mid-tenth century (Amand de Mendieta and Rudberg, *Basile*, 27–29); B8 [Pasquali's y] = Vat. gr. 1857, probably the beginning of the fourteenth century (Amand de Mendieta and Rudberg, *Basile*, 72); E6 [Pasquali's O] = Oxford, Bodleian, Barocci gr. 228, end of tenth/beginning of eleventh century (Amand de Mendieta and Rudberg, *Basile*, 138–41); and G2 [Pasquali's G] = Genoa, Franzoniana, gr. 17, later tenth century (?) (Amand de Mendieta and Rudberg, *Basile*, 128). The manuscripts with note no. 3 are A3 and B8 (Pasquali's F and y), dated tenth and fourteenth century, respectively.

90. Roberts, "Re-Translation."

91. S 9^{v}–10^{r}.

> (1) That is, **since they were ignorant of God Almighty, they did not posit** an intellected/conceivable cause (*ʿilla mafhūma*) for the generation of **the universe** (*al-kull*), (2) but rather that which they built upon what preceded corresponds to their ignorance, from the beginning, of an origin (*aṣl*). (3) And so some among them **had recourse to material causes** (*al-asbāb al-hayūlānīya*) **and made the cause of the universe the world's elements** (*isṭiqsāt*); (4) and some of them made it **bodies** that are indivisible and **without parts,** and they made masses and paths (*ajrām wa-masālik*) comprise **the nature of the visible things.**

Ibn al-Faḍl's translation, based on both the original Greek and the Anonymous Translation, reads:[92]

> (١) ولمّا جهلوا الله تعالى، لم يطلقوا تقدّم وجود علة عاقلة للكل، (٢) لكنهم تكلّموا على ذلك بما ضلّوا فيه لضلالهم في المبدأ العنصري. (٣) فمنهم من لجأ إلى الأسباب الهيولانية وجعل علة الكل استقصات العالم (حاشية حوالي ٣ سطور)، (٤) ومنهم من تصوّر وتخيّل أن طبيعة المبصرات تألفت من أجسام لا تتجزّأ، ومن الملاء والخلاء.

> (1) And **since they were ignorant of God Almighty, they did not posit** the prior existence of an intelligent cause (*ʿilla ʿāqila*) of **the universe,** (2) but in speaking on that topic they erred as they did because of their error concerning the original/elemental principle (*al-mabdaʾ al-ʿunṣurī*).[93] (3) And so some of them **had recourse to the material causes and made the cause of the universe the world's elements** [*marginal note of about 3 lines*];[94] (4) and some imagined and fantasized[95] that **the nature of the visible things** was composed of **bodies without parts,** and of plenum and void (*al-malāʾ wa-l-khalāʾ*).[96]

A comparison of these translations reveals that both translators, but especially Ibn al-Faḍl, were attentive to the technical terms Basil used. First, we may note that Ibn al-Faḍl took over much of the text of this passage directly from the Anonymous Translation (boldface). These verbatim overlaps include some general terminology, in particular "cause" (*ʿilla* for *aitia*), "universe" (*al-kull* for *ta hola*), "the

92. **D** 2–3.

93. I translate this clause somewhat loosely. A literal translation would begin "but they spoke about that by [speaking about the issue] concerning which they erred because of their error . . ."—syntax that is natural in the Arabic but awkward in English.

94. This note will be discussed below.

95. *taṣawwara wa-takhayyala:* Ibn al-Faḍl has moved and modified the Anonymous Translation's *takhayyalūhā* (which is the first word after the passage quoted, beginning Basil's next thought somewhat awkwardly with *takhayyalūhā inna hādhihi l-ajsām* . . .) so that in Ibn al-Faḍl's translation both *taṣawwara* and *takhayyala* govern not only the claim about atoms and molecules and pores but also the subsequent passage (not quoted here) on the dynamics of this atomic origin, which Basil goes on to describe. This brings Ibn al-Faḍl's translation more in accord with Basil's Greek, where the subsequent passage on dynamics is expressed in infinitive clauses governed by ἐφαντάσθησαν.

96. Ibn al-Faḍl's syntax, more than the Anonymous Translator's, continues the sentence, like Basil's Greek (even though Amand de Mendieta and Rudberg punctuate it as a new sentence), with further erroneous beliefs.

world" (*ʿālam* for *kosmos*), "the visible things" (*al-mubṣarāt* for *ta horata*). They also include some terminology specific to Aristotelian physics: "material causes" (*al-asbāb al-hayūlānīya* for *hylikai hypotheseis*) and "elements" (*isṭiqsāt* or *istiqṣāt*, the standard loanword for *stoicheia*).

Many of Ibn al-Faḍl's changes are primarily stylistic improvements to the Arabic for clarity and show a general tendency to produce a less literal, more idiomatic Arabic text. At one point in this passage, however, Ibn al-Faḍl has corrected a substantive error relating to technical terminology, by changing the Anonymous Translation's "intellected (*mafhūma*) cause" to "intelligent (*ʿāqila*) cause," where Basil has clearly written "intelligent cause" (αἰτίαν ἔμφρονα). Aside from making God, usually considered beyond comprehension, into something that can be "understood," the Anonymous Translation had missed, or at least weakened, the point of the passage, which is that the world did not arise out of mindless matter, but rather out of a First Cause with mental capacity.[97] Ibn al-Faḍl's remedy uses a word formed from the root of *ʿaql*, the standard term for "mind" and used to describe God's mind in Arabic Neoplatonism.[98] This is not to say it is an otherwise uncommon word—far from it—but only that it is an apt choice, compared with other potential translations for *emphrōn*, like *fāhim* (understanding), *ʿālim* (knowing), *nāṭiq* (rational), or even *ḥāzim* (prudent). Ibn al-Faḍl's choice of translation was not without precedent: the ninth-century Arabic translation of Galen's treatise *The Soul's Faculties* by Ḥubaysh—nephew and student of Ḥunayn ibn Isḥāq—renders the Greek word *emphrōn* using the Arabic *ʿāqil*.[99]

Even minor stylistic changes can offer hints as to Ibn al-Faḍl's conceptual vocabulary. In the next clause of Basil's text (number 2), about the errors deduced from ignorance of the correct premise, both Arabic translations inverted the order of the Greek for the sake of clarity, beginning with *ta ephexēs syneperanan*, "they [logically] concluded the things that follow." The Anonymous Translation is quite literal, with *bali lladhī banawhu ʿalā mā taqaddama*, "rather that which they built upon what preceded [i.e., the premise]." Although Basil's *symperainō*, "conclude," does not literally refer to building or construction, the senses of completing something and of reaching conclusions by means of logic are both part of its semantic range, and "building" has the same sense of accomplishment.[100] Ibn al-Faḍl moves further from this sense with his *takallamū ʿalā dhālika*, "they spoke about that."

97. An "intellected" or noetic cause does at least contrast with a material cause.

98. For example, Fārābī, *Virtuous City*, 1.1.10, ed. and trans. (modified) Walzer, *Al-Farabi on the Perfect State*, 74–77 = Dieterici 11.

99. Galen, *That the Soul's Faculties Follow upon the Mixtures of the Body*, §4, ed. in Helmreich et al., 2:43$_9$; Arabic translation ed. Biesterfeldt, 17$_{22}$; cited by *Glossarium*, Galen.An-virt.3075. Ḥubaysh's translation was made from Ḥunayn ibn Isḥāq's Syriac translation; Biesterfeldt, 9, 16. In this passage, Galen is quoting Plato's description of how a developing soul becomes "intelligent" (*Timaeus* 44b).

100. See LSJ s.v., I and II.2.

The result is clearer Arabic, but this reference to "speech" (*kalām*) also bears a particular connotation of theorizing—for example, as applied to the Muslim practitioners of *kalām,* the *mutakallims*. This term was also used by Christians, including Ibn al-Faḍl, for their own theologians; for example, Gregory of Nazianzos's Byzantine epithet "the Theologian" is often rendered in Arabic as *al-mutakallim fī l-lāhūt,* "the one who speaks about divinity." But in the present context, where Basil is denouncing wrongheaded opinions of certain philosophers, especially atomists, the connotation of the Muslim *mutakallims*, many of whom believed in some form of atomism, was, from an eleventh-century perspective, quite apt.

Ibn al-Faḍl's revisions also reveal particular attentiveness to the terminology of physics and the natural philosophical ideas being expressed and referenced. This allows us to infer how he interpreted the passage; that is, we may read his translation as interpretation. In the same clause (number 2), Basil, remarking on what led the philosophers to their erroneous conclusions, suggests that they reached their conclusions "fittingly"—namely, because their process of arriving at that conclusion (*symperainō*) accords with "their original ignorance" (ἀλλ' οἰκείως τῇ ἐξ ἀρχῆς ἀγνοίᾳ). In other words, their erroneous conclusions correspond to the fact that they were ignorant from the start. In the Anonymous Translation, the same passage says that the philosophers' conclusions "correspond to their ignorance, from the beginning, of an origin" (*yuḍāhī jahlahum mina l-ibtidāʾi bi-aṣlin*), apparently translating *ex arches* ("original" or "from the beginning") both in the sense that the philosophers were ignorant from the beginning and that their ignorance concerns the beginning, or "origin." This "doublet," in which the translator offers two distinct translations for a single word in the original text, suggests an uncertainty about which is Basil's intended meaning.[101] This is reasonable. After all, the passage is all about the "origin" of the universe, so it is somewhat counterintuitive to see Basil playing with this meaning by labeling the philosophers' ignorance with a term that more naturally applies to what they are ignorant *of:* the origin of the universe (God). The Anonymous Translator is hedging.

Ibn al-Faḍl chose to eliminate the ambiguity by opting for one of the two senses. For him, the thinkers' error arose "because of their error concerning the original/elemental starting point" (*li-ḍalālihim fī l-mabdaʾi l-ʿunṣurī*). As usual, Ibn al-Faḍl has produced tighter, crisper Arabic than the Anonymous Translator. Ibn al-Faḍl's rendering also clarifies the question of causation: no longer is the statement about a "correspondence" between their ignorance and their conclusions, but rather their ignorance, or for Ibn al-Faḍl their "error" (another sense of Basil's *agnoia*), is a *cause* of their erroneous conclusions. Ibn al-Faḍl has thus reinterpreted Basil's phrase "their original (*ex archēs*) error" by specifying that their error was to think that the origin of the physical world is the elements themselves, rather than God.

101. For doublets in Greek-Arabic translation, see Tuerlinckx, "Le lexique," 482–85.

To do this, Ibn al-Faḍl interprets Basil's *ex archēs* not according to the syntax—which would suggest that the error *is* original—but according to the expected sense, that the error *concerns* the origin (of the world). This has the effect of making the train of thought more logical: (1) the thinkers were ignorant of the original cause, God; (2) their conclusions were erroneous because of their ignorance concerning that original cause; then sentences 3 and 4 go on to describe examples of such erroneous conclusions. It is possible that this interpretation was suggested to Ibn al-Faḍl by the Greek text he had in front of him: by changing just one letter (*ex archēs* to *ep' archēs*), the modern critical edition of Basil's text could be made to read "their error *concerning* the starting point."[102] Still, it was certainly a choice with respect to the Anonymous Translation he was revising. At the same time, by speaking of "error" instead of "ignorance," Ibn al-Faḍl has made it possible to read his Arabic Basil as saying that a positive error, and not just ignorance, is to blame. These were subtle but deliberate choices to present ancient philosophers as adopting erroneous premises that doomed their inquiry, inevitably producing erroneous conclusions.

But what exactly were their erroneous premises? Let us look more closely at the phrase in question, *al-mabda' al-ʿunṣurī*, "the original/elemental starting point." Ibn al-Faḍl's use of *mabda'* for "starting point" or "principle" (*archē*), rather than the Anonymous Translation's "beginning" (*ibtidā'*), is standard in Aristotelian physics in Arabic. Isḥāq ibn Ḥunayn's translation of Aristotle's *Physics* translates *archē* in this sense as *mabda'*.[103] Ibn al-Faḍl's choice of *ʿunṣurī* to describe the starting point is perhaps more unexpected. The straightforward Arabic word for "origin" was *aṣl*, and indeed this option was already available to Ibn al-Faḍl in the Anonymous Translation. Why speak of an "*ʿunṣurī* starting point" instead?

The basic sense of *ʿunṣur* is "origin"; a medieval Arabic lexicon defines *ʿunṣur* as a synonym of *aṣl*.[104] But it had taken on a particular set of meanings in Arabic philosophy. In Greek-Arabic translations, *ʿunṣur* is used to translate the Greek *stoicheion*, "element," and sometimes *hylē*, "matter," or *sōma*, "body," especially when the context is the four (or five) elements. Consider the work of the ninth-/tenth-century scholar, scientist, and translator Qusṭā ibn Lūqā of Baʿlabakk (in present-day Lebanon), a Byzantine Christian of Greek origin active in Baghdad

102. τῇ ἐξ/ἐπ' ἀρχῆς ἀγνοίᾳ. The editors, Amand de Mendieta and Rudberg, do not list this as a variant attested by any of the eight manuscripts they used for their edition.

103. Aristotle, *Physics* 1.1, 184a13; Arabic ed. Badawī, 1_{11}. When Aristotle uses *archē* in the more straightforward sense of "beginning," as in "beginning of life," translators sometimes used *ibtidā'*; e.g., *Generation of Animals* 355b35; Arabic (probably from Syriac) ed. Brugman and Drossaart Lulofs, 64_{11} (on the heat within animal bodies, on which see ch. 8, §1, pp. 235, 238–39); *Meteorology* 2.2, 355b35; Arabic (possibly from Syriac) ed. Schoonheim, $71_{537-538}$; cited by *Glossarium*, Arist.Phys.00371, Arist.Gener-anim.0038, and Arist.Meteor.0318, respectively.

104. *Lisān* s.v. *ʿnṣr*.

and Armenia who wrote in Arabic.[105] In his translation of the doxographical work *Epitome on Philosophers' Physical Doctrines* ascribed to Plutarch (often called the *Placita philosophorum*), Qusṭā uses *ʿunṣur* to translate words referring to Aristotle's fifth element (*stoicheion* and *sōma*), Thales of Miletos's primordial formless matter (*hylē*) that in his theory plays a role analogous to the elements, and Anaximander's "error" in speaking of the stuff out of which the universe is made (*hylē*), which he called "the indefinite," but denying the universe an efficient cause.[106] In all of these examples, *ʿunṣur* refers to the basic stuff out of which the world is made, especially with reference to the world's genesis.

For more precision, we may turn to Avicenna, who offers a definition of *ʿunṣur* as part of an account of various ways of speaking about the material substrate of physical bodies. In the physics portion of the *Healing*, he explains that *hayūlā* ("matter" or "material") may be referred to using various terms: *hayūlā* in a restricted sense, insofar as it potentially receives forms; "subject," insofar as it has actually received a form; "matter" (*mādda*), insofar as all forms have it in common as the thing in which they inhere; the loanword from the Greek word for "element" *isṭiqiss*, insofar as it is the simple unit into which composite bodies can, at least theoretically, be analyzed; and *ʿunṣur*, insofar as it is the original component out of which a physical body is composed.[107] As Avicenna himself acknowledges, the last two definitions, "element" and *ʿunṣur*, are quite similar: element is the simple part into which a composite body may be analyzed, while *ʿunṣur* is the simple part out of which a composite body may be composed. At least in an Aristotelian framework, these would seem to be two directionally different ways of referring to the same concept.

So an *ʿunṣur* is a basic unit or element out of which the universe is made. And though we looked to Qusṭā ibn Lūqā and Avicenna to learn this, a reader of Ibn al-Faḍl's translation of Basil's *Hexaemeron* could simply have glanced at the margin at this point, where there was a note, probably written by Ibn al-Faḍl himself (to whom it is ascribed by some manuscripts, though in others it is anonymous). The note briefly glosses terms for matter, including *ʿunṣur*. It reads:[108]

يجب أن يُعْلَم أنّ اسم الهيولى يخترع لها بحسب تدرجها في المعاني، فلأنّها قابلٌ[١] للكل تسمى مادّةً، و<. . .> عنصراً، وبالصور البعدية تسمى عظماً[٢]، وبالتهيؤات[٣] تسمى هيولى، وبقبول الصور موضوع يسمى[٤] غير متناه[٥].

[١]قابلٌ: د ق؛ قابلة: ذ [٢]تسمى عظماً: تالف في ذ [٣]وبالتهيؤات: د ذ؛ والتهيؤات: ق [٤]موضوع يسمى: د ذ ق؛ أي: يسمى موضوعاً [٥]متناه: ذ؛ منتهاه: د؛ متنهاءٍ: ق

105. Swanson, "Qusṭā."

106. Diels, *Doxographi* (Greek)/Daiber, *Aetius Arabus* (Arabic): 305a5/15$_{2}$, 333a21/26$_{12}$, 349a7/33$_{4}$, 275a29/3$_{8}$, 278a3/4$_{4}$; cited by *Glossarium*, Ps-Plut.Placita.3208, 3207, 3208, 3202, 3203.

107. Ibn Sīnā, *Shifāʾ*, Physics 1.2.6, ed. and trans. McGinnis, 1:15. My description of Avicenna's definitions is a close paraphrase of McGinnis's translation.

108. **D** 2–3, **E** [2]–[3], **Q** 4$_{16}$–5$_{1}$. **B** and **D** leave the note anonymous, calling it simply a *ḥāshiya,* while **E** and **Q** call it *ḥāshiya li-Ibn al-Faḍl;* all of them present the text in-line with the main text.

> It should be known that the noun "material" (*hayūlā*) has a range of meanings.[109] In that it is a receptacle[110] of the universe (*al-kull*), it is called matter (*mādda*) and <. . .>[111] element (*ʿunṣur*); by virtue of [its association with] forms (*ṣuwar*) with extension, it is called magnitude; by virtue of [its association with] dispositions (*tahayyuʾāt*),[112] it is called *hayūlā;* and by virtue of receiving forms, it is called an infinite substrate.[113]

The note as it survives appears to have been distorted in the process of copying, but we can still make out its general sense. This discussion of terms for matter, besides underscoring Ibn al-Faḍl's (or at least his later readers') interest in the Arabic terminology of natural philosophy, coincides roughly with Avicenna's discussion in defining *ʿunṣur* as a term for an aspect of matter.

Now we are in a position to return to Ibn al-Faḍl's translation itself and the question posed above: what does he mean by "*ʿunṣurī* starting point"? As we have just seen, Avicenna defines *ʿunṣur* as matter insofar as it is the original component out of which a physical body is composed. Avicenna frames the discussion where that definition appears as articulating what counts as a "starting point" or "principle" (*mabdaʾ* ~ *archē*) of a physical body. There are two main types: matter (*hayūlā*) and form (*ṣūra*). So the terms, including *ʿunṣur,* that each refer to matter with a different valence are really a list of the ways in which matter can be a "starting point" of physical bodies. An "*ʿunṣurī* starting point" would then be one of the simple components (such as the elements fire, water, air, and earth) that serve as the "starting points" or "principles" for physical bodies. A further indication that Ibn al-Faḍl had the elements in mind when he used the term *ʿunṣurī* is that the passage goes on to refer to "the elements" using the Greek loanword *istiqṣāt,* from

109. Literally, "is contrived for/applied to it [i.e., *hayūlā*] according to its [i.e., *hayūlā*'s] gradation in meanings."

110. The word *qābil* is typically used as an adjective to translate δεκτικός, "receptive," but it also appears as a substantive to translate δεξαμενή, "receptacle" or "vessel," in Qusṭā ibn Lūqā's translation of the *Placita philosophorum* (pseudo-Plutarch), ed. Diels, *Doxographi,* 317a4–5; Daiber, *Aetius Arabus,* 20_3.

111. There may be a lacuna here between *wa-* and *ʿunṣur,* since we would expect the definition of *ʿunṣur* to be different from the definition of *mādda.* This lacuna might contain the verb that explains the recurring preposition *bi-* in the following clauses.

112. Cf. Ibn Sīnā, *Shifāʾ*, Physics 1.2.17, ed. and trans. McGinnis, 1:21 (translation modified): when something (e.g., organic matter) undergoes change (e.g., from a non-human to a human), the privation that is in it before the change (e.g., its being non-human) "is not absolute privation, but a privation that has a certain mode of being, for it is privation of a thing along with a predisposition (*tahayyuʾ*) and preparedness in some determinate matter (*mādda muʿayyina*)," i.e., a predisposition to become the thing that it has not yet become.

113. Reading *yusammā mawḍūʿan ghayra mutanāhin* instead of the manuscripts' *mawḍūʿun yusammā ghayra mutanāhin.*

stoicheion (sentence 3).[114] In other words, here in Ibn al-Faḍl's translation, the word *ʿunṣurī* makes perfect sense if we read it in the context of Avicenna's definition: "*ʿunṣurī* starting points" are the primordial elemental components out of which all material bodies are composed. These components are material components. So Basil's expression has been transformed in Ibn al-Faḍl's translation to tie it more closely to what follows. The foolish philosophers, ignorant of God, produced erroneous theories about the cause of the universe because they were wrong about "material starting points," or "elemental starting points"; that is, they believed that the universe originated in some sort of material or elemental cause (e.g., elemental building-blocks colliding and combining to form larger, more complex bodies). This led them to form the sorts of theories that the text—in Basil's original and in both Arabic translations—goes on to relate.

This brings us to how Ibn al-Faḍl translated the end of this passage (sentence 4): "And some imagined and fantasized that the nature of the visible things was composed of bodies without parts, and of plenum and void." The Anonymous Translation translates most of the technical terms in this sentence with Arabic technical terms, and Ibn al-Faḍl consistently adopts those terms (although he changes the word order to accord better with the sense of the Greek than the Anonymous Translation's strict adherence to the Greek word order).

The first physical theory this passage refers to is atomism. Both Arabic translations indicate awareness of the physical theory behind Basil's words. Basil speaks of "bodies uncuttable (*atoma*) and without parts (*amerē*)," and the Anonymous Translation reproduces this aptly and literally as "bodies that are indivisible and without parts" (*ajsām lā tanqasim wa-lā tatajazzaʾ*). Ibn al-Faḍl revises this by removing "indivisible": "bodies (that are) without parts (*ajsām lā tatajazzaʾ*)." After all, the crucial question in atomism had become not whether one could *in practice* continue to divide matter into smaller and smaller subdivisions, but whether at some point one reached entities that did not have parts at all, which both Epicureans and *kalām* atomists claimed.[115] So again here we can detect a small act of interpretation, as Ibn al-Faḍl clearly considered it less important and redundant to call the minimal parts "indivisible." Now, as already mentioned, in *kalām* physics the smallest entities are not *bodies* without parts, but rather "*parts* without parts." Whether because he did not want to stray too far from the original, or because the language of *kalām* atom-

114. In a marginal note discussed in the following chapter (§1, p. 235 and n. 17), Ibn al-Faḍl uses the term *ʿanāṣir* (plural of *ʿunṣur*) to refer to elements (perhaps because he is directly quoting an Arabic translation of Philoponos). But here instead he follows the Anonymous Translation—whose text for this sentence he has reproduced almost verbatim—in translating "elements" by means of the standard loanword from Greek (though he spells it differently). Ibn al-Faḍl uses the Greek loanword for "element" elsewhere in his translation as well, e.g., in his translation of Basil, *Hexaemeron*, 4, at the beginning (**D** 49).

115. For the development of this distinction, see Long and Sedley, *Hellenistic Philosophers*, 1:42–43.

ism was not foremost in his mind, Ibn al-Faḍl did not go so far as to change Basil's "bodies" (*sōmata*) to "parts" (which would have produced the *kalām* formula "parts without parts") but rather kept with the Anonymous Translation's "bodies" (*ajsām*).[116]

Ibn al-Faḍl's omission of "uncuttable" or "indivisible" contrasts with the interest that one Byzantine reader of Basil showed for the equivalent Greek term *atoma*. In the same tenth-century Genoa manuscript of Basil's *Hexaemeron* already mentioned,[117] there is a marginal note in Greek explaining the word *atoma*. As now preserved, the note is missing one or more lines, but the missing portion (italicized within square brackets below) can be reconstructed once we realize that the note is a modified quotation from John of Damascus's *Dialectica*.[118] The note reads:

> "Atom" is said in four [changed to: three] senses. (1) That which cannot be cut or divided is called "atom," such as the point, the present moment, and the unit/monad, which are also called "devoid of quantity." (2) That which is difficult-to-cut is also called "atom," that is, what is difficult to [*cut, such as the diamond and the like. (3) "Atom" is primarily applied to that which can be cut but does not*] preserve its prior species after the cutting. For example Peter can be divided into soul and body. But neither the soul on its own is a complete man or a complete Peter, nor the body. Among philosophers it is this last [sort of atom] that is talked about; it signifies the subsistent entity (*hypostasis*).[119]

The note almost entirely follows the short recension of John of Damascus's *Dialectica;* the main difference is that it speaks of only three meanings of the word "atom," whereas John of Damascus speaks of four. (Even this difference may be illusory, depending on how we reconstruct the note.) These definitions are entirely within the Aristotelian framework—naturally, given that John of Damascus was largely an Aristotelian. None of the definitions addresses the atomist position directly. The closest is the first definition: conceptually indivisible like a geometric point. If we interpret Basil's use of the word *atoma* according to this first definition, it refers, as Basil surely intended, to the claim that physical bodies are *composed* of such conceptually indivisible things. Still, the overall effect of the note is to shift away from discussing the atomism that Basil has brought up. Thus the Byzantine reader who wrote this note, though attentive to the word *atoma* (which Ibn al-Faḍl, by contrast, omitted in his translation), ended up rather further from atomism—the physical thesis that all macroscopic bodies are composed of indivisible, microscopic bodies—by emphasizing (following John of Damascus) the final definition, which refers to a

116. I am grateful to Asad Ahmed for pointing out this discrepancy.

117. See p. 209 and n. 41 above.

118. John of Damascus, *Dialectica*, §3 (short recension) = §11 (long recension), ed. Kotter, 81.

119. G2 = Genoa, Franzoniana, gr. 17, fol. 3^{v}–4^{r}, apparatus to Basil, *Hexaemeron*, 1.2 οἱ δὲ ἄτομα, ed. Amand de Mendieta and Rudberg, 4_{7}; Cataldi Palau, "Complemento," 349 (scholion E). I intend to publish a re-edition of this note.

standard Aristotelian way to conceptualize an individual. Ibn al-Faḍl's translation, on the other hand, preserves Basil's clear and deliberate reference to atomism.

So far, Ibn al-Faḍl's translation and the Anonymous Translation have been quite similar in substance, with only subtle differences. But when it comes to describing "molecules and pores," the translations are quite different. The Anonymous Translator does not attempt to explain these "pores" or "passageways," simply rendering the phrase literally as *ajrām wa-masālik,* "masses and paths."[120] This translation is similar but not identical to the way Ḥunayn ibn Isḥāq rendered the phrase "molecules and pores" in his translation of Galen's treatise *On the Elements.* In the passage cited earlier in which Galen derides Asklepiades for "his miraculous molecules and pores," Ḥunayn wrote "masses" (*ajrām*) for "molecules" (but "gaps," *furaj,* for "pores").[121]

By contrast, Ibn al-Faḍl translates the same phrase as *al-malāʾ wa-l-khalāʾ*, "plenum and void." This rhyming phrase is a standard pairing in Arabic Aristotelianism, referring to space respectively full and devoid of matter. For example, Avicenna, in the logic portion of his *Deliverance* (*Najāt*), uses the phrase *al-malāʾ wa-l-khalāʾ* in an example of the contradiction between rational thought and imagination: even though rationally we (as good Aristotelians who deny the possibility of actual infinity) know that the universe is finite, we cannot help but imagine either an infinite plenum (*malāʾ*) or infinite void (*khalāʾ*) beyond the outermost edge of a finite universe.[122] Al-Ghazālī's famous attempt to refute the "philosophers" (completed in 1095 CE) uses the phrase *al-malāʾ wa-l-khalāʾ* for a similar purpose.[123]

Ibn al-Faḍl's translation thus implies his own interpretation, which eliminates the notion of discrete molecules and reads the "pores" as referring to the concept of empty space, or "void"—something that Aristotelians held to be as impossible as atoms. Ibn al-Faḍl's Arabic still fits Basil's general rhetorical purpose here, to ridicule (non-Aristotelian) ancient physical doctrines, but the meaning is quite different. No longer is there a reference to the array of physical theorists, from Straton of Lampsakos to Epicurus to Asklepiades of Bithynia and perhaps Herakleides of Pontus, who wielded the terms "molecules" and "pores." In its place is plenum and void, expressed in a rhyming phrase familiar from contemporary Arabic Aristotelianism.

120. *jirm* is a technical term of philosophy as well; e.g., Ibn Sīnā, *Ishārāt,* Physics 2.1.13, ed. Dunyā, 2:197 (*jirmīya*).

121. Galen, *K. Jālīnūs fī l-istiqṣāt,* ed. Sālim, 125.

122. Ibn Sīnā, *Najāt,* Logic 94.3, 107.1, ed. Dānešpažūh, $106_{6\text{–}10}$, 116_{3}; trans. Ahmed, 83, 89. Already al-Kindī used these terms together (glossing them as *jism* and *farāgh,* respectively); *First Philosophy, fann* 2, ed. Abū Rīda, 1:109, ¶1. By contrast, al-Fārābī, making a point about our misleading intuition similar to Avicenna's, pairs void (*khalāʾ*) and body (*jism*): *al-Amkina al-mughliṭa,* ed. al-ʿAjam, in Fārābī, *Manṭiq,* 2:161; cited by Rashed, "Lost Treatise," 34.

123. *Tahāfut al-falāsifa,* ed. Dunyā, 111–12. Likewise al-Kindī, *On First Philosophy,* 4.8, trans. Kindī, *Philosophical Works,* 16.

Was this an error on Ibn al-Faḍl's part? Unlikely. If he had wanted a literal translation for Basil's phrase, he had a perfectly acceptable one right in the Anonymous Translator's "masses and paths" (*ajrām wa-masālik*). It would have been hard to replace these two plural words with words in the singular by accident.

I would argue on the contrary that Ibn al-Faḍl knew exactly what he was doing. He was replacing a reference to physical theories that had become obscure with something of much more contemporary relevance. To do so, he was not doing great violence to the text but was only reading it through the lens of someone trained in the tradition of Aristotle and Galen. Galen himself equated Asklepiades' "molecules and pores" with Epicurean atoms and void, as mentioned earlier. Even if this characterization did not do justice to Asklepiades, it might have seemed plausible in the eleventh century to read Basil this way: the erroneous philosophers believed in atoms, on the one hand, and both plenum and void, on the other. In any case, Ibn al-Faḍl's reading is much more conservative than that of his contemporary, the Byzantine philosopher and rhetor Psellos. In his Greek commentary on this very same passage of Basil's *Hexaemeron,* Psellos seems to have reinterpreted the phrase entirely by reading the word "pore" (*poros*) as the homophonous Greek word for "stone" (*pōros*).[124]

As for the existence of void, this question was still very much alive. Aristotelian commentators like Simplikios and Philoponos discussed it at length. Avicenna devoted considerable attention to refuting the existence of void (in any meaningful sense).[125] Practitioners of *kalām* debated whether void existed between atoms.[126]

So by translating Basil's "molecules and pores" as "plenum and void," Ibn al-Faḍl updated the text for a contemporary audience without changing the sense too drastically from the perspective of the tradition in which he was working. We could almost see it as an *explanatory* translation, a paraphrase (the latter being a standard way to explicate a philosophical text in Greek).[127] It certainly indicates that Ibn al-Faḍl felt confident enough in his philosophical training to interpret a Byzantine ecclesiastical text through the lens of Arabic Aristotelian terminology.

Byzantine engagement with ancient and late antique thought has traditionally been viewed as insular and concerned only with recycling older doctrines. The foregoing analysis of this passage of Ibn al-Faḍl's translation suggests that at least on the periphery, Byzantines brought their familiarity with Arabic authors to bear on their reading of the Greek tradition.

124. I intend to discuss this curious reinterpretation in a future publication.

125. Ibn Sīnā, *Shifā'*, Physics 2.8, ed. and trans. McGinnis, 177–200.

126. Dhanani, *Physical Theory,* 71–89.

127. See, e.g., Themistios's paraphrases of Aristotle (*Commentaria in Aristotelem Graeca* 5.1–5).

5 CONCLUSION

In his preface to pseudo-Kaisarios's *Questions and Answers,* one of the useless questions Ibn al-Faḍl lists concerns "the difference between prime matter (*hayūlā*) and substrate (*mawḍū ʿ*)."[128] But if we are to believe the manuscripts of Ibn al-Faḍl's translation of Basil's *Hexaemeron* that ascribe the note on the meanings of *hayūlā* quoted above to Ibn al-Faḍl,[129] then we are forced to conclude that Ibn al-Faḍl was interested in precisely this question.

Ibn al-Faḍl professed to embrace a Christian paradigm to the exclusion of all other philosophical frameworks (as we saw in chapter 4). Accordingly, his starting point for thinking about the natural world as it arose in his Byzantine Christian translation program was the church fathers. This is not to say that he was narrowly dogmatic or restricted himself to what the Bible or other textual authorities said about physics. The Cappadocian Fathers themselves had received a Greek philosophical education, including ancient physics; this is what allowed them to adapt and refute ancient theories for their own purposes. The evidence in this chapter shows that Ibn al-Faḍl continued this tradition, showing a marked interest in ancient philosophers, whose doctrines contemporary Byzantine scholars continued to study. At the same time, Ibn al-Faḍl's translation choices show the influence of Arabic Peripatetics like Avicenna on his conceptual vocabulary, in physics just as in logic. In short, Ibn al-Faḍl's Christian paradigm for thinking about nature was not as independent of the outside world and the questions it generated as he presented it.

128. Question no. 4. See ch. 4, §6, p. 146.

129. See n. 108 above.

8

COSMOLOGY

What lies beyond the earth, in the sky above our heads? How does the world of human experience relate to the rest of the world that exists? What are stars? How far away are they? How long has the universe existed? How did it come into being? Or if it has always existed, how can that be? And what is it all made of? Is it all one big material continuum? Can there be space without matter? Is the universe infinitely large, or limited in its extent? How large is it? How is it all arranged?

These are the sorts of questions posed by modern cosmologists.[1] They have probably been discussed in some form within every human culture ever to exist. In the ancient Greek tradition, Aristotle was only one in a long line of authors who sought to answer these questions in a rigorous way, but for medieval cosmology he was the most important. For the first millennium and a half of the Common Era, Aristotle's cosmological paradigm was dominant, even as subsequent authors revised and refined it.[2]

Aristotle's universe had no beginning and no end. The earth was at its center, and concentric spheres, each the domain of one of the seven planets (including the sun and moon), surrounded the earth. Below the lowest sphere (belonging to the moon), things changed and decayed and came into being, but the celestial spheres—of the moon and above—were perfectly regular and orderly in their uniform circular motion, always had been, and always would be.[3] Aristotle also thought that the

1. Wright, *Cosmology*, 1–3.
2. Ancient cosmological models: Gregory, "Astronomy."
3. Wright, *Cosmology*, 28.

universe had an "unmoved mover" as its cause.[4] Aristotle's teacher Plato also exerted a strong influence over the late antique and medieval tradition. Platonic cosmology looms large in the hexaemeral literature, from Philo of Alexandria to Basil of Caesarea and beyond.[5] By far most influential in this regard was Plato's *Timaeus;* especially influential concepts included Plato's principle that God is good and his division between the intelligible, changeless, eternal realm and the perceptible realm that was subject to constant generation and decay.[6]

In this chapter we will consider two marginalia by Ibn al-Faḍl addressing two quite different cosmological questions: first, what is the sky made of, and, second, was our world created in time or has it always existed?

1 THE SKY'S ELEMENTS

What exactly is the sky? What is it made of? This was an old question. In the ancient Greek tradition, it was bound up with the broader question of what fundamental building-blocks were combined to produce the macroscopic bodies detected by ordinary sense-perception. The pre-Socratic philosopher Empedocles (ca. 495–435 BCE) was known for his belief that natural bodies were constituted from four elements. Aristotle considers him to be the originator of the four-element theory.[7]

Aristotle himself accepted that terrestrial bodies were made of the four elements fire, air, water, and earth. His physics, however, led him to conclude that celestial bodies had to be made of a fifth element. For Aristotle, the tendency of heavy bodies to fall and lighter ones to rise could be explained by a natural upward or downward tendency of each of the four elements. Since heavenly bodies appeared to move in a circle around the earth, he reasoned, they could not be made of elements with a natural upward or downward motion. Instead, they were made of a fifth element that naturally moved in uniform circular motion around the earth. Positing a fifth element also allowed Aristotle to explain why the celestial bodies were not subject to change and decay like terrestrial bodies: the fifth element was something more stable, "more divine."[8]

Aristotle's theory of a fifth element was not universally accepted. The Stoics subscribed to the four-element theory.[9] Aristotelian commentators took

4. Aristotle, *Metaphysics* Λ, 1072a25: ὃ οὐ κινούμενον κινεῖ, which causes circular motion and is God (1072b30).

5. Robbins, *Hexaemeral Literature,* ch. 1.

6. Robbins, 3–5. See also Zeyl and Sattler, "Plato's *Timaeus.*"

7. Aristotle, *Metaphysics* A.4, 985a31–33; trans. KRS², 286; cited by Parry, "Empedocles," §1.

8. Aristotle, *On the Heavens,* 1.2, 269a32.

9. Long, *Hellenistic Philosophy,* 156. See also Long and Sedley, *Hellenistic Philosophers,* 1:280 = fragments 47A (Stobaeus on Chrysippus) and 47B (from Diogenes Laertius), as well as the rest of §47.

various positions on the fifth element, some critiquing Aristotle's theory, others defending it.[10]

This centuries-long conversation about elements is part of the background of Basil's discussion of the natural world in his *Hexaemeron.* Indeed, Basil ridicules precisely this conversation as empty speculation. In his first homily, Basil enumerates various answers to the question of what the sky is made of. Four elements? A fifth and otherwise unknown element?[11] Without mentioning Aristotle, his school, or any of his followers by name, Basil goes on to summarize Aristotle's reasoning in favor of his theory of a fifth element:

> [The four elements] have their own natural motion in a straight line, light bodies upwards and heavy bodies downwards. Now this motion upwards and downwards is not the same as circular motion; there is the greatest possible difference between straight and circular motion. Since their motion is so various, say [those who believe in a fifth element], so too must their essences vary.

This roughly summarizes Aristotle's argument in *On the Heavens* 1.2. Basil continues to paraphrase Aristotle: it is hard to imagine how a composite of elements straining against each other, each tending to move in a straight line, would "produce an even and spontaneous motion." (This parallels Aristotle's thinking in *On the Heavens* 1.2, 268b30–269a3 and 269a24–31.) Such reasoning, continues Basil, led "the inventors of the fifth nature of body" to "reject the ideas of their predecessors," and so "they needed their own hypothesis." But, he concludes, there will always be someone else who comes later to reject this theory in favor of his own.[12]

Despite the attention he lavishes on spelling out the reasoning behind this last theory, Basil's ultimate purpose is to ridicule all these positions as entirely speculative, taking no stand of his own on the issue.[13] He concludes that we should "leave them to be refuted by each other" and be content with what Moses said: "God made the sky and the earth."[14] No wonder, then, that Basil mocks the originators of doctrines on the elemental makeup of the sky as "the sages of this world"[15] and leaves them nameless, for why bother name the authors of so much nonsense, who are, as Basil says, fit only to refute each other?

10. Sorabji, *Philosophy of the Commentators,* 2:357–74.

11. Callahan, "Greek Philosophy," 41.

12. Basil, *Hexaemeron,* 1.11, ed. Amand de Mendieta and Rudberg, 18_{12}–19_{24}; trans. (modified) Basil-NPNF, 57–58.

13. On his refusal to commit to a theory about the sky's material composition, see Callahan, "Greek Philosophy," 44.

14. Basil, *Hexaemeron,* 1.11, ed. Amand de Mendieta and Rudberg, 20_{1-3}; trans. based on Basil-NPNF, 58.

15. σοφοῖς τοῦ κόσμου ~ *ḥukamāʾ al-ʿālam: Hexaemeron,* 1.11, ed. Amand de Mendieta and Rudberg, 18_{13}; **B** 21_{6}. Ibn al-Faḍl's use of *al-ʿālam* (not *al-dunyā*) is typical. Cf. the beginning of one of his marginalia on Basil's *Hexaemeron,* **B** 21_{24}: "those of the world claim . . ." (*ahl al-ʿālam yazʿamūn*).

But Ibn al-Faḍl was not willing to leave them unnamed. In his retranslation of Basil's *Hexaemeron*, he wrote this note:[16]

(١) الذين قالوا إن السماء من < بعض؟> العناصر الأربعة أصحاب الرّواق وابتدقليس[1]. (٢) وحكى يحيى النحوي أنّ افلاطن[2] وثامسطيوس[3] كانا يزعمان أنّها من العناصر الأربعة، إلا أن[4] <الطبيعة؟> النارية هي الغالبة[5] عليها، وليست نارية محرقة[6]، لكنها بمنزلة النار[7] الغريزية[8] التي في الأبدان. (٣) وأمّا مَن قال إنّها طبيعة[9] خامسة، فهم أرسطاطاليس[10] ومن تابعه[11]. (٤) وقد قال[12] آخرون إنّ الفلك من النار والهواء والماء دون الأرض، (٥) ولم يزل الخلف بينهم.

[1]وابتدقليس: ب د ق؛ وابندقليس: ذ؛ والمقصود: انبدقليس، أي امبدقليس [2]افلاطن: ب د ق؛ افلاطون: ذ، ومن المحتمل أن هذا من تصحيح «ذ» [3]وثامسطيوس: ب د ق؛ وثامسطوس: ذ [4]أن: ب د ق؛ —ذ [5]الغالبة: ذ ق؛ الغاية: د؛ وفي ب، أقرأ إمّا «الغاية» وإمّا «الغايرة» [6]محرقة: د ذ ق؛ تحرقه: ب؛ وقد يبدو أنّ في د «تحرقه» أيضاً [7]النار: د ذ ق؛ النا: ب [8]الغريزية: د ذ ق؛ العزيزية: ب [9]طبيعة: د ذ ق؛ طبيعية: ب [10]أرسطاطاليس: ب د ق؛ ارسطوطاليس: ذ، وكأن هذا من تصحيح «ذ» أيضا [11]تابعه: ب د ق؛ تبعه: ذ [12]وقد قال: ب د ق؛ وقال: ذ

(1) Those who said that the sky is made up of <one of?> the four elements are the Stoics and Empedocles. (2) John the Grammarian [i.e., Philoponos, d. ca. 570] narrates that Plato and Themistios claimed that it is [made] of the four elements (*ʿanāṣir*),[17] except that the fiery <nature?>[18] predominates[19] and is not fiery [in the sense of] burning, but is of the same degree as (*bi-manzilat*) the innate fire (*al-nār al-gharīzīya*) that is in bodies. (3) As for those who said that it is a fifth nature, they are Aristotle and his followers. (4) Others have said that the heavenly sphere is [made] of fire, air, and water, without earth. (5) And the variance[20] among them still continues.

Ostensibly, Ibn al-Faḍl is simply elaborating on Basil's point. Basil says the (unnamed) philosophers are only fit to refute each other, and Ibn al-Faḍl has enumerated various mutually contradicting doctrines of the philosophers. But this very enumeration underscores his interest in those doctrines and those philosophers. While Basil's text has the effect of contrasting the vain complexity of philosophical speculation with the simplicity of scriptural truth, Ibn al-Faḍl's marginal note emphasizes the natural philosophical discussion for which the scriptural passages—and Basil's homily—provide an opportunity. The discussion that Basil had declared dead in the fourth century was, as Ibn al-Faḍl casually remarks, still alive in the eleventh.

16. **B** 21_{11-18}, **D** 16_{5-11}, **E** 14_{10-16}, **Q** 26_{6-13}; begins at Basil, *Hexaemeron*, 1.11, ed. Amand de Mendieta and Rudberg, 18_{19} ἐπεισήγαγον.

17. While just a few lines above, in the translation of Basil's text, the word for "elements" is *istiqṣāt*, from Greek *stoicheion*, the word used here in the comment is *ʿanāṣir*. Cf. Basil, *Hexaemeron*, 1.2, discussed in ch. 7, §4, pp. 226–27 and n. 114, where he also uses *istiqṣāt* to translate Basil's "elements."

18. Neither *ʿunṣur* nor *isṭaqis* is feminine. Supplying *ṭabīʿa*, which is feminine, is recommended by the subsequent reference to *ṭabīʿa khāmisa*.

19. Following **EQ**'s *al-ghāliba ʿalayhā* instead of **D**'s *al-ghāya ʿalayhā*. **E** tends to make corrections, but **Q**'s agreement suggests this was not the case here.

20. By comparison to the nearly identical phrase in another note by Ibn al-Faḍl on Basil's *Hexaemeron* (on the stars, part D.ix; see ch. 9, §2, pp. 277–78 and n. 146), perhaps this word (*khulf*) should be emended to *khilāf*, "dispute."

A closer look at this brief marginal note sheds light on Ibn al-Faḍl's relation to the Greek and Arabic philosophical tradition. Ibn al-Faḍl's note, without emendation, says that Empedocles believed the sky was made of the four elements. It would be reasonable to associate Empedocles with a four-element theory of matter; this was the Aristotelian tradition's view of Empedocles, probably reflecting Empedocles's own doctrines. But the specific claim that Empedocles believed that the *sky* was made of the four elements does not appear to be substantiated by the tradition. As Peter Kingsley has argued, Empedocles believed that there were four elements—earth, water, fire, and air, the last of which, using the Greek of his day, he called *aithēr* (as opposed to *aēr,* which meant "mist" at the time)—but that the sky is made out of air (*aithēr*).[21] Furthermore, two reports specifically about what Empedocles thought the sky was made of appear to be quite at odds with Ibn al-Faḍl's note. Achilles Tatius (third century CE?), in the introduction to his commentary on the cosmological poem *Phenomena* by Aratus (fl. third century BCE), reports that Empedocles thought the sky was a "clear" or "icy" (κρυσταλλώδη) aggregate of something "ice-cold" or "frosty" (παγετώδους).[22] This could have been read to imply that the sky is made of frozen *water* in Empedocles's view. A different report, from pseudo-Plutarch, suggests instead that Empedocles thought of the sky as air or mist crystallized by fire.[23] Neither report justifies the claim that Empedocles's sky was made of four elements. Yet another report, again from pseudo-Plutarch, describes Empedocles's cosmogony as a series of elements being separated off from a primordial mix: *aithēr,* fire, earth, and water. But even this report clearly states that the sky was formed from *aithēr,* not all four elements.[24] Finally, a sky made of four elements seems to have little to do with the doctrines ascribed to Empedocles in the Arabic tradition.[25]

I therefore propose emending Ibn al-Faḍl's note. As transmitted in the manuscripts I have consulted, the note ascribes to the Stoics and Empedocles the doctrine that the sky is made of "the four elements" (*al-ʿanāṣir al-arbaʿa*), but the addition of a single word, which could have been dropped by a scribal error, would make Ibn al-Faḍl's note say "*one of* (*baʿḍ*) the four elements." With this emenda-

21. Kingsley, *Ancient Philosophy,* chs. 2–3. See also Burnet, *Early Greek Philosophy,* 228–29.

22. Maass, *Commentariorum in Aratum reliquae,* 34_{25}–35_{2}; cited by Diels-Kranz, 1:293 (Empedocles no. 51).

23. Ps.-Plutarch (see *OCD*^{3}, s.v. "Aëtius [1]"), 2.2.2, in Ritter and Preller, *Historia,* 138 = no. 170c; cited by Burnet, *Early Greek Philosophy,* 237. The later tradition tended to replace Empedoclean *aithēr* with *aēr:* Kingsley, *Ancient Philosophy,* 19–20.

24. Fragment 365 = ps.-Plutarch, 2.6.3; trans. Kingsley, "Notes on Air," 28; cf. KRS^2, 299. See Kingsley, *Ancient Philosophy,* 29–31.

25. De Smet, *Empedocles Arabus,* 107, 151: *ʿunṣur* in the Arabic Empedocles means something like Plotinian "noetic matter" (*Enneads* 2.4).

tion, Ibn al-Faḍl's note would become consistent with Empedocles's attested doctrine that the sky is made of a single element.

Ascribing the belief that the sky is made of all four elements to the Stoics also appears to be only loosely related to the doxographical tradition. As far as we know from surviving fragments of Stoic works, the Stoics held that the stars, or the celestial sphere containing the stars, were made of fire.[26] If Ibn al-Faḍl's original text—by the emendation I have tentatively suggested—actually ascribed to the Stoics the belief that the sky is made of *one* of the four elements, then his statement would be perfectly consistent with a Stoic doctrine that the sky is made of fire. On the other hand, leaving the text unchanged, we may again conclude that Ibn al-Faḍl, or his source, is simply inferring, from the general Stoic belief in the four elements as the fundamental building-blocks of the material world, that the Stoics also believed that the sky in particular was made of four elements.

Ibn al-Faḍl's note turns next to a doctrine of Plato and Themistios, that the sky is made of earth, water, air, and a special kind of fire. For this report about Plato and Themistios, he cites his source: John Philoponos, the sixth-century Christian philosopher of Alexandria whom we have already encountered as a commentator on Aristotle (in chapters 6 and 7). Philoponos was a major influence on medieval Arabic philosophers. His now-lost treatise *Against Aristotle on the Eternity of the World* directly and indirectly provided Muslims, Christians, and Jews with sophisticated arguments in support of the proposition, central to monotheisms of the Mediterranean and the Middle East, that the world had a beginning in time.[27] (We will return to this issue in the following section.) Psellos and Symeon Seth were among Ibn al-Faḍl's contemporaries who read (and excerpted) *Against Aristotle.*[28] Ibn al-Faḍl himself excerpted Philoponos in his own works.[29] Ibn al-Faḍl evidently considered the thought of a philosopher like Philoponos inseparable from the task of reading a "religious" text like Basil's homilies.

The passage of Philoponos that Ibn al-Faḍl is citing may not be extant in the original. A related statement about Plato, however, appears in Philoponos's extant

26. They considered this to be a special fire and called it *aithēr,* but they did not consider it to be a fifth element like Aristotle's *aithēr.* See Long and Sedley, *Hellenistic Philosophers,* 1:275, 280, 286–87 = fragments 46D3, 47B2, and commentary on §47.

27. The treatise survives only in fragments, collected in Philoponos, *Against Aristotle,* trans. Wildberg. Philoponos: Wildberg, "John Philoponus." His influence on Islamicate Muslims and Jews: Davidson, "John Philoponus"; *EI*², s.v. "Yaḥyā al-Naḥwī"; D'Ancona, *EI*³, s.v. "Aristotle and Aristotelianism," §1.2. Philoponos in the Byzantine tradition: Tatakis, *La philosophie,* 171 (index under "Philopon"); Podskalsky, *Theologie und Philosophie,* 99–102.

28. Rashed, "Problem of the Composition," 40–41.

29. In his *Book of Benefit,* a passage from Philoponos, *Against Aristotle:* Rashed, "Problem of the Composition," 37–38. In his *Joy of the Believer,* from Philoponos, *Against Proklos:* Wakelnig, "Al-Anṭākī's Use." See also Treiger, "ʿAbdallāh."

Exegetical Discourses on the Cosmogony of Moses, conventionally known to modern scholars as *On the Creation of the World* (*De opificio mundi*).[30] In that treatise, Philoponos compares what Plato, Aristotle, and Moses (Genesis) have to say about the substance of the sky: Plato, he reports, believed that "the firmament" is made up of the four elements but that the heavenly bodies are mostly made of fire.[31]

Philoponos, and through him Ibn al-Faḍl himself, was drawing on and participating in the Greek doxographical tradition. The qualified four-element theory of the sky ascribed by Philoponos to Plato and Themistios is consistent with the theory Plato lays out in the *Timaeus* in which earth, fire, water, and air are the basic building-blocks of the visible world; as John Callahan points out, Plato's reasoning there is similar to what Basil says is the justification of people who hold this theory.[32] The qualified version—that the fourth element, fire, is a special kind of fire—is quite similar to what Simplikios, wishing to harmonize Aristotle with Plato, says *Aristotle* believed.[33]

The notion of an elemental fire, to be distinguished from fire that burns, and its association with the heat generated by living beings, had a long history. Plato says that the fire that does not burn but rather emits "a gentle light" is similar to "the pure fire within us" (he says this as part of describing his theory of vision).[34] Similarly, Aristotle equates the heat (*thermon*) of living bodies with breath or spirit (*pneuma*) and says that it is "analogous to the element of the stars," that is, *aithēr*, Aristotle's fifth element.[35] For Aristotle, starting from the observation of this difference between burning heat and vital heat, it was an advantage of his fifth-element theory that it could explain the difference.[36] In the Hellenistic period it was standard in medicine to refer to "innate heat" as a source of and impetus to life in organisms. Cleanthes (304–233 BCE), Zeno's successor as head of the Stoic philosophical school in Athens, extrapolated from this notion that the whole universe was sustained by a sort of "vital heat," starting a debate among Stoic thinkers about the nature of this "vital heat," identified with a type of fire—namely, "designing fire" (*technikon pyr*)," a generative sort of fire as opposed to the ordinary, destructive "undesigning" (*atechnon*) sort of fire. The special "designing" quality of the first was, according to Stoicism's

30. *CPG* 7265; ed. Reichardt. The text survives in a single eleventh-century manuscript, Vienna, ÖNB, theol. gr. 29 (fols. 61^{v}–141^{v}), which also contains, inter alia, Philo's *De opificio mundi*.

31. Philoponos, *De opificio mundi* 3.5, ed. Reichardt, 117–18.

32. Plato, *Timaeus* 31b–32c; Callahan, "Greek Philosophy," 41.

33. Simplikios, *In Aristotelis De caelo Commentaria*, on 270a3, ed. Heiberg, 85_{31}–86_{7}; trans. Sorabji, *Philosophy of the Commentators*, 2:365–66. Harmonizing: Sorabji, 2:17–18.

34. Plato, *Timaeus* 45B; trans. Cornford, *Plato's Cosmology*, 152.

35. Aristotle, *On the Generation of Animals* 2.3, 736b30–737a1; Solmsen, "Vital Heat." See also Bos, "Pneuma."

36. Longrigg, "Elementary Physics," 213 and n. 8.

founder Zeno (335–262 BCE), a trait shared by the stars.[37] Philoponos himself distinguishes between "elemental fire," which is life-giving warmth, and "flame" (an excessive concentration of elemental fire).[38]

The language Ibn al-Faḍl uses to communicate this aspect of Philoponos's report has close affinities to the contemporary Arabic philosophical tradition, in particular the phrase "the innate fire that is in bodies" (*al-nār al-gharīzīya allatī fī l-abdān*). It appears almost verbatim in Avicenna's treatment of logic in his *Deliverance,* where he incidentally uses an example concerning "the innate/vital warmth that is in bodies."[39] Avicenna also wrote a medical treatise *On the Difference between Vital and External Heat.*[40]

This is clearly the notion to which Ibn al-Faḍl's note (quoting Philoponos) is referring (though it is ascribed to Plato and Themistios). What is striking is the close verbal similarity of Ibn al-Faḍl's phrase to Avicenna's in referring to the physiological concept of a human body's innate warmth (a familiar concept in Galenic medicine and encountered in Avicenna's medical works as well). This similarity may derive directly from an Arabic translation of Philoponos from which Ibn al-Faḍl is quoting, or it may be Ibn al-Faḍl's own choice of language. Either way, it shows his inclination to bring terms and concepts known to him from reading Arabic philosophy, and in this case perhaps medicine, to a discussion of this Byzantine church father's text. Yet again, Arabic philosophical terminology was part of how he thought about and taught a Byzantine ecclesiastical classic.

On the other hand, Ibn al-Faḍl's approach to Basil's discussion of philosophers' views on the sky's substance is not far from the contemporary Byzantine tradition. In the same tenth-century Greek manuscript of Basil's *Hexaemeron* in Genoa already mentioned in the previous chapter, there is a Greek marginal note related to this part of Ibn al-Faḍl's note. It appears beside an earlier passage in Basil's *Hexaemeron* and likewise lists theories about the material makeup of the sky (numbered to illustrate the parallels with Ibn al-Faḍl's note): (1) one element, either (a) fire or (b) water in an "icy vault" (attributed to Empedocles), (2) four elements, (3) a fifth element. The note then concludes that squabbling over such matters is pointless (corresponding to part 5 of Ibn al-Faḍl's note). Nothing in the note corresponds to part 4 of Ibn al-Faḍl's note, and Ibn al-Faḍl's note contains more

37. Cleanthes and medicine: Long and Sedley, *Hellenistic Philosophers,* 1:287, focusing on fragment 47C. Zeno: fragment 46D, trans. Long and Sedley, 1:275. The translations of these Stoic terms are theirs. See also Long, *Hellenistic Philosophy,* 155.

38. Philoponos, *De opificio mundi* 1.6, ed. Reichardt, 13–15.

39. Ibn Sīnā, *Najāt,* Logic 145.4, ed. Dānešpažūh, 161_{12}–162_{1}; trans. (modified) Ahmed, 128.

40. Gutas, *Avicenna,* 538 (text GMed 18), whose translation of the title I follow. Manuscripts: ibid., 519. This text was brought to my attention by a lecture on Avicenna's works that Dimitri Gutas delivered at the University of California, Berkeley, 18 September 2014.

attributions of the theories. Otherwise they are quite similar.[41] The similarity is due in part to Basil, who mentions both the four-element and the fifth-element theory of the sky,[42] but perhaps also to their participation in a shared doxographical tradition. It is possible that Ibn al-Faḍl read some version of this Greek note in the Greek manuscript he had before him.

The Greek scholiast and Ibn al-Faḍl both felt the need to elaborate on a debate that Basil claimed was pointless. This is partly because Basil's dismissal is a bit disingenuous, for he too has a position: he holds that the sky is composed of four elements.[43] This implies a position on the more general question that the debate about the sky represents—namely, whether the celestial is like or unlike the terrestrial. Basil implies that one material world encompasses the celestial and terrestrial; the sky is made of the same ordinary matter as the sublunar world. Philoponos, in a passage that we know Ibn al-Faḍl read because he quotes it elsewhere, adhered to this same physical theory.[44] Thus Basil, like Philoponos after him, rejects Aristotle's doctrine that the heavens are entirely unlike earthly things, not made of the four ordinary elements of which earthly things are made, but of a fifth element.

This view is consistent with their position that the world is not eternal, since Aristotle explicitly linked his theory of a fifth element with the world's eternality in *On the Heavens* 1.3 by arguing that "the body that moves in a circle" (i.e., the fifth element) is not only weightless (269b30–31) but also "unoriginated and incorruptible" (270a14), meaning it has no beginning or end and so is "eternal" (ἀΐδιον, 270b1–5).[45] A created world was not necessarily incompatible with a fifth element, though; al-Kindī, for one, accepted Aristotle's fifth element but argued against the eternity of the world.[46]

From reading Philoponos, Ibn al-Faḍl would have known that this debate was alive in Philoponos's time. But medieval philosophers, including Avicenna in the tenth century, continued to challenge the Philoponian argument that the celestial is analogous to the terrestrial, and so corruptible and noneternal.[47] In the eleventh century, then, it was important to know the debate, so that one could engage in it oneself.

41. Pasquali, "Doxographica," 200 = no. 22, on Basil, *Hexaemeron*, 1.7, ed. Amand de Mendieta and Rudberg, 14_{10} Ὥστε μὴ ζήτει (or perhaps on a point a few lines below).

42. Basil, *Hexaemeron*, 1.11.

43. Basil, *Hexaemeron*, 1.11. Ed. and trans. Giet, 131 n. 1: this is Plato's position.

44. For Philoponos's position on this, see the fragment discussed by Rashed, "Problem of the Composition"; the fragment is quoted by Ibn al-Faḍl, as Rashed discovered.

45. See Philoponos, *On Aristotle, Physics* 1.4–9, trans. Osborne, 25 n. 18 (introduction); Philoponos, *Against Aristotle*, trans. Wildberg.

46. Catarina Belo, *EI*^{3}, s.v. "Elements."

47. Rashed, "Problem of the Composition," 41–46.

2 INFINITY AND THE ETERNITY OF THE WORLD

This brings us to a hot-button issue of medieval cosmology: Is the world eternal? Has it always existed? Pagan philosophers often answered yes, but to many Jewish, Christian, and Muslim thinkers, this thesis was unacceptable. In the sixth century, Philoponos wrote two treatises detailing proofs that the world could not be eternal, one framed as a refutation of Aristotle (lost except for fragments), and the other as a refutation of the fifth-century philosopher Proklos, *diadochos* of the Athenian Academy.[48] Philoponos's work was to become a key source and inspiration for refutations of the eternity of the world in Arabic and Greek cosmology.[49]

Aristotle had argued that an *actual* infinity was physically impossible but a potential infinity was unproblematic. He also held that an infinity could never be traversed.[50] But at the same time he believed that the world had always existed. The infinity of time that this implied did not bother him because in his view it was not an actual infinity, since only one moment in time exists in actuality; past and future times exist only potentially, not actually.[51]

Philoponos took several approaches to attacking this line of reasoning. He argued that the world's pre-eternity would mean that infinite days had been traversed in order to reach the present, violating Aristotle's doctrine that an infinity cannot be traversed. He also objected that the various planets would each have revolved around the earth (in the Ptolemaic universe) an infinite number of times, but that each planet takes more or less time to complete a single revolution, so that one planet completes x times as many revolutions as another planet in the same space of time, making its total revolutions x times as many—a conclusion that Philoponos considered absurd when applied to infinite quantities. In a similar vein, he argued that the total number of (immortal) souls existing at present would have to be infinite (assuming that human beings had always existed along with the world).[52]

Subsequent arguments for and against the eternity of the world sought to deal with these and other problems with infinity. Maximos the Confessor (sixth–seventh century), drawing on Philoponos, also argued against the eternity of the world.[53] The Muslim philosopher al-Kindī (ninth century) argued that the notion of an infinite body was incoherent, and then concluded that this also meant that

48. *Against Aristotle,* fragments, trans. Wildberg; *De aeternitate mundi contra Proclum,* ed. Rabe.

49. Davidson, "John Philoponus."

50. The following survey of arguments about infinity and the eternity of the world is based on McGinnis, "Avicennan Infinity," 200–211.

51. McGinnis, "Avicennan Infinity," 200–201.

52. McGinnis, 202–3, 206–8; see also Sorabji, "Infinity." Philoponos's other approaches responding to more recent arguments: Golitsis, *Les commentaires,* 124–27.

53. Shchukin, "Matter as a Universal."

time could not be infinite.[54] Al-Fārābī (d. 950) also wrote at least one work on the topic, now lost.[55] On the other hand, the scientist and mathematician Thābit ibn Qurra (d. 901), a Sabian of Ḥarrān active in Baghdad, argued that an actual infinity was, in fact, possible.[56] But most adhered to a version of Aristotle's position that it was impossible.[57] Avicenna took an intermediate position, arguing that an *essentially ordered* infinite set of things all existing at once was impossible, where "essentially ordered" means that the set has an order inherent in its members (such as each inch of length in a long pole). In this view, an infinitely long pole could never exist, but infinitely many souls—which may be lined up in an arbitrary order (e.g., by birthdate) but have no order that is essential to them—could. This modification of Aristotle's position helped Avicenna argue for the eternity of the world.[58] The persistence of this Aristotelian doctrine famously led al-Ghazālī, like Philoponos, to pen his own refutation.[59] This issue was no less a concern in contemporary Constantinople, where the Byzantine philosopher John Italos, formally condemned in the 1070s and '80s for allegedly believing in the eternity of the world (among other things), likewise wrote a refutation of this doctrine emphasizing the world's corruptibility.[60]

Not only a narrow circle of philosophers took an interest in the world's beginning and arguments for its eternity. Ibn al-Faḍl's Syrian contemporary Abū l-ʿAlāʾ al-Maʿarrī (who, as already mentioned, may have been Ibn al-Faḍl's teacher of Arabic philology)[61] attests to the currency of this question in wider elite circles. In his virtuosic poetry collection *Requiring What Is Not Required,* Abū l-ʿAlāʾ includes a number of lines rejecting the eternity of the world, for example:

54. McGinnis, "Avicennan Infinity," 204–6; Shamsi, "Question"; al-Ālūsī, "Dalīl al-Kindī" (cited by al-Ālūsī and al-Hāshim in their edition of al-Ḥillī's *Asrār* [Beirut, 2005], 141 n. 5; I owe this reference to Asad Ahmed). Al-Kindī argued against the eternity of the world in part 2 of his book on metaphysics, *On First Philosophy,* as well as in three shorter works on the subject: ed. Abū Rīda, 1:97–162, 186–92, 194–98, 201–7; trans. Adamson and Pormann, 3–72.

55. *On Beings That Change* (*Fī l-mawjūdāt al-mutaghayyira*). See Rashed, "Al-Farabi's Lost Treatise"; Janos, "Al-Fārābī, Creation ex nihilo."

56. McGinnis, "Avicennan Infinity," 206–8. Sabians: van Bladel, *Arabic Hermes,* ch. 3.

57. For Yaḥyā ibn ʿAdī's more radical rejection of the claim that there are infinite numbers, see McGinnis, "Avicennan Infinity," 209–11.

58. McGinnis, "Avicennan Infinity," 218–19.

59. *Tahāfut al-falāsifa,* §§1–2.

60. John Italos, *Quaestiones quodlibetales* 71 ("On the fact that the world is corruptible and that there will be a resurrection"), ed. Joannou, 120–25; see Kraft and Perczel, "John Italos" (with a new critical edition and translation).

61. See ch. 1, p. 15.

> My belief is not in the eternity of stars,
> nor is my doctrine the pre-eternity of the world.[62]

At the same time, as R. Kevin Lacey observes, he seems to allude to an unorthodox belief in the eternity of the world in several other lines, such as the following:

> Establishing when this sun was born eludes you;
> reason reports that it was before time.[63]

Whatever Abū l-ʿAlāʾ may have believed, the repeated motif suggests he expected it to resonate with his elite literary audience.[64] Another man of letters seeking to impress Abū l-ʿAlāʾ wrote a long letter to the poet in which, at one point, he notes that the notorious atheist Ibn al-Rāwandī wrote various heretical books including one arguing for the eternity of the world.[65]

There is considerable evidence that Ibn al-Faḍl took more than a casual interest in the question of the eternity of the world—a question that he answered with a firm negative. In his *Book of Benefit* (*Kitāb al-manfaʿa*), he quotes or paraphrases an argument of John Philoponos against the eternity of the celestial bodies (also cited by Ibn al-Faḍl's Greek-speaking contemporary Psellos): the celestial bodies are visible, therefore tangible, therefore composite, therefore corruptible, therefore have a beginning in time.[66] Ibn al-Faḍl's *Joy of the Believer* (*Bahjat al-muʾmin*), a collection of 365 questions and answers on philosophical and exegetical issues, gives great prominence to the issue of the world's creation, especially in the first set of 100 questions. This set opens (no. 1) with an argument that the world is created (*mubdaʿ*), and continues with two more questions about the Creator's choice of when to create the world (nos. 2–3). Several more questions deal with the apparent incompatibility between God's impassibility and the transition from the world's nonexistence to existence (nos. 7–9). Two others consider how the material world could have been formed from nothing with no preexisting matter out of which God could form it (nos. 10 and 22). Finally, two other questions (nos. 11 and 16)

62. Maʿarrī, *Luzūmīyāt*, ed. Zand, 2:320, line 13; trans. Lacey, "Syncretistic Perspective," 127: *wa-laysa ʿtiqādī khulūda l-nujūmi * wa-lā madhhabī qidama l-ʿālami.*

63. Maʿarrī, *Luzūmīyāt*, ed. Zand, 2:261, line 5; trans. (modified) Lacey, "Syncretistic Perspective," 128: *wa-mawlidu hādhī l-shamsi aʿyāka ḥadduhu * wa-khabbara lubbun annahu mutaqādimu.*

64. Lacey ("Syncretistic Perspective," 128) views statements favoring eternity as representing his true belief.

65. Ibn al-Qāriḥ, *Epistle* to Abū l-ʿAlāʾ al-Maʿarrī, 3.9, ed. and trans. van Gelder and Schoeler in Maʿarrī, *Epistle of Forgiveness*, 1:24.

66. Rashed, "Problem of the Composition," 38, 58. A sketch of this argument is also known from Simplikios (= Philoponos, *Against Aristotle*, fragment 59, trans. Wildberg, 74–75). Psellos used Philoponos's argument in a short treatise (*Syllogisms on the Soul*) also adduced (and printed in full) by Rashed.

offer demonstrations that the world and the four elements (*arkān*) are created in time (*muḥdath*).[67] Ibn al-Faḍl clearly read widely in the literature on the eternity of the world, a point underscored by Elvira Wakelnig's observation that the quotations ascribed in manuscripts of the text to "Yaḥyā ibn ʿAdī al-Naḥwī" are in fact references to Yaḥyā al-Naḥwī, that is, John Philoponos—in particular, to his *Against Proklos on the Eternity of the World*.[68]

This tradition is part of the context in which Ibn al-Faḍl wrote a marginal note about the eternity of the world beside his Arabic version of Basil's *Hexaemeron*. The basic question of whether the universe has a beginning had also been a central concern for Basil and his exegetical predecessors.[69] Already in his first homily, as he reads the opening line of Genesis—"In the beginning God made the sky and the earth"—it is foremost in his thoughts. This "beginning" is, for Basil, a resounding refutation of any theory asserting that the world is pre-eternal or was formed spontaneously out of elements or dust or other preexisting matter. He dismisses the argument for the world's pre-eternity from the circular motion of the heavenly bodies by pointing out that our inability to discern where a circle began is no proof that it didn't begin somewhere. Ultimately he rests his case on Scripture: for Basil, the opening words of Genesis are unambiguous and irrefutable.[70]

Here Ibn al-Faḍl inscribed in the margin an extended refutation of a purported proof of the eternity of the world that Basil had not even considered. The purported proof is presented as a paraphrase, and its refutation as a direct quotation, but the latter is probably also an abridged adaptation of Ibn al-Faḍl's source, a method that he used in his *Joy of the Believer*.[71] The point that Ibn al-Faḍl makes in his marginal note is the same as Basil's, but by introducing a philosophical argument, he implicitly shifts authority from Scripture to the power of human reason to elucidate this pressing cosmological problem. He begins by introducing the argument for the eternity of the world that is to be refuted:[72]

67. Ibn al-Faḍl, *Joy of the Believer*, Cairo COP Theol. 112, pp. 2–27. The contents of the first set of 100 are summarized (using a different manuscript) by Wakelnig, "Al-Anṭākī's Use," 293. Wakelnig also quotes and discusses several of these arguments against the eternity of the world.

68. In questions 14, 49, 60: Wakelnig, "Al-Anṭākī's Use," 294, 297–310.

69. Philo of Alexandria rejects the world's eternity on the grounds that such a doctrine exalts the creation to the rank of the Creator and denies Providence: *De opificio mundi* 7–11.

70. Basil, *Hexaemeron*, 1.2–3.

71. See Wakelnig's analysis of question 49, in which she shows that Ibn al-Faḍl excerpted from Philoponos's *Against Proklos*, producing a text that is an Arabic version of the original Greek but abridged in such a way that an altogether different point is emphasized: Wakelnig, "Al-Anṭākī's Use," 303–7. See also n. 86 below.

72. The full note is **B** 12_{13}–13_{12}, **D** 5_{3}–6_{5}, **E** $[4]_{⌂5}$–$[5]_{⌂6}$, **Q** 8_{14}–10_{10}; begins at Basil, *Hexaemeron*, 1.3, ed. Amand de Mendieta and Rudberg, 7_{3} φύσει. To facilitate discussion, I divide the text into several parts (A–D). Throughout, I am indebted to Harvey Lederman and Asad Ahmed for a number of suggestions.

إن شيعة الأباطيل والمشغوفين بالأضاليل استدلوا[1] على سرمدية العالم بما تصوروه[2] من تزيد[3] الأعداد والأزمان والحركات والأشخاص، وتنقُّص المقادير والأعظام بالقسمة لا إلى نهاية[4]. وقالوا: ما كانت هذه الأمور بالتي[5] تكون على هذه الصفة، لولا أن العالم سرمدي. ثم يفسّرون ذلك فيقولون: للزمان معنى غير المتناهي في الاتصال، والأعظام والمقادير في القسمة، وللعدد[6] في ذلك.

[1]استدلوا: د ذ ق؛ يستدلوا: ب [2]تصوروه: د ذ ق؛ تصوره: ب [3]تزيد: ب د ق؛ تزايد: ذ [4]لا إلى نهاية: ب ذ ق؛ "لا" إلى نهاية: د؛ وأظن أن المقصود: إلى لا نهاية [5]بالتي د ذ ق؛ التي: ب [6]في القسمة، وللعدد: تالف في «ذ» حتى منتصف كلمة «للعدد»

(A) The partisans of absurdities and those fascinated by errors inferred the pre- and post-eternality (*sarmadīya*) of the world from what they imagine in the way of the (1) increase of numbers,[73] time-intervals, movements, and individuals, and (2) the reduction of measures (*maqādīr*) and magnitudes (*aʿẓām*), by infinite division. They said: "These matters wouldn't be the things which fit this description if the world were not pre- and post-eternal." (3) They then explain, saying: "Time-interval (*zamān*) has the sense of that which is infinite in continuity; and magnitudes and measures [have the sense of that which is infinite] in division; and likewise (?) for number."

The anonymous opponents argue that the world must be eternal because (1) there exist things that increase infinitely, like numbers, and (2) there exist things that divide infinitely, like measures and magnitudes. This is clearly the sketch of a proof, and not a very satisfying one. Ibn al-Faḍl, of course, has no interest in promoting the plausibility of such arguments.

The idea seems to be that if infinite processes like increase and division ad infinitum take place in the world, the world itself must be infinite. In particular, if the universe contains objects of finite magnitude, and objects of finite magnitude are infinitely divisible, then it contains objects that are in a sense "infinite" and so might be said to "contain infinity." But if the universe "contains infinity" then it must be infinite itself. And what else does it mean for the universe to be infinite than for it to exist eternally? This is still not a proof, but it may be the sort of reasoning that motivated the proof to which Ibn al-Faḍl refers.

In reconstructing the argument that Ibn al-Faḍl wishes to refute, it may help to consider al-Kindī's reasoning on the relation between corporeal and temporal infinity. As already mentioned, al-Kindī would have agreed with Ibn al-Faḍl that the world is finite and created in time. In his book *On First Philosophy*, after offering a proof that body cannot be infinite in actuality, nor "any quantity" (*lā . . . shayʾun min al-kammīyāt*), al-Kindī offers the following corollaries. First, he concludes that time, which, like the size of a body, is also a quantity, cannot be infinite. Second, presumably for those who think his earlier proof is only applicable to corporeal, not temporal extension, he says that "things predicated of something finite (*al-ashyāʾ . . . al-maḥmūla fī l-mutanāhī*) are necessarily finite" and concludes that "everything predicated of body, be it quantity, place, motion, or time . . . is also finite. Since body is finite, the world must be finite, and likewise its

73. *aʿdād*, i.e., natural numbers.

every attribute." In short: time is predicated of body, and so the time belonging to the finite body of the whole world must be finite.[74]

It is difficult to make out what exactly Ibn al-Faḍl's opponents were arguing, but it seems to have involved a step that was something like the converse of al-Kindī's argument. Whereas al-Kindī argued that the world's corporeal finitude implied its temporal finitude, the opponents might have argued that the world's corporeal *infinity* (infinite divisibility) implied its temporal infinity (eternity). Although al-Kindī rejected the eternity of the world, his reasoning may have inspired those who defended it to devise a demonstration modeled partly on his.

Whatever the proof was, it clearly assumed (in A.2) that measures and magnitudes are infinitely divisible. This is closely related to the question of whether *bodies* are infinitely divisible. Aristotle holds that physical bodies, like mathematical bodies, are infinitely divisible (*Physics* book 6), though elsewhere he suggests that bodies composed of matter and form cannot be infinitely divided and still maintain their form (book 3).[75]

However we may imagine the relation of the proof Ibn al-Faḍl has in mind to specific aspects of the philosophical tradition, Ibn al-Faḍl's presentation of it is certainly rich in the relevant philosophical terminology (e.g., eternality, time-intervals, infinity, division, continuity, magnitude), as is the rest of his note. One set of terms, *miqdār* (~ μέτρον) and *ʿiẓam* (~ μέγεθος), which I have been translating as "measure" and "magnitude," seems redundant. These two terms are typically used synonymously by Arabic Aristotelians as two different translations for the same Greek word, *megethos*. Isḥāq ibn Ḥunayn (son of the more famous translator Ḥunayn ibn Isḥāq), in his translation of Aristotle's *Physics*, renders *megethos* as *ʿiẓam*, while the Aristotelian commentator Abū ʿAlī Ḥasan ibn al-Samḥ (d. 1021), in his explication of this passage, uses the word *miqdār* to refer to Isḥāq's *ʿiẓam*.[76] In Ibn al-Faḍl's description of a "proof" for the eternity of the world, the synonymity of the two terms *miqdār* and *ʿiẓam* is further suggested by the fact that they occur as a pair. On the other hand, in the refutation of the proof, they are not always paired and may be meant to refer to two slightly different concepts, such as spatial coordinates (measures) versus quantities extended along them (magnitudes).

The rest of Ibn al-Faḍl's note consists of two anonymous quotations from a refutation of the argument in part A, one short (B), the other longer (C–D). He presents the short one as follows:

74. Kindī, *On First Philosophy*, ed. Abū Rīda, 1:116, ¶¶4–6; trans. (modified) Shamsi, "Question," 54–55.

75. Glasner, "Ibn Rushd's Theory," 9–14.

76. E.g., at 187b8 and 187b33, ed. Badawī, *Arisṭūṭālīs: al-Ṭabīʿa*, 1:37–38, 39. Abū ʿAlī's death date: ibid., 1:*taṣdīr* p. 20.

وقد أفسد رأيهم هذا وأبان غباءه[١] بعضُ المتكلمين، بأن[٢] قال إنّ الكمية[٣] المتّصلة ليس يتهيّأ فيها أنْ يكون الشيء الذي[٤] ليس بمتناهٍ[٥] في إحدى جهتيه، غير الشيء الذي ليس بمتناهٍ[٦] في جهتيه جميعاً، وذلك أنّه قد يمكننا[٧] أن نتوهَّم خطّاً[٨]، في إحدى جهتيه ذا[٩] نهاية، وغير متناهٍ[١٠] في الجهة الأخرى، وإن كان ذلك غير طبيعي[١١]. فأمّا في الكمية المنفصلة، فذلك[١٢] غير ممكن أن يُتوهّم توهُّماً فقط، فضلاً عن أن يكون بالحقيقة.

[١]غباءه: صححته؛ عداده: ب د ق؛ اعداده: ذ [٢]بأن: د ذ ق؛ فان: ب [٣]إنّ الكمية: تالفة في ذ [٤]الذي: د ذ ق؛ —ب [٥]بمتناهٍ: ق؛ بمتناهي: ب د ذ؛ وفي «ق» كأن الناسخ أو من بعده محا «هي» وكتب «ه» في مكانه. [٦]بمتناهٍ: ذ ق؛ بمتناهي: ب د؛ في «ق» مُحِيَ «هي» وكُتِبَ «ه». [٧]يمكننا: ب د ذ؛ يمكنّا: ق [٨]خطّاً: ب ذ ق؛ خطٌّ: د [٩]ذا: ب ذ ق؛ ذاء: د [١٠]متناهٍ: ذ؛ متناهي: ب د؛ متناهـ[[ي]]: ق (بالمحو، ومع ذلك أضيف تنوين كسر على غير يد الناسخ). [١١]طبيعي: ذ ق؛ طبيعياً: ب د [١٢]فذلك: د ذ ق؛ فلذلك: ب

(B) One of the *mutakallims* has undermined their opinion and made clear its stupidity[77] by saying: (1) It is not possible in the case of the continuous quantity for the thing which is infinite on one of its two sides to be different from the thing which is infinite on both of its sides. That is, it may be possible for us to imagine a line which is finite on one side but infinite on the other, even if that is unnatural. (2) As for the case of the discrete quantity, it is not possible even to imagine it, to say nothing of its truly being.

The anonymous *mutakallim*—a word, in both Christian and Muslim contexts, for a dialectician, often a theologian—seems to argue that it is not possible for a quantity to be infinite on one side and finite on the other, or perhaps that a quantity infinite on one side and finite on the other is *equivalent* to (commensurate with) one that is infinite on both sides.[78] If the quantity is (1) continuous, it is conceivable for it to be infinite on only one side (for example, we can imagine a ray), but physically impossible. If the quantity is (2) discrete, it is not even conceivable for it to be infinite on one side and finite on the other.

This may be intended to falsify the first premise of the opponents' argument (A.1).[79] Discrete quantity is a genus whose species include numbers, time-intervals, movements (e.g., planetary revolutions), and individuals. The claim that a discrete quantity must be either infinite on both ends or infinite on neither (B.2), then, implies that all these specific discrete quantities (which, as one counts them, all begin with one: one individual, one day, etc.), while they may increase indefinitely, cannot conceivably be actually infinite: one cannot imagine *infinite* people. After all, this would contravene the Aristotelian rule against actual infinities.[80] The first premise (A.1) has thus been falsified. The role of the continuous quantity (B.1) in this argument seems to be rhetorical: it is a familiar case that may seem more difficult to prove than the discrete case (B.2); the latter is thus made to look self-evident.

77. Reading *ghabāʾahu* for *ʿidādahu* ("its like": *Lisān* s.v. *ʿdd*) or *aʿdādahu* ("its numbers").
78. As suggested by Asad Ahmed.
79. I owe this observation to Harvey Lederman.
80. McGinnis, "Avicennan Infinity," 201; Sorabji, "Infinity."

The longer quotation that now follows concentrates on the argument that the infinite divisibility of continuous quantities (like measures and magnitudes) implies the eternity of the world (A.2). The *mutakallim* begins with the case of measures.

وقال أيضاً: ليس كما يقال في المقادير إنّها تنقسم دائماً بغير نهاية، كذلك يقال في الكون، إنّه يكون بغير نهاية. وذلك أنّ المقادير يقال إنّها تنقسم بلا نهاية، ليس بأنّه ممكن أن يحتمل انقسام بالفعل بلا نهاية، ولا بأنّ انقسامها لا يكون لها انقطاع ولا سكون بالفعل، فإن هذا[١] ليس هو لها[٢] بالقوة فضلاً[٣] عن أن يكون لها بالفعل. لكن إن تَوَهَّمَ متوهمٌ أنّها قد انقسمت دائماً، لم[٤] تنتهِ[٥] القسمة إلى نقط الأجزاء التي لا أجزاء لها ولا أبعاد[٦]، لكن يكون كلما[٧] يخرج من القسمة ذا أبعادٍ[٨] لا محالة، فَمِن أجل أنّ لها أبعاداً يقال إنّها يحتمل أنْ تنقسم أيضاً، فتكون منقسمة لا غير منقسمة. فعلى هذه الجهة يقال بالمقادير إنّها منقسمة بلا نهاية، وإنّ قسمتَها لا تقف[٩] بالقول ولا بالتوهم، إذ[١٠] كانت الأجزاء التي تخرج من الأجزاء ذوات أبعاد، ومع هذا فإن التجزئة التي تكون بالفعل قد تقف وتنتهي اضطراراً.

[١]هذا: د ذ ق؛ 'هذا': ب [٢]لها: ب د؛ –ذ ق [٣]فضلاً: ذ؛ فضلٌ: ب د [٤]لم: ب د ق؛ ولم: ذ؛ الاثنان يجوزان نحويّاً، ولكن كلاهما يعطي للجملة معنى خاصّ، وذلك أنّ «ولم» يعني أنّ ما يلي هو من توهُّم المتوهم وجواب الشرط «إن توهم متوهم. . .» يبدأ بالقول «فمن أجل أن»؛ أمّا «لم»، فمعناه أنّ ما يلي إنّما هو جواب الشرط «إن توهم متوهم. . .» [٥]تنتهِ: ذ؛ تنتهي: ب د؛ تنتهـ[ـي]]: ق (بالمحو). [٦]أبعاد: ذ؛ ابعاداً: ب د [٧]كلما: ب د ق؛ كل ما: ذ؛ والمقصود: كلُّ ما [٨]أبعادٍ: ذ ق؛ ابعاداً: ب د [٩]تقف: +لا: ذ ق (وفي «ق» كأنه أضيف بعد نسخ النص على يد الناسخ لأنه فوق طرف حرف فاء كلمة «تقف») [١٠]إذ: د ذ ق؛ اذا: ب

(C) And he also said: (1) Saying that measures (*maqādīr*) are divisible (*tanqasim*) continually ad infinitum is not like saying that the universe (*al-kawn*) exists infinitely. (2) This is because one says that measures are divisible (*tanqasim*) ad infinitum not in the sense that it is possible that they admit of actual division ad infinitum, or that their division actually goes on without interruption or rest. (3) For this cannot even potentially happen to them, to say nothing of happening in actuality. (4) But if one were to imagine that they were perpetually divided, the division wouldn't reach points (*nuqaṭ*) of the parts without parts or dimensions (*abʿād*); but rather everything that emerges from the division necessarily has dimensions. (5) Because [the parts resulting from a division] have dimensions, it is said that they too admit of division, such that they are divisible, not indivisible. (6) It is in this sense that it is said that measures are divisible ad infinitum, and that their division does not stop in speech[81] or imagination, since the parts which emerge from the parts contain dimensions. (7) Nevertheless the partitioning which occurs in actuality may be forced to stop and come to an end.

The *mutakallim* proceeds by arguing that the statements "measures divide infinitely" (= *d*) and "the universe exists infinitely" (= *e*) are not analogous (1) because *d* is only true *conceivably* (4–6), not actually (2) or even potentially (3). (It is assumed that by "*e*" one means "actually *e*.") In other words, even if one concedes that "actually *d*" implies "actually *e*," one may show that "actually *d*" is false (7), and thereby refute the proof (since then "actually *e*" has not been shown), even if "potentially *d*" or "conceivably *d*" is true.

Finally, the *mutakallim* makes a similar argument, also addressing the claim that *d* implies *e* (A.2), though now the text speaks of magnitudes instead of measures:

81. *bi-l-qawl.* Perhaps emend to *bi-l-qūwa,* "in potentiality."

فإن كان[١] انقسام الأعظام دائماً بلا نهاية، إنّما قوامه بالوهم والقوة، على أنّ الأجزاء التي تخرج بالتجزئة ذوات أبعادٍ[٢]، على أنّ تجزئتها بالفعل لا[٣] تقف ولا تنتهي؛ و(إن) كان[٤] كون الأشياء، والأشياء نفسها منقسمة، ليس بأنّها[٥] كائنة بالقوة، والقوة فقط، لكن على[٦] أنّها كائنة بالفعل، فليس تنقسم إذاً الأعظام[٧] بلا نهاية.

[١]كان: ب د ذ؛ —ق [٢]أبعادٍ: ذ ق؛ ابعاداً: ب د [٣]لا: ب د؛ ولا: ذ ق [٤]وإن كان: ذ؛ وكان: ب د ق [٥]بأنّها: ب د؛ لأنّها: ذ؛ انها: ق [٦]على: د ذ ق؛ 'على': ب [٧]تنقسم إذاً الأعظام: ذ؛ إذاً الأعظام تنقسم: ب د ق، إلا أن في «ق» كتبت لفظة «إذاً» فوق سين لفظة «فليس».

(D) (1) If the division of magnitudes is continual without end, then it occurs [only] conceivably and potentially, (2) in that the parts that emerge by partitioning have dimensions, (3) in that their partitioning in actuality does not stop or end. And if[82] (4) the generation of things—the things themselves being divisible—is [meant] not in the sense that [they] are generated potentially and only potentially, but in that they are generated in actuality, then (5) magnitudes do not therefore divide ad infinitum.

Parts of magnitudes also have dimension, suggesting you could go on splitting them forever (2–3), but this infinite division is only *conceivable* and *potential* (1); it can never be realized in actuality. This is because (as Aristotle argued) the magnitude could never be in a state of *actually* having been divided infinitely many times, only of having been divided finitely many times with infinitely many *potential* divisions left to be made. But potential divisions do not actually exist (4), so magnitudes cannot be said to divide infinitely in actuality (5).[83]

The note concludes (D.5): "Magnitudes do not therefore divide ad infinitum." This is only the conclusion of this last portion of the refutation (D). But the implication is that the refutation is complete, for parts C and D each argue that a continuous quantity is not infinitely divisible *in actuality*, referring to the continuous quantities as "measures" and "magnitudes," respectively. Since part B had already taken care of the case of discrete quantities, now both of the opponent's premises (A.1 and A.2) have been falsified, meaning that the purported proof of the eternity of the world collapses.

The particular proof that Ibn al-Faḍl reproduces seems to consider the infinite divisibility of measures and magnitudes to be different from one another: measures are infinitely divisible only conceivably (not actually or potentially), while magnitudes are infinitely divisible conceivably and potentially (but not actually). Why? The answer is not clear to me, but it is worth noting that the proof's statement that measures cannot even potentially divide infinitely (C.2–3) is followed by a line of argument that would seem to suggest that imaginary division reaches a point where the parts that emerge have spatial extent but can no longer be conceivably *divided*, such that the claim that these smallest parts are "divisible" is only true insofar as it means that it has spatial extent (C.4–6).

82. The "if" may be an emendation from **E**, which reads *wa-in kāna*, against **BDQ**'s *wa-kāna*.

83. This is the standard Aristotelian distinction between being able to divide a line indefinitely (at each stage, there are always further divisions to be made) and being able to divide it infinitely (which would result in an actual infinity, something Aristotle wished to avoid). I thank Harvey Lederman for clarifying this point. See Sorabji, "Infinity," 211, 213.

This is reminiscent of the medieval Peripatetic theory of *minima naturalia*. This theory is a bit like Epicurean atomism (in which the world is made up of atoms that are indivisible but nevertheless have internal parts), especially in the claim that even the *mental* division of matter reaches a threshold beyond which it cannot continue.[84] But crucially, the theory rejects the concept of atoms, instead arguing that the world is an Aristotelian continuum, except that there is a minimum scale beyond which no continuous physical body can be divided without perishing.

The theory of *minima naturalia* takes its inspiration from Aristotle's own remarks, but it was only cogently articulated and defended after him. For some time it was thought that this developed version of the theory only appeared in the Latin West during the thirteenth century, but Ruth Glasner showed that already in the twelfth century Averroes (Ibn Rushd) had a developed theory of *minima naturalia*. Jon McGinnis has recently shown that Avicenna, in the tenth century, did too.[85]

Thus we may imagine that Ibn al-Faḍl's source for this refutation of the eternity of the world subscribed to such a theory of *minima naturalia*. Given Ibn al-Faḍl's decision not to name his source, it may well be non-Christian.[86]

But we can put aside the question of Ibn al-Faḍl's source and its ideological commitments. The fact remains that where Basil is content to dismiss the eternality of the world on the grounds that it stands in contradiction to Scripture, Ibn al-Faḍl elected to provide his reader with a proper refutation. His long note engages the threatening argument on its own, rather than scriptural, terms—much like Philoponos.[87] This suggests that unlike Basil, he did not consider the scriptural proof sufficient.[88] Ibn al-Faḍl's choice to sketch a purported proof of the world's eternity and a refutation of it in the margins of Basil's text suggests a concern to confront those who were not content to accept the literal meaning of the Judeo-Christian Scripture. Such an audience of doubters might have been Christians, but they might also have been people for whom the Mosaic books were at best of limited authority, such as Muslims. To this end, Ibn al-Faḍl was willing to draw on a more recent philosopher's work to bolster what should have been an entirely authoritative text, the work of a church father.

84. See ch. 7, p. 215.

85. Glasner, "Ibn Rushd's Theory"; McGinnis, "Small Discovery." I thank Asad Ahmed for referring me to McGinnis's work on the subject.

86. Cf. Ibn al-Faḍl's quotation from Philoponos's *Against Proklos* (cited above, n. 71), where, as Wakelnig has shown, Ibn al-Faḍl is most interested in asserting a point made not by Philoponos but in fact by Proklos: Wakelnig, "Al-Anṭākī's Use," 306–7. Elsewhere in the same book, Ibn al-Faḍl was willing to cite pagan philosophers by name (ibid.), but those cases are all doxographical; when presenting a pagan philosopher's position *as his own*, perhaps he did not wish to advertise it.

87. I owe this observation to Maria Mavroudi.

88. Philo of Alexandria (first century BCE–first century CE) had insisted that "in the beginning" cannot refer to the beginning of time: *De opificio mundi*, §26.

In this way, we see that Ibn al-Faḍl's educational and intellectual program not only stressed the need to focus on valuable, rather than worthless, questions, as Ibn al-Faḍl himself argued in the preface to his translation of pseudo-Kaisarios's *Questions and Answers* (as we saw in chapter 4). He was also prepared to confront pesky philosophical questions, when they arose, in philosophical terms. His marginal note on the eternity of the world, being sketches of arguments rather than formal argumentation, may, for all its Arabic philosophical vocabulary, seem like unsatisfying evidence for engagement with philosophy. But I would argue that these sketches are unmistakable traces of just that. Perhaps they are notes that Ibn al-Faḍl then used as he presented this material in more detail to students; or perhaps they are notes taken down by a student listening to him explain. We may imagine a student asking, after reading Basil's passage, how to respond to the argument that Aristotle's infinite division implies an eternal world, and Ibn al-Faḍl's impatient reply: "Well look, there are plenty of misguided people who will make this argument. But this has already been refuted in the following way . . ."

9

ASTRONOMY

We now move to an illustrious science: astronomy.[1] In late antique and Byzantine education, astronomy had a special place, at least in theory, in the curriculum. This curriculum of higher education began with the trivium—grammar, dialectic (valid argumentation), and rhetoric—and moved on to the quadrivium (ἡ τῆς μαθηματικῆς τετρακτύς): arithmetic, geometry, music, and astronomy.[2] The anonymous textbook *Logic and Quadrivium* of 1007–1008 thus covers logic and these four subjects, ending with astronomy.[3]

In the Hellenic tradition, the discipline of astronomy, concerned with observing, predicting, and explaining the changing positions of heavenly bodies, was closely associated with astrology. The English derivatives of the Greek words *astronomia* and *astrologia* refer to very different disciplines today, but in antiquity and the Middle Ages the disciplinary distinction was much hazier.

A good astrologer was also an astronomer, and an astronomer who wished to put his knowledge to practical use was often an astrologer. Astrology—the correlation of terrestrial conditions and events with celestial configurations—was the most prominent practical application of astronomical observation and theory. If one posited a relationship between the celestial and the terrestrial, then the relationship could be inferred by repeated simultaneous observations; then, by pre-

1. The following rapid survey of Byzantine and Islamic astronomy and astrology is based on Neugebauer, *History;* Tihon, "L'astronomie"; Mavroudi, *Byzantine Book,* 396–400; Magdalino, "Byzantine Reception"; Magdalino and Mavroudi, *Occult Sciences;* Morelon, "General Survey"; Morelon, "Eastern Arabic Astronomy."

2. *ODB,* s.vv. "Curriculum," "Quadrivium."

3. See ch. 6, p. 186, n. 34.

dicting future celestial configurations (a task at which ancient and medieval astronomers excelled), one could predict future terrestrial conditions. The process was very similar to modern weather forecasts: a set of parameters (air pressure, humidity, etc.), presumed relevant, are measured repeatedly and correlated with the parameters one wishes to predict (temperature, precipitation, cloud cover). Weather predictions are often wrong, but they are right or nearly right often enough to be taken seriously.[4]

Thus the influential Hellenistic astronomer Ptolemy, active in Alexandria in the second century CE, was also an astrologer.[5] His *Handy Tables* (Πρόχειροι κανόνες) present values for various parameters useful for calculating planetary positions.[6] This text was very popular in the subsequent tradition, often corrected and adapted.[7] Ptolemy scrutinized such astronomical observations in two complementary ways.

First, in his *Mathematical Treatise* (Σύνταξις μαθηματική), conventionally known as the *Almagest,* Ptolemy laid out his mathematically precise model to account for planetary motions within the framework of Aristotelian physics.[8] In the geocentric Ptolemaic cosmos, celestial bodies were supposed to move in uniform circular motion, as Aristotle had posited.[9] The planets did so, each in their own concentric sphere centered on the earth. But Ptolemy, like his predecessors, needed to explain why the planets (from Greek *planēs,* "wanderer") do not in fact move uniformly from the perspective of an observer on the earth but instead exhibit retrograde motion at regular intervals. Building on his predecessors, Ptolemy devised his famous mathematical model combining epicycles, the deferent, and the equant. This model was excellent at predicting planetary positions but was deeply unsatisfying to later astronomers working within the Ptolemaic paradigm because it seemed to violate the *physical* laws upon which it claimed to be based (in particular the uniform circular motion of celestial bodies).[10] This influential theory would nonetheless serve as the starting point for the further development of astronomical theories for over a thousand years. In another book, the *Planetary Hypotheses* (which survives only partially in Greek but is preserved in Arabic in full),[11] Ptolemy

4. I owe this comparison between ancient astrology and modern meteorology to Maria Mavroudi.

5. Tihon, "L'astronomie," 604–5. For Ptolemy, see now Feke, *Ptolemy's Philosophy.*

6. A critical edition is in progress, with the first pair of volumes published: *Ptolemaiou Procheiroi kanones 1a,* ed. Tihon; *Ptolemaiou Procheiroi kanones 1b,* ed. Mercier.

7. Tihon, "L'astronomie," 605.

8. Ptolemy, *Almagest,* ed. Heiberg; trans. Toomer.

9. See ch. 8, §1, p. 233.

10. Bouché-Leclercq, *L'astrologie,* 111; Saliba, "Arabic versus Greek Astronomy," 329–38.

11. Of the two books of the *Planetary Hypotheses,* only the first part of book 1 survives in Greek: Ptolemy, *Opera astronomica minora,* ed. Heiberg, 69–145. The German translation of the Arabic provided by Heiberg (111–45) includes book 2 but omits the second part of book 1. See Goldstein, "Arabic Version," 3–4; Sezgin, *Geschichte des arabischen Schrifttums* (hereafter *GAS*), 6:94; Morelon, "General Survey," 7.

sought to offer a physical account of the cosmos consistent with the geometrical models of the *Almagest*, arguing, for example, that the planetary spheres are concentric, each packed inside the next.[12]

Second, in his astrological *Tetrabiblos* (a.k.a. *Apotelesmatika*), Ptolemy laid out the terrestrial effects of the sort of celestial motion that his *Handy Tables* helped predict.[13] This science, which he calls "prognostication through astronomy" and we call astrology,[14] required knowledge of the special traits of each planet and zodiacal sign, as well as the effects of whole configurations of multiple planets. As Ptolemy explained, no one doubts that the greatest celestial body, the sun, has a great effect on terrestrial life (seasons, agriculture, and so on), so why shouldn't we imagine that the smaller celestial bodies have a smaller but still noticeable effect on terrestrial life?[15]

Ptolemy's contemporary Vettius Valens, active in Antioch ca. 152–162 CE, produced an influential treatise on astrology, the *Anthologies*, with many specific examples of horoscopes.[16] Ancient Greek horoscopes otherwise survive mainly in papyri.[17]

Still, Graeco-Roman intellectuals were far from unanimously approving of astrology. In his defense of astrology, Ptolemy was responding to a philosophical tradition of critiquing astrology, a tradition that continued after him as well. Philosophers effectively distinguished between "hard" and "soft" astrology, where soft astrology is the doctrine that the planets and stars are merely *signs* indicating possible future events, and hard astrology is the doctrine that they not only serve as signs but also *cause* events.[18] It was this causal claim that raised the most objections. For example, the Neoplatonist philosopher Plotinos (active in Alexandria and Rome, d. 269–270), who rejected hard astrology, was amenable to soft astrology in principle, even if he objected to some of the details of astrology as it was practiced.[19] Plotinos's student Porphyry (d. ca. 305) and later the Neoplatonist philosopher Proklos (d. 485) may even have written commentaries on Ptolemy's *Tetrabiblos*.[20]

The objection that (hard) astrology implies determinism continued to be prominent (along with astrology's association with worship of the planets as gods) in the writings of the late antique Christian authors most influential on the later

12. Ptolemy, *Planetary Hypotheses*, 1.3, summarized by Goldstein, "Arabic Version," 4.

13. Ptolemy, *Tetrabiblos* [= *Apotelesmatika*], ed. Hübner; ed. and trans. Robbins. Both names are attested in the manuscript tradition. Porphyry wrote an Εἰσαγωγὴ εἰς τὴν Ἀποτελεσματικὴν τοῦ Πτολεμαίου. See Hübner, xxxvi–xxxviii.

14. Ptolemy, *Tetrabiblos*, 1.1, line 1, ed. Hübner, 3. See also Robbins, xi.

15. Long, "Astrology," 178–83.

16. Ed. Pingree.

17. Neugebauer and van Hoesen, *Greek Horoscopes;* supplemented by Baccani, *Oroscopi greci*.

18. Here I adopt the terminology of Long, "Astrology," 170 n. 19.

19. Long, "Astrology," esp. 170 n. 19, 174, 178–83, 187.

20. Long, 187.

Byzantine tradition, the Cappadocian Fathers (fourth century) and John Chrysostom (d. 407), and especially Basil's *Hexaemeron,* homily 6.[21] Basil provides a classic refutation of astrology, arguing that it is impracticable, theoretically implausible, and morally unacceptable: (1) it is impossible for astrologers to measure the exact moment of a birth and the exact positions of the planets with the precision that they claim; (2) in any case, it is absurd to posit a causal relationship between things so manifestly unrelated as the positions of heavenly bodies and a newborn's fate; and (3) belief in astrology implies belief in a determinism that sweeps away all moral responsibility.[22]

Nevertheless, throughout late antiquity the Greek astronomical tradition, including astrology, thrived. Around 320 CE, Pappos of Alexandria wrote a commentary on Ptolemy's *Almagest.*[23] Theon of Alexandria (fourth century) wrote commentaries on the *Handy Tables*—an elementary *Small Commentary*[24] and the more advanced *Great Commentary*[25]—and the *Almagest.*[26] His commentary on book 3 of the *Almagest* was edited by his daughter, the philosopher Hypatia, before 415 CE.[27] Further annotations and observations produced in subsequent centuries in and around Alexandria, at least until the sixth century, are also preserved in Byzantine manuscripts.[28] Meanwhile, this same tradition was cultivated in late antique Syria (certainly by the fifth century) by authors, usually Christian, writing in Greek and Syriac, and in Sassanian Mesopotamia and Iran.[29]

In the early seventh century, Stephen of Alexandria, working in Constantinople, wrote a commentary on Ptolemy's *Handy Tables* (if we believe the ascription in some manuscripts) in the tradition of Theon's elementary *Small Commentary,* focusing on how to use the tables, but updated to use tables calculated for Byzantion (Constantinople)—and enhanced with instructions for calculating the date of Easter.[30] This commentary is dated by its astronomical examples to the

21. Riedinger, *Die Heilige Schrift,* 14–15, 39–45, 47–49, 53–57.

22. Basil, *Hexaemeron,* 6.5–7.

23. Ed. Rome, vol. 1; for the date, see p. XIII.

24. Ed. and trans. Tihon.

25. Ed. and trans. Mogenet and Tihon.

26. In Ptolemy and Theon, *Claudii Ptolemaei Magnae constructionis,* ed. Camerarius; books 1–4 in Pappos and Theon, *Commentaires,* ed. Rome, vols. 2–3. Books 3 and 11 are lost except for a fragment of book 3. See Tihon, "L'astronomie," 605 n. 10.

27. Tihon, "L'astronomie," 605–6 and n. 11; Pappos and Theon, *Commentaires,* ed. Rome, 2:317 n. 1; 3:807.

28. Tihon, "L'astronomie," 606 n. 11.

29. Pingree, "Greek Influence," 34–35; cited by Tihon, "L'astronomie," 607 n. 15. For the Syriac, see also Ptolemy, *Ptolemaiou Procheiroi kanones 1b,* ed. Mercier, 186–87. Note in Vat. gr. 190 written ca. 462 in Apameia: Mercier, 189.

30. *Le commentaire aux Tables faciles,* ed. and trans. Lempire; the first volume has been published. Tihon, "L'astronomie," 607–8.

610s, mainly 618–619, but the ascription to Stephen of Alexandria is not consistent in the manuscripts, some of which ascribe it to his contemporary Emperor Heraclius (r. 610–641).[31] This has opened the door to questioning Stephen's authorship of the text.[32] In any case, it was certainly produced in Constantinople at the beginning of the seventh century under the emperor Heraclius.[33] As Paul Magdalino emphasizes, support for astronomy from "the pious emperor Heraclius" should make us reconsider narratives that pit Byzantine piety and emphasis on orthodoxy against cultivation of Hellenic science, especially "occult sciences" like astrology.[34] Magdalino reads the inclusion of Easter calculations along with the tables as a sign that this was astrology-astronomy in the service of Christian orthodoxy.[35]

Because of the state of research into Byzantine astronomy, very little is known about the composition of new Greek astronomical works—in the modern sense that excludes astrology—in the rest of the seventh and eighth centuries. However, Ptolemaic astronomical texts were certainly studied and copied in this period—that much we may infer from the fact that the Greek manuscript tradition preserved the *Handy Tables,* the *Almagest,* and Theon's commentaries on them in relatively complete form. In 1987 Alexander Jones warned against "pronounc[ing] confidently on what Byzantine astronomers did not know" when so many Byzantine astronomical manuscripts awaited study.[36] This warning is still valid today.

Despite the paucity of eighth-century sources and the attempt of later Byzantine sources to sully the name of the iconoclast emperor Constantine V (r. 741–775), it is possible to discern that he was a patron of astronomy-astrology (as well as alchemy). In Constantinople, interest in astronomy and astrology continued in the late eighth century, though we lack the details; the famous *Horoscope of Islam* ascribed to Stephen of Alexandria must date to "the end of the eighth century," when its list of "predicted" caliphs ceases to be accurate.[37]

At the same time, there is evidence that Byzantine astronomy and astrology were also being practiced under Muslim rule in the eighth century. The Maronite (Syrian Chalcedonian Monothelete) Christian Theophilos of Edessa (ca. 695–785) served as astrologer to the Abbasid caliph al-Mahdī (r. 775–785). His astronomical-astrological works survive mainly in Greek, many probably written in Greek originally, though at least some were originally written in Arabic (or at least the

31. Neugebauer, *History,* 2:1045–46; Tihon, "L'astronomie," 608.

32. Neugebauer was ambivalent: *History,* 1:1045–46. Roueché ("Stephanus the Alexandrian Philosopher" and elsewhere) challenged Stephen's authorship. The commentary's editor argues that Stephen was probably its author: Lempire, 1:3–6. See further Roberts, "Framing," n. 17.

33. Magdalino, *L'orthodoxie,* 35.

34. Magdalino, 36.

35. Magdalino, 37.

36. Jones, *Eleventh-Century Manual,* 19.

37. Neugebauer, *History,* 1:1050; Magdalino, *L'orthodoxie,* 50–51.

surviving Greek versions of some texts were translations from Arabic, even if the Arabic from which they were translated might itself have been the result of translation from the original Greek).[38] This suggests that there were others like Theophilos, who presumably learned astrology from teachers who likewise used Greek.

Theophilos represents the continuation of the Byzantine astronomical and astrological tradition in eighth-century Syria. As the new Muslim rulers encountered this philosophical and scientific tradition, they, like other rulers, found it useful for their own purposes and so patronized and supported it by granting individual non-Muslim scholars like Theophilos stipendiary positions at court and other financial support. At first these scholars continued to work and teach from Greek, Syriac, and Middle Persian texts. Eventually, as Arabic-speaking Muslims who did not know these languages wished to study this Byzantine and Syrian philosophical and scientific curriculum, demand grew for the same texts to be translated into Arabic.

And so beginning in the eighth century scholars in the Islamic world, mostly non-Muslims (usually Christians like Theophilos), translated texts of astrology and astronomy as part of this curriculum from Greek, Syriac, and Middle Persian into Arabic. Their patrons, usually in Baghdad, were caliphs, Muslim scholars, and others who wished to read and teach astronomical works in Arabic. Indeed, as Dimitri Gutas has argued, astrology and astronomy were major parts of the Greek-Arabic translation movement of the eighth to tenth century.[39]

The core of the astronomical curriculum translated into Arabic and subsequently revised, retranslated, and annotated was Ptolemy's *Handy Tables*,[40] *Almagest*,[41] *Planetary Hypotheses*,[42] and *Tetrabiblos*.[43] Prominent among the translators, correctors, and annotators who in the process created an Arabic technical vocabulary for astronomy and astrology were scholars whom we have already encountered: the Nestorian Christian Ḥunayn ibn Isḥāq of Ḥīra (808–873), his son Isḥāq ibn Ḥunayn (d. 910–911), the Byzantine Chalcedonian Christian Qusṭā ibn Lūqā (Κώστας ὁ Λουκᾶ) of Baʿlabakk (d. ca. 912–913),[44] and the Sabian mathematician Thābit ibn Qurra of Ḥarrān (d. 901)—all of them active in Baghdad. The established corpus of mathematical texts necessary for understanding Ptolemy's

38. Mavroudi, *Byzantine Book*, 397; Mavroudi, "Occult Sciences," 87 n. 148.

39. Gutas, *GTAC*.

40. Sezgin, *GAS*, 6:95–96, 102.

41. Sezgin, 6:88–89. Thābit ibn Qurra revised an eighth-century translation and a new translation by Isḥāq ibn Ḥunayn.

42. Sezgin, *GAS*, 6:94–95. The extant Arabic version was revised by Thābit ibn Qurra.

43. Sezgin, 7:43–44. It was first translated into Arabic in the eighth century; Ḥunayn ibn Isḥāq produced a revised translation. Thābit ibn Qurra wrote commentaries on parts of the *Tetrabiblos*. See also Burnett, *EI*[3], s.v. "Astrology."

44. See ch. 7, §4, pp. 224–25.

astronomy was also translated into Arabic by these same non-Muslim scholars.[45] Greek commentaries on Ptolemy were also translated; for example, though the Arabic translation of Theon's commentary on the *Almagest* does not survive, we know it existed in the ninth century because the ninth-century philosopher al-Kindī quotes it in his astronomical work, *On the Greatest Art* (*Kitāb fī l-ṣināʿa al-ʿuẓmā*).[46] New Arabic commentaries on the *Almagest*, by Thābit ibn Qurra and Qusṭā ibn Lūqā among many others, were also produced.[47]

The Arabic astronomical tradition that built on these translations (along with Persian and Indian traditions)[48] incorporated (1) observation and prediction of astral positions; (2) the use of these for "practical" astrological purposes; and (3) theoretical attention to the physical arrangement of the universe. Astral sciences in general were referred to broadly as "the science of the stars" (*ʿilm al-nujūm*). Astrology, when specified precisely, was known as "the science of the verdicts of the stars" (*ʿilm aḥkām al-nujūm* or *ʿilm al-aḥkām*). (Other practical applications in the Islamic world include calculating the times of the five daily prayers performed by Muslims, ascertaining the direction of Mecca for prayer, and regulating the calendar.)[49] Finally, the term *ʿilm al-hayʾa*, the "science of the configuration" of the cosmos, came to refer, especially in the eleventh century and later, to that part of astronomy concerned with how the universe *actually* is and moves rather than simply mathematical devices that allow astronomers to predict *apparent* celestial motion.[50]

We have abundant evidence about who practiced astronomy and astrology in the Islamic world, largely thanks to the biographical and bibliographical information preserved in three interrelated biographical dictionaries that happen to have survived.[51] It should be stressed that these sources are crucial for our knowledge of not only Muslim scientists, but also non-Muslims working in Arabic, like Thābit, Qusṭā, and Ḥunayn.[52] If only we had such bio-bibliographical sources for their Byzantine counterparts!

Many Arabic-speaking intellectuals in the ninth through eleventh centuries (and later) devoted considerable energy to astronomy and astrology. They con-

45. Morelon, "Eastern Arabic Astronomy," 21.

46. Morelon, 23.

47. Sezgin, *GAS*, 6:90–94.

48. Saliba, "Role," 47 and n. 20.

49. Morelon, "General Survey," 15; King, *Astronomy in the Service*, with Saliba's review.

50. Ragep, *EI*^{3}, s.v. "Astronomy."

51. Ibn al-Nadīm, *Fihrist* (completed in 987–988 CE, ed. Sayyid, trans. Dodge); Ibn al-Qifṭī (d. 1248), *Tārīkh al-ḥukamāʾ* (al-Zawzanī's epitome of 1249, ed. Lippert); and Ibn Abī Uṣaybiʿa (d. 1270), *ʿUyūn al-anbāʾ fī ṭabaqāt al-aṭibbāʾ* (ed. Riḍā).

52. I owe this observation, and the contrast with the situation for Byzantine sources, to Maria Mavroudi.

ducted observations, at first to verify and correct Ptolemy's tables but also, and especially later, to inquire into and critique his theoretical models and devise new ones.[53] The Abbasid caliphate invested heavily in building scientific institutions dedicated, among other things, to such observation. Besides funding translations and technical scholarship, we know that al-Maʾmūn (r. 813–833) set up observatories in Baghdad and just outside Damascus in order to observe the position of the sun for a whole year (831–832).[54]

Among those we know worked on astronomy in the ninth century is Abū Jaʿfar Muḥammad ibn Mūsā al-Khwārizmī (ca. 800–ca. 847), the famous mathematician best known for his work on algebra, who also worked for al-Maʾmūn. His influential astronomical *Sind-India Tables* (*Zīj al-Sindhind*) were much annotated and updated by subsequent astronomers.[55] Another was Ḥabash al-Ḥāsib (mid-ninth century), an astronomer from Marw (Khurāsān in eastern Iran) who worked for al-Maʾmūn. He based his *Damascene Tables* (*al-Zīj al-Dimashqī*) on observations carried out in Damascus and Baghdad. Just as Stephen of Alexandria's commentary on the *Handy Tables* incorporated new Christian concerns (the date of Easter), so too Ḥabash's *Damascene Tables* dealt with a crucial new calendrical consideration: the visibility of the new moon, since the lunar calendar used by Muslims begins each lunar month on the first day that the new moon is (theoretically) visible.[56]

Among ninth-century intellectuals, Ptolemy's translators Thābit ibn Qurra and Qusṭā ibn Lūqā should also be mentioned as astronomers in their own right. Qusṭā ibn Lūqā wrote an *Introduction to Theoretical Astronomy*.[57] Thābit ibn Qurra wrote works on the physical model of Ptolemy's *Planetary Hypotheses* and other astronomical issues. Like Ḥabash, he also carried out mathematical work on the visibility of the new moon.[58]

Thābit was one of a number of ninth-century astronomers who worked in Baghdad for the three sons of Mūsā ibn Shākir al-Munajjim (a Khurāsānian astrologer hired by al-Maʾmūn during his residence in Marw), known as the Banū Mūsā (Sons of Mūsā). Of the three, Muḥammad (d. 873) was most interested in astronomy.[59] He

53. Morelon, "Eastern Arabic Astronomy," 25.

54. Morelon, "General Survey," 8–9.

55. Sezgin, *GAS*, 6:140–43. The name: *EI*², s.v. "Sindhind." The original text does not survive but can be partially reconstructed from the Latin translation (by Adelard of Bath) of a later recension (made by al-Majrīṭī, d. 1007), and from Ibn al-Muthannā's commentary (preserved only in a Hebrew translation by Abraham ibn Ezra, twelfth century) on al-Khwarizmī's *Zīj*.

56. Morelon, "Eastern Arabic Astronomy," 31–34.

57. *Kitāb al-madkhal ilā l-hayʾa* or simply *Kitāb al-hayʾa*. This work is discussed further below; see p. 281, especially nn. 151–52; Morelon, "Eastern Arabic Astronomy," 25.

58. Morelon, "Eastern Arabic Astronomy," 25, 34–46.

59. Saliba, "Early Arabic Critique," 123–24.

wrote a treatise (only partially extant) critiquing Ptolemy's attempt to square his geometrical models of the cosmos with Aristotelian physics.[60]

Arabic astronomical work—observational and theoretical—continued into the late ninth, tenth, and eleventh centuries (and beyond). A prominent example is al-Battānī (d. 929). A Muslim, as his given name (Muḥammad) indicates, who lived most of his life in Raqqa (in Syria), he came from a family of Sabians of Ḥarrān (like Thābit), and so he was often given the additional appellations al-Ḥarrānī al-Ṣābī. He carried out an observational program for thirty years in Raqqa and produced the *Sabian Tables* (*al-Zīj al-Ṣābī*).[61]

As the Abbasid caliphate disintegrated and in Baghdad came under the control of the Buyids, state investment in such astronomical observations continued. In Rayy, near Tehran, the Buyid governor Fakhr al-Dawla (d. 997) commissioned astronomers to build an observatory consisting of an enormous, partially underground sextant (of the sort whose traces can still be seen today in Ulugh Beg's observatory established in 1420 outside of Samarqand).[62]

Although I have passed over Arab interest in Indian astronomy and astrology for the sake of brevity, it was certainly present from the beginning and continued. Thus, for example, the central Asian polymath al-Bīrūnī (973–ca. 1050), who worked on astronomy and composed the *Tables of Masʿūd* (*al-Qānūn al-Masʿūdī*), used his knowledge of Sanskrit to draw on Sanskrit astronomical works.[63] And though I have focused entirely on the eastern Islamic world, the Islamic West was also very active in astronomy. The eleventh-century Andalusian astronomer al-Zarqālī (a.k.a. al-Zarqālluh, d. 1100) especially stands out.[64]

We have returned to Avicenna (d. 1037) again and again in chapters 6–8, and here yet again we must mention the great philosopher. For along with logic, physics, and other philosophical subjects, his interests included astronomy. He wrote on Ptolemaic astronomy in the *Healing* (*al-Shifāʾ*) and various other works.[65] In his work *On Observational Instruments*, he described a new device that greatly improved the precision of measurements of celestial positions.[66]

Finally, the *Doubts against Ptolemy* by the astronomer and mathematician Abū ʿAlī al-Ḥasan ibn al-Haytham (965–1039) has often been identified as an important stage in the development of Arabic theoretical astronomy. Ibn al-Haytham

60. Saliba, "Early Arabic Critique," 123–24; see also n. 136 below.

61. Battānī, *Opus*, ed. Nallino. Morelon, "General Survey," 9–10; Morelon, "Eastern Arabic Astronomy," 46.

62. Morelon, "General Survey," 10–11, 14–15; *EI*², s.v. "Fakhr al-Dawla."

63. Morelon, "Eastern Arabic Astronomy," 51–52.

64. See §2, p. 274 below.

65. Sezgin, *GAS*, 6:276–80.

66. Morelon, "General Survey," 12.

served at the court of the Fatimid caliph al-Ḥākim (r. 996–1021) in Cairo.[67] His *Doubts*—building, as George Saliba has argued, on the work of predecessors like the eldest of the Banū Mūsā, Muḥammad ibn Mūsā ibn Shākir—critiqued Ptolemy's intellectually unsatisfying physical model of the cosmos and pushed for the development of a more physically coherent alternative.[68]

Although we needn't continue past the 1050s, the survey could go on. Organized astronomical activities continued right through the Seljuk and then Mongol conquests of the Middle East, most famously at the observatory founded in Marāgha in Azerbaijan by the non-Muslim Mongol ruler Hulagu (d. 1265).[69]

In the Islamic world, then, astronomy was seldom neglected. This was at least in part because of private and state interest in its practical application: astrology.[70] Islamic philosophers, scientists, theologians, and jurists debated the validity, morality, and legality of astrology.[71] Al-Kindī embraced astrology as part of the natural world, while al-Fārābī and Avicenna rejected it.[72] As among ancient and medieval Greek writers, Hellenic-pagan and Christian, so too in Arabic the debate continued to center around determinism, free will, and moral responsibility.[73] Some astrologers working in Arabic have already been mentioned. Others include Māshāʾallāh, a Jewish astrologer who helped cast the horoscope for the city of Baghdad in 762 when it was founded as the new Abbasid capital by the caliph al-Manṣūr; the highly influential Khurāsānian (eastern Iranian) astrologer Abū Maʿshar al-Balkhī (ninth century);[74] al-Battānī, who wrote a commentary on Ptolemy's *Tetrabiblos;* al-Qabīṣī, who worked in Aleppo for the Ḥamdānid ruler Sayf al-Dawla (r. 945–967) and wrote an *Introduction to Astrology;* al-Bīrūnī, who also wrote an astrological introduction; and Ibn al-Faḍl's Muslim contemporary active in Fatimid Cairo, the physician Ibn Riḍwān (d. 1061), another commentator on Ptolemy's *Tetrabiblos.*[75]

We have seen that Christians, including the Greek-speaking Byzantine Qusṭā ibn Lūqā, were deeply involved in astronomical teaching and research in the

67. Hodgson, *Venture,* 2:18, 168; *EI*², s.v. "Ibn al-Haytham."

68. Saliba, "Early Arabic Critique," 116 and nn. 10–11; Saliba, "Arabic versus Greek Astronomy," 329, 333–34.

69. Morelon, "General Survey," 13–14.

70. Saliba, "Role."

71. Saliba, "Role," 46–47.

72. Burnett, *EI*³, s.v. "Astrology," §1.

73. Burnett, *EI*³, s.v. "Astrology," §1. This was one of al-Fārābī's main concerns: Janos, *Method,* 44–57, esp. 50. Avicenna (*Réfutation de l'astrologie,* ed. Michot) refuted astrology above all (but not exclusively) on epistemological grounds—namely that it is not built up from first principles as a science should be but rather assigns characteristics to planets and constellations arbitrarily. I owe these two references to an anonymous reviewer.

74. Burnett, *EI*³, s.v. "Abū Maʿshar."

75. Burnett, *EI*³, s.v. "Astrology," §1.

Islamic world. What about astronomy and astrology in the Byzantine Empire itself?

In the ninth century, especially with the activity of John the Grammarian (d. before 867) and Leo the Mathematician (d. after 869), and in the tenth and eleventh centuries, the evidence points to sustained Byzantine interest in the astral sciences.[76] The Greek manuscript tradition likewise attests to the study of Ptolemaic astronomy and astrology. Extant ninth-century Greek astronomical manuscripts of Ptolemy and Theon include uncial manuscripts dated to the reigns of Emperors Leo V (r. 813–820) and Leo VI (r. 886–912).[77]

Moreover, there are scraps of evidence that scholars in the Byzantine Empire took an interest in the work of astronomers in the caliphate. A set of annotations in Greek astronomical manuscripts of the thirteenth century and later mention observations that can be dated to 829–830 and 906–907; Magdalino has pointed out that these dates are precisely when Byzantine embassies to the caliphate took place, and that further considerations place the first set of observations in Damascus at just the time when the caliph al-Maʾmūn was there and his observatory there was active. Magdalino argued that the observations were made not by Arab astronomers, as historians of science have tended to assume, but by Byzantine astronomers who were part of those embassies.[78]

Byzantine astronomers and astrologers also had access to some Arabic texts in Greek translation. From the Greek manuscript tradition of Greek translations of the astrologer Abū Maʿshar (787–886), it seems likely that Abū Maʿshar was known in Greek in the mid-tenth century.[79] For the eleventh century, there is considerable evidence that Byzantines were well acquainted with Arabic astronomy and astrology.[80] For example, Byzantine annotations on the *Almagest* from ca. 1032 use observations performed in Baghdad under the Abbasid caliph al-Maʾmūn (r. 813–833), as well as the astronomical tables of an Arab astronomer Ἀλήμ, which Edward Kennedy, followed by Joseph Mogenet, identified (on the basis of the astronomer's name) with Ibn al-Aʿlam's (d. 985) *ʿAḍudian Tables* (*al-Zīj al-ʿAḍudī*), which survive only in fragments.[81] Whatever the merits of this identification, the broader point that the Byzantine annotations draw on Arabic astronomy still stands. Likewise, a Greek astronomical manual produced at Constantinople around 1060–1072 used Arabic astronomical material from the ninth

76. Magdalino, *L'orthodoxie*, chs. 3–4.

77. Tihon, "L'astronomie," 609–10.

78. Magdalino, "Road to Baghdad," 209–10; Mavroudi, *Byzantine Book*, 396–97.

79. Mavroudi, *Byzantine Book*, 398, citing Pingree's work on the manuscript tradition.

80. Mavroudi, *Byzantine Book*, 399–400.

81. Mogenet, "Une scolie"; Tihon, "L'astronomie," 611 n. 35; Mavroudi, *Byzantine Book*, 399; Tihon, "Science," 195–96. On the text: Sezgin, *GAS*, 6:216; Kennedy, "Survey," 134, no. 70. Jones (*Eleventh-Century Manual*, 16) cast doubt on this identification.

and tenth centuries: Ibn al-Muthannā's (tenth-century) commentary (known from the Hebrew translation) on al-Khwārizmī's *Sind-India Tables* and Ḥabash al-Ḥāsib's *Damascene Tables*.[82] Ibn al-Faḍl's contemporary Symeon Seth—himself from Antioch and bilingual in Greek and Arabic—cultivated astronomy and astrology (among other disciplines) in Constantinople.[83] The astronomical tables (*zīj*es) of al-Khwārizmī and Ḥabash were sources for an eleventh-century Greek astronomical treatise (dated by the observations it contains to 1072 or later, probably before 1086).[84] The general impression one gets is that Byzantines continued to be interested in astronomy and astrology and sought the most up-to-date works and data on the subject as they became available, even when those works and data were expressed in Arabic.

This rapid survey makes clear that in the world Ibn al-Faḍl inhabited, astronomy and astrology were widely practiced and often highly prestigious. Their practitioners and patrons included Sabians, Jews, Christians, and Muslims, writing in Greek, Syriac, Arabic, and Persian. As we shall see, Ibn al-Faḍl may not have been an astronomer himself, but he was informed enough about astronomy to participate in a venerable tradition of critiquing the ancient science.

1 TRANSLATING ASTRONOMICAL TERMINOLOGY

A passage on astronomy in Ibn al-Faḍl's retranslation of Basil's *Hexaemeron* allows us to observe his attention to Arabic astronomical terminology. In his first homily, Basil mocks astronomers for wasting their labor on the irrelevant details of cosmic positions and movement:[85]

> Ἤπου αὐτοῖς ἡ περιουσία τῆς τοῦ κόσμου σοφίας προσθήκην οἴσει ποτὲ τῆς χαλεπῆς κατακρίσεως, ὅτι οὕτως ὀξὺ περὶ τὰ μάταια βλέποντες, ἑκόντες πρὸς τὴν σύνεσιν τῆς ἀληθείας ἀπετυφλώθησαν. Ἀλλ' οἱ τῶν ἄστρων τὰ διαστήματα καταμετροῦντες καὶ τοὺς ἀειφανεῖς αὐτῶν καὶ ἀρκτῴους ἀπογραφόμενοι καὶ ὅσοι περὶ τὸν νότιον πόλον κείμενοι τοῖς μέν εἰσι φανεροί, ἡμῖν δὲ ἄγνωστοι, καὶ βόρειον πλάτος καὶ ζῳδιακὸν κύκλον μυρίοις διαστήμασι διαιροῦντες, καὶ ἐπαναφορὰς ἄστρων καὶ στηριγμοὺς καὶ ἀποκλίσεις καὶ πάντων τὴν ἐπὶ τὰ προηγούμενα κίνησιν δι' ἀκριβείας τηρήσαντες, καὶ διὰ πόσου χρόνου τῶν πλανωμένων ἕκαστος τὴν ἑαυτοῦ περίοδον ἐκπληροῖ, μίαν τῶν πασῶν μηχανὴν οὐκ ἐξεῦρον πρὸς τὸ τὸν θεὸν ἐννοῆσαι.

82. Jones, *Eleventh-Century Manual*, 12–13; Mavroudi, *Byzantine Book*, 399–400. See also Pingree, *EI*², s.v. "ʿIlm al-hayʾa," section on "The Sindhind tradition" (3:1137); and n. 55 above.

83. Magdalino, "Byzantine Reception," 46–53. For the possibility that he was Ibn al-Faḍl's teacher, see ch. 1, p. 14.

84. *Methods of Computing Various Astronomical Hypotheses:* Jones, *Eleventh-Century Manual* (date discussed on p. 11; title ed. and trans. pp. 30–31).

85. Basil, *Hexaemeron*, 1.4, ed. Amand de Mendieta and Rudberg, 7_{11}–8_{5}; trans. based on Basil-NPNF, 54.

> (1) Perhaps abundance of wisdom about this world will one day add to their harsh condemnation, since, gazing so keenly at worthless things, they were willingly blinded to comprehension of the truth. (2) But those who measure the distances of the stars, who note down both those that are always visible and Arctic and those that lie around the South Pole and are visible to some but unknown to us, (3) and who divide northern latitude and the zodiacal circle into countless intervals, (4) who observe precisely the stars' succedents, stations, cadents, and the movement of all according to the foregoing, and how much time each of the planets takes to complete its period—(5) of all these contrivances not a single one have they discovered for knowing God.

Thus Basil suggests that the astronomers will not only be punished on the Day of Judgment for their failure to recognize the true god; they will also incur additional punishment for willfully ignoring God while devoting themselves so assiduously to astronomical trivialities. To drive home his point, Basil pronounces a barrage of technical terms to describe some of the trivial information that astronomers collect.

In the modern astronomical model, the earth and other planets revolve around the sun, and the moon revolves around the earth. To a viewer on the surface of the earth, however, it seems very much like the earth is standing still while a great celestial orb carrying all the fixed stars rotates around it. Meanwhile, the sun, moon, and planets other than the earth, though following this same daily rotation of the celestial orb, also undergo a slower (apparent) motion, along a circle called the ecliptic that loops around the celestial orb with the earth at its center. The ecliptic is tilted with respect to the equator. Though they are not always precisely on it, the sun, moon, and planets stay close to it, roughly within a band or "belt" called the zodiac.

This is what Basil is referring to when he says that the astronomers divide the zodiac into "countless intervals": they are dividing up this band that wraps around the celestial orb. In particular, they typically divided the zodiac into twelve equal intervals, or "places." The intervals are "countless" because astronomers divide each "place" into 30 degrees (or 360 degrees for the whole zodiac), each degree into 60 "minutes," each minute into 60 "seconds," and so on ad infinitum in the sexagesimal system used by ancient astronomers.[86] He also refers to the division of "northern latitude," that is, into degrees (30 degrees north, 60 degrees north, etc.).[87]

And this is just the beginning. Astronomers also measure the distances (*diastēmata*) of northern and southern stars. This probably refers to the distances of stars from the earth, which Ptolemy discusses in his *Planetary Hypotheses*.[88] This

86. Summarized by the Sāmānid secretary active in Bukhārā (in present-day Uzbekistan) Abū ʿAbdallāh Muḥammad ibn Aḥmad al-Khwārizmī al-Kātib (tenth century; not to be confused with the ninth-century mathematician and astronomer Abū Jaʿfar Muḥammad ibn Mūsā al-Khwārizmī) in his *Mafātīḥ al-ʿulūm*, 6.2, ed. van Vloten, 215_{12}–216_{2}.

87. The reference might be to latitude relative to the ecliptic, rather than relative to the earth's equator.

88. Morelon, "General Survey," 7; see also n. 155 below.

is how Ibn al-Faḍl seems to have interpreted it, as we shall see. It could also refer to planetary positions, which are measured in terms of two *angular* distances (using polar coordinates). As for the stars, here Basil means the fixed stars, the stars that seem to travel in a circle around the earth's axis once a day. Basil casually makes reference to the fact that while we can see many of them, there are others—at least according to astronomers—that we cannot see, visible only from the Southern Hemisphere. He is perhaps mocking the astronomers even in this, since it may have seemed absurd to Basil's audience that astronomers would busy themselves about imaginary stars that they couldn't even see.

Astronomers, continues Basil, take special care in their observations of succedents (*epanaphorai*), stations (*stērigmoi*), and cadences (*apokliseis*). These terms are particularly technical astrological terms, used in the interpretation of a horoscope.

The first, "succedents," and third, "cadences," refer to subsets of the zodiac. Although we typically think of the twelve "places" as the zodiacal signs Aries, Taurus, Gemini, and so on, this was only one possible subdivision into twelve equal places—namely, the one that begins at the vernal equinox (i.e., the sun's position along the zodiac at the time of the vernal equinox). But astrologers often needed to start at a different point—namely, the ascendant, the point along the zodiac that was rising at the eastern horizon at the moment when a horoscope was cast. If we number the twelve places beginning with the place starting at the ascendant, then the 1st, 4th, 7th, and 10th were the *cardinal places*. The four places that each followed (or "succeeded") a cardinal place were called *succedent places*—namely, the 2nd, 5th, 8th, and 11th. The remaining four places, that is, the places that each preceded a cardinal place, were called the *cadent places*—namely, the 3rd, 6th, 9th, and 12th.[89] Being able to identify the succedent and cadent places was an important part of casting a horoscope. For example, in discussing how to interpret a birth-horoscope, Ptolemy says that a planet exerts a stronger influence when it is in a succedent (under certain conditions).[90] Ptolemy's younger contemporary Vettius Valens speaks of determining whether a planet is "in a cardinal, succedent, or cadent place."[91]

Basil's term "cadences" (ἀποκλίσεις) is not found in Ptolemy's *Tetrabiblos*, but it is very similar to the Ptolemaic term "cadent place" (ἀπόκλιμα). On the other hand, Vettius Valens speaks of a planet being "in cadence" (ἐν ἀποκλίσει) as a synonym for being "in (one of the) cadent places" (ἐν . . . τοῖς ἀποκλίμασιν).[92]

89. Bouché-Leclercq, *L'astrologie*, 273–74; Beck, *Brief History*, 43; *OED*, s.v. "succedent" A.2, and "cadent (2)" no. 2. See also Qabīṣī (tenth century), *Introduction to Astrology*, 1.55–56, ed. and trans. Burnett et al., 46–49.

90. *Tetrabiblos*, $3.4_{219-220}$, ed. Hübner, 179; ed. and trans. Robbins, 238 (3.3.3).

91. *Anthologies*, 2.2.2, ed. Pingree, 55_{18}.

92. *Anthologies*, 2.2, sentences 10 and 4, respectively, ed. Pingree, 56_{11}, 55_{23}. For other similar examples, see ibid., 473 (index).

This suggests that Basil may have been drawing on his knowledge of Vettius Valens's astrological manual, whether direct or indirect.[93]

Basil's list also includes "stations." This refers to the points where the planets would, as viewed from earth, stop in their movement along the zodiac and turn back. This phenomenon was, as mentioned, a major part of what Ptolemy's astronomical system, with its epicycles, was designed to explain, and he incorporated stations into his astral prognostication (astrology) as well. In particular, he says that planets are more or less powerful depending on what part of their epicycle they are in, either moving in the same direction as the motion of the celestial sphere or in the opposite direction.[94] The turning points between these motions with or against the celestial sphere are the stations. So while the term was not only used in astrology, Basil again might have referenced it with astrology in mind.

After these astrological references—references that could be made only by someone with considerable exposure to technical astrological literature—Basil mentions a more neutral astronomical parameter: planetary period (*periodos*), or how long it takes for a planet to go all the way around the zodiac. The moon takes about a month, the sun takes a year, and so on. These periods could also have an astrological significance because they were part of predicting conjunctions and oppositions of planets, and planetary positions more generally.

In short, even though Basil does not emphasize astrology in this passage, his attack on astronomy closely associates astronomy with astrology. Moreover, Basil was erudite enough to refer intelligently to astrological concepts that would be entirely opaque to a nonspecialist. Although a nonspecialist might well have heard of the planets or poles or periods or latitudes, this was probably not the case with succedents, cadents, and stations.

Before moving to the Arabic translations, it should be noted that Byzantine readers took great interest in this passage. This is shown by a series of seven Greek marginal notes appearing in some manuscripts of Basil's *Hexaemeron* beside this passage alone.[95] Some of them are quite long. They explain (1) what it means to measure the distances of the stars (namely, the distances *between* individual fixed stars); (2) the stars that are always (northern), never (southern), and sometimes visible (those in between); (3) how stars that are always visible to us in the north are never visible to those in the south and vice versa; (4) "northern latitude"; (5) the zodiac and what Basil means when he says that astronomers divide it "into

93. Alternatively, Basil's use of *apoklisis* instead of *apoklima* may be independent of Vettius Valens, since it may simply reflect linguistic development: it was common for Greek verbal nouns originally referring abstractly to the verb's action (ending in -σις) to take on the additional meaning of a concrete instance or result of the action.

94. Bouché-Leclercq, *L'astrologie*, 111–23.

95. Ed. Pasquali, "Doxographica," 196–99, nos. 8–14. Nos. 8–11 are in G2 and E6 (Pasquali's G and O). Nos. 12–14 are in all four manuscripts Pasquali used, on which see ch. 7, p. 220, n. 89.

countless intervals"; (6) succedent, cadent, and *stērigma* ("support, foundation," rather than *stērigmos*, "station");[96] and (7) the planets and their periods.

In other words, they seek to explain the astronomical terms used by Basil in much the way that I have just sought to do above. The manuscripts containing these marginalia date from the tenth to the fourteenth century.[97] Thus they attest to a continued interest among Byzantine readers of Basil in understanding the elementary astronomy and astrology behind Basil's critique. As we shall see, this is an interest that Ibn al-Faḍl shared—to the point of drawing on at least one of these Greek notes in his own marginal note on the passage.

Not only Ibn al-Faḍl but also the Anonymous Translator was attentive to astronomical terminology. As will become apparent, however, both translators ignored or did not understand the more obscure astrological jargon, replacing it with other astronomical terminology.

The Anonymous Translation renders Basil's passage on astronomers as follows:[98]

ولعلّ زيادة حكمتهم في العالم تصير زيادة في الحكومة الصعبة عليهم في[١] وقتٍ من الأوقات، إذ[٢] كانوا قد نظروا إلى الباطل نظراً[٣] هكذا حادّاً، ثم[٤] عمِهوا[٥،٦] عن فهم الحق. ولكن هؤلاء[٧] الذين مسحوا مقادير النجوم وأبعادها، وأثبتوا ما هو منها دائم[٨] الظهور وجنوبي، وعرفوا ما يقرب منها من[٩] القطب القبلي[١٠] مما هو ظاهر لقوم آخرين[١١]، ونحن لا نعلم به، وما في الجانب الشمالي، وما قسموه من أبعاد[١٢] نطاق فلك[١٣] البروج، وما عرفوه من مطالع النجوم ووقوفها وميلها، وما استقصوه في ذكر الحركة المتوجهة إلى قدّام، وفي كم من المدّة يقطع كل كوكب من الكواكب المتحيّرة التائهة جُملة الفلك. مع هذا كله مما تعبوا فيه، لم[١٤] يجدوا حيلة عرفوا بها الله.

[١]في: س؛ وفي: پ غ [٢]إذ: س؛ إذا: پ غ [٣]نظراً: س غ؛ نظروا: پ [٤]ثم: س؛ —پ غ [٥]عمِهوا: س غ؛ عميوا: پ [٦]+[[هو]]: غ، وإن هذا يعني أن طول السطر في أصل «غ» كان: «عن فهم الحق ولكن هاولا الذين مسحوا مقادير النجوم وابعادها واثبتوا منها ما»، أو نصف ذلك، لأن بعد ذلك نقرأ «هو» [٧]هؤلاء: پ س؛ هاولا: غ [٨]ما هو منها دائم: س (وعند ابن الفضل)؛ منها ما هو دائم: پ غ [٩]من: پ غ؛ إلى: س [١٠]القبلي: س (وفي ترجمة ابن الفضل)؛ الجنوبي: پ غ [١١]لقوم آخرين: پ غ؛ لآخرين: س [١٢]أبعاد: پ غ؛ —س [١٣]فلك: پ غ؛ —س [١٤]لم: س؛ ولم: پ غ

(1) **And perhaps their excess of wisdom about the world** will become an excess in the hard judgment against them[99] sometime, since they had contemplated the **worthless** so keenly, then strayed from **understanding the truth.** (2) But these men, **who measured** the magnitudes (*maqādīr*) of the stars (*nujūm*) and their **distances** (*abʿād*); **and established which of them is perpetually visible and southerly;** and came to know which of them is near **to the South Pole** (*al-quṭb al-qiblī*) among those which are **visible to others** while we do not know of them; what is **on the northern side;**[100] (3) the **intervals**

96. The note (Pasquali, "Doxographica," 198, no. 13) says that the succedent is "the rising part of the ascendant Zodiacal sign"; the cadent is "the first [part]"; and the *stērigma* is "the intermediate [part]."

97. See ch. 7, p. 220, n. 89.

98. Homily 1, *faṣl* 1: **G** 4^{v}_{01}–5^{r}, **P** 10^{v}, **S** 12^{v}. The readings in **W** 11^{v}–12^{r} (not given in the apparatus) follow **P**'s readings.

99. *ʿalayhim:* the judgment is both "against" them and difficult "for" them.

100. The Anonymous Translation and Ibn al-Faḍl's translation both depart from the Greek here. This may be in part due to a variant reading in a Greek exemplar used, such as βορείῳ πλάτει for βόρειον πλάτος.

(*abʿād*) of the belt (*niṭāq* ~ ζώνη) of **the orb**[101] **of constellations** [i.e., the Zodiac] which **they divided;** (4) the **rising-places** (*maṭāliʿ*) **of the stars, their stopping** (*wuqūf*), **and their declination** (*mayl*) which they came to know; what **they examined** concerning the mentioning of **the progressive motion, and in how long a period each of the wandering,** straying (*tāʾiha*) **stars traverses** the totality of the celestial orb—(5) in spite of all these efforts, **they did not find a contrivance** (*ḥīla*) by which they came to know **God.**

As usual, Ibn al-Faḍl's translation draws heavily on the Anonymous Translation, while replacing its overall sentence structure with his much clearer constructions and revising or replacing much of the phrasing. Ibn al-Faḍl adopted most of the Anonymous Translator's renderings of astronomical terms, but his divergences are telling. Ibn al-Faḍl's translation reads:[102]

ولعلّ زيادة حكمتهم في العالم تمتري لهم في بعض الأحايين وافر العذاب ووخيمه، إذ كان نظرهم في الباطل ثاقباً[١]، وفي فهم الحق مظلماً[٢]. نعم والذين[٣] مسحوا أبعاد الكواكب، وأثبتوا ما هو منها[٤] دائم[٥] الظهور وجنوبي، وما[٦] هو منها قريب من القطب القبلي، ظاهرٌ[٧] لقوم آخرين، ومستترٌ عنّا في الجانب الشمالي، وقسموا فلك البروج[٨] بعدّة[٩] أبعاداً، ورصدوا مطالع النجوم ووقوفها وميلها، واستقصوا النظر[١٠] في الحركة المتوجهة إلى قدّام، وفي[١١] كم من[١٢] المدّة يقطع كل كوكب من الكواكب المتحيرة فلكه، (حاشية حوالي ثلاثين سطرا) ولم يجدوا حيلةً يتوصلون[١٣] بها إلى معرفة الله تبارك وتعالى[١٤].

[١] ثاقباً: ذ ق؛ ثاقب: ب د [٢] مظلماً: ذ ق؛ مظلم: ب د [٣] والذين: د ذ ق؛ الذين: ب [٤] ما هو منها: ب د ق؛ منها ما هو: ذ [٥] دائم: د ذ ق؛ دائماً: ب [٦] الظهور وجنوبي، وما: تالف في ذ [٧] ظاهرٌ: ذ؛ ظاهراً: ب د ق [٨] في الجانب الشمالي، وقسموا فلك البروج: ب د ق؛ وقسموا الجا[نب الشمالي] وفلك البروج: ذ [٩] بعدّة: أو: بُعْدَه [١٠] النظر: تالف في ذ [١١] وفي: د ذ ق (إلا أن في د خطاً من ميم في السطر الذي فوقه يدخل السطر بعد الواو فقد يبدو أنه ألِف)؛ وافي: ب [١٢] من: د ذ ق؛ في: ب [١٣] حيلةً يتوصلون: ب د ق؛ تالف في ذ [١٤] تبارك وتعالى: د ذ ق؛ [[تعالى]] تبارك وتعالى: ب

(1) **And perhaps their excess of wisdom about the world** will bring about[103] for them at some time abundant and harmful torment, since their contemplation of the **worthless** was penetrating (*thāqib*), but of **understanding the truth,** murky (*muẓlim*). (2) And furthermore, those **who measured**[104] the **distances** of the stars (*kawākib*), **and established which of them is perpetually visible and southerly,** and which of them is near **to the South Pole, visible to others,**[105] and hidden from us **on the northern side.**[106] (3) And **they divided** the **orb of constellations** [*falak al-burūj*, i.e., the zodiac] by a number of **intervals,** (4) and they observed the **rising-places** (*maṭāliʿ*) **of the stars, their stopping** (*wuqūf*), **and their declination** (*mayl*); and **they examined** by contemplation **the progressive motion, and in how long a period** (*fī kam min al-mudda*) **each of the wandering**[107] **stars traverses** its celestial orb.

101. *falak;* not all manuscripts include this word.

102. **B** 13–14, **D** 6–7, **E** [5]–[7], **Q** 10–12.

103. *tamtarī,* literally "extract" or "draw out": *Lisān* s.v. *mry.*

104. *masaḥa,* which can mean many things ("wipe," "rub," "anoint"—like the Messiah, *al-masīḥ*) but here means "to measure." *Lisān* s.v. *msḥ:* "*misāha:* measurement of land . . . To *masaḥa* land . . . means to measure it."

105. Ibn al-Faḍl has eliminated the superfluous words *mimmā huwa* between "South Pole" and "visible to others."

106. See n. 100 above.

107. Ibn al-Faḍl omits the Anonymous Translation's following word, *tāʾiha,* "straying."

[*Marginal note of about 30 lines.*][108] (5) But **they did not find a contrivance** (*ḥīla*) **by which** they might attain knowledge of **God** Blessed and Exalted.

The Anonymous Translator and Ibn al-Faḍl render "stations" (*stērigmoi*) as *wuqūf,* literally a planet's "stopping." Now, this is a fairly straightforward translation of the Greek even for someone who does not know astronomical terminology. And while al-Qabīṣī's *Introduction to Astrology* uses *maqām* as the technical term for "station," it also uses the verb "stop" (*waqafa*) in defining stations.[109]

The most specialized jargon that Basil referenced has been distorted in the process of translation: "succedents" (*epanaphorai*) and "cadences" (*apokliseis*) have become, in the Anonymous Translation, *maṭāliʿ* and *mayl.* While both of these Arabic words are technical terms in Arabic astronomy, they mean quite different things from the Greek terms they are meant to translate. The word *maṭāliʿ* can mean the "rising-places" or "rising-times" of a star. It also has a more specialized use—not intended here, to judge from context—of "co-ascension."[110] The term *mayl* also has a less technical and a more technical sense. The less technical sense is "inclination"; al-Qabīṣī says of Mercury in his *Introduction to Astrology* that "its nature *inclines* to whichever of the planets and signs mixes with it."[111] The more technical sense is the astronomical term "declination," the angular distance from the equator to a star or planet.[112]

Clearly these terms have little to do with the two sets of zodiacal "places"—succedents and cadents—described above. Nor are they at all related to the terms for these "places" used by al-Qabīṣī's *Introduction to Astrology: mā yalī l-awtād* (succedents) and *al-sawāqiṭ ʿan al-awtād* (cadents).[113] From a linguistic perspective, however, it is straightforward to see why the Anonymous Translator chose these

108. This note will be discussed in §2 below. The estimate of thirty lines is from **Q.**

109. 3.27, ed. and trans. Burnett et al., 100–101: planets can be "at their second station (*maqām*), which is the place where they stop (*taqif*) in retrogression."

110. Al-Khwārizmī al-Kātib, *Mafātīḥ,* 6.2, ed. van Vloten, 219: "The *maṭāliʿ* of the 'right orb' [*al-falak al-mustaqīm,* i.e., the celestial sphere that shares the earth's axis] are the parts of the equinoctial [i.e., the circle on the celestial sphere corresponding to the earth's equator] that rise with the arcs of the ecliptic (*falak al-burūj*)." See also Naṣīr al-Dīn al-Ṭūsī's (1201–1274 CE) *Tadhkira fī ʿilm al-hayʾa* [= *Memoir on Astronomy*], 3.7.1, ed. and trans. Ragep, 1:282.

111. 2.31, ed. and trans. Burnett et al., 78–79: *yamīlu ṭabʿuhu ilā mā māzajahu mina l-kawākibi wa-l-burūj* (emphasis added).

112. Al-Khwārizmī al-Kātib (*Mafātīḥ,* 6.2, ed. van Vloten, 216_{4-5}) defines *mayl* as "the distance of the sun or the planets from the equinoctial" (*al-mayl huwa buʿd al-shams aw al-kawākib min muʿaddil al-nahār*). The "equinoctial" is the circle on the celestial sphere corresponding to the earth's equator; see the previous page, where al-Khwārizmī says that when the sun reaches the circle called by this name, the day is equal to the night. See also Ṭūsī, *Memoir on Astronomy,* 2.3.2, 2.3.6, ed. and trans. Ragep, 1:112–15. I have followed Ragep's translations of terms.

113. Qabīṣī, *Introduction to Astrology,* 1.56, ed. and trans. Burnett et al., 48–49.

words. *Epanaphora,* like *anaphora,* can mean "rising,"[114] so choosing the astronomical term "rising-places" might seem fitting, especially to a translator who knew that *epanaphora* did *not* mean "ascendant" (ὡροσκόπος, *ṭāliʿ*). Likewise, *mayl,* literally an "incline," is a fairly literal translation of *apoklisis,* which can mean "slope."[115] At the same time, it is certainly a term with strong astronomical associations.

Ibn al-Faḍl took over these two terms from the Anonymous Translation, probably because he too did not know enough astrology—or at least had not received sufficient astrological training in Greek—to recognize Basil's jargon. And so he kept the Anonymous Translation's renderings, which, after all, still reproduced Basil's rhetorical purpose: to stress the many pointless parameters astronomers measure.

While he may not have been especially well-versed in *Greek* astrology, Ibn al-Faḍl seems to have been familiar, at least on a basic level, with Arabic astronomical terms, to judge from the parts of the Anonymous Translation that he revised.

Thus Ibn al-Faḍl has replaced the Anonymous Translation's *nujūm* (stars, sg. *najm*) with *kawākib* (planets/celestial bodies, sg. *kawkab*), where Basil had used a form of the word *astēr.* The words *najm* and *kawkab* were closely linked; in the astronomical context, the medieval Arabic lexicon *Lisān al-ʿarab* defines *nujūm* as referring either to "all the *kawākib*" or specifically to the Pleiades.[116] Historically, *kawkab* seems to be the earlier word for a celestial body,[117] while *najm* probably acquired it from the verb *najama,* which means "to rise (*ṭalaʿa*) and appear (*ẓahara*),"[118] but already in the early Islamic period, the two words seem to have been roughly synonymous. Nevertheless, in astronomical-astrological literature, the two words tended to be used in different ways. *Najm* supplied a name for the discipline, *ʿilm al-nujūm* (astronomy) and *aḥkām al-nujūm* (astrology), and so for the name of its practitioner as well (*munajjim*). On the other hand, astronomical-astrological texts themselves tended to refer to particular heavenly bodies and classes thereof, like the fixed and wandering stars, as *kawākib.*[119] In this way, Ibn al-Faḍl's revision represents a choice between two words that were synonymous in ordinary parlance, in favor of the word used in astronomical-astrological texts in the sort of context that Basil is evoking: Basil is referring to the distances of particular, though unspecified, stars—and so the word most consistent with astronomical literature here would be Ibn al-Faḍl's *kawākib.*

Likewise, Ibn al-Faḍl modifies *al-kawākib al-mutaḥayyira al-tāʾiha,* at the end of the passage, by omitting the last word. (Here the Anonymous Translation is

114. LSJ s.v. ἐπαναφορά III.
115. LSJ s.v. ἀπόκλισις I.
116. *Lisān* s.v. *njm.*
117. *Lisān* s.v. *kwkb: al-kawkabu maʿrūfun.*
118. *Lisān* s.v. *njm.*
119. For examples, see Roberts, "Crossing Paths," 285–92.

using the word *kawākib* precisely as astronomers would.) "The wandering stars," *al-kawākib al-mutaḥayyira,* was a standard astronomical term, while the expression produced by the Anonymous Translation's doublet for πλανωμένων—"wandering, straying" (*al-mutaḥayyira al-tā'iha*)—is not.[120] A subtle change in the translation has produced a text that resonates better with Arabic astronomical vocabulary.

Another example is the word for "zodiac." The Anonymous Translation refers to it as *niṭāq falak al-burūj* (or, in one manuscript, *niṭāq al-burūj*). The term *niṭāq* (belt) is equivalent to the Greek ζώνη, which can be used in the sense of ζῴδιον, the zodiac.[121] *Falak* means "(celestial) orb." And the *burūj* are the zodiacal places Aries, Gemini, and so on. This phrase—"the belt of the orb of the zodiacal places"—is used in astronomical-astrological texts.[122] Ibn al-Faḍl eliminated the word *niṭāq*, leaving simply *falak al-burūj*. This too was a standard way to refer to the zodiac or ecliptic in Arabic astronomy.[123] One might think of it as a sort of shorthand, since it is referring to a circle (the ecliptic) using a word for "orb" (*falak*). In any case, this was standard practice, and *falak al-burūj* was probably more common than the bulkier *niṭāq falak al-burūj*. In this case, then, both translations are using a standard astronomical phrase. The Anonymous Translator, as usual, has preferred a phrase that makes close reference to Basil's Greek (*niṭāq*, referring to the same "belt" as Basil's ζῳδιακόν). Meanwhile, Ibn al-Faḍl has opted for the more concise phrase that perhaps more immediately invokes the meaning because of its common usage. The choice to do so here suggests that he felt comfortable enough with basic astronomical terminology to make this revision with confidence.

Ibn al-Faḍl's decisions *not* to revise may be revealing as well. The phrase that both translations use to render Basil's "South Pole" is *al-quṭb al-qiblī*.[124] What is striking about the phrase is its evidently Muslim connotations. Literally it means something like "the pole (that lies) in the direction of prayer." The Christian direction of prayer (*qibla*) is (and was) to the east, whereas for the earliest Muslims it

120. Roberts, "Crossing Paths," 285–92. For doublets, see ch. 7, p. 223, n. 101. Another example in this same passage is the Anonymous Translation's *masaḥū maqādīra l-nujūmi wa-ab'ādahā*, where *miqdār* reemphasizes the second half of the compound word καταμετροῦντες. Ibn al-Faḍl removes this redundant vagueness, leaving only the more precise *ab'ād*.

121. LSJ s.v. ζώνη III.2.c.

122. Thus al-Qabīṣī speaks of the "*niṭāq falak al-burūj*" in his *Introduction to Astrology* (*Kitāb al-madkhal ilā ṣinā'at aḥkām al-nujūm*), 1.6, ed. Burnett et al., 20. I thank Asad Ahmed for alerting me to the technical sense of *niṭāq* and the related term *minṭaqa*.

123. E.g., Khwārizmī, *Mafātīh*, 6.2, ed. van Vloten, 215_{12}.

124. Some manuscripts of the Anonymous Translation read *al-quṭb al-janūbī* instead (**PW**). Since *qiblī* is the more unexpected reading (*lectio difficilior*), and since Ibn al-Faḍl's translation has it as well, we may conclude that the Anonymous Translation probably had it too originally, at least in the version available to Ibn al-Faḍl.

seems to have been Jerusalem, as for the Jews, at first, and then Mecca soon afterward (within two years of the *hijra*, according to Muslim tradition).[125] From the point of view of Syria and Iraq, Mecca was roughly to the south, whence, presumably, *qiblī* came to mean "southern."[126] Ibn al-Faḍl could have chosen to revise this by using a more neutral term for "southern," such as *janūbī* (as indeed a copyist of the Anonymous Translation did at some point, to judge from the manuscript tradition). Instead Ibn al-Faḍl chose to keep *qiblī*, perhaps because this term with Muslim origins had become a standard designation whose etymology failed to trouble him.

2 THE STARS, BYZANTINE MARGINALIA, AND AN ARABOPHONE BYZANTINE ASTRONOMER

We now turn to a marginal note that Ibn al-Faḍl wrote beside this very passage—a note that demonstrates that he also drew directly on the Byzantine (Greek) commentary tradition in how he approached Basil's cosmological homilies. This lengthy note on astronomy, though originally written in the margin, is (like his other "marginalia") preserved in manuscripts as an in-line note labeled "a marginal note by Ibn al-Faḍl." It appears just as Basil finishes his list of the pointless parameters astronomers like to measure and before he concludes by returning to his initial point, that astronomers, for all their observations and calculations, know nothing about God. The positioning of Ibn al-Faḍl's note in the extant manuscripts would lead one to expect it to focus on astronomy—and indeed that is the case.[127]

Picking up on Basil's references to astronomical concepts, Ibn al-Faḍl briefly discusses a number of points: fixed stars, the earth's roundness, and the precession of the equinoxes (A); astronomers all contradict each other (for example, on the question of whether each planet has its own orb), so we should turn away from them to focus on Scripture and the salvation of souls (B–C); the planets and their names (D); the sun's movement and the purported naming of the planets after ancient peoples (E); and a book by the Byzantine-Arab astronomer Qusṭā ibn Lūqā where astral distances are discussed (F).

Ibn al-Faḍl thus moves methodically through various astronomical terms, concepts, and debates suggested by Basil's denunciation of astronomers. As with many of Ibn al-Faḍl's other marginalia, they read like teaching notes that would aid him

125. *EI*², s.v. "Ḳibla, i"; Liritzis and Vassiliou, "Sunrise Day," 525–26.

126. The linguistic phenomenon may be related to one of the most important tasks of an astronomer working for Muslim patrons: calculating, for a given location, the direction of Mecca. See n. 49 above.

127. This note (unlike most if not all of Ibn al-Faḍl's other marginalia) has previously appeared in print, in Cheikho, "Makhṭūṭāt," 678–79. Until now it has received little further attention.

in answering questions that students reading this passage of Basil's *Hexaemeron* might ask. The note begins:[128]

الكواكب التي تظهر لقوم دون قوم، هي الكواكب الثابتة، ومن هاهنا¹ استدلّوا على أن شكل الأرض كريّ. وإنّما سُمِّيَتْ ثابتةً لا أنّها² غير متحركة، بل لأنّها بطيئة³ السير، وذلك أنّها تقطع الدرجة على رأيهم الضالّ في مائة سنة.

¹هاهنا: ب د ق؛ ههنا: ذ ²أنّها: ب د ق؛ لأنّها: ذ ³بطيئة: ذ ق؛ بطيت: ب د؛ بطئة: شيخو

> (A) The stars which appear to some people but not to others are the fixed stars (*al-kawākib al-thābita*). From this, [astronomers] inferred that the shape of the earth is spherical (*kurī*). Now, they were called "fixed" not because they are unmoving, but rather because their motion is slow; that is, they traverse one degree, according to their erring opinion, in a hundred years.

Here Ibn al-Faḍl is responding to the first astronomical activity Basil mentioned when he spoke of "those who measure the distances of the stars, who note down both those that are always visible and Arctic and those that lie around the South Pole and are visible to some but unknown to us."[129] In particular, he explains Basil's implicit allusion to the fixed stars by naming the fixed stars explicitly and saying that *they* are the stars that fit Basil's definition, for they are the stars that only some can see (i.e., because some northern stars cannot be seen in the south and vice versa).

Next, Ibn al-Faḍl moves to issues raised by the astronomical literature at least in part in connection with the fixed stars, issues that Basil had not even alluded to: the earth's roundness and the precession of the equinoxes. For "they" (astronomers) inferred that the earth is spherical from the fact that the fixed stars are visible only to some. Ibn al-Faḍl is referring here to Ptolemy's argument that the earth is curved not only in the east-west direction (as demonstrated by the later observation times of the same eclipse when viewed from further east) but also in the north-south direction (because as one moves northward, southern stars disappear behind the horizon).[130]

Ibn al-Faḍl does not dispute this claim here but instead moves on to another astronomical doctrine—namely, that the fixed stars are not as fixed as they may appear. He is not here referring to the trivial observation that the orb of the fixed stars appears to rotate around the earth once daily. Instead, he is referring to the very subtle motion of the fixed stars relative to their ordinary daily motion known as the precession of the equinoxes: the gradual change in the position of the sun at the vernal equinox (which we may call "the position of the vernal equinox" for short, relative to the fixed stars).

128. The entire note is at **B** $13_{\triangle 6}$–$14_{\triangle 12}$, **D** 6_{18}–7_{18}, **E** $[6]_{4\text{-}\triangle 1}$, **Q** 11–12, beginning at Basil, *Hexaemeron,* 1.4, ed. Amand de Mendieta and Rudberg, 8_4, at ἐκπληροῖ. I occasionally record Cheikho's reading as well, but not systematically.

129. See §1 above, pp. 263–64, part 2 of quotation.

130. Ptolemy, *Almagest,* 1.4.

Ptolemy held that the precession of the equinoxes was the result of a gradual motion of the heavenly sphere containing the fixed stars relative to the vernal equinox, which he considered to be fixed and unmoving.[131] Basing himself on the observations of Hipparchus, Ptolemy estimated that the fixed stars shifted or "precessed" one degree every hundred years.[132] This is precisely the figure given by Ibn al-Faḍl: "They traverse one degree . . . in a hundred years."

While indicating Ibn al-Faḍl's interest in Ptolemaic astronomy, this figure also suggests that his astronomy was not entirely up-to-date. Ptolemy's figure for precession had been corrected by al-Battānī (d. 929 CE), who found that it was 1 degree per 66 years.[133] The anonymous eleventh-century Byzantine astronomical treatise mentioned above, based as it is on Arabic sources, gives al-Battānī's figure of 1 degree per 66 years.[134] Ibn al-Faḍl, by contrast, gives Ptolemy's outdated figure.

If Basil was mocking astronomer-astrologers when he spoke of them concerning themselves with stars they cannot even see, and measuring trivial parameters, this is not the approach Ibn al-Faḍl's note takes. Instead, he presents these Ptolemaic theories in almost neutral tones, his opposition revealed only when he describes Ptolemaic precession as "their erring opinion." It seems that Ibn al-Faḍl's concern so far is primarily to elucidate the astronomical concepts that Basil mocked, even if he distances himself from them.

Ptolemy's *Almagest* was not the last word on precession. Ptolemy had thought that not only the vernal equinox but also the solar apogee—the point along the ecliptic where the sun is farthest from the earth—was constant and unmoving year after year. But al-Battānī discovered that the sun's apogee does not remain constant relative to the vernal equinox *but precesses along with the fixed stars.* In Islamic Spain, al-Zarqālī (d. 1100 CE) refined this picture with further observations revealing that the solar apogee *also* moves, at a much slower rate, relative to the *fixed stars*—that is, its movement relative to the vernal equinox is slightly different from that of the fixed stars.[135]

These discoveries heightened the sense that Ptolemy's physical model of the cosmos had to be revised or replaced. In a ninth-century astronomical work most likely written by Muḥammad ibn Mūsā ibn Shākir (one of the famous Banū Mūsā active in Baghdad) and known only from a later excerpt, objections are raised—on physical as well as geometrical grounds—to the theory that the daily motion of the heavens as well as precession can all be accounted for by the motion of several concentric heavenly spheres.[136]

131. Rome, "Les observations," 153.

132. Ptolemy, *Almagest,* 7.2, ed. Heiberg, 15_{15-18}; trans. Toomer, 328.

133. Battānī, *Kitāb al-Zīj al-Ṣābī,* §52 end, ed. Nallino, 3:192_{4-5}.

134. Jones, *Eleventh-Century Manual,* 19; see also n. 84 above.

135. Rome, "Les observations," 153. Rome's "1 degree per 299 years" should read "1 degree per 279 years."

136. Saliba, "Early Arabic Critique," with ed. and trans. of the excerpt. The text is apparently not extant but was quoted by Quṭb al-Dīn al-Shīrāzī in his *Faʿaltu fa-lā talum* as part of his elucidation of the *Tadhkira fī ʿilm al-hayʾa* of his teacher Naṣīr al-Dīn al-Ṭūsī.

If precession of the equinoxes caused a problem for the Ptolemaic model of concentric spheres moving each other, surely the corrections of al-Battānī and later al-Zarqālī would have shaken it even more fundamentally. After all, if the solar apogee generally moves along with the fixed stars and *also* moves slightly relative to them, then what exactly is embedded in what? Muḥammad ibn Mūsā (d. 873) was writing too early to benefit from al-Zarqālī's work, and probably from al-Battānī's as well; in any case he died before the publication of the first edition of al-Battānī's only extant work, his famous *Zīj* (after 880 CE, before February 901 CE).[137] Still, the ninth century was clearly a time when the Ptolemaic cosmos was being increasingly questioned on the basis of theory and observation. It is likely that these various critiques were interrelated.[138]

In any case, these texts would have been well known in astronomical circles by the eleventh century. Even if those circles did not include Ibn al-Faḍl, it seems that such critiques of Ptolemy articulated in Arabic might be at the background of Ibn al-Faḍl's comments as he continues his note:

وما أحسن ما قال القدّيس باسيليوس[1] إن اختلاف آراء الفلاسفة الضال وَتَضَادُّهُم[2] يغنينا عن المناقضة لهم. وذلك أن طائفة منهم تزعم أن أفلاك الكواكب مركوزة فيها، وقال آخرون: الكواكب متحركة دون الأفلاك، وقال قومٌ: هما[3] جميعاً متحركان، وقال قومٌ آخرون إنّه لا أفلاك لها، وإن الكواكب هي التي تتحرك[4] لا في أفلاك.

[1]باسيليوس: د ذ ق؛ باسليوس ب [2]وَتَضَادُّهُم: وتضادهم: ذ ق وشيخو؛ وتضاددهم: ب د [3]هما: ب د ق وشيخو؛ ــ ذ [4]تتحرك: د ذ ق؛ تحرك: ب

(B) How well Saint Basil put it when he said that the difference in the opinions of the erring philosophers and their mutual contradiction relieves us of the task of refuting them! (i) Some of them claim that the planetary orbs (*aflāk al-kawākib*) have [planets] implanted in them. (ii) Others say: the planets (*kawākib*) move below the orbs. (iii) Yet others say: they both move. (iv) Others say that [the planets] have no orbs but that the planets are themselves what move, not in orbs.

Here Ibn al-Faḍl first reiterates Basil's frequent refrain that philosophers' disagreements eliminate the need to refute them.[139] He then enumerates several physical models meant to explain how exactly the celestial orbs are responsible for the motion of the planets. The first is that each of the (seven) planetary orbs has a planet (including the sun and the moon) embedded in it. Thus the motion of each planetary sphere would cause the motion of each planet by carrying the planet along with it. The second theory seems to be that the planets are *not* implanted in orbs but rather move below their corresponding orbs. The third is that each planet has a corresponding orb but can move independently of that orb; such a theory

137. Preface to the *Zīj* by Nallino, 1:xxxii. Battānī's second edition of the text includes two observations made in Antioch in 901 CE.

138. This would fit the view of ninth-century Arabic astronomy proposed by Saliba, "Early Arabic Critique," 116.

139. A standard Christian argument against Hellenic philosophy, this approach is based on an argument made by the Skeptics: Karamanolis, *Philosophy*, 36.

might, for example, propose that the component of a planet's motion progressing parallel to the ecliptic was due to the planetary orb but that the planet also moved away from and toward the ecliptic, and additionally retrogressed and progressed, within that orb (this could be an attempt to describe the physical reality behind epicycles). Finally, the fourth theory Ibn al-Faḍl enumerates is that the orbs have no physical reality at all but that instead the planets move on their own.

In listing these various doctrines, Ibn al-Faḍl's ostensible purpose is to mock them as mutually contradictory, an attitude very much in line with Basil's approach. Still, by summarizing these positions here, he betrays enough interest in the cosmological models under debate to have read or heard about them and to have copied, translated, or summarized what he read in the margin. The models he describes correspond, at least somewhat, to known ancient theories. For example, Plato, in the *Timaeus,* proposed a model in which the fixed stars are implanted in an orb but the planets (and sun and moon) move independently below that orb.[140]

It is also worth noting that Ibn al-Faḍl's translation of Basil's passage subtly hints at Ibn al-Faḍl's own attraction to some of these models over others: where the Anonymous Translation refers to each planet traversing the whole celestial orb (*al-falak*), Ibn al-Faḍl's translation speaks of each planet traversing *its own orb* (*falakahu*).[141] This would suggest that he would favor one of the first three theories, with orbs corresponding to each planet, over the fourth. So even while Ibn al-Faḍl may express hostility toward astronomical theorizing, he seems at least implicitly to have his own preferred astronomical model.

All the same, as he proceeds, Ibn al-Faḍl continues to emphasize the need to reject astronomers' views and turn instead to Scripture for guidance:

كذا[1] قد[2] جرى أمرهم في ترتيب أفلاك الكواكب المتحيرة، وكون السماء وغير ذلك من أمر الموجودات. وهذا دليل على بُعدهم من الحقّ، وإذا كانت حالهم هذه الحال، فلا وجه للميل إلى مذاهبهم، بل الرضوخ للكتاب الإلهي فهو أنفع، وفي خلاص النفس من الأضاليل فهو أبلغ.

[1]كذا: ذ ق، وشيخو؛ كذى: ب د   [2]قد: د ذ ق؛ "قد": ب

(C) Thus did they proceed concerning the arrangement of the planetary orbs,[142] the generation (*kawn*) of the sky, and other such issues concerning the existent beings. This demonstrates their distance from the truth, and if this is the case with them, there is no reason for inclining towards their ways of thinking (*madhāhib*)—but rather [there is every reason for] submission to the Divine Book, for it is more beneficial, and [for concentrating] on the salvation of the soul from errors, for it is more lasting.

140. Gregory, "Astronomy," 101–4.

141. See §1 above, pp. 263–64, part 4 of the quotation.

142. Literally, "orbs of the wandering stars." Thus here he specifies what was only implicit in part B, that he is talking about the orbs of the *planets,* not the orb of the fixed stars.

One of Basil's broader points in the first homily is that Moses, as author of the book of Genesis, gives us all the cosmological knowledge that we need. Here Ibn al-Faḍl seems enthusiastically to concur, as he emphasizes that astronomical speculations are in vain and that one should accept the scriptural account of the cosmos and in any case focus one's efforts on the salvation of the soul rather than these debates that are so irrelevant to that awesome task. This position is quite consistent with the views expressed in the prefaces to his translations, especially in the preface to pseudo-Kaisarios's *Questions and Answers* (see chapter 4, §6).

Here we also see a subtler aspect of Ibn al-Faḍl's intellectual program and its context. He is not only saying that we should ignore astronomers because the Bible has all the truth we need. He is also saying that because astronomers get it all wrong, we *should not be tempted* to accept their views: "There is no reason for inclining towards their ways of thinking." From this we may conclude that Ibn al-Faḍl's audience might in fact have been tempted to listen to astronomers precisely because they seemed, in fact, to get so much right. The famous eleventh-century Muslim theologian and philosopher al-Ghazālī refers to this phenomenon directly when he observes that philosophers and especially mathematicians win over many people to their false cosmological views because of their astounding ability to prove certain things like mathematical theorems.[143] Indeed, astronomers could be quite impressive in their ability to predict celestial events like eclipses, so perhaps Ibn al-Faḍl's rhetorical strategy here is meant to counteract the impression that such successes extend even to those of their claims that were not so easy to verify. Perhaps Ibn al-Faḍl is referring to such a claim when he writes of astronomers' interest in "the generation of the sky": the claim that the celestial spheres have always existed, as Aristotle had concluded from what he took to be the uniform circular motion of the cosmos (see chapter 8).

At this point, Ibn al-Faḍl's note, having concluded one discussion, rather abruptly begins to describe the "wandering stars," or planets (including the sun and moon):

والكواكب المتحيرة سبعة، وإنّما سُمِّيَتْ متحيرة لمخالفة سيرها لسير الفلك ورجوعها كالحائر، هكذا تزعم هذه الطائفة. وهذه أسماؤها: زحل والمشتري والمريخ والشمس وعطارد والزهرة والقمر[1]. أمّا زحل فيقطع فلكه في ثلثين سنة، والمشتري في اثنتى عشرة[2] سنة، والمريخ في سنتين ونصف، والشمس وعطارد والزهرة في سنة واحدة، والقمر في شهر. وقد ذكر قومٌ آخرون أن مَسِيرَها على غير هذا النظام، ولم يزل الخلاف بينهم.

[1]زحل والمشتري . . . والقمر: ب د، وشيخو؛ وجاءت القائمة بدون واو الربط في «ذ» و«ق»: زحل المشتري المريخ الخ. [2]اثنتى عشرة: ذ؛ ا‹ثـ›نتى عشر‹ة›: ق؛ اثنى عشر: ب د

(D) (i) And the wandering stars [planets] are seven; (ii) indeed, they were called the wandering [or "confused": *mutaḥayyir*] stars (iii) because their motion is contrary to

143. Ghazālī, *al-Munqidh min al-ḍalāl,* trans. Khalidi, in Khalidi, *Medieval Islamic Philosophical Writings,* 68–69.

the motion of the celestial orb (iv) and because they turn back like one confused (*ḥāʾir*)—so claims this faction. (v) These are their names: (vi) Saturn (*zuḥal*), Jupiter (*al-mushtarī*), Mars (*al-mirrīkh*), the Sun (*al-shams*), Mercury (*ʿuṭārid*), Venus (*al-zuhara*), the Moon (*al-qamar*). (vii) As for Saturn, it traverses its celestial orb in thirty years; Jupiter [does so] in twelve years;[144] Mars in two and a half years; the Sun and Venus and Mercury in one year; the Moon in a month. (viii) Another group mentioned that their motion follows a different arrangement—(ix) and the disagreement among them still continues.

Here he offers the standard introduction to the wandering stars: they are seven in number and are called wandering because they move relative to the fixed stars, sometimes in retrograde motion (at the "stations" discussed in Basil's passage). He then gives their standard Arabic names and their periods. In doing so, he speaks of completing a period using the same language as his translation, saying that a planet "traverses its orb" (*yaqṭaʿ falakahu*), in contrast, as just discussed, to the Anonymous Translation, which speaks of traversing *the* celestial orb (*al-falak*).

At the same time, he continues to distance himself from astronomical doctrines. After explaining why the wandering stars are so called, he interjects, "so claims this faction," presumably meaning the astronomers. And after listing the planetary periods, he refers vaguely to a different "arrangement" of planetary motion, concluding—just as in his note on what the sky is made of[145]—with almost identically phrased emphasis on the continued bickering among specialists: "The disagreement among them still continues."[146]

The first disavowal (D.iv) seems a bit forced. After all, he is not even disavowing an astronomical doctrine here, only an etymological explanation for the term "wandering stars"; in this sense the disavowal should probably be read more broadly to refer to the model that gives the planets their name, in particular that of the celestial orb contrary to which the planets often move. And in the very next line, his note sounds matter-of-fact as he lists the planets' names.

This abrupt back-and-forth, between disavowal and neutral description, is best explained as a feature of notes to oneself. These notes might have aided Ibn al-Faḍl in responding to questions arising in connection with the astronomical content of Basil's passage. They did not therefore need perfectly smooth transitions but were more like bullet-point lists, each bit dealing with a different aspect—and perhaps drawn from a different source.

144. In a refutation of the world's eternity in *Tahāfut al-falāsifa*, al-Ghazālī refers to the same figures for the periods of Saturn and Jupiter; see Hillier, "Al-Ghazālī's Argument," 85 n. 33.

145. See ch. 8, §1, p. 235; that note on qualities appears later in the text than the one currently under discussion.

146. The two phrases differ only by a single letter: the note on the sky has *khilāf*, where this note on stars has *khulf*.

Indeed, the impression that Ibn al-Faḍl's note on astronomy was gathered from different sources is strengthened by the observation that part D, just presented above, is an adapted translation of one of the Greek notes appearing in at least four Greek manuscripts of Basil's *Hexaemeron,* beside the very same passage.[147] The Greek note, first added to a copy of Basil's text in the tenth century or earlier, remarks that (i) there are seven wandering stars, (ii) also known as wanderers (*planētai*) (iii) because of their contrary motion (iv) and their changing location (relative to the fixed stars), which suggests they are not "implanted (ἐμπεπῆχθαι) in the sky" like the fixed stars. Only this last item (iv) is substantively different from Ibn al-Faḍl's note, especially because Ibn al-Faḍl omitted the final contrast between the planets and the fixed stars (though earlier in his note, B.i, he had mentioned a theory that the planets are "implanted," *markūza,* not in a single orb like the fixed stars but rather each in their own orb).

The Greek note continues with a detailed list of the planets (v–vi), providing three names for most of the planets (the epithet, followed by the "Hellenic" and "Egyptian" names) and including a digression on the early and erroneous distinction between the morning and evening star. It also reports an alternative Egyptian planetary order. Ibn al-Faḍl's note is much more succinct at this point, simply listing the planets using their standard Arabic names.

Ibn al-Faḍl lists the planets not in the order of the Greek note but rather in the alternate "Egyptian" order. This does not necessarily mean that Ibn al-Faḍl derived his list from that Egyptian order, since it is one of the standard orders. Indeed, it is very similar to Ptolemy's order, only with Venus and Mercury swapped (a typical variation in planetary orders); crucially, Ibn al-Faḍl, unlike the Greek note but like Ptolemy, places the Sun in the middle of the list. Ptolemy's order continued to be standard in contemporary Byzantine astronomy: Symeon Seth, in his Greek *Synopsis of Physics,* follows it in his list of the planets.[148]

This standardization is also reflected in the straightforward presentation of planetary order in both Ibn al-Faḍl's note and Symeon Seth's account. By contrast, the Greek note, which continued to be transmitted at least until the fourteenth century, attests to a different emphasis: by preserving alternate orders and names, it suggests an interest in the history of the discipline. In Ibn al-Faḍl and Symeon Seth, that history is flattened: planetary order has become, at least as they present it, a simple fact.

Finally, the Greek note ends with (vii) the planetary periods of the Moon, Sun, Venus, and Mercury and (viii) the remark that the identical periods of the last

147. Ed. Pasquali, "Doxographica," 198–99, no. 14 (the seventh of those summarized above in §1), at Amand de Mendieta and Rudberg, 8_3 καὶ διὰ. For the four manuscripts, see ch. 7, p. 220, n. 89.

148. §32, in Delatte, *Anecdota,* 2:38–39.

three explains "why [their order is inconsistent]"[149]—probably referring to the different planetary orders already mentioned (which involve permutations of the Sun, Venus, and Mercury). Ibn al-Faḍl's note includes this same information about periods but supplements it with the omitted periods of Saturn, Jupiter, and Mars. As for the final remark about inconsistent order (missing from three of the four manuscripts containing the Greek note and fragmentary in the oldest of the four), Ibn al-Faḍl has adapted it to imply not only divergent theories (viii) but also empty controversy among astronomers (ix).

This is where the Greek note ends, but Ibn al-Faḍl's note continues:

وذكر أصحاب التعاليم أنّ حركة الشمس ليست كحركة الفلك المحيط بها، بل متحركة حركة تحدث شكلاً معوَّجاً[١]. وذكروا أنّ هذه الأسماء قديمة لأُناسٍ قدماء. أمّا زحل فكان[٢] ملكاً[٣] على المصريّين، أمّا المشتري فعلى الأسيريين[٤]، وأمّا الشمس فعلى الافريغون (كذا)، وأمّا القمر فعلى الصقالبة[٥]، وأمّا المريخ فعلى الأتراكي (كذا)، وأما عطارد فكان مؤدَّباً[٦].

[١]شكلاً معوَّجاً: ذ ق؛ شكلٌ معوجٌ: ب د   [٢]فكان: د ذ ق؛ +[[الشمس]]: ب   [٣]ملكاً: ذ؛ ملكـ'ا': ق ؛ ملكٌ: ب د   [٤]الأسيريين: ذ؛ الاسيريون: د ق؛ الاسيريوا: ب   [٥]الصقالبة: ب د ذ؛ السقالبة: ق   [٦]مؤدَّباً: ب ذ ق؛ مودبٌ: د

(E) (i) The mathematicians mentioned that the sun's motion is not like the motion of the orb that surrounds it, but that instead its motion produces [i.e., traces out] a bent shape. (ii) They mentioned that these names are ancient, belonging to ancient people: Zuḥal [Saturn] was a king of the Egyptians; al-Mushtarī [Jupiter], of the Assyrians; the Sun, of the Phrygians (?); the Moon, of the Slavs; al-Mirrīkh [Mars], of the Turks; and ʿUṭārid [Mercury] was a cultivated man.[150]

Ibn al-Faḍl does not challenge the statement about the sun's motion, and rather than leave it anonymous, he ascribes it to the "mathematicians," a label that seems neutral, not pejorative. Given that his previous sentence (D.ix) referred to the continuing disagreement between astronomers, it seems that here yet again his note has shifted abruptly to a different tone and subject—perhaps from a different source.

Ibn al-Faḍl then ends his note by shifting to yet another topic:

وأمّا أبعاد الكواكب من الأرض فقد ذكره قسطا ابن[١] لوقا في المدخل إلى الفلسفة.

[١] ابن: ب د ق؛ بن: ذ

(F) And as for the distances of the stars/planets from the earth, Qusṭā ibn Lūqā mentioned it in his *Introduction to Philosophy.*

Here again, he is clearly responding to Basil's text, which had said that astronomers measure the "distances of the stars"; here in the note Ibn al-Faḍl uses the same Arabic to render this phrase as in his own translation (*ab ʿād al-kawākib*), distinct here from the Anonymous Translation (*maqādīr al-nujūm wa-ab ʿādahā*).

149. Pasquali supplied the last phrase from the Greek note's source for this line.

150. This final identification recalls the Arabic legends about Hermes, for which see van Bladel, *Arabic Hermes,* esp. chs. 4–5.

In this final line of Ibn al-Faḍl's note, there is no longer any trace of Basil's aim of critiquing and dismissing astronomy.

Throughout the note, Ibn al-Faḍl has been discussing astronomy without revealing his sources. As we have seen, part of his note must derive from Greek marginalia in a Byzantine copy of Basil's *Hexaemeron*. Here in the final line, Ibn al-Faḍl explicitly refers the reader to what seems to be a work on astronomy. Rather than list the distances of the stars himself, he cites a specific book by the astronomer and physician Qusṭā ibn Lūqā (ninth/tenth century), an Arabic-speaking Byzantine Chalcedonian Christian of Greater Syria like Ibn al-Faḍl himself. The way Ibn al-Faḍl cites the book suggests that he had seen it or read it.

Which book was it? The bibliographers Ibn al-Nadīm, Ibn al-Qifṭī, and Ibn Abī Uṣaybiʿa do not mention a book with this exact title in their entries on Qusṭā, but they do mention the sort of book that Ibn al-Faḍl might have had in mind. Ibn al-Qifṭī says that Qusṭā wrote an *Introduction to Theoretical Astronomy and the Movements of the Orbs and Stars.*[151] Ibn al-Nadīm says he wrote an *Introduction to Astronomy.*[152] These two titles may refer to a single work by Qusṭā.[153] A work by Qusṭā on theoretical astronomy (*hayʾa*)—probably to be identified with this work mentioned by the bibliographers—is preserved in a manuscript in Oxford; part of it is also to be found in a manuscript in Damascus.[154]

If this is the book Ibn al-Faḍl meant, why does his note call the book by an unattested title that does not refer at all to the book's subject matter, neither *hayʾa* (theoretical astronomy) nor *ʿilm al-nujūm* (astronomy or astrology)? One possible explanation is that his original marginal note *did* refer to an *Introduction to Theoretical Astronomy,* but that the last word of the title (which is also the last word of his entire marginal note) was distorted in transmission, with "theoretical astronomy" (*al-hayʾa*) becoming "philosophy" (*al-falsafa*). The two Arabic words do not look very similar, but if part of the word *hayʾa* had been damaged (not unlikely for the last word in a marginal note, which might have been written at the edge of a page), it is not so difficult to see how a later scribe might have interpreted the first three letters and last two letters of *al-hayʾa* as the beginning and end of *al-falsafa*—

151. *Kitāb al-madkhal ilā l-hayʾa wa-ḥarakāt al-aflāk wa-l-kawākib:* Ibn al-Qifṭī, ed. Lippert, 262_{17}–263_{1}. Ibn Abī Uṣaybiʿa lists a similar title that probably refers to the same work (*Kitāb fī l-hayʾa wa-tarkīb al-aflāk*): ed. Riḍā, $330_{⌂9}$. (Not in Ibn al-Nadīm.)

152. *Kitāb al-madkhal ilā ʿilm al-nujūm:* Ibn al-Nadīm, ed. Sayyid, $2{:}294_{2-3}$ = Flügel 295. Also listed by Ibn Abī Uṣaybiʿa, ed. Riḍā, $330_{⌂3-⌂2}$. (Not in Ibn al-Qifṭī.)

153. So suggests Saliba, "Early Arabic Critique," 119–20. Since Ibn Abī Uṣaybiʿa lists both Ibn al-Nadīm's title and a modified version of Ibn al-Qifṭī's title, it is possible that Ibn Abī Uṣaybiʿa, has transformed one work into two.

154. Oxford, Bodleian, Arabic MS Arch. Seld. 11, no. 2; Damascus, Ẓāhirīya Library, 4489. Sezgin, *GAS*, 6:181–82; supplemented and corrected by Saliba, "Early Arabic Critique," 119–20, who noted (n. 23) that the text was to be published by Régis Morelon.

especially in a manuscript lacking diacritical dots, and especially if the word *hayʾa* had been stretched, as final words often are in Arabic manuscripts. Alternatively, perhaps Ibn al-Faḍl really did mean to refer to a work by Qusṭā, otherwise unattested, called the *Introduction to Philosophy.* This title would suggest a compendious work beginning with logic and perhaps including a section on astronomy, not unlike the anonymous Byzantine *Logic and Quadrivium* of 1007–1008. Either way, Ibn al-Faḍl is clearly referring to a work or part of a work by Qusṭā that would have been technical enough to provide "distances of stars," a method for measuring them, or both.

Again in contrast to Basil's purpose of critiquing and mocking astronomy as a pointless discipline, Ibn al-Faḍl's apparently approving or at least neutral citation of Qusṭā ibn Lūqā leaves a different impression: in this note, he is simply providing information about where to find a certain type of astronomical parameter—indeed, precisely the parameter with which Basil began his ridicule of astronomy: "the distances of the stars." Basil's description (and Ibn al-Faḍl's translation of it) probably refers (as the reference to Qusṭā certainly does) to the linear distance between the earth and a given planet, as mentioned. It might also refer to the arc-distance between stars or planets relative to some reference point like the ecliptic. Both sorts of astral distances are discussed by Ptolemy.[155]

Ibn al-Faḍl's purpose was not to subvert Basil. Instead, as already mentioned, his note makes most sense if we read it as teaching notes or explanatory textual notes, much like the Greek annotations in Byzantine manuscripts of the *Hexaemeron:* without endorsing astronomy, they nevertheless indicate that readers wished to know what Basil was talking about—and that a learned translator like Ibn al-Faḍl sought to provide that background, even for a discipline Basil condemned. Such solicitude for the curious reader suggests that Ibn al-Faḍl considered at least some astronomical questions worth asking, or at least unavoidable. Why else would he refer the reader to a book containing astronomical parameters?

Ibn al-Faḍl's note thus began with an emphasis on the internal contradiction of astronomy but quickly shifted to providing straightforward astronomical background to Basil's critique. Ibn al-Faḍl defined "fixed stars," then mentioned precession, which he considers to be an error (A). He stressed Basil's point that natural philosophers all contradict each other by mentioning several divergent theories about the motion of the planets and the question of whether they are "implanted" in the celestial orbs (B), then declared this to be vain speculation that should be

155. *Almagest:* mostly arc-distances, but also linear distances, e.g., "of the moon" (5.13), "of the sun" (5.15); trans. Toomer, 29. In the *Planetary Hypotheses,* Ptolemy discusses the distances of the planetary spheres (each distance referred to in the Arabic translation as a *buʿd*) and his corresponding calculations for the sizes of the planets; 1.2.4–5, trans. (from Arabic) Goldstein, "Arabic Version," 7–8, manuscript reproduction at 31.

abandoned in favor of Scripture (C). But then he nevertheless continued to describe astronomy, adapting a Greek note in his exemplar to present a list of the planets and their periods (D). Apparently drawing on a different source (or sources), he then referred to the doctrine of a specific group (the Ptolemaic "mathematicians," in contrast to Peripatetic "natural philosophers") on the sun's motion and reproduced mythology associated with each of the planets' names (E). Finally, he concluded with a quick memorandum about the astronomical content of a book by a specific practitioner of astronomy, the Byzantine Christian Qusṭā ibn Lūqā.

3 ASTROLOGY

Clearly Ibn al-Faḍl, like Basil himself and the Byzantine scholars who annotated Greek copies of Basil's homilies, took an interest in astronomy. The astronomical issues he mentions, especially the question of precession, were of interest to contemporary astronomers writing in Arabic. Why then was he, like Basil, so hostile to astronomers? The answer lies in the intimate connection between the pure science of astronomy and its practical application, astrology, in antiquity and the Middle Ages. Al-Battānī, in addition to his "strictly astronomical" work, had written a commentary on Ptolemy's astrological *Tetrabiblos*, as already mentioned. Al-Zarqālī (eleventh century) also wrote an astrological treatise on the influences of the heavenly bodies on earthly events. Astronomers and astrologers were usually one and the same.[156]

As for Ibn al-Faḍl's attitude toward astrology, we do not need to divine it, since two works of his dealing with the topic survive and have been recently translated into English and annotated by Samuel Noble: an *Essay Containing Ideas Useful for the Soul*,[157] whose first part concerns astrology, and a very brief *Refutation of Astrology*.[158]

Furthermore, one of Ibn al-Faḍl's annotations on a translation shows that he felt very strongly about astrology. As we saw in chapters 5–6, Ibn al-Faḍl's *Garden*, a translation of the *Loci communes*, contains many brief comments that were almost certainly written by Ibn al-Faḍl himself.[159] One of these comments is a rejection of astrology.

In the section of the *Garden* on education, we read:[160]

156. Saliba, "Role."

157. Ed. Sbath, *Vingt traités*, 131–48; trans. Noble, "ʿAbdallah," 174–84. I use Noble's translation of the title.

158. Ed. and trans. Graf, "Die Widerlegung," 340–42; trans. Noble, "ʿAbdallah," 184–86.

159. See ch. 5, §1, and ch. 6, §3.

160. Ibn al-Faḍl, *Garden*, *bāb* 17 (*fī l-adab* ~ περὶ παιδείας καὶ φιλοσοφίας καὶ παίδων ἀνατροφῆς), **V** 118^r; **S** 299^v–300^r = *Loci communes*, 17.29/35, ed. Ihm, 411.

وقال افلاطن: كل علم يبعُد من العدل وغيره[١] من الفضائل فقد ظهر خُبْثاً كُلّيّاً لا حكمة.

[١]وغيره: س؛ وعبره: ف

Plato said: Every science (*ʿilm* ~ ἐπιστήμη) that is distant from justice and the other virtues has shown itself to be total wickedness, not wisdom.

Plato is saying that knowledge that fails to aim at justice or some other good end is not wisdom but wickedness: knowledge on its own is not morally good, not even neutral, but bad. *Epistēmē* and *ʿilm* mean "knowledge" or "science," but they need not refer to the specialized study of natural phenomena as the modern English word "science" must. This saying certainly makes no mention of astronomy or astrology.

Nor, it should be mentioned, does the context from which this quotation was taken have anything to do with astrology. It is an excerpt from Plato's *Menexenus*, a dialogue mostly consisting of Socrates delivering a hypothetical speech for the Athenian war dead. Astrology is not mentioned anywhere in the dialogue, and indeed, the only mention of science at all is this single quotation, which is pronounced as a sort of proverb to explain why bodily beauty and strength is discordant with cowardice (just as knowledge must aim at virtue to be wisdom, so too bodily beauty and strength must be directed at virtuous deeds to be praiseworthy).[161]

Nevertheless, Ibn al-Faḍl's response to this saying makes clear that he read it as a reference to the dangers of technical, specialized natural science not founded on the pursuit of the good. In particular, this made him think of astrology:

شرح: إنّ أصحاب علم الأحكام الذين يرفعون الفضيلة عن فاعلها، واالرذيلة[١] أيضاً، بإسنادِهم هذين وما شاكلهما من سائر الأمور إلى الكواكب، وجَعْلِهم إيّاها السبب فيها، يسمعون هذه القضية الكلية المُوجبة الصادقة، فإن أوجبوا لها نُطقاً، فيَبِسَ[٢] النطقُ، إذ كان يوجب أموراً تنكرها عقولنا نحن الذين نكابد مضارّ الجسم، فلا[٣] يكاد يصفو، أَفَجا<ءَ>نا بسببه؛ وإن حكموا عليها بأنّها أجرام غير ناطقة، وأنّ علة العلل، تقدّس اسمه، المُحرِّك لها <هـ>ـو الذي[٤] خصّها بهذه الأدلّة، فقد غَرِقُوا في بحرٍ[٥] الشناعة غاية الغَرَق والسلم.

[١]واالرذيلة: س؛ في الرذيلة: ف [٢]فيَبِسَ: ف؛ فبيس (أي فَبَئِسَ): س [٣]فلا: س؛ ولا: ف [٤]<هـ>ـو الذي: والذي: س؛ الذي: ف [٥]بحر: ف؛ بحرا: س [٦]والسلم: وقد يكون المقصود: والشَّنَع.

Commentary: The practitioners of the science of verdicts [i.e., astrology], who remove virtue from its agent and also vice by attributing both [virtue and vice] and other similar things to the stars and making them the cause of those things, hear this true, affirmative, universal proposition.[162] If they affirm (1) that [the stars] have rationality, then rationality is barren, since it would affirm things denied by the minds of those of us who struggle against the drawbacks of body, which is far from being pure—and now it comes to us with the cause of it?[163] And if [astrologers] judge (2) that [the stars] are non-rational bodies and that the cause of causes, hallowed be

161. Plato, *Menexenus* 246e4–247a2; cited by Ihm, 411.

162. Here we have yet another example of his predilection for using the technical terms of Arabic logic, even when, strictly speaking, unnecessary.

163. *a-fa-jāʾanā bi-sababihi*, perhaps meaning that body (here a celestial body) is supposed to be providing the cause of rationality (?).

> his name, who causes them to move <is the one> who endowed them with these [prognostic] indicators (*adilla*),[164] then they have become immersed in a sea of repugnance, end of story (*wa-l-salām*).

Ibn al-Faḍl begins with the objection to astrology that astrology implies determinism, which eliminates moral responsibility by ascribing good and bad deeds not to the agent but to the stars. As we have seen, this objection is predominant in the ancient and medieval anti-astrological tradition.

He then proceeds with the dialectic: either the stars are rational beings or they are not. If astrologers say that stars are rational, then it is rationality in name only, bearing no rational fruit. The text is not quite clear to me at this point, but Ibn al-Faḍl seems to explain this statement by saying that the verdicts of the stars make no sense to anyone who seeks to control bodily impulses by means of higher rationality. (This reading is supported, as we shall see, by Ibn al-Faḍl's *Refutation of Astrology.*) On the other hand, if the astrologers say that stars are not rational but are caused to move and given their portentous powers by God, then their position is even more repugnant. Presumably this is because then God would be the cause of evil and an abettor of those who fail to control their bodily passions.[165]

This note is particularly striking because it is a very specific response to a general aphorism about knowledge. Plato's broad remark about the wickedness of knowledge not directed toward justice and the good made Ibn al-Faḍl think immediately of astrology—apparently for him the ultimate example of an immoral science.

What made astrology so repugnant to him? If we turn to his two essays refuting astrology, we see that his approach in the first part of his *Essay Containing Ideas Useful for the Soul* contains a classic argument against determinism,[166] similar to what we just saw in his note on Plato's saying in the *Garden.* He sets out to refute three different positions: (1) "that human affairs are determined by the stars," (2) that God causes evil, and (3) that events happen by chance without God's providence.[167] His arguments dealing with the first focus on preserving human agency, whose necessity means that the stars cannot be the cause of "virtues and vices." (In the process, he showcases a syllogism and references Aristotle's *Ethics* and *Physics.*)[168]

164. Burnett, *EI*³, s.v. "Astrology": "Arabic astrologers use the word *dalla* ('to indicate or guide') for the action of the stars."

165. Such a reading is supported by a similarly worded passage in Ibn al-Faḍl's *Refutation of Astrology,* §4, ed. Graf, "Die Widerlegung," 342; trans. (modified) Noble, "ʿAbdallah," 186: "that God, may his name be sanctified, who, as the religious laws and philosophers agree, is good and pure, is the cause of evils because he is the one who created the stars and gave them these properties."

166. ¶¶2–6, ed. Sbath, *Vingt traités,* 132–35; trans. Noble, "ʿAbdallah," 174–76.

167. ¶2, trans. Noble, "ʿAbdallah," 174.

168. ¶¶4–5, trans. Noble, "ʿAbdallah," 175. On Ibn al-Faḍl's sources for Aristotle's works here, including Nemesios's *On the Nature of Man* (sometimes perhaps via John of Damascus), see ibid., 175–76 nn. 12–16 (printed on p. 318).

In other words astrology (at least "hard" astrology) implies determinism, which would mean no human agency. So determinism, and thus (hard) astrology, must be misguided.

But for a better sense of what made Ibn al-Faḍl think that astrology epitomized *immoral* and not merely misguided or false knowledge, his other essay, the *Refutation of Astrology,* offers a clue. In it, he begins by declaring that astrology is "Satanic," then presents five arguments to demonstrate that it is irrational and "incompatible with what the definitions of philosophy affirm" (§0).[169] Here Ibn al-Faḍl is yet again using technical philosophical terms: "definition" (*ḥadd*) and "affirm" (*awjaba*) are both standard terms in Arabic logic. Interestingly, the arguments he presents go beyond the usual objection that astrology implies determinism, though that objection also makes an appearance (in §4). Instead, he is mainly concerned with astrology's moral premises. His argument is as follows.

Astrologers all agree that wealth and the enjoyment of food, drink, and other pleasures constitute good fortune, whereas philosophers say the opposite is true, that deprivation and sadness lead one toward contemplation and so are in truth good fortune (§1).[170] "The philosopher is he who resembles God," and the only way to resemble God is to practice renunciation in this world, including poverty and other states that astrologers consider to be misfortune; the one who is absorbed in pleasures is, as Galen said in his *Ethics,*[171] like the worm and the pig—which can hardly be considered good fortune (§2). Humans have three souls, according to philosophers: the intellecting, immortal soul in the brain, the irascible soul in the heart, and the appetitive soul in the liver; the last two we share with animals, and so the astrologers, who associate good fortune with the pleasurable satisfaction of desires, consider the most fortunate human being to be the one who most closely resembles beasts (§3). Also, if the stars determine everything about our character and traits, then there is no personal responsibility (§4). For understanding his way of thinking, his last point is telling: astrologers "believe that man will only die when the degree of the ascendant loses the two lucky (stars) and acquires the two unlucky (stars); but jurists (*aṣḥāb al-sharʿ*) and philosophers agree that the beginning of every good man's good fortune is the moment of his dissolution (*ḥalāla*) from this defective body (*hādhā l-jasadi dhī l-āfāt*),[172] since he frees himself from the company of beasts and joins the spiritual beings (*rūḥānīyīn*)" (§5).

169. I use paragraph numbers to refer to this text, although Graf's edition has none. I call the first line the *title,* the following paragraph §0 (the proem), then the rest of the paragraphs I number §1, §2, §3, etc., to correspond to Ibn al-Faḍl's phrases *wa-l-wajh al-thānī, wa-l-wajh al-thālith,* etc.

170. For the close ties between the Byzantine concepts of philosopher and monk, see ch. 4, n. 35.

171. Lost in the Greek, this book survives in an Arabic epitome, where the relevant passage is at the end of *maqāla* 1 (as noted by Daiber, "Graeco-Arabica," 4 and n. 6), ed. Kraus, "Kitāb al-Akhlāq," 34 ¶2. See also Noble, "ʿAbdallah," 185 n. 37 (printed on p. 320).

172. *Lisān* s.v. *ʾwf.* Cf. Graf: "von diesem vergänglichen Leibe."

4 CONCLUSION

Ibn al-Faḍl was not an astronomer-astrologer, nor, we may surmise, did his sessions with his teachers of Greek involve astrological texts. And yet to teach a text of Christian exegesis, Basil's *Hexaemeron*, and present it to the readers of his revised translation, he needed to have a basic sense of this prestigious science.

In continuing Basil's tradition of *learned* critique of astronomy and astrology, Ibn al-Faḍl was not alone. Instead, his marginalia can be seen quite tangibly as part of the Byzantine commentary tradition upon which he drew to produce his own notes on the astronomy referenced by Basil's text.

We see here a tradition in action: not mindlessly assenting to the words of authority but working generation after generation to preserve the tradition through rational exertion. Basil's dismissal of astronomy's vanity was not enough for Ibn al-Faḍl, for in his day too, mathematicians, natural philosophers, and just about anyone who wished to know his or her chances to lead a prosperous and pleasant life remained captivated by the stars. But at the same time, he had no wish to dispense with astronomy altogether. Instead, for Ibn al-Faḍl, the problem with stargazing—even if one did not embrace determinism at the cost of free will and moral responsibility—was that it could distract one from truly worthwhile pursuits and produce an immoral, worldly obsession with pleasure and material comfort. And so Ibn al-Faḍl read about the stars and strove to convince others to conceive of the heavens in a pious way consistent with Basil's exposition, and to shun the way of the pigs and the worms.

10

A SHARED SCHOLARLY CULTURE

Reading Ibn al-Faḍl's Arabic marginalia and translations has brought a whole tradition of philosophical education into greater focus. It has also allowed us to perceive how Ibn al-Faḍl read that tradition. For him, philosophy as practiced by the likes of Empedocles, Plato, Aristotle, Proklos, Philoponos, al-Fārābī, and Avicenna was neither harmless nor entirely worthless. Instead, ancient and contemporary philosophy was at the same time dangerous and indispensable. For how could one hope to think without it? How could one begin to articulate, let alone assent to the truth which it was the duty of all believers to proclaim? Confronted with fallacious arguments directed against the truth, how, without philosophy, could one overcome them? If to philosophize was to approach divinity, then how could one hope to be saved in a manner befitting the followers of a human god, a god-human, whose very humanity was precisely what allowed his followers to become like him and so like God and so be saved?

But it was dangerous too. Without guidance, without a moral compass, it was easy to become mired in the errors and led astray by the sophistries that had accumulated over the centuries.

And so this learned deacon at the edge of the Byzantine Empire in Antioch-on-the-Orontes applied himself to translating texts of whose authority there could be no doubt, whose benefit to the mind and the soul was beyond question: the works of divine men whose sanctity the Byzantine Church—one, holy, universal, and apostolic—had long recognized, the fathers of the church. It was no coincidence that these texts were some of the same texts being translated at the same time by Georgians around Antioch, for Chalcedonian Christians in northern Syria (and elsewhere in the Byzantine Empire) were carrying out parallel parts of a single project to implement in their own languages a Byzantine ecclesiastical curriculum being promoted by Byzantine churchmen, backed by the wealth and prestige of something they called the Roman Empire.

Many of these texts had already been available in Arabic before Ibn al-Faḍl retranslated them, just as many had been available in Georgian before the Athonites Euthymios and George did their work. And yet even these retranslations were something new. They were clearer. They were more palatable to refined Arab ears. Sometimes they dazzled. With the irresistible rhythm and tempered pitch of the great orators—Chrysostom, Basil, Gregory—whose periods they rendered, these new Arabic translations mediated their divine thoughts for those raised on Syria's new tongue, yes, but also their divine Hellenic voices, trained in Attica and Antioch, that they might again be heard by the banks of the Orontes.

In retranslation as in other things, Ibn al-Faḍl and his Georgian colleagues were thoroughly Byzantine. Constantinople's elite—devoted to the saints who helped and protected them and infused their privileged world with meaning, and thirsty for the Attic prose that filled their days and nights with delight like a mountain spring or a holy hymn or a boat ride on the Bosphorus—consumed volumes and volumes of Metaphrastic lives. These saints' lives, dressed in Attic attire, unfolding in accordance with the ancient rules of Greek rhetoric, were metaphrases, "translations" from low- to high-style Greek, of preexisting saints' lives. The stories they told were nothing new. But the deeds and miracles that had once been rattled off in the humble parataxis of popular storytelling were now sung in a manner congruous with their holiness, like bones shining from within a reliquary. For Symeon the Metaphrast and his team, for Emperor Basil II, for Patriarch John III Polites of Antioch,[1] and for generations of elite Byzantine readers, this was a worthy literary achievement. In replacing old, perfectly usable translations with finer stuff, Ibn al-Faḍl and other Antiochian translators were, in their own languages (and with two sources, the earlier translation and the original Greek), doing much the same.

This metaphrastic purpose was not among the motives that Ibn al-Faḍl chose to emphasize in his translations' prefaces, though it was implicit in the Arabic rhymed prose of the prefaces themselves. Instead he offered weightier justification for his tireless efforts: not only the wishes of his patrons and the authority of the translated Christian texts but also and especially the utility of these texts as a replacement and antidote for the pointless and dangerous questions preoccupying Christians of his day, questions covering a wide array of topics, from grammar and philology to logic, arithmetic, geometry, physics, and metaphysics. These topics together make up a significant portion of what, in antiquity and the Middle Ages, was called philosophy.

1. Kontouma ("Jean III," 139) has argued that John III Polites, patriarch of Antioch (996–1021), was associated with Byzantine Metaphrastic circles.

Ibn al-Faḍl's marginalia have allowed us to qualify his disavowal of philosophy. These marginalia attest to Ibn al-Faḍl's educational agenda: his effort to use authoritative Byzantine Christian texts, in his new and updated Arabic translations, to teach students to think about a range of subjects belonging to a "secular" education: grammar (Greek and Arabic), logic, and more advanced disciplines such as physics, cosmology, and astronomy.

Thus Ibn al-Faḍl recommended ignorance of philosophy while in his own marginalia (drawing on Byzantine marginalia and the Arabic Aristotle) he demonstrated abundant familiarity with a variety of philosophical topics and clearly expected his students and readers to do the same. In this, he was a product of the scholarly culture of his time, shared with Jewish, Christian, Muslim, Sabian, and other peers writing in Greek, Syriac, Arabic, Armenian, Georgian, and Persian. This culture was at once rational and dogmatic, open-minded and partisan: parochial in its axioms, universal in its conclusions, unquestioningly loyal and "religious" in aspiration, critical and "scientific" in execution.

1 METHOD AND MADNESS

For a concrete sense of this shared scholarly culture, let us consider another eleventh-century scholar, the Sunni Muslim "reviver of religion" (*mujaddid*) Abū Ḥāmid al-Ghazālī (1058–1111). Al-Ghazālī is perhaps best known for his attack on the doctrines of "the philosophers,"[2] such as the world's pre-eternity, but his engagement with ancient philosophy was complicated. In his autobiographical narrative *Deliverer from Error* (*al-Munqidh min al-ḍalāl*), al-Ghazālī describes that he was overcome by an epistemological crisis: how could he know that Islam was the true religion? The ensuing period of skepticism, he explains, convinced him to study several systems of knowledge that he regarded as potential paths to the truth: Muslim theology (*kalām*), Shiite esotericism (*bāṭinīya*), Avicennan philosophy (*falsafa*), and finally direct experience of the divine (Sufism). It is easy to take his attacks on "philosophers" at face value and suppose that he rejected the Aristotelian tradition as a whole, seeking to replace it with a fundamentalist return to the Qur'an, Hadith, Muslim theology, and Islamic law. And yet al-Ghazālī followed the great Aristotelian philosopher Avicenna when it came to topics covered by philosophy. Indeed, al-Ghazālī was one of a number of Sunni scholars who in the eleventh century systematically incorporated Avicenna's philosophy into Sunni Muslim theology.[3] In his magnum opus on worship, customs, vices, and virtues—the ambitiously titled *Revival of the Religious Sciences*—al-Ghazālī's account of

2. Arberry, *Revelation*, 61.

3. Wisnovsky, "One Aspect." Avicennan philosophy in later Islamic legal education: Hodgson, *Venture*, 2:48–49.

"mystical cognition and eschatology" is essentially Avicennan, as Alexander Treiger has shown, except that al-Ghazālī fastidiously replaced key Avicennan (philosophical) terms with other words.[4] This is not to diminish what al-Ghazālī was trying to do: break free from the doctrinal baggage of the ancient philosophical tradition and its terminology while grounding his system of knowledge and thought in the Qur'an and the words and deeds of Muḥammad. It is simply to observe that to undertake this project, he deliberately drew on the philosophical system in which, by his own account, he had been trained—just like Ibn al-Faḍl.

This phenomenon was not restricted to the Islamic world or Arabic-speaking scholars. Niketas Stethatos (d. ca. 1090), a Byzantine theologian and monk at the Stoudite Monastery in Constantinople, ostensibly opposed "external learning" in a number of his works.[5] In his masterful *Life* of his spiritual teacher Saint Symeon the New Theologian (ca. 949–1022), Stethatos describes Symeon's confrontation with the sophistical attacks of the high patriarchal official Stephen of Alexina, whose book learning and "sharp tongue" are no match for Symeon's humility and divinely granted wisdom.[6] Stethatos himself was involved in a polemical exchange with a certain "sophist" Gregory who had critiqued something Stethatos had written about the soul and the "paradise of the mind." On the other hand, Stethatos wrote philosophical works on free will, moral action, and the faculties of the soul. Perhaps unsurprisingly, Stethatos covered in his works a range of topics that maps closely onto Ibn al-Faḍl's translations, including fifteen exegetical homilies on the hexaemeron (the six-day creation narrative of Genesis), questions and answers (*erōtapokriseis*), three "centuries" of "chapters" (*kephalaia*) on ascetic practice, nature, and knowledge, and a liturgical poem (*kanōn*) on Saint Nicholas. (He also wrote, and is perhaps better known for, polemical treatises against the Jews, against the addition of the *filioque* to the Latin creed, and against the Latin and Armenian use of unleavened bread for the Eucharist—the last two being part of the controversy between the Byzantines and the Latins that came to a head in 1054.)

Plenty of others worked assiduously on "religious" and "secular" topics, apparently without seeing any need to make a point of rejecting the latter. The Nestorian priest, monk, and physician of Baghdad Ibn al-Ṭayyib (d. 1043), whom we encountered in chapter 6 as the author of a commentary on Porphyry's *Eisagoge,* wrote not only on Aristotelian logic and metaphysics (*theologia*) but also on biblical exegesis, canon law, and Christian theology.[7] This does not seem to have bothered him. Nor does it seem to have troubled the prolific Miaphysite Christian philosopher Yaḥyā ibn ʿAdī of Tikrit, Iraq (893–974), to study, teach, and write on

4. Treiger, *Inspired Knowledge.*
5. Beck, *Kirche,* 535–38.
6. §74ff., ed. and trans. Greenfield, 166ff.
7. Graf, *GCAL,* 2:160–77.

philosophy in Baghdad, with Nestorian and Muslim teachers (Mattā ibn Yūnus and al-Fārābī), while at the same time producing Christian theological and apologetic works.[8]

Much the same could be said about the Rabbanite Jewish scholar Saʿadya Gaon (882–942). Saʿadya (Saʿīd ibn Yūsuf al-Fayyūmī in Arabic) was from Egypt but also studied in Palestine and eventually became the chief scholar (*gaʾon*) at the academy in Sūrā (on the Euphrates near Kufa and some 180 km south of Baghdad). He translated the Hebrew Bible into Arabic with commentary and was also a grammarian, rabbinic jurist, theologian, and philosopher. He wrote primarily in Judeo-Arabic (Arabic written in Hebrew script) and so, we may surmise, for other Arabophone Jewish scholars. Deeply involved in disputes over doctrine and authority within his own confessional community and in defending Jewish doctrine from outside attacks, he was also well acquainted with Arabic philosophical literature (including Muslim *kalām*) and used this knowledge for confessional purposes.[9]

Ibn al-Faḍl, al-Ghazālī, and others like them sought to preserve what they found coherent and useful for their purposes while jettisoning the rest. Because their own habits of thought were a result of the ancient philosophical system, they could hardly jettison very much of it in practice. From the outside, this might look like nothing more than dressing up blindly accepted dogma in rational garb, but for them it was quite different; it was a quest for truth and an understanding of the world, seen and unseen, using the best tools available to them: sense-perception, intellect, and history. And history, for them, included revelation.

This sort of approach to systems of knowledge was not without precedent. The effort to embark on a new intellectual path has often led writers to disavow their own intellectual roots. One can see it in the way Plato's polemic against the "sophists" may mislead readers into exaggerating the difference between the likes of Protagoras and Plato's teacher Socrates—a difference that the later Platonic tradition had a vested interest in amplifying. One can see it in how Aristotle reviews and rejects the physical doctrines of his predecessors while adopting and adapting their ideas; or in early Christian theories about the mind, body, and cosmology, heavily indebted to Stoics, Platonists, and Aristotelians but often framed as something new, rooted in the Gospels and the letters of Paul.

8. Graf, *GCAL*, 2:233–49; Endress, *Works;* Wisnovsky, "New Philosophical Texts"; Wisnovsky, "MS Tehran."

9. His works include a commentary on the occult properties of the letters of the Hebrew alphabet, which Sarah Stroumsa ("Wondrous Paths") has argued should be understood in the wider context of similar interests among Ismailis. Such an interest is attested for eleventh-century Byzantium as well: Ierodiakonou, "Greek Concept," 110–16.

For Ibn al-Faḍl and other medieval scholars, this selective approach was intentional. As al-Ghazālī explained, the problem was not philosophers' methods but only some of their doctrines, which they propounded, he said, with fallacious arguments that broke their own rules but nevertheless impressed some people because they were associated with the prestige of the philosophical, especially mathematical, methods.[10] Learning the methods was a step toward wisdom; accepting philosophers' doctrines uncritically, madness.

2 TWIN PAIDEIAS

The foundation for this scholarly culture's existence and perpetuation was the conceptual separation of twin curricula. Let us call the pair "inner" and "outer" learning, to paraphrase the Byzantine distinction between "our own" (Christian) paideia and paideia "from outside" (non-Christian, usually pagan).[11] The inner curriculum was particular to each religious confession and consisted of what are often called religious texts. The outer curriculum was common to elite scholars of all confessions and was made up of philosophical texts that are typically called secular. Using this terminology, we can say that Ibn al-Faḍl's educational agenda focused on inner texts but presupposed outer learning and deliberately linked it to the inner texts he translated; and that intellectuals like Ibn al-Faḍl and al-Ghazālī largely shared the same outer curriculum, even though their inner curricula were quite different.

Inner and outer were hardly as segregated from each other as confessional rhetoric declared. On the contrary, they were closely integrated. As Ibn al-Faḍl makes plain, the inner curriculum only made sense with the outer, for the inner was born in part from the outer.

Inner and outer were also mutable over time. Ibn al-Faḍl and his fellow Christian scholars inherited their curricula from the late antique elite men who came to be known as fathers of the church. But much had changed over the centuries. The specifics of the "secular" curriculum had shifted somewhat, and the literary canon studied by the likes of Gregory of Nazianzos and Julian had been partly displaced by Gregory himself, and Chrysostom, and others. Saints' lives and the Old and New Testaments offered edifying narratives alongside the Homer that Byzantine schoolchildren still read. The Athenian orators had been partially pushed aside by the new orators of Antioch (Chrysostom and his pagan teacher Libanius) and Cappadocia (Basil and Gregory). Many of the old classics remained.

There was also plenty of synchronic variation between individual scholars cultivating these curricula. The reading lists and the traditions of reading in Constantinople

10. *Munqidh*, trans. Khalidi, in Khalidi, *Medieval Islamic Philosophical Writings*, 69.

11. For these twin curricula in Byzantium, see Podskalsky, *Theologie und Philosophie*, 19–20, 40.

were not precisely the same as in Ibn al-Faḍl's Antioch, or in Baghdad, or among Chalcedonians, Miaphysites, or Nestorians. But the similarities are more striking: religious specialists like Ibn al-Faḍl or al-Ghazālī were drawing on the same Graeco-Roman heritage, whose cultivation was necessary in order to prove one's intellectual merits and credibly defend one's views about what mattered—about God, the cosmos, and the good life human beings ought to strive for. They each used that heritage differently, applying it to different inner curricula, and came to different conclusions, but for each the heritage itself was indispensable.

These twin curricula were passed down from teachers to students. This process is mostly invisible to us. Translation programs like Ibn al-Faḍl's are a rare opportunity to glimpse a snapshot (albeit faded and damaged by the passage of time) of the educational process. And if we set Ibn al-Faḍl's translations in the context of Greek-Syriac-Arabic translation from the eighth to the eleventh century, we realize that together these snapshots form a larger picture, in which the twin curricula, inner and outer, are intertwined.

The outer curriculum shared by Ibn al-Faḍl and his non-Christian peers had been translated into Arabic in the previous centuries. The Greek- and Syriac-speaking non-Muslims who were called upon by Muslim patrons to translate Aristotle, Galen, Ptolemy, and other philosophical, scientific, and technical texts into Arabic did not appear ex nihilo.[12] They were the old learned elite that had lived on in the new Muslim polity, bearers not only of their useful linguistic knowledge but of the curriculum itself.[13] Arab Muslims who wished to study Greek learning at first depended on non-Muslim scholars even to identify the texts relevant to their patrons' interests and to find a Greek or Syriac exemplar; translation was at the end of a longer process.

At the same time, these non-Muslim scholars, mostly Christians, had close ties to their own religious communities and often wrote works on "religious" topics such as theology, canon law, and the defense of Christian doctrines (including those of their own particular Christian confessions). These included famous translators like the Nestorian Christians Timothy I (Katholikos, 780–823) and Ḥunayn ibn Isḥāq (809–873) and the Chalcedonian Christian Qusṭā ibn Lūqā (d. ca. 912–913).[14] Timothy I, chief prelate of the Nestorian Church and its representative before the Abbasid caliph in Baghdad, was involved in the translation of Aristotle's *Topics* from Syriac into Arabic for the caliph al-Mahdī (r. 775–785); he also wrote Syriac works on canon law and Christian doctrine. Educated in Aristotelian philosophy and patristics, Timothy's Syriac accounts of his own disputations with Muslims at court show him using Aristotelian logic and scriptural evidence (the

12. Gutas, *GTAC*, ch. 6.
13. Tannous, "Syria," part I.
14. Graf, *GCAL*, 2:30–32, 114–18, 122–29.

Bible and the Qur'an) to defend Christian doctrine against Muslim objections.[15] The famous Aristotelian and Galenic translator Ḥunayn also wrote a refutation of a purported proof of Muḥammad's prophethood, in which he argued that in order to discern the true religion one needed logic, history, and supernatural signs.[16] Qusṭā, whom we have met as an astronomer and translator, also wrote a world chronicle (beginning with the creation of the world) and, like Ḥunayn, wrote a refutation of Muslim arguments for Muḥammad's prophethood, in which he used explicitly Aristotelian logic and refered to medicine and astrology (as evidence that knowledge of unseen things comes not only from God through revelation but also from human arts).[17] Lesser-known translators did much the same, with careers embracing "secular" and "religious" texts.[18] Thus the same scholars who provided the outer curriculum to Muslim-Arab patrons were also bearers and builders of their own Christian inner curricula.

From the eighth to the tenth century, translation into Arabic focused on the outer curriculum because non-Muslims were for the most part still teaching both inner and outer curricula in Greek, Syriac, and other learned languages of the territories taken in the seventh century by the Arab Muslim conquerors. Arabic translations were made mainly of works that Muslims were interested in studying; these typically excluded the Christian inner curriculum. Beginning around the tenth century, as elite non-Muslim communities gradually shifted to using Arabic as their own language of education and eventually even liturgy, inner curricula were translated into Arabic as well.[19]

As we have seen in the case of Ibn al-Faḍl, this process of translating and retranslating the inner curriculum reveals the close ties between the inner, Christian curriculum and the outer, ancient philosophical curriculum always hovering in the background. A glance at other Chalcedonian Christian translators active at

15. Gutas, *GTAC*, 61–69; Heimgartner and Roggema, "Timothy I."

16. Roggema, "Ḥunayn."

17. Swanson, "Qusṭā."

18. Graf, *GCAL*, 2:111, 118, 119–20, 129–30. Timothy's colleague and supporter Abū Nūḥ al-Anbārī (ninth century), who, according to Timothy, was primarily responsible for the *Topics* translation, wrote Arabic theological treatises on God's unicity (*tawḥīd*) and triplicity (*tathlīth*), a polemical work against the Qur'an, and a hagiographical *Life* of the Nestorian saint John of Daylam (d. 738, syriaca.org/person/825): Swanson, "Abū Nūḥ." Ḥabīb-ʿAbdîšoʿ ibn Bahrīz, Nestorian bishop of Harran, then Mosul, translated philosophical works for the caliph al-Maʾmūn (r. 813–833) and also wrote a polemical work refuting Miaphysite and Chalcedonian Christology. Ḥunayn's son and collaborator Isḥāq ibn Ḥunayn (d. 910–911)—whose translation of Aristotle's *Physics* we encountered in chapter 7—also wrote theological works (as well as poetry and belles lettres) and produced a translation of Nemesios's *On the Nature of Man* (ascribed by him to Gregory of Nyssa). The physician Gabriel ibn ʿUbaydallāh (d. 1006) of the Nestorian Bukhtīshūʿ (Boktîšoʿ) family of Jundīshāpūr wrote on the harmony of philosophy and prophecy, the Eucharist, and the Jewish failure to acknowledge the coming of the Messiah.

19. Mavroudi, "Greek Language"; Treiger, "Christian Graeco-Arabica," esp. 201.

Antioch suggests that in this Ibn al-Faḍl was no exception.[20] Recall that Antonios of Saint Symeon translated, among other texts, John of Damascus's *Dialectica* and *Exposition of Faith.* Though an inner text in the sense that it was composed by someone who was venerated as a saint, the *Dialectica* is best seen as a part of the Aristotelian logical tradition.[21] The *Exposition of Faith* likewise tracks other parts of the outer curriculum, such as astronomy and even astrology, quite closely. The *protospatharios* Ibrāhīm ibn Yūḥannā of Antioch (d. 1025 or later) translated Christian saints' lives as well as orations by Gregory of Nazianzos, whose works constantly grapple with and adapt the outer curriculum, and an excerpt from the *Divine Names* of pseudo-Dionysios the Areopagite on good and evil.[22] The *Divine Names,* as part of the Dionysian Corpus, was intimately linked to the thought of the pagan Neoplatonist Proklos, whose works were more advanced (and so less read) components of the outer curriculum. Nearby, in Fatimid Damascus, Ibn Saḥqūn translated the entire Dionysian Corpus into Arabic in 1009. He also translated a Greek liturgical book.[23]

These translation programs reflect not only the tastes and interests of their Arabic-speaking audiences but also the preexisting (and continuing) traditions on which they drew. We may thus conclude that elite scholars of the eastern Mediterranean and Near East around the turn of the millennium cultivated a "common core" shared by a wide range of scholars alongside a closely related curriculum internal to each religious confession. There were of course other texts internal to each religious culture. Many of these had little to do with the ancient philosophical heritage. But for those with an elite education who engaged with some of the same theological, physical, ethical, and logical questions that had exercised ancient philosophers, thinking about their own religious traditions was simply impossible to separate from the ancient curriculum that was still taught from Gibraltar to the Bosphorus to the Oxus and beyond.

3 WEST OF SAMARQAND

Ibn al-Faḍl and scholars like him should let us lay to rest the old narrative of intellectual history that saw the rise of Christianity and then Islam in late antiquity and

20. On their translations, mentioned here, see Treiger, "Christian Graeco-Arabica," 203–7, esp. 206–7. Now see also Roggema and Treiger, *Patristic Literature,* chs. 5–8 (by H. Ibrahim, J. Mugler, A. M. Roberts, and J. Glynias, respectively).

21. See ch. 6, pp. 184–85.

22. Lamoreaux, "Ibrāhīm."

23. Treiger, "New Evidence"; Treiger, "Arabic Version"; Bonmariage and Moureau, "*Corpus Dionysiacum Arabicum* I"; Bonmariage and Moureau, "*Corpus Dionysiacum Arabicum* II"; Parker and Treiger, "Philo's Odyssey"; Treiger, "Christian Graeco-Arabica," 193.

the Middle Ages as lethal blows to philosophy and science.[24] This Enlightenment-era notion pitting religion against science has gradually seen its pieces chipped away over the years. Now we know that fourth-century pagan and Christian elite men were more similar to each other than they were different,[25] that Muslims were deeply interested in the Greek classical heritage,[26] that al-Ghazālī's full-throated critique of philosophy did not spell the end nor even a decline of science and philosophy in the Islamic world. Ibn al-Faḍl did not study and teach philosophy in spite of theology but precisely because of it. Religion was a powerful motivation to study Aristotle and Plato and to know something about the pre-Socratics and the atomists lest their latter-day followers go unrefuted. Truth and morality may have started with "faith"—assent to certain axioms—but for anything beyond that one required thought, and a tradition of thought to guide it.

Seen in a wider context extending beyond his fellow Arabic-speaking Chalcedonian Christians, Ibn al-Faḍl represents an era and an attitude toward knowledge past and present. He and his fellow scholars portrayed themselves as adhering strictly to their own particular religious traditions, and in a sense they did. But this adherence led them enthusiastically to adapt aspects of ancient philosophy, engage in rational inquiry, and take interest in each other's arguments. This mutual interconfessional interest was ostensibly for polemical purposes only, but there can be no doubt that even in this polemical mode they learned from one another, more often, I imagine, than was desirable to disclose.

This confluence of intellectual traditions and attitudes, this spirit of critical inquiry with a moralizing force, took many forms at various times and places. But it is a recognizable pattern in western Eurasian thought. This is the proper context in which to see the cultural and intellectual rebirths, the renaissances and revolutions, ascribed to western Europeans of the twelfth or fifteenth or seventeenth century.[27] Perhaps in culture and thought (rather than commerce or military might), what has seemed like a phoenix rising out of the ashes will turn out to have been the wandering fringes of a flock of migratory birds.

24. Mavroudi, "Classical Tradition."
25. Elm, *Sons*.
26. Rosenthal, *Classical Heritage;* Gutas, "Graeco-Arabic."
27. Treadgold, *Renaissances;* Jones, *Good Life*.

BIBLIOGRAPHY

MANUSCRIPTS USED FOR IBN AL-FAḌL'S (AND OTHER) TRANSLATIONS

Basil, *Hexaemeron:* **B**/ب = Beirut BO 479 | **D**/د = Damascus OP ar. 142 | **E**/ذ = Damascus OP ar. 149 | **Q**/ق = Dayr al-Mukhalliṣ 114 || Anonymous Translation: **G**/غ = Vat. Borg. ar. 153 | **P**/پ = Paris ar. 134 | **S**/س = Sinai ar. 270 | **W**/و = Cairo COP Theol. 139 (= Graf 380 = Simaika 431)

Book of the Garden. See *Loci communes.*

Isaac the Syrian: **A**/أ = Sinai ar. 350 | **J**/ج = Jerusalem, Holy Sepulcher, ar. 24 | **Ṭ**/ط = Vat. Sbath 646 | **V**/ڤ = Vat. Sbath 649

John Chrysostom, *Homilies on Genesis:* Jerusalem, Holy Sepulcher, ar. 35

John Chrysostom, *Homilies on Hebrews:* **A**/أ = Paris ar. 96 | **B**/ب = Paris ar. 95 | **S**/س = Sinai ar. 303 | Dayr al-Ḥarf 7 | Sinai ar. 156, fols. 247r–248r (preface)

John of Damascus, *Statement on Correct Thought:* Sinai ar. 352 | Vat. ar. 79 (with Ibn al-Faḍl's brief prefatory creed)

John of Thessaloniki, *Encomium to Saint Demetrios:* **A**/أ = Sinai ar. 350 | **B**/ب = Sinai ar. 352

Loci communes = *Book of the Garden* (*Kitāb al-Rawḍa*): **S**/س = Sinai ar. 66 | **V**/ڤ = Vat. ar. 111

Maximos, *Chapters on Love* (possibly trans. Ibn al-Faḍl): Vat. Sbath 176

Maximos, *Disputation with Pyrrhos:* Jerusalem, Holy Sepulcher, ar. 12 | Vat. ar. 125

Psalter: **V**/ڤ = Vat. ar. 4 | **Y**/ي = New Haven, Yale Beinecke, ar. 349 || patristic extracts commenting on the Psalms: Vat. ar. 145 | New Haven, Yale Beinecke, ar. 349 (preface)

Pseudo-Kaisarios, *Questions and Answers:* **Q**/ق = Cairo COP Theol. 112 | **Ṭ**/ط = Vat. Sbath 45

Sophronios, *Synodical Letter*, adaptation = *Book of Proof* (*Kitāb al-Burhān*): **M**/م = Jerusalem, Holy Sepulcher, ar. 12 | **Ṭ**/ ط = Vat. Sbath 44

PRIMARY SOURCES

ACO[2] = *Acta Conciliorum Oecumenicorum*, 2nd ser. Ed. Rudolf Riedinger. 3 vols. in 8. Berlin, 1984–2016.

Alexander of Aphrodisias. *Commentaire perdu à la Physique d'Aristote: Les scholies byzantines; Édition, traduction et commentaire.* Ed. and trans. Marwan Rashed. Berlin, 2011.

Ammonios. *Ammonii Hermei Commentaria in Librum peri Hermeneias. Magentini Archiepiscopi Mytilenensis in eundem enarratio.* Ed. Aldus Manutius. Venice, 1503.

———. *In Porphyrii Isagogen sive quinque voces.* Ed. Adolf Busse. Berlin, 1891.

Anaxagoras. *Anaxagoras of Clazomenae: Fragments and Testimonia.* Ed. and trans. Patricia Curd. Toronto, 2007.

———. *The Fragments of Anaxagoras.* Ed. and trans. David Sider. Meisenheim am Glan, 1981.

Aristotle. *Aristotle's Meteorology in the Arabico-Latin Tradition.* Ed. Pieter L. Schoonheim. Leiden, 2000.

———. *Arisṭūṭālīs: al-Ṭabīʿa. Tarjamat Isḥāq b. Ḥunayn, maʿ shurūḥ Ibn al-Samḥ wa-Ibn ʿAdī wa-Mattā ibn Yūnis wa-Abī l-Faraj ibn al-Ṭayyib.* Ed. ʿAbd al-Raḥmān Badawī. 2 vols. Cairo, 1964–1965.

———. *Fī l-nafs: Arisṭūṭālīs.* Ed. ʿAbd al-Raḥmān Badawī. Cairo, 1954.

———. *Generation of Animals: The Arabic Translation Commonly Ascribed to Yaḥyâ ibn al-Biṭrîq.* Ed. J. Brugman and H. J. Drossaart Lulofs. Leiden, 1971.

———. *Manṭiq Arisṭū.* Ed. ʿAbd al-Raḥmān Badawī. 3 vols. 1948–1952.

al-Ashʿarī. *Die dogmatischen Lehren der Anhänger des Islam = Maqālāt al-islāmīyīn wa-ikhtilāf al-muṣallīn.* Ed. Heinrich Ritter. 2 vols. Istanbul, 1929–1933.

Basil of Caesarea. *Exegetic Homilies.* Trans. Agnes Clare Way. Washington, DC, 1963.

———. *Homélies sur l'Hexaéméron.* Ed. and trans. Stanislas Giet. 2nd ed. Paris, 1968.

———. *Homilien zum Hexaemeron.* Ed. Emmanuel Amand de Mendieta and Stig Y. Rudberg. Berlin, 1997.

[Ps.-]Basil of Caesarea. *Sur l'origine de l'homme: Hom. X et XI de l'Hexaéméron.* Ed. and trans. Alexis Smets and Michel van Esbroeck. Paris, 1970.

[Ps.-]Basil of Caesarea and [Ps.-]Gregory of Nyssa. *Auctorum incertorum vulgo Basilii vel Gregorii Nysseni: Sermones de creatione hominis, Sermo de Paradiso.* Ed. Hadwiga Hörner. Leiden, 1972.

Basil-NPNF = Basil of Caesarea. *Letters and Select Works.* Trans. Blomfield Jackson. Nicene and Post-Nicene Fathers, 2nd ser., 8. Ed. Philip Schaff. New York, ca. 1894.

al-Battānī, Abū ʿAbdallāh Muḥammad b. Sinān. *Opus Astronomicum/Kitāb al-Zīj al-Ṣābiʾ.* Ed. Carlo Alfonso Nallino. 3 vols. Milan, 1899–1907.

Christopher of Mytilene. *Versuum variorum collectio cryptensis.* Ed. Marc De Groote. Turnhout, 2012.

Constantine VII Porphyrogennetos. *The Book of Ceremonies.* Trans. Ann Moffatt and Maxeme Tall. 2 vols. Canberra, 2012.

———. *Le livre des cérémonies.* Ed. A. Vogt. 2 vols. in 4. Paris, 1935–1940.

Cougny, Edme, ed. *Epigrammatum Anthologia Palatina, cum Planudeis et appendice nova epigrammatum veterum ex libris et marmoribus ductorum.* 3 vols. Paris, 1864.

Cramer, J. A., ed. *Anecdota Graeca e codd. manuscriptis bibliothecarum Oxoniensium.* 4 vols. Oxford, 1835–1837.

Daiber, Hans, ed. *Aetius Arabus: Die Vorsokratiker in arabischer Überlieferung.* Wiesbaden, 1980.

Daphnopates, Theodore. *Correspondance.* Ed. and trans. Jean Darrouzès and L. G. Westerink. Paris, 1978.

Delatte, Armand, ed. *Anecdota atheniensia.* 2 vols. Paris, 1927–1939.

Dexippos. *In Aristotelis categorias commentarium.* Ed. Adolf Busse. Berlin, 1888.

Diels-Kranz = Diels, Hermann, and Walter Kranz, eds. *Die Fragmente der Vorsokratiker.* 6th ed. 3 vols. Berlin-Charlottenburg, 1951–1952.

Diogenes Laertius. *Diogenis Laertii Vitae philosophorum.* Ed. Miroslav Marcovich. 3 vols. Stuttgart, 1999–2002.

Ps.-Dionysios the Areopagite. *Corpus Dionysiacum II: Pseudo-Dionysius Areopagita; De coelesti hierarchia, De ecclesiastica hierarchia, De mystica theologia, Epistulae.* Ed. Günter Heil and Adolf Martin Ritter. 2nd ed. Berlin, 2012.

Dionysios Thrax. *Ars grammatica.* Ed. Gustav Uhlig. Leipzig, 1883.

Elias. *Eliae in Porphyrii Isagogen et Aristotelis Categorias commentaria.* Ed. Adolf Busse. Berlin, 1900.

Ps.-Elias. *Pseudo-Elias (Pseudo-David): Lectures on Porphyry's Isagoge.* Ed. L. G. Westerink. Amsterdam, 1967.

Elias of Nisibis. *Liber sessionum sive disputatio inter Eliam metropolitam Nisibenum et vezirum Abū 'l-Qāsim al-Ḥusayn ibn ʿAlī al-Maġribī et Epistola eiusdem Eliae Nisibeni ad vezirum Abū 'l-Qāsim missa.* Ed. Nikolai N. Seleznyov. Moscow, 2018.

al-Fārābī. *Al-Farabi on the Perfect State: Mabādiʾ ārāʾ ahl al-madīna al-fāḍila.* Ed. and trans. Richard Walzer. Oxford, 1985.

———. *Al-Farabi's Commentary and Short Treatise on Aristotle's De interpretatione.* Trans. Fritz W. Zimmermann. London, 1981.

———. *Al-Manṭiq ʿind al-Fārābī.* Ed. Rafīq al-ʿAjam and Majid Fakhry. 4 vols. Beirut, 1986–1987.

———. *Sharḥ al-Fārābī li-kitāb Arisṭūṭālīs fī l-ʿibāra.* Ed. Wilhelm Kutsch and Stanley Marrow. 2nd ed. Beirut, 1971.

Galen. *Galens Traktat "Dass die Kräfte der Seele den Mischungen des Körpers folgen" in arabischer Uebersetzung.* Ed. Hans Hinrich Biesterfeldt. Wiesbaden, 1973.

———. *Institutio logica.* Ed. Karl Kalbfleisch. Leipzig, 1896.

———. *Institutio logica.* Trans. John Spangler Kieffer. Baltimore, 1964.

———. *Kitāb Jālīnūs fī l-istiqṣāt ʿalā raʾy Abuqrāṭ.* Trans. Ḥunayn ibn Isḥāq al-ʿIbādī. Ed. Muḥammad Salīm Sālim. Cairo, 1986.

———. *On the Elements According to Hippocrates.* Ed. Phillip De Lacy. Berlin, 1996.

———. *Opera omnia.* Ed. C. G. Kühn. 20 vols. Leipzig, 1821–1833.

———. *Scripta minora.* Ed. G. Helmreich, J. Marquardt, and I. Müller. 3 vols. Leipzig, 1893.

al-Ghazālī, Abū Ḥāmid. *Tahāfut al-falāsifa.* Ed. Sulyamān Dunyā. Cairo, 1972.

Gregory of Nazianzos. *Discours 42–43.* Ed. and trans. Jean Bernardi. Paris, 1992.

Gregory of Nazianzos and Ambrose of Milan. *Funeral Orations.* Trans. Leo P. McCauley et al. Washington, DC, 1953.

Gregory of Nyssa. *In hexaemeron.* Ed. Hubertus R. Drobner. Leiden, 2009.

———. *Quae supersunt omnia.* Ed. George H. Forbes. 2 vols. Burntisland, 1855–1861.

Halkin, François, ed. *Douze récits byzantins sur Saint Jean Chrysostome.* Brussels, 1977.

Heiberg, J. L., ed. *Anonymi logica et quadrivium.* Copenhagen, 1929.

Hero of Alexandria. *Pneumatica et Automata.* Ed. W. Schmidt. Leipzig, 1899.

Hilgard, Alfred, ed. *Scholia in Dionysii Thracis Artem grammaticam.* Leipzig, 1901.

al-Ḥillī, Jamāl al-Dīn al-Ḥasan ibn Yūsuf ibn al-Muṭahhar. *Al-Asrār al-khafīya fī l-ʿulūm al-ʿaqlīya: Al-Ṭabīʿīyāt.* Ed. Ḥusām Muḥyī l-Dīn al-Ālūsī and Ṣāliḥ Mahdī al-Hāshim. Beirut, 2005.

Ibn Abī Uṣaybiʿa. *ʿUyūn al-anbāʾ fī ṭabaqāt al-aṭibbāʾ.* Ed. Nizār Riḍā. Beirut, [1965].

Ibn al-ʿAdīm, Kamāl al-Dīn. *Bughyat al-ṭalab fī tārīkh Ḥalab.* Ed. Suhayl Zakkār. Beirut, 1988.

Ibn al-Nadīm. *The Fihrist of al-Nadīm: A Tenth-Century Survey of Muslim Culture.* Trans. Bayard Dodge. New York, 1970.

———. *Kitāb al-Fihrist.* Ed. Ayman Fuʾād Sayyid. 2 vols. London, 2009.

Ibn al-Qifṭī. *Inbāh al-ruwāt ʿalā anbāh al-nuḥāt.* Ed. Muḥammad Abū l-Faḍl Ibrāhīm. 4 vols. Cairo; Beirut, 1986.

———. *Ta'rīḫ al-Ḥukamā'.* Ed. Julius Lippert. Leipzig, 1903.

Ibn al-Sikkīt. *Iṣlāḥ al-Manṭiq.* Ed. Aḥmad Muḥammad Shākir and ʿAbd al-Salām Muḥammad Hārūn. Cairo, 1949.

Ibn al-Ṭayyib, Abū l-Faraj ʿAbdallāh. *Arabic Logic: Ibn al-Ṭayyib's Commentary on Porphyry's Eisagoge.* Trans. Kwame Gyekye. Albany, 1979.

———. *Tafsīr Kitāb Īsāghūjī li-Furfūriyūs.* Ed. Kwame Gyekye. Beirut, 1975.

Ibn ʿArabī. *Al-Futūḥāt al-makkīya.* Ed. Aḥmad Shams al-Dīn. 9 vols. Beirut, 1999.

Ibn Rushd. *Talkhīs manṭiq Arisṭū.* Ed. Jīrār Jihāmī. 7 vols. Beirut, 1992.

Ibn Sīnā. *Al-Ishārāt wa-l-tanbīhāt li-Abī ʿAlī ibn Sīnā, maʿ sharḥ Naṣīr al-Dīn al-Ṭūsī.* Ed. Sulaymān Dunyā. 4 vols. in 3. Cairo, 1957–1968.

———. *Al-Najāt min al-gharaq fī baḥr al-ḍalālāt.* Ed. Muḥammad Taqī Dānešpažūh. Tehran, [1985].

———. *Al-Shifāʾ.* Ed. Ibrāhīm Madkūr. 28 vols. Cairo, 1952–1983.

———. *Avicenna's Deliverance: Logic.* Trans. Asad Q. Ahmed. Oxford, 2011.

———. *The Metaphysics of the Healing.* Ed. and trans. Michael E. Marmura. Provo, UT, 2005.

———. *The Physics of the Healing.* Ed. and trans. Jon McGinnis. 2 vols. Provo, UT, 2009.

———. *Réfutation de l'astrologie.* Ed. and trans. Yahya Michot. Beirut, 2006.

Ibn Taymiyya. *Darʾ taʿāruḍ al-ʿaql wa-l-naql.* Ed. Muḥammad Rashshād Sālim. Riyadh, 1991.

Isaac I Bedjan = Isaac of Nineveh. *De perfectione religiosa.* Ed. Paul Bedjan. Paris; Leipzig, 1909.

Isaac I_{eng} Wensinck = Isaac of Nineveh. *Mystic Treatises.* Trans. A. J. Wensinck. Amsterdam, 1923.

Isaac I_{gr} Pirard = Isaac of Nineveh. *Ἀββᾶ Ἰσαὰκ τοῦ Σύρου, Λόγοι ἀσκητικοί.* Ed. Marcel Pirard. Mount Athos, 2012.

Isaac II.4–41 Brock = Isaac of Nineveh. *"The Second Part," Chapters IV–XLI.* Ed. Sebastian Brock. 2 vols. Louvain, 1995.

Isaac III Chialà = Isaac of Nineveh. *Terza collezione.* Ed. and trans. Sabino Chialà. 2 vols. Louvain, 2011.

Isaac III Hansbury = Isaac of Nineveh. *Spiritual Works.* Ed. and trans. Mary T. Hansbury. Piscataway, NJ, 2016.

JChrys-NPNF-Gal-etc. = John Chrysostom. *Homilies on Galatians, Ephesians, Philippians, Colossians, Thessalonians, Timothy, Titus, and Philemon.* Nicene and Post-Nicene Fathers 13. Ed. Philip Schaff. New York, 1889.

JChrys-NPNF-John/Heb = John Chrysostom. *Homilies on the Gospel of St. John and the Epistle to the Hebrews.* Nicene and Post-Nicene Fathers 14. Ed. Philip Schaff. New York, 1890.

John of Damascus. *Commentarii in epistulas Pauli.* Ed. Robert Volk. In *Die Schriften,* vol. 7. Berlin, 2013.

———. *Contra imaginum calumniatores orationes tres.* Ed. Bonifaz Kotter. In *Die Schriften,* vol. 3. Berlin, 1975.

———. *Die Schriften des Johannes von Damaskos.* Ed. Bonifaz Kotter. 7 vols. Berlin, 1969–2013.

———. *Expositio fidei.* Ed. Bonifaz Kotter. In *Die Schriften,* vol. 2. Berlin, 1973.

———. *Institutio elementaris, Capita philosophica (Dialectica).* Ed. Bonifaz Kotter. In *Die Schriften,* vol. 1. Berlin, 1969.

John Italos. *Quaestiones quodlibetales.* Ed. Perikles Joannou. Ettal, 1956.

Jones, Alexander, ed. and trans. *An Eleventh-Century Manual of Arabo-Byzantine Astronomy.* Amsterdam, 1987.

Ps.-Kaisarios. *Die Erotapokriseis.* Ed. Rudolf Riedinger. Berlin, 1989.

Khalidi, Muhammad Ali, ed. *Medieval Islamic Philosophical Writings.* Cambridge, 2005.

al-Khwārizmī al-Kātib, Abū ʿAbdallāh Muḥammad b. Aḥmad b. Yūsuf. *Liber Mafâtîh al-Olûm explicans vocabula technica scientiarum tam Arabum quam peregrinorum.* Ed. G. van Vloten. Leiden, 1895.

al-Kindī, Yaʿqūb ibn Isḥāq. *The Philosophical Works.* Trans. Peter Adamson and Peter E. Pormann. Oxford, 2012.

———. *Rasāʾil al-Kindī al-falsafīya.* Ed. Muḥammad ʿAbd al-Hādī Abū Rīda. 2 vols. Cairo, 1950–1953.

Leo VI. *Homiliae.* Ed. Theodora Antonopoulou. Turnhout, 2008.

Leontios. *Das Leben des Heiligen Gregorios von Agrigent.* Ed. Albrecht Berger. Berlin, 1995.

———. *A Translation of Abbot Leontios' Life of Saint Gregory, Bishop of Agrigento.* Trans. John R. C. Martyn. Lewiston, NY, 2004.

Lisān = Ibn Manẓūr. *Lisān al-ʿarab.* www.baheth.info.

al-Maʿarrī, Abū l-ʿAlāʾ. *The Epistle of Forgiveness, with the Epistle of Ibn al-Qāriḥ.* Ed. and trans. G. J. H. van Gelder and Gregor Schoeler. 2 vols. New York, 2013.

———. *Al-Luzūmīyāt, aw Luzūm mā lā yalzam.* Ed. ʿAzīz Zand. 2 vols. Cairo, 1891–1895.

———. *Muʿjiz Aḥmad: Sharḥ Dīwān Abī l-Ṭayyib al-Mutanabbī.* Ed. ʿAbd al-Majīd Diyāb. Cairo, 1986–1988.

Maass, Ernst, ed. *Commentariorum in Aratum reliquae.* Berlin, 1898.

Malalas, John. *Chronographia.* Ed. Ioannes Thurn. Berlin, 2000.

Maximos the Confessor. *Capitoli sulla carità.* Ed. A. Ceresa-Gastaldo. Rome, 1963.

———. *Selected Writings.* Trans. G. C. Berthold. London, 1985.

Ps.-Maximos the Confessor. *Erste kritische Edition einer Redaktion des sacro-profanen Florilegiums Loci communes.* Ed. Sibylle Ihm. Stuttgart, 2001.

Niketas Stethatos. *The Life of Saint Symeon the New Theologian.* Ed. and trans. Richard P. H. Greenfield. Cambridge, MA, 2013.

Nikomachos of Gerasa. *Introductionis arithmeticae libri II.* Ed. Richard Gottfried Hoche. Leipzig, 1866.

———. *Kitāb al-madkhal ilā ʿilm al-ʿadad/Ṯābit ibn Qurra's arabische Übersetzung der Ἀριθμητικὴ Εἰσαγωγή des Nikomachos von Gerasa.* Ed. Wilhelm Kutsch. Beirut, [1959].

Orestes of Jerusalem. *Historia et laudes ss. Sabae et Macarii.* Ed. I. Cozza-Luzi. Rome, 1893.

Orion of Thebes. *Etymologicon.* Ed. F. W. Sturz. Leipzig, 1820.

Pappos of Alexandria and Theon of Alexandria. *Commentaires sur l'Almageste.* Ed. Adolphe Rome. 3 vols. Rome, 1931–1943.

Petit, Françoise, ed. *Catenae graecae in Genesim et in Exodum.* 2 vols. Turnhout, 1977–1986.

———, ed. *La chaîne sur la Genèse: Édition intégrale.* 4 vols. Louvain, 1991–1996.

Philoponos, John. *Against Aristotle on the Eternity of the World.* Trans. Christian Wildberg. London, 1987.

———. *De aeternitate mundi contra Proclum.* Ed. Hugo Rabe. Leipzig, 1899.

———. *De opificio mundi.* Ed. Walter Reichardt. Leipzig, 1897.

———. *On Aristotle, Physics 1.4–9.* Trans. Catherine Osborne. London, 2009.

Photios. *Bibliothèque.* Ed. and trans. René Henry. 9 vols. Paris, 1959–1991.

Porphyry. *Isagoge et in Aristotelis Categorias commentarium.* Ed. Adolf Busse. Berlin, 1887.

———. *Opuscula tria.* Ed. August Nauck. Leipzig, 1860.

Psellos. *De Gregorii Theologi charactere iudicium.* Ed. Paulus Levy. Leipzig, 1912.

———. *De operatione daemonum.* Ed. Jean François Boissonade. Nuremberg, 1838.

———. *Michael Psellos on Literature and Art: A Byzantine Perspective on Aesthetics.* Ed. Charles Barber and Stratis Papaioannou. Notre Dame, 2017.

———. *Orationes funebres, volumen I.* Ed. Ioannis Polemis. Berlin, 2014.

———. *Psellos and the Patriarchs: Letters and Funeral Orations for Keroullarios, Leichoudes, and Xiphilinos.* Trans. Anthony Kaldellis and Ioannis Polemis. Notre Dame, 2015.

———. *Theologica I.* Ed. Paul Gautier. Leipzig, 1989.

———. *Theologica II.* Ed. L. G. Westerink and John Duffy. Munich; Leipzig, 2002.

Ptolemy. *Almagest.* Trans. G. J. Toomer. London, 1984.

———. *Apotelesmatika* [= *Tetrabiblos*]. Ed. Wolfgang Hübner. Leipzig, 1998.

———. *Opera astronomica minora.* Ed. J. L. Heiberg. Leipzig, 1907.

———. *Ptolemaiou Procheiroi kanones 1a: Les tables faciles de Ptolémée; Tables A1–A2: Introduction, édition critique.* Ed. Anne Tihon. Louvain-la-Neuve, 2011.

———. *Ptolemaiou Procheiroi kanones 1b: Ptolemy's Handy Tables; Tables A1-A2: Transcription and Commentary.* Ed. Raymond Mercier. Louvain-la-Neuve, 2011.

———. *Syntaxis mathematica* [= *Almagest*]. Ed. J. L. Heiberg. 2 vols. Leipzig, 1898–1903.

———. *Tetrabiblos.* Ed. and trans. Frank Egleston Robbins. Cambridge, MA, 1940.

Ptolemy and Theon of Alexandria. *Claudii Ptolemaei Magnae constructionis, id est perfectae coelestium motuum pertractationis, lib. 13. Theonis Alexandrini in eosdem Commentariorum lib. 11.* Ed. Joachim Camerarius. Basel, 1538.

al-Qabīṣī. *The Introduction to Astrology.* Ed. and trans. Charles Burnett, Keiji Yamamoto, and Michio Yano. London; Turin, 2004.

al-Qalqashandī. *Ṣubḥ al-aʿshā fī ṣināʿat al-inshāʾ.* 14 vols. Cairo, 1913–1922.

Rabe, Hugo, ed. *Prolegomenon sylloge.* Leipzig, 1931.

Sbath, Paul, ed. *Vingt traités philosophiques et apologétiques d'auteurs arabes chrétiens du IXᵉ au XIVᵉ siècle.* Cairo, 1929.

Severus ibn al-Muqaffaʿ. *History of the Patriarchs of the Egyptian Church/Taʾrīkh baṭārikat al-kanīsa al-miṣrīya.* Ed. Yassā ʿAbd al-Masīḥ and O. H. E. Burmester. Cairo, 1943–.

Simplikios. *In Aristotelis De caelo Commentaria.* Ed. J. L. Heiberg. Berlin, 1894.
Sophronios and ʿAbdallāh ibn al-Faḍl. *Kitāb al-Burhān fī tathbīt al-īmān.* Ed. Jurays Saʿd Khūrī. Jerusalem, 2015.
Stephen of Alexandria. *Le commentaire astronomique aux Tables faciles de Ptolémée attribué à Stephanos d'Alexandrie.* Ed. and trans. Jean Lempire. Louvain, 2016–.
Sturz, F. W., ed. *Etymologicum Graecae linguae Gudianum et alia grammaticorum scripta e codicibus manuscriptis nunc primum edita.* Leipzig, 1818.
Symeon the New Theologian. *Hymnen.* Ed. Athanasios Kambylis. Berlin, 1976.
Theon of Alexandria. *Le grand commentaire de Théon d'Alexandrie aux Tables faciles de Ptolémée.* Ed. Joseph Mogenet and Anne Tihon. 3 vols. Vatican City, 1985–1999.
———. *Le petit commentaire de Théon d'Alexandrie aux Tables faciles de Ptolémée.* Ed. and trans. Anne Tihon. Vatican City, 1978.
Theon of Smyrna. *Expositio rerum mathematicarum ad legendum Platonem utilium.* Ed. Eduard Hiller. Leipzig, 1878.
Theophanes. *The Chronicle of Theophanes Confessor.* Ed. and trans. Cyril Mango and Roger Scott, with the assistance of Geoffrey Greatrex. Oxford, 1997.
Theophrastos. *Theophrastus of Eresus: Sources for His Life, Writings, Thought, and Influence.* Ed. and trans. William Fortenbaugh et al. 2 vols. Leiden, 1993.
Theophylact of Ochrid. *Theophylacte d'Achrida, Lettres.* Ed. Paul Gautier. Thessaloniki, 1986.
al-Ṭūsī, Naṣīr al-Dīn. *Memoir on Astronomy (al-Tadhkira fī ʿilm al-hayʾa).* Ed. and trans. F. Jamil Ragep. 2 vols. New York, 1993.
van den Ven, Paul, ed. *La vie ancienne de S. Syméon Stylite le jeune (521–592).* 2 vols. Brussels, 1962–1970.
Vettius Valens. *Anthologiarum libri novem.* Ed. David Pingree. Leipzig, 1986.
V.Nich.Sion = *The Life of Saint Nicholas of Sion.* Ed. and trans. Ihor Ševčenko and Nancy P. Ševčenko. Brookline, MA, 1984.
al-Wāḥidī, Abū l-Ḥasan ʿAlī ibn Aḥmad. *Mutanabii Carmina cum commentario Wahidii/Dīwan Abī Ṭayyib al-Mutanabbī, wa fī athnāʾ matnihi sharḥ al-imām al-ʿallāma al-Wāḥidī.* Ed. Friedrich Dieterici. Berlin, 1861.
Yaḥyā of Antioch. *Cronache dell'Egitto Fāṭimide e dell'impero Bizantino, 937–1033.* Trans. Bartolomeo Pirone. Milan, 1998.
———. *Histoire de Yaḥyā ibn Saʿīd d'Antioche* [pt. 2]. Ed. Ignace Kratchkovsky. Trans. Françoise Micheau and Gérard Troupeau. Patrologia Orientalis 47.4. Turnhout, 1997.
Yāqūt al-Rūmī. *Muʿjam al-buldān.* 5 vols. Beirut, 1977.

SECONDARY LITERATURE

Abbreviations of journal titles are from Dumbarton Oaks' Byzantine publications.

Adamson, Peter. *Al-Kindī.* Oxford, 2007.
———. "On Knowledge of Particulars." *Proceedings of the Aristotelian Society* 105 (2005): 257–78.
Ahmed, Asad Q. "Post-Classical Philosophical Commentaries/Glosses: Innovation in the Margins." *Oriens* 41.3–4 (2013): 317–48.
Ahmed, Asad Q., and Margaret Larkin. "The *Ḥāshiya* and Islamic Intellectual History." *Oriens* 41.3–4 (2013): 213–16.

Alfeyev, Hilarion. *The Spiritual World of Isaac the Syrian*. Kalamazoo, 2000.

Allen, Pauline. "Pseudo-Caesarius." In di Berardino, *Patrology*, 99–100.

———. *Sophronius of Jerusalem and Seventh-Century Heresy: The Synodical Letter and Other Documents*. Oxford, 2009.

Alpi, Frédéric. "Le paysage urbain d'Antioche sur l'Oronte dans les sources syriaques anciennes." In *Les sources de l'histoire du paysage urbain d'Antioche sur l'Oronte*, ed. Catherine Saliou, 149–57. Paris, 2012.

al-Ālūsī, Ḥusām Muḥyī l-Dīn. "Dalīl al-Kindī fī ḥudūth al-ʿālam al-mustanid ʿalā tanāhī jirm al-ʿālam." *Majallat al-aqlām* 8 (1967): 141–49.

Amand de Mendieta, Emmanuel, and Stig Y. Rudberg. *Basile de Césarée: La tradition manuscrite directe des neuf homélies sur l'Hexaéméron; Étude philologique*. Berlin, 1980.

Anderson, Jeffrey C. "Cod. Vat. gr. 463 and an Eleventh-Century Byzantine Painting Center." *DOP* 32 (1978): 175–96.

Anrich, Gustav. *Hagios Nikolaos: Der Heilige Nikolaos in der griechischen Kirche: Texte und Untersuchungen*. 2 vols. Leipzig, 1913–1917.

Antioch-on-the-Orontes. 5 vols. Princeton, 1934–1972.

Aouad, Maroun, et al. "Les manuscrits de philosophie en langue arabe conservés dans les bibliothèques du Liban—Protocole—Catalogue raisonné des manuscrits de philosophie en langue arabe de la Bibliothèque Saint-Paul de Harissa (première partie)." *MUSJ* 61 (2008): 189–341.

Arberry, A. J. *Revelation and Reason in Islam*. London, 1957.

Assemani, Giuseppe Simone, and Stefano Evodio Assemani. *Bibliothecae Apostolicae Vaticanae codicum manuscriptorum catalogus*. 3 vols. Rome, 1756–1759.

Assemani, Stefano Evodio. *Bibliothecae Mediceae Laurentianae et Palatinae codicum manuscriptorum orientalium catalogus*. Florence, 1742.

Atiya, Aziz S. *Al-Fahāris al-taḥlīlīya li-makhṭūṭāt Ṭūr Sīnā al-ʿarabīya/Catalogue raisonné of the Mount Sinai Arabic Manuscripts*. Alexandria, 1970.

———. "St. John Damascene: Survey of the Unpublished Arabic Versions of His Works in Sinai." In *Arabic and Islamic Studies in Honor of Hamilton A. R. Gibb*, ed. George Makdisi, 73–83. Leiden, 1965.

Baccani, Donata. *Oroscopi greci: Documentazione papirologica*. Messina, 1992.

Bacha, Constantin, and Louis Cheikho. "ʿAbdallāh ibn al-Faḍl al-Anṭākī." *Al-Mashriq* 9 (1906): 944–53.

Balthasar, Hans Urs von. *Kosmische Liturgie: Das Weltbild Maximus' des Bekenners*. 2nd ed. Einsiedeln, 1961.

Barnes, Jonathan. "Syllogistic in the anon Heiberg." Chap. 5 in Ierodiakonou, *Byzantine Philosophy*, 97–137.

Basta Donzelli, G. "Del 'Tieste' di Diogene di Sinope in Diog. Lae. VI, 73." *StItalFCl*, 2nd ser., 37 (1965): 241–58.

Baur, Chrysostomus. "Chrysostomus in Genesim." *ThQ* 108 (1927): 221–32.

———. *S. Jean Chrysostome et ses oeuvres dans l'histoire littéraire*. Louvain, 1907.

Beck, Hans-Georg. *Kirche und theologische Literatur im byzantinischen Reich*. Munich, 1959.

Beck, Hildebrand. *Vorsehung und Vorherbestimmung in der theologischen Literatur der Byzantiner*. Rome, 1937.

Beck, Roger. *A Brief History of Ancient Astrology.* Oxford, 2007.
Bedke, Andreas. *Anthropologie als Mosaik: Die Aufnahme antiker Philosophie durch Gregor von Nyssa in seine Schrift De hominis opificio.* Münster, 2012.
Bennett, David. "Abū Isḥāq al-Naẓẓām: The Ultimate Constituents of Nature Are Simple Properties and Rūḥ." Chap. 8 in *Abbasid Studies IV,* ed. Monique Bernards, 207–17. Cambridge, 2013.
———. "The Spirit of Ahypokeimenonical Physics: Another Side of Kalām Natural Philosophy." PhD diss., University of California, Los Angeles, 2011.
Berryman, Sylvia. "Ancient Atomism." In *SEP.*
———. "The Evidence for Strato of Lampsacus in Hero of Alexandria." Chap. 6 in *Strato of Lampsacus: Text, Translation, and Discussion,* ed. Marie-Laurence Desclos and W. W. Fortenbaugh, 277–91. New Brunswick, NJ, 2011.
Bertaina, David. "Science, Syntax, and Superiority in Eleventh-Century Christian-Muslim Discussion: Elias of Nisibis on the Arabic and Syriac Languages." *Islam and Christian-Muslim Relations* 22.2 (2011): 197–207.
Bettiolo, Paolo. "Syriac Literature." In di Berardino, *Patrology,* 407–90.
BHG = Halkin, François, ed. *Bibliotheca Hagiographica Graeca.* 2nd ed. Brussels, 1909. 3rd ed. Brussels, 1957.
BHGNovAuct = Halkin, François, ed. *Bibliotheca Hagiographica Graeca: Nova Auctarium.* Brussels, 1984.
Binggeli, André. "Early Christian Graeco-Arabica: Melkite Manuscripts and Translations in Palestine (8th–10th Centuries AD)." *Intellectual History of the Islamicate World* 3.1–2 (2015): 228–47.
Black, Deborah L. *Logic and Aristotle's Rhetoric and Poetics in Medieval Arabic Philosophy.* Leiden, 1990.
Blank, David. "Ammonius." In *SEP.*
Bobzien, Susanne. "Ancient Logic." In *SEP.*
Bonmariage, Cécile, and Sébastien Moureau. "*Corpus Dionysiacum Arabicum:* Étude, édition critique et traduction des *Noms Divins* IV, §1–9, Partie I." *Le Muséon* 124.1–2 (2011): 181–227.
———. "*Corpus Dionysiacum Arabicum:* Étude, édition critique et traduction des *Noms divins* IV, §1–9, Partie II." *Le Muséon* 124.3–4 (2011): 419–59.
Booth, Phil. *Crisis of Empire: Doctrine and Dissent at the End of Late Antiquity.* Berkeley, 2013.
Bos, Abraham P. "Pneuma as Quintessence of Aristotle's Philosophy." *Hermes* 141.4 (2013): 417–34.
Bottini, Laura. "The *Apology* of al-Kindī." In *CMR,* 1:585–94.
Bouché-Leclercq, Auguste. *L'astrologie grecque.* Paris, 1899.
Brentjes, Sonja. "Teaching the Sciences in Ninth-Century Baghdad as a Question in the History of the Book: The Case of Abū Yūsuf Yaʿqūb b. Isḥāq al-Kindī (d. after 256/870)." *Intellectual History of the Islamicate World* 5.1–2 (2017): 1–27.
Brill's New Pauly. 16 vols. Leiden, 2002–2010.
Brock, Sebastian. "An Early Syriac Life of Maximus the Confessor." *AB* 91 (1973): 299–346.
———. "The Syriac Commentary Tradition." In Burnett, *Glosses,* 3–18.

———. "Syriac Manuscripts Copied on the Black Mountain, near Antioch." In *Lingua Restituta Orientalis: Festgabe für Julius Assfalg*, ed. Regine Schulz and Manfred Görg, 59–67. Wiesbaden, 1990.

Brown, Peter. "A Dark-Age Crisis: Aspects of the Iconoclastic Controversy." *EHR* 88, n. 346 (1973): 1–34.

———. *Power and Persuasion in Late Antiquity: Towards a Christian Empire*. Madison, WI, 1992.

———. "The Saint as Exemplar in Late Antiquity." *Representations* 2 (1983): 1–25.

Bulliet, Richard W. *Conversion to Islam in the Medieval Period: An Essay in Quantitative History*. Cambridge, MA, 1979.

Burnet, John. *Early Greek Philosophy*. London, 1892. 4th ed. London, 1930.

Burnett, Charles, ed. *Glosses and Commentaries on Aristotelian Logical Texts: The Syriac, Arabic, and Medieval Latin Traditions*. London, 1993.

Cabouret, Bernadette, Pierre-Louis Gatier, and Catherine Saliou, eds. *Antioche de Syrie: Histoire, images et traces de la ville antique*. Lyon, 2004.

Callahan, John F. "Greek Philosophy and the Cappadocian Cosmology." *DOP* 12 (1958): 29–57.

Canard, Marius. *Histoire de la dynastie des H'amdanides de Jazîra et de Syrie*. Paris, 1953.

Canart, Paul, ed. *La Bible du patrice Léon: Codex Reginensis Graecus 1*. Vatican City, 2011.

Cataldi Palau, Annaclara. "Complemento a 'Doxographica aus Basilius-scholien' di G. Pasquali." *Revue d'histoire des textes* 17 (1987): 347–51.

Chamberlain, Michael. *Knowledge and Social Practice in Medieval Damascus, 1190–1350*. Cambridge, 2002.

Cheikho, Louis. *Kitāb al-makhṭūṭāt al-ʿarabīya li-katabat al-naṣrānīya/Catalogue des manuscrits des auteurs arabes chrétiens*. Beirut, [1924].

———. "Majālis Īliyā Muṭrān Niṣībīn." *Al-Mashriq* 20 (1922): 33–44, 112–22, 267–72, 366–77, 425–34.

———. "Al-Makhṭūṭāt al-ʿarabīya fī khizānat kullīyatinā al-sharqīya: Aʿmāl al-ābāʾ (tatimma)." *Al-Mashriq* 7 (1904): 676–82.

Cheynet, Jean-Claude. "Basil II and Asia Minor." In *Byzantium in the Year 1000*, ed. Paul Magdalino, 71–108. Leiden, 2003.

———. "Michel Psellos et Antioche." *ZRVI* 50–51 (2013): 411–22.

Chialà, Sabino. "Due discorsi ritrovati della Quinta parte di Isacco di Ninive?" *OCP* 79 (2013): 61–112.

Chittick, William. "Ibn Arabi." In *SEP*.

Ciggaar, Krijna Nelly. *Western Travellers to Constantinople: The West and Byzantium, 962–1204: Cultural and Political Relations*. Leiden, 1996.

CMR = Thomas, David, et al., eds. *Christian-Muslim Relations: A Bibliographical History*. 15 vols. Leiden, 2009–2020.

Codices Chrysostomici Graeci. 8 vols. Paris, 1968–.

Cohen, S. Marc. "Aristotle's Metaphysics." In *SEP*.

Condylis-Bassoukos, Hélène. *Stéphanitès kai Ichnélatès, traduction grecque (XIe siècle) du livre Kalīla wa-Dimna d'Ibn al-Muqaffaʿ (VIIIe siècle)*. Leuven, 1997.

Connor, Carolyn L. "Hosios Loukas as a Victory Church." *GRBS* 33.3 (1992): 293–308.

Conrad, Lawrence. "Ibn Buṭlān in Bilād al-Shām: The Career of a Travelling Christian Physician." In *Syrian Christians under Islam: The First Thousand Years*, ed. David Thomas, 131–57. Leiden, 2001.

Cook, Michael. *Commanding Right and Forbidding Wrong in Islamic Thought.* Cambridge, 2000.

Cooperson, Michael. *Classical Arabic Biography: The Heirs of the Prophets in the Age of al-Ma'mūn.* Cambridge, 2000.

Cornford, Francis MacDonald. *Plato's Cosmology: The Timaeus of Plato Translated with a Running Commentary.* London, 1937.

Cotsonis, John. "The Contribution of Byzantine Lead Seals to the Study of the Cult of the Saints (Sixth–Twelfth Century)." *Byzantion* 75 (2005): 383–497.

Courtonne, Yves. *Saint Basile et l'hellénisme: Étude sur la rencontre de la pensée chrétienne avec la sagesse antique dans l'Hexaméron de Basile le Grand.* Paris, 1934.

CPG = *Clavis Patrum Graecorum.* Ed. Maurice Geerard. 5 vols. Turnhout, 1974–2003.

Crone, Patricia. "Excursus II: Ungodly Cosmologies." Chap. 6 in *The Oxford Handbook of Islamic Theology*, ed. Sabine Schmidtke, 103–29. Oxford, 2016.

Cross, F. L., and E. A. Livingstone, eds. "Evergetinos, Paul." In *The Oxford Dictionary of the Christian Church*, 3rd rev. ed. Oxford, 2005.

Dagron, Gilbert. "Formes et fonctions du pluralisme linguistique à Byzance (IXe–XIIe siècles)." *TM* 12 (1994): 219–40.

———. "Minorités ethniques et religieuses dans l'Orient byzantin à la fin du Xe et au XIe siècles: L'immigration syrienne." *TM* 6 (1976): 177–216.

Dagron, Gilbert, and Denis Feissel. "Inscriptions inédites du Musée d'Antioche." *TM* 9 (1985): 421–61.

Dagron, Gilbert, and J. Marcillet-Jaubert. "Inscriptions de Cilicie et d'Isaurie." *BTTK* 42 (1978): 373–420.

Daiber, Hans. "Graeco-Arabica Christiana: The Christian Scholar 'Abd Allāh ibn al-Faḍl (11th c. AD) as Transmitter of Greek Works." In Reisman and Opwis, *Islamic Philosophy*, 3–9.

Darrouzès, Jean. "Le mouvement des fondations monastiques au XIe siècle." *TM* 6 (1976): 159–76.

———. *Recherches sur les Offikia de l'église Byzantine.* Paris, 1970.

Davidson, Herbert A. "John Philoponus as a Source of Medieval Islamic and Jewish Proofs of Creation." *JAOS* 89.2 (1969): 357–91.

de Blois, François. "*Naṣrānī* (Ναζαραῖος) and *ḥanīf* (ἐθνικός): Studies on the Religious Vocabulary of Christianity and of Islam." *Bulletin of the School of Oriental and African Studies* 65.1 (2002): 1–30.

De Giorgi, Andrea U. *Ancient Antioch from the Seleucid Era to the Islamic Conquest.* Cambridge, 2016.

Del Re, Niccolò, and Maria Chiara Celletti. "Nicola (Niccolò), vescovo di Mira, santo." In *Bibliotheca Sanctorum*, 9:923–48. Rome, 1967.

de Smet, Daniel. *Empedocles Arabus: Une lecture néoplatonicienne tardive.* Brussels, 1998.

Desreumaux, Alain. "La paléographie des manuscrits syriaques et araméens melkites: Le rôle d'Antioche." In Cabouret, Gatier, and Saliou, *Antioche*, 555–71.

Dhanani, Alnoor. "The Impact of Ibn Sīnā's Critique of Atomism on Subsequent *Kalām* Discussion of Atomism." *Arabic Sciences and Philosophy* 25.1 (2015): 79–104.
———. "Kalām Atoms and Epicurean Minimal Parts." In *Tradition, Transmission, Transformation*, ed. F. Jamil Ragep, Sally P. Ragep, and Steven John Livesey, 157–71. Leiden, 1996.
———. *The Physical Theory of Kalām: Atoms, Space, and Void in Basrian Muʿtazilī Cosmology*. Leiden, 1994.
di Berardino, Angelo, ed. *Patrology: The Eastern Fathers from the Council of Chalcedon (451) to John of Damascus (750)*. Trans. Adrian Walford. Cambridge, 2006. Orig. publ. Genoa, 2000.
Diels, Hermann, ed. *Doxographi graeci*. Berlin, 1879.
Diez, Ernst, and Otto Demus. *Byzantine Mosaics in Greece: Hosios Lucas and Daphni*. Cambridge, MA, 1931.
Djobadze, Wachtang. *Archeological Investigations in the Region West of Antioch on-the-Orontes*. With contributions by M. Hendy, N. Lowick, C. Mango, D. M. Metcalf, and H. Seyrig. Wiesbaden, 1986.
———. *Materials for the Study of Georgian Monasteries in the Western Environs of Antioch on the Orontes*. Louvain, 1976.
Doens, Irénée. "Nicon de la Montagne Noire." *Byzantion* 24 (1954): 131–40.
Dörrie, Heinrich, Margarete Altenburger, and Uta Schramm, eds. *Gregor von Nyssa und die Philosophie*. Leiden, 1976.
Downey, Glanville. "Nikolaos Mesarites: Description of the Church of the Holy Apostles at Constantinople." *TAPS*, n.s., 47.6 (1957): 855–924.
Drobner, Hubertus R. "Gregory of Nyssa as Philosopher: *De anima et resurrectione* and *De hominis opificio*." *Dionysius* 18 (2000): 69–102.
Dvornik, Francis. *The Ecumenical Councils*. New York, 1961.
Dyobouniotes, C. I. "Κοσμᾶ Βεστίτωρος ἀνέκδοτα ἐγκώμια εἰς Χρυσόστομον." *Ἐπ.Ἑτ.Βυζ.Σπ.* 2 (1925): 55–83.
———. "Κοσμᾶ Βεστίτωρος ἀνέκδοτον ἐγκώμιον εἰς Ἰωάννην τὸν Χρυσόστομον." *Ἐπ.Ἑτ.Βυζ.Σπ.* 16 (1940): 151–55.
———. "Λόγος ἀνέκδοτος εἰς τὴν ἀνακομιδὴν τοῦ λειψάνου Ἰωάννου τοῦ Χρυσοστόμου." *Ἐπ.Ἐπ.Θεο.Σχο.Παν.Ἀθη.* 1 (1925): 306–19.
———. "Νικήτα Παφλαγόνος ἐγκώμιον εἰς Ἰωάννην τὸν Χρυσόστομον." *Θεολογία* 12 (1934): 53–68.
Eger, Asa. "(Re)Mapping Medieval Antioch: Urban Transformation from the Early Islamic to Crusader Periods." *DOP* 67 (2013): 95–134.
Ehrhard, Albert. *Überlieferung und Bestand der hagiographischen und homiletischen Literatur der griechischen Kirche von den Anfängen bis zum Ende des 16. Jahrhunderts*. 3 vols. Leipzig, 1937–1952.
EI[2] = *Encyclopaedia of Islam*. 2nd ed. Leiden, 1960–2008.
EI[3] = *Encyclopaedia of Islam*. 3rd ed. Leiden, 2007–.
El Cheikh, Nadia Maria. *Byzantium Viewed by the Arabs*. Cambridge, MA, 2004.
Elm, Susanna. "Priest and Prophet: Gregory of Nazianzus's Concept of Christian Leadership as Theosis." In *Priests and Prophets among Pagans, Jews, and Christians*, ed. Beata Dignas, Robert Parker, and Guy G. Stroumsa, 162–84. Leuven, 2013.
———. *Sons of Hellenism, Fathers of the Church: Emperor Julian, Gregory of Nazianzus, and the Vision of Rome*. Berkeley, 2012.

Endress, Gerhard. *The Works of Yahyā ibn ʿAdī: An Analytical Inventory.* Wiesbaden, 1977.
Falcon, Andrea. "Aristotle on Causation." In *SEP.*
Faultless, Julian. "Ibn al-Ṭayyib." In *CMR,* 2:667–97.
Fedwick, Paul J. *Bibliotheca Basiliana Universalis: A Study of the Manuscript Tradition, Translations, and Editions of the Works of Basil of Caesarea.* 5 vols. Turnhout, 1993–2004.
Féghali, Paul. "ʿAbdallāh ibn al-Faḍl al-Antākī et le commentaire de l'Évangile de Saint Jean." *Parole de l'Orient* 34 (2009): 95–111.
Feke, Jacqueline. *Ptolemy's Philosophy: Mathematics as a Way of Life.* Princeton, 2018.
Floridi, Luciano. "Scepticism and Animal Rationality: The Fortune of Chrysippus' Dog in the History of Western Thought." *Archiv für Geschichte der Philosophie* 79.1 (1997): 27–57.
Flusin, Bernard. "Le panégyrique de Constantin VII Porphyrogénète pour la translation des reliques de Grégoire le Théologien (*BHG* 728)." *REB* 57.1 (1999): 5–97.
Gacek, Adam. *Arabic Manuscripts: A Vademecum for Readers.* Leiden, 2009.
Gautier, Paul. "La Diataxis de Michel Attaliate." *REB* 39.1 (1981): 5–143.
Géhin, Paul. "Les collections de *Kephalaia* monastiques: Naissance et succès d'un genre entre création, plagiat et florilège." In *Theologica minora: The Minor Genres of Byzantine Theological Literature,* ed. Antonio Rigo, Pavel Ermilov, and Michele Trizio, 1–50. Turnhout, 2013.
Georr, Khalil. *Les Catégories d'Aristote dans leurs versions syro-arabes.* Beirut, 1948.
Giannakis, Elias. "The Structure of Abū l-Ḥusayn al-Baṣri's Copy of Aristotle's *Physics.*" *Zeitschrift für Geschichte der arabisch-islamischen Wissenschaften* 8 (1993): 251–58.
Gigante, Marcello. "Su un insegnamento di Diogene di Sinope." *StItalFCl,* 2nd ser., 34 (1962): 130–36.
Gil-Tamayo, Juan Antonio. "Hex: Apologia in Hexaemeron." In *The Brill Dictionary of Gregory of Nyssa,* ed. Lucas Francisco Mateo Seco and Giulio Maspero, trans. Seth Cherney, 387–89. Leiden, 2010.
Glasner, Ruth. "Ibn Rushd's Theory of *minima naturalia.*" *Arabic Sciences and Philosophy* 11.1 (2001): 9–26.
Glossarium Graeco-Arabicum: A Lexicon of the Mediaeval Arabic Translations from the Greek. Ed. Gerhard Endress. telota.bbaw.de/glossga.
Goitein, S. D. *A Mediterranean Society: The Jewish Communities of the Arab World as Portrayed in the Documents of the Cairo Geniza.* 6 vols. Berkeley, 1967–1993.
Goldstein, Bernard R. "The Arabic Version of Ptolemy's Planetary Hypotheses." *TAPS* 57.4 (1967): 3–55.
Golitsis, Pantelis. *Les commentaires de Simplicius et de Jean Philopon à la Physique d'Aristote: Tradition et innovation.* Berlin, 2008.
———. "Un commentaire perpétuel de Georges Pachymère à la Physique d'Aristote, faussement attribué à Michel Psellos." *BZ* 100.2 (2008): 637–76.
Goossens, Godefroy. *Hiérapolis de Syrie.* Louvain, 1943.
Graf, Georg. "Die Widerlegung der Astrologen von ʿAbdallāh ibn al-Faḍl." *Orientalia,* n.s., 6 (1937): 337–46.
———. *Geschichte der christlichen arabischen Literatur.* 5 vols. Vatican City, 1944–1953.
———. *Verzeichnis arabischer kirchlicher Termini.* 2nd ed. Louvain, 1954.
Gregory, Andrew D. "Astronomy." Chap. 6 in *A Companion to Science, Technology, and Medicine in Ancient Greece and Rome,* ed. Georgia L. Irby, 1:96–113. Chichester, UK, 2016.

Griffith, Sidney H. *The Church in the Shadow of the Mosque: Christians and Muslims in the World of Islam.* Princeton, 2008.

Grumel, Venance. *La chronologie.* Paris, 1958.

———. "Le patriarcat et les patriarches d'Antioche sous la seconde domination byzantine (969–1084)." *EO* 33, no. 174 (1934): 129–47.

Grumel, Venance, V. Laurent, and Jean Darrouzès, eds. *Les regestes des actes du Patriarcat de Constantinople.* 7 vols. Paris, 1932–1979.

Gutas, Dimitri. "Aspects of Literary Form and Genre in Arabic Logical Works." In Burnett, *Glosses,* 29–76.

———. *Avicenna and the Aristotelian Tradition: Introduction to Reading Avicenna's Philosophical Works.* 1988. 2nd ed. Leiden, 2014.

———. "Classical Arabic Wisdom Literature: Nature and Scope." *JAOS* 101.1 (1981): 49–86.

———. *Greek Thought, Arabic Culture: The Graeco-Arabic Translation Movement in Baghdad and Early ʿAbbāsid Society, 2nd–4th/8th–10th centuries.* London, 1998.

———. *Greek Wisdom Literature in Arabic Translation: A Study of the Graeco-Arabic Gnomologia.* New Haven, 1975.

———. "Introduction: Graeco-Arabic Studies from Amable Jourdain through Franz Rosenthal to the Future." *Intellectual History of the Islamicate World* 3 (2015): 1–14.

Hacken, Clara ten. "The Description of Antioch in Abū al-Makārim's *History of the Churches and Monasteries of Egypt and Some Neighbouring Countries.*" In *East and West in the Medieval Eastern Mediterranean: Antioch from the Byzantine Reconquest until the End of the Crusader Principality*, vol. 1, ed. Krijna Ciggaar and D.M. Metcalf, 185–216. Leuven, 2006.

Haddad, Rachid. *La Trinité divine chez les théologiens arabes: 750–1050.* Paris, 1985.

———. *Manuscrits du couvent Saint-Sauveur (Saïda).* Beirut, 1972.

Halm, Heinz. *The Fatimids and Their Traditions of Learning.* London, 1997.

Harvey, Alan. *Economic Expansion in the Byzantine Empire, 900–1200.* Cambridge, 1989.

Hatlie, Peter. *The Monks and Monasteries of Constantinople, ca. 350–850.* Cambridge, 2007.

———. "The Politics of Salvation: Theodore of Stoudios on Martyrdom (*Martyrion*) and Speaking Out (*Parrhesia*)." *DOP* 50 (1996): 263–87.

Hausherr, Irénée. "Dogme et spiritualité orientale." In *Études de spiritualité orientale,* 145–79. Rome, 1969.

Hava, J.G. *Al-Farāʾid al-durrīya: ʿArabī inglīzī/al-Farâʾid Arabic-English Dictionary.* Beirut, 1970.

Heimgartner, Martin, and Barbara Roggema. "Timothy I." In *CMR,* 1:515–31.

Hibbs, Darren. "Was Gregory of Nyssa a Berkeleyan Idealist?" *British Journal for the History of Philosophy* 13.3 (2005): 425–35.

Hill, Jonathan. "Gregory of Nyssa, Material Substance, and Berkeleyan Idealism." *British Journal for the History of Philosophy* 17.4 (2009): 653–83.

Hillier, Harold Chad. "Al-Ghazālī's Argument for the Eternity of the World in Tahāfut al-falāsifa (Discussion One, Proofs 1 and 2a) and the Problem of Divine Immutability and Timelessness." *Journal of Islamic Philosophy* 1.1 (2010): 62–84.

Hitti, Philip K. *History of Syria, including Lebanon and Palestine.* 1st ed. London, 1951.

Hodgson, Marshall G.S. *The Venture of Islam.* 3 vols. Chicago, 1974.

Honigmann, Ernst. *Die Ostgrenze des byzantinischen Reiches.* Brussels, 1935.

Hörandner, Wolfram. "Literary Criticism in 11th-Century Byzantium: Views of Michael Psellos on John Chrysostom's Style." *International Journal of the Classical Tradition* 2.3 (1996): 336–44.

Huby, Pamela. *Theophrastus of Eresus: Sources for His Life, Writings, Thought, and Influence; Commentary*, vol. 2: *Logic*. With contributions on the Arabic material by Dimitri Gutas. Leiden, 2007.

Hugonnard-Roche, Henri. *La logique d'Aristote du Grec au Syriaque: Études sur la transmission des textes de "l'Organon" et leur interprétation philosophique*. Paris, 2004.

Hunger, Herbert. *Die hochsprachliche profane Literatur der Byzantiner*. 2 vols. Munich, 1978.

Ibrahim, Habib. "Some Notes on Antonios and His Arabic Translations of John of Damascus." Chap. 5 in Roggema and Treiger, *Patristic Literature*, 158–79.

Ierodiakonou, Katerina, ed. *Byzantine Philosophy and Its Ancient Sources*. Oxford, 2002.

———. "The Greek Concept of *Sympatheia* and Its Byzantine Appropriation in Michael Psellos." In Magdalino and Mavroudi, *Occult Sciences*, 97–117.

———. "Psellos' Paraphrasis on Aristotle's *De interpretatione*." Chap. 7 in Ierodiakonou, *Byzantine Philosophy*, 157–81.

Ierodiakonou, Katerina, and Börje Bydén. "Byzantine Philosophy." In *SEP*.

Inwagen, Peter van, and Meghan Sullivan. "Metaphysics." In *SEP*.

Jacoby, David. "Silk Economics and Cross-Cultural Artistic Interaction: Byzantium, the Muslim World, and the Christian West." *DOP* 58 (2004): 197–240.

Janin, Raymond. *Géographie ecclésiastique de l'Empire byzantin*. Paris, 1953–1981.

———. "Les églises byzantines: St. Nicholas à Constantinople." *EO* 31, no. 168 (1932): 403–18.

Jankowiak, Marek. "The Invention of Dyotheletism." *StP* 63 (2013): 335–42.

Janos, Damien. "Al-Fārābī, Creation ex nihilo, and the Cosmological Doctrine of *K. al-Jamʿ* and *Jawābāt*." *JAOS* 129.1 (2009): 1–17.

———. *Method, Structure, and Development in al-Fārābī's Cosmology*. Leiden, 2012.

Jenkins, Romilly J. H., and Cyril Mango. "A Synodicon of Antioch and Lacedaemonia." *DOP* 15 (1961): 225–42.

Jones, Matthew L. *The Good Life in the Scientific Revolution: Descartes, Pascal, Leibniz, and the Cultivation of Virtue*. Chicago, 2008.

Kalvesmaki, Joel. "Evagrius in the Byzantine Genre of Chapters." Chap. 10 in *Evagrius and His Legacy*, ed. Joel Kalvesmaki and Robin Darling Young, 257–87. Notre Dame, 2016.

Karamanolis, George. *The Philosophy of Early Christianity*. Durham, UK, 2013.

Kashouh, Hikmat. *The Arabic Versions of the Gospels: The Manuscripts and Their Families*. Berlin, 2011.

Kassel, R., and C. Austin. *Poetae Comici Graeci*. 8 vols. Berlin, 1984–2001.

Kavvadas, Nestor. *Isaak von Ninive und seine Kephalaia Gnostika*. Leiden, 2015.

Kazhdan, Alexander. *A History of Byzantine Literature*. In collaboration with Lee F. Sherry and Christine Angelidi. 2 vols. Athens, 1999–2006.

Kazhdan, Alexander, and Alice-Mary Talbot. *Dumbarton Oaks Hagiographical Database*. www.doaks.org/research/byzantine/resources/hagiography-database.

Keating, Sandra Toenies. "Abū Rāʾiṭa l-Takrītī." In *CMR*, 1:567–81.

Kennedy, Edward Stewart. "A Survey of Islamic Astronomical Tables." *TAPS* 46.2 (1956): 123–77.

Kennedy, Hugh. "Antioch: From Byzantium to Islam and Back Again." In *The City in Late Antiquity*, ed. John Rich, 181–98. New York, 1992.

———. "From Polis to Madina: Urban Change in Late Antique and Early Islamic Syria." *Past and Present* 106 (1985): 3–27.

———. "The Melkite Church from the Islamic Conquest to the Crusades: Continuity and Adaption in the Byzantine Legacy." In *The 17th International Byzantine Congress, Major Papers*, 325–42. New Rochelle, NY, 1986.

Kessel, Grigory. "Isaac of Nineveh's *Chapters on Knowledge*." In *An Anthology of Syriac Writers from Qatar in the Seventh Century*, ed. Mario Kozah et al., 253–80. Piscataway, NJ, 2015.

Kessel, Grigory, and Nikolai N. Seleznyov. "Bibliography of Syriac and Christian Arabic Studies in Russian, 2018." *Hugoye: Journal of Syriac Studies* 22.1 (2019): 295–305.

Key, Alexander. *Language between God and the Poets: Maʿnā in the Eleventh Century*. Oakland, 2018.

Khalifé-Hachem, Élie. "Isaac de Ninive." In *Dictionnaire de spiritualité, ascétique et mystique*, ed. Marcel Viller, F. Cavallera, and J. de Guibert, 7:2041–54. Paris, 1971.

Kinberg, Leah. "What Is Meant by *Zuhd*." *Studia Islamica* 61 (1985): 27–44.

King, David A. *Astronomy in the Service of Islam*. Aldershot, 1993.

Kingsley, Peter. *Ancient Philosophy, Mystery, and Magic: Empedocles and Pythagorean Tradition*. Oxford, 1995.

———. "Notes on Air: Four Questions of Meaning in Empedocles and Anaxagoras." *CQ*, n.s., 45.1 (1995): 26–29.

Koikylides, Kleopas M. *Κατάλογος ἀραβικῶν χειρογράφων τῆς Ἱεροσολυμιτικῆς Βιβλιοθήκης*. Jerusalem, 1901.

Kontouma, Vassa. "The *Fount of Knowledge* between Conservation and Creation." Chap. 5 in *John of Damascus*.

———. "Jean III d'Antioche (996–1021) et la *Vie de Jean Damascène* (BHG 884)." *REB* 68 (2010): 127–47.

———. *John of Damascus: New Studies on His Life and Works*. Farnham, 2015.

Kotter, Bonifaz. *Die Überlieferung der Pege Gnoseos des Hl. Johannes von Damaskos*. Ettal, 1959.

Kotzabassi, Sofia. "Miscellanea Palaeographica." *Parekbolai* 5 (2015): 135–43.

Kraft, András, and István Perczel. "John Italos on the Eternity of the World." *BZ* 111.3 (2018): 659–720.

Kraus, Paul. "Kitāb al-Akhlāq li-Jālīnūs." *Majallat Kullīyat al-Ādāb* (Cairo) 5 (1937): 1–51.

Krause, Karin. "Göttliches Wort aus goldenem Mund: Die Inspiration des Johannes Chrysostomos in Bildern und Texten." In Wallraff and Brändle, *Chrysostomosbilder*, 139–67.

Krausmüller, Dirk. "Enhypostaton: Being 'in Another' or Being 'with Another'? How Chalcedonian Theologians of the Sixth Century Defined the Ontological Status of Christ's Human Nature." *VChr* 71.4 (2017): 433–48.

KRS² = Kirk, G. S., J. E. Raven, and M. Schofield. *The Presocratic Philosophers: A Critical History with a Selection of Texts*. 2nd ed. Cambridge, 1983.

Kupreeva, Inna. "Qualities and Bodies: Alexander against the Stoics." *Oxford Studies in Ancient Philosophy* 25 (2003): 297–344.

Lacey, R. Kevin. "An 11th Century Muslim's Syncretistic Perspective of Cosmology: Abū al-ʿAlāʾ al-Maʿarrī's Philosophical Poetic Reflections in *Luzūm mā lā yalzam* on [the] Make-Up and Dynamics of the Universe." *MW* 85.1–2 (1995): 122–46.

Lackner, Wolfgang. "Ein angebliches Enkomion des Chrysostomos auf Gregor von Nyssa (*BHG*[3] 717c)." *AB* 86 (1968): 5–9.

———. "Ein hagiographisches Zeugnis für den Antapodotikos des Patriarchen Germanos I. von Konstantinopel." *Byzantion* 38.1 (1968): 42–104.

Ladner, Gerhart B. "The Concept of the Image in the Greek Fathers and the Byzantine Iconoclastic Controversy." *DOP* 7 (1953): 1–34.

———. "The Philosophical Anthropology of Saint Gregory of Nyssa." *DOP* 12 (1958): 59–94.

Lagerlund, Henrik. "Medieval Theories of the Syllogism." In *SEP*.

Lameer, Joep. *Al-Fārābī and Aristotelian Syllogistics: Greek Theory and Islamic Practice*. Leiden, 1994.

Lamoreaux, John C. "Ibrāhīm ibn Yūḥannā al-Anṭākī." In *CMR*, 2:611–16.

Lampe = Lampe, G. W. H. *A Patristic Greek Lexicon*. Oxford, 1961.

Lang, Uwe Michael. "The Christological Controversy at the Synod of Antioch in 268/9." *JTS* 51.1 (2000): 54–80.

Langermann, Y. Tzvi. "Islamic Atomism and the Galenic Tradition." *History of Science* 47.3 (2009): 277–95.

Leigh, Robert Adam. "On Theriac to Piso, Attributed to Galen." PhD diss., University of Exeter, 2013.

Lemerle, Paul. *Cinq études sur le XI*[e] *siècle byzantin*. Paris, 1977.

———. *Les plus anciens recueils des miracles de saint Démétrius*. 2 vols. Paris, 1979–1981.

Lentin, Jérôme, and Jacques Grand'Henry, eds. *Moyen arabe et variétés mixtes de l'arabe à travers l'histoire*. Louvain, 2008.

Le Strange, Guy. *Palestine under the Moslems: A Description of Syria and the Holy Land from A.D. 650 to 1500*. London, 1890.

Lettinck, Paul. "Ibn Sina on Atomism: Translation of Ibn Sina's Kitab Al-Shifa, Al-Tabi'iyyat I: Al-Sama' Al-Tabi'i Third Treatise, Chapter 3–5." *Al-Shajarah: Journal of the International Institute of Islamic Thought and Civilization* 4.1 (2014): 1–51.

Lewin, B. Review of *Iṣlāḥ al-Manṭiq*, by Ibn al-Sikkīt, ed. Aḥmad Muḥammad Shākir and ʿAbd al-Salām Muḥammad Hārūn. *Oriens* 3.2 (1950): 325–28.

Liritzis, Ioannis, and Helen Vassiliou. "Does Sunrise Day Correlate with Eastern Orientation of Byzantine Churches on Significant Solar Dates and Saint's Days? A Preliminary Study." *BZ* 99.2 (2006): 523–34.

Long, A. A. "Astrology: Arguments pro and contra." In *Science and Speculation: Studies in Hellenistic Theory and Practice*, ed. Jonathan Barnes and Jacques Brunschwig, 165–92. Cambridge; Paris, 1982.

———. *Hellenistic Philosophy: Stoics, Epicureans, Sceptics*. 2nd ed. Berkeley, 1986.

Long, A. A., and David N. Sedley. *The Hellenistic Philosophers*. 2 vols. Cambridge, 1987.

Longrigg, James. "Elementary Physics in the Lyceum and Stoa." *Isis* 66.2 (1975): 211–29.

Louth, Andrew. "Isaac of Nineveh." In di Berardino, *Patrology*, 225–28.

———. "John of Thessalonica." In di Berardino, *Patrology*, 118–21.

———. "Maximus the Confessor." In di Berardino, *Patrology*, 135–53.

LSJ = Liddell, Henry George, and Robert Scott. *A Greek-English Lexicon*. Revised by Henry Stuart Jones. 9th ed. Oxford, 1996.

MacDonald, Duncan B. "Ibn al-ʿAssāl's Arabic Version of the Gospels." In *Estudios de erudición oriental: Homenaje á D. Francisco Codera*, 375–92. Zaragoza, 1904.

Magdalino, Paul. "The Byzantine Reception of Classical Astrology." In *Literacy, Education, and Manuscript Transmission in Byzantium and Beyond,* ed. Catherine Holmes and Judith Waring, 33–57. Leiden, 2002.

———. *L'orthodoxie des astrologues: La science entre le dogme et la divination à Byzance, VIIe–XIVe siècle.* Paris, 2006.

———. "The Road to Baghdad in the Thought World of Ninth Century Byzantium." In *Byzantium in the Ninth Century: Dead or Alive?* ed. Leslie Brubaker, 195–213. Aldershot, 1998.

Magdalino, Paul, and Maria Mavroudi, eds. *The Occult Sciences in Byzantium.* Geneva, 2006.

Mango, Cyril. "The Date of Cod. Vat. Regin. Gr. 1 and the 'Macedonian Renaissance.'" *ActaIRNorv* 4 (1969): 121–29.

Martin-Hisard, Bernadette. "La Vie de Georges l'Hagiorite (1009/1010–29 juin 1065): Introduction, traduction du texte géorgien, notes et éclaircissements." *REB* 64.1 (2006): 5–204.

———. "La Vie de Jean et Euthyme et le statut du monastère des Ibères sur l'Athos." *REB* 49.1 (1991): 67–142.

———. "Le patriarche Pierre III d'Antioche (1052–1057), son pseudo-successeur Jean IV/Denys et le Géorgien Georges l'Hagiorite († 1065)." *Νέα Ῥώμη: Rivista di ricerche bizantinistiche* 4 (2007): 177–215.

Martini, Aemidius, and Dominicus Bassi. *Catalogus codicum graecorum bibliothecae Ambrosianae.* Milan, 1906.

Matthews, John. *The Journey of Theophanes: Travel, Business, and Daily Life in the Roman East.* New Haven, 2006.

Mauropous, John. *Iohannis Euchaitorum Metropolitae quae in codice Vaticano graeco 676 supersunt.* Ed. Paul Lagarde. Göttingen, 1882.

Mavroudi, Maria. "Arabic Words in Greek Letters: The Violet Fragment and More." In Lentin and Grand'Henry, *Moyen arabe,* 321–54.

———. *A Byzantine Book on Dream Interpretation: The Oneirocriticon of Achmet and Its Arabic Sources.* Leiden, 2002.

———. "Greek Language and Education under Early Islam." Chap. 11 in *Islamic Cultures, Islamic Contexts: Essays in Honor of Professor Patricia Crone,* ed. Behnam Sadeghi et al., 295–342. Leiden, 2014.

———. "Licit and Illicit Divination: Empress Zoe and the Icon of Christ Antiphonetes." In *Les savoirs magiques et leur transmission de l'Antiquité à la Renaissance,* ed. Véronique Dasen and J.-M. Spieser, 431–60. Florence, 2014.

———. "Occult Sciences and Society in Byzantium: Considerations for Future Research." In Magdalino and Mavroudi, *Occult Sciences,* 39–95.

———. "Translations from Greek into Latin and Arabic during the Middle Ages: Searching for the Classical Tradition." *Speculum* 90.1 (2015): 28–59.

Mayer, August. "Psellos' Rede über den rhetorischen Charakter des Gregorios von Nazianz." *BZ* 20.1 (1911): 27–100.

McGinnis, Jon. "Avicennan Infinity: A Select History of the Infinite through Avicenna." *Documenti e studi sulla tradizione filosofica medievale* 21 (2010): 199–222.

———. "A Small Discovery: Avicenna's Theory of Minima Naturalia." *Journal of the History of Philosophy* 53.1 (2015): 1–24.

Mercati, Giovanni. "Origine antiochena di due codici greci del secolo XI." *AB* 68 (1950): 210–22.
Merlan, Philip. *From Platonism to Neoplatonism.* 1953. 3rd ed. The Hague, 1968.
Michel, Anton. *Humbert und Kerullarios.* 2 vols. Paderborn, 1924–1930.
Michot, Yahya. "Vanités intellectuelles . . . L'impasse des rationalismes selon le rejet de la contradiction d'Ibn Taymiyyah." *Oriente moderno,* n.s., 19.3 (2000): 597–617.
Mingana, Alphonse. *Catalogue of the Mingana Collection of Manuscripts Now in the Possession of the Trustees of the Woodbrooke Settlement, Selly Oak, Birmingham.* 4 vols. Cambridge, 1933.
Mioni, Elpidio. *Introduzione alla paleografia greca.* Padua, 1973.
Mogenet, Joseph. "Une scolie inédite du Vat. gr. 1594 sur les rapports entre l'astronomie arabe et Byzance." *Osiris* 14 (1962): 198–221.
Moore, Paul. *Iter Psellianum: A Detailed Listing of Manuscript Sources for All Works Attributed to Michael Psellos.* Toronto, 2005.
Morelon, Régis. "Eastern Arabic Astronomy between the Eighth and the Eleventh Centuries." Chap. 2 in Rashed, *Encyclopedia,* 1:20–57.
———. "General Survey of Arabic Astronomy." Chap. 1 in Rashed, *Encyclopedia,* 1:1–19.
Morris, Rosemary. *Monks and Laymen in Byzantium, 843–1118.* Cambridge, 1995.
Mullett, Margaret. *Theophylact of Ochrid: Reading the Letters of a Byzantine Archbishop.* Brookfield, VT, 1997.
Nasrallah, Joseph. *Catalogue des manuscrits du Liban.* 4 vols. Harissa; Beirut, 1958–1970.
———. *Histoire du mouvement littéraire dans l'Église melchite du Ve au XXe siècle.* Louvain, 1979–1996.
———. "La liturgie des patriarcats melchites de 969 à 1300." *OC* 71 (1987): 156–81.
Nesbitt, John, and Werner Seibt. "The Anzas Family: Members of the Byzantine Civil Establishment in the Eleventh, Twelfth, and Thirteenth Centuries." *DOP* 67 (2013): 189–207.
Neugebauer, Otto. *A History of Ancient Mathematical Astronomy.* 3 vols. Berlin, 1975.
Neugebauer, Otto, and H. B. van Hoesen. *Greek Horoscopes.* Philadelphia, 1959.
Noble, Samuel. "ʿAbdallah ibn al-Fadl al-Antaki." Chap. 7 in Noble and Treiger, *Orthodox Church,* 171–87.
———. "The Doctrine of God's Unity According to ʿAbdallāh ibn al-Faḍl al-Anṭākī." *Parole de l'Orient* 37 (2012): 291–301.
———. "Saint Nicholas." Unpublished edition of Ibn al-Faḍl's preface to and translation of Andrew of Crete's *Encomium to Saint Nicholas,* 21 October 2013.
Noble, Samuel, and Alexander Treiger. "Christian Arabic Theology in Byzantine Antioch: ʿAbdallāh ibn al-Faḍl al-Anṭākī and His Discourse on the Holy Trinity." *Le Muséon* 124 (2011): 371–417.
———, eds. *The Orthodox Church in the Arab World, 700–1700: An Anthology of Sources.* DeKalb, IL, 2014.
*OCD*³ = *The Oxford Classical Dictionary.* Ed. Simon Hornblower and Antony Spawforth. 3rd ed. Oxford, 1996.
ODB = *The Oxford Dictionary of Byzantium.* Ed. Alexander Kazhdan et al. Oxford, 2005.
OED = *Oxford English Dictionary.*
Oikonomides, Nicolas. "The First Century of the Monastery of Hosios Loukas." *DOP* 46 (1992): 245–55.

O'Keefe, Timothy. "The Ontological Status of Sensible Qualities for Democritus and Epicurus." *Ancient Philosophy* 17.1 (1997): 119–34.Omont, Henri. *Catalogue des manuscrits grecs des bibliothèques de Suisse: Bâle, Berne, Einsiedeln, Genève, St. Gall, Schaffhouse et Zürich.* Leipzig, 1886.

Ostrogorsky, George. *History of the Byzantine State.* Trans. Joan Hussey. Rev. ed. New Brunswick, NJ, 1969.

Pagoulatos, Gerasimos P. *Tracing the Bridegroom in Dura.* Piscataway, NJ, 2008.

Papadopoulos, Chrysostomos. *Ἱστορία τῆς Ἐκκλησίας Ἀντιοχείας.* Alexandria, 1951.

Papaioannou, Stratis. *Michael Psellos: Rhetoric and Authorship in Byzantium.* Cambridge, 2013.

Parker, Emily, and Alexander Treiger. "Philo's Odyssey into the Medieval Jewish World: Neglected Evidence from Arab Christian Literature." *Dionysius* 30 (2012): 117–46.

Parry, Kenneth. *Depicting the Word: Byzantine Iconophile Thought of the Eighth and Ninth Centuries.* Leiden, 1996.

Parry, Richard. "Empedocles." In *SEP.*

Pasquali, Giorgio. "Doxographica aus Basiliusscholien." *NachrGött,* 1910, 194–228.

Peers, Glenn. *Subtle Bodies: Representing Angels in Byzantium.* Berkeley, 2001.

Peeters, Paul. "Histoires monastiques géorgiennes." *AB* 36–37 (1922): 5–318.

Perczel, István. "Finding a Place for the *Erotapokriseis* of Pseudo-Caesarius: A New Document of Sixth-Century Palestinian Origenism." *ARAM Periodical* 18–19 (2006–2007): 49–83.

Peters, Curt. "Eine arabische Uebersetzung des Akathistos-Hymnus." *Le Muséon* 53 (1940): 89–104.

Philias, Georgios. "Eucharistie et prières diverses transmises sous le nom de Jean Chrysostome dans la tradition liturgique de l'Eglise Orthodoxe." In Wallraff and Brändle, *Chrysostomosbilder,* 99–109.

Philippidis-Braat, A. "L'enkômion de Saint Démétrius par Jean de Thessalonique." *TM* 8 (1981): 397–414.

Pinakes: Textes et manuscrits grecs. pinakes.irht.cnrs.fr.

Pingree, David. "The Greek Influence on Early Islamic Mathematical Astronomy." *JAOS* 93.1 (1973): 32–43.

Podskalsky, Gerhard. *Theologie und Philosophie in Byzanz.* Munich, 1977.

Quasten, Johannes. *Patrology.* 3 vols. Utrecht, 1950–1960.

Räisänen, Heikki. "Marcion." In *A Companion to Second-Century Christian "Heretics,"* ed. Antti Marjanen and Petri Luomanen, 100–124. Leiden, 2008.

Ramelli, Ilaria. *The Christian Doctrine of Apokatastasis: A Critical Assessment from the New Testament to Eriugena.* Leiden, 2013.

Rapp, Claudia. *Holy Bishops in Late Antiquity: The Nature of Christian Leadership in an Age of Transition.* Berkeley, 2005.

Rashed, Marwan. "Al-Farabi's Lost Treatise *On Changing Beings* and the Possibility of a Demonstration of the Eternity of the World." *Arabic Sciences and Philosophy* 18.1 (2008): 19–58.

———. "The Problem of the Composition of the Heavens (529–1610): A New Fragment of Philoponus and Its Readers." In *Philosophy, Science, and Exegesis in Greek, Arabic, and Latin Commentaries,* ed. Peter Adamson, Han Baltussen, and M. W. F. Stone, 2:35–58. London, 2004.

Rashed, Roshdi, ed. *Encyclopedia of the History of Arabic Science*. 3 vols. London, 1996.

Rassi, Juliette. "Le 'Livre de l'abeille' (al-Naḥlah) de Macaire ibn al-Zaʿīm, témoin de l'échange des cultures." *Parole de l'Orient* 32 (2007): 211–57.

Reinert, Stephen W. "The Muslim Presence in Constantinople, 9th–15th Centuries: Some Preliminary Observations." In *Studies on the Internal Diaspora of the Byzantine Empire*, ed. Hélène Ahrweiler and Angeliki E. Laiou, 125–50. Washington, DC, 1998.

Reisman, David, and Felicitas Opwis, eds. *Islamic Philosophy, Science, Culture, and Religion: Studies in Honor of Dimitri Gutas*. Leiden, 2012.

Rescher, Nicholas. "Al-Kindī's Sketch of Aristotle's *Organon*." *New Scholasticism* 37.1 (1963): 44–58.

Richard, Marcel. "Le traité de Georges Hiéromoine sur les hérésies." *REB* 28.1 (1970): 239–69.

Richter-Bernburg, Lutz. "Eine arabische Version der pseudogalenischen Schrift *De Theriaca ad Pisonem*." PhD diss., Göttingen, 1969.

Riedinger, Rudolf. "Die Nachkommen der *Epistula synodica* des Sophronios von Jerusalem (a. 634; CPG 7635)." *Römische Historische Mitteilungen* 26 (1984): 91–106.

———. *Pseudo-Kaisarios: Überlieferungsgeschichte und Verfasserfrage*. 1969.

Riedinger, Utto. *Die Heilige Schrift im Kampf der griechischen Kirche gegen die Astrologie: Von Origenes bis Johannes von Damaskos; Studien zur Dogmengeschichte und zur Geschichte der Astrologie*. Innsbruck, 1956.

Ritter, Heinrich, and Ludwig Preller. *Historia philosophiae graecae*. Ed. Eduard Wellmann. 8th ed. Gotha, 1898.

Robbins, Frank Egleston. *The Hexaemeral Literature: A Study of the Greek and Latin Commentaries on Genesis*. Chicago, 1912.

Roberts, Alexandre M. "Being a Sabian at Court in Tenth-Century Baghdad." *JAOS* 137.2 (2017): 253–77.

———. "Byzantine-Islamic Scientific Culture in the Astronomical Diagrams of Chioniades on John of Damascus." In *The Diagram as Paradigm: Cross-Cultural Approaches*, ed. Jeffrey Hamburger, David Roxburgh, and Linda Safran. Washington, DC, forthcoming.

———. "The Crossing Paths of Greek and Persian Knowledge in the 9th-Century Arabic 'Book of Degrees.'" In *Le vie del sapere in ambito siro-mesopotamico dal III al IX secolo*, ed. Carla Noce, Massimo Pampaloni, and Claudia Tavolieri, 279–303. Rome, 2013.

———. "Framing a Middle Byzantine Alchemical Codex." *DOP* 73 (forthcoming).

———. "A Re-Translation of Basil's Hexaemeral Homilies by ʿAbdallāh ibn al-Faḍl of Antioch." Chap. 7 in Roggema and Treiger, *Patristic Literature*, 198–240.

———. "Writing and Reading Greek on the Pages of Arabic Translations of Byzantine Christian Classics." In *Language Multiplicity in Byzantium and Beyond*, ed. Claudia Rapp, Emilio Bonfiglio, and Ekaterini Mitsiou. Vienna, forthcoming.

Roggema, Barbara. "Ḥunayn ibn Isḥāq." In *CMR*, 1:768–79.

———. "Job of Edessa." In *CMR*, 1:502–9.

Roggema, Barbara, and Alexander Treiger, eds. *Patristic Literature in Arabic Translation*. Leiden, 2020.

Rome, A. "Les observations d'équinoxes de Ptolémée: Ptolémée et le mouvement de l'apogée solaire." *Ciel et terre* 59.5–6 (1943): 141–55.

Rosenthal, Franz. *The Classical Heritage in Islam.* Trans. Emile Marmorstein and Jenny Marmorstein. New York, 1975.

Roueché, Mossman. "Stephanus the Alexandrian Philosopher, the *Kanon,* and a Seventh-Century Millennium." *JWarb* 74 (2011): 1–30.

Rousseau, Philip. *Basil of Caesarea.* Berkeley, 1994.

Sakkelion, Ioannes. "Κωνσταντίνου Ζ' Πορφυρογεννήτου ἐπιστολὴ πρὸς Γρηγόριον τὸν τῆς Θεολογίας Ἐπώνυμον." *Δελτ.Ἑτ.Ἑλλ.* 2 (1885): 261–65.

Saliba, George. "Arabic versus Greek Astronomy: A Debate over the Foundations of Science." *Perspectives on Science* 8.4 (2000): 328–41.

———. "Early Arabic Critique of Ptolemaic Cosmology: A Ninth-Century Text on the Motion of the Celestial Spheres." *Journal for the History of Astronomy* 25 (1994): 115–41.

———. Review of *Astronomy in the Service of Islam,* by David A. King. *Isis* 86.1 (1995): 97–98.

———. "The Role of the Astrologer in Medieval Islamic Society." *BEODam* 44 (1992): 45–67.

Samir, Samir Khalil. "Bibliographie du dialogue islamo-chrétien (2e partie: auteurs chrétiens arabes, XIe et XIIe siècles)." *Islamochristiana* 2 (1976): 201–42.

———. "Bibliographie du dialogue islamo-chrétien (corrigenda et addenda des auteurs arabes chrétiens des XIe et XIIe siècles)." *Islamochristiana* 5 (1979): 300–311.

———. "Quelques notes sur les termes *rūm* et *rūmī* dans la tradition arabe: Étude de sémantique historique." In *La nozione di "Romano" tra cittadinanza e universalità,* 461–78. Naples, 1984.

Sauget, Joseph-Marie. *Premières recherches sur l'origine et les caractéristiques des synaxaires melkites (XIe–XVIIe siècles).* Brussels, 1969.

Sbath, Paul. *Al-Fihris: Catalogue de manuscrits arabes.* 3 vols. Cairo, 1938–1939.

Schellewald, Barbara. "Chrysostomos und die Rhetorik der Bilder im Bema der Sophienkirche in Ohrid." In Wallraff and Brändle, *Chrysostomosbilder,* 169–92.

Sedley, David N. "Hellenistic Physics and Metaphysics." Chap. 11 in *The Cambridge History of Hellenistic Philosophy,* ed. Keimpe Algra et al., 355–411. Cambridge, 1999.

Seleznyov, Nikolai N. "Jacobs and Jacobites: The Syrian Origins of the Name and Its Egyptian Arabic Interpretations." *Scrinium* 9.1 (2013): 382–98.

SEP = Zalta, Edward N., ed. *Stanford Encyclopedia of Philosophy.* plato.stanford.edu.

Serikoff, Nikolaj. "*Rūmī* and *Yūnānī*: Towards the Understanding of the Greek Language in the Medieval Muslim World." In *East and West in the Crusader States: Context, Contacts, Confrontations,* vol. 1, ed. Krijnie Ciggaar, Adelbert Davids, and Herman Teule, 169–94. Leuven, 1996.

Ševčenko, Ihor. "Re-reading Constantine Porphyrogenitus." Chap. 11 in *Byzantine Diplomacy,* ed. Jonathan Shepard and Simon Franklin, 167–95. Aldershot, 1992.

Sezgin, Fuat. *Geschichte des arabischen Schrifttums.* 17 vols. Leiden, 1967–2015.

Shamsi, F. A. "The Question of World's Eternity in Al-Kindī's Book of Metaphysics." *Hamdard Islamicus* 12.3 (1989): 49–69.

Shchukin, Timur. "Matter as a Universal: John Philoponus and Maximus the Confessor on the Eternity of the World." *Scrinium* 13.1 (2017): 361–82.

Shehaby, Nabil. *The Propositional Logic of Avicenna: A Translation from al-Shifāʾ: al-Qiyās with Introduction, Commentary, and Glossary.* Dordrecht, 1973.

Shields, Christopher. "Aristotle." In *SEP.*

Sidarus, Adel. "Ibn al-Rāhib." In *CMR,* 4:471–79.

Siegal, Michal Bar-Asher. "Shared Worlds: Rabbinic and Monastic Literature." *HTR* 105 (2012): 423–56.
Simonetti, Manlio. "Sabellio e il sabellianismo." *Studi storico-religiosi* 4.1 (1980): 7–28.
Sivers, Peter von. "Taxes and Trade in the ʿAbbāsid Thughūr, 750–962/133–351." *Journal of the Economic and Social History of the Orient* 25.1 (1982): 71–99.
Smith, Robin. "Aristotle's Logic." In *SEP*.
Solmsen, Friedrich. "The Vital Heat, the Inborn Pneuma, and the Aether." *JHS* 77.1 (1957): 119–23.
Sorabji, Richard. "Infinity and the Creation." Chap. 9 in *Philoponus and the Rejection of Aristotelian Science*, ed. Richard Sorabji, 207–20. 2nd ed. London, 2010.
———, ed. *The Philosophy of the Commentators, 200–600 AD: A Sourcebook*. 3 vols. London, 2005.
———. *Time, Creation, and the Continuum: Theories in Antiquity and the Early Middle Ages*. Ithaca, NY, 1983.
Stern, S. M. "Ibn al-Samḥ." *JRAS* 1–2 (1956): 31–44.
Street, Tony. "Arabic and Islamic Philosophy of Language and Logic." In *SEP*.
Stroumsa, Sarah. "'Wondrous Paths': The Ismāʿīlī Context of Saadya's 'Commentary on *Sefer Yeṣīra*.'" *Bochumer Philosophisches Jahrbuch für Antike und Mittelalter* 18 (2015): 74–90.
Studer, Basilio. "Andrew of Crete." In di Berardino, *Patrology*, 161–63.
———. "John of Damascus." In di Berardino, *Patrology*, 228–37.
Studtmann, Paul. "Aristotle's Categories." In *SEP*.
Swanson, Mark N. "Abū Nūḥ al-Anbārī." In *CMR*, 1:397–400.
———. "Qusṭā ibn Lūqā." In *CMR*, 2:147–53.
———. "Yaḥyā ibn Saʿīd al-Anṭākī." In *CMR*, 2:657–61.
Tannous, Jack. "In Search of Monotheletism." *DOP* 68 (2015): 29–67.
———. "Syria between Byzantium and Islam: Making Incommensurables Speak." PhD diss., Princeton University, 2010.
Tarchnišvili, Michael. *Geschichte der kirchlichen georgischen Literatur*. Ed. Julius Assfalg. Vatican City, 1955.
Tatakis, Basile. *La philosophie byzantine*. 2nd ed. Paris, 1959.
Thomson, Robert W. *Saint Basil of Caesarea and Armenian Cosmology: A Study of the Armenian Version of Saint Basil's Hexaemeron and Its Influence on Medieval Armenian Views about the Cosmos*. Louvain, 2012.
Tihon, Anne. "L'astronomie byzantine (du Ve au XVe siècle)." *Byzantion* 51.2 (1981): 603–24.
———. "Science in the Byzantine Empire." Chap. 7 in *Medieval Science*, ed. David C. Lindberg and Michael H. Shank, 190–206. Cambridge, 2013.
Tinnefeld, Franz. "Michael I. Kerullarios, Patriarch von Konstantinopel (1043–1058): Kritische Überlegungen zu einer Biographie." *JÖB* 39 (1989): 95–127.
Todt, Klaus-Peter. "Antioch in the Middle Byzantine Period (969–1084): The Reconstruction of the City as an Administrative, Economic, Military, and Ecclesiastical Center." In Cabouret, Gatier, and Saliou, *Antioche*, 171–90.
———. "The Greek-Orthodox Patriarchate of Antioch in the Period of the Renewed Byzantine Rule and in the Time of the First Crusades (969–1204)." In *Tārīkh kanīsat Anṭākiya li-l-Rūm al-Urthūdhuks: Ayyat khuṣūṣiyya?* 33–53. Tripoli, Lebanon, 1999.

———. "*Notitia* und Diözesen des griechisch-orthodoxen Patriarchates von Antiocheia im 10. und 11. Jahrhundert." *Orthodoxes Forum* 9 (1995): 173–85.
———. "Region und griechisch-orthodoxes Patriarchat von Antiocheia in mittelbyzantinischer Zeit (969–1084)." *BZ* 91.1 (2001): 239–67.
———. *Region und griechisch-orthodoxes Patriarchat von Antiocheia in mittelbyzantinischer Zeit und im Zeitalter der Kreuzzüge (969–1204)*. 2 vols. Wiesbaden, 1998.
Todt, Klaus-Peter, and Bernd Andreas Vest. *Syria*. 3 vols. (continuous pagination). Vienna, 2014.
Trapp, Erich. *Lexikon zur byzantinischen Gräzität, besonders des 9.–12. Jahrhunderts*. Vienna, 1994–2017.
Treadgold, Warren. *The Nature of the Bibliotheca of Photius*. Washington, DC, 1980.
———, ed. *Renaissances before the Renaissance*. Stanford, 1984.
Treiger, Alexander. "ʿAbdallāh ibn al-Faḍl al-Anṭākī." In *CMR*, 3:89–113; additions and corrections, 5:748–49.
———. "The Arabic Version of Pseudo-Dionysius the Areopagite's *Mystical Theology*, Chapter 1: Introduction, Critical Edition, and Translation." *Le Muséon* 120 (2007): 365–93.
———. "Avicenna's Notion of Transcendental Modulation of Existence (*taškīk al-wuǧūd, analogia entis*) and Its Greek and Arabic Sources." In Reisman and Opwis, *Islamic Philosophy*, 327–63.
———. "Christian Graeco-Arabica: Prolegomena to a History of the Arabic Translations of the Greek Church Fathers." *Intellectual History of the Islamicate World* 3 (2015): 188–227.
———. "The Earliest Dated Christian Arabic Translation (772 AD): Ammonius' Report on the Martyrdom of the Monks of Sinai and Raithu." *Journal of the Canadian Society for Syriac Studies* 16 (2016): 29–38.
———. "From Theodore Abū Qurra to Abed Azrié: The Arabic Bible in Context." In *Senses of Scripture, Treasures of Tradition*, ed. Miriam Lindgren Hjälm, 11–57. Leiden, 2017.
———. "Greek into Arabic in Byzantine Antioch: ʿAbdallāh ibn al-Faḍl's 'Book of the Garden' (*Kitāb ar-Rawḍa*)." In *Ambassadors, Artists, Theologians: Byzantine Relations with the Near East from the Ninth to the Thirteenth Centuries*, ed. Zachary Chitwood and Johannes Pahlitzsch, 223–34. Mainz, 2019.
———. *Inspired Knowledge in Islamic Thought: Al-Ghazālī's Theory of Mystical Cognition and Its Avicennian Foundation*. London, 2012.
———. "New Evidence on the Arabic Versions of the Corpus Dionysiacum." *Le Muséon* 118 (2005): 219–40.
Trizio, Michele. "A Late Antique Debate on Matter-Evil Revisited in 11th-Century Byzantium: John Italos and His *Quaestio* 92." In *Fate, Providence, and Moral Responsibility in Ancient, Medieval, and Early Modern Thought: Studies in Honour of Carlos Steel*, ed. Pieter d'Hoine and Gerd Van Riel, 383–94. Leuven, 2014.
Troupeau, Gérard. *Catalogue des manuscrits arabes*, pt. 1, *Manuscrits chrétiens*. 2 vols. Paris, 1972–1974.
———. "Les églises d'Antioche chez les auteurs arabes." In *L'Orient au coeur: En l'honneur d'André Miquel*, ed. Floréal Sanagustin, 319–27. Paris, 2001.
———. "Les églises et les monastères de Syrie dans l'œuvre d'Abù al-Makàrim." *MUSJ* 58 (2005): 573–86.

Tuerlinckx, Laurence. "Le lexique du moyen arabe dans la traduction des discours de Grégoire de Nazianze: Présentation de quelques traits caractéristiques et étude des doublets." In Lentin and Grand'Henry, *Moyen arabe*, 473–88.

Vallance, J. T. *The Lost Theory of Asclepiades of Bithynia*. Oxford, 1990.

van Bladel, Kevin. *The Arabic Hermes: From Pagan Sage to Prophet of Science*. Oxford, 2009.

van Esbroeck, Michel. "Les sentences morales des philosophes grecs dans les traditions orientales." In *L'eredità classica nelle lingue orientali*, ed. Massimiliano Pavan and Umberto Cozzoli, 11–23. Rome, 1986.

van Ess, Josef. *Theologie und Gesellschaft im 2. und 3. Jahrhundert Hidschra: Eine Geschichte des religiösen Denkens im frühen Islam*. 6 vols. Berlin, 1991–1997.

Varghese, Baby. "The Byzantine Occupation of Northern Syria (969–1085) and Its Impact on the Syrian Orthodox Liturgy." *Parole de l'Orient* 40 (2015): 447–67.

Vasiliev, A. A. *Byzance et les Arabes*. Brussels, 1935–1968.

Viano, Cristina. "Le commentaire d'Olympiodore au livre IV des *Météorologiques* d'Aristote." In *Aristoteles chemicus: Il IV libro dei "Meteorologica" nella tradizione antica e medievale*, ed. Cristina Viano, 59–79. Sankt Augustin, 2002.

Vollandt, Ronny. *Arabic Versions of the Pentateuch: A Comparative Study of Jewish, Christian, and Muslim Sources*. Leiden, 2015.

———. "Beyond Arabic in Greek Letters: The Scribal and Translational Context of the Violet Fragment." Appendix 1 in *The Damascus Psalm Fragment: Middle Arabic and the Legacy of Old Ḥigāzī*, by Ahmad Al-Jallad, with a contribution by Ronny Vollandt. Chicago, forthcoming.

von Staden, Heinrich. "Teleology and Mechanism: Aristotelian Biology and Early Hellenistic Medicine." In *Aristotelische Biologie: Intentionen, Methoden, Ergebnisse*, ed. Wolfgang Kullmann and Sabine Föllinger, 183–208. Stuttgart, 1997.

Wakelnig, Elvira. "Al-Anṭākī's Use of the Lost Arabic Version of Philoponus' *Contra Proclum*." *Arabic Sciences and Philosophy* 23.2 (2013): 291–317.

Walbiner, Carsten-Michael. "Preserving the Past and Enlightening the Present: Macarius b. al-Zaʿīm and Medieval Melkite Literature." *Parole de l'Orient* 34 (2009): 433–41.

Walker, Paul E. "A Byzantine Victory over the Fatimids at Alexandretta (971)." *Byzantion* 42 (1972): 431–40.

Wallraff, Martin, and Rudolf Brändle, eds. *Chrysostomosbilder in 1600 Jahren: Facetten der Wirkungsgeschichte eines Kirchenvaters*. Berlin, 2008.

Wannous, Ramy. "Abdallah ibn al-Faḍl: Exposition of the Orthodox Faith." *Parole de l'Orient* 32 (2007): 259–69.

Watts, Edward Jay. *City and School in Late Antique Athens and Alexandria*. Berkeley, 2006.

Wehrli, Fritz. *Herakleides Pontikos*. In *Die Schule des Aristoteles: Texte und Kommentare*, vol. 7. Basel, 1953.

Wessel, Susan. "The Reception of Greek Science in Gregory of Nyssa's *De hominis opificio*." *VChr* 63.1 (2009): 24–46.

Wildberg, Christian. "David." In *SEP*.

———. "Elias." In *SEP*.

———. "John Philoponus." In *SEP*.

———. "Olympiodorus." In *SEP*.

Wisnovsky, Robert. "MS Tehran—Madrasa-yi Marwī 19: An 11th/17th-Century Codex of Classical *falsafah,* Including 'Lost' Works by Yaḥyā ibn ʿAdī (d. 363/974)." *Journal of Islamic Manuscripts* 7.1 (2016): 89–122.

———. "New Philosophical Texts of Yaḥyā ibn ʿAdī: A Supplement to Endress' Analytical Inventory." In Reisman and Opwis, *Islamic Philosophy,* 307–26.

———. "One Aspect of the Avicennian Turn in Sunnī Theology." *Arabic Sciences and Philosophy* 14 (2004): 65–100.

Wöhrle, Georg, ed. *The Milesians: Thales.* Trans. Richard McKirahan, with the collaboration of Ahmed Alwishah and an introduction by Georg Wöhrle and Gotthard Strohmaier. Berlin, 2014.

Wright, M. R. *Cosmology in Antiquity.* London, 2013.

Zayat, H. "Vie du patriarche melkite d'Antioche Christophore (m. 967) par le protospathaire Ibrahīm b. Yuhanna." *Proche-Orient Chrétien* 2 (1952): 11–36, 333–66.

Zeyl, Donald, and Barbara Sattler. "Plato's *Timaeus.*" In *SEP.*

GENERAL INDEX

Abraham ibn Ezra, 259n
Abramios (monk), translation of Isaac of Nineveh, 67
Abū l-ʿAlāʾ, 16, 154; teaching of Ibn al-Faḍl, 15
Abū l-ʿAlāʾ Ṣāʿid ibn al-Ḥasan, 15
Abū Bakr al-Rāzī. *See* al-Rāzī, Abū Bakr
Abū l-Faḍl Salāma ibn al-Mufarraj, patronage of Ibn al-Faḍl, 13
Abū l-Fatḥ ʿĪsā ibn Idrīs/Darīs: learning of, 138–39, 140; patronage of Ibn al-Faḍl, 13–14, 138–39, 140
Abū l-Ḥasan Simʿān (Symeon), 13, 142
Abū l-Khayr Mīkhāʾīl (Michael), 13, 142
Abū l-Makārim, description of Antioch, 26
Abū Maʿshar al-Balkhī (astrologer), 261, 262
Abū Naṣr Nikephoros: as *kouboukleisios*, 141–42, 143; patronage of Ibn al-Faḍl, 141–42
Abū Nūḥ al-Anbārī, *Topics* translation, 295n
Abū ʿUthmān al-Dimashqī, translation of Porphyry's *Eisagoge*, 189
Abū Zakariyāʾ ibn Salāma, patronage of Ibn al-Faḍl, 14, 127, 130
accidents: Basil of Caesarea on, 189, 206; in *Book of the Garden*, 198–99; John of Damascus on, 205
Achilles Tatius, 236
Adelard of Bath, 259n
agapē, Maximos the Confessor on, 57, 104
Agapios (patriarch of Antioch), 25
Ahmed, Asad, 151n; on syllogisms, 192n
Aimilianos (patriarch of Antioch), 23
aithēr, Stoic, 237n
Alexander of Aphrodisias, on void, 217–18
Alexandria: Christianity/Hellenism synthesis of, 2; Greek commentary tradition of, 182; Ptolemaic commentary in, 255–56
Amand de Mendieta, Emmanuel, 221n
Ammonios (Alexandrian exegete), 58n, 216; four *prosdiorismoi* of, 197
Anaxagoras, on matter, 207
Andrew of Crete: as deacon, 69; encomium for Basil of Caesarea, 97; in homiliaries, 94; as ideal bishop, 69–70; life of, 69; liturgical poetry of, 70; and Monotheletism, 69
—*Encomium to Saint Nicholas*, 105; elite audience of, 106; Ibn al-Faḍl's preface to, 68–69; Ibn al-Faḍl's translation of, 35, 68, 71, 96; manuscript tradition of, 84, 112
Anemas, Nicholas, 92
angels: corporeality/incorporeality of, 78, 210–14; form of, 174n; multiplication of, 46; pro-icon arguments for, 211n; substance of, 58, 213; subtle bodies of, 211–12, 213, 214
animals, domesticated, 146n. *See also* logic, dog
annotations, Ibn al-Faḍl's, 1, 2, 4, 14, 41, 80, 151–52; in Arabic book culture, 151; Arabic morphology in, 179; Arabic philosophy and, 154, 236, 239; Arabic terminology in, 152; on

Arabic philologists in, 156; Arabic phonetics in, 155–56; on Arabic syntax, 154–55; Aristotle's *On Interpretation* in, 196; articulate speech in, 159n; on astrology, 283–85; authorship of, 152–53, 162; causes in, 203–4; clerical audience for, 135; comparative linguistics in, 158; "deficient nouns" in, 159; on education, 157–63; erudition in, 197–98; grammar in, 153, 154–56, 159–60, 198–99; Gregory of Nazianzos in, 154–55; Gregory of Nyssa in, 199; John Chrysostom in, 156; on language, 153, 154; logic in, 194–99; nature in, 161; "On Honoring One's Parents," 196; "On Law," 194–96; "On Old Age and Youth," 198–99; organization of, 152; philosophy in, 161–63; premises in, 194–96; propositions in, 196–98; rationality in, 195, 199; on science, 283–84; self-knowledge in, 162, 163; substance in, 198–99; syllogism in, 195; title of, 134; vocabulary glosses in, 168; voice in, 158–60; witnesses in, 194–96
—preface, 132–36; commanding and forbidding in, 135; patristic texts in, 135; salvation in, 134; Trinity in, 133–34; universal substance in, 133–34
Book on Love (possible translation by Ibn al-Faḍl), 57
Brock, Sebastian, 29; on Isaac, 65, 66
Bydén, Börje, 186
Byzantine Empire: Arabic-speakers of, 180; christological debates of, 49; dating system of, 9–10, 30; expansion of, 2; Galen's influence in, 217; intellectual mobility within, 3; map of, *xiv*; monotheists of, 82; Muslim defeat of, 49; relations with Muslim states, 3
Byzantine literature, reckoning of dates in, 9–10, 118. *See also* educational curriculum, Byzantine; literary culture, Byzantine

Caesarius. *See* Kaisarios; Pseudo-Kaisarios
Cairo, Fatimid, 3
calendar: in Arabic astronomy, 259; in Georgian manuscripts, 118. *See also* chronology, Byzantine
caliphs, Abbasid: as imams, 169; loss of power, 260; scientific institutions of, 259, 262
Cappadocian fathers: on astrology, 255; in Byzantine ecclesiastical curriculum, 87; in catenae, 87; Greek philosophical education of, 231; Hellenic paganism and, 35; Ibn al-Faḍl's translations of, 34–35, 49; on matter, 201. *See also* patristic fathers
catenae (biblical exegesis), 87–88; on Genesis, 88n
cause(s): in *Book of the Garden*, 203–4; God as, 43; intelligent, 221
causes, Aristotelian: efficient, 202, 203; final, 202–3, 204; formal, 202, 203; material, 202; models in, 204; tools in, 204
celestial bodies: Ibn al-Faḍl's terminology for, 270; positions of, 265, 266; terrestrial effects of, 252–53, 254; visibility of, 243. *See also* astronomy; planets
celestial orb, 271; carrying of fixed stars, 264; ecliptic of, 264, 271, 276; effect on planetary motion, 275–76; planets' traversal of, 278; rotation of, 264
Chalcedonian Church: Armenians in, 29; Georgians in, 29, 109; Syriac-speakers in, 29; under Islamic rule, 22n. *See also* Christians, Chalcedonian; theology, Chalcedonian
Cheikho, Louis, 24n
Cheynet, Jean-Claude, 21n, 26n
Chialà, Sabino, 65, 66
Christianity: intellectual energy of, 149, 150; legitimacy of, 131; non-Christian learning in, 149; polytheism accusations against, 178; pre-Islamic, 135; synthesis with pagan culture, 62–63
Christianity, Byzantine, 2–3; Ibn al-Faḍl's engagement with, 1, 231
Christianity, Graeco-Roman: cultural commonality with paganism, 297; patristic articulation of, 38
Christians, Chalcedonian: of Antioch, 19, 71, 85; conflict with other Christians, 21; dispute with Nestorians, 141; dogma of, 49–56; languages of, 30; liturgies of, 29, 35–38; local traditions of, 22; loyalty to Byzantine Empire, 71; Melkites, 22–23; as participants in Byzantine ecclesiastical tradition, 288; use of Byzantine liturgy, 29
Christians, Melkite, 8; in Byzantine culture, 23; as term for Middle Eastern Chalcedonian Dyothelete Christians, 22–23
christological debates: Dyotheletism in, 50; John Chrysostom in, 41; John of Damascus in, 53–56, 177–78; John of Thessaloniki's, 76–81, 170–72; Maronites in, 52; Miaphysites in, 49, 52, 68, 81; Monotheletes in, 49; pro-Chalcedonian, 49, 51–56; Sophronios of Jerusalem in, 49, 50, 163, 164–65. *See also* God; hypostasis; Jesus Christ

Christopher (patriarch of Antioch), murder of, 26n
Christopher of Mytilene, on John Chrysostom, 92–93
chronology, Byzantine: indiction cycles in, 9, 10, 118. *See also* calendar
Chrysippos: logical dog of, 190–94; Stoic logic of, 182
Church of Cassian (Antioch), 25–26
Church of Episkopoi (Evrytania), Saint Nicholas frescoes of, 70
Church of Holy Wisdom (Kiev), Saint Nicholas frescoes of, 70
Church of Holy Wisdom (Ohrid), frescoes of, 93–94
Cleanthes, on heat, 238
comparative linguistics, Arabic-Greek, 158–60
Connor, Carolyn, 62n
Constantine I (emperor): tomb of, 100
Constantine V (emperor): patronage of astronomy-astrology, 256
Constantine VII Porphyrogennetos (emperor): *Book of Ceremonies*, 99–100, 108; on John Chrysostom's relics, 98; translation of relics, 99
Constantine IX Monomachos (emperor), 24, 117–18
Constantine X Doukas (emperor), 107–8
Constantinople: governing class of, 21; interest in astronomy, 256; metaphrastic circle of, 289; middle Byzantine transformation of, 3; reading traditions of, 293; sacred processions of, 99–100; ties to Byzantine Antioch, 18
Cook, Michael, 135
corporeality: of angels, 78, 210–14; Demetrios on, 210; of world, 245–46
cosmogony, Hellenic theories of, 43. *See also* creation
cosmology: Basil of Caesarea's, 42–44; in Genesis, 277; in Hexaemeron Corpus, 48; Ibn al-Faḍl's, 4, 233; likeness to God in, 46–47; of material world, 219; medieval, 232; modern, 232. *See also* creation; sky; universe
cosmology, Arabic: eternity of world in, 241–50; infinity in, 242
cosmology, Aristotelian, 232–33; Basil's use of, 234; four elements in, 233–34, 236; infinity in, 241, 247
cosmology, Greek, 130; Epicurean, 167; eternity of world in, 241–50; Platonic, 233
Cotsonis, John, 106, 107n
Council of Nicaea, Second: on angels' bodies, 211
creation: in Basil's *Hexaemeron*, 42–44, 188–89, 219–30; in *Encomium to Saint Demetrios*, 76, 77, 78, 81; errors concerning, 227; fifth element and, 240; God's role in, 201; hexaemeral narrative of, 42–48; Ibn al-Faḍl's terminology for, 224–27; of land animals, 190; material premises of, 219–30, 221; Moses on, 234; place of man in, 46; preexisting matter in, 243; time in, 243–44. *See also* cosmology; hexaemeral narratives; universe
culture, Byzantine: Arabic authors in, 230; classical tradition in, 149; decorative programs, 96; elite, 101; Melkite Christians in, 23; patristic fathers in, 39, 92; saints in, 96–101. *See also* ecclesiastical culture, Byzantine; literary culture, Byzantine
culture, Georgian: elite defense of, 109. *See also* book culture, Georgian
curiosity, human, 81

Dagron, Gilbert, 30
Dahrī *aṣḥāb al-ṭabā'i'* (materialists), 208
Damascus, observatory of, 259, 262
deduction, disjunctive, 192n
Demetrios, Saint: on angels' bodies, 212; Chalcedonian teachings of, 166, 170; on corporeality, 210, 212; doctrinal refutations by, 74–82, 136, 165, 170; encomia for, 108; fame of, 74; feast day of, 108; on hypostasis, 76, 78–79, 81–82; Ibn al-Faḍl's interest in, 74; iconography of, 106–7; manuscript attestations, 108; miracles of, 74, 108, 137, 138; on Nicene Trinity, 136; popularity of, 103; as "the Prizewinner," 72–73; as soldier-saint, 105, 107; as teacher, 136; as teacher-soldier, 108; veneration in Constantinople, 107, 108. *See also* John of Thessaloniki, *Encomium to Saint Demetrios*
Democritus: atomism of, 205; on division of matter, 214; on void, 218
demons: in *Encomium to Saint Demetrios*, 77; Maximos the Confessor on, 58; monastic struggle with, 60n
density, simplicity and, 212
Dexippos, *prosdiorismoi* of, 197
dialectic, Aristotelian, 182
Diogenes Laertius, 216
Diogenes of Sinope, physics of, 216
Dionysian Corpus, translations of, 296
Dionysios the Areopagite. *See* Pseudo-Dionysios the Areopagite
Dionysios Thrax, *Art of Grammar*, 159–60, 171

physics, Stoic: bodies in, 205–6; four elements of, 237; qualities in, 207; void in, 218. *See also* Stoicism
piety, rational, 139
Pinakes (online database), Greek manuscripts listed in, 83–84, 85
planets: Egyptian order of, 279; influence of, 265; motion of, 275–78, 282; names of, 272, 278, 283; orbs of, 272, 275; order of, 279–80; revolutions of, 241; spheres of, 232, 254; stations of, 265, 266, 269, 278; traversal of celestial orb, 278. *See also* astrology; astronomy; celestial bodies
plants, names of, 280
Plato: allegory of the sun, 44n, 139; Byzantine Greek pronunciation of, 11; on elements, 237, 238; on firmament, 238; on fixed stars, 276; on physical bodies, 214–15; polemic against sophists, 292; on science, 284. Works: *Menexenus*, 284; *Phaedrus*, 59n; *Republic*, 44n; *Timaeus*, 233, 276
Platonism, likeness to God in, 45–46
plenum, Basil of Caesarea on, 221, 227, 229–30
Plotinos: on astrology, 254; encomium for Demetrios, 108; on matter, 236n
Plutarch, on qualities, 207
Porphyry: on Ptolemy, 254; on universal substance, 133–34; universal utterances of, 147n
—*Eisagoge*, 160; Abū ʿUthmān al-Dimashqī's translation of, 189; Arabic commentary translations, 183–84; commentaries on, 187; theory of predication in, 183; translated commentaries on, 183–84
prayer, Muslim direction for, 271–72
prefaces, Ibn al-Faḍl's, 4, 13, 36; biblical exegesis, 123; praise of saints, 123; purposes of, 123, 180. *See also* annotations; translations
—Andrew of Crete, 68–69
—*Book of the Garden*, 132–36; commanding and forbidding in, 135; patristic texts in, 135; praise of God in, 133–34; salvation in, 134; Trinity in, 133–34; universal substance in, 133–34
—Gospel lectionary, 37–38
—Isaac's *Ascetic Homilies*, 13, 123, 140–43, 144; address to Isaac, 141, 142; clothing metaphors of, 143; existence of God in, 141; materiality/spirituality in, 142–43; perfume metaphors of, 140, 142; rhyme in, 140; sun metaphor of, 142; versions of, 140–43
—John Chrysostom on Hebrews, 143–45; avoidance of error in, 144; hypostasis in, 144
—John of Thessaloniki, 136–40; audience of, 140; christology of, 138; clothing metaphors of, 136–38, 139; dichotomies in, 136; hypostasis in, 138; purpose of, 140; rationality in, 139
—"Melkite" epistolary, 37, 143–46
—Psalter, 124–32
—Pseudo-Kaisarios, 123, 145–49; Christian/non-Christian debate in, 146–49; circular numbers in, 146; distraction from scripture in, 147, 149, 251, 277; Gregory of Nazianzos in, 148; lists of questions, 146–47, 149; motives for, 148, 149; non-Christian learning in, 149; patristic texts in, 147–48, 149; profane learning in, 148; science in, 146, 149; substance in, 147
—Pseudo-Maximos. See *Book of the Garden*; prefaces, *Book of the Garden*; *Loci communes*
Proklos (Neoplatonist), 296
prophetologion, Ibn al-Faḍl's translation of (possible), 35, 38
propositions: modality of, 196; negative, 197–98, 199; without quantifiers, 196–97
Protagoras, 292
Psalter: Arabic, 36–37; for Arabophone Christians, 131; in Byzantine education, 37; Greek patristic commentaries on, 36
Psalter, Ibn al-Faḍl's, 56; benefit for Christians, 131; corrected, 130; emotional reading of, 128; garden metaphor for, 129, 134
—preface, 124–32; ascription of, 124; Chalcedonian Dyothelete terms in, 127–28; Christian legitimacy in, 131; creation in, 129; fragrance tropes in, 126; Gregory of Nazianzos in, 125, 128; high Arabic style of, 130; hypostasis in, 126, 128, 129; longing for God in, 131; paired synonyms in, 128; particulars/universals in, 130; Peripatetic philosophy in, 131–32; preexisting matter in, 130; purpose for translation, 128–29, 130, 131; recensions of, 124, 127; recompense from God in, 126; rhyming prose of, 128; Socrates in, 128, 129; substance in, 129
Psellos (philosopher and rhetor): commentary on Basil, 230; correspondence of, 23; as drawing on Philoponos, *Against Aristotle*, 237, 243; on Gregory of Nazianzos, 91; on John Chrysostom, 91; on literary models, 91–92; on Monastery of Saint Symeon, 27; paraphrases of Aristotle, 185. Works: *Improvised Discourse to Pothos the Vestarches*, 91; *The Styles of Gregory the Theologian, Basil the Great, Chrysostom, and*

ARABIC INDEX

* based on a proposed emendation
( ) Greek word cited as likely basis or equivalent for an Arabic word
¶ paragraph number when numbered, otherwise counting from top of Arabic text on that page

GREEK INDEX

INDEX OF MANUSCRIPTS

ar. = Arabic; gr. = Greek; or. = oriental; syr. = Syriac

Athos
- Iviron, Georgian
  - 45: 116n176
  - 84: 116n175, 117n180
- Skētē Kausokalybion, Kyriakou 3: 94–95, 94n45, 95n47

Basel, Universitätsbibliothek AN III 13: 88

Beirut, B[ibliothèque] O[rientale de l'Université Saint-Joseph]
- 479 [= Basil *Hex.* **B**]: 9n12, 179n100, 188–89, 190n53, 190–94, 206–7, 225n108, 234n15, 235, 244n72, 244–49, 268n102, 273n128, 273–81
- 545: 63n134

Birmingham, Mingana, Christian Arabic Add. 220: 38n18

British Museum. *See* London, British Museum

Cairo, C[optic] O[rthodox] P[atriarchate]
- Theol. 112 [= Ps.-Kaisarios **Q**]: 41n31, 145n63, 145–48, 194n66, 244n67
- Theol. 139 [= Basil *Hex.* **W**]: 267n98

Damascus
- [Greek] O[rthodox] P[atriarchate of Antioch and All the East,] ar.
  - 142 [= Basil *Hex.* **D**]: 9n12, 190n53, 190–94, 206–7, 221n92, 225n108, 227n114, 235, 244n72, 244–49, 268n102, 273n128, 273–81
  - 149 [= Basil *Hex.* **E**]: 9n12, 10n22, 190n53, 190–92, 206–7, 225n108, 235, 244n72, 244–49, 268n102, 273n128, 273–81
- Ẓāhirīya Library, 4489: 281n154

Dayr al-Banāt. *See* Lebanon, Dayr al-Banāt

Dayr al-Ḥarf. *See* Lebanon, Dayr al-Ḥarf

Dayr al-Mukhalliṣ. *See* Lebanon, Dayr al-Mukhalliṣ

Florence, [Biblioteca] Laurenziana
- or.
  - 99: 39n24
  - 396: 70n171
- gr.
  - 4.27: 220n89, 266n95, 266–67
  - 87.5: 201n1

Genoa, [Biblioteca] Franzoniana, gr. 17: 209n41, 209–10, 220n89, 239–40, 240n41, 266n95, 266–67

Ḥarīṣā. *See* Lebanon, Ḥarīṣā

Founded in 1893,
UNIVERSITY OF CALIFORNIA PRESS
publishes bold, progressive books and journals on topics in the arts, humanities, social sciences, and natural sciences—with a focus on social justice issues—that inspire thought and action among readers worldwide.

The UC PRESS FOUNDATION
raises funds to uphold the press's vital role as an independent, nonprofit publisher, and receives philanthropic support from a wide range of individuals and institutions—and from committed readers like you. To learn more, visit ucpress.edu/supportus.